SCIENCE STEALING THE FIRE OF THE GODS AND HEALING THE WORLD

Art As Evidence Of Science:
The Exhibits Of The Museum Of The Creative Process

CAN THE UNCONSCIOUS BE A NATURAL SCIENCE PHENOMENON?

COULD THIS UNCONSCIOUS HAVE MEASURABLE AND GRAPHICALLY PORTRAYABLE DIMENSIONS?

COULD RELIGIONS SIMPLY BE DISCOVERIES OF THIS SCIENTIFIC PHENOMENON?

Normative Publications Vol. 4

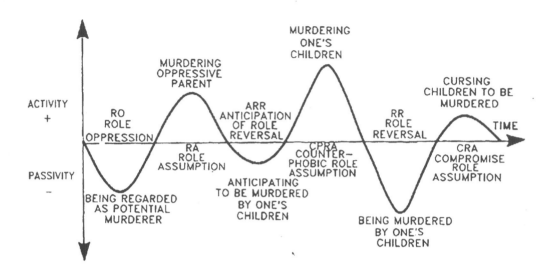

COULD THIS BE THE NEW WAY OF TALKING ABOUT MORALITY AND BEHAVIOR?

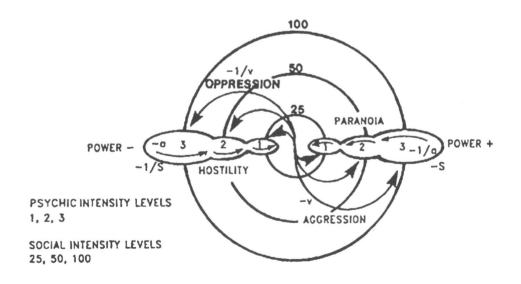

SCIENCE STEALING THE FIRE OF THE GODS AND HEALING THE WORLD

Art As Evidence Of Science:
The Exhibits Of The Museum Of The Creative Process

Introducing a scientific breakthrough:
the Conflict Resolution Process
as the Universal Harmonic, the Unit of the Moral Science

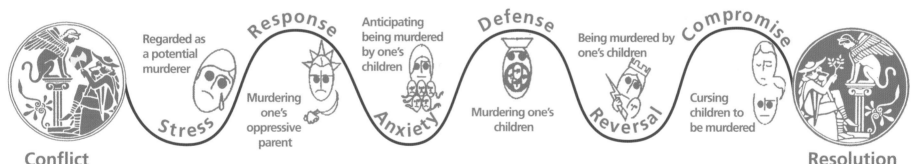

Conflict

Passivity
Antagonism
Alienation

Regarded as a potential murderer

Response

Stress

Murdering one's oppressive parent

Anticipating being murdered by one's children

Anxiety

Defense

Murdering one's children

Being murdered by one's children

Reversal

Compromise

Cursing children to be murdered

Resolution

Activity,
Cooperation
Mutual respect

A companion to the textbook:

MORAL SCIENCE
The Scientific Interpretation Of Metaphors

PRINTED IN CHINA

FIRST PRINTING, 2011

ISBN 978-0-615-48507-2

INSTITUTE OF CONFLICT ANALYSIS

AND THE MUSEUM OF THE CREATIVE PROCESS AT THE WILBURTON INN

257 WILBURTON DRIVE

MANCHESTER, VT 05254

WWW.ARTTOSCIENCE.ORG

Every philosophy and science has its way of impacting our world. This book is about the Moral Science. It clarifies values and beliefs, placing them on a scientific foundation. The world needs it. We are in the midst of a war whose nature is philosophical; it is a war about values and beliefs fought without an awareness of the scientific nature of values.

To deal with the cultural conflicts of our times we need conceptual clarity in the definition of fairness and justice. The attack of 9/11, the collapse of the World Trade Center represents the collapse of the modern Tower of Babel, and reflects the difficulty we have in agreeing on values. This disaster and the ensuing war of faiths or values will not end until the world has conceptual clarity on the nature of moral values. Only then shall we be able to reach a moral consensus and attain a permanent peace.

The good news brought about by this book is that science elucidates the nature of the mind and of morality. Moral Science introduces a concept that completes the unfinished task of religions in their pursuit of peace as the state of conflict resolution. It clarifies that morality does not stem from the supernatural but from the natural human unconscious struggling to adjust to the stressors of life by resolving conflicts. Science discovers the unconscious adjustment process manifest in all stories as the formal transformation of emotions from a state of passivity to one of activity, a state of antagonism to cooperation and a state of alienation to that of mutual respect. It is that simple.

This transformative process connects the emotions in every story; we identify it as the plot of stories, the unfolding of a predictable and universal mental adjustment mechanism. Science interprets art and metaphors, shifting from the content of stories to what is universal in all stories, the plot of stories, the unconscious as a palpable Conflict Resolution.

Religions also discovered this universal process as a progression of adaptive stories with alternative choices of formal resolutions. They evolved norms of family roles, and increasingly abstract representations of the process attributing it to divinities. The Greek Olympian religion chose mastery and identified the process with the 12 Olympian gods. India discovered cooperation with a multiplicity of gods and finally with Buddha. Judea discovered mutual respect and defined the one god of monotheism. Religions represent ways of resolving conflicts with different values, norms and authority figures. Science integrates religions as complementary discoveries of the process.

Thus Moral Science clarifies the origin of moral order as the unconscious adjustment to stress and reconciles the religions as the alternative paths to conflict resolution. Religions are merely complementary partial discoveries of the underlying Conflict Resolution Process. They have mystified and deified the process. Science shifts the focus from the content of the stories and the individual resolution to the universal process demystifying and reconciling the religions of the world promoting the scientific message, the complete set of values, the three principles that resolve conflict in every story: mastery, cooperation and mutual respect.

By validating the process with the evidence advanced in this book science establishes the foundation for the healing of the world. The unifying language has many practical benefits and advantages. But foremost science frees the world from being mesmerized and captive to dated cultural resolutions, their norms and divinities. Science, with natural law integrates the diverse moral laws leading to insights, and clarity to define optimal power management. Leaders may now have confidence in effectively introducing moral reason where faiths have failed to bring about peace. Reason reconciles the sacred faiths while recognizing their respective limitations.

The Moral Science is relevant for our times of religious conflicts. Military interventions, brutal confrontations of power, do not lead to conflict resolution because power alone does not alter people's belief systems. What is needed is enlightenment, understanding the nature of moral order. Science has the answers to the mysteries of psychology and religion. The new science integrates them both into the science of moral order, the Science of Conflict Resolution.

Barack Obama is a president who inspires, educates, and enlightens; he recognizes the advantages of moral values beyond religions. That is why the science of moral reason is timely and of particular usefulness in our times. Obama is seeking change, conflict resolution, but the world is caught between the norms of civil rights and the sacrosanct values, norms and gods of many religions. America, to lead the world, must reconcile paradigms. With the help of the Moral Science we can move beyond the many religion-based moralities and free the world from its uncertainty. The secret to an effective nation and a harmonious globalization hinges on our capacity to understand the difference between stories we believe in and the unifying process underlying all stories. We must be clear on the nature of the partial resolutions we invented and conflict resolution as the innate formula of our minds.

This book assists this search for meaning and peace by interpreting metaphors with scientific principles. May the Moral Science assist the public and President Obama to promote a spirit of mastery, cooperation and mutual respect and to find in science the validation of his heroic struggle for change.

ACKNOWLEDGEMENTS

All four of my children have contributed in the development of the concepts and the art exhibits during their school and college years. The four Levis children have been my research assistants. Each one has been associated with one art exhibit conceived as a parent child science project. My eldest daughter, Tajlei ("Thalia"), helped me with the Sculptural Trail upon her Bat Mitzvah as our Bible study activity. The trail started as the Bible Walk; it retraced the history of the Bible with a series of commemorative signs with inscriptions of events, dates, and quotations. We planted them chronologically in the fields surrounding our VT home.

This project inspired the Sculptural Trail at first focusing on the Biblical story, but then the trail expanded to include stations for the era of the pagan religions preceding the Bible and then stations beyond the biblical era illustrating abstract concepts on the scientific nature of the unconscious Conflict Resolution Process. The trail then ended retracing the history of religions as discoveries of the Moral Science as a shift in paradigms from the stories we believe in to the plot of stories as a scientific phenomenon that resolves conflict.

Now the trail begins with the Easter Island Head as the Wizard, the author of all stories with a tear in his eye wandering 'why is the world unhappy in spite of all my stories?' The answer is given by a scale standing next to him, representing science: 'The secrets are in what is universal in all stories, instead of believing them, we should examine the nature of the plot of stories.' This answer is confirmed at the end of the trail where the creative process is celebrated with the abstract sculptures depicting the process and the principles of conflict resolution.

My daughter Melissa ("Moey") helped with another theoretical and artistic project. She was very interested in the metaphor testing and helped me in the development of some of the tests. She continued using them for personal insights and for working through some of her emotions; I have five books completed with her scales and metaphors. She was also active in promoting the project among her peers and spent a summer in a workshop of personal development in VT. One of the murals of the Sanctuary is her own case study contrasted to that of another student who participated in that summer camp training experience. Moey composed a drama with music, 'Eureka', very educational in nature and eventually another, 'Inn-trouble', very entertaining, about the family's adventures in inn-keeping. But she was so good with music and so dramatic in her thinking that she eventually found her identity in music, theater and education of young people through the use of creativity.

My eldest son, Oliver, helped me with the Gorski Retrospective. We created the sequences of interrelated canvases during one of his high school science projects. He became friends with Henry Gorski and the three of us had several opportunities to get familiar with the bridging of art and science by interpreting his symbolic language. We also enjoyed a close personal relationship with the artist. Oliver gravitated to being an outdoorsman. He chose to become an organic farmer and leader of a wellness-focused educational farming community.

Eli ("Max") is the youngest of my four children, but the one who has sustained interest in our research project in psychology as his career choice. Max suggested to me the analysis of the Wizard of Oz story. He insisted that we see the movie and read the book. Together we worked on the formal analysis of the metaphors of the story. Max remained interested in the project and conducted two clinical research studies utilizing the two tests of my battery while in grammar and then in high school. The first was the analysis of the plot of stories by utilizing the *Animal Metaphor Test* to identify the formal relation binding feelings in the sequences of associations constituting the totality of the Conflict Resolution Process. The other was the use of my personality inventory, the Relational Modality Evaluation Scale or REMS, to test the inheritance of personality types.

Max has also attended international conferences with me, such as the World Parliament of Religions in Cape Town, South Africa, the Institute of Religion in the Age of Science conference at Star Island, NH, the annual Conflict Resolution Conference in St. Petersburg, Russia, and many others. He befriended my fellow scholars and participated in the delivery of training at the Wilburton, where he conducted guided tours of the exhibits.

Max continued his studies on the subject of psychology and religion at Columbia as an undergraduate, then at Harvard's Divinity School as a graduate student. Being spiritual and interested in conflict resolution as peace, he has spent time in Israel's East and West Banks studying cultures, Islam and Judaism. He and I have collaborated in the completion of this volume.

I wish to thank Kevin Metcalfe, my technical artistic and typesetting associate in this project. For more than two years Kevin and I have worked typesetting this manuscript. Kevin has been helpful, patient and diligent. He has also been involved with the display of the Henry Gorski Retrospective. He has energized the project and has adopted a Gorski canvas, *Kafka I*, as his Facebook identity image. He has sought to do justice not only to the ideas of the Formal Theory but to the art of Henry Gorski.

I also want to thank Mark O. Puryear, who took the initiative to promote the work of Henry Gorski, associated with the promotion of the concepts of the Formal Theory by organizing exhibitions of his artwork. The first exhibit was in Rutland's Chaffee Art Center. It was identified as 'Stealing the Fire of the Gods.' The exhibit in Burlington's 'Arts Alive' space is identified as 'Art as Evidence of Science.'

Editing the manuscript has been my responsibility and I have to apologize to the readers for not completing this job in a timely fashion as I wished to go to press as soon as possible. This critical aspect of the publication will be addressed before going to print with a major publishing house.

TABLE OF CONTENTS

THREE EXHIBITS ILLUSTRATE THE UNIT PROCESS
EXHIBIT #1 THE METAPHORIA MURALS
Six murals demonstrate the formal structure of the Conflict Resolution Process
Review of the first exhibit
1. Three Creation Stories: Revealing the whole and the parts.
2. The Flag of the United Metaphors: Order in the universe of cultural metaphors
3. The Physics of Metaphysics and of Relational Modalities; Religions as natural science phenomena
4. My Metaphors, Myself: Identifying the personal Conflict Resolution Process by utilizing the *Conflict Analysis Battery*.
5. The Evolution of Cultural Metaphors: The integration of religions as the dialectic of discoveries
6. The Scientific Interpretation of Metaphors: From Art to Science
EXHIBIT #2 THE GORSKI RETROSPECTIVE
Deciphering the symbolic language of the unconscious
Six objectives of the exhibit
Making sense of the meaning of life; a joint venture of an artist and a scientist
The unit process as the object and formal analysis as the method for the study of the social sciences
The formal analysis of symbolic languages demonstrates the manifestation of a universal order
Figurative Expressionism

DISCUSSION OF THE EXHIBIT AS THREE TOPICS
TOPIC #1: THE RETROSPECTIVE AS THREE ACTS OF A DRAMA
The Formal Analysis of the Gorski Retrospective
The sequences of conflict resolution
Act one: personal and political quests for meaning
Pain-things, role oppression (RO) and expressing hostility and anger at the untrustworthy authorities, role assumption (RA)
Act two: Eros versus agape
Temptation and anxiety, anticipation of role reversal (ARR) versus defense as the counter-phobic role assumption (CPRA):
Act three: illusions of kisses and the reality of the cross
Accepting the responsibilities of a creator, Role Reversal (RR) and finding peace of mind, Compromise Role Assumption (CRA)
Review of the drama

TOPIC#2: THE PHYSICS AND LOGIC OF THE CRP
Formal Analysis of symbolic languages
Formal distinctions
Identification of the six separate role-states in each thematic period
Organization of the sequences as interrelated into a dramatic lifetime process.
The unconscious thought process as a natural science phenomenon
The physiology of conflict resolution

Symbolic distinctions as formal and physical constructs and formulas
Energetic ideas, cathexis
The ten levels of formal analysis, the Formal Analysis Profile, FAP
Level 1, the formal analysis of symbolic systems:
Level 2-10 the physics of the process: the equivalence between psychological concepts and the constructs and the formulas of physics
Conclusions

TOPIC #3: Three Focus Studies on the function of the CRP
FOCUS STUDY #1: The Healing Function as illustrated by Gorski's evolving self-portrait sequence
FOCUS STUDY #2: The Normative Compliance Function as illustrated by Gorski's religious paintings and his faith-based gender portrayals.
FOCUS STUDY #3: The Norm-Changing Function as illustrated by comparing the works of Gorski and Francis Bacon.
DISCUSSION OF SYMBOLIC DISTINCTIONS
The anthropology of conflict resolution as the evolution of normative para-digms
Science reconciles religions to the scientific understanding of conflict and the determination of norms

EXHIBIT #3 THE WIZARD OF OZ STORY
THE SCIENTIFIC INTERPRETATION OF METAPHORS
The integration of social science disciplines into the Moral Science
The interpretation of four metaphors clarifies the four social sciences:
1. The Yellow Brick Road as the epistemology of patterns.
2. The four characters as psychology's diagnostic categories
3. The killing of the witch as the discipline of psycho-education.
4. The unveiling of Oz as the demystification of religion and morality.

CHAPTER TWO: RELIGION
STEALING THE FIRE OF THE GODS: Religions Integrated as Complementary Discoveries Of The Conflict Resolution Process
THE EVOLVING NATURE OF RELIGIONS
Science integrates religions as partial and complementary discoveries of the process
The Sculptural Trail establishes continuity between religions as the progression to justice and to abstraction
The sculptural exhibit presents science integrating religions into a continuum of moral discoveries ushering in the Moral Science
• Genesis
• Monotheism
• The Ten Commandments
• The four children of the Haggadah ceremony
History and design of the Sculptural Trail

PREFACE

PREPARED BY WWII TO FACE 9/11

I was born in 1937 in Athens, Greece, the second of three sons to a wealthy Jewish family. The big formative influence in my childhood years was experiencing the conflicts of WWII, the Nazi persecution of the Jews, and the cruelties of the Greek Civil War that followed upon the end of the occupation of Greece. My early memories were witnessing Athens in ruins, tragic losses: 96% of the Greek Jewish community perished in gas chambers; my good friend, teacher and father died in 1944, victim of the war years; my loving grandfather was killed by the communists for possessing a British passport.

These early experiences generated in me the need to understand cultural conflicts and the meaning of it all and to eventually intervene as a healer. My keen interest on the subject is reflected in my preoccupations. In 1956 I graduated high school with the prize-winning essay of the class about the history of the Jewish Diaspora. In 1964, upon finishing medical school, I wrote a play, 'The Argives', dramatizing the genocidal War of Troy, as a metaphor for World War II.

While writing this play I came to recognize a pattern that is repeated in the five generations of the Greek Creation story. The periodicity of this pattern impressed me as evidence of a scientific order underlying human behavior. The study of the pattern became the focus of my research during my psychiatric career. I identified it as both a scientific and a moral order or conflict resolving entity. It reflected the unconscious organization of emotions as an adjustment mechanism, but it also had the characteristics of a natural science phenomenon. I identified the pattern as the mental oscillation, an emotional dialectic, present in all samples of creativity, as the plot of stories.

My career as a psychiatrist, clinician, researcher, trainer has been driven by the study of this entity. In 1970 I established a private research and training clinical practice in Hamden, CT, the Center for the Study of Normative Behavior, PC. In 1988 I published two volumes: *Conflict Analysis, the Formal Theory of Behavior, a Theory and its Experimental Validation*, and *Conflict Analysis Training, a Program of Emotional Education.* In my theoretical treatise, *Conflict Analysis, the Formal Theory*, I described this periodic natural science phenomenon as a six-role-state, an emotional dialectic guided by three formal operations. The pattern was the unconscious as a predictable, physiological adjustment response to stress. It was also the unit of the social sciences, which allows us to bridge psychology and moral order with the rigorous sciences, transforming psychology into the Moral Science.

In 1987 aware of the pioneering nature of my formal conceptualization of the unconscious, its validation through the *Conflict Analysis Battery* and its relevance as a concise program of emotional education, I acquired the Wilburton Inn in Manchester, VT. My objective was to deliver from there the training program, *Creativity and Power Management*. I incorporated the Inn as Art to Science Inc., and gradually installed there an art collection to illustrate the scientific and conflict resolving or moral nature of the creative process as a universal phenomenon. The exhibits constitute now the Museum of the Creative Process. The Museum features five permanent "Art as Evidence of Science" exhibits, which clarify the nature of the process.

In 2002 I retired from my Connecticut practice to focus on the delivery of the training program in Vermont fulfilling my mission of establishing an educational resort dedicated to the scientific study of behavior. Since retirement I completed two more volumes: *Science Stealing the Fire of the Gods and Healing the World* consisting of the presentation of the five art exhibits of the Museum of the Creative Process and Moral Science, the *Scientific Interpretation of Metaphors*, consisting of essays about the Formal Theory, and case studies it reports on my clinical work.

These volumes, case studies from my practice and the Inn's exhibits, demonstrate, illustrate and validate the concept of the creative process as the scientific moral paradigm. These publications complete the readiness for the delivery of *Creativity and Power Management* as a standardized program suitable for the classroom and the clinical settings.

The program combines conceptual clarity leading to the integration of knowledge, the humanities: psychology and religion with the sciences; it imparts both enlightenment and personal insights. It addresses the educational mission of the integration of the humanities and the sciences, the delivery of self knowledge and the study of moral values. Accordingly it certainly can serve the college age population providing the core curriculum integrating the humanities and the sciences. It could be effective preparing school age population satisfying their needs for emotional and moral education. As a wellness educational program it should be available for the general public. It has been shown to be effective in the treatment of psychiatric patients providing a clear diagnostic assessment and the method to study therapy outcome.

I refer to the unit process as the *Teleion Holon*, the Perfect Universe, which is Aristotle's concept for the structure of Greek tragedies as scientific and moral totalities. This is the name also of an edifice dedicated to the delivery of the research and training program. It will be the home of the Institute which will manage the ongoing research on the Formal Theory, curate the art exhibits of the Museum of the Creative Process and inform the public with its web site, ArtToScience.org.

The Museum and its function

The challenge for me as a scientist was not only to conduct research but also to convincingly present my findings to the public. I explored conveying my observations on the creative process as the universal, rational and moral order entity, the unit of the social sciences, through the study of art exhibits. The exhibits, like clinical case studies, illustrated the process in its multiple manifestations, bridging art and science.

The art exhibits validate the scientific and moral nature of behavior. This volume illustrates the museum exhibits as studies of the creative process exemplifying the formal interpretation of metaphors into units of the Universal Harmonic. The Harmonic meaningfully connects parts into totalities of conflict resolution in each of the five exhibits. The process binds fragments into units. The exhibits demonstrate clearly the nature of the Creative Process. They confirm the definition of the unconscious as a periodic directional phenomenon, the unit of the social sciences, the scientific integrative moral paradigm.

The first three exhibits deliver information on the science of the process

• The six Metaphoria Murals, each composed of six tiles, impart the impression that the process has a distinct six-part structure with a conflict resolution or moral direction.

• The Henry Gorski Retrospective illustrates the process integrating the disparate canvases of the artist's lifetime into meaningful sequences of conflict resolution, themselves integrated into a three act dramatic totality.

• The 12 panels of the Wizard of Oz tale interpret the four key metaphors of the story: the Yellow Brick Road, the characters walking it, killing the witch and humbling the Wizard. These are presented as metaphors of the alternative manifestations of the unit corresponding to the four disciplines of the social sciences: epistemology, psychology, therapy and morality. Thus the versatile unit is shown to integrate the four disciplines into the Moral Science.

The fourth exhibit pertains to the formal analysis of religions:

• The Sculptural Trail integrates the religions of the world as dialectically connected discoveries of alternative ways of resolving conflict, gradually making us conscious of the unconscious as the abstract and unifying process. The process is the ultimate moral paradigm.

The fifth and last exhibit illustrates the educational program:

• Murals of students and patients' creativity, a collection of standardized metaphors generated with the help of the *Conflict Analysis Battery*, are shown to lead to self discovery; they illustrate how we can identify the personal way of resolving conflict, achieving accurate self assessment and facilitating making optimal adjustments.

The Museum exhibits are not about admirable art; they are about admirable science. Art is not displayed to celebrate artistry with individual aesthetically pleasing statements. Art is presented holistically as sequences of formal transformations to establish the Conflict Resolution mechanism occurring in the mind of the artist as well as in the mind of the observer.

The exhibits identify the mental process as the perfect, or scientific, foundation of psychological and moral order. They bind reason and moral order, integrating religion and psychology, the humanities and the sciences into the Moral Science. The Harmonic becomes established as the unit order of the Moral Science. The Museum exhibits illustrate and validate the thesis advanced in Conflict Analysis the Formal Theory: the unconscious mind proceeds predictably along the suggested path of an emotional dialectic to conflict resolution that is moral order, a natural science phenomenon totally independent of religions.

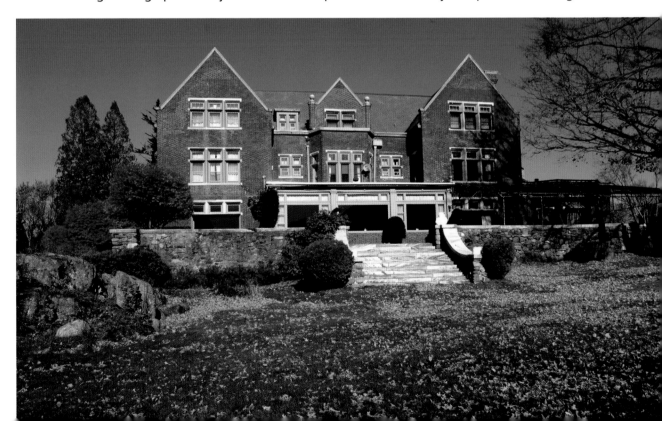

THE SCOPE OF THE BOOK: RELIGION VERSUS SCIENCE

The discovery of the scientific moral paradigm
This volume is the sequel of *Conflict Analysis, the Formal Theory of Behavior*. The Formal Theory advanced that behavior is the study of a physical entity with a moral outcome. The physical structure of the process consists of six emotions, in formal relation to each other, progressing predictably along three formal operations from a conflict to its resolution. This process reflecting the organization of ideas in any sample of creativity, a circumscribed entity, has been conceptualized using the physics of the pendulum and the logic and math of the equilibrial trays of a scale. This entity has been identified as formally interrelated emotions with natural science measurable dimensions having a conflict resolution or moral function and adjustive outcome.

A new way of looking at art validates the formal theoretical thesis, the science of moral order
The Formal Theory and its experimental validation utilizing an assessment battery have been articulated in the first two volumes of the Normative Publications. They validated the process merely as a scientific phenomenon, not as a moral order one. The task of this volume is to validate Formal Theory's assumption that the unconscious is a conflict resolving, hence moral and natural science entity. The validation is delivered by examining the formal organization of the symbolic representation of emotions by viewing art exhibits. Beyond just validating the science the exhibits validate the Moral Science. They establish that morality is generated by the unconscious and not by religious revelation. This volume introduces art exhibits as evidence of the underlying scientifically established moral order.

The art exhibits demonstrate the universality of the unit Conflict Resolution Process as the holistic way of looking at art and the scientific way of looking at behavior. With some help the visitor of the exhibits detects this emotional dialectic spontaneously resolving conflicts underlying all samples of creativity; we know the dialectic as the plot of stories, also as the creative process. Now these familiar concepts are interpreted as a natural science emotional dialectic represented by a sine curve, the Universal Harmonic, the ultimate manifestation of a natural science based moral order. The exhibits explore the method of formal analysis by identifying the process and thus validating the theory. The process is present in all samples of creativity. We may conclude that the unit order is the motivational force driving all behavior in the pursuit of conflict resolution/moral order as the quest for personal adjustment, for meaning, and social justice.

This book is an unusual art book. It is not about fine arts. It is about the new way of looking at art reconciling art and science, psychology and morality by identifying the unconscious as a conflict resolving or homeostatic adaptational entity. The five art exhibits of the Museum of the Creative Process illustrate the holistic way of looking at art by detecting the Conflict Resolution Process integrating emotions as parts into conflict resolution totalities.

The totalities are graphically portrayed as a sine curve, the Universal six-role-state Harmonic. By identifying the postulated process as the harmonic in all exhibits, the exhibits confirm the unconscious organization of emotions as the six-role state dialectic process, the scientific unit of moral order. The point being established here is that moral order is a natural science phenomenon independent of religions. One of the exhibits emphasizes in particular that the religions of the world pioneered insights in the scientific phenomenon and science is coming to complete their mission by identifying the perfect nature of the unconscious conflict resolving mechanism.

Moral reason redefines meaning and the pursuit of justice as a physiological natural science entity. Moral reason amounts to the six role state dialectic organizing emotions as predictably transformed from chaos to order, the moral direction of compromise through change of attitude, social change, justice, and catharsis. All thoughts, all social sciences, all aspects of psychology and religion may be interpreted as measurable natural science units of conflict resolution.

The new concept represents a paradigm shift in the social sciences. Methodologically it represents a shift from propositional logic to relational logic by considering the interrelation of items within a totality. (See the volume of the Formal Theory and Joshua Royce.) Phenomenologically the shift presents a change from the many stories we believe in that divide the public, to identify the nature of what is universal in all stories, the plot of stories, as a scientific meaningful and measurable phenomenon. This orderly universal process is the unconscious having a distinct structure, the formal organization of emotions and the distinct function of resolving conflicts, a natural science moral task. This entity besides conforming to relational logic principles is shown to abide by the laws of the two equilibrial periodic phenomena of physics: the pendulum oscillation and the balance of the trays of a scale.

The exhibits demonstrating the universal manifestation of the unit order confirm the correctness of the formal thesis. They confirm the unit order organizing the chaotic field of behavior and religion and establish this order as stemming from the unconscious, organizing meaningfully and logically emotions in all samples of creativity. The mental unit order is like a magnet redirecting random associations like shards of metal around its magnetic polarity making visible the power field as a system with a beginning, middle and a moral north, its end.

The validations of the Formal Theory confirm it as the Moral Science. The exhibits demonstrate that morality is a natural science phenomenon totally independent of religions. Morality is shown to originate in the psychological conflict-resolving unconscious as a process that abides by the laws of the rigorous sciences. It is the unit and the measuring rod of the social sciences. It transforms emotions, diagnostic categories, religions, gods, any story into quantifiable, graphically portrayable purely natural science phenomena.

The clear manifestation of this elusive order is a development of pivotal importance in the history of science and religion. The exhibits demonstrate the object for the study of behavior, the circumscribed emotional transformative dialectic of the process and the formal analysis of emotions as the method for its study. The art exhibits validate the concept of the unconscious as a predictable natural science phenomenon that is both physically structured and morally directed. Moral Science reconciles the humanities psychology and religion and the rigorous sciences. Hence this publication represents a major scientific breakthrough ushering in the era of moral reason, of the moral psychology.

The process, a periodic phenomenon, becomes the Unit of the Social Sciences, the common denominator of all samples of creativity. The Unit Process complies with rigorous scientific laws, clarifies personality diagnostic categories as alternative ways of resolving conflict, which can be measured with a new assessment technology; the formal principles provide clarity on how to optimally resolve conflict as the science-based moral values. This unconscious process becomes the atomistic unit of the social sciences. This Unit moral order integrates the social sciences into the exact Moral Science.

My reward, meaning and service
The process is the unit entity integrating moral order and psychology into a natural science moral order-creating phenomenon. With the validation of the discovery of moral order as a

natural science phenomenon originating in the unconscious as the adjustment response to stress my quest for meaning of my childhood years has come to a happy conclusion. This mechanical and moral physiological homeostatic process explains the origin of all moral order and provides the world objectivity on the scientific nature of religions.

A process of research that began in my childhood WWII years has led to insights on the nature of behavior that are timely to deal with the developments of the post Cold War-era identified with the events of 9/11. Religion-based prejudice and conflicts scarred my childhood and have continued into my retirement years. I know that my research can contribute new insights into understanding what is happening to individual and cultural psychology. Science finally makes us aware of our psychological nature of social adjustment, freeing us from clinging to dated explanations. A scientific paradigm provides insights into the nature of religious paradigms, which have not evolved since the times of Abraham. They still determine the norms defended by the clergy structuring our domestic relations. Science allows us to become objective on the nature of the moral thought process underlying our beliefs. Science commands the ultimate moral order as optimal power management beyond our glorious epics and scriptures.

Science introduces clarity, objectivity, and consensus on moral matters. The new Moral Science delivers the enlightenment necessary to rise beyond the wars of genders and the wars of faith. It provides us with evidence on the nature of moral order. Science makes it easier to settle our differences, domestic and religious conflicts, and our personal and cultural dilemmas. The new concepts integrate religion and psychology with science. They lead the public to enjoy creativity as both entertaining and healing, both as spirituality and as science; the concepts deliver the scientific secrets of "living happily ever after."

A Simple Demonstration of the Process
Albert Levis, a case study, Mural #4 (pp. 82-83), 'My Metaphors, Myself" a sample formal analysis validating the process while delivering self-discovery
By now you know my case study as a person affected by certain childhood experiences dedicating his career to conducting research pursuing a general synthesis. Well you can see how my metaphors, generated with the *Conflict Analysis Battery* help us to understand my emotions integrated by metaphors into a logical but also moral/dramatic conflict resolution sequence validating the theory. 'My Metaphors Myself' is a mural, the fourth out of twelve displayed in the Sanctuary, validating the unit process.

The method of this validation experiment proceeds first with the creation of diverse exercises completed independently of each other following the instructions in the workbook of the Formal Theory. The next phase is inserting the images/metaphors into the six-role-state Conflict Resolution Process template integrating the tests as the personal dialectic of emotions into a dramatic totality. Is the ensuing sequence relationally validating the premise?

The preface has introduced my story/case study and I am pleased with how the images reflect the interrelation of my emotions. The sequence corresponds to my development from my childhood to the present. The mural shows how my metaphors reconstruct my drama as a three-act play and sum up my life's pattern. The reader too knowing my life's story can appreciate how the metaphors capture the conflict resolution pattern in a minimalist fashion.

This mural illustrates how the Conflict Resolution Process integrates the metaphors generated with the help of the workbook. Six tests, as six illustrated metaphors, are interrelated as the six emotions or role states on the suggested Conflict Resolution template. The six role states/emotions:

stress, response, anxiety, defense, reversal and compromise are captured by particular exercises and are in the predicted formal relation to each other. Together the images provide continuity reconstructing the personal dramatic sequence of emotions accurately reflecting the personal story as a conflict resolution or drama.

Each role state is illustrated with a metaphor capturing the role related emotion.
Stress, depicting a Conflictual Memory from my Childhood, presents my family hiding from the war of metaphors, symbolized as the war between ideologies and religions of WWII.
My response, portrayed by the *Mask Test*, presents my identity as that of a Pinocchio, the wooden puppet, whose nose grows as he lies. The puppet is persecuted by the whale of cultural metaphors. I recall lying about my name, hiding my Jewish identity, identifying my self as Nikolas Theologopoulos to protect myself from deportation.

My anxiety role state, my emotional state, identified by the Behind the Transparent Mask, presents my Pinocchio in the stomach of that whale, my being swallowed in the world of metaphors, talking to the father figure, Geppetto, the carpenter, the creator of the puppet. The wooden puppet tells its creator that he knows the secret to becoming a real child by freeing himself from the strings that manipulate him as a puppet, by using the formal interpretation of metaphors.

The defense role state, identified by the *Animal Metaphor Test*, presents Oedipus solving the riddle of the Sphinx, offering her the branch of an olive tree and stating: 'I know the answer to your riddle but please don't jump off the cliff. Let us be partners.' Getting along with a "sphinx" allows this version of Oedipus to enjoy an equitable, respectful relation with women, guaranteeing a good domestic partnership.

My role reversal image, generated by the Dream

Metaphor Test, portrays the Levis family offering hospitality to the guests of the Wilburton Inn. This is my dream coming true as I am introducing to the public the wisdom of the scientific interpretation of metaphors exemplified by a family that collaborates.

The final image of the mural illustrates my compromise role generated by the Short Story Metaphor Test, as the reconciliation of art and science presented metaphorically as the Judaic fiddler on the roof of a Greek temple. The image is surrounded by the flags of the nations of the world waving in the same direction reflecting symbolically peace in the world as the reconciliation of all cultural metaphors. The image of the fiddler on the roof, the reconciliation of faith and reason refers to the reconciliation of my two identities, my Judaic passion for justice and my Grecian arrogance of using reason to explain everything.

The images integrated into a dramatic totality present the adventures of a child who does not want to be a puppet and who finds the way to be truly a rationally thinking caring human.

Act one: The trauma/stress of the war of metaphors and my response as a Pinocchio, a puppet who wants to be a human child running away from the killer whale of metaphors.
Act two: the child's anxiety/hope for meaning in the context of the scientific paradigm leads to the defense as solving the riddle of the Sphinx by responding with cooperation and respect of partners.
Act three: The reversal or outcome of the adventure, a family can function together, here delivering hospitality.
The compromise, presents my philosophy: a fiddler on the roof of a Greek temple, celebrating the reconciliation of faith and reason, my two cultural identities but also reconciling the flags/paradigms/cultural metaphors of all nations.

Ultimate validation
The metaphors of the mural demonstrate the Conflict Resolution Process as the key interrelation between the inception of the story and its conclusion as a conflict resolution. The Stress role state represents the conflict of the War of Metaphors defined as passivity, antagonism and alienation. The Compromise role state should represent the resolution state defined as mastery, cooperation and mutual respect. Well, if we examine the two role states in this mural we may enjoy the thrill of a validation and affirmation of the theoretical assumption as a prophetic statement. The stress state describing the 'War of Metaphors' is completed with the Compromise role state as the resolution of the conflict between metaphors, art and science, the paradigms of nations. Indeed, It represents the reconciliation of the scientific and cultural paradigms as the wreath/halo around the structure of the sanctuary.

Hence, the mural clarifies the dialectic of my emotions, while validating the theory. The mural/drama illustrates a conflict resolution; the war of metaphors finds its resolution in the reconciliation of metaphors validating the formal method of interpreting the process. This is the pattern that has motivated me and determined my behaviors, my quest for meaning. The mural also illustrates the analytical technology and the moral unconscious. This mural then reflects my sense of completing my life's work with this set of books introducing the scientific theory of behavior as the Moral Science, integrating psychology and moral order with science.

Art/the creative process in this sample is instrumental in validating science, the underlying predictable formal relational pattern of a set of emotions. The speed of validation of science combined with the generation of personal insights exemplifies the effectiveness of the emotional moral education program based on tapping creativity for self-discovery and for integration of knowledge.

DEMYSTIFYING RELIGION BY FORMALIZING THE UNCONSCIOUS

Historically religions and science have been locked into a struggle of incompatible alternatives, faith versus reason. The Formal Theory cancels this dichotomy by recognizing that faith is reason since religions constitute complementary quasi-scientific solutions of conflict resolution. The formal thesis claims that conflict resolution is manifested in all samples of creativity, stories or metaphors, as the distinct organization of emotions as formally interrelated symbolic transformations, hence religions can be understood as conflict resolutions.

The new science reduces stories, including religions, to what is universal in all stories, their plot, and identifies the plot of stories as the measurable and graphically portrayable formal transformations of the Conflict Resolution Process. It integrates psychology with morality and reconciles the two with the rigorous sciences, physics and math, excluding religion from this equation. According to the Formal Theory religions are forerunners of the exact Science of Conflict Resolution, the Moral Science, but they are metaphorical explanations of the process.

The Moral Science shifts focus from the concrete stories people believe in, like idol-worshipers, to what is universal in all stories, the plot of stories, as the abstract scientific moral paradigm, the unit of the Conflict Resolution Process, the calculus of power management. This paradigm reconciles morality and reason. It allows using one's thinking to understand one's emotions and relational choices and consequences, the calculus of power management; this approach to moral order amounts to respecting moral order as science, while emancipating humanity from religions and their divisive concrete moral paradigms.

Religions have discovered the unconscious process, but have mystified it and deified it. The Moral Science demystifies the process as a natural science energetic phenomenon abiding by the laws of the rigorous sciences. The process is reduced to the calculus of power management, and this calculus is a set of simple formulas. The unit has a clear psychological and physiological function. The unconscious resolves conflicts following a roller-coaster six-part emotional sequence. It is an equilibrial mechanism processing stressors and sustaining one's emotional balance, the status quo, the rest state, by processing stress-energy and thus improving emotional stability and social adjustment.

The Moral Science implies quantification, measurement and the existence of units and measuring rods for moral order. Religions are measurable natural science phenomena. The new science has a measurable unit entity, the Conflict Resolution Process; it also has a measuring rod, the unit process applied to circumscribed samples of the person's creative process utilizing a self-assessment instrument, the *Conflict Analysis Battery*. The unconscious is the moral mental heartbeat and the Battery is science's stethoscope.

The Nature of the Unconscious

The unconscious has a clear function. It helps the individual to reduce differences between oneself and one's normative community. Conflict resolution defines moral order as the transformation of social and emotional chaos or power differentials to order; it transforms injustice to justice, emotions as stressors, be that guilt and or hostility and resentment to compromise, peace. The process assists the individual to modify conflict incurring personal attitudes but it also addresses rectifying societal injustice.

The unconscious is then the mediator managing relations between the individual and his environment. It is a moral sociological psychological physiological mechanism, an equilibrial homeostatic process, but also an orderly scientific entity and the origin of all morality and of all social change.

The Moral Science regards religions as partial discoveries of this unconscious process. They establish conflict resolutions as societal norms sanctified by the deified unknown. They evolved along the history of civilization as a progression of discoveries of conflict resolution improving domestic relations. They have also evolved in their redefinitions of the metaphysical divine; gradually gods have been reduced to a single force and then into a transformational process.

We end up therefore having religions progressing toward justice in domestic relations and toward abstraction of the deified underlying mechanism; hence religions have been progressing spontaneously toward science. The Formal Theory goes a step beyond by formalizing the process and by identifying conflict resolution as the calculus of power management. Religions represent solutions of the calculus for distinct values of the formulas' variables. The new theory delivers the successful completion of the universal mission of religions.

Of significance in this final conceptual position is that morality is based on science and physiology but not on dogma, theistic revelation. Morality is then independent of religious dogma and implicit to the physiology and psychology of the unconscious. Religions represent bad science, but they are good attempts at science surpassing in their insights 20th century's science of psychology.

The unconscious Conflict Resolution Process is then the natural science moral order entity, the scientific moral paradigm as the unit of the social sciences. Religions will be respected as pioneers of the Science of Conflict Resolution, as discoveries of alternative and complementary ways of resolving conflict by using metaphors, parables, and mythic explanations. Religions as metaphors or stories are now interpreted into natural science measurable phenomena by analyzing the formal structure of emotions in stories. What is significant in the study of religions is that through formal analysis they are integrated among themselves and reconciled with science and psychology.

One exhibit, the Sculptural Trail in the History of Love, examines the history of religions as an evolutionary continuum completed by religions ushering in the Moral Science, the Science of Conflict Resolution. Science explains the inner need for an emotional equilibrium and the outer constraints of normative standards also as a relational order. The inner dialectic resolves emotional conflicts but also addresses cultural ones. The resolutions target incremental differentiation in personal integrity and in interpersonal justice. The psychic and the social phenomena are understood through the same scientific constructs and formulas.

The Moral Science completes the trend to abstraction and puts an end to religions' self-righteousness, their claims as the absolute moral authorities. Traditionally religion has ended where science begins, i.e. the Darwinian scientists pronounced God dead or recognized him as a delusion. The Moral Science objects to this summary dismissal of religions and gods. The Moral Science respects religions but continues their explorations. Science begins where religions culminate in their historical evolution to identify meaning. Science begins where religions give up in finding meaning metaphorically. Physics deciphers metaphors and metaphysics. Science clarifies justice in norms in the area of domestic relations, and clarifies abstraction on the nature of the unconscious process.

The Formal Theory respects religions as forerunners of science, but demystifies them as metaphors, as particular discoveries of the scientific nature of the process; it integrates them into a continuum of resolutions as evolving norms promoting increased fairness in domestic relations and increased abstraction in the attributes of the divine. The theory disrespects religions' arbitrariness in establishing norms and in deifying the process. Their norms are unjust and immoral, and their definitions of the divine are incorrect and concrete. Science retains for itself the role of the ultimate moral authority. It defends a standard and from there it can and must scrutinize religions, demystify and dedeify the simplistic understanding of the complexities of the human unconscious. Science has as its objective the rational definition of moral order and the merger of morality with psychology and science.

Science ends the confusion on norms and gods. It integrates religions as measurable conflict resolutions constituting a progression to fairness and abstraction finally reaching the desirable level of justice and science; here we find clarity in the nature of justice and the formal nature of the creative process. Science identifies the optimal way, the fairest way of resolving conflicts and the most abstract way of defining the nature of god as the unconscious process.

The exhibits of the Museum of the Creative Process demonstrate the unconscious moral mechanism organizing emotions along the predictable dialectic, which defines both the nature of justice in relations and the abstract nature of the process. Science then advances from metaphors, or stories, art, to pure abstractions, constructs and formulas. It addresses religions as the era of metaphors ushering in Moral Science as the era of the formal interpretation of metaphors.

The validations attest to the manifestation of moral order as the universal dialectic organizing emotions in all samples of creativity. The search for God ends with the discovery of the formulas underlying human thought. The Conflict Resolution Process explains the wisdom anthropomorphized as God to correspond to a set of formulas transforming chaos to order, entropy to negative entropy, responsible for the predictability of insight, enlightenment, wisdom and civilization.

The Moral Science therefore puts a happy end to humanity's search for meaning. Meaning is about the Universal Harmonic, the unconscious as a conflict resolution mechanism improving conceptual clarity on the nature of social and mental order. The research concludes that psychology is an exact science featuring the following:
• Behavior abides by the purely rigorous epistemology using scientific constructs and formulas from the realms of physics and logic;
• The constructs allow formal distinctions, which help to identify a new set of diagnostic categories, the syndromal relational modalities.
• The measuring rod of behavior is an assessment instrument combining a theory-based personality inventory with a set of projective techniques.
• The theory clarifies moral values as the scientific principles of conflict resolution. Finally
• Science is the foundation for a well-developed concise and comprehensive emotional and moral educational program that may be used in therapy and also as a training program in the classroom.

Science challenges religion and psychology
Moral Science is presented as a fully articulated and validated package of theoretical information, with applications, testimonials and validations ready for clinical and educational implementation. It is a bold statement of a well argued and defended conceptual position challenging simultaneously psychology and religion, academia and spiritual traditions, seeking to put an end to the mighty schools of agnostic psychology and the sacrosanct moralistic belief systems.

The sudden occurrence of a challenger of academic authorities and powerful religions reminds us of the birth of the fully developed Athena from Zeus's head. The release of a fully articulated Moral Science is like the birth of the wise warrior who sprang from Zeus's head ready to stand her ground armed with a helmet, shield and javelin to defend the city of fairness and wisdom from abusive authorities like Zeus, the aggressive and paranoid chief of the Olympians.

The news about the Moral Science might sound apocalyptic, stunning, and unabashedly arrogant. But the theory was not born with capricious intent or pretentious attitude. Behind this sudden overwhelming pronouncement rests the suffering of humanity subject to endless strife between religions and a dose of personal suffering caused by the religious strife of the Holocaust; then the theory was not born overnight. The process of gestation has been my lifetime of research and clinical work, of hypotheses and testing, conducted with self-restraint in communicating findings prematurely or in a fragmented fashion. I have worked methodically on these concepts, and techniques for the last forty years pursuing my intuitions to their formulation, validation, illustration and integration.

The Moral Science began with the observation of patterns, the study of method in their analysis, the development of testing instruments for the experimental validation of hypotheses, the clinical testing of the theory, and the illustration of the concept through art exhibits. The work was self-published as the textbook: *Conflict Analysis, the Formal Theory of Behavior* and the workbook: *Conflict Analysis Training*, containing the complete personality assessment battery in 1988. Those publications are followed presently, 23 years later with two books corroborating evidence validating the theory; the current book contains information on the art exhibits of the Museum of the Creative Process, the next volume '*Moral Science, the Scientific Interpretation of Metaphors*' reports on clinical case studies.

The delay in communication of the progression of findings has allowed the development of the moral theory to its validations into a science. The information, applications, explanations and educational techniques have matured. The entire theory now has reached the critical mass to be shared as the full body of knowledge, a well-reasoned argument. This research work has the potential of becoming the definitive science of behavior.

The set of publications theory and testing, exhibits and case studies, represents a cohesive development departing from the observation of patterns that repeat to the postulation of a unit conflict resolving structure with a moral function that is measurable. The Moral Science embraces psychology and moral order bound in this single entity.

The set of four volumes coming suddenly to the attention of the public reminds not only of the birth of Athena from Zeus's head but also of the Promethean challenge to the moral leadership of Zeus. Prometheus stole the fire of the gods to give it to the mortals. This myth corroborates the struggle between religion and science in the service of humanity. The birth of Athena is a metaphor of the birth of wisdom or insight departing from religion's head. The deed of Prometheus and the birth of Athena connect science and religion as adversaries who yet are interrelated. They remind us of Science's double affront to the ruling moral normative authorities. The Olympian Gods are apt metaphors of the authoritarian and cruel rule of religions and of associated political and academic authorities defending partial insights and dated moral paradigms.

The Moral Science represents a rebellion against the cruel and paranoid moral authorities resisting change; it seeks justice as the reformation of concepts and norms. The new science, the child of the Gods, is the challenger of the Gods and of the authorities in the social sciences. The metaphors concur that mortals may fight the Gods for their rights. The Formal Theory though respectful seeks to emancipate the humans from dictatorial religious and academic institutions. Moral Science is committed to struggle with religions and academia in order for the truth to prevail. It is not easy to free humanity from the reign of uninterpreted metaphors revered and worshiped as truths, as faiths, as idols, usurping humans' capacity to reason.

Words spoken are symbols or signs (symbola) of affections or impressions (pathemata) of the soul (psyche); written words are the signs of words spoken.

As writing, so also is speech not the same for all races of men. But the mental affections themselves, of which these words are primarily signs (semeia), are the same for the whole of mankind, as are also the objects (pragmata) of which those affections are representations or likenesses, images, copies (homoiomata).—Aristotle, On Interpretation, 1.16a4 (Wikpedia, Hermeneutics, 2011)

2. HEIDEGGER In The Origin of the Work of Art, Heidegger explains the essence of art in terms of the concepts of being and truth. He argues that art is not only a way of expressing the element of truth in a culture, but the means of creating it and providing a springboard from which "that which is" can be revealed. Works of art are not merely representations of the way things are, but actually produce a community's shared understanding. Each time a new artwork is added to any culture, the meaning of what it is to exist is inherently changed.

Heidegger begins his essay with the question of what the source of a work of art is. The artwork and the artist, he explains, exist in a dynamic where each appears to be a provider of the other. "Neither is without the other. Nevertheless, neither is the sole support of the other."[1] Art, a concept separate from both work and creator, thus exists as the source for them both. Rather than control lying with the artist, art becomes a force that uses the creator for art's own purposes. Likewise, the resulting work must be considered in the context of the world in which it exists, not that of its artist.[2] In discovering the essence, however, the problem of the hermeneutic circle arises. In sum, the hermeneutic circle raises the paradox that, in any work, without understanding the whole, you can't fully comprehend the individual parts, but without understanding the parts, you cannot comprehend the whole. (Wikipedia, Heidegger, 2011)

THE METAPHOR OF PROMETHEUS
SCIENCE AS PROCESS CHALLENGING RELIGION AS THE CONTENT OF MANY STORIES

Two metaphors introduce the significance of this set of books: 'the key that unlocks all doors' versus the 'myth of Prometheus.' Metaphors are useful in conveying parallel complex phenomena with simpler, familiar and more meaningful alternatives. I present here two metaphors to convey the significance of this research communication with the simplicity of familiar notions.

The first metaphor: The process as 'the Master Key to Knowledge', a metaphor that introduces the notion of science into the study of behavior.
The first metaphor presents the Formal Theory identifying the unit of the Conflict Resolution Process as the master key to knowledge; the process unlocks the secrets of all the social sciences, moral and psychological realms. The master key is the scientific unit of the social sciences integrating them into the Moral Science. This concept makes clear the secrets to living happily ever after. It is the unit order that explains epistemology, psychology of development and personality types, assessment and self-knowledge, wisdom and insights. Moral values are the scientific principles of moral order.

The metaphor of the master key to knowledge defines the process as the unit order, the integrative paradigm reconciling art and science, also psychology and religion into the Moral Science. It is Aristotle's Teleion Holon, the secret order of the Perfect Universe. It is the process as the measuring rod for wisdom. We can understand God and integrate the religions of the world into one easy-to-understand universal order.

The second metaphor: The myth of Prometheus addresses the relevance of the Moral Science.
The metaphor of Prometheus alludes to the antagonistic relationship between science and religion. I am introducing the Promethean myth, the struggle between a caring hero and an uncompromising

cruel Zeus to illustrate the struggle that science has to fight to undertake the rethinking of religions as well as of psychology for the benefit of the public. The Prometheus story and that of the Moral Science is about the drama of a paradigm shift struggling with the cultural institutions resisting innovation. Though the many religions are contradicting each other and fighting perennial wars with each other humanity views them as sacred. They are all protected constitutionally as the ultimate freedom of faith but also by a convention, Political Correctness.

The evidence of science is conveyed in the art exhibits of the Museum of the Creative Process. These illustrate and validate the postulation that morality is a physiological homeostatic and unconscious conflict resolution natural science phenomenon. This evidence is compounded with statistical analysis of data generated from an assessment battery: the relational modalities evaluation scale and of the metaphor projective tests.

Science places morality and psychology on the same scientific foundation. It shows that religions are pure natural science phenomena. We no longer need revelation, dogma to account for moral order. Science frees humanity from the mystique of religions as dated social contracts; it frees us from the contradictory injunctions generating more conflicts than harmony in our globalized society. We no longer need to subject ourselves to religions' normative regulations of behavior to achieve social conformity and civilization. Contradicting the powers of the day science addresses religions as measurable and predictable natural science phenomena.

Stealing the Fire of the Gods is about formulas demystifying religion and demonstrating that moral order stems from the unconscious as the process, the Universal Harmonic that organizes our emotions and behaviors meaningfully and adaptively. Moral Science like Prometheus steals the fire, religions' privilege of righteousness and immunity to criticism. Science by demonstrating that the underlying moral order is a physiological homeostatic mechanism that has natural science dimension, substitutes metaphysics and makes religions vulnerable to analysis and criticism. Religions are normative structurings of roles and power in systems.

By revamping the conceptualization of the unconscious as both a natural and a moral phenomenon the process can help to avert religious and philosophical wars by establishing moral consensus. Science based consensus grants and guarantees freedom from conflict. Conceptual correctness replaces political correctness, dogma and metaphysics.

While the 'master key metaphor' simply informs on the power of science without considering its impact and relevance for religion and morality, the Promethean story dramatizes the conflict between religion and science. The metaphor of the master key does not clarify the underlying power struggle between gods and mortals.

It is important to recognize the nuance between the master key and the notion of science stealing the fire, the two metaphors of the process, to appreciate the relevance of this book for our times of confusion on moral values. The Promethean fire is not a metaphor of the CRP concept, but of the power struggle for knowledge, justice, survival, warmth, food, sexuality and creativity, which characterizes the attempt of science to replace the uncaring egocentric territorial imperialistic religions. Science is pertinent to the current politics of religion as humans need to redefine morality to free the mortals from religions' dictatorial jurisdiction.

Prometheus' background: Three brothers as the anthropomorphized dialectic process: Prometheus, Epimetheus, and Atlas, (Forethought, Afterthought, and the totality of a myth as the wisdom of symbolic universes).

Prometheus was one of the Titans, a family of giants in Greek mythology, who ruled the earth until overthrown by Chronos' children, the Olympians. Prometheus ("forethought") was the son of the Titan Iapetus and of either the sea nymph Cly-

mene or the goddess Themis. Epimetheus ("afterthought") and Atlas were his brothers; Hesione, daughter of the Titan Oceanus, was his wife. Prometheus was considered the wisest of his race; he was credited with the creation of humans and with giving them fire, food and various types of skills and knowledge.

Wikipedia on Prometheus
Prometheus was the champion of the underprivileged and the protector of humankind
1. When Zeus and the other Olympian gods rebelled against the Titans, Prometheus sided with the gods and thus won their favor. Prometheus played a decisive role in the Titanomachy, securing victory for Zeus and the other Olympians. He later held Zeus' aching head so that Hephaestus (Vulcan) could split it open and release the goddess Athena. To show her gratitude, Athena taught Prometheus astronomy, mathematics, architecture, navigation, metalwork, writing, and other useful skills. He later passed this knowledge on to humans.
2. Prometheus is alleged to have created humans by shaping lumps of clay into small figures resembling the gods. Athena admired these figures and breathed on them, giving them life. Zeus disliked the creatures, but he could to uncreate them. He did, however, confine them to the earth and denied them immortality.
3. Prometheus was given the task of determining how sacrifices were to be made to the gods. He cut up a bull and divided it into two portions. One contained the animal's flesh and skin, but these were concealed beneath the bull's stomach, the least appetizing part of the animal. The other consisted of the bones, wrapped in a rich layer of fat. Prometheus then asked Zeus to choose a portion for himself, leaving the other for humans. Fooled by the outward appearance of the portions, Zeus chose the one containing the bones and fat. Prometheus thus ensured that humans got the best choice. Angered by this trick, Zeus punished humans by withholding fire from them so that they would have to live in cold and darkness and eat meat raw.

4. Prometheus, a wise craftsman, felt sorry for humans, so he taught them various arts and skills including navigation, writing, and architecture and gave them fire. Prometheus promptly went to Olympus, stole a spark of fire from Hephaestus, and carried it back to humans.
5. Zeus discovered what Prometheus had done and punished him by chaining the god to a rock on a mountain peak. Every day an eagle tore at Prometheus' body and ate his liver, and every night the liver grew back. Because Prometheus was immortal, he could not die, but he suffered endlessly.
6. Prometheus remained chained and in agony for thousands of years. The other gods begged Zeus to show mercy, but he refused. Finally, Zeus offered Prometheus freedom if he would reveal a secret that only he knew. Prometheus told Zeus that the sea nymph Thetis would bear a son who would become greater than his father. This was important information. Zeus, who desired Thetis, arranged for her to marry a mortal.
7. Zeus sent Hercules to shoot the eagle that tormented Prometheus and to break the chains that bound him.
8. Zeus ordered Hephaestus to create a woman from clay, and he had the winds breathe life into her. This woman was Pandora. He sent her as a gift to Prometheus' brother Epimetheus, who married her despite warnings from Prometheus not to accept any gift from Zeus. Pandora brought with her a box containing good and evil. When Pandora opened the box, she released sorrows into the world and Zeus thus gained his revenge on humankind. Aeschylus includes information about Pandora's box as containing hope, associated with Prometheus inspiring hopes to live in the hearts of men.
9. Aeschylus composed a trilogy on the myth of Prometheus. He introduced the drama of this evolving relationship between Prometheus and Zeus in the trilogy of Prometheus Bound, Prometheus Unbound and Prometheus the Fire-Giver.
Trilogies are compounded conflict resolutions.
(Wikipedia, Prometheus, 2010)

Three partial conflict resolutions in each of the three dramas coalesce into a higher order resolution. Here we see the protagonists Prometheus and Zeus reconciled. Our book is a trilogy as well. Its three chapters use the myth as the metaphor for the struggle between science and religion, leading to their reconciliation and integration into the Moral Science.

• This book begins with Prometheus Bound. In this tragedy Prometheus becomes the benefactor of humanity, while every character in the drama decries the Olympian as a cruel, vicious tyrant. Prometheus asserts that Zeus had wanted to obliterate the human race, but that he stopped him. The first chapter is about science, information about the unit process.
• Fragmentary evidence indicates that Heracles, as in Hesiod, frees the Titan in the trilogy's second play, Prometheus Unbound. In our second chapter we talk about how science integrates religions and completes their task of attaining happiness as conflict resolution.
• It is apparently not until Prometheus reveals the secret of Zeus' potential downfall that the two reconcile in the final play, Prometheus the Fire-Bringer. In the third chapter we talk about education, the program of Creativity and Power Management.

The traits of a hero, the features of a scientific moral process
1. Prometheus wrestled with gods to prevail in favor of the young and deprived. He consistently protected the next generation from abusive parental authorities. This choice was opposing the Greek gods who were antagonistic to their offspring, killing or oppressing children. First he was protective of the Olympians from their cruel Titan parents. He fought the Titans to protect Zeus during the Titanomachy. Then he is portrayed as the creator of humans from clay.
2. He created the humans and gave them food, wisdom, crafts and education and finally fire. He stole the fire from the Olympians who were interested in the undoing of the humans.

3. He favored humans over the Olympians securing food from them by fooling the gods with deceptive offering.
4. Prometheus suffered the ultimate torture of being attacked nightly by an eagle, a punishment earned for selflessly procuring the fire of the gods for the mortals.
5. Then he endured with his brother Epimetheus the woman named Pandora; she is her box, the blessings and curses of a domestic partner with the hope for love versus the potential of many conflicts. Hope as conflict resolutions and love prevailing in the relationship is the challenge to Prometheus and to science.

Prometheus' profile describes the positive attitude of the process that spontaneously resolves conflict. It has the features of caring and wrestling for a good cause. It pertains to the evolution of a paradigm shift in the Greek culture from the original antagonistic paranoid relationships characterizing the Cosmogony to one of cooperation and respect. The names Prometheus (forethought) and Epimetheus (afterthought) reveal that the story of this hero is about self-awareness that is wisdom on the nature of relations. Atlas is about the symbolic universe of a story, the mythos. We may therefore equate the three brothers with the dialectic of science, informing gods on negative predictable patterns in need of reform.

In the conflict between Prometheus and the Olympians we detect a metaphor about the struggle between science and religion. Here we have a struggle for normative transformation. Thus, in his role in favor of the humans and his struggles with gods, Prometheus is like the Judaic hero, Israel, "the one who wrestles with God," and in his suffering a daily torture he is a Jesus figure subjected to an alternative crucifixion for the benefit of humans. We may therefore adopt Prometheus as the appropriate metaphor for the role of science in its dramatic battle with religion toward the empowerment and emancipation of humans from archaic religions' and their imperfect and incomplete conflict

resolutions. Unlike Jesus, Prometheus is observed to resolve his conflicts with the Olympians and to prevail in his role of fire giver, offering mortals enlightenment.

Prometheus represents a paradigm shift and normative change for the Greek culture, the beginning of the transformation of the Greek antagonistic father-son relationship prevalent in the Greek cosmogony. Prometheus, the creator, the fire- and knowledge-giver introduces a new model of relating or resolving conflicts.

Zeus remained the cruel infanticidal parent, wishing the undoing of humans; he meant to deprive the mortals of immortality, fire and food. Furthermore, he endowed the myth-brothers with Pandora, a woman who could bring hope but also despair. We may think of Prometheus as wrestling with the gods introducing cooperation and mutual respect in domestic relations but being tested by the gods in power management, dealing with women wisely.

Prometheus was also an educator. He combined forethought with afterthought with educating humans with the sciences he received from Athena. He could predict but also teach. He shared with Zeus the fate of antagonistic relating predicting his potential demise by a wife with a killer child. This knowledge was useful and Zeus took the initiative to avert this fate by avoiding the woman and also by changing his antagonistic relation toward Prometheus as reflected in his releasing him from his bondage.

The metaphor of Prometheus emphasizes the antagonistic relationship between science and religion
Science like Prometheus is stealing the fire of the gods. Religions discovered alternative ways to resolve conflict but science knows conflict resolution as a true and comprehensive phenomenon. 'Moral Science' confirms Formal Theory's assumption on the nature of the unconscious studying the creative

process by examining the relevance of the process for the scientific understanding of both religion and the psychology of relationships.

Science, the new Prometheus, is fighting self-righteous and arrogant religion by interpreting metaphors correctly as conflict resolutions. Science is evoking the respect for the unit process presented in each chapter by discussing the art exhibits of the Museum of the Creative Process. The unit is demonstrated integrating the religions as moral discoveries of partial truths into the total truth of the scientific process. Science reaches a compromise with religion, the moral education of the general public as a civil right.

The dramatization of the Moral Science volumes by identifying the three chapters as parallel to the Promethean trilogy

The Moral Science books on the interpretation of metaphors utilize the Promethean story as a metaphor for the dramatic organization of information on the Conflict Resolution Process. The Promethean metaphor unfolds in three phases: the nature of the fire; stealing the fire from the gods; and giving the fire to the mortals. Each phase corresponds to one of the three chapters of the new books presenting the Moral Science unfolding by sequencing information as a conflict resolution in the relationship between science versus religion. The three chapters illustrate the three successive phases of the conceptual developments utilizing the Promethean metaphor.

THE OUTLINE OF THE BOOK AND THE EXHIBITS OF THE MUSEUM OF THE CREATIVE PROCESS

The Promethean metaphor binds the exhibits as a conflict resolution experience, as the trilogy of a Greek drama, demonstrating the process under observation. The three chapters of this book, Science, Religion and Education, integrate the Museum exhibits into a dramatic progression that clarifies the significance of this scientific discovery for the world of the humanities.

The three chapters utilize the five art exhibits of the Museum of the Creative Process to illustrate the scientific nature of moral order. The exhibits are metaphors interpreted as conflict resolution phenomena. Each exhibit is complementary to the others in the study of the interpretation of metaphors.

• In the first chapter I present the nature of the fire as the science of the process: the exhibits here present evidence that the unconscious Conflict Resolution Process (CRP) is a purely scientific entity. There is no discussion of religions in this section but what is conveyed is that science understands conflict resolution.
• In the second chapter, Science completing the scientific discoveries of religions steals their fire, the leadership position; science becomes the supreme moral authority to which now religions become accountable. The process intergrates religions as partial discoveries of the conflict resolution mechanism and as an incomplete progression to the ultimate knowledge of wisdom. Science having the answers that escapes religions brings the evolution of religions to the missing wisdom that helps them to resolve their conflicts.
• In the third chapter science/Prometheus gives the fire; it delivers wisdom in a program of emotional education as the scientific study of moral psychology. This moral education departs from the study of the unit order integrating the humanities and the sciences. It continues by understanding religions and clarifying moral values, it continues with creativity for self-discovery and

skills development. This integration of insight and enlightenment can heal the world and bring peace on earth.

1) SCIENCE: The science of the CRP is the fire of the gods.

In this first chapter three exhibits establish the scientific foundation of the moral process. The six Metaphoria Murals present and analyze the unit order. The Unit is exemplified in the Gorski Retrospective and its applications are summed up in the twelve Wizard of Oz Panels.

The Metaphoria Murals: The Metaphoria Murals illustrate and validate the structure and function of the conflict resolution phenomenon. The process as a scientific unit order is introduced detecting patterns that repeat in the Greek creation stories. Twelve hand-painted murals of samples of creativity echo the regularities of the Conflict Resolution Process as the Universal Harmonic. The colorful Murals demonstrate the universality of the process as the structure of the thought process in 12 different stories, each mural composed of six tiles corresponding to the six role-states. Five of the murals analyze stories from mythology and religion. Seven represent clinical case studies with metaphors generated by trainees and patients utilizing the workbook of the Formal Theory, Conflict Analysis Training, to elicit samples of creativity and their interpretation for self-discovery.

The Gorski Retrospective: Historically the first exhibit was a collection of paintings that I used as the model case study in the introduction of the Formal Theory textbook. The Retrospective presents the formal relations between one hundred canvases to illustrate the process of conflict resolution. The Gorski Retrospective focuses on the grammar and syntax of symbolic languages, issues pertaining to the discipline of epistemology. This exhibit established the holistic way of looking at art as the philosophy of the Museum of the Creative Process. The pattern is then explored in detail examining the formal progression of the artist's canvases, his lifetime work as the path to personal growth, insight and wisdom.

The Wizard of Oz Panels: The process is the unifying reference behind the metaphors of the Wizard of Oz story. The four central metaphors of this story pertain to the four disciplines of the social sciences: epistemology, psychology, personal transformation and morality. Hence, the process is introduced as the integrative paradigm of the social sciences and the unit order of the new Moral Science.

2) RELIGION: Science is 'stealing the fire of the gods' by understanding moral order better than religions. The process as the true nature of moral order is stealing the credibility of religions, the fire of the gods.
The Sculptural Trail retraces the history of moral paradigms and religions as the evolution of awareness of the underlying Conflict Resolution Process. The Trail does so as six cycles of discoveries on the nature of the unconscious. The process indeed is validated by integrating the epics of the goddess and the scriptures of the one God, into the six role dialectic continuum of interrelated conflict resolutions. In the sculptural trail the Conflict Resolution Process guides the integration of religions and the completion of their evolution into the Moral Science.

The science of the process takes morality beyond where religions have gone in conceptualizing the underlying order. The trail through stories and magic leads to the discovery of the scientific process, defining meaning and leading to moral consensus.

3) EDUCATION/ HEALING: giving the fire to the mortals corresponds to delivering information to the public about the demystified nature of moral order.
The book's third chapter addresses the delivery of moral and emotional education in the classroom.

Self-knowledge, moral values and enlightenment are emancipated from the authorities, the high priests, doctors and educators. Science, having stolen the fire of the gods, can now deliver this as wisdom to the mortals. The viewing of the exhibits and the tapping of creativity for self-discovery become two segments of an emotional education program that can lead to insights and enlightenment. This program could be delivered in the classroom.
Indeed we advocate Moral and Emotional Literacy, an education including enlightenment and insights as a civil right.

The Case Study Murals present the significance of the delivery of this emotional education program, *Creativity and Power Management*, through the use of the *Conflict Analysis Battery*. This is a self assessment instrument that leads to for self-discovery and self-help. It targets moral and emotional literacy. The seven Murals present the Universal Harmonic reconstructed with personal metaphors. The Harmonic identifies how a person resolves conflict and how to improve one's patterns of adjustment and relating.

The significance of science entails a change in the relationship between those controlling the power of knowledge and the beneficiaries of knowledge, the public. Moral Science introduces the socialism of knowledge, effectively demystifying moral order and redistributing the power of moral judgment. Science proclaims a revolution, the fire, enlightenment, may empower the masses to think clearly outside of the cultural/narrow boxes of traditional religions.

There is a dramatic element implicit in the Moral Science and its relevance for our times. Science has the answers to the mysteries of psychology and moral order. Art illustrates the Harmonic and attests to the scientific nature of the human spirit, challenging the way we think about behavior and religion. Science clarifies that religions have discovered this process, mystified and

deified it, and thus have impeded their effectiveness toward a universal moral order. The Moral Science now reconciles psychology and religion with science, and redefines morality with the potential for the world to arrive at a moral consensus terminating the war of moral paradigms and finding peace and prosperity for all.

The Formal Theory entails social changes across the board. It popularizes knowledge, demystifies the established authority of religions, entails changes across the prevailing views and practices in education, therapy and catechism. Though it is about conflict resolution, it is bound to generate conflict by challenging the current powers in charge of defining faith for all believers. Like Prometheus, it challenges the way we think about psychology, morality, religion, politics, the psyche and god. It changes the way we teach, conduct therapy, manage power across gender relations and the way we conduct politics today.

Science stealing the fire and giving it to the mortals emancipates believers from the reign of uninterpreted metaphors that hold them captive. It introduces objectivity, this generates moral consensus and integrates religions based on their evolution. Science suggests a new civil right: emotional and moral literacy as the education of the public on the nature of the process by understanding the moral or meaningful interpretation of metaphors, hence also of religions. Science completes the task of religions by clarifying the origin of moral order and the nature of the divine. The happy ending in the conflict between science and religion is the integration of psychology and morality leading to the increase of meaning on the nature of life.

ABSTRACT:
AN OUTLINE OF THE CONCEPTS

PROMETHEUS STEALING THE FIRE: THE META-
PHOR OF SCIENCE CHALLENGING RELIGION

The discovery of the scientific and moral nature of the unconscious is dramatized in this volume with the metaphor of Prometheus 'stealing the fire of the gods.' The drama unfolds with the organization of its information in three acts. The contents represent a conflict, the relation between science and religion, finding gradually its resolution in the triumph of science identifying the exact nature of moral order leading to the emancipation of the world from the cruel tyranny of its many gods.

Science, like Prometheus, is stealing the fire, the moral authority, the normative power of religions, their capacity to identify right from wrong, by showing that religions' are simply incomplete and inaccurate discoveries of the unconscious, a natural science phenomenon. But religions are respected as pioneers of science as moral discoveries. Their norms, which evolved through the history of civilization based on politically motivated criteria in making distinctions on right and wrong increased in fairness and their attributions of the divine increased in abstraction. The new Moral Science in contrast to religions makes distinctions on fairness in relations and on the attributes of the divine that are founded on the principles of rigorous method; it completes the mission of religions by identifying the natural science basis of moral order and by seeking the cooperation of religions toward the healing of the world.

The three chapters of this book present three concepts corresponding to the Promethean myth's trilogy by Aeschylus; they represent together the three acts of the old drama:
The first act/chapter is about our hero, science; it identifies the scientific nature of the 'fire' as the demystified concept of the divine; the fire corresponds to the scientific understanding of the underlying emotional dialectic of the unconscious Conflict Resolution Process.

The second act/chapter is about the hero dueling with the gods and demystifying religions by 'stealing the fire of the gods.' It retraces their evolution as a progression of discoveries of the Conflict Resolution Process, a natural science phenomenon. Religions/resolutions evolved as a sequence of normative restructurings of family relations, and as the redefinitions of the divine, as insights on the scientific process. The religions are integrated as the drama of the healing the world by identifying the scientific entity as the unit of the social sciences.

The third chapter/act is 'on education' as the hero/science 'delivering the fire to the mortals.' It identifies a program of emotional and moral education, a scientific catechism, informing the general public by providing enlightenment, personal insights and skills in power management.

Chapter One: On 'The Fire Of The Gods' as the Science of the Unit Process; Psychology and Moral Order are integrated into the Science of Conflict Resolution, the Moral Science
The first chapter on science as the 'fire of the gods' features three art exhibits introducing the scientific study of the creative process as the Conflict Resolution Process, the unit order of psychology. The three art exhibits demonstrate and validate the unconscious as both moral and scientific, thus ending the perennial struggle between the humanities, morality and psychology versus the sciences.

Evidence validates Formal Theory's assumptions on the nature of the unconscious, the Conflict Resolution Process.
• We observe this entity manifested as organizing emotions and actions, and their respective symbols into dramatic totalities in all samples of creativity as an emotional dialectic. We know the process as the plot and moral of stories and observe it unfolding in samples of creativity as the conflict resolving dialectic.

• The process/plot of stories has a distinct structure with the moral function of resolving conflicts. The structure consists of six formally interrelated emotions or role states: stress, response, anxiety, defense, reversal, and compromise. The moral function is guided by three equilibrial operations: passivity is transformed to activity, antagonism to cooperation and alienation to mutual respect.

• The dialectic structure of emotions is the object of study of psychology. The method of study is the formal analysis of the transformation of emotions in every story as a symbolic language leading obligatorily from a conflict to its resolution.

• The Conflict Resolution Process is the unconscious physiological faculty monitoring emotional wellbeing and social homeostasis; it reflects the need for serenity, stability and social permanence. It is the principle psychic motivational force determining the organization of emotions, psychological reality, and the corresponding sociological reality into dramatic or emotional adjustment totalities.

• The process is identified as a periodic natural science equilibrial entity that we conceptualize with the clear language of physics and logic. It is the unit integrating the social science disciplines and the rigorous sciences into the Moral Science.

• The unconscious as a natural science periodic phenomenon abides by the laws of the rigorous sciences, in particular, the law of conservation of energy, the equilibrial laws of the pendulum oscillation, the Simple Harmonic Motion, and the laws of the equilibrial scale, (the Kleinian Group of four formal operations).

• The Conflict Resolution Process as a natural science periodic phenomenon is graphically portrayable as a six-part harmonic or sine curve function of time. Its cross-section is a system of concentric circles, the Power Field in which we can graphically depict displacements, behaviors and emotions as interrelated constructs.

• The process integrates psychology and morality with science by identifying the unconscious as a homeostatic physiological conflict resolving/moral order natural science phenomenon.

• The process is the unit of the social sciences. It integrates epistemology, diagnosis, assessment, therapy and moral order into the Science of Conflict Resolution, the exact Moral Science.

• All psychological, sociological, and moral order phenomena such as art and religions are natural science entities with measurable graphically portrayable relational and physical dimensions.

• Clinically the process and relational scenarios correspond to syndromal relational modalities.

• We recognize a set of four key wellness diagnostic categories; these as natural science phenomena are measurable.

• An assessment instrument has been developed that accurately detects the physical dimensions of the relational modalities.

• This unconscious corrects inner and outer imbalances as the inspired pursuit of or abidance to justice as the ideal conflict resolution.

• The unconscious as a Conflict Resolution Process automatically addresses normative deviations by either complying to norms or changing them in order to reduce personal and social conflict.

• The three conflict resolution operations correspond to science based moral values.

Chapter Two: On 'Stealing the Fire of the Gods' as Science Integrating Religions as Partial and Com-plementary Discoveries of the Unit Process

The second chapter on religion as 'stealing the fire of the gods' uses a sculptural trail through the history of love. The trail integrates the religions of the world as partial but complementary discoveries of conflict resolution into the totality of a complete dramatic and abstract Conflict Resolution Process. The trail begins with the era of magic, continues with the epics of matriarchy as evolving norms, includes the scriptures of patriarchy and ends with the celebration of the Moral Science healing the world.

The trail presents religions evolving as a sequence of restructurings of domestic relations representing partial and complementary discoveries of the Conflict Resolution Process. Religions evolved in terms of fairness in conflict resolution in domestic relations and in terms of abstraction as the attributions defining the divine. The process is shown to be the origin of all moral order. The evolution of religions and gods is thus completed with the Science of Conflict Resolution, the Moral Science; it clarifies the scientific conditions for the just restructuring of domestic relations and the most abstract redefinition of God coinciding with the scientific process.

• Psychology and moral order have been misunderstood as separate entities. Psychology, driven by homeostasis inspires the need for moral order. Religions are conflict resolutions, rationalizations regulating domestic relations. In a paranoid way all order is attributed to divine figures as external ethical authorities.

• Religions represent psychological, sociological physiological homeostatic adjustments to stress generated by the unconscious six-role process. Aristotle identified this dramatic moral transformation with what Romans translated into *deus ex machina*, the moral phase of Greek tragedies: an emissary of gods introduces the verdict for the fate of the hero.

• Stressors generate strong responses.
• Responses generate anxiety as anticipations or prophecies of role reversal.
• Anxieties motivate one's defenses.
• The defenses elicit the hero's role reversal.
• The reversal is offset by his making compromises. The prophetic or paranoid response of the anxiety state fulfilled the mind invents rationalizations on the nature of external authorities. The conflicted person negotiates terms in his compromise response.

• The Moral Science introduces the conditions for social justice or conflict resolution as determined by the formulas of science. These qualify the divine. God is equated with the equilibrial principles and energetic transformations implicit in the unconscious Conflict Resolution Process. The process is the unit of the social sciences. Moral values are the three principles of conflict resolution: passivity transformed to activity, antagonism to cooperation and alienation to mutual respect.

• Religions are normative institutions. Their norms have evolved as partial and complementary discoveries of the three formal operations of the unconscious process. Greece identified mastery, India cooperation and Judea mutual respect as the key principles of conflict resolution.

• Religious philosophies reflecting the personal philosophies of humans have the same characteristics as human psychology in espousing four alternative ways of resolving conflict. Religions are liable to the human relational psychopathologies.

• Religions relational characteristics determine moral distinctions as norms generating conflict in the public's mind for deviations from them.

• Religions' norms evolved in fairness of resolving gender role conflicts by restructuring domestic and parent child relationships. Religions also progressed toward abstraction in their attributions on the nature of the divine. Yet religions have neither achieved complete fairness in domestic relations nor have they achieved clarity on the nature of the divine.

• Science completes the mission of religions as conflict resolution in the realm of domestic relationships and in conceptualizing the divine as the universal unconscious Conflict Resolution mechanism.

• Religions as regulatory moral authorities determining normative behavior have immense political power in generating personal and cross-cultural conflicts. As political institutions with diverse definitions of the normative or acceptable behavior, religions are accountable to the public, to secular law and to the principles of the Moral Science. Science and secular law attain the role of the legitimate moral or normative authorities.

Chapter Three: On Giving the Fire to the Mortals, on Moral and Emotional Education by Studying *Creativity and Power Management*
The third chapter on education as Prometheus 'giving the fire to the mortals' is illustrated with a science associated educational program. An exhibit of seven case studies utilizing *Creativity and Power Management* illustrates the effectiveness of this program. 'Power Management' is a concise and comprehensive moral and emotional education based on the study of the creative process for enlightenment, insight and clarity of moral values. This program has educational, diagnostic and therapeutic functions and may be introduced into the classroom but also used as a standardized therapy. Moral education is advocated as a civil right, the right to learn to interpret metaphors for personal enlightenment and insights.

• The moral and emotional readiness of the student has been neglected by contemporary education due to the lack of conceptual clarity on matters of behavior and to avoid the ethical and normative politics of religions.

• The development of the Moral Science entails

that education on psychology and moral order represents factual, science-based information that is crucial to fulfill education's traditionally defined mission statement first, of the integration of art and science, second of delivering self-knowledge and third, offering clarity on moral values.

• Science makes moral and emotional education informative, personally relevant, apolitical and safe for delivery in the classroom. It defeats agnosticism by introducing meaning that is moral direction, which integrates meaningfully the encyclopedically delivered knowledge.

• *Creativity and Power Management* is a model concise and comprehensive program of emotional and moral education combining educational, diagnostic and therapeutic and skills development components.

• The program utilizes the exhibits of the Museum of the Creative Process to educate on the process introducing scientific concepts and formulas, diagnostic categories of wellness, assessment methods, and clarity on moral values. It also utilizes the *Conflict Analysis Battery* as a self-assessment instrument leading to personal insights and growth.

• The program completes the objectives of education by clarifying the scientific nature of the unconscious as the Conflict Resolution Process, thus bridging the humanities and the sciences, offering enlightenment, self-knowledge as insights in one's relational modality, and clarity of values by identifying the principles of conflict resolution as appropriate changes in power management.

• The critical need for the education of the public on emotional and moral matters entails a new civil right, the right for emotional and moral literacy. Scientific information may and must be delivered as a program of moral and emotional education to offset the public's vulnerability to narrow theistic paradigms regulated by traditional unfair norms of moral order.

Conclusion
The volume is completed addressing the genesis of religions as physiological sociological political conflict resolving movements.

• Religions begin with novel normative solutions of sociological conflicts sponsored by heroic and charismatic individuals discovering new ways in resolving conflicts.

• Resolutions endorsed by their communities become the new norms, the institutionalized conflict resolving orders.

• Religions serve several functions: they stabilize societies by giving societies norms of acceptable behavior. Religions assist the individuals to qualify as members of a values sharing community; they are self-monitoring and self-healing.

• Cultures and religions support inequitable distribution of power to members of the family. Thus they discriminate and manage power arbitrarily generating domestic and cross-cultural conflicts.

• Religions representing inequitable politicized power positions in the domestic institution, and limited understandings of the nature of the divine defend partial interpretation or solutions as universal moral order misleading the public and thus generating cross cultural and intra-cultural pathology.

• The Moral Science determines that religions need to become aware of the scientific moral order and become accountable to science's principles of conflict resolution and to secular law as the proper normative moral authorities.

• Therefore religions must become correct their communications to the public both in terms of norms and in terms of the definitions of the divine.

INTRODUCTION

THE UNCONSCIOUS AS THE CONFLICT RESOLUTION PROCESS: RECONCILING PSYCHOLOGY AND RELIGION WITH SCIENCE

The field of psychology has suffered from the lack of clear conceptual language with the consequence of loss of relevance and effectiveness. Dynamic, emotions based analytic approaches have been abandoned in favor of medical models, the study of the brain and of chemistry to manage behavior. The Formal Theory addresses this deficiency by introducing conceptual clarity on the nature of the unconscious as an emotional operational system that has structure and direction, periodicity and meaning. The task of the mind is adaptational growth.

The attributes of the new unconscious as an orderly conflict resolving mechanism rediscover Aristotle's description of the plot of stories as the Teleion Holon, the Perfect Universe.

The process having manifestations and identities across the social sciences is the integrative paradigm bridging psychology and moral order with the rigorous sciences. This order manifested in the formal organization of emotions in the plot of stories, is a pattern readily identifiable and measurable. The structure and function of the mental operations as a moral order defines morality as conflict resolution based on science.

In *Conflict Analysis, the Formal Theory of Behavior and Conflict Analysis Training*, (Normative Publications, 1988), I introduced the notion that the unconscious, manifested in all samples of creativity, has a distinct natural science structure with the moral function of resolving conflicts. The unconscious as the Conflict Resolution Process was identified as the homeostatic function helping the person to automatically adjust to stressful experiences by completing a sequence of emotional operations.

The scientific structure and the moral function of the unconscious originally observed by studying patterns that repeat in the Greek Cosmogony, (the Greek Creation stories), was confirmed experimentally in samples of the creative process studied through the *Conflict Analysis Battery*, a self-assessment instrument. This battery using creativity for self-discovery tasks confirmed that the unconscious has a distinct structure and a moral, conflict resolution function thus validating the assumptions on the process as a natural science moral order entity.

Two current volume, Science Stealing the Fire of the Gods and Healing the World, and Moral Science, the Scientific Interpretation of Metaphors, introduce art as evidence of science. The current volume presents the five exhibits of the Museum of the Creative Process illustrating and demonstrating the process and its relevance as the scientific moral paradigm. The exhibits validate 'Conflict Analysis, the Formal Theory of Behavior' and confirm it as the exact Moral Science or the Science of Conflict Resolution.

Moral Science understands the unconscious as a scientific, conflict resolving homeostatic mechanism, the unit of the social sciences. This concept allows us to conceptualize psychology and moral order as inherently integrated, giving new meaning to behavior and religion. The innate conflict resolving mechanism seeking social adjustment becomes the building block of the social sciences.

The new books comprehend religions as discoveries of alternative ways of resolving conflict. Religions, as discoveries of conflict resolution are the forerunners of science. Religions, though commanding immense spiritual and political power on the minds of the public and though being central in the history of civilizations, have escaped scientific analysis. The two books introducing the unit process reconcile religion and psychology with science. The process is the object and formal analysis the method for the scientific analysis of behavior and religion. Formal Analysis identifies religions as measurable and graphically portrayable natural science entities of conflict resolution.

The unconscious process is the foundation for a new psychology that clarifies something that traditional dynamic psychology has missed; morality represents the driving force of the unconscious. Religions have recognized this emotional need, this unconscious striving for morality, and they have harnessed it by introducing several alternative normative pathways for the individual's societal adjustment.

Religions, have introduced a succession of alternative ways to resolve conflict. They evolved along the restructuring of the domestic relations providing the normative reference for emotional and social stability. From the jungle to the ultimate civilization religions have redefined the family system as the normative or acceptable structure of domestic relations.

The norms evolved from favoring the one or other gender and from one parent child alliance to another. In all their paradigms they have not understood the imperative of fairness for all members of the family institution and they have not understood the unifying abstract order behind all moral systems. The family system even in our times is not equalitarian, free of prejudice and inequities and god is still conceived as represented by multiple philosophies. Religions understand the universality of moral order but do not recognize it as a psychological phenomenon; they attribute it to external magical supernatural authorities.

Science now completes this evolution of normative paradigms by introducing the conditions for the complete and fairest structuring of relations for all the members of the core social entity, the family institution. The scientific definition of morality entails different normative injunctions than those suggested by religions. Scientific morality entails justice for all, the fair social adjustment of all the members of the family in order to achieve peace as the optimal long lasting conflict resolution. Science respects the process as the universal moral order, the redefinition of the divine.

The discovery of the unconscious as a natural science periodic and moral order physiologic, homeostatic phenomenon reconciles reductionism/science and determinism/moral purpose. We avail now simplicity and objectivity in the conceptualization of moral order and all the social sciences. The simplicity is due to introducing constructs and formulas of science into the study of behavior; science identifies new diagnostic categories of wellness as formal alternative ways of resolving conflict; it allows us to devise a simple technology for assessment by sampling creativity for self-discovery, and revamping the realms of moral and emotional education.

While psychology becomes the Science of Conflict Resolution, religions are identified as ideologies and philosophies advocating particular ways of resolving. The new unconscious formalizes the moral drive and the pathway to the perfect state of social justice; it demystifies religions and extricates the world from their divisive theisms.

Science respects religions as partial and complementary discoveries of morality and social justice; science criticizes religions for deifying the unconscious process, for lacking insights in their limitations, for deliberately supporting inequitable norms as social justice, and as responsible of generating serious socio- and psychopathologies, one of them being the perpetual cross cultural strife leading to wars in the name of God.

Moral Science, the scientific understanding of moral order completes the outstanding task of religions; it does so by identifying what is missing from religions for them to become fair, just and effective role models for all members of the family and society. Science identifies the conditions of perfect or optimal conflict resolution and enables us to unify the many religions, to reconcile them among themselves, to integrate religion/morality and psychology, to revamp moral paradigms, to reconceptualize psychology and rethink education.

The Moral Science provides a unified moral paradigm that reconciles religions into a universal and clearly defined spirituality based in the appreciation of creativity. Science identifies norms for successful domestic relations as the equitable social adjustment for all members of the family. Religions discriminating gender roles fail to deliver optimal conditions for effective societal relations. The new science also provides a technology that delivers a user friendly emotional education. *Creativity and Power Management* is a model concise and comprehensive program of emotional and moral education that can be introduced in the classroom to deliver enlightenment, personal insights, and to practice skills of power management.

This education offers the public improved understanding of moral order, of the psyche and of the divine; it provides the public with enlightenment and personal insights. Besides educating the public on the nature of moral values this new education provides skills in interpreting metaphors and in managing power. This conceptual development and emotional education program can free the world from the divisiveness of moral paradigms and it can provide rational people with a language to reach moral consensus and to benefit from the improved psychology, and its related technologies.

The publication of this volume is of considerable significance in the conceptualization of behavior. It introduces pivotal integration of information, reconciling religion, morality and psychology with the natural sciences. It delivers applications of the theory as an educational reform; with these conceptual and technological developments humanity crosses the last frontier of knowledge. The Moral Science rethinks psychology and religion. Practically it revamps psychology and reforms education. But here we may address its political relevance. It ushers moral consensus that may facilitate conflict resolution and the attainment of peace in the world. The new field of study demystifies religion, humanizes creativity as a science-based universal spirituality and as the personal and societal path to healing.

The Moral Science can change the political conflicts based on religious distinctions. As religions are demystified and continuity is established between the diverse faiths, emotions will dissipate and reason will prevail and inspire the public to the science based set of conflict resolution and power management moral values. The traditional moral paradigms will loose their monopolistic moral authority of generating distinctions and conflicts in the minds of the public. Norms will be redefined, communications improved, psychological insights will help to evolve self-knowledge and proper power management reducing related psychological and cross-cultural conflicts.

THE KEY METHODOLOGICAL ASSUMPTION:
A PARADIGM SHIFT FROM THE STORIES WE BELIEVE IN, TO SCIENCE, THE CONFLICT RESOLUTION PROCESS, THE UNIVERSAL PLOT OF STORIES

The Easter Island head is the Wizard, who has written all the stories of the world. He has a tear of blood running down his cheek and is wondering 'How come after all my stories the world is not living happily ever after?' Next to him stands a scale, representing science, and science tells the Wizard 'Don't despair, the secrets to happiness are in all stories; but instead of believing them see what is universal in all stories, the plot of stories.'

From the Sculptural Trail at the Museum of the Creative Process

The key assumption of the Formal Theory on the nature of the unconscious

The key assumption of the Formal Theory is a shift of paradigms from the content of stories to what is universal in all stories, their plot. This theory suggests that the unconscious unfolds as a predictable conflict resolution natural science mechanism, captured in the plot as a sequence of emotions, helping the person to adjust to change, the stressors of every day living.

The Conflict Resolution Process has been the assumption formulated in *Conflict Analysis, the Formal Theory of Behavior*, published in 1988. The present volumes, '*Stealing the Fire of the Gods*' and '*Moral Science, the Scientific Interpretation of Metaphors*' introduce art exhibits and clinical case studies, essays validating the Formal Theory by providing evidence on the scientific and moral nature of the unconscious. Both volumes study the creative process as manifested in a number of art exhibits and rediscover in each one of them the underlying mental logic, the formal transformation of emotions from a state of conflict to that of a resolution following the pathway described in the Formal Theory.

The exhibits demonstrate the emotional dialectic uniting parts into perfect totalities of conflict resolution. All exhibits illustrate this formal transformation connecting emotions unfolding unconsciously along six predictable steps changing one's attitude from passivity to activity, from antagonism to cooperation and from alienation to mutual respect. This mental oscillation is portrayed as a sine curve, which we identify as the Universal Harmonic, *(Table #1, pp 76-77)*.

Lack of consensus on the nature of the psyche and of moral order

Religions detected the underlying order in relations. They mystified it and deified it, attributing the need for resolution and justice to external forces, the magic of gods and goddesses. On the other hand, psychology demystified and despiri-tualized the psyche as a biological unconscious, demonized as a set of conflict arousing drives, sexuality and aggression rather than a peace loving homeostatic mechanism. Current research seeks neuropsychological control centers for moral values. Thus neither religions nor contemporary psychology have understood the moral and natural science nature of the process as a holistic emotional phenomenon. They missed identifying the unconscious process as the morality generating motivational natural science equilibrial faculty.

The exhibits show the process uniting fragments/emotions/symbolism art into meaningful totalities of conflict resolution. They demonstrate the structure of the six-role-state thought process: stress-response, anxiety-defense, reversal-compromise, and its moral/conflict resolving function determined by the three formal operations transforming emotions or attitudes from conflict as passivity, antagonism and alienation to resolution as mastery, cooperation and mutual respect.

The volumes validate the Formal Theory into the Moral Science. Hence while the first set of volumes were about the Formal Theory and its assessment the second set is about using art as evidence of science leading to validating the Formal Theory into the exact Moral Science. The two new volumes, '*Stealing the Fire*', and '*Moral Science*', examine the relevance of the orderly process for the integration of religions and science, but also of morality, psychology and the rigorous sciences into the definitive Moral Science. We recognize that both psychology and religion address the same object, the unconscious, but have come to different interpretations on its nature.

Concluding, the two upcoming Moral Science volumes introduce art as evidence of science validating the conceptual innovation on the nature of the unconscious as the unit Conflict Resolution Process, the scientific moral paradigm.

This validation provides answers to the public perplexed about the divisive influence of inspirational religions and the agnostic amoral positions of psychological literature. The Moral Science with constructs and formulas, simple predictive syndromal relational diagnostic categories of wellness, user friendly assessment methods and a set of formal operations as the universal guiding moral values, reconciles, integrates, enlightens, and definitively revamps the field of the social sciences.

Identifying the unconscious as the unit of the social sciences, a moral and scientific phenomenon

The Conflict Resolution Process is shown to be a universal, predictable, measurable, moral periodic entity, the unit of the social sciences, and the origin of all emotional and moral order. The unconscious is moral because it automatically advances to resolution as a compromise, as the personal adjustment to the normative social environment.

The unconscious is a natural science phenomenon because it is a formal entity and an energetic quantity in equilibrial oscillation. This phenomenon pertains to the dialectic power balance between the individual and the social environment. The internal need to adjust to normative requirements by resolving one's differences represents the origin of all motivation and of all moral order. Moral order as norms regulates individual liberties but also allows the rethinking of the norms as preordained regulations.

The totality and its components: six role states guided by three formal operations

Conflict resolution is known as the plot of stories and as the moral of stories. It is identified as 'dike' or justice and catharsis in Greek tragedies, as the 'happy ending' in movies and as 'living happily ever after' in fairy tales. The exhibits explain this order by introducing Formal Analysis revealing how emotions evolve predictably from a conflict to its resolution along six steps: Stress, response, anxiety defense, reversal and compromise. These emotions are interrelated by three formal operations.

Formal Analysis identifies these six role states and measures the three formal operations transforming the emotional states in the process to the resolution of a conflict. The sequence of role-states or emotions is completed within the circumscribed entity of a story. The six-role process is the unit of the social sciences, the foundation of the scientific and moral psychology. *See Art to Science tables, pages 76 and 77. Also see murals #1, 2 and 3, pp 74-79*

Aristotle's perfect universe or Teleion Holon

Aristotle in *Poetics* studied the dramatic process as the Teleion Holon, the perfect universe of Greek tragedies (Aristotle/ Butcher, 1961). He also described it as the continuity of action, which he identified as a role state sequence beginning with hubris, followed by an adventure, leading to the recognition and the reversal of fortune, entailing a punishment and act of expiation as catharsis. He identified the process with the discovery of moral order, the apparition on the stage of the emissary of the gods, the *deus ex machina*, who delivers the verdict on the fate of the hero. Formal Theory's Conflict Resolution Process continues the Aristotelian reasoning conceiving the dramatic process as a natural science/energetic and formal order phenomenon. This is conceptualized by scientific constructs and formulas. This meaningful transformative entity is the building block of the humanities; it is the unit natural science phenomenon that reconciles all the social sciences including religion and psychology with the rigorous sciences.

The process as a natural science phenomenon has clear scientific characteristics. It abides by a rigorous epistemology with the constructs and formulas of physics and logic. The process as a conflict resolution mechanism is qualifiable; the ensuing typology of conflict resolution alternatives

corresponds to personality wellness diagnostic categories, the syndromal relational modalities. Art, creativity is the manifestation of the process and creativity may be tapped for diagnostic purposes to identify one's personality type. The scientific principles of conflict resolution clarify moral values as the formal characteristics of patterns. Thus epistemology, psychology, assessment, therapy, and moral order are united in the formal organization of emotions and behaviors, the core psychic dialectic or dynamic, the unit process of the social sciences.

The Moral Science: determinism and reductionism coincide in the process

The Formal Theory suggested that the moral process is a formal and energetic phenomenon. The new studies demonstrate that it manifests in all symbolic systems, all ideational universes, giving them their structural organization and the moral and dramatic direction of the plot of stories. This structure and this moral direction accounts for the plot of stories organizing ideas in all samples of creativity be that literature, drama, religions and psychological phenomena. We refer to it as determinism. With the Moral Science determinism is shown to coincide with reductionism, science. Morality needs not be supported by metaphysical influences.

The unit as the integrative paradigm of the social sciences

The unconscious as the core natural science moral order entity, the unit periodic phenomenon, integrates psychology with moral order and with the rigorous sciences into the Science of Conflict Resolution, the Moral Science. The process as the unit of the social sciences unifies our perceptions of psychological and moral reality. The formal analysis identifying the process provides objectivity on the contentious subjective issues on the nature of religion and psychology. The process being the scientific foundation of all psychological and moral order, psychology and religions have known it only partially, indeed only metaphori-

cally. The scientific process revamps psychology, sociology, morality and religion, and rethinks education and psychotherapy.

Definition of the process as the unit of the social sciences

The Moral Science identifies the origin of all moral order and all psychological thought as a purely scientific and readily observable phenomenon, the creative or Conflict Resolution Process. Psychological and religious phenomena become measurable natural science conflict resolution entities. The process, a simple trigonometric equation, graphically charted as an oscillation, explains the unconscious resolving conflicts, a moral order phenomenon along a totality that is perceived as the meaningful context of emotions evolving to their proper completion.

The first three exhibits validate the concept by presenting the structure of this simple adaptive physiological mechanism as consisting of six role states/emotions guided by three formal operations and graphically represented as a simple six part harmonic or sine curve. The six states and emotions process a conflict whatsoever through a series of three passivity and activity phases. The inception of the conflict is identified with the state of stress countered by the personal response; the response evokes a state of anxiety, as anticipations of a role reversal, countered by a state of defense, or counter-phobic role assumption; defensiveness leads to the anticipated state of powerlessness, the role reversal or reversal of fortune, the fulfillment of the prophecy or anticipatory state; the reversal is followed by the final state, the resolution of the conflict, through the compromise.

These three dialectic transformations of emotions as states of passivity turned around to states of activity are determined by the three formal operations: reciprocity, negation and correlation. So the mind departs from a conflict defined as passivity, antagonism and alienation, to achieve resolution, the end state, defined as mastery, co-operation and mutual respect. These three formal operations as a whole transform the person's emotions as associations leading to the moral conflict resolution outcome of the unconscious process.

This totality represents a one directional transformation of emotions, organized along six formally interrelated role states. It begins elicited by any stress defined as the individual's normative deviation, the experience of oppression, or transgression. The sequence unfolds as an emotional oscillation leading to the compromise change of attitude restoring the disturbed state of rest, or peace of mind. The individual rests finding the acceptable compromise in his /her relations with the cultural norm. The unconscious, the Conflict Resolution Process then, is an equilibrial entity that monitors emotions and relations.

The six role state process unfolds as the formally interrelated states of one key action. Aristotle identified it as the continuity of action. This key action is determined by the eliciting conflict or stress. Continuity manifests in one choice action state transformed in the reciprocal, passive and active forms, the opposites, cooperative and antagonistic forms, and the correlative forms, the alienation versus mutual respect. These transformations unite past, present and future into the unit process.

Relevance of the unit order in the interpretation of metaphors

The new science provides the Conflict Resolution Process as a clear concept on how the mind responds to stress. The unit process is a predictable and measurable entity, which we can identify as the new way of interpreting any sample of creativity, be that looking at the unconscious, at behavior, at art, and religion. This entity is the universal interpretation of metaphors or stories. It completes the quest for meaning aspired for by religions; it revamps psychology, and rethinks education. With this unit order science provides the

answers to the riddle of the humanities as they are transformed to a natural science.

This unit process, the unconscious as a moral and natural science phenomenon, bridges the humanities and the rigorous sciences integrating them into the rigorous Moral Science, or the Science of Conflict Resolution. The bridging of the humanities and the sciences is of extraordinary theoretical and also practical relevance for the sciences but it is also relevant for our times.
• In the field of behavior it clarifies the principles of dynamic psychology by revamping epistemology, diagnosis, assessment and moral thinking.
• It addresses the emotional and moral needs of the student by integrating the humanities and the sciences, psychology and morality, thus providing enlightenment, personal insights, and skills in power management within the classroom.
• Politically it addresses contending with religious fundamentalism

Because knowledge has been fragmented into meaningless encyclopedic informational overload, the new perspective integrating information through the emotional processing of information reinforces meaning and thoughtfulness. The new science integrates the fragments of what we have known as psychology and moral order, science and the social disciplines, the psyche and God. The new concept, a universal process that has been given many names by theologians, psychologists, scholars, philosophers and prophets throughout the history of civilization, that has been studied separately in many disciplines, is finally clarified with universality and conceptual simplicity.

Science now introduces objectivity on the nature of the psyche and god in the place of subjectivity and conjecture characterizing our current understandings of the human condition. Science using the process transforms the social sciences and promises to heal the world.
The exhibits validate the formal hypothesis
The hypothesis being the definitions of the process

spelled above as the six-role state, and three formal operations entity, the museum exhibits represent data that validate the theory. The exhibits are testimonials of the process as it occurs in a great number of symbolic universes. Empirically we already know this emotional process as the plot and the moral of stories. We reviewed how Aristotle detected it in Greek tragedies as the continuity of action evolving dramatic totalities into the Teleion Holon, the perfect universe of emotions. We validate this theory by observing the physical structure and moral function of the plot of stories, in detail or as overviews of the harmonic in the five exhibits. Observing them we witness the suggested dialectic of emotions by contrasting the beginning and the end of stories. Conflict corresponding to a state of passivity, antagonism and alienation is compared to resolution as the state of mastery, cooperation and mutual respect.

The Moral Science unit entity integrates psychology and moral order

Observing predictability confirms that we are dealing here with a natural science entity that abides by the laws of periodic phenomena like the pendulum oscillation and the equilibrial scale.
The conclusion from this scientific discovery is very significant. The unconscious adjusts to stress spontaneously following a meaningful flow of emotions, the path to restoration of an emotional equilibrium. This moral reaction as predictable and measurable entails that morality coincides with science, that determinism/moral order is reconciled with reductionism/science, and that the process, the core mental phenomenon as a periodic entity, bridges the humanities with the sciences.

Given these validations we may conclude that the Conflict Resolution Process, CRP, now is the scientific definition of the unconscious and the origin of all psychological and moral order as the social adjustment reflex. Accordingly this process, an innate homeostatic mechanism becomes the unit of the social sciences integrating them as partial views of behavior into the exact Moral Science, or the Science of Conflict Resolution.

IMPACT OF MORAL SCIENCE IN THE STUDY OF RELIGION

Issues Around the Scientific Study Of Religion

1. Science questions religions as the expert moral authorities

This book is about science understanding the moral process. Religions, our venerable institutions, have evolved discovering metaphorically the scientific process. Science completes the series of discoveries and integrates the religions with psychology into the natural science of Conflict Resolution. Religions as the trusted moral authorities have regulated human behavior by determining norms as criteria of generating conflicts and inspiring resolutions. They generate conflicts by setting norms of what is sinful and what virtuous behavior. Deviation from the acceptable conduct places weights on the trays of the mental scale, tipping the equilibrial state and triggering the cycle of compensatory behaviors. Religions have effectively guided behavior toward what they have viewed as moral that is acceptable or normative conduct.

Religions as moral authorities have had the role of guiding the public to virtuous conduct. Yet as partial discoveries of the process, unbeknownst to them, they have been systematically misleading the public by claiming to represent the total truth. Their moral authority identified with revelation from God, has empowered clergy to introduce normative determinations of right and wrong generating intense and at times counterproductive mental and cross-cultural conflicts. Hence the scientific discovery identifying the conditions for conflict resolution as mastery, cooperation and mutual respect is pertinent in evaluating religious norms, which emphasize merely one type of resolution rather than another. Science, introducing the set of scientific criteria for conflict resolution, differs from religions, which have only a set of metaphors influencing their values and the issues of normative determinations.

2. Science questions religions' normative power

Religions generate conflicts by regulating norms arbitrarily. We may examine the impact of these norms on the public; we may also study the political evolution of norms and determine the potential modifications that can reduce religion generated cultural and personal conflicts and pathology. Such conflicts plague individuals and the world today. We are helpless in contending with these powerful institutions because everyone is spiritual and it is difficult to challenge religions without having an alternative moral platform. We respect religions and feel resigned with their imperfections, but now the Moral Science can understand the generation of conflicts and can address their imperfections providing the science based moral alternative. Science is no longer agnostic and amoral; on the contrary we may have faith in the Moral Science as it reconciles the religions of the world with each other with psychology and science.

3. Science questions religions as partial but complementary discoveries of the Conflict Resolution Process

Religions, ahead of psychology, pioneered insights on this mental process as philosophies of conflict resolution. Religions represent partial and complementary discoveries of the natural science conflict resolution phenomenon; they progressed as stories along alternative paths to conflict resolution in family relations; they also evolved increasingly fair norms regulating behavior, as acceptable family role relations, (from the Olympic gods' rules we advance to the fairness of the Ten Commandments), and increased abstraction on the nature of divinities, the role models of their ethics, (from polytheism and paganism they evolved to monotheism and pure philosophies as in Buddhism). But religions evolved intuitively and responding to political developments with metaphors of the process without grasping the scientific nature of moral order, the underlying psychic mechanical emotional process. Below we examine three religions and detect how they differ in that each placed emphasis on one of the three principles of conflict resolution, mastery, cooperation and mutual respect, and accordingly mystified and deified the process as alternative civilizations, divinities, role models determining respective norms and value systems.

1. The Greek Olympian religion presents conflict resolution as the mastery of men over women as conveyed in the Homeric Epics, the *Iliad* and the *Odyssey*; it identified moral order inspired and directed by the Olympian gods, twelve deities exemplifying the Greek version of optimal family relations. This civilization favored antagonistic relations and evolved the political institutions of democracy and the competitiveness of the Olympic games.

2. India in the Upanishads discovered primarily the operation of cooperation and invented the hundreds of deities of the Hindu religion, which evolved into the pure philosophy of Buddhism, promoting the virtue of cooperation as the suppression of desires. This values direction led to a culture of coexisting casts, the yogi traditions of enduring pain and self-discipline, and the non-violent protestation political style.

3. Judea chose primarily the mutual respect operation leading to the father son Covenant justified in the worship of the one loving father figure. Indeed God in Judaism had no spelling and no name but only a description; he was identified as 'who was, is and will be', a definition that coincides with the elusive dialectic of the Conflict Resolution Process. This culture led to theocracy, the literature of the bible, the preoccupation with law as the elucidation of moral reason.

Science reconciles religions and completes their mission

The Moral Science respects religions as forerunners of the underlying scientific order as each has discovered an aspect of the unconscious conflict resolution mechanism. It integrates them as a sequence of interrelated discoveries into the totally abstract domain of knowledge, the Science of Conflict Resolution. Science at the same time critiques religions as incomplete perceptions of the truth and hence as misleading the public identifying themselves as representing the total truth. The formal method demystifies the religions of the world and integrates them with psychology, ethics and with the rigorous disciplines of logic, mathematics and physics into the exact Moral Science.

The implication from the studies of the art exhibits is that science completes the unfinished task of religions and of psychological research elucidating the nature of the psyche/unconscious as an oscillation coming to the rest state identifying rest with finding God, or conforming to the norms of religious traditions. God has been equated with the psychic center of normative gravity, see Gorski's canvas 'The scientific proof of the metaphysical existence of God.'

Science now changes the center of gravity, which varies for each religion, by clarifying the three equilibrial operations and the six role process. The conclusion is that science understands moral order better than religions and hence religions become accountable to science as the supreme moral authority. The Moral Science makes us simply conscious of the moral unconscious and releases us from divisive story telling speculations and the respective conflict generating distinctions advanced by religions.

The conceptual advantages of the Moral Science
This science of the process delivers multiple practical benefits to the study of behavior.

• Methodologically it delineates the objet for the study of behavior as circumscribed, the unfolding of a story as a drama, and it introduces the analytical method for the study of this object, the Formal Analysis of emotional transformations along the pathway of the resolution.
• The scientific unconscious leads to clarity on

psychological matters. This conceptual development increases the meaningfulness of the social sciences as it identifies rationality and moral purpose coinciding in the unconscious operations as the need to adjust to societal norms as the definition of stress. The process revamps psychodiagnosis introducing four alternative ways of resolving conflict, the four relational modalities, pertaining to wellness.

• The process manifesting itself in all samples of creativity, an assessment instrument, the *Conflict Analysis Battery*, has been developed which taps creativity for self-discovery; it accurately identifies one's relational modality and ensuing need for changes.

• The assessment of the process is the basis for a user-friendly psycho-educational program: *Creativity and Power Management*. This program may be delivered in the classroom as a concise and comprehensive emotional education. The program revamps education first by bridging the humanities and the rigorous sciences, then allowing self-knowledge and clarity of values.

• Moral values are no longer based on revelation or dogma; they are the three scientific principles of conflict resolution leading to resolution defined as mastery, cooperation and mutual respect.

Moral Science addresses the religious conflicts of our times
The implication of establishing the scientific foundation of behavior and morality is that it leads to moral consensus, which diminishes the cultural conflicts and potential wars based on religious normative and theistic differences. The discovery of the process addresses the moral conceptual problems of our times symbolized by Islamic fundamentalism and the sexual abuses of Catholic clergy.

The collapse of the magnificent World Trade Cen-

ter accomplished by the suicidal bombers, Islam's idealistic youth in the name of God is very disturbing. So is the scandalous behavior of catholic clergy internationally. The Moral Science provides clear insights about the cause of these behaviors. They are related to conflict generating religious teachings, norms evoking conflicts and processing of conflicts adversely affecting the health of both clergy and of the vulnerable public. The moral problems of our times are addressed legalistically in the cases of the catholic clergy and militarily in the case of the Islamists. They are not understood as sociological, psychological conceptual problems; the good news is that viewed from the scientific perspective these problems are intelligible and manageable. A good theory helps to make all religious institutions accountable to science and the public, hence that they become respectful of reason and laws regulating relations instead of relying on dogma.

Moral Science understands religions; it has the capacity to diagnose and heal
The discovery of the moral process and the new science is of great political, psychological and educational significance. It can generate consensus among scientists of behavior, reconcile believers of all religions and atheists as it defines the nature of moral order objectively. It thus deal effectively with fanaticism by diminishing the arbitrary influence of religions on behavior and politics. The current disposition in dealing with these moral aberrations has been singling out the individuals as responsible for antisocial behaviors rather than understanding the underlying dynamics of the religious institutions and recognizing the nature of the problem as evoked by doctrinaire teachings and normative determinations of the religious traditions themselves.

Science eliminates the notion of Political Correctness and makes religions accountable
Heeding the insights of science, religions may no longer enjoy immunity from analysis and criticism. They lose the self-righteous legitimacy of the

doctrine of Political Correctness. The Moral Science shifts the nature of morality from the stories people believe in as the sacred truth, to the plot of stories as an adjustment mechanism; religions evolved different norms of what is acceptable. These norms evoke conflicts and resolutions. We need to revisit the nature of the evolution of their conflict-generating norms. The public must confront their respective religious institutions and ask the religious authorities to act responsibly, to manage their messages as conflict evoking pathogenetic norms.

Addressing religions' responsibilities for conceptual reform toward achieving moral integrity
Religions introduce norms to regulate behaviors. Norms arouse conflicts by forbidding or praising behaviors. They generate conflicts similar to those of eating disorders inspired to young people who seek to abstain from food to conform to the norm of thinness. It is culturally induced norms that generate eating conflicts, which lead to the obsession with food, manifested in cyclic binging and purging.

• Similarly sexual abstinence norms generate conflicts, which lead to cyclic sexual indulgence and abstinence. The transgressive Catholic clergy are merely the victims of the respective conflict-generating sexuality vilifying norms and belief system of the Catholic Church obsessed with humility translated as equating sexuality with sinful conduct.

• Islamist teachings introduce distinctions that prohibit individuals to question faith or criticize the prophet. Some clergy motivate individuals to express their devotion and faith through self-sacrifice in the direction of political Islamist prevalence. The intensification of this distinction, respect of God through self-sacrifice, motivates people, who cannot think freely or negotiate to prove their sincerity by committing atrocities. The inequity between genders and the prohibition of freedom of expression are pathology inducing

norms, which influence acting out rather than pursuing a rational reasoning conflict resolving process in a mutually respectful manner.

While the Abrahamic religions polarize thinking about gender distinctions and behaviors generating conflicts and pathology, Buddhism encourages meditation and freedom from conflictual preoccupations. Science addresses processing conflicts freely within certain conflict-resolving pathway.
(Discussion continued on chapters 2 and 3.)

A thesis advanced on the Abrahamic family as the unfinished drama of domestic relations: Judaism's father son covenant versus the Messianic faiths' mother-child alliance
The pivotal episode in religious history was the accomplishments of the Abrahamic family. It evolved the father-son Covenant, an enormous historically significant conflict resolution development, resolving the adversarial father-son relation of the Greek Creation, of the five generations of patricides and infanticides. The father-son relationship has been affected by the role of wives.

In Greece, wives did not trust their husbands and handed the murder weapon to their youngest to kill the resented abusive spouse and father. In Judaism, women, starting with Sarah trusted their husbands and they implored God to give them offspring to dedicate to the temple, (as in the case of childless Hannah). Sarah, we may assume, seeking to empower her son Isaac, encouraged him to respect his father; Abraham, tested his son's loyalty threatening a live sacrifice to God. Sarah and Isaac passed the trust test and made history.

The trust emanating from this act inspired the father-son covenant of monotheism; but this father-son covenant had a major shortcoming. It violated the rights of women who were left outside the male-to-male alliance with adverse

consequences for the future of gender relations. Women became second-class citizens losing their civil rights; politically victimized, they pursued changes.

The Messianic religions evolved as a rebellious reaction to the oppressiveness of male, father-son dominated, Judaism as the mother-child counterpart alliances. Originally Christianity was conceived as the political normative movement of protecting women pregnant out of wedlock, as well as women who were sexually active. Jesus stood as the hero opposing stoning of women. Then later Islam emerged as the institution identified with protecting Hagar and her child, Abraham's first born, Ishmael. The core mother child alliance is symbolized in Islam's emblem of the Crescent and the Star, the Mother, the Moon Goddess, embraces her child as the star.

The Messianic religions emerged as sponsoring support for women, protecting pregnant women sexually active non-pregnant women, as well as the abandoned or widowed. So we may consider the Messianic religions politically as an emergence of the feminist cause of the mother-child alliance, offsetting the father-son alliance/covenant. In addition, Greco-Roman cultural values brought awareness to the vain pleasures of life influenced the rights of women and lessened the strict Judaic theistic norms.

The two Messianic religions, established to protect the rights of oppressed and discriminated women gradually became even more authoritarian and oppressive of women's rights than Judaism. Christianity evolved norms of asexuality particularly adopted by the Catholic Church, while Islam evolved as the religion of powerful, polygamous, authoritarian devout men and oppressed and sequestered women, controlled by the norm of unquestioning abidance to faith. Two very different Messianic normative resolutions evolved respectively regulating women's sexuality and gender relations.
(Discussion continued in Chapters 2 and 3.)

Moral Science challenges religion

The science of moral reason is timely in addressing the conflicts of all three Abrahamic religions as unresolved gender relations caused by the inequities of that family. The world is suffering from Catholicism's demonization of sexuality, threatening the mental wellness of the clergy and the faithful as witnessed by the widespread abuse of children by emotionally and sexually deprived priests. Similarly Islamic masculine authoritarianism and the frustrated oppressed mother is conducive of the children's upbringing with idealism of self sacrifice with hostile intent.

Science intervenes here by demonstrating that natural law underlies the diverse faiths and by pointing to the condition of mutual respect as a requirement in resolving conflicts. The public may opt for moral reason in addressing its conflicts recognizing religions' limitations and the multiple advantages of a unified Moral Science. The public may reduce the rigidity of religions' self-righteousness by modifying the power that religions command in establishing pathogenetic normative distinctions, such as the discrimination of women and the unquestioning, uncritical worship of deified humans.

Science clarifies the interrelation of psychology and sociology, of moral systems and the scientific disciplines. In doing so it increases the purity of abstraction in the field of psychic and moral order. We avail scientific objectivity in the realms of psychology and morality/ethics. Science provides enlightenment, rational understanding of the nature of moral order, conceptual consensus on moral matters and educates on the nature of individual and institutional power management. Enlightenment and insight can disarm fanatics and guide the public to wisdom, to new adjustments and eventually the end of prejudice, of the wars of faith, the misconduct of the clergy and of the general religion generated psychopathologies.

This study, interpreting metaphors by recognizing the underlying process, gives scientists the methodology for conducting research and gives the public a new unifying rational moral paradigm. The unit of behavior has meaning and natural science dimensions. It inspires spirituality and enables us to attain practical objectives. We may all address the task of dealing with normative issues in order to help all members of the family and all citizens of the world evolve fairness in the resolution of their conflicts. We may all enjoy the ultimate spirituality as justice promoted and affirmed through the arts.

The world is bound to find in science the set of dependable concepts defining the nature of the psyche, of cultures, and of justice. The process, the unit of moral order, points us all to the path of the ultimate self-discovery and enlightenment. The clarity of the new language increases the chances of the public communicating effectively, paving the way to the healing of the world.

The Sculpture of the Abrahamic Family by Judith Brown (above) illustrates a milestone in the history of family relations. The three Pharaoh figures represent the three patriarchs. The four diminutive women represent the four matriarchs. The two large birds represent the concubines.

The composition conveys the development of mothers trusting fathers with their children. The troubling aspect of this development is the inequity between genders. Women surrender too much of their power. Could this family power structure be considered as the moral paradigm of our times? We may understand the Messianic religions as the rightful response of women, in alliance with their sons, countering the father-son covenant.

LITERATURE REVIEW:
FORMAL ANALYSIS OF TEXTS ILLUSTRATING THE SHIFT OF PARADIGMS FROM THE CONTENT OF STORIES TO THE PROCESS

There have been several approaches seeking to bridge the conceptual gap between physical reality and metaphysics, science and religion. Science has been identified with the Darwinian natural science biological evolutionary model used to confront religions' naïve model of creation and to negate rather than understand theism. Other 'sciences' have been used, the philosophical, economic, and psychological disciplines, to understand the mind and religion. The fact is that the social sciences like psychology, sociology and anthropology, have escaped the status of becoming rigorous disciplines.

The perspective we are reviewing presents science emerging from the domain of philosophy. Here we are not interested in most representatives of the social sciences who have contributed insights on religion, philosophers like Nietzsche, Kant, and Husserl, psychologists like Freud and Jung, political philosophers like Hegel and Marx, sociologists like Max Weber and Emile Durkheim. We are interested in a small group of thinkers who focused their research on the same object of study as the Formal Theory, the organization of ideas in the analysis of texts. This is the school associated with Frankfurt and is represented by scholars who originally collaborated at that university. Most active in the years leading up to WWII, this group of thinkers speculated on the conceptual bridging of science and religion, but ultimately failed.

Nevertheless, we may benefit from reviewing the speculations of this school's thinkers so as to appreciate the differences conferred in the field by the Formal Theory. These two perspectives share interest in the analysis of the same object of study, analysis of ideas in a text. While the Frankfurt School identified structural patterns, other thinkers, like Derrida, have questioned these findings.

THE FORMAL THESIS:
THE OBJECT AND THE METHOD
(see table 1 on page 39)

There are two differences between the Frankfurt and the formalist or the Aristotelian approaches. Aristotle in his *Poetics* and the formalists in their attempt to create a science like the Formal Theory recognized a discreet order. The Formal Theory innovates in the field of textual interpretation by identifying the object of moral organization of thought and also the scientific method for the study of texts.
• The object is the creative process as a distinct circumscribed, well delineated, conflict-resolving structure, inherently with a moral outcome.
• The method used for its analysis is two rigorous science equilibrial models, one of physics, the Simple Harmonic Motion, the other of logic, the equilibrial laws of the trays of a scale.
The object of choice and the scientific models of analysis are key differences between the formal and the non-formal, propositional, the Frankfurt approach to analysis of texts.

The Formal Theory addresses the systematic organization of ideas as a homeostatic unconscious adjustment mechanism. This mechanism, the Conflict Resolution Process, organizes thoughts along the moral direction of three formal operations defining moral order as conflict resolution. Individuals differ in the ways of resolving conflict along these three operations. The Religions discovered like individuals alternative ways of resolving conflicts. So individuals and cultures differ along the formal operations of mastery, cooperation and mutual respect, besides the symbolic choices that differentiate the content of stories.

The Formal Theory reduces behavior to a predictable psychological moral natural science periodic phenomenon representing the unconscious as a homeostatic, physiologic process that seeks to restore the optimal tension level in the psyche by adjusting the individual's conduct and attitude.

Thus the Formal Theory represents a structuralist/formalist theoretical position with a clear object and analytical method in the study of ideas. It is addressing the formal and energetic interpretation of a text as the object of study. It differs from the other approaches as it conceptualizes the text as unit entities of moral/conflict resolving directions following a set of scientific phenomena reducing behavior to predictable formal and energetic transformations.

Wikipedia on Formalism
'Formalism is a school of literary criticism and literary theory having mainly to do with structural purposes of a particular text. In literary theory, formalism refers to critical approaches that analyze, interpret, or evaluate the inherent features of a text. These features include not only grammar and syntax but also literary devices such as meter and tropes. The formalist approach reduces the importance of a text's historical, biographical, and cultural context.

Formalism rose to prominence in the early twentieth century as a reaction against Romanticist theories of literature, which centered on the artist and individual creative genius, and instead placed the text itself back into the spotlight, to show how the text was indebted to forms and other works that had preceded it. Two schools of formalist literary criticism developed, Russian formalism, and soon after Anglo-American New Criticism. Formalism was the dominant mode of academic literary study in the US at least from the end of the Second World War through the 1970s, especially as embodied in Rene Wellek and Austin Warren's Theory of Literature (1948, 1955, 1962).

Russian Formalism refers to the work of the Society for the Study of Poetic Language (OPOYAZ) founded in 1916 in St. Petersburg (then Petrograd). Eichenbaum's 1926 essay "The Theory of the 'Formal Method'" (translated in Lemon and Reis) provides an economical overview of the ap-

TABLE 1: OBJECT AND METHOD FOR THE STUDY OF MORAL PSYCHOLOGY:
Contrasting two approaches, formal and propositional, in the conceptual integration of science and religion

Methodology Structure versus Deconstruction	Frankfurt school Propositional method and Hegelian Dialectics	Aristotle's Poetics Relational method without scientific models, basic principles of formal logic	Levis' Formal Theory Distinct structure accounted for by two scientific models 1. Physics of the pendulum, with conservation of energy, the constructs formulas of the Simple Harmonic Motion 2. Piagetian, Kleinian group of formal operations
The object of study Totality in the text, the story versus the plot of stories	Texts without closure, no concept of totality. Theories introduce multiple distinctions: linguistic, grammatical, historical, political, economic, sociological, philosophical, and psychological. Texts consist of multiple unrelated fragments that cannot be unified to integrate science and moral order.	Greek tragedies: continuity of action integrates episodes into meaningful totalities: hero's hubris, peripetia, recognition and reversal, dike, catharsis, *deus ex machina*, are integrated into the 'Teleion Holon' or 'perfect universe.'	Study of texts as the finite dialectic of emotions leading the restoration of equanimity, the rest state or homeostasis. All samples of creativity have the same dramatic structure, the moral plot of stories, a six role-states three formal operations structure: Stress, response, anxiety, defense, reversal and compromise lead to catharsis. This is the unconscious as a natural science and moral order unit entity.
End product concepts	Theories as the end product of philosophy, disunity of parts, lack of integration, of concepts i.e. Structuralism versus deconstruction Communicational Intersubjectivity Aporia Alienation	Moral end: Endelechy, Relational transformations *Deus ex machina*, Catharsis, all concepts referring to moral end	The creative process as a circumscribed dramatic equilibrial totality, leading to conflict resolution or moral order, coincides with increased order or negative entropy in the service of homeostasis as normative adjustment. The Conflict Resolution Process, the Unit entity of the social sciences, a periodic moral order phenomenon, the Universal Harmonic, is the integrative paradigm
Capacity to Unify the social sciences Psychology Religion Science	Theories disunited, divided disciplines, Husserl, Hegel and Marxist postulations, unconscious as Freudian Oedipal dynamics Multiple disunited theories of psychology and religion Something missing: duality of reason and moral principles	Aristotle united Sciences as a philosopher without availing technological conceptual integration. His theories embraced the sciences: metaphysics and ethics, poetics, politics and physics.	The six role-states are intertransformable emotions, conserved energies, and forms closed into natural science units of moral order. The unit integrative paradigm is constructs and formulas, diagnostic categories, assessment testing, moral values. The unit integrates the social science disciplines: epistemology, psychology, assessment, therapy, education and religion as natural science and moral order phenomena into the Moral Science. The Conflict Resolving Process reconciles religions among themselves with psychology and science. Creativity affirms morality and spirituality.

proach the Formalists advocated, which included the following basic ideas:

• *The aim is to produce "a science of literature that would be both independent and factual," which is sometimes designated by the term poetics.*
• *Since literature is made of language, linguistics will be a foundational element of the science of literature.'*

The Formal Theoretical structure

This Wikipedia article needs to be modified to include the Aristotelian perspective as defining formalism as we have referred to in his treatise on drama, the Poetics; of course the Formal Theory departs from the Teleion Holon as the purely formal theoretical perspective and continues with the scientific understanding of the process as an equilibrial phenomenon.

The Formal Theory identifies in texts the universal structure of the unconscious entity as consisting of a sequence of six emotions or role states: stress, response, anxiety, defense, reversal and compromise, directed by three mandatory formal operations: passivity is transformed to activity, antagonism to cooperation and alienation to mutual respect. The role states correspond to formally interrelated emotions, energies, ideas constituting a well-organized symbolic universe, a dramatic totality. This emotional moral entity, the unconscious, is a natural science measurable, qualifiable and quantifiable, graphically portrayable phenomenon abiding by the laws of the rigorous sciences.

This entity is the homeostatic equilibrial mechanism of the unconscious operating as a unit periodic phenomenon restoring the rest state when a stressor generates a conflict that disturbs it. Conflict resolution, finding the rest state, consists then of emotions or ideas, as forms and energies different from the state of conflict. Resolutions scientifically represent formal transformations but also energetic transformations. The energy

being conserved is merely upgraded by the process into a higher quality energetic organization. Moral order is this upgrading of energy experienced as an attitude change, improved sense of meaning and defined as conflict resolution.

The Formal theoretical phenomenon is measurable utilizing a new assessment instrument, the *Conflict Analysis Battery.* This is a self-assessment instrument; it measures the personal conflict resolution process. It is diagnostic, therapeutic and educational. It can be used to validate the theory as it confirms the formal pathways of transformation of emotions, from passive to active, from antagonistic to cooperative and from alienation to mutual respect.

The *Conflict Analysis Battery* consists of a relational personality inventory and a set of projective techniques that lead a person to identify his relational modality and also to generate metaphors of conflict resolution symbolically reflecting the relational choices. The statistical analysis of the test results of the inventory validates the range of alternative formal pathways to resolution, the four relational modalities.

The Formal Theory identifies the psychological, physiological moral entity as a universal natural science phenomenon. This is the unit of the social sciences. It may be used to understand psychology and religions. This concept is pertinent to the study of psychology leading to the identification of wellness personality typology, diagnostic categories of conflict resolution. The same typology may be applied and rediscovered in examining religions.

Religions as discoveries of conflict resolution

According to the Formal Theory religions represent complimentary discoveries of the scientific unconscious mental process. Religions have progressed in abstraction, with increasingly fairer norms and simplified and empowered role models, the divinities of the respective religions.

The evolution of religions is completed upon the discovery of the Science of Conflict Resolution, the Moral Science. The science provides information for the optimal resolution of conflicts. The Moral Science understands the unconscious, the Conflict Resolution Process as a natural science phenomenon. Psychology and religion become integral aspects of this science.

HYPOTHESIS: SAMPLE ANALYSIS OF TEXTS CONTRASTING CONTENT VERSUS FORM OR STRUCTURE

Three case studies of Formal Theory's method of interpretation of a text

The Formal Theory interprets the meaning of a text by identifying its structure or plot as a sequence of six emotions propelled by three formal transformations. This structure connecting emotions in a text may be identified in any symbolic universe as six formally interrelated ideas or role states. We identify in the text a conflict, which may be viewed in the context of norms unfolding in the story as the polarizing element beginning with a normative deviation and concluded with normative conciliation or adjustment; the text then is conceptualized as a process restoring the rest state of the author resolving a conflict and sustaining homeostasis.

The thesis to test here is the assumption that the formal theoretical totality may be observed in any text as having a beginning, middle and an end. Its parts, the six role states, are in distinct formal relation to each other. The process has a moral conclusion coinciding with the progression from the initial to the final role-state so that the resolution is in formal relation to the initial role-state, its inception.

The plot of stories, art of one artist, drama, movies, simple texts like metaphors and even ideas promoting a theory, may be used to illustrate and demonstrate the universality of the conflict resolution process. As a way of interfacing theories I am presenting below formal analysis of three theoretical texts to contrast the two methodological approaches in theory making. The sample analyses confirm the process underlying all samples of creativity as presented on a research topic as a universal mechanism.

FINDINGS - THE MORAL AND PHYSICAL STRUCTURE OF THE THOUGHT PROCESS

We recognize the innate homeostatic equilibrial mechanism as having the features of the unit periodic phenomenon. This process is a structure; it is a formal structure and it may be subsumed in the tradition of formalism though it differs from the specific schools mentioned above.

Three case studies: Formal Analysis of texts shifts the focus from the content of three stories/theories to the plot of stories, the universal Conflict Resolution Process.

Clarifying the plot as a formal emotional process. Samples of formal analysis interpret the theoretical articles as objects of analysis. The ideas are integrated as interrelated emotions, as manifestations of the formal analytical six role-state process.

All sample texts are standardized as articles about the theorists stemming from the same source, the Wikipedia. The first is an article from Wikipedia about Derrida's theory of deconstruction.

Derrida's deconstruction

Derrida questions structuralism/formalism and hence the formal perspective. Derrida rigorously pursues the meaning of a text to the point of undoing the oppositions on which it is apparently founded, and to the point of showing that those foundations are irreducibly complex, unstable or impossible (*Wikipedia, Derrida*, 2011).

Wikipedia on Derrida:

"Deconstruction generally attempts to demonstrate that any text is not a discrete whole but contains several irreconcilable and contradictory meanings; that any text therefore has more than one interpretation; that the text itself links these interpretations inextricably; that the incompatibility of these interpretations is irreducible; and thus that an interpretative reading cannot go beyond a certain point. Derrida refers to this point as an aporia in the text, and terms deconstructive reading 'aporetic.' J. Hillis Miller has described deconstruction this way: "Deconstruction is not a dismantling of the structure of a text, but a demonstration that it has already dismantled itself. Its apparently-solid ground is no rock, but thin air."

The formal analysis presents the text of the article as Derrida's evolution from a conflict to its resolution as following the six role state three formal operations dynamic, overlooking the content of his argument.

Stress (existential normative discomfort, state of passivity, antagonism and alienation)

"Derrida began speaking and writing publicly at a time when the French intellectual scene was experiencing an increasing rift between what could broadly be called 'phenomenological' and 'structural' approaches to understanding individual and collective life. For those with a more phenomenological bent the goal was to understand experience by comprehending and describing its genesis, the process of its emergence from an origin or event. For the structuralists, this was precisely the false problem, and the 'depth' of experience could in fact only be an effect of structures, which are not themselves experiential."

Response (as the related intellectual initiative)

"It is in this context that in 1959 Derrida asks the question: Must not structure have a genesis, and must not the origin, the point of genesis, be already structured, in order to be the genesis of something? In other words, every structural or 'synchronic' phenomenon has a history, and the structure cannot be understood without understanding its genesis."

Anxiety (questioning distinctions: synchronic or diachronic?)

"At the same time, in order that there be movement, or potential, the origin cannot be some pure unity or simplicity, but must already be articulated—complex—such that from it a "diachronic" process can emerge.

This originary complexity must not be understood as an original positing, but more like a default of origin."

Defense: (action to address anxiety)

"Derrida refers to it as iterability, inscription, or textuality. It is this thought of originary complexity, rather than original purity, which destabilizes the thought of both genesis and structure, that sets Derrida's work in motion, and from which derive all of its terms, including deconstruction."

Reversal (outcome of conceptual actions)

"Derrida's method consisted in demonstrating all the forms and varieties of this originary complexity, and their multiple consequences in many fields. His way of achieving this was by conducting thorough, careful, sensitive, and yet transformational readings of philosophical and literary texts, with an ear on what in those texts runs counter to their apparent systematicity (structural unity) or intended sense (authorial genesis)."

Compromise (normative rethinking of the field, end of disagreement, reconciliation with theorists, mastery, cooperation and mutual respect)

"By demonstrating the aporias and ellipses of thought, Derrida hoped to show the infinitely subtle ways that this originary complexity, which by definition cannot ever be completely known, works its structuring and destructuring effects" (Norris, 1987).

The sample conflict resolution analysis presents the six role-states as a predictable emotional sequence concluded with a resolution as the moral end, or normative reconciliation. The six role-states are in formal relation to each other as passivity to activity, antagonism to cooperation and alienation to mutual respect. He started in conflict with theories, his normative deviation, experiencing passivity, antagonism and alienation, and evolved a theory as his conflict's resolution, a normative reconciliation characterized by relief based on the conditions of mastery, cooperation and mutual respect.

While the content of the text follows Derrida's search for meaning addressing rationally a philosophical maze of concepts, complexity of propositions, the formal analysis of the text connects the underlying emotions of the author into a smooth continuum starting with a conflict and completed with its resolution validating the assumption of the formal transformation of role-states

The second analysis examines Habermas' dilemma

The quest for meaning in the school of Frankfurt has continued with contemporary 'Theory of Communicative Action', a book by Juergen Habermas published in 1981 in two volumes, the first subtitled *Reason and the Rationalization of Society (Handlungsrationalität und gesellschaftliche Rationalisierung)* and the second, *Lifeworld and System: A Critique of Functionalist Reason (Zur Kritik der funktionalistischen Vernunft)*. His thesis is a concept developed by him, communicative reason, which is distinguished from the rationalist tradition in that it considers the site of rationality to be the structures of interpersonal linguistic communication rather than the structure of either the cosmos or the knowing subject. The theory of communicative action has been deemed one of the most important theoretical works to have come out in the second half of the 20th century.

Habermas argues that the key to liberation is rather to be found in language and communication between people. The study of reason has

traditionally belonged to philosophy, and philosophical reason can most simply be defined as an unpacking of reason's experience of itself.[1] However, philosophers have so far been unable to define reason any better than by saying that it is "good" thinking codified in language.
The following is the formal analysis of the Wikipedia article on Habermas; formal analysis of the article about Habermas' theory of communicative action reflects his inability to integrate the two realms of discourse but leading to a compromise, a pragmatic theory (*Wikipedia, Habermas,* 2011).

Stress, (state of passivity, antagonism and alienation)
Referring to Richard Rorty.

Response, (state of activity)
Habermas agrees with the postmodernist position that a philosophical world view has become untenable and that there can no longer be a totalizing abstract knowledge. Yet Habermas argues that it does not then follow that an empirically tested theory of rationality could not be universal.

Anxiety, (state of passivity)
With this failure of the search for ultimate foundations by "first philosophy" or "the philosophy of consciousness."

Defense, (state of activity)
An empirically tested theory of rationality must be a pragmatic theory based on science and social science.

Reversal, (state of passivity)
This implies that any universalist claims can only be validated by testing against counterexamples in historical (and geographical) contexts - not by using transcendental ontological assumptions.

Compromise, (state of activity, cooperation and mutual respect)
This leads him to look for the basis of a new

theory of communicative action in the tradition of sociology. He starts by rereading Max Weber's description of rationality and arguing it has a limited view of human action. Habermas argues that Weber's basic theoretical assumptions with regard to social action prejudiced his analysis in the direction of purposive rationality, which purportedly arises from the conditions of commodity production.

A second cycle of thoughts repeats the conflict resolution process:

Stress, (state of passivity, antagonism and alienation)
Taking the definition of action as human behavior with intention, or with subjective meaning attached, then Weber's theory of action is based on a solitary acting subject and does not encompass the coordinating actions that are inherent to a social body.

Response, (state of activity)
This 'purposive rational action' is steered by the "media" of the state, which substitute for oral language as the medium of the coordination of social action.

Anxiety, (state of passivity)
An antagonism arises between these two principles of societal integration:

Defense, (state of activity)
one being language, which is oriented to understanding and collective well being, and the other "media", which are systems of success-oriented action.

Reversal, (state of passivity)
Following Weber, Habermas sees specialization as the key historical development,

Compromise, (state of activity, cooperation and mutual respect)* which leads to the alienating effects of modernity, which 'permeate and frag-*

ment everyday consciousness.

The third sample formal analysis examines Stanley Fish's comments on Habermas
Stanley Fish is known for his work on interpretive communities, an offshoot of reader-response criticism that studies how the interpretation of a text by a reader depends on the reader's membership in one or more communities defined by acceptance of a common set of foundational assumptions or texts. Theoretical work can be viewed as an explanation of how meaning is possible in the context of a particular interpretive community, even if one accepts the deconstructionist position that no single privileged reading of any text exists.

He is addressing accordingly the position promoted by synthetic scholar, Jurgen Habermas in a New York Times editorial. According to Stanley Fish 'What is missing for reason' is the smooth conceptual integration of science and psychology/moral order. Presenting the difference between formal analysis and other conceptualizations I analyze S. Fish's critique of Habermas as a six-step Conflict Resolution Process. The process may be seen to unfold twice:

Stress as problem detected, (state of passivity, antagonism and alienation)
The path to meaning is the missing step between Habermas' respect of religion with reservations and criticism of liberalism as pointless… What secular reason is missing is self-awareness. It is "unenlightened about itself" in the sense that it has within itself no mechanism for questioning the products and conclusions of its formal, procedural entailments and experiments.

Response to the problem, (state of activity)
"Post-metaphysical thinking," Habermas contends, "cannot cope on its own with the defeatism concerning reason which we encounter today both in the post-modern radicalization of the 'dialectic of the Enlighten-

ment' and in the naturalism founded on a naïve faith in science."

Anxiety or hope, (state of passivity)
"he structures of argumentative speech, which Habermas identifies as the absence of coercive force, the mutual search for understanding, and the compelling power of the better argument, form the key features from which

[Defense, (state of activity)]
intersubjective rationality can make communication possible.

Reversal, (state of passivity)
Action undertaken by participants to a process of such argumentative communication

Compromise, (state of activity, cooperation and mutual respect)
can be assessed as to their rationality to the extent which they fulfill those criteria.
Habermas makes the assumption about identity that we learn who we are as autonomous agents from our basic relations with others (*Fish*, 2011).

DISCUSSION: THE ADVANTAGES OF FORMAL ANALYSIS

Two methods present the alternative perspectives in addressing the challenge of interpreting meaningfully ideational phenomena, texts. The above sample formal analysis exercises exemplify the two approaches in interpreting reality. Frankfurt philosophers use theories or content versus the Formal Theory interpreting the process, or the plot of stories. These approaches correspond methodologically respectively to the propositional versus the relational methods.

The Frankfurt thinkers address content issues with speculative postulations on the nature of behavior and moral order. The Formal Analysis in stark contrast examines the plot of their theoretical stories overlooking the theories but examining the interrelation of parts as emotions in conflict resolution totalities.

The Frankfurt philosophical movements associated with Husserl, Adorno, Habermas, Fish, etc exemplify speculations on the nature of the mental process. The many theories developed in the content of Derrida's, Habermas' and then Fish's texts vary as syllogisms. The European theorists of the mid century have been seeking science as rationalizations on sociological and political foundations, or grammatical linguistic observations. Their theories have been subjected to extensive discussions; deconstruction is one of them; arguments are very nuanced and difficult to follow as one theorist expands on another theorist's distinctions.

These theories advanced philosophical, ideological, intellectual, axiomatic distinctions generating a maze of argumentation and neologisms like post metaphysical thinking, post-modern radicalization, intersubjective rationality, argumentative communication, communicative action, etc. These series of assumptions are of questionable validity and causality but in the final analysis admittedly they have failed to bridge rationality and moral thought or religion.

According to Fish, the Formal Theory would represent a new interpretive community. We argue here that it is more than another interpretive approach and its community. We claim that it represents the objectivity of science, that it is not merely intersubjective, but truly objective as a phenomenon observable by all researchers and the naïve public.
While axiomatic theorizing is speculative the formal analytical method differs in two distinct ways.
• First, the object of analysis is a circumscribed text, a dramatic conflict resolution totality.
• Second the analysis of this text consists in identifying a universal process unfolding as a unit entity, repeated at every sample of discourse

pertaining to the structure of emotions. The emotions six-role states pertain to the emotions of the theoretician and not to his content-based ideas. They account for the author's homeostatic emotional unconscious reasoning process. Unlike the ideational arguments of the propositional method the formal analysis identifies the universal unconscious, the physiologic homeostatic mechanism that is by definition adjustment or morally directed. What also is new here is that this process abides by the rigorous laws of science.

What we observe then is that the Formal Theory's universal unit phenomenon organizes emotional, moral reality at various levels in accordance with science. It deals with emotions in all symbolic realms, i.e. theoretical discourse, sociological phenomena, artistic creations and cultural phenomena. It understands religions as natural science phenomena.

Formal Theory's features
(Table one, the object and method of Formal Analysis)
The Formal Theory rediscovers the Aristotelian conceptualization of the dramatic process as a Teleion Holon, a perfect universe, identifying the universal structure of the plot of stories as a natural science equilibrial phenomenon. This order consisting of interrelated states in continuity of action, a natural science universal moral order mechanism, becomes the unit of the social sciences, integrating them into the Moral Science.

Unlike the dense propositional content of communicative action, formal analysis identifies the emotional continuity as a six-role process, whose role states are in consistent formal relationship to each other within a totality. This entity introduces meaning to the thought process in the samples of textual analysis quoted above. The Formal Theory is thus validated by introducing emotional continuity in the authors' ideational postulations.

We may conclude on the advantages of the Formal conceptualization of behavior. Unlike following the content of the theoretical argument and dealing with the looseness of speculative assumptions, meaningful only to the members of a school of theorists but not articulated in a language that is meaningful to the public, the formal analysis introduces an intelligible simple set of formally interrelated states, focuses on the emotions of the author, following the associations as the goal directed restoration of his equanimity, peace within the respective normative society of thinkers.

Then we may conclude that the Formal Theory offers a process that is universal and that explains the emotions of the author following scientific principles. The Conflict Resolution Process confers objectivity to the analysis. It is totally independent of the content, which is of hypothetical nature and totally subjective, though promoting rational explanations.

The Formal versus propositional theories
The Formal Theory differs in the choice of object and method from other theories of moral psychology. The formal analysis focuses on the emotions of the thinker rather than his theoretical rationalizations. The formal interpretation focuses on the formality of emotions and dissociates itself from the content of his rationalizations.

1. The theory departs from the rationalist propositional method to introduce the relational method as formal operations connecting emotions as parts into transformative totalities of conflict resolution.

2. The object of its study changes from text content with linguistic distinctions to address the author's emotional process as the plot or formal connection of ideas or states within a circumscribed totality.

3. The substance of parts is not intellectual ideational distinctions but emotions as energies and as forms in their symbolic representations as role states.

4. The Formal Theory departs from the multiple axiomatic or arbitrary distinctions to consider only one distinction, the emotional continuity as a physical, physiological, psychological and moral entity.

5. Interpersonal identity is shaped by the formal nature of relations as interactional patterns transmitted across generations within every culture.

6. Descriptive distinctions are replaced by Formal Relational measurable, qualifiable, quantifiable graphically portrayable distinctions. Employing these criteria we differentiate personal as well as cultural relational dispositions and patterns. Sociological, cultural and individual systems have dimensions and physical constructs in relationship to each other.

EQUIVALENT CONCEPTS:

the promethean fire

the unconscious

the atomistic unit of the so- cial sciences

art and science

the conflict resolution process

trigonometric formulas

the teleion holon

the sine curve

THE SCIENTIFIC MORAL PARADIGM
measurable, graphically portrayable

the perfect universe

relational modalities

THE MENTAL HEARTBEAT

the creative process

religions

the Universal Harmonic

civilizations

THE PSYCHE

God

the plot of stories

Genesis

the dramat- ic process

six days
seven shakras

CHAPTER ONE: SCIENCE

THE PROMETHEAN FIRE: THE CONFLICT RESOLUTION PROCESS AS THE SCIENTIFIC MORAL PARADIGM

THE CONCEPT OF THE PROCESS

The first chapter, the hubris of this book as a drama, introduces the concept of the Promethean fire; it corresponds to placing morality on a scientific foundation and declaring its superiority to revealed morality, religions. In this chapter we identify the nature of the fire as science demystifying the magic of moral order by understanding it as a simple natural science psychological homeostatic phenomenon. This amounts to recognizing that science is the expert moral authority. The moral process is reduced to the secure path to social adjustment. Meaning of life's mysteries is explained as the mechanics of the physiologic automatic method of resolving conflicts.

Deciphering faith with the discovery of the process science challenges religion. The book begins with three exhibits demonstrating the scientific nature of the process abbreviated as the CRP. Scientific rationality contradicts religions' claim that morality is based on revelation; hence refuting the notion that faith is above reason.

The exhibits show that the unconscious in all samples of creativity is a natural science phenomenon that manifests in the unfolding dialectic of the Conflict Resolution Process. In every circumscribed sample of creativity, associations and emotions are shown to be in a distinct formal relation to each other along the unit process; incidentally, we already know this process as the plot and of the moral of stories.

The object and the method to study the moral unconscious

The story is the object of study and formal analysis is the scientific method to study the unconscious and to understand both behavior and moral order. What we identify is a predictable transformation of emotions. The exhibits confirm the universality of this conflict resolving mechanism as the reflection of the unconscious homeostatic response to stress. This universal organizing entity is the unit of the social sciences. It integrates the social sciences into the cohesive and comprehensive Moral Science.

In this chapter we study the structure of the process and its formal direction observing the mental dialectic; it is organizing data meaningfully as predicted in the definition of the process. Three exhibits allow us to examine the concept, identify its physical structure and moral function, as the formal interrelation of ideas/emotions/symbols in the circumscribed entity of a story whatsoever.

Conflict as the deviation from a norm, resolution as normative conciliation or change

Conflict is evoked by experiencing or initiating a deviation from a norm; the resolution process reduces the distress of inner conflict, be that guilt for a transgression or hostility for being victimized. Responding to the deviation the person automatically protests or conforms to the norm as the two alternatives on the paths to resolution. The Conflict Resolution Process then is an emotional and a moral natural science physiological, psychological mechanism, the psychic adjustment response to stress. The conflict is resolved as the individual either conforms to or changes the normative environment. The choices are to either comply to or to wrestle with the societal rules/norms.

In either case the unconscious seeks the restoration of the rest state. Associations evolve spontaneously managing emotions elicited by the stressor. The creative process is a healing mechanism; it restores the mental equilibrium and assumes the social norm as one's identity. Conforming versus wrestling the person may pursue four distinct paths to healing. The four alternatives correspond to the typology of alternative personality diagnoses, the relational modalities. Personality types are characteristic of the individual.

We diagnose the personal type of resolution as the individual's relational modality utilizing the *Conflict Analysis Battery* combining projective tests with an inventory; the two ways of measuring confirm the diagnosis of a relational pattern. The projective tests use creativity tasks generating metaphors. The Relational Modality Evaluation Scale, a relational personality inventory test, accurately identifies a person's relational modality. The metaphor projective tests confirm the diagnostic impression derived from the inventory test. The relational pattern is projected in the associations of one's samples of creativity. While the content of one's stories may vary the plot of such stories, remains characteristic of the individual.

The unconscious as an emotional dialectic

In the first chapter, defining the nature of the fire, we examine the process of conflict resolution as the physiological emotional adaptive mechanism, the scientific essence of all human thought. The study confirms the use of the creative process as the object and its formal analysis as the proper method to study behavior. We analyze the process as metaphors, representative samples of creativity, to identify the predictable six-role state and three formal operations dialectic of the person's emotions.

The physics and logic of the mental phenomenon

The process has the natural science structure of an equilibrial formal and energetic oscillation abiding by the laws of the rigorous sciences; it consists of a six-role state sequence of interrelated energetic states or emotions, guided by three formal operations. This process is shown to be an equilibrial natural science phenomenon abiding by the laws of the Simple Harmonic Motion and the laws of the balance of a scale. (Formal Analysis Profile FAP 155-156)

The process's function is moral as a universal normative adaptive response. The process is the essence of human adjustment as the reduction of conflict, evoked by the deviation of the individual from what is acceptable or normative. Technically moral or conflict resolution order is described as the state of mastery, cooperation and mutual respect. These end states are pursued by three formal operations automatically transforming conflict or chaos to resolution or order. Moral reason is generated in the dialectic unfolding of the process. Moral order coincides with resolution as conformity to norms or alternatively the changing of norms.

The many identities of the process
The process is an emotional periodic phenomenon, the unit of the social sciences.
• It is epistemology's constructs and formulas, the clear language of physics, logic and math.
• It is psychology's unconscious manifested clinically as four syndromal diagnostic categories, as alternative ways of resolving conflicts; these are wellness diagnostic categories.
• It is psycho-assessment's measuring rod manifested in all samples of creativity as conflict resolving symbolic universes.
• It is the religions' moral paradigms integrated as complementary discoveries of aspects of the unit process.

The process entity then, constructs of science, modalities as diagnostic categories, metaphors for assessment purposes and moral paradigms are the many aspects of the unit of the social sciences. The process is then the unit entity integrating the disciplines into the Science of Conflict Resolution, the exact Moral Science.

The history of the concept
Behavior never became a science for lack of an object and for faulty or improper methods for its analysis. Now the creative or conflict resolution process represents any creation as the object of study and formal analysis as the method to study psychological as well as moral order phenomena. The Conflict Resolution Process becomes the scientifically defined object for the study of behavior; it is the unconscious as a purely formal and physical entity that can be isolated and studied.

The publication of Conflict Analysis, the Formal Theory of Behavior in 1988, pioneered the reconceptualization of the unconscious. The Freudian conflict generating primitive, biologically determined, irrational unconscious was redefined as a physiological, psychological, relational, rational, adaptive, conflict resolving, moral order and natural science entity. The unconscious from a conceptually perplexing antisocial, sexually obsessed and aggressive drive was transformed to the Conflict Resolution Process, a natural science moral order unit entity.

The Formal Theory reduced the perplexing unconscious to a simple peace loving harmonic, the mental heartbeat, the plot of stories, the unit periodic phenomenon of all the social sciences, elegantly integrating them with the rigorous disciplines into the exact Moral Science. It is not surprising that religious/pious people greet each other using the word peace, 'Shalom' implying the essence of the mental function, conflict resolution.

Cultures and philosophers have observed this process and have attributed its qualities to magical and/or metaphysical entities. They have equated the process with the psyche and God as tangible anthropomorphized entities. The unconscious natural science process related to creativity and spirituality has been observed as the six days of creation and the day of rest in Genesis, as six chakras and the seventh over one's head, and as

the three acts of a Greek tragedy as sequences of 'pathos and drasis' leading to the emotional spiritual growth identified with catharsis. The process has been redefined, deified and mystified as the psyche and God.

Aristotle was the first philosopher/scientist to analyze the emotional experience as a mechanism. He described the structure and the function of the process accurately in the *Poetics* as the continuity of action of Greek tragedies. According to Aristotle the process has a beginning, middle and a moral, cathartic end. It relationally unites role states: the initial hubris, the ensuing adventure, the recognition of the hero leading to the reversal of fortune, followed by justice and catharsis. This cycle of events consist of interrelated emotions, 'pathos' as suffering, and 'drasis' as actions. He identified this entity as the 'Teleion Holon', the 'perfect universe', where perfection corresponded to a scientific predictable totality, with the proportionate organization of ideas. He observed this process in all symbolic universes of Greek drama. He described the pursuit of justice with the apparition of the messenger of the Olympian gods, the *deus ex machina*, announcing their verdict, determining the fate of the protagonist, the hero, inducing catharsis or relief to the audience.

The Formal Theoretical thesis originates with my detecting a pattern that was repeated across the five generations of the very cruel Greek Creation stories, the Cosmogony. Eventually I identified it organizing associations in all samples of creativity along a six role state dialectic of emotions. The study of that periodic pattern led me to research the physical structure and the conflict resolution or moral function of the unconscious. The Formal hypothesis of a six role and three formal operations entity expanded Aristotle's phenomenological analysis of drama. The dramatic process became the Conflict Resolution Process, a pure formal and natural science energetic entity, having a dialectic structure and a moral conflict resolving function. This pattern was identified as a natural science entity that was predictable and measurable; hence formulas governed psychology and morality, the psychic and the divine.

The process as a scientific entity
In *Conflict Analysis, the Formal Theory of Behavior*, I identified the mental periodic phenomenon with two equilibrial systems, one of physics, the Simple Harmonic Motion, the other of logic and mathematics, the laws governing the equilibrial operations of the trays of a scale. This equivalence allowed the introduction of the constructs and formulas of the two natural science phenomena into the study of the unconscious organization of emotions. This development identified that a psychological and moral order periodic phenomenon abides by the laws of equilibrial systems and hence that we can bridge, using this entity as the unit of the social sciences, the soft with the rigorous sciences. (See page 153-154.)

Differences between the mind and machines
The equation of the mind and the mechanical phenomena needs clarification. There are differences between the mental and the mechanical phenomena.
• First, the mental equilibrial system like a machine transforms energy; but unlike machines the mind transforms an energetic quantity from conflict to resolution that is from disorder/chaos or entropy to order or negative entropy; the mind upgrades order or energy.
• Second, the mechanical periodic equilibrium is a cyclic periodic entity that is reversible. The pendulum goes back and forth virtually forever. The mental process is irreversible; action is one directional, it seeks the restoration of the equilibrial rest state as the transformation of unstable to a stable or negative entropy state. Upon the transformation of energy the mental oscillation stops. The emotional rest state represents conflict resolution as the restoration of the coveted homeostatic state, the individual's psycho-social adjustment.

• Third, the process is innate; it is determined by the software of the unconscious fully operational at birth. We may infer that the mind is like a computer, which upon its inception is delivered as neurological hardware bundled with conflict resolution normative adjustment software. (See page 151.)

The unconscious as the integrative paradigm
The definition of the unconscious as a natural science phenomenon accounted simultaneously for psychological phenomena such as the syndromal nature of emotions and thoughts, sociological phenomena, like the cultural diversity of ways of resolving conflict, and the cross generational transmission of patterns. It accounted for the plot and the moral of stories, also the origin of religion as the systemic experience of the processing of emotions generating the yearning for meaning and providing the inspiration of moral explanations. It explained the state of rest, peace of mind and peace in the world as representing the actualization of conflict resolution.

The unconscious as the origin of moral order
While the first set of publications, the Formal Theory and its training program, introduced the discovery of the process and its many applications in psychology, the second set of publications on the Moral Science presents its relevance for the study of religions as a moral order phenomenon. The set of the Moral Science books test the thesis of the Formal Theory on the nature of the unconscious as the origin of moral thought. They present the exhibits of the Museum of the Creative Process as evidence establishing that moral order is a natural science phenomenon, totally independent of revelation and theistic Genesis.

Religions are scientific discoveries of aspects of the Conflict Resolution Process
Religions are merely stories about resolving conflict. They use metaphors. Metaphors are interpreted as particular types of resolution. Hence religions discovered partially the under-

lying natural science process. Their discoveries advanced alternative ways of resolving conflict between the members of the family institution. Resolutions followed the process's three formal operations: mastery, cooperation and mutual respect. Religions as discoveries of conflict resolution evolved gradually dialectically but also independently of each other in many different locations of the world. This progression is documented in the sculptural trail retracing the history of the family institution. (Exhibit #4 The Sculptural Trail.)

Religions evolved resolutions as particular norms regulating dealings in the area of domestic relations generating covenants delineating gender relations. Many religions contributed to the evolution of the institution of the family as we know it today by discovering intuitively alternative ways of resolving. In Greece men assumed mastery over women; men chose cooperation and compliance to women in India and mutual respect between father and son but not between men and women in Israel. The discoveries of these religions are complementary not contradictory versions of conflict resolution.

The historical problem has been that religions as partial discoveries of the process, and accounting it theistically have professed their resolutions to represent the entire truth about the nature of moral order and have discouraged alternative belief systems. Religions from the scientific perspective may be considered as misleading the public with arbitrarily determined resolutions.

Prometheus steals the fire as the metaphor of science usurping the moral authority of religions
Formal Theory's rational and moral unconscious process introduces reason in the area of moral order. It demystifies metaphysics as the physics of the moral process. The science of the process integrates religions and advances them to the Moral Science. Science thus corrects the moral impasse of the Abrahamic religions by promoting

conflict resolution in domestic relations emphasizing the need for the missing mutual respect between genders, between men and women bound in the marital relationship and outside of it. The understanding of the creative process as a multi-operational conflict resolution mechanism reconciles and integrates the religions of the world into an evolutionary continuum of restructured domestic relationships.

Concluding, the scientific moral paradigm contradicts the metaphysical origin of moral order as well as the social justice of religious normative paradigms. Science completes the quest of religions for peace and moral order or justice by identifying the abstract nature of conflict resolution. Science in this process integrates psychology with morality. Moral order is defined as the abstract calculus of power management, conflict resolution, leading optimally to the equitable distribution of power to all systemic participants.

PRINCIPLES OF THE FORMAL ANALYTICAL METHOD

Formal Theory's methodology: the object and the method for the study of behavior
Conflict Analysis, the Formal Theory of Behavior ushered in the scientific definition of the unconscious and *Conflict Analysis Training*, the companion volume contributed the *Conflict Analysis Battery*, a user friendly self assessment. The battery allowed the experimental validation of the theory.

The Formal Theory changes the object and the method for its analysis in the study of behavior. It studies the creative process analytically as a mechanism, interpreting metaphors scientifically, instead of examining their contents literally. The object of study of the Formal Theory is the plot of stories, not their content, and the method is formal analysis of symbolic ideas/emotions rather than the validation or refutation of their con-

tent. This object and method lead conclusively to the study of behavior and moral order as patterns that are measurable and that are moral as resolving conflict.

The Formal Theory studies the creative process, the formal relation of ideas in stories as symbolic ideational and emotional systems identifying the structure of the process as a distinct six-role state and three formal operations pattern with the function of conflict resolution. This outcome is the physiological, psychological and sociological adjustment to stress. The formal analysis of symbolic systems identifies this mental dialectic as the object of study and the two natural science periodic phenomena, the Simple Harmonic Motion and the equilibrial scale, as providing the method for the scientific analysis of behavior. Thus the theory placed Conflict Resolution, moral order, on a scientific foundation and defined the process as the unit integrating the social sciences into the rigorous Moral Science.

The process entity, the emotional and ideational dialectic is intrapsychic but also interpersonal. It is between the individual's inner emotions as a sequence of states but this sequence manifests as actions interpersonally affecting the individual's relations with others. The result is in the individual either resolving his conflicts in his own play of ideas and emotions or alternatively projectively confronting or conforming to societal norms interactively. Inner change may accompany social change as the individual challenges the norms of the system.

Three conceptual fallacies on the scientific research on the nature of morality/religion
The two Moral Science volumes explore humanity's history of insights on the nature of the psyche and God, the two poorly understood philosophical spiritual concepts, by reconciling them in the analytical study of the process. The new science reconciles the multiplicity of religious explanations and psychological theories

that have polarized our views by integrating the two domains of knowledge into a continuum studying the nature of the unconscious.

The split between religion and psychology has been caused by three methodological fallacies in the scientific study of the mind.

• **The first fallacy has been the separation of the psychological from the moral;** morality has been equated with determinism, the pursuit of a moral end, determined by God, revelation, hence moral order has been dismissed by 'science' as metaphysical. Following the separation of moral order and psychology, scientists, psychologists and theologians, have divided the field of behavior into the two unrelated fields of psychology and religion.

• **The second fallacy has been scientists' inappropriate use of the object of study, the content of stories.** For example, Genesis, a scriptural story of mythic nature, has been interpreted literally by both parties debating its veracity. Positive or negative theories are totally misplaced debating Genesis as a critical point for the existence or refutation of God. Theistic thinkers have been concrete in the choice of object and method of study of moral order; they chose the content of stories as the literal interpretation of the stories advanced by the scriptures. Scientists chose as the alternative to literal belief in the content of the stories the scientific scrutiny of reality dismissing the content of stories seeking mechanistic models to explain moral order.

Biology has contributed evidence contradicting the assumptions of the biblical creation story. New biologists examine the brain to identify emotions and moral order. This split between moral order attributed to god as revealed in the scriptures and psychological order as identified in the study of the brain still divides the literalists or true believers from the atheists or the agnostics. It is a mistake to debate the veracity of myths and primitive rationalizations as the way of refuting moral order and religions. Morality exists as a universal phenomenon even if the veracity of the content of stories is accepted or refuted. Religions are a universal phenomenon totally independent of the story of Genesis. According to the Formal Theory both groups are wrong in their respective explanations; they have chosen the wrong object of study and the wrong method for its analysis. Moral order is about conflict resolution; it is nor about gods and it is not about creation.

• **The third fallacy is related to the choice of proper method for the analysis of the object in studying moral order.** The appropriate object, the plot of stories, needs the appropriate method as the Formal Analysis of associations. The appropriate 'scientific' analysis of systems of ideas and emotions are the disciplines of the rigorous sciences, physics, logic and mathematics. The Formal Theory introduces the rigorous sciences in the analysis of symbolic universes examining the formal and energetic structure of ideas and emotions in systems of conflict resolution.

Genesis as a sample of formal theoretical interpretation

Genesis is a typical story needing formal analysis. We identify it as a metaphor of the mental dialectic process leading to conflict resolution. Genesis, meaning Creation, has captured metaphorically the six-part process with a creation story of six days, leading to the day of rest. The metaphor describes accurately the six-role state unit structure leading to the resolution of a conflict as the structure of the unconscious process. Genesis then is vindicated as a correct insight in the nature of the process and the nature of the unconscious. Judaism advanced several metaphors on the scientific nature of the process and of moral order: the one God, the Ten Commandments, the personality types of the children of the Haggadah as alternative ways to resolve conflict, etc.

Integrating psychology and morality with science

The conclusions of both creationists and evolutionists, new versions and old, are mute and irrelevant on methodological grounds as both perspectives have missed examining the proper object, the emotional structure of the process as a formal continuum. Both parties of the long debate have wasted energy in debating the issue passionately. They have erred. They have failed by not using the appropriate object and method for the analysis of the object of moral order, the emotions generated by experiencing conflicts and seeking resolutions.

We repeat the Formal Theory postulates the object is the creative process, and the method of analysis, the formal organization of ideas or emotions in the context of the closed system of a conflict resolution. The Formal Theory chooses the appropriate object of analysis: the story, any creative process, and the appropriate method, the formal analysis of distinctions reflecting emotions. The studies of the art exhibits analyze stories to identify the process as the relational structure of ideas as orderly distinctions manifested as forms and energies. Distinctions shape the symbolic language of emotions following the predictable six-role state, three formal operations energetic pathway.

The formal methodological perspective unifies psychology and morality by studying the unconscious as determined by an inner moral imperative, the adjustment of the individual to the societal norms. This concept defines the individual in terms of the psychic moral order generating and perpetuating or altering the social order pursuing justice as one's homeostatic rest state. The pathway of resolutions identifies personality types as the range of alternative ways of resolving conflict. It also identifies religions as measurable conflict resolution ideational and relational psychological and sociological phenomena.

The propositional and the relational method

Methodologically we recognize two approaches in the analysis of phenomena: the relational and the propositional. Methodology as a science evolved from propositional, axiomatic reasoning to the abstract relational logic of formal analysis. The propositional perspective consists of arbitrary postulations, multiple assumptions or stories, on the nature of behavior. It examines causality. Contemporary psychology recognizes the medical, neurological, behavioral, cognitive and chemical models or stories on the nature of behavior. Similarly, religions are stories or explanations, the many dogma-based definitions on the nature of moral order and of the divine or higher authority.

The formal analytical method is a shift from propositional or axiomatic thinking to relational reasoning, from concrete to abstract thinking. In the relational method deductions do not depend on the veracity of the assumptions made, the content of stories, but on the interrelation of parts into totalities. i.e. in Genesis the content of the six day of creation is propositional method, the interrelation of days as a progression of interrelated emotions is the relational approach of analysis. There is a cause-effect relationship between stress and response, anxiety and defense, etc, it is the relational operations seeking equilibrial balance. If an actor commits a hubris, the consequence is a punishment. Alternatively if he completed a social contribution he may expect a reward. One expects and acting defensively one finds what one has expected as deserved. The process is completed with a compromise or proportionate resolution.

Instead of dogma, we identify the plot of stories as the universal formal relational structure leading to a conflict resolution inherent in the systemic organization of emotions and related symbolic constructions. Formal relations are the scientific foundation of psychology and morality.

The logic of formal relations generates wider deductions or more meaningful explanations than propositional thinking. It is the science of method that dictates that instead of axiomatic thinking, accepting the credibility of stories, we must identify and measure their formal dimensions as internal systemic transformations leading to quantifiable and qualifiable resolutions. The evidence of the process is conveyed in the spontaneous associations following the predicted organization balancing emotions as power choices following the logical necessity leading to the predictable conflict resolution outcome.

CONCEPTUALIZATIONS OF THE THOUGHT PROCESS: PIAGET AND FREUD
The Piagetian epistemology:
The Kleinian group of four equilibrial operations

The process has been identified by many psychologists, but incompletely. The Unit Conflict Resolution Process is the homeostatic response of the unconscious, averting setbacks following the dialectic of three one directional formal equilibrial transformations (Piaget/ Garcia, 1989). This directedness underlies all symbolic systems. The exhibits validate the theory by demonstrating the irreversibility of this unconscious process. They illustrate this order, organizing associations along the predicted formal structure and moral function (Brainerd, 1978).

The Formal Theory postulates the use of relational method in the study of the Unit process. It regards the mental and moral order as an equilibrial mechanism abiding by the laws of logic and physics. The relational method is illustrated by the scale, whose balance is determined by the Kleinian group of four formal operations (Klein/ Hedrick, 1932). Piaget introduced the formal operations in the study of the thought process as an equilibrial system, but he used this model in a very different way than the Formal Theory. He identified the formal principles in the capacity of the mind to conserve unemotional cognitive abstract constructs as fully reversible mental operations.

The four formal equilibrial operations, Felix Klein's group of equilibrial operations
The disturbance of the state of rest is identified by the formal operation of the Kleinian system, the identity operation, I, identity. Identity corresponds to the initial change of the symbolic balance. It is the stress state. The operations of reciprocity, R, opposition, N, and correlation, C, restore the balance of the system.

$$I = NRC$$

The formal interrelation of the six role states is determined by three formal conflict-resolving operations: passivity is turned to activity, antagonism to cooperation and alienation to mutual respect.
1. These mental operations are the equilibrial principles of the trays of a scale where any added weight, I, identity operation, disturbing the balance is countered by three alternative operations restoring the balance as follows:
2. N for negation: cooperation, removing the added weight from the same tray, undoing the disturbance, corresponds to transforming antagonism to cooperation,
3. R for reciprocity: mastery as placing a weight to the opposite tray, reciprocating the change, corresponds to transforming a state of passivity to one of activity,
4. Finally C, for correlative, corresponds to mutual respect, shifting the weight on the fulcrum, correlating a small change to a bigger one, corresponds in psychology of relations to transforming alienation to mutual respect.

The three corrective formal operations: reciprocity leading to mastery, negation leading to cooperation and correlation transforming alienation to mutual respect, restore the emotional balance like the placement of the weights restores the equilibrial balance of the scale. The end state fulfills the inner need of the person complying or protesting to the external stress evoking norms. The Moral Science reduces the psyche and god

to a set of trigonometric formulas. Ideational phenomena correspond to natural science conflict resolutions, the alternative solutions of the formulas of physics and logic, generated by different values of the variables involved.

For the Simple Harmonic Motion as the physics of the mental dialectic, see the Wizard of Oz exhibit, panel #2.

We need to clarify three key differences with the Piagetian use of the formal operations.
• First, the formal operations conserve and transform energy, an emotional and energetic quantity, not only abstract entities like the Piagetian constructs of time, volume and space.
• Second, the formal operations occur unconsciously and upon one's birth or conception, not consciously and at later developmental phases as suggested by Piaget.
• Third, the formal operations proceed irreversibly as the mind is targeting restoration of an inner balance, conflict resolution, as the desirable end state of the equilibrial process. The mind departs from conflict, defined as passivity, antagonism and alienation, and pursues conflict resolution, defined as the state of activity, cooperation and mutual respect. The mental process is one directional as it proceeds toward resolution, the recapturing of the state of rest; it does not allow for reversibility as Piaget postulated. The mind commands progress toward the comfort zone of the rest state.

Formalization of the psychoanalytic structural model
The formal theoretical Unit allows the reconceptualization of the Freudian structural model into a dynamic totality. The Formal Theory using the purely formal concept of a role-state integrates Freud's structural model into a dynamic totality, the Conflict Resolution Process. Thus, the formal theoretical Unit reconciles the fragmented phenomenological structural constructs of psychoanalysis. The static constructs of the id, ego and

superego are translated into the three formally interrelated passivity-activity cycles of the Unit of the Conflict Resolution Process.

Freud's id, ego and superego represent fragments of the process as separate entities, competing in controlling the person (Freud/ Strachey, 1977). He identified the id as the reality of the drives, in conflict with the ego, as the realistic processor of the impulsive drives, and the superego as the faculty of moral injunctions.

Freud's unconscious, compartmentalized into three agencies, may be reconceptualized as a unit process through the holistic integration of parts into a totality, the formal thought system.

• The Freudian id, for instance, is seen to correspond to the stress-response cycle. The Freudian drives are interpreted in relational terms, not as biological states. They represent the stress/ trauma and its reciprocal, the response, transgression or hubris, as two reciprocally related role-states. These are also identified as the states of Role Oppression and Role Assumption.

• The Freudian ego, as the system of anxieties and defenses, may be seen to coincide with Formal Theory's second cycle, representing the formally interrelated role-states identified as Anticipated Role Reversal and Counterphobic Role Assumption, anxiety and defense.

• The Freudian superego may be seen to coincide with the third cycle of the mental totality, Formal Theory's Role Reversal and Compromise Role Assumption; the conflict resolution cycle discovers moral order. Formal Theory identifies moral order as the unconscious objective of this holistically integrated process.

This process, though totally intrapsychic, manifests itself interpersonally, and allows the transmission of structured role systems across generations. The moral structure of the totality is only obvious pro-vided we examine the six role dramatic sequence in its entirety as determined by the formal transformation of a key role-state.

The Formal Theory views this role sequence evolving progressively from its relational inception as a conflict initiated by a role relational stress to which the person reacts, reciprocates with a response. The initial disturbance, the Role Oppression is followed by a Role Assumption.

This cycle elicits the inner/outer conflict cycle, the ego states of anxiety and defense, as the hero's state of Anticipated Role Reversal elicits his/her Counterphobic Role Assumption behavior. This second cycle represents the externalization of the internal conflicts.

This elicits the third cycle as the sociological experience of Role Reversal as punishment, and of the compromise as the hero's revenge or expiation.

The Formal Theory organizes this dramatic totality into a trigonometric formula that is valid for any value of its variables. That is, for any dramatic action of the hero, for any role choice in a relational system as a whole, there is a particular role system that applies.

Transference versus relational modalities

The two main operational distinctions in the course of resolving conflict, passivity versus activity, cooperation versus antagonism, determine alternative ways of resolving conflict. The finite spectrum of two alternative formal operations provides four relational solutions. The combinations of these two operations represent the range of the four key syndromal diagnostic personality patterns: dominant-cooperative, dominant-antagonistic, submissive-cooperative and submissive-antagonistic as the new, purely relational personality diagnoses. These syndromal entities account for a person's experience of reality both during wellness and during psychopathology.

The two retrospective art exhibits, the Gorski canvases and the cultural sculptures, address the relational modality issue by showing how both the artist, and the moral philosophies of the world evolved in their relational approach dialectically from modality to modality in the course of their historical evolution.

Case studies address the issue of relational syndromes

Relational diagnosis redefines the Freudian transference as the innate inclination toward one relational modality. Indeed the relational pattern as transference is identified much more accurately through analysis of one's artwork than the ruminations of a patient on the couch. The free associations from the couch are less easy to objectify than the associations generated through Metaphor exercises and the Relational Modality Evaluation Scale, RMES. Samples of creativity, reveal the subtle relational structure of one's unconscious thinking precisely and it is a great advantage that the client is doing the analysis and interpretation of the pattern rather than the therapist.

Thus while conceptually we shift from transference to relational modalities, practically the *Conflict Analysis Battery* replaces the couch. Psychological testing, sampling creativity for self-discovery, is a cost-effective alternative to psychoanalysis. It is the express and accurate way to access self-knowledge and personal transformation without incurring the dependency relationship with a therapist. The battery preempts the need for a therapist to evolve insights as the trainee may become self-aware on his own. This allows the patient to restructure one's own relational pattern simply by analyzing one's creativity tasks. Creativity-generated insights accurately reveal the structure of one's unconscious thinking and implicitly entail the need for the corrective restructuring of one's relational pattern.

The importance of context in examining a system: Psychoanalysis Oedipus Complex versus the Formal Theory's Conflict Resolution Process

Oedipus, according to Freud, represents the drive of libido and aggression. Oedipus according to the Formal Theory is the hero of an entire drama, including the episode of arrogance to be followed by the episodes of punishment and expiation. The propositional method is exemplified in Psychoanalytic Theory's fundamental hypothesis, founded on Freud's observation of the Oedipal incident in the Greek tragedy, as a universal instinctive mechanism underlying all psychological phenomena. Freud arbitrarily and incorrectly chose an incident in a play as the total truth about the human condition overlooking this incident's context in the total play of Oedipus Rex as a conflict resolution entity.

The relational method studies the predictable, internal organization of ideas in a story as parts of any given totality. The Formal Theory recognizes the circumscribed entity of a story, as a drama, as a sequence of formally interrelated events leading to conflict resolution. In contrast to Freud's propositional or axiomatic method, the Formal Theory examines the Oedipal incident in the context of the entire tragedy as a dramatic totality with a beginning, middle and a conclusive moral end. We examine the tragedy as a cause-effect formal or causal interrelation of parts into the conflict resolving totality.

In this context the Oedipal episode, a son killing his father, is the hubris incident of the dramatic plot in balance or formal relation with the rest of the play's segments: the adventure, the role reversal, the recognition, and finally deke or justice as the resolution of the story imparting the feeling of expiation or catharsis. All dramas have both a psychological and a sociological function; i.e. the patricidal and incestuous hero is punished and such conduct is denounced admonishing the culture of the dangers of a close mother child relationship antagonistic to the paternal authority.

Greece grew to distrust the mother son relationship and this is dramatically portrayed in Orestes, who with the help of his sister Electra, killed his unfaithful mother Klitemnestra, Perseus decapitated the Medusa, while Heracles, the hero battling mythic monsters was defeated by his jealous wife.

Formal Analysis of psychoanalytic concepts
The Formal Theory interprets and reconciles the multiple psychoanalytic hypotheses

The Formal Theory explains findings of other theories and integrates the multiple theories of psychoanalysis into a unified theory of behavior: the structural model, transference relational psychology, etc. are accounted for by the formal definition of the unconscious.

Psychoanalysis consists of a number of independent and unintegrated axomatic postulations. The Formal Theory reconciles the diversity of parallel assumptions into the study of the unconscious as a single assumption, that of a unit Conflict Resolution Process. The relational method integrates the diversity of non-relational psychoanalytic theories.

1. On the nature of the unconscious

The Formal Theory changes the object and method of the study of the unconscious. It revamps the nature of the Freudian unconscious from a biological negative drive to a dynamic adjustment process of six interrelated emotions seeking normative compliance or normative change. The unconscious is not Freud's sexual and violent 'Oedipal complex', methodologically a propositional statement. Instead the Formal Theory shifts the focus from the story to the dramatic process of the circumscribed entity of a play, the Teleion Holon, adopting the relational method, the consideration of the formal relation of parts, the six emotions in their formal predictable restructuring from a conflict to a resolution. The object of study of the unconscious is conflict resolution totalities. This unconscious process is the unit order, organizing emotions and social reality as deviation from norms.

2. On the structural model

The application of this method identifies Freud's structural model, the id, ego, and super ego system as equivalent to Formal Theory's six role states linked by three formal operations into the Conflict Resolution Process. The emotions are a series of formal inter-transformations of one key role. The plot leads a conflict to its resolution, moral order, catharsis, as a natural science phenomenon. According to the Formal Theory the six emotions bound by three formal operations lead to resolution as the definition of moral order.

This pattern is reduced into a set of six formal transformations of one verb, or action: murdering characterizing five generations of the Greek Creation stories.

Stress: The child is perceived as a potential murderer and oppressed,

Response: the child responds by murdering his father. Anxiety: The child becoming a father is anxious anticipating being murdered in return by his children and Defense: a father murders his children counter phobically;

Reversal: the father is murdered by his children and

Compromise: The dying father curses his children to be murdered in their own turn.

The Freudian Structural model is rediscovered as the formal dialectic of the six emotions or role states. The process reconciles then the id ego and super ego aspects of the model into a formal continuum that progresses to meaning and social growth. Emotions, associations, role states, symbolic transformations reflect the continuity from a conflict to its resolution.

Id is the stress response phase,
ego the anxiety defense cycle and
super ego is the moral phase, the resolution, as a reversal and compromise attitude change.

3. The model of unconscious drives

The Oedipal Complex is a cultural path to resolution. The drives of libido and thanatos correspond to the Grecian Oedipal dynamics representing the dominant antagonistic way of relating polarizing interpersonal relations within the family system. This relational modality is characteristic of all Greek culture's social systems: mythology, Olympic competition, democratic political institution, dramatic play writing competitions, etc.

4. Freud's relational model, transference

Transference is accounted for by Formal Theory's genetically determined syndromal relational modalities (Mitchell/ Black, 1995). These are a set of four wellness diagnostic categories. Research demonstrates the formal alternatives dominance versus subordinacy, cooperation versus antagonism, as reflecting four alternative ways of resolving conflict. Relational modalities are personality types determined genetically and not by developmental circumstances and formative relations.

5. Psychoanalysis energetic model

The formal unit order reconciles Freud's energetic model, ideas as cathexis, with the physics of equilibrial systems, energies intertransformed but upgraded, and with morality as emotions transformed to self-improvement by facilitating attitude change. Catharsis is about resolution of conflict as spirituality coinciding with release from antagonism, alienation and passivity. This unconscious process is present in all creativity as the plot of stories, binding emotions, behaviors, as dynamic and kinetic energies, progressing to negative entropy, catharsis as resolution or moral order. The process is a natural science energetic and formal entity abiding by the laws of natural science equilibrial systems.

6. Psychoanalysis as a therapeutic modality

Freud was never able to measure behavior and validate his theories experimentally. He collected free associations on the couch; in contrast to that we have the *Conflict Analysis Battery*, an entire theory based assessment. The Formal Theory identifies the formal operations as the variables in samples of creativity to identify and measure relational modalities.

7. Therapy as interminable

Freud's psychoanalysis as a therapeutic modality has been considered interminable. Formal Theory introduces a manual-driven time limited, standardized psychotherapy that integrates the psychotherapeutic modalities of art therapy, cognitive, experiential, and behavior modification. The Formal model of psychotherapy, *Creativity and Power Management*, consists of a concise program of emotional education that can be delivered in the classroom. Therapy outcome can be monitored with the inventory and the metaphor testing as we show in the murals 11 and 12.

8. Religions

Freud explained religions as cultural tribal Oedipal phenomena. The Formal Theory considers religions as partial and complementary conflict resolutions. They are indeed discoveries of conflict resolution that are formally interrelated to each other.

The volumes on the art exhibits and case studies present this mental entity manifested in art exhibits as symbolically cohesive systems. These systems are natural science predictable and universal phenomena abiding by the laws of conservation of energy and of the laws of two equilibrial phenomena, the Simple Harmonic Motion and the balance of the trays of a scale. The symbolic system consists of six formal transformations of one key action, see table following mural one.

Examples of symbolic systems:
Greece versus Judea

In the Greek creation stories the action is murdering and its six formal variations, whereas in the Judaic/Biblical culture the role in the patriarchal generations is one of trust, faith versus distrust.
Stress: The person is oppressed perceived and treated as a potential murderer by his father.
Response: The person responds by becoming the murderer of his own father, committing patricide in collaboration with his mother.
Anxiety: The murderer cursed by his father antici-

pates to be murdered by his own children.
Defense: The scared murderer counter-phobically murders preemptively his children; a father commits infanticide.
Reversal: The offensive, defensive father is murdered by his children with the help of their mother, his wife.
Compromise: The dying hero resigned curses his children to be murdered in their turn by their own children.

In the Biblical cross-generational relations the specific role choice and symbolic system binding members of the family and mental states energizing individuals is the opposite behavior to Greek culture's murdering and paranoia or distrust. The key role of the Judaic system of relations was established upon Abraham's testing his family evolving from distrust to total trust by testing loyalty through the staged sacrifice of Isaac. The family, his wife and son passed the test transforming the father son and mother relationship from Oedipal and antagonistic dynamics to those of the Judaic father son mother covenant. Implicit in this system is mutual respect in the father son relationship. But while this choice emphasizes model resolution, the overall process in biblical family relations started with the conflict of distrust by testing partners gradually leading to trusting relationships.

Unresolved conflicts in the Abrahamic family shifted to the man/woman power differential and sibling rivalries, motivated by competitive drive to become the father's favorite son and hence his heir and successor. The role-state forming the cultural pattern evolved from murdering one's rival sibling to cheating or testing one's partner and eventually resolving the sibling rivalries with fairness and forgiveness.

The symbolic system of testing, mistrusting, started with God testing Adam and Eve. Adam and Eve failed the test. Their children similarly failed when Cain killed his brother, Abel.

Abraham tested his wife and son, threatening the sacrifice of Isaac, by attributing this request to God. Sarah passed the test, but died of grief at the thought of her son being sacrificed. Isaac passed the test by complying to his father's request. In his turn, Isaac was tested by his wife Rebecca and his son Jacob, who conspired to deceive him and win his blessings reserved for his brother Esau. Jacob, having cheated his father in his turn, was tested by the angel of God with whom he had to wrestle before encountering his cheated brother, Esau. He was also cheated by Laban, his father-in-law, who substituted Rachel, the daughter promised to Jacob, with Leah her sister; Jacob was cheated by his many sons pretending that Joseph, his favorite with the multicolored coat, was killed by animals; they showed him as evidence the bloodied garment; the truth was they had abandoned Joseph who found his way to Egypt. The concept of testing escalated as Levi and Simon deceived the citizens of Sechem telling them they would allow the marriage of their sister Dinah, who had been raped by one of them, if they were circumcised. Jacob's children attacked and killed the men of Sechem while they were disabled as warriors. Joseph tested by his brothers tested them again in Egypt planting items in their bags of food (*Dershowitz*, 2001).

The Judaic conflict of testing or distrusting versus trusting the love relationship between siblings that started with the failure in the relationship between Cain and Abel must be seen in the context of the series of sibling relations concluded successfully with Joseph testing and forgiving his jealous brothers and granting them the status of equal power as leaders of the twelve tribes of Israel. Job is a key Judaic cultural hero who endured tests of his faith in God.

The six-role system is a natural science phenomenon
The six role states of the chosen relational distinctions are conveyed in the symbolism of a key action identified by one verb. The passive active

forms of any symbolic system, from murdering to distrusting, become a predictable system of role states in formal relation to each other constituting an energetic system that is conserved. This system has the properties of two equilibrial natural science phenomena. It can be conceptualized as a mechanical natural science periodic oscillation. While the forms evolve formally from passive to active, antagonistic to cooperative and alienation to mutual respect, these forms are also energies transformed from passivity as emotions to activities as behaviors and finally to insights as inner meaning; in physics this state is identified as negative entropy, (entropy meaning chaos). The mental process then is both a system of formally interrelated emotions and a directional transformation determined by the need for the rest state. The rest state coincides with the moral end, a goal, which gives closure to the periodic phenomenon. This transformation consists in diminishing unstable energy, transforming it into resolutions corresponding to positive rather than negative emotions. These goals are achieved in the completed three-cycle mental harmonic.

The nature of meaning: the process connects parts into dramatic and adjustive totalities
The Formal Theory's relational method examines stories as composed of the process' six segments and three formal operations as a sequence of emotions/episodes constituting the complete unit process. The formal entity integrates all these episodes as interrelated leading by necessity to the moral end as the conflict's resolution or social normative conciliation. The exhibits demonstrate this simple entity, the creative process, to integrate parts into totalities of meaning or conflict resolution, contributing internal and external growth, insights and enlightenment. The exhibits represent the scientific interpretation of metaphors by qualifying and quantifying conflict resolution. The exhibits complement each other in demonstrating how the process, the plot of stories has a clear structure and function.

The process as the unit of the social sciences
The six-role state unit process is a predictable conflict resolution mechanism. The conflict resolution process defines moral order as the physiological and psychological restoration of the rest state. The unit is serving homeostasis. No matter how much adversity or conflict we depart from, we end up at the state of resolution, compromise, abstraction, peace, rest, corresponding to the reconciliation of opposites, murdering with celebrating life, distrust with trust pleasure with pain.

It is important to learn to observe the mental harmonic integrating fragments into meaningful totalities because the dramatic totality is the object for the scientific study of psychology and of moral order. The art exhibits illustrate and validate this assumption of the Formal Theory. They demonstrate that the unconscious thought process has the six role-state and three formal operations structure and the conflict resolution moral function. This finding entails that this process is the universal harmonic, the unit of the social sciences integrating them into the exact Science of Conflict Resolution, the Moral Science.

Humans have valued this process; they have acquired it as art and worshiped it as divinities. They cherish it as philosophies and respect authors as social heroes. Creators are exalted. Yet it is the unconscious mind that is the artist of all symbolic universes. It is the unit process that unfolds in the histories of gods, in all literature, drama and music. But little or no attention has been paid by scientists to this universal order underlying all creativity. The Museum does not present art as an end to itself. It presents art to identify the transformational process. The process is the object for the study of psychology and of the social sciences.

The new theory introduces the process as the object of study of behavior and formal analysis as the appropriate method for its study. The object, the creative process, and the method, the formal relation of associations in any story or sample of creativity as a symbolic universe, are the phenomena to observe in the exhibits. We may overlook the individual creations for their aesthetic qualities. (See the table of the Greek Creation Story as a Metaphor of the Process).

Our object for analysis is what we know as the plot of stories. The Formal Theory claims that plots have the six role-state structure, bound by three formal operations. The assumption is that the ideas in a story are in a formal relationship to each other as a cascade of three formal transformations predictably unfolding from a conflict to its resolution. This unit order rediscovered in each exhibit attests to the predictability of the mental or moral phenomenon as a symbolic universe or totality and also that this totality is abiding by the laws of the rigorous sciences.

The claim is that this sequence of ideas represents the mental heartbeat, the unit of the social sciences. This entity is what we have been missing in our evolution from the myriad religions of the world and the many theories of behavior to the universality of a moral psychology that is all encompassing, the unified theory of behavior.

The six role-state sequence unfolds automatically and unconsciously. By identifying it, we become aware of the unconscious as interrelated emotions and actions, a sequence concluded upon reaching the desired state of conflict resolution. Thus the unit process is an emotional roller coaster, a dramatic experience with its ups and downs. It is hence the simple equilibrial response to stress as the homeostatic mental faculty that restores the emotional balance. Moral order stems from the need to offset the disturbance of one's rest state by converting stress to compromise. This is the objective of the process manifested as the universal plot of stories.

The nature of meaning as reconciling opposites, making distinctions and reconstituting dualities into unities

The six role-state sequence is the methodological foundation of the Formal Theory. This entity describes how the mind constructs moral order or meaning by first splitting the atom of a symbolic system through a key role distinction and how it proceeds to reconstitute the atom healing it from the discomfort of the split. For example, in the Greek creation myth the distinction is murdering and being murdered. The process thus follows: stress as being regarded as a potential murderer; response as murdering one's father; anxiety as the anticipation of being murdered by one's children; defense as counter-phobically murdering one's children, reversal as being murdered by one's children; and finally compromise, cursing one's children to be murdered.

This pattern evolves to resolution, worshiping Athena, the virgin mother. This distinction and resolution are characteristic of the Greek culture. The resolution evolved gradually with repetitions of the pattern until its resolution in the fifth generation, when the conflict became a resolution and the core paradigm of many Greek cultural institutions The Greek resolution of personal and cultural conflicts attained the value of cooperative antagonism, characteristic of the institutions of democracy, the Olympic games, the pursuit of excellence in works of art and especially dramatic competitions.

The depth of meaning as the many functional identities of the unit order

The six states represent the evolution of the distinction across three formal, obligatory transformations: reciprocity, opposition and correlation. The three formal and irreversible transformations organize the unconscious thought process and transform the emotions as role-states. Emotions/associations evolve by necessity from the state of conflict to that of resolution by turning the state of awareness from passivity to activity, antago-

nism to cooperation and alienation to mutual respect.

This formal series of transformations, the mental heartbeat, is the principle concept of the Formal Theory. It is introduced as the Universal Harmonic, the Conflict Resolution Process and the Unit of the social sciences. Religions have grasped this universal order as moral justice or spirituality, which they have attributed to gods. Psychology examined the process as the unconscious. In literature we know it as the plot of stories and in theatrical plays as the dramatic scenario. In clinical situations we recognize the sequence of six emotions and behaviors as a syndrome and distinguish four relational modalities as diagnostic categories.

Validation of symbolic distinctions

The six role sequence is generated by the making of any distinction whatsoever, as by the notion of an action represented by any verb. The verb is then declined according to a mental grammar and syntax along the set of six interrelated role or emotional states determined by the three mandatory formal operations. The six role-states created by the distinction unfold as an automatic equilibrium-restoring and justice-promoting mechanism completed upon the three formal transformations of the state of stress to the state of compromise. The validation of this unit order is in showing that the initial and end role-states of a symbolic universe, as it unfolds in any sample of creativity, are in a particular formal relation to each other as opposites, reciprocals and correlatives. The sequence, leading to the correction of a distinction as a disturbance, establishes the moral conclusion and confirms justice as a universal order.

Distinctions and resolutions are the theme illustrated by the Museum's exhibits

In the Gorski Retrospective we see the generation of distinctions and resolutions through the use of the symbolic system of the mouth representing the evolution of his feelings/ attitude: from hostility to reconciliation, from lust to spirituality and from alienation to self-acceptance.

In the Sculptural Trail we see the distinctions evolve in the realm of family relations across many cultures finding a sequence of resolutions. Distinctions evolved from the conflicts between matriarchy and patriarchy, father and son, and mother-child alliance, to the outstanding reconciliation of the genders and of the loving husband wife children relationship.

The Conflict Resolution Process is the innate healing mechanism that characterizes the human mind. It is the foundation of the social sciences. It is the sequence of these ideas as a continuum of formal transformations, which accounts for both personal and cultural patterns.

THE GRAPHIC REPRESENTATION OF THE PROCESS

THE SINE CURVE, THE UNIVERSAL HARMONIC OR THE TELEION HOLON

ITS CROSS SECTION, THE POWER FIELD

THE CONCENTRIC CIRCLES AS THE SOCIAL OR NORMATIVE SYSTEM

THE CONCENTRIC ELLIPSES AS THE PSYCHIC OR EMOTIONAL SYSTEM

NORMATIVE DEVIATION AS DISPLACEMENT = S

EMOTIONS AS ACCELERATION = a

BEHAVIOR AS VELOCITY = v

EMOTIONS AND ACTIONS AS INTERTRANSFORMABLE ENERGIES

RESOLUTIONS

AS RESTRUCTURINGS OF THE SOCIAL AND EMOTIONAL ORDER

AND

AS THE UPGRADING OF INNER ORDER OR MEANING

THE GRAPHIC PORTRAYAL OF THE PROCESS

The graphic portrayal of the mental oscillation as the Universal Harmonic, a sine curve of three oscillations and its cross section as a set of concentric circles, the Power Field (Levis, 1977).
The six-role sequence, a trigonometric entity, is presented graphically as a sine curve or harmonic. It has the three-dimensional appearance of a molecule of DNA, a tendril or a corkscrew. Its cross section is a circle and for the purpose of identifying intensity we use a set of three concentric circles. Both the harmonic and the circles are calibrated according to the intensity of the individual relational choices. The position of the individual on the circle as a sociological reference may be indicated by an ellipse or a set of concentric ellipses. Vectors within the circle represent behaviors; vectors within the ellipses represent emotions.

THE UNIVERSAL HARMONIC AS A SINE CURVE
The unit entity is an equilibrial system unfolding in time as a periodic event. It is a three cycle sine curve or harmonic. Its characteristics coincide with those of the Simple Harmonic Motion; the mental oscillation parallels the pendulum oscillation.
The cross section of the harmonic consists of concentric circles. The concentric circles indicate normative layers as the range of displacements, S. Vectors within them reflect the individual's normative deviation, velocity, v. Ellipses on polar opposites of the circles indicate the psychic system and vectors within them indicate emotions as accelerations.

stress, response, anxiety, defense, reversal and compromise

THE THREE-CYCLE MENTAL OSCILLATION

THE POWER FIELD AS A SET OF CONCENTRIC CIRCLES AND ELLIPSES
circles = social system;
ellipses = individual system

ACTIVITY

The diagram rediscovers the Yin Yang presentation of balance as a measurable psycho-social natural science equilibrial system, the Power Field.

PASSIVITY

Passivity and activity are reciprocal vectors.

COOPERATION

ANTAGONISM

Antagonism and cooperation are opposite vectors.

ALIENATION

MUTUAL RESPECT

Alienation and mutual respect are vectors indicative of the increase or reduction of tension by affecting the diameter of the circle

The formal process is also seen as an energetic transformation, which in the triple oscillation upgrades energy from chaos to order. The process then is a formal and energetic entity manifested in the organization of ideas in a story that we can now study utilizing the natural sciences rigorous method, constructs and formulas.
The mental process, however, differs from the mechanical process in one critical way: the ultimate transformation of energies. The mind completes the function of resolution by stopping the mental oscillation upon transforming kinetic/behavioral and dynamic/emotional energy to

meaning. In contrast to the mind, the mechanical pendulum motion continues its oscillation until its energy is dissipated or downgraded. In spite of this difference, the mental process abides by the physics of Simple Harmonic Motion. This equivalence provides the mental oscillation with the language of the sciences, a language that is reliable, valid and which provides the predictability and measurability attained by the rigorous sciences of logic, math, and physics.

There is equivalence between the key constructs of the Simple Harmonic Motion, SHM, and the Conflict Resolution Process, CRP:
status shift = normative displacement, S
emotions = acceleration, a
behaviors = velocity, v
Each of these constructs abides by the trigonometric formulas of the Simple Harmonic Motion. See Panel 3 of the Wizard of Oz Exhibit.

The harmonic is the timeline of the mental oscillation
The Formal Theoretical method measures metaphors as the formal interrelation of ideas in a story along the unit harmonic. We identify the formal interrelation of ideas as six role-states and place the respective emotional states on the peaks and valleys of the three-cycle oscillation. Calibrating these peaks and valleys, we can measure art and graphically portray the intensity and quality of emotions in any given context. The meaning of ideas is thus reduced to totalities of conflict resolution with a specific graphic representation and measurement.

By identifying the process as a periodic phenomenon in the realms of psychology and moral order behavior acquires a new object and a new method for its scientific analysis. It acquires the constructs and formulas of the rigorous sciences for its conceptualization and measurement. The object of study, the succinct and circumscribed sample of creativity, may now be represented by the harmonic as an entity with measurable dimensions. This entity allows us to detect the personal choices in resolving conflicts and to measure accurately a conflict resolution scenario of a given personality or culture as one of four alternative ways of resolving conflict, the four relational modalities.

The relational model of the Formal Theory circumvents the confusion of the diversity of cause-effect propositional models of study characterizing the many theories of psychology and religion. Propositional distinctions cannot be quantified or presented graphically as they are not interrelated; they are deprived of an anchoring context encompassing a universe of events. The relational method gives this context as the scientific foundation to both psychology and morality explaining simultaneously the one-directional outcome of the thought process as the mandatory formal processing of emotions from a conflict to its resolution.

The Harmonic as the template of evolving emotions

The exhibits demonstrate the simple harmonic as the template of six role-states integrating emotions revealing the formal structure of samples of creativity. Each sample is shown to consist of the six interrelated emotions: stress, response, anxiety, defense, reversal and compromise connected to each other as units of the conflict resolution continuum. The exhibits illustrate this harmonic, integrating canvases, sculptures and the individual metaphors of each mural into the respective symbolic universes.

Science describes moral order as having the characteristics of two natural science phenomena: the Simple Harmonic Motion of the pendulum oscillation and the equilibrial balance of the trays of a scale. The moral mental process then acquires the epistemology, laws, constructs and formulas governing these two well-researched natural science phenomena. Thus moral behavior now may be measured along the formal relational dimensions of the scale and along the physical parameters of the pendulum oscillation.

The physics of psychological concepts, status, behaviors and emotions

The exhibits of the Museum illustrate the abstractions about the process advanced in Conflict Analysis, the Formal Theory of Behavior. The abstract process, as a harmonic corresponds to the trigonometric formula of the pendulum variables. Emotions, behaviors and power positions correspond to the constructs of acceleration, velocity and displacement of the harmonic motion. These constructs are captured graphically as a circumscribed three-cycle harmonic, a succinct sine curve, shown to underlie all art exhibits.

The museum exhibits illustrate and demonstrate the harmonic as a six role-state process, a syndrome or totality of interrelated emotions. The role-states or emotions are in formal relation to each other along the three formal operations. They constitute a quantum of conserved energy manifested symbolically as emotionally charged ideas, associations, predictably inter-transformed into the sequence of patterned emotions and action. The symbols of the emotions and actions in the formal order constitute the system we can call the "symbolic universe" of a story.

The exhibits confirm that art presents the equilibrial physiological forces of the unconscious abiding by the formulas of science. The exhibits demonstrate how creativity, and hence all art, is the healing pathway serving the restoration of the emotional state of rest. These exhibits then put an end to the metaphysical quandary on the nature of moral behavior.

The Museum exhibits exemplify the simple harmonic uniting emotions as formally interrelated ideas or role-states leading predictably to conflict resolution. The variety of symbolic languages enlivens the abstract trigonometric formulas of the harmonic. The impersonal unemotional formulas are coming to life with the intense emotions of any symbolic system. The imagery explains the process predictably evolving from a conflict to its

resolution. The artwork breaths life into the abstract formulas of physics and logic. The harmonic of six emotional states conveys the emotions as a drama with beginning and an end. The harmonic becomes the template organizing symbolic systems as emotions; it makes the scientific process emotionally meaningful.

The three exhibits are reiterations of the Simple Harmonic

The contribution of the exhibits is to demonstrate that all symbolic universes are reducible to this dramatic six role state processing of emotions. The evolving images of the many art exhibits validate the concept of the unconscious as the modifiable unit of the Conflict Resolution Process. The exhibits make the point of the universality and the variability of the process. They affirm that the arts identify the physical dimensions of a harmonic entity that is physiological, moral, meaningful and aesthetically pleasing. Science helps to reinforce the notion that art is the orderly language of emotions.

As we rediscover this process in all exhibits and in all phases of conflict resolution in each exhibit, we arrive at the important conclusion that here is overwhelming evidence confirming the assumptions of the Formal Theory. The dialectic process is an entity that is predictable and measurable. The art illustrates how the unconscious again and again organizes images meaningfully into dramatic entities, the units of conflict resolution. The exhibits demonstrate that this dialectic of ideas and emotions is a moral natural science phenomenon. They identify the harmonic of conflict resolution, the circumscribed process, as the atomistic unit of the social sciences.

The conflict resolving entity the six-part harmonic is manifested in the simplest and quietest mental dialogues. It unfolds in our dreams and samples of our creativity. It is the Teleion Holon, the perfect dramatic universe of Aristotle, the mental heartbeat, the compass of emotional thinking, which seeks resolution as the moral north. Resolution is therefore a mental necessity; creativity is like breathing, a vital physiological operation helping the adjustment of a person in this world of norms and conflicts.

The exhibits demonstrate the function of the unconscious as a faculty that transforms conflicts into resolutions as a moral and natural science phenomenon. They make us conscious of the unconscious process as an organizing entity abiding by the laws of the rigorous sciences. The student of behavior finds in the three formal transformations the method to study the process. There he identifies the natural laws governing the human unconscious.

The harmonic is the constant element studied in the exhibits. Though the harmonic stays the same the imagery changes in every work of art. The imagery/symbolic universes consist of the formal transformations of a key role choice. The transformations constitute the symbolic universe of a resolution. The key role state determines the symbolic language of the particular universe. Each exhibit is a natural science phenomenon defined by the key preoccupation determining the thematic continuity integrating the artwork of any exhibit. The formal operations qualify the dimensions of the process.

The trigonometric process as the measuring rod or yardstick of psycho-social reality

The predictable structure of the process allows it to become the measuring rod or yardstick of behavior. We recognize this process in each exhibit confirming the structure and function of the unconscious mechanism. The Harmonic becomes the scientific interpretation of metaphors, of all clinical samples of behavior; it becomes the key to interpreting dreams, analyzing plays, demystifying religions, integrating canvases, sculptures, and episodes of murals and panels into meaningful totalities. The simple language of logic and physics provides the constructs to simplify the complex language of psychology and religion, indeed of all the humanities. Science departs from the diversity of religions, art canvases, cultural stories, to capture the elegant simplicity of the Universal Harmonic.

The art exhibits introduce the holistic perspective of viewing creativity manifested as an orderly conflict resolving entity. Creativity tapped through the assessment technology, the metaphor creation testing of the *Conflict Analysis Battery*, confirms that mental associations evolve predictably and obligatorily from a conflict to its resolution along the six role-state sequence compelled by the three formal operations. The exhibits validate this Moral Science periodic phenomenon as abiding by the universal laws of science and as providing qualitative and quantitative data.

The scientific interpretation of metaphors: physical and emotional characteristics of the unit
The exhibits show the Universal Harmonic being circumscribed, having a beginning (conflict, normative deviation), middle (internalization of the conflict) and end (moral or socialized resolution, normative conciliation). They clarify that the mind operates as an equilibrial entity like the pendulum oscillation and like the trays of a scale. The energetic difference between mind and machines is due to the fact that the mental process is irreversible; it evolves into the direction of the rest state, the improved state of mind. The exhibits show that the mind is oscillating between power positions, balancing attitudes but completing resolution only upon achieving the states of mastery, cooperation and mutual respect. Resolving, making compromises, is contingent upon the individual experiencing mastery but with deference to his/her partners. This attitude is described in the qualifications of cooperation and mutual respect.

The formal analysis allows us to interpret metaphors scientifically. We can translate associations in a story, be those emotions, behaviors, or symbols of those, into formal operations and energetic transformations having a predictable structure and function. The process is energetic and formal. Therefore we may use the constructs and formulas of the natural sciences based on the premise of the conservation of energy and the requirements of the completed formal transformation. So the exhibits show the manifestation of the human mind abstracted into a predictable harmonic, the dialectic of emotions, as simplicity, the natural science orderly pattern, meaningfully binding the complexity and diversity of many samples of any symbolic universe.

The art exhibits demonstrate the coincidence of science, physiology and psychology with morality, identified as conflict resolution, confirming this moral order as defined by the clear language of the rigorous sciences. This language is introduced to bind disparate samples of creativity into the meaningful justice process; deviance is always corrected bringing about catharsis or role modeling. The images and metaphors of the Museum's exhibits confirm the discrete order of conflict resolution made visible as the Universal Harmonic. In the Harmonic we identify the distinct, rigorous phenomenon that is equally clear to all, admirers of art, scientists and religious people.

Moral order as a natural science phenomenon
The Museum exhibits study the creative process as metaphors of the Conflict Resolution mechanism, a measurable six-step and three-formal operations conflict resolution entity; this is a formal structure of emotions, the natural science phenomenon. This definition clarifies the object for the study of behavior, the method of its analysis, and its key function, conflict resolution, as the essence of unconscious thinking. The process represents the particular cultural or individual response to stress as a phenomenon with clear relational and physical dimensions. Conflict resolution has a physiological, psychological and spiritual function but it is also a natural science

phenomenon that by definition has physical dimensions and graphic portrayal.

The creative process, presented in the art exhibits, reflects the stream of unconscious thought, to abide by the laws of the natural sciences. In its universality it is the measuring rod of emotional sensitivities and behavioral responses. The process measures symbolic systems, metaphors, as conflict resolutions and since metaphors are art, the process measures art. All art is metaphors and all metaphors are measurable natural science phenomena.

The significance of this periodic process, following a pathway and targeting a moral outcome, conflict resolution, is enormous. This entity becomes the scientific and moral order unit of the social sciences. A natural science phenomenon integrates art and science, the humanities and the rigorous disciplines into the Moral Science and has inspirational spiritual but also practical value. The consequence is that all observers of behavior can identify the same measurable conflict resolution phenomenon as the circumscribed entity of a story, and agree about morality as the reductionist nature of this determinist or moral evolution of associations.

The unit as the integrative paradigm of the social sciences

The Formal Theory's unit order has vast significance for the social sciences, revamping the way we conceptualize morality, psychology, and deliver therapy and education. This physiologic entity accounts for the organization of reality in units of resolution or emotional adjustment. Conflict resolution is the path of reconciling opposites into oneness as the path to abstract thinking. Accordingly:
• This unit bridges art and science, moral order and psychology. It connects the field of religion with the science of psychology, both dealing with conflict resolution.
• It allows the introduction of rigorous language into behavior.

• It allows the introduction of new diagnostic categories for the well person as four relational modalities, four alternative ways of resolving conflict.
• It allows the creation of a new assessment and therapeutic instrument, the *Conflict Analysis Battery*, to assist the individual in identifying one's pattern of resolving and how to modify his/her responses.
• It reconciles the religions among themselves as alternative modalities of resolving conflict. The conflict resolution principles are moral values but also the dimensions of the process. The process ushers us from religions to the reverence of order as the evolving disorder.

The Formal Theory regards this unit as a malleable entity reflecting both psychological and cultural/moral dimensions. It demystifies religion and psychology. This entity is the origin of religions and formulated and normatively calibrated by religions. Unlike other natural sciences we are dealing with a directional phenomenon. Resolution is the buoyancy of the need to rise above conflict and find peace of mind and peace in the world.

The unit order is the integrative paradigm not only of psychology and religion but of all the social sciences: epistemology, psychology, assessment/psychoeducation, and ethics/morality. The validation of the premises of the Formal Theory compels change in the other social sciences; it establishes the Moral Science as the authority on matters of morality and psychology. The Harmonic integrates the four social science disciplines:

• Epistemology becomes rigorous as science introduces into the study of behavior and morality constructs, formulas and graphic representation.
• Psychology acquires formal diagnostic categories, the relational modalities, syndromes of interrelated emotions and behaviors. This is a major departure in a field dominated by the Diagnostic Statistical Manual consisting of non-dynamic empirical and descriptive symptom-focused diagnostic categories. These medical model diagnoses deprive the public of insights into the psychology of wellness. The new categories connect choices and consequences into four relational categories that help the public to evolve insights, self-knowledge but also to understand psychology as moral.
• Assessment evolves to identify the object of measurement as the unit process. The *Conflict Analysis Battery* is a psycho-assessment instrument composed of both a relational inventory and projective techniques. The battery reconstructs and measures the process as the personal symbolic universe. The approach to assessment is radically different. It is a self-assessment. The person may find out about oneself without the help of a clinician as insights are about factual knowledge, relations, patterns of relating concealed by symbolism, revealing to the creator their deeper significance.
• Morality/ethics: This equilibrial conflict resolving process is the essence of moral order as it negotiates the individual and environmental influences as the conditions to establish peace or rest. Balancing an outer change with a corresponding inner change is the act of compromise, which corresponds to the change from a negative to a positive attitude. This human response to stress is our capacity to change internally and also to make external changes, to heal and to grow.

Morality has been determined by religions establishing what is acceptable, just or normative behavior. Now morality beyond historical covenants and conventions is determined by the principles of conflict resolution. Traditional normative behaviors culturally determined, need to adjust to the better resolutions of conflict as dictated by science. Religions' norms have untill now determined social justice. Religions need to readjust their ways of resolving conflict based on the new set of norms. And they do deviate from the optimal or scientifically determined optimal resolutions.

The process as the origin of moral order

The exhibits validate Formal Theory's Conflict Resolution Process. They demonstrate the universality of a harmonic that follows the formal organization of associations confirming that the mind proceeds along the path to conflict resolution. The conflict resolution is the happy ending as well as the tragic conclusion of stories. It is the keywords of peace and justice. It coincides with the definition of moral order. The exhibits demonstrate moral order in multiple samples of creativity as a periodic phenomenon, a natural science entity. The Formal Theory thus identifies the formal and natural science organization of resolving conflict as the physiologic origin of moral order.

Spirituality as the awareness of the atomistic unit of behavior

Conflict resolution, as the emotional and sociological adjustment to change, is not only a physiological, but also a spiritual motivational entity; the conflict resolution entity is generated by the unconscious organization of associations defined physiologically as the homeostatic response to stress. The unconscious seeks to maintain equilibrial balance averting the sense of loss and pain by attaining a resolution, the pursuit of continuity through a pleasurable compromise; we know it as the happy ending or "happily ever after." This unit restructures emotional and symbolic systems to address outer change with inner change, the change of attitude. The process of closure inspires emergence and confidence in evolution.

This process establishes the unconscious as innately seeking adjustment and defines moral order as a predictable struggle between the individual and his environment's norms. It shows that the outcome is an equilibrial process allowing personal and societal changes. This process allows us to understand psychology and morality as the continuum of social and emotional adjustment. Resolution is the Nirvana point, the center of gravity totally capturing the spirit and motivating behavior.

The emotional, motivational process captures subjectivity and translates it into the objectivity of the sciences. The social sciences and morality demystified by the imperative of conflict resolution become natural science phenomena. Unlike emotionally sterile psychology, we recognize that the Moral Science is about values that are inspirational, spiritual, and which promote a scientific understanding of justice as the normative dialectic between the individual and the societal constraints. The new knowledge is important for the world as the means to a unifying moral theory of behavior. The religions of the world are part of this science.

Understanding conflict resolution is being enlightened and inspired by the positive outcome of the mental process as the equilibrial tool of progress. The process is the compass of creativity pointing to progression as justice. This book of science does not diminish spirituality but on the contrary, it legitimizes it as a natural science phenomenon. It also empowers this concept by promoting emotional education, the study of the scientific interpretation of metaphors, as the civil right to moral and emotional literacy, and the means of letting spirituality as creativity become the path to self-healing, personal and cultural growth. The world is consumed by conflicts that the process can resolve.

As the world becomes a global homogeneous culture it needs to clarify its belief systems and reconcile religions, psychology and science rather than blindly follow metaphors that are divisive and misleading in terms of the nature of justice as the incomplete partial resolutions of domestic relations as identified by the various cultures of the world.

The Sculptural Trail retraces the history of religions and respective cultures to demonstrate that they constitute complementary discoveries of resolutions as increments of social justice. The trail presents the incomplete evolution of religions at an impasse now that is overcome by science. The trail achieves reconciliation of all religions and with science and psychology as the ultimate objective of enlightenment. Science comprehends and completes humanity's journey of moral discoveries to clarify the secrets to happily ever after as the principles of conflict resolution.

The exhibits validate the spiritual/moral nature of the scientific phenomenon. The spiritual process is the meaningful equivalent to the hallowed concepts of God and the psyche. We can associate the process with a clear understanding of the inherent goodness of the psyche and God but also with profound understanding of the dramatic process departing from conflict prior to achieving its resolution.

RECONCILING SCIENCE AND RELIGION

Religions as philosophies of conflict resolution

It is Formal Theory's position that religions are alternative ways of resolving conflict. They have been inspired by human beings who unconsciously responded to societal needs for the reduction of interpersonal and intrapsychic conflict. Stories revealed to philosophers and prophets are reflections of the unconscious mind seeking stability to offset social adjustment issues, crises of a lifetime redefining social justice. Religions began especially addressing issues of domestic relations. Father son relations were the most conflict-arousing issues of domestic relations. We see the mythic conflict played out in both the Greek Cosmogony and the Biblical Abrahamic family in each finding different solutions for infanticidal intent. Both cultures evolved resolutions establishing stable family institutions.

Religions set the norms and covenants regulating gender relations and domestic roles

Religions are personal and cultural normative responses to societal stressors like the father son relationship. Moral orders established societal norms unconsciously projected to metaphysical authorities. It is this process, the ongoing normative adjustment to social stressors attributed to moral authorities that has invented religions as the evolving images of the goddess and of god.

Science shows that both personalities and religions are measurable entities of conflict resolution. People and religions resolve conflict following three formal operations leading to variations in resolutions. Resolutions have evolved following the personality of the religion's prophet or philosopher. Both personalities and religions favor alternative ways of resolving conflict. For this reason the world has been divided by value systems in wide variance to each other.

Moral order, the pursuit of conflict resolution, is the principle motivational force of behavior.
Science now has the challenge of integrating the many images of god, the multiple religions. It accomplishes that by showing that morality and psychology are united aspects of the same phenomenon, the unconscious thought process. These have been artificially divided as the secular and the pious view of the unconscious, neither grasping the thought process as a natural science nor moral order phenomenon. Science discovers now that moral order, the pursuit of conflict resolution, is the principle motivational force of behavior.

Religions have been pioneers of conflict resolution, yet they are guilty of misleading the public both with inequitable norms and by attributing moral authority to heroes deifying partial knowledge of the process as universal truths. So science now is rightfully upstaging religions and current theories on psychology by introducing the rigorous study of the morality bound unconscious.
Religions pioneered psychological explanations, which have evolved in abstraction

Religions evolved to address the stressful social reality by introducing norms, laws and moral imperatives to stabilize the man-woman and parent children as well as sibling to sibling relationships in the evolving family institution. Progress may be viewed as a trend to fairer conflict resolution in the realm of domestic relations and a trend toward greater abstraction on the nature of the divine figures (see Chapter two and follow the Sculptural Trail). The Moral Science completes religions' path to abstraction by identifying the process as the unit order represented by the Universal Harmonic. Religions, as the authorities and monopolies of morality, and psychology as the empirical description of behavior become integrated into the unifying Moral Science.

The art exhibits demonstrate the Harmonic as ubiquitous. It is the process connecting meaningfully disparate art pieces, a diversity of otherwise contradictory creations, into the perfection of a predictable, measurable, meaningful scientific phenomenon. This orderly entity is nothing less than the unconscious and its projection on the cosmos.

Psychic origination of moral order, becoming conscious of the unconscious
Moral conscience and God thinking, psychology and religion, coincide. They are generated in the organic system of the six role state sequence of the emotional motivational unconscious process. Attributive and conciliatory moral rationalizations are generated upon the three-cycle Conflict Resolution Process. The cycle of reversal and compromise evoke conflict resolution as the willingness to change one's attitude by acknowledging a superior authority.

By definition the state of role reversal introduces the anticipated as fulfilled in reality; reversal is the self-fulfillment of one's prophecy; every person is a prophet convinced in his beliefs. The reversal is then perceived as deserved justice inflicted on the transgressor, or reward to the good person, as just magically occurring outcomes. The spontaneous and predictable developments are

hence attributed to external moral authorities, the divine guardians of moral order and justice, societal imaginary friends.

Religious thinking is an integral part of the creative process' third cycle. Role reversal leads to compromise, the activity role state associated with introducing concessions, resolutions, laws, rituals and thanksgiving. The role state of compromise formulates a new attitude, promoting wisdom and respect for an external moral authority. The formal perspective views the reversal and compromise cycle as the adjustive social response component of the six role ideational mechanism. Aristotle's *deus ex machina* is a manifestation of the morality generating unconscious reversal and compromise components. This may be identified as the spiritual or attitude change segment of the process.

Religions represent the compromise thinking on the power balance between the individual and the society/cosmos. Explanations rationalize factors restoring the psychic equilibrium as a change of attitude in the language of the symbolic choice of the thinker's system. This is the cycle we also identify with self-awareness and conscience. Freud identified it as the super ego without connecting it formally to the id and ego as interrelated role states.

Principles of the Moral Science
The Formal Theory redefines the object and method of study as the formal structure of associations and emotions in stories, the plot of stories, the stream of associations as sampled in exercises of creativity; the secrets of moral order are in the formal and physical analysis of the unconscious projected in the clear structure of the plot of stories; thus instead of the propositional truth or untruth of assertions as conveyed in stories of religions we study the formal interrelations between role states, emotions or symbols thereof with the help of the science of physics and the logic of relations. The underlying science

process represents the origin of moral order as the physiological adaptive mechanism.

The process then is demonstrated as the origin of moral order. The unconscious generates the stories. Religions are stories reflecting the unconscious moral order and the level of awareness of this order. The stories describe gods reflecting the individual's relational make up; gods are associations, figments of the human dramatic imagination complying versus rebelling at the norms of a social system.

We can find the secrets of moral order in the formal analysis of small samples of creativity simply by generating metaphors; this is the method of self-evaluation used in the *Conflict Analysis Battery*. The interpretation of metaphors may be used as evidence in the spontaneity of moral self-monitoring (religious) thought. Instead of looking for god in the sky, the science of relations and the physics of equilibrial systems identify moral order in the formal structure of symbolic universes. This order is universal. It is a system of formally interrelated energetic ideas in the process of conflict resolution, a predictable transformation that we can use to validate the abidance of ideational equilibrial systems to the constructs and formulas of the rigorous sciences.

The advantages of abstraction
Methodologically the Formal Theory shifts the object and method of analysis in the study of behavior. Instead of disputing the content of stories questioning the existence of God, Formal Analysis recognizes what is universal in all stories, their conflict resolution structure as a natural science internal moral equilibrial process entailing recognition of the laws of science in the operations of the mind.

The practical consequences are immense. Accordingly a story is a set of formally interrelated symbolic distinctions and energetic transformations. The energetic quantity manifested as emotions are conserved in the totality of the story as a conflict resolution. The plot of stories, a process of equilibrial transformations, predictably departs from a conflict or chaos, unstable energy, to arrive to a resolution or order, an emotionally restful or energetically stable state following the distinct path to compromise.

The exhibits present art as evidence of the Moral Science
The Moral Science volumes demonstrate the manifestation of the Conflict Resolution Process, the new object and method for the study of moral order in all samples of creativity. The exhibits of the Museum of the Creative Process demonstrate the two characteristics of the process: the first is that it consists of an equilibrial three cycle, six-role-state emotional oscillation, pointed to the direction of social adjustment coinciding with the concept of moral order; the second is that the process as the evolution of associations is directed by three motivational formal operations transforming conflict to resolution and redefining moral order as passivity turned to its reciprocal, activity; antagonism to its opposite, cooperation, and finally alienation to its correlative, mutual respect.

The exhibits illustrate the two characteristics as a universal harmonic, a sine curve, an emotional rollercoaster of six role states in formal relation to each other within the totality of symbolic systems as units of conflict resolution. They demonstrate the presence of this process in all samples of creativity. They validate the formal interrelation of emotions in units of conflict resolution. The conclusion is that there can be no psychology separate from moral order and no psychological and moral order separate from science.

Hence moral order and all religions and all psychological phenomena are about the unconscious natural science dialectic of emotions. The process of conflict resolution is physiological, psychological and sociological. The process leads the individual to cope with the normative environment by either adjusting to it or by challenging it but in either case achieving resolution as the upgrading of the psychic systemic order and the culture's system of justice.

Conclusion: The Conflict Resolution Process is the scientific moral paradigm
Science departing from the past misperceptions on the nature of the unconscious identifies the Conflict Resolution Process as a natural science energetic and emotional mechanism bridging the moral and the scientific aspects of the unconscious. The process, a mental adjustment mechanism, is recognized as a universal orderly ideational, formal, energetic, measurable periodic phenomenon. This is a motivational entity, as the mind wishes to achieve a homeostatic state, rest, and social justice by completing the Conflict Resolution Process; the process is the key motivational unconscious mental force.

With the help of this construct as the unit of the social sciences we can understand the psyche in samples of creativity with the ease of feeling the pulse throbbing in one's wrist. With this definition of the unit we also can readily identify the nature of moral direction with the certainty of looking at a compass pointing to the magnetic north as the manifestation of a non metaphysical moral order.

The mental physiological mechanism is the common denominator of the humanities and the sciences integrating diversity of knowledge into the simple harmonic of the Conflict Resolution Process, CRP. The ambiguity of the traditional paradigms is replaced by the certainty of science binding psychology and morality into a pure science terminating humanity's struggle with contentious and divisive speculations on the nature of moral order. Religions introduced theistic explanations of moral justice. Science reclaims moral order as founded on natural law. Formal causality is the foundation of all moral law.

The unit moral order, a natural science measurable and predictable phenomenon, is the key to the moral and scientific interpretation of metaphors. The formal analysis is applicable to stories, creativity and religions as natural science dimensional phenomena. The analysis transforms moral complexity to the factual objective criteria of the conflict resolution process. The process allows enlightenment and insight to bridge the divide between the humanities and the rigorous sciences.

People, instead of being divided by many moral stories, can be reconciled by understanding the universal plot of stories as the unit moral order; religions are merely solutions of the moral calculus of Power Management. Science demystifies religions as particular ways of resolving conflict and accordingly particular norms, the acceptable types of resolutions in interpersonal relations. Science restructures relations and norms and reduces conflict by introducing the optimal and equitable distribution and management of power.

Rehabilitating morality with respect and distance from religions

20th century rational humanism, psychoanalysis and communism, discarded religion as irrational and immoral. Like Toto, who unveiled the fraudulent Wizard of Oz, rational humanism rejected religion and ostracized it from the world of conceptual legitimacy. Moral Science, in contrast to rational humanism, introduces conceptual correctness that demystifies religions respectfully.

Moral Science has pulled back the curtain of religious magic, revealing the dialectical evolution of moral paradigms throughout history. Over time, norms of justice have become morea abstract, shaping and reshaping soceital values and concepts of divinity. Behind the curtain of the Wizard of Oz, science discovers continuity among the messages of revelation evolving from Moses' Ten Commandments, to Aristotle's perfect universe, the Teleion Holon and finally Moral

Science's Formal Analysis Profile, the ten formulas of logic, math and physics identified by the Formal Theory.

The explanations on moral order began with creation stories, imaginative speculations on the cosmic order and evolved gradually to the current level of complete abstract thinking identifying the formulas organizing our emotions as orderly symbolic universes. Formulas revealed by science clarify the mind managing conflicts; the moral calculus deals with temptations by respecting the conditions for optimal structuring of individual needs and interpersonal realities.

The political and ethical consequences of the scientific moral theory of behavior

The unconscious is a mechanical equilibrial natural science ideational phenomenon. The mental moral pulse is an equilibrial mechanism aligning the individual polarities with the societal magnetic field and vice versa. The moral unconscious is the compass guiding the individual to modify the societal order according to an evolving awareness on the nature of social justice. For instance, Jesus sought to reform the normative handling of women pregnant out of wedlock. As an individual he was able to change this norm rather than allow it to prevail. Prophets have been political reformers that became worshiped rather than merely respected.

The formal theoretical position challenges the norm of political correctness as fostering methodological and conceptual incorrectness. This challenge entails the need for normative changes in the conduct of research and the politics of expressing one's opinion without being labeled prejudiced. Science usually prevails. The new theory represents the power of scientific discovery confronting traditional normative conceptions that do disservice to the truth and ultimately to humanity. Science, like Prometheus, is stealing the fire of the gods and the academic establishment, minor deities, to heal the world from its

confusion on the nature of moral order. Is this a crime or a necessary reform?

In this chapter science establishes the moral unconscious as the universal authority on values. Here we start with a conceptual position that should prevail on the traditional normative standards. The position is a hubris in the outset. Can science prevail on the traditional definitions of moral order? We know from the trilogy of Aeschylus that change in the relationship of Prometheus and Zeus occurred following the test of his capacity to foretell. The dramatic struggle is now between the Formal Theory's capacity to foretell and the academic establishment's willingness to test the claim and to approve its correctness. We may anticipate a contemporary struggle between science and traditional psychology and religion, and between scientists and philosophers before we achieve moral consensus on the findings of the Formal Theory.

The new science respects religions as forerunners of science. Religious norms have introduced inequitable distribution of power to the members of domestic relations and by extension to all other models of organizational hierarchies. These norms were innovative at certain evolutionary phases of history but have become obsolete and inappropriate in our times of expanded awareness on the nature of the universe; civilizations have evolved requiring rethinking of norms on civil rights and gender relations.

While science respects religions as pioneers, it also challenges the status quo of religions' dogma and frozen norms, value systems and definitions of the divine. Dogma and norms are counterproductive, distorting the truth and enforcing inequitable relations polarizing the public and generating unnecessary personal and cross-cultural conflicts, upsetting mental health and peace in the world. The new science, like Prometheus, must fight a battle with the religions as the well-established empirical theories of behavior before it receives the legitimacy of its rigorous perspective. Summing up the insights advanced in this chapter we may acknowledge the following as the features of the process, the unit of the social sciences.

Ten features of the Conflict Resolution Process

1. The unconscious is defined as the adaptive response to stress, a sequence of emotions that transform conflict to resolution by changing a person's attitude. This emotional processing of information is universal. It is the mental heartbeat, a periodic pattern. It unifies psychology, sociology and morality.

The emotional process has a distinct structure of six emotions guided by three formal operations. The process has a function: conflict resolution or emotional social adjustment. We know it as the plot or moral of stories.

The process integrates psychology and moral order coinciding as the essence of human motivation, the need for normative adjustment, a simple unconscious emotional process predictably seeking the restoration of normative compliance or social acceptance.

2. The unconscious is a natural science phenomenon defined by rigorous constructs and formulas with clear graphic representation. The pattern is a natural science equilibrial phenomenon comparable to the pendulum oscillation and the equilibrial trays of a scale. The language of these phenomena, physics and logic, become applicable to the social sciences and introduce rigorous conceptual language into the study of morality and psychology, thus transforming the field of the humanities into that of a natural science.

3. The process clinically manifests as a syndrome of emotions and behaviors. We recognize four wellness diagnostic categories, the relational modalities, as four alternative ways of resolving conflict. Each modality has different scenarios and predictable consequences. Knowledge of these diagnostic categories is beneficial to the individual. It clarifies patterns of interpersonal relations accounting for emotions and behaviors. These diagnostic categories pertain to wellness.

4. The *Conflict Analysis Battery* is a self-assessment instrument. It combines an inventory with a set of projective techniques. The inventory contains a questionnaire of four relationally determined choices, leading to identify one's relational modality. The projective techniques tap the creative process, generating metaphors for self-discovery. The self-assessment is user-friendly, allowing everyone to learn about themselves, their respective strengths and weaknesses.

5. The unconscious resolving conflict is the origin of all moral order and the religions of the world are philosophies of conflict resolution now completed into the Science of Conflict Resolution, the Moral Science. The identification of the process generates moral consensus on the nature of moral order. It reconciles people of faith and agnostics.

6. Religions are partial but complementary discoveries of the natural science unconscious mechanism almost corresponding to scientific discoveries. Science completes religions' search for the divine identifying the definitive and abstract natural science moral order as the Conflict Resolution Process. The unit process integrates all religions as a continuum of metaphors of conflict resolution.

7. The process unifies psychology with morality and religion. Both deal with adaptive strategies of conflict resolution. Psychology addresses the conflict resolution in general while religions address it within narrow normative choices. Religions establish norms for models of relating that evolved in historical periods. Psychology studies the entire range of conflict resolutions independently of period related norms. Science makes us conscious of the natural science unconscious and makes us deliberate in the pursuit of the optimal ways of resolving conflict.

8. The relevance of the theory is in its applications in psychotherapy and in education. The advantages in understanding the psyche are multiple; we can identify our modality and measure the personal process. We can also identify the relational modalities of our cultures and religions sampling their symbolic languages and universes. We may assess their relational modalities.

9. *Creativity and Power Management* is a concise and comprehensive program of emotional education utilizing the training manual containing the *Conflict Analysis Battery*. The program combines cognitive, psychoeducational, diagnostic and therapeutic objectives. Power Management education may be delivered in the classroom and in therapy.

The education starts with cognitive information, the study of the exhibits, as a new way of looking at art, identifying how the process integrates art and science recognizing the features of conflict resolution as the essence of meaning and purpose. The middle segment is experiential, it uses creativity for self discovery by identifying the personal way of resolving conflicts, self-knowledge. Insight clarifies moral values as the principles of resolving conflict and managing power. The third segment of the program addresses skills development in the field of power management.

10. The political role of the process entails the civil right of individuals to emotional literacy; that is, to interpret and understand metaphors, both cultural and personal, as alternative types of conflict resolution.

THREE EXHIBITS ILLUSTRATE THE UNIT PROCESS

The exhibits are samples of creativity always concluded by rectifying injustices. The mental process restores the sense of rest in the individual after an emotional disturbance. The exhibits illustrate the process, the plot of stories as a scientific and moral mechanism. In them we detect the circumscribed dialectic conflict resolution entity presented metaphorically. Observing these exhibits we come to respect the mental equilibrial process as the unit of moral order as how the mind guides the individual to adjust to changes and comply or rebel with the norms of his culture.

The exhibits establish that the process has the features of science: universality, predictability, qualification, quantification and graphic representation. The pattern is analyzed as a natural science entity and rediscovered in each of the three exhibits:

1) The Metaphoria Murals exhibit departs from the observation of the conflict resolution pattern that repeats itself across five generations of Greek gods.
2) The Henry Gorski Retrospective presents the pattern as five conflict resolutions in the five sequences of canvases.
3) The metaphors of the Wizard of Oz Panels identify the pattern in the story's four key metaphors examining the process as the integrative paradigm of four social sciences.

These exhibits demonstrate the discovery that moral order is a scientific universal moral order phenomenon totally independent of religions. The exhibits demonstrate that this entity has a distinct six role state structure, and then that the six roles or emotions are bound into a conflict resolution by three formal transformations. The exhibits represent the structure of the Universal Harmonic and its moral function as resolving conflicts. This is the unit process of the social sciences. It transforms the unintegrated social disciplines into the Moral Science.

The three art exhibits also validate this structure and its conflict resolving direction as the unit of moral order as a periodic entity, a natural science phenomenon. This entity describes the structure and function of the unconscious as the ideas of a story unified by its plot into the Aristotelian continuity of action. The three exhibits validate the six-role process accounting for the continuity in symbolism, emotions, energy and formal operations.

The first chapter's three exhibits introduce knowledge on the creative process as the scientific moral paradigm. The evidence on the nature of the process is presented by studying the orderly organization of emotions or associations in the first three art exhibits. These exhibits identify the six-role and three formal operations pattern in six murals, they rediscover it in the 100 canvases of the Henry Gorski Retrospective, and study it extensively as the integrative paradigm in the four key metaphors of the Wizard of Oz. The exhibits confirm the universality of the orderly process as the unconscious response to stress.

The exhibits validate the formal dialectic representing the physiological response to stress as an equilibrial phenomenon with the distinct structure of the six role states and the moral or conflict resolution function following three formal operations transforming conflict to resolution. These three operations represent the universal science based moral values.

The Metaphoria exhibit: Six murals introduce the pattern as a six-role totality. Two murals identify the pattern as observed consisting of six role states connecting emotionally the episodes observed in the Greek creation stories. One depicts the episodes of Kronos' life cycle. Another mural portrays the metaphors as repeated in the five generations of the Creation stories and the pattern as modified from art to science and as transmitted across generations and cultures. The Abrahamic religions are identified in a third mural as alternative ways of resolving conflict and as subject to scientific scrutiny. Three other murals present the process integrating personal and cultural metaphors as formally interrelated into units of resolution. Six more murals illustrate the process integrating experimentally generated metaphors into identifying the personal dramatic conflict resolution. These are studied in the third chapter as exhibit #5.

The Gorski Retrospective unites the artist's lifetime canvases as a continuum of conflict resolutions making the canvases meaningful and explaining the emotional and spiritual ongoing growth of the artist.

The twelve Wizard of Oz panels represent a detailed study of the metaphors of the story as corresponding to the core concepts of four social sciences. Each metaphor pertains to the manifestation of the process as the order in the discipline. The process is the constructs and formulas of epistemology, the diagnostic categories of psychology, the experimentally derived assessment protocols, and finally the set of moral insights that have inspired religions to the public.

This exhibits sums up the findings of the textbook: *Conflict Analysis, the Formal Theory of Behavior* by demonstrating the process as the unit of the social sciences integrating them into the Moral Science.

EXHIBIT #1
THE METAPHORIA MURALS

Six murals demonstrate the formal structure of the Conflict Resolution Process

The Sanctuary of the Unit is a square building whose four walls support two exhibits. There are murals on the interior walls and graphic designs on the exterior ones. Each wall supports three wall hangings. There are then 12 individual displays on each side of the walls: 12 murals of hand painted tiles inside and 12 Wizard of Oz graphic design panels outside, a study of the metaphors of the story of the Wizard on the outside. The murals inside represent 12 individual stories to study the process while the panels outside present the in-depth study of only one story. Each wall of the sanctuary is dedicated to the study of one of the social science disciplines:

• Epistemology, the natural science of the unit Conflict Resolution Process, on the South wall of the building;

• Psychology, the discipline of the typology of personality, wellness diagnostic categories, as alternative ways of resolving conflicts, is featured on the East wall;

• Psycho-education and therapy as attitude transformation and emotional education is featured on the North wall; and

• Morality and religion as the exaltation of the unit process on the West wall of the building.

Each mural is six feet long by four feet high comprised of six square tiles that present the six role-states of the conflict resolution mechanism. In most of the murals each one of the six tiles is marked with one of the six role states: stress, response, anxiety, defense, reversal and compromise, to remind the viewer that the exhibit is about the universality of the structure of the

unconscious process. Each mural pieces together the six fragments of the conflict resolution totality reconstructing the personal or cultural drama unfolding predictably as the unit process.

For many years I came north to Vermont from Connecticut carrying the individual tiles of the murals as artist Kim Salander from Norwalk, Connecticut completed them. After six years the exhibits and the Sanctuary of the Unit of the Conflict Resolution Process were completed.

The first six murals of the exhibit pertain to cultural stories as conflict resolution phenomena. The second half of the murals presents case studies (reviewed as exhibit #5) applying the technology of creation and analysis of metaphors for self-discovery and personal growth.
The construction of the personal case study murals follows a simple pattern. The trainees start with the creation of metaphors using the *Conflict Analysis Battery*. Their exercises are interrelated to reconstruct the personal Conflict Resolution Process. The Metaphoria Murals present their meaningfully integrated metaphors validating the Universal Harmonic.

Review of the first exhibit

The six murals of the first exhibit clarify the nature of the creative process as a natural science moral order psychological and physiological mechanism. At the end of this first exhibit the viewer may be clear on the integrative power of the new concept. It bridges the sciences and the humanities, psychology and religion, assessment and cultural evolution, finally it informs on the scientific aspects of the process and the graphic portrayal of the entity.
Mural 1, of the three cosmogony stories presents their interpretation as discoveries of the dialectic in three cultures.
Mural 2, the united metaphors of the world are shown integrated in a new flag; they are united by being reduced to the unit process, which gives them their individual dimensions.

Mural 3, clarifies the psychology and sociology of the Abrahamic religions; it offers clarity on cultural and personality variations but also accounts for the socio-psychological differences characterizing the three Abrahamic religions. These religions are integrated as relational modalities and the Mosaic Law is simplified into the natural science laws of equilibrial systems.
Mural 4, 'Creativity for self discovery' illustrates the reconstruction of the personal relational pattern by organizing one's set of metaphors. This mural clarifies the ease of the assessment process using creativity for scientific analysis and measurement of personal choices
Mural 5, integrates six prominent cultures as formally interrelated to each other into an evolutionary conflict resolution continuum. This process shows evolution in resolutions characterized by increased fairness in relations and increased abstraction on the nature of the divine.
Finally mural 6 clarifies the dramatic normative differences between four key cultures: Mexico and India versus Judea and Greece.

MURAL 1: THREE CREATION STORIES PRESENTING THE STRUCTURE AND FUNCTION OF THE UNCONSCIOUS

The observation of periodicity of a pattern in the Cosmogony, the Greek Creation story inspired me the Formal Theory. In this pattern I detected the syndromal nature of the unit process. The cross-generational transmission of the pattern, featured in Mural 2, helped me to recognize the six role-states of the creative process as a universal pattern of conflict resolution and as an equilibrial phenomenon.

Mural #1 illustrates the analysis of the process interpreting the lifetime creation story of Chronos as a sequence of interrelated events completing the six-part transformation of conflict to a resolution. The Greek creation drama provides clear imagery for the role states of the six formally interrelated transformations of the key behavior: 'murdering.' The cyclic process of the formal transformations of this key concept illustrates well the nature of the formal symbolic universe.

The mural also alludes to the Biblical Genesis (Greek for Creation), the six days of creation of the universe as the metaphor of the six role-state process. Sabbath, the day of rest corresponds to the state of resolution. Genesis then qualifies as the creative process manifested through the six role-state composition of all symbolic universes; this interpretation validates the scriptural use of the process as the unit of the moral construction of reality. All creations have a structure and a function: they progress to conflict resolution.

The metaphorical use of the process as a unit entity is more appropriate and pertinent to the biblical story as addressing the scientific foundation of moral order. This interpretation is more meaningful than the two traditional interpretations: the creationists in defense of moral order have been advocates of the literal acceptance of the story, while the evolutionists have considered it as a metaphor of the creation of the cosmic universe. Both interpretations have failed to recognize the metaphorical identification of the structure and function of the creative process. The role of Genesis as a key structure determines its utilization as the unit of moral order, and of conflict resolution as the universal moral dialectic, the unit of meaning and of all the social sciences.

The mural identifies an additional creation story, the oriental yin yang as the evolution of balance between opposites: male versus female, earth and sky, etc. In this tradition we also encounter the system of six states; here it is the six chakras aligned along the spine, a seventh, spirituality, above one's head. The six chakras refer to distinctions associated with physical and emotional needs, sources of social and personal conflict. They connect conflict and resolutions alluding to the six erogenous areas of functioning of the body. Their alignment integrates physiologi-

cal and sociological integration into a spiritual continuum of adjustment to personal needs and social realities based on the cultural philosophy of self-restraint, a particular way of power management.

In each of these creation stories we can detect the dialectical pattern of six states that lead toward a spiritual seventh step, the Sabbath, a correlate of the cathartic seventh chakra. This trend attests to a consensus about the structure of the Universal Harmonic. In Greece, it is identified as drama of power struggles between the members of the family. In Judea, the drama is celebrated with respect for a universal order founded on a God or moral order of benevolent and mindful social justice. In the Orient, the philosophy is one of individual surrender to a universal order as the internal containment of multiple conflict-generating needs.

Thus, moral order with alternative centers of gravity is conceived intuitively and given different explanations fitting the culture's favorite dramatic story as the key role shaping transactions of the respective cultural system. In Greece, an individualistic culture, murdering stands out, introducing the norm of antagonistic or competitive relations. In Judea the norm is trust between father and son. The norm is inspired by the theocratic monotheistic culture by trusting God, the Creator. This role state permeates the culture as an emotion binding God to man by a covenant, inspiring the formal operation of mutual respect. This disposition has introduced the norm of trust between fathers and sons as partners and has resolved the antagonism permeating the Greek culture. In the Orient, a community conscious culture, the norm focuses on the holistic harmonious balance of individual desires versus societal needs.

The process from the scientific language perspective is seen to pertain to six emotions, or energetically charged states: these are the sequence

of stress, response, etc. These, as energetic inter-transformations, are propelled or guided automatically by three formal operations along the homeostatic, physiologically determined resolution of conflict or equilibrial balance. These operations are dictated by the need for rest, the restoration of the equilibrium. We distinguish them as mastery versus passivity, cooperation replacing antagonism, and mutual respect healing alienation. The energetic outcome is identified as entelechy, the state of rest coinciding with the restructuring of emotions as increased internal order.

MURAL 2: THE FLAG OF THE UNITED METAPHORS OF THE WORLD REFLECTING THE NATURAL SCIENCE DIMENSIONS OF METAPHORS AND THEIR GRAPHIC PORTRAYAL

This mural presents the American flag as the flag of the united metaphors of the world. The flag allows the graphic representation of the Universal Harmonic along two time references: the cross-section of the harmonic presents the placement of cultural resolutions as metaphors with relational dimensions independent of the time element. The flag in its stripes allows the representation of the cultural stereotypes unfolding predictably along the six role sequences.

The stars section presents the cross section of the mental pendulum oscillation as the 'power field' integrating the cultural metaphors of the world, religions, and ideologies along a set of cardinal references, passivity versus activity, power on the right and powerlessness on the left reciprocally related, and cooperation versus antagonism distinguished by clockwise versus counterclockwise vectors. These distinctions allow us to identify the range of relational or attitudinal dimensions. The striped section of the flag represents the Universal Harmonic, the unit of the social sciences, and reflects the graphic representation of the six-role state process. It addresses its cross-generational transmission on the left and the cross-cultural differences on the right.

The power field allows us to give dimensions to each cultural resolution as representing a values solution. The metaphors' place indicates the sociological emotional complement of each culture in the simplified language of the graphic representation of the culture. We detect two elements in each metaphor depicted: first, its sociological place on the circumference, which refers to the power choices of the culture, and second its vector, reflecting the emotional complement of the cultural choice.

The sine curves represent much information, but principally the restructuring of the unit process across generations and across cultures. The mural's intent is to convey the scientific nature of the process and the ease with which we can use its graphic representation to convey the characteristics of each culture in a new clear conceptual language that enlightens by simplifying their complex nature.

The second mural allows interpreting metaphors as alternative ways of resolving conflict identified as having natural science dimensions. The function of this mural is critical in illustrating the graphic representation of emotional and sociological phenomena as totalities of conflict resolution along a path of necessary transformative steps or emotions and energies. The path is predictable, measurable, and graphically portrayable.

MURAL 3: THE PHYSICS OF METAPHYSICS AND OF RELATIONAL MODALITIES REFLECTING THE RANGE OF RELATIONAL MODALITIES AND UNDERLYING FORMAL DISTINCTIONS

This mural highlights moral law coinciding with scientific or natural law. The central image presents Rembrandt's Moses holding the tablets with the Ten Commandments interpreted into the three principal formal operations transforming conflict to resolution: Passivity is transformed to activity, antagonism to cooperation, and alienation to mutual respect.
On the left and right of the Moses revelation

image we see the scientific essence of the Ten Commandments as formulas of logic on the left, pertaining to the laws of the equilibrial scale, and of physics on the right, pertaining to the laws of the Simple Harmonic Motion. The lower sequence of tiles illustrates the three Abrahamic religions: Christianity, Judaism and Islam. They represent the range of alternative conflict resolutions corresponding to three alternative relational modalities. The text provides sociological explanations of the respective religions. These religions then are diagnosed as complementary relational modalities and respectively as alternative configurations of the core family system. They represent psychologically and sociologically determined alternative relational responses to stress. Science accounts for the variations of cultural resolutions of conflict.

While mural one clarified the six-role structure of the Conflict Resolution Process, the third mural introduces the three formal operations leading to the range of formal alternative resolutions of any conflict determining cultural and also personality typology identified as syndromal behaviors. The third mural shows how the unit entity is the foundation of the three Abrahamic religions, but also of the range of diagnostic categories of a wellness based view of psychology. It explains cultural and personality typology founded on relational differences. There are four choices: cooperative and antagonistic forms of dominance, or cooperative and antagonistic forms of subordinacy. Religions evolved like the personalities of individuals, as choices caused by relational alternatives in resolving conflict.

The mural demystifies the metaphysics of religions by promoting awareness of the physics of relational modalities. This mural connects religion and psychology, sociological and psychological influences as having natural science dimensions.

MURAL 4: MY METAPHORS, MYSELF, THE EXPERIMENTAL VALIDATION OF FORMAL THEORY'S ASSUMPTION ON THE UNCONSCIOUS AS A CONFLICT RESOLUTION MECHANISM

Mural 4 introduces the use of creativity for self-discovery. The personal system of conflict resolution as a harmonic or template is captured or reconstructed by the metaphor testing of the Conflict Analysis Battery. The mural clarifies the correspondence of tests and role-states reflecting the organization of personal emotions into the dramatic totality of the creator's Conflict Resolution Process.

The mural presents my metaphors as these evolved in my first attempt of completing the assignment. 'My Metaphors Myself', presents my personal metaphors integrated in the unit process as revealing my dramatic life story. The story reflects my journey beginning with the cultural conflicts of my childhood and how I puzzled them through as a Pinocchio, finding out how the wooden puppet can become human, how Oedipus can solve the riddle of the Sphinx interpreting metaphors, how I reached my dream, the family offering hospitality at the Wilburton Inn, and how my story comes to completion as the compromise, the conciliation between art and science, presented as a fiddler on a roof surrounded by the flags of nations, the metaphors of the reconciled faiths of the world. This image illustrates the conflict resolution reconciling my two identities, the Judaic passion for justice and the Greek arrogance of pursuing reason.

The captions of the mural explain the correspondence between each role state and a specific test of the Conflict Analysis Battery.

Stress is portrayed in the Conflictual Memory Test and the Portraits of the Family.

Response is reflected in the choices of the Transparent Mask Test.

Anxiety is portrayed in the second *Transparent Mask,* displaying one's hidden feelings.

Defense is elicited by the *Animal Metaphor* and *Fairy Tale Metaphor* tests.

Reversal is captured in the *Dream Analysis* and the *Intensified Animal Metaphor Test.*

Compromise is elicited by the autobiographic *Short Story Metaphor.*

The mural begins with the role of stress illustrated by my *Conflictual Memory Test.* It reflects my childhood experiences of the WWII as the war of the metaphors. I experienced it as a Jew and a citizen of Greece. In this scene my family is seeking safety huddled together during a bombardment. The image presents symbolisms of all the cultures involved in the conflict. It illustrates stress as passivity, antagonism and alienation. The sixth image illustrates the role state of Compromise; it presents the resolution of the conflict of metaphors as a scene of the core integration of art and science as the Jewish fiddler on the roof of a Greek temple. The fiddler symbolizes faith, the temple Greek rationality or science. The metaphors of the cultures of the world as the many flags, wave around this core image of art and science reconciled. The flags are the united metaphors of the world respected as equal celebrating the new era of peace inspired by the integration of science and religion.

This mural, besides reflecting my personal story, presents a validation of the theory by demonstrating how the testing process helps to resolve conflict as a triple formal transformation. The mural starts from a conflictual metaphor depicting stress and ends with a short story corresponding to the compromise. Here we see the validation as the formal relation connecting the beginning and the end segments, the mural presents how the process transforms passivity, antagonism and alienation to resolution as mastery, cooperation and mutual respect.

MURAL 5: OUR CULTURAL METAPHORS AS A CONTINUUM OF EVOLVING MORAL ORDER

Mural five depicts the formal interrelation of the six matriarchal religions, the epics of the goddess, as gender wars. The epics are integrated into the dialectic continuum of the conflict resolution process. Each culture is represented by the image of a heroine of one of the classic epics. Mexico's Quatlique, Greece's Helen of Troy as a Sphinx, India's Kalli, Japan's Geisha, Mesopotamia's Ishtar, and Christianity's Virgin Mary. Thus the mural retraces religions as moral battles and discoveries of conflict resolution integrated into an overarching harmonic. The dialectic of conflict resolutions gradually leads towards a more stable restructuring of the family institution.

In the world of religions, men finally prevailed over women by suppressing women's aggressive sexual behavior, like that of Helen of Troy, Ishthar of Mesopotamia and Eve of the Judaic Bible.

Six discoveries, conflict resolutions, restructure family relations as normative changes in domestic relations. The six role-state cultural Harmonc presents how moral thinking evolved dialectically from concrete interpretations of reality, myth making creation stories, to the abstract understanding of moral order in the Mosaic Laws. Yet the world has not achieved the ultimate abstractions of the Moral Science. The new era's conflicts and resolutions unfold in the sculptural trail exhibit. There we see how the Moral Science completes the quest of religions for peace on earth, complete and fair conflict resolution.

Mural five presents the evolution of cultural paradigms from matriarchy to patriarchy as conclusive gender wars. Matriarchy is illustrated in the three lower tiles: stress, Mexico's murderous Quatlique, anxiety, masterful Kali and consort Siva stepping on the inner child, and reversal, seductress Ishtar of the Gilgamesh epic. Patriarchy is presented empowered in the top three tiles: response, Greece defeating the Sphinx as

Helen of Troy, the impersonation of a woman as the fight/flight response, defense, Japan's Sun Gods replacing India's Moon goddess with an accommodating geisha, and compromise, Israel's Messianic religions' mother child alliance prevailing over the biblical father son covenant.

The inception of the series is the Mexican matriarchy, illustrated by the cruel mother earth as an eagle devouring a snake. This image corresponds to the mythic mother demanding live blood sacrifice from her son to avert the impending fifth destruction of the universe, as conveyed in the monumental Aztec calendar. The concluding image of this mural presents the Messianic mothers in alliance with their offspring demonstrating the conflict resolution in the evolution of civilizations. Again passivity, antagonism and alienation of the initial stress state, the Aztec civilization, is transformed to mastery, cooperation and mutual respect of the Messianic religions, upon the concluding compromise state.

MURAL 6: FROM ART TO SCIENCE

The mural portrays four cultural relational responses to the same stressor: the apple as the symbol of temptation. The four relational alternatives reflect the cultural dimensions as diametrically opposite and reciprocal to each other. The second part of the mural illustrates how the art of these metaphors is interpreted as the abstractions of science: graphs capture the relational differences of the four cultural alternatives.

The mural juxtaposes four cultures around the distinctions of power and powerlessness, cooperation and antagonism. On the power side of the field, Israel and Greece, represent the dominant cooperative versus the dominant antagonistic ways of resolving conflicts and on the powerless side India and Mexico represent respectively the submissive cooperative and antagonistic modalities.

The murals exhibit is discussed in detail in the companion volume, *Moral Science: The Scientific Interpretation of Metaphors*. We can distinguish four relational modalities comparing the cultures' respective metaphors of managing power, as dealing with temptation, four formally related variations of the apple metaphor.

On the right side of the power field we recognize the Judaic and the Greek cultures. The Jews were trained in the norm of respecting the apple as the forbidden fruit of knowledge. So the image illustrates Adam telling Eve that the apple is forbidden. The Greek metaphor presents the apple of discord cast to evoke conflict by being inscribed 'to the fairest.' We see the three goddesses seeking to own the golden apple reminding us of the very competitive Greek culture, home of the Olympics and of Democracy.

On the left side of the power field we see two cultures illustrating submission, the avoidance of power by the mortals. In India men are stubbing themselves conquering the drive for pleasure, while the inflated apple of desires is respected as a sacred cow. This culture represents the submissive cooperative resolution. The Aztec culture regards the live heart of a sacrificial victim as the apple of the gods illustrating the submissive antagonistic relational resolution.

These metaphors are represented as natural science phenomena by the juxtaposed graphs. The longitudinal harmonic and its cross section with vectors signify the combination of a social power choice and the associated emotions.

EXHIBIT #1: THE METAPHORIA MURALS

THE STRUCTURE AND FUNCTION OF THE CONFLICT RESOLUTION PROCESS:

1. Three Creation Stories:
   Revealing the whole and the parts.

2. The Flag of the United Metaphors:
   Order in the universe of cultural metaphors

3. The Physics of Metaphysics and of Relational Modalities:
   Religions as natural science phenomena

4. My Metaphors, Myself:
   Identifying the personal CRP by utilizing the *Conflict Analysis Battery.*

5. The Evolution of Cultural Metaphors:
   The integration of religions as the dialectic of discoveries

6. The Scientific Interpretation of Metaphors:
   From Art to Science

1. THREE CREATION STORIES REVEAL HOW THE MIND PROCEEDS FROM CHAOS TO ORDER FROM CONFLICT TO RESOLUTION

Three creation stories the Greek cosmonogy the Oriental yin-yang and the Bibles six days of creation have an identical structure The Formal Theory suggests that this structure, the Conflict Resolution Process, is the unit of unconscious moral order.

Hun-tun, Chinese for chaos, was divided into two interactive entities, the *yin*, the earth below, and the *yang*, the sky above. The Greek creation also started with the interaction of the Earth below and the Sky above.

RESPONSE

RESPONSE: Mother Earth armed Chronos, her youngest son, with a flint sickle. Chronos castrated his father. Father Sky's severed phallus falling on the water was transformed into the beautiful Aphrodite.

DEFENSE

DEFENSE: Upon their birth, out of fear of being killed by them, Chronos devoured the Olympian children.

COMPROMISE / REST

COMPROMISE: Dying Chronos cursed Zeus to be killed in his turn by his child. Zeus, scared of this predicament, swallowed his wife Metis as soon as she became pregnant. A few months later Hephestus, the smith, opened his skull and Zeus' daughter Athena emerged. His screams and curses shook the universe.

REST: Athena was born dressed like a warrior to protect herself from men and the curse of being killed by her children. Yet Athena was raped by Hephestus and had a son, Erichthonius, whom she promptly got rid of by putting him in foster placement. Having come of age, to appease his mother, Erichthonius built her a temple on the Acropolis. Athena, reassured gave to Athens her olive tree and her owl.

STRESS

STRESS: Following their union, Father Sky threw his children into Tartarus-Hell, to the dismay of his wife, Mother Earth.

ANXIETY

ANXIETY: Dying Father Sky cursed Chronos to be killed in his turn by his children, the Olympians. Chronos panicked at the sight of his children.

OUTCOME

OUTCOME: Mother Rhea hid her youngest, Zeus, from his father. Zeus grew up, freed his brothers, Hades and Poseidon, and the three killed their father. Hades hidden in his helmet of darkness, disarmed Chronos, Poseidon with his trident pinned him down and Zeus finished him off with a lightning bolt.

The first mural illustrates the Greek creation stories as a sequence of interrelated events completing the six-part transformation of conflict to a resolution. It alludes to Genesis resolving conflict metaphorically as a six-part continuum leading to the Sabbath, the day of rest. The Greek creation drama provides clear imagery of the cyclic process summed up in six transformations of one key behavior: 'murdering.' This periodic phenomenon allows us to introduce scientific conceptualization into the study of behavior. It is the orderly, formal and moral sequencing of thoughts present in all samples of creativity.

Mural 1: THREE CREATION STORIES REVEAL HOW THE MIND PROCEEDS FROM CHAOS TO ORDER – FROM CONFLICT TO RESOLUTION

The Greek cosmogony, the Oriental yin-yang, Hinduism's six chakras and the Bible's six days of creation, have an identical structure.
The Formal Theory suggests that this structure, the Conflict Resolution Process, is the unit of unconscious moral order.
Hun-tun, Chinese for chaos, was divided into two interactive entities, the yin (the earth below), and the yang (the sky above).
The Greek creation also started with the interaction of the Earth below and the Sky above.

RESPONSE: Mother Earth armed Chronos, her youngest son, with a flint sickle. Chronos castrated his father. Father Sky's severed phallus falling on the water was transformed into the beautiful Aphrodite.

DEFENSE: Chronos devoured the Olympian children upon their birth because of his fear of being killed by them.

COMPROMISE: Dying Chronos cursed Zeus to be killed in turn by his child. Zeus, scared of this predicament, swallowed his wife Metis as soon as she became pregnant. A few months later, Hephaestus, the smith, opened his skull, and Zeus' daughter Athena emerged. His screams and curses shook the universe.

STRESS: Following their union, Father Sky threw his children into Tartarus (Hell), to the dismay of his wife, Mother Earth.

ANXIETY: Dying Father Sky cursed Chronos to be killed in his turn by his children, the Olympians. Chronos panicked at the sight of his children.

ROLE REVERSAL: Mother Rhea hid her youngest, Zeus, from his father. Zeus grew up, freed his brothers, Hades and Poseidon, and the three killed their father. Hades, hidden in his helmet of darkness, disarmed Chronos, Poseidon with his trident pinned him down, and Zeus finished him off with a lightning bolt.

REST: Athena was born dressed like a warrior to protect herself from men and the curse of being killed by her children. Yet Athena was raped by Hephastus and had a son, Erichthonius, whom she prompty got rid of by putting him in foster placement. Having come of age, to appease his mother, Erichthonius built her a temple on the Acropolis. Athena, reassured, gave Athens her olive tree and owl.

ART: THE GREEK CREATION STORY AS A METAPHOR

CYCLE 1

The first cycle introduces the conflict:

1. Role Oppression/Stress:
A child, Chronos, is perceived by Uranus, Father Sky, as a threat, his siblings are tossed into Tartarus, a place as far below the Earth as the sky is above.

2. Role Assumption/Response:
The child is armed by his protective mother with a scythe and he uses it to kill his father. Chronos severs his father's penis as he is sleeping and tosses it into the sea where it is transformed into Aphrodite.

CYCLE 2

In the second cycle the conflict is internalized:

3. Anticipation of Role Reversal/Anxiety:
The child, Chronos, becomes a man who now in his turn is afraid of his children since his father cursed him to the same predicament.

4. Counterphobic Role Assumption/Defense:
Chronos, married to Rea, is afraid that his children, the Olympians, will murder him. To protect himself, he swallows the children when they are born. Enraged, his wife hides one of them, Zeus, and gives Chronos a stone to swallow instead.

CYCLE 3

In the final cycle the conflict is resolved:

5. Role Reversal/Reversal:
Zeus gave his father an emetic potion and Chronos regurgitated Poseidon and Hades. Zeus, in collaboration with these siblings, kills Chronos.

6. Compromise Role Assumption/Compromise:
The dying Chronos curses Zeus to in turn be killed by his children.

Formal Analysis and validation of the Conflict Resolution Process:
First, the Formal Theory advances the thesis that the unconscious mind proceeds from a conflict to a resolution in the course of six role-states/emotions. In the Greek creation story the verb, action, and distinction is 'to murder.' Validating the six role structure, the evoked sequence unfolds as a series of six verb forms: being murdered by one's father, murdering the father, anticipating being murdered by one's children, murdering one's children, being murdered by one's children and finally, cursing one's children to be murdered in turn.
Second, the Formal Theory advances the thesis that conflict resolution occurs with the completion of three formal operations: passivity, antagonism and alienation are transformed to mastery, cooperation

and mutual respect. The conflict that began with a child being murdered by the father concludes with the murdered father cursing his son to the same fate, i.e. to be murdered by his children. Does this outcome validate the assumption of resolution as mastery, cooperation and mutual respect?
As a means of validation, let us discuss each of the three formal operations:
• Transformation of passivity to activity:
In the compromise role assumption, the father curses his son, representing a state of activity.
• Transformation of antagonism to cooperation:
In Greek culture antagonism is not converted to cooperation. In Judaic culture there is a transformation of the father-son relationship. Abraham, the father, does not kill his son, demonstrating a resolution based on the discovery of cooperation and mutual respect.

Instead of cursing his son, Abraham blesses Isaac.
• Transformation of alienation to mutual respect:
In the Greek culture, alienation is not transformed to mutual respect, but there is respect for a universal order governing father-son relationships. As Chronos curses Zeus, he is making the observation that he too will be murdered by his child as has happened before in the several generations of the Greek creation story.

In the Judaic culture, we experience an evolution in the father-son relationship. Abraham establishes the father-son covenant, mutual respect. This is an example of the progression in the quality of conflict resolution across cultures. In the Museum's art exhibits we see the progression to resolution in sequential phases of samples of creativity.

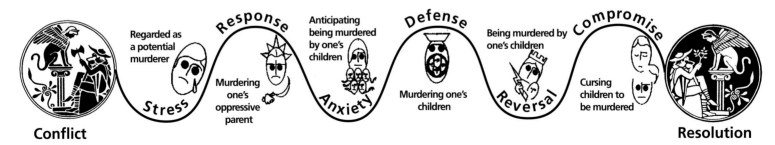

Conflict — Regarded as a potential murderer — **Stress** — Murdering one's oppressive parent — **Response** — Anticipating being murdered by one's children — **Anxiety** — Murdering one's children — **Defense** — Being murdered by one's children — **Reversal** — Cursing children to be murdered — **Compromise** — **Resolution**

PASSIVITY • ANTAGONISM • ALIENATION

MASTERY • COOPERATION • MUTUAL RESPECT

SCIENCE: THE SIX ROLE-STATE CONFLICT RESOLUTION PROCESS AND ITS EXPERIMENTAL VALIDATION

CYCLE 1

Role Oppression, the Stress state marks the inception of the conflict as determined by the role state's distinction.

- Clinically we identify this state using the *Conflictual Memory Test*. The memory depicts the most traumatic experience one remembers. This conflict is the formative experience determining the rest of the role-states as the shift from a conflict to its resolution.
- All dialogues in a metaphor test are in a formal relation to each other completed with a resolution. Stress or role oppression state corresponds to the first exchange. It is the formative, normative deviation. The opening statement determines how the story unfolds in a conversation or in a story.

Role Assumption corresponds to the response behavior or emotion.

- Clinically we determine the response state using the *Transparent Mask Test*; it reflects the individual's identity as a role choice related to the stress state.
- Formally the response is reciprocal to the stress experience.
- This is the second transaction in a conversation or story.

CYCLE 2

Anticipated Role Reversal corresponds to the anxiety state. It is formally related to the role assumption or response behavior.

- This state defines anxiety as anticipation of reciprocities, as fears of a Role Reversal, the reversal of the role assumed.
- Clinically this state is identified using the *Second Mask*, portraying feelings revealed as the first mask becomes transparent.
- Formally this state corresponds to the opposite emotions portrayed in the first mask.
- The anxiety state is reflected in the third sentence of a dialogue. This exchange alludes to fears and concerns about the future.

Counterphobic Role Assumption or Defense corresponds to behaviors seeking to avert the anxiety, the fears of role reversal.

- Counterphobic behaviors and emotions are reciprocal or opposite of the anxiety state.
- Clinically this is identified using the *Animal Metaphor Test* reflecting a person's choice of mastery response.
- This state is reflected in the fourth statement or association of a dialogue or story as introduced in the *Animal Metaphor Test.*

CYCLE 3

Role Reversal is the downturn state of a reality that has been anticipated and finally comes true. It is the fulfillment of the self-fulfilling prophecy that has actually been elicited by the counterphobic behavior.

- Reversal emotional state is opposite to the counterphobic role assumption.
- Assessment wise it is identified using the *Dream Metaphor Test*; it is also manifested in the Intensified *Animal Metaphor Test*
- It is the fifth statement in a dialogue or story.

The Compromise Role Assumption corresponds to the behavior or emotion as a response or attitude to a reality that is generalized from a particular to a general audience. It represents an attitude change; a reconciliation or lack of it as a philosophy of life; it represents an abstraction.

- The compromise is the correlative to the role Reversal state.
- It is identified clinically using the *Short Story Metaphor.*
- It is the sixth statement in a dialogue or story and the conclusion; the dialogue may continue beyond the sixth statement when there is difficulty for the person to make a concession and resolve a conflict.

CYCLE 1 TESTS:
Conflictual Memory Test
Transparent Mask Test

CYCLE 2 TESTS:
Second Mask
Animal Metaphor Test

CYCLE 3 TESTS:
Dream Metaphor Test
Short Story Metaphor

Conflict

Resolution

PASSIVITY • ANTAGONISM • ALIENATION

MASTERY • COOPERATION • MUTUAL RESPECT

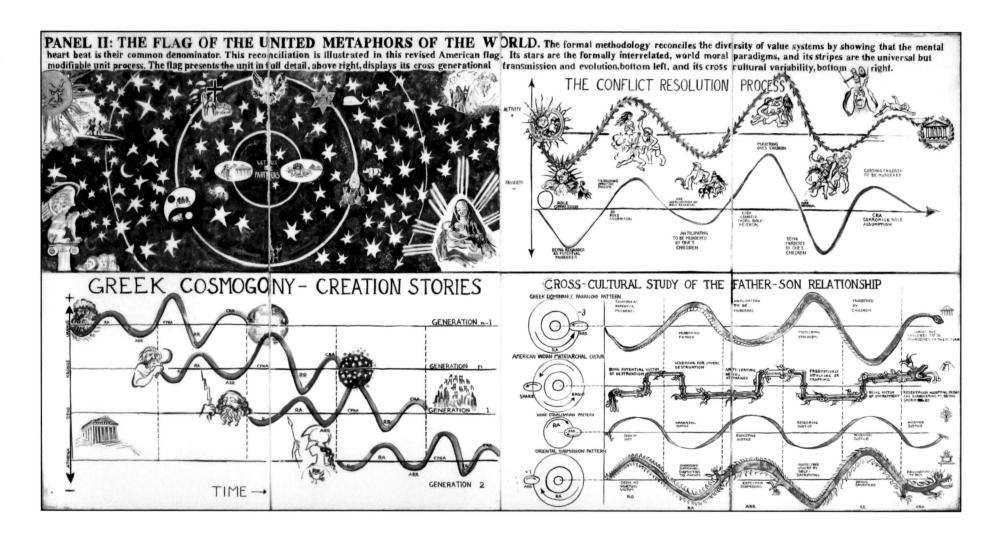

PANEL II: THE FLAG OF THE UNITED METAPHORS OF THE WORLD. The formal methodology reconciles the diversity of value systems by showing that the mental heart beat is their common denominator. This reconciliation is illustrated in this revised American flag. Its stars are the formally interrelated, world moral paradigms, and its stripes are the universal but modifiable unit process. The flag presents the unit in full detail, above right, displays its cross generational transmission and evolution, bottom left, and its cross cultural variability, bottom right.

This mural presents the American flag as the flag of the united metaphors of the world. The striped section of the flag represents the Universal Harmonic, the unit of the social sciences, and reflects the graphic representation of the six role process. It is addressing its cross-generational transmission on the left and the cross-cultural differences on the right. The stars section presents the cross section of the unit as the power field integrating the cultural metaphors of the world, religions, and ideologies along their relational or attitudinal dimensions.

Mural 2: THE FLAG OF THE UNITED METAPHORS OF THE WORLD

The formal methodology reconciles the diversity of value systems by showing that the mental heartbeat – the Unit – is their common denominator. This reconciliation is illustrated in this revised American flag.

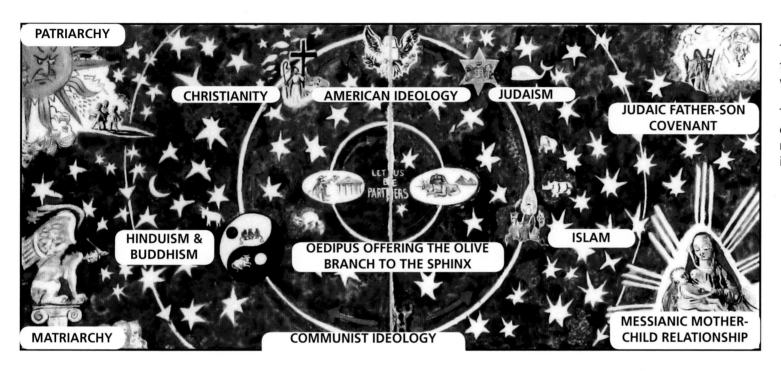

The stars of the flag are the formally interrelated, world moral paradigms.

The stars present the cultural and ideological metaphors in their formal interrelationship.

The stripes of the flag are the universal, but modifiable, unit process

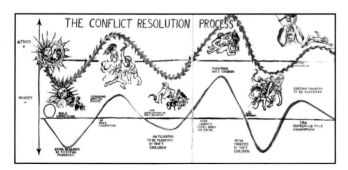

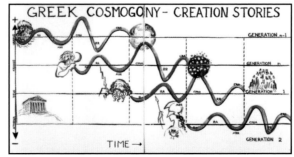

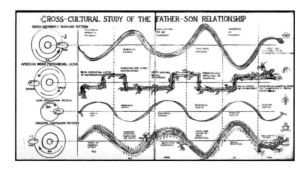

The flag presents the unit in full detail as the evolution from art to science.

The flag displays the unit in its cross-generational transmission and evolution.

The flag shows the unit's cross-cultural variability.

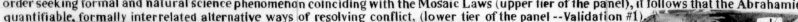

3. THE PHYSICS OF METAPHYSICS AND OF RELATIONAL MODALITIES.

If the Conflict Resolution Process is a moral order seeking formal and natural science phenomenon coinciding with the Mosaic Laws (upper tier of the panel), it follows that the Abrahamic religions are quantifiable, formally interrelated alternative ways of resolving conflict, (lower tier of the panel -- Validation #1).

THE PROCESS IS FORMAL INTERTRANSFORMATIONS TOTALITY, a formal equilibrial system, illustrated by the trays of a scale with the difference that the unconscious tips the scale toward resolution, that is activity over passivity, cooperation over antagonism, and respect over alienation.

Opposites: cooperation (a) plus antagonism (-a) cancel each other out: $a + (-a) = 0$

Reciprocals: activity (a) times passivity (1/a) yields the unit: $(a) \times (1/a) = 1$

THE CONFLICT RESOLUTION PROCESS IS THE UNIT OF MORAL ORDER, like the Mosaic Laws. It mandates deliberate conflict resolution as the transformation of passivity to activity, (moderation), of antagonism to cooperation, and of alienation to respect.

$E = mc^2$

THE PROCESS IS A CONSERVED ENERGETIC MODALITIES INTER-TRANSFORMATIONS TOTALITY like the pendulum oscillation. It is abiding by the laws of physics, but unlike the pendulum the process upgrades order, that is it increases negative entropy.

CHRISTIANITY ILLUSTRATES THE SUBORDINACY SYNDROME. Jesus, the son of an unwed mother, espoused cooperation, non-violence, asexuality and even willingness to sacrifice himself: the relational choice of surrender and hope.

JUDAISM ILLUSTRATES THE ASSERTIVENESS SYNDROME Jacob, the favored son of a powerful mother is assertive, both in extracting blessings from his father and wrestling with God. Becoming empowered as Israel, he is respectful of his discriminated brother Hesau and a fair judge for his wives and sons. The Passover Seder's querying sons illustrate the four relational modalities, those of the wise, wicked, simple and the quiet alternatives and reinforce the desirability of assertiveness and respect.

ISLAM ILLUSTRATES THE DOMINANCE SYNDROME. Mohammed espoused dominance as the relational choice attributed to Ishmael, the first born of Abraham and Hagar, a wife banished to the desert. As unjustly deprived, this son could feel justified to pursue justice by dominating his peers, the relational choice of controls and anxiety.

This mural highlights Moses holding the tablets of the Ten Commandments. In them are inscribed the three principal formal operations transforming conflict to resolution. On the left and right we see the Commandments have scientific essence; they are formulas of logic and physics. Below we see the three Abrahamic religions as alternative conflict resolutions corresponding to alternative relational modalities. The text provides sociological explanations of the respective religions which represent psychologically and sociologically determined alternative relational responses to stress.

Mural 3: THE PHYSICS OF METAPHYSICS AND OF RELATIONAL MODALITIES

The upper tier of the mural presents the CRP as a moral order and natural science phenomenon. The three formal operations driving the process coincide with the Mosaic Laws. It follows that the Abrahamic religions are alternative ways of resolving conflict. The Unit redefines the unconscious abstractly as an order-upgrading mechanism processing ideas along three morally-directed formal operations. It is transforming passivity to activity, antagonism to cooperation, and alienation to mutual respect.

The process is a sequence of formal transformations. It is an equilibrial system illustrated by the balance of a scale. The unconscious tips the scale toward resolution, transforming passivity to activity, antagonism to cooperation, and alienation to mutual respect. Opposites: cooperation + antagonism cancel each other out.
Reciporcals: Activity x passivity yields the unit.

The Conflict Resolution Process is the unit of moral order. It mandates deliberate conflict resolution as the transformation of passivity to activity, of antagonism to cooperation, and of alienation to repect. The universal laws of morality, coincide with the Ten Commandments.

The process is a sequence of energetic transformations, like those of the pendulum oscillation. It abides by the laws of physics, but unlike the pendulum, the process upgrades order; it increases negative entropy.

Christianity illustrates the subordinacy syndrome. Jesus, the son of an unwed mother, espoused cooperation, non-violence, asexuality, and self-sacrifice: the relational choices of surrender and hope; the submissive-cooperative syndrome.

Judaism illustrates the assertiveness syndrome. Jacob, the favored son of a powerful mother, is assertive. He extracts blessings from his father and wrestles with God. Becoming empowered as Israel, he is respectful of his discriminated brother Hesau, and a fair judge for his wives and sons. The Passover Seder's querying sons illustrate the four relational modalities; those of the wise, wicked, simple, and the quiet alternatives. The Judaic values reinforce the desirability of assertiveness and respect, qualities of cooperative dominance.

Islam illustrates the dominance syndrome. Mohammed espoused dominance, the relational choice attributed to Ishmael. Ishmael was the first born son of Abraham and Hagar. Hagar and Ishmael were banished to the desert. Feeling unjustly deprived, Ishmael could feel jusitified in dominating peers and rivals. This relational choice is experienced as anxiety and controls, the characteristics of dominant-antagonism.

4. MY METAPHORS, MYSELF: 1983

Validation #2: Here six metaphor creation tests help to reconstruct the personal six-role Conflict Resolution Process. The experimentally derived sequence validates the theory by showing that parts are formally interrelated within the dramatic totality. This totality also tells how its author, Dr. Levis, evolved from a stress, "The War of the Metaphors", through his response, anxiety, defense, reversal, to the compromise of "The Reconciliation of the Metaphors"

2. RESPONSE is identified by the MASK TEST which reveals a person's identity. I chose the image of the runaway Pinocchio, the wooden puppet lying about his identity, fleeing the killer whale of hot ideologies pursuing naive consumers.

4. DEFENSE is identified by the ANIMAL METAPHOR TEST. Here the Formal Theory Oedipus is offering the Sphinx an olive branch, conflict resolution, as the new answer to the everlasting riddle on the nature of man.

6. COMPROMISE is identified by the SHORT STORY TEST. My Judaic passion for justice and my Greek respect for reason as the fiddler on the temple roof unite the world metaphors in the cosmic dance of a universal moral order.

1. STRESS is identified by the MEMORIES TEST. It represents my recollection of World War II as "The War of the Metaphors", the war of multiple cultural conflicts endangering everybody's survival.

3. ANXIETY is identified by the BEHIND THE MASK TEST. It presents Pinocchio trapped in the stomach of the killer whale with his creator, Geppetto. My Pinocchio is showing to a puzzled Gepetto the unit of the Conflict Resolution Process which has transformed him into a true human.

5. ROLE REVERSAL is identified by the DREAM TEST. It presents the daydream of my family working as a team delivering hospitality and wisdom to fellow travelers on the patio of my Art to Science Project, the Wilburton Inn.

Mural 4 introduces the use of creativity for self-discovery. The personal system of conflict resolution as a harmonic or template is captured or reconstructed by the metaphor testing of the Conflict Analysis Battery. The mural clarifies the correspondence of tests and role-states reflecting the organization of personal emotions into the dramatic totality of the creator's CRP. The text of the mural captions explain the correspondence between each role state and a specific test of the *Conflict Analysis Battery*.

Mural 4: MY METAPHORS, MYSELF: 1983

Here, six metaphor creation tests help to reconstruct the personal six-role Conflict Resolution Process. The experimentally derived sequence validates the theory by showing that parts are formally interrelated within the dramatic totality. This totality also tells how its author, Dr. Albert Levis, evolved from a stress, "The War of Metaphors," through his response, anxiety, defense, reversal, to the compromise of "The Reconciliation of the Metaphors."

RESPONSE is identified by the TRANSPARENT MASK TEST, which reveals a person's identity. I chose the image of the runaway Pinocchio, the wooden puppet lying about his identity, fleeing the killer whale of hot ideologies pursuing naive consumers.

DEFENSE is identified by the ANIMAL META-PHOR TEST. Here, the Formal Theory Oedipus is offering the Sphinx an olive branch-- Conflict Resolution--as the new answer to the everlasting riddle on the nature of man.

COMPROMISE is identified by the SHORT STORY TEST. My Judaic passion for jus-tice and my Greek respect for reason as the fiddler on the temple roof unites the world metaphors in the cosmic dance of an univer-sal moral order.

STRESS is identified by the MEMORIES TEST. It represents my recol-lection of World War II as "The War of the Metaphors," the war of multiple cultural conflicts endangering everybody's survival.

ANXIETY is identified by the BEHIND THE MASK TEST. It presents Pinocchio trapped in the stomach of the killer whale with his creator, Geppetto. My Pinocchio is showing the Unit of the Conflict Resolution Process to Geppetto. This discovery has trans-formed him from a pup-pet into a true human.

ROLE REVERSAL is identi-fied by the DREAM TEST. It presents the daydream of my family working as a team delivering hospital-ity and wisdom to fellow travelers on the patio of the Art to Science Project, the Wilburton Inn.

5. OUR CULTURAL METAPHORS AS A CONTINUUM OF EVOLVING MORAL ORDER: 1986 Validation #3: From Matriarchy to Messianism
the Process Integrates the Religions of the World into a Continuum of Ever-Improving Family Relations.

2. RESPONSE: Greece's Oedipus, outwitting and dominating the Sphinx monster and marrying his mother represents *PATRIARCHY*'s Greek snake man rising to power over women.

4. DEFENSE: The moral ascendance of men over women is reflected in the sacredness of snakes, flying dragons and feathered serpents, gradually identified with the worship of the sun and the single male god.

6. COMPROMISE: Christianity's virgin mother and self-sacrificial child, Islam's crescent and star, reflect the shift of power balance from Judaism's father-son Covenant to *MESSIANISM*'s mother-infant spiritual alternative.

1. STRESS: The Mexican eagle immobilizing and devouring a snake represents *MATRIARCHY*'s omnipotent mother intimidating her weak partners and children.

3. ANXIETY: Women return to power through Hinduism's moral discovery of cooperation. Six-armed Siva is the cooperative man stepping on a child-like self. His own sexuality is cancelled.

Mother-Kali is dominating and nurturing son Siva. She is the cooperative mother-child solution. In his turn

5. REVERSAL: The comeback of women as seductive Eve reducing Adam to a charmed snake backfired on women. It evoked the father-son alliance; a monotheistic male dominated moral order.

Mural five depicts the interrelation of the pagan religions as the epics of the goddess. This harmonic integrates cultural resolutions of domestic conflicts which lead to the formation of the stable family institution. The mural retraces the formal interrelation of religions as moral discoveries of conflict resolution integrated into a six role-state sequence. The discoveries of the conflict resolution process are presented as restructuring and rethinking family relations and the moral philosophies as normative changes in domestic relations. The six role-states present how moral thinking evolved from concrete interpretations of reality to the abstract understanding of the Moral Science and the ensuing era of moral reason and enlightenment.

Mural 5: OUR CULTURAL METAPHORS AS A CONTINUUM OF EVOLVING MORAL ORDER

From matriarchy to messianism, the process integrates the religions of the world into a continuum of ever-improving family relations.

RESPONSE: Greece's Oedipus, outwitting and dominating the Sphinx monster and marrying his mother represents **Partiarchy's** Greek snake man rising to power over women.

DEFENSE: The moral ascendance of men over women is reflected in the sacredness of snakes, flying dragons, and feathered serpents, gradually identified with the **worship of the sun** and the single male god.

COMPROMISE:Christianity's Virgin Mother and self-sacrificial child, Islam's crescent and star, reflect the shift of power balance from Judaism's father-son Covenant to **Messianism's** mother-infant spiritual alternative.

STRESS: The Mexican eagle immobilizing and devouring a snake represents **Matriarchy's** omnipotent mother intimidating her weak partners and children.

ANXIETY: Women return to power through **Hinduism's** moral discovery of cooperation. Six-armed Kali is dominating and nurturing her partner Siva. Siva is the cooperative partner in his turn stepping on his inner child-like self, corresponding to cancelling his sexual desires.

REVERSAL: The comeback of women as seductive Eve reducing Adam to a charmed snake backfired on women. It evoked the father-son alliance; the **monotheistic** male dominated moral order.

The mural portrays four cultural relational responses to the same stressor: the apple as the symbol of temptation. The four relational alternatives reflect the cultural dimensions as diametrically opposite and reciprocal to each other. The second part of the mural illustrates how the art of these metaphors is interpreted as the abstractions of science: graphs capture the relational differences of the four cultural alternatives.

Mural 6: FROM ART TO SCIENCE IN THE SEARCH FOR A BETTER PARADIGM

Insights in the great world cultures are easily yielded by constrasting their respective variation of dealing with temptation as reflected in their Apple Metaphors. The graphs reflect how these may be portrayed and quantified scientifically as alternative restructurings of power.

Mexican Indian Culture

Submissive Antagonistic Mode
Human sacrifice to the Gods.
Man is the apple to be plucked.

Judaic Culture

Dominant Cooperate Mode
Forbidden Fruit
Mosaic Law

Oriental Culture

Submissive Cooperative Mode
Sacred cows as an exaggeration of the forbidden fruit, exaggerated self restraint leading to inflicting pain on oneself.

Greek Culture

Dominant Antagonistic Mode
Competitiveness is acceptable
The Apple of Discord

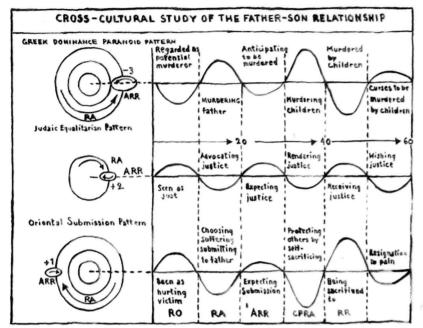

CROSS-CULTURAL STUDY OF THE FATHER-SON RELATIONSHIP

Physic's constructs of displacement (S), velocity (v) and acceleration (a) are equivalent to Formal Theory's status (S), behaviors (v) and emotions (a). Clockwise vectors correspond to cooperation, counterclockwise to the opposite, antagonism. Whole numbers correspond to activity states, fractions to reciprocal passivity states.

Physics constructs of displacement (s), velocity (v), and acceleration (a), are equivalent to Formal Theory's status (s) behaviors (v) and emotions (a).

Clockwise vectors correspond to cooperation, counterclockwise to the opposite, antagonism. Whole numbers correspond to activity states, fraction to reciprocal passivity states.

FOUR DISTINCT PERSPECTIVES FOR RAISING THE PENDULUMBALL OF HUMANITY

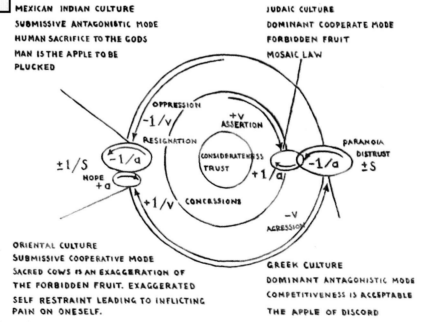

MEXICAN INDIAN CULTURE
SUBMISSIVE ANTAGONISTIC MODE
HUMAN SACRIFICE TO THE GODS
MAN IS THE APPLE TO BE PLUCKED

JUDAIC CULTURE
DOMINANT COOPERATE MODE
FORBIDDEN FRUIT
MOSAIC LAW

ORIENTAL CULTURE
SUBMISSIVE COOPERATIVE MODE
SACRED COWS IS AN EXAGGERATION OF THE FORBIDDEN FRUIT. EXAGGERATED SELF RESTRAINT LEADING TO INFLICTING PAIN ON ONESELF.

GREEK CULTURE
DOMINANT ANTAGONISTIC MODE
COMPETITIVENESS IS ACCEPTABLE
THE APPLE OF DISCORD

THE FORMAL ANALYSIS OF
THE HENRY GORSKI RETROSPECTIVE

September 11 —
October 12, 2009
at the Chaffee Art Center,
Rutland, Vermont

**Commemorating 9/11
by recognizing the
creative process as the
scientific moral paradigm**

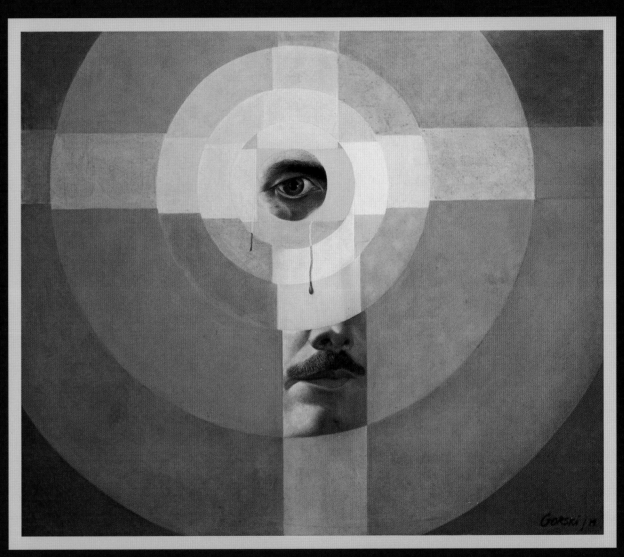

SCIENCE STEALING THE FIRE OF THE GODS AND HEALING THE WORLD

The Mathematical Proof
of the Metaphysical Existence of God (1973)

"God, above, is kissing Adam, below. Graphic configuration of the fixed laws of nature, of God, indicate order emerging from chaos, a triumphant reaching out for love and expectation of love in return. Although the title is facetious, there is joy implied in the presentation of Adam's profile in the lower part of the painting, looking upward toward the outstretched mouth of God emerging from the complete circle. The circle above symbolizes unity and understanding and being in power. The profile of man looking upward symbolizes hope and aspiration and knowing that even if he is fixed there by mathematical, universal laws, it is still a pretty wonderful state to exist in." Henry Gorski

Dr. Albert Levis in the amphitheater at Epidaurus

HENRY GORSKI

Excerpt from an article, "Artist Gorski and his 'Pain-things' (Maurer, New Haven Register, 1968)

"Gorski, who has taught in New Haven at the Paier School of Art, the Creative Arts Workshop, [and Southern Connecticut State University], was born in 1918 in Lackawanna, New York, a town packed with people from nearly every nationality. His family lived in what could be called the Polish ghetto. In the 1930's columnist and broadcaster Walter Winchell called it the melting pot of America and claimed more races and nationalities lived there than in New York City.

"His father worked as a railroad repairman and also owned a tavern. All types of men came into his father's tavern and would sit there for long stretches drinking beer. They were perfect models. Exhausted from working all day they might sit motionless for a half an hour at a time. Gorski made sketch after sketch of those men, somber paintings of working men.

"Gorski, graduated from the Albright School of Art of the University of Buffalo where he met his wife, Bernie. She is an artist and craftsman in her own right and has exhibited widely. Her main interest is in textiles, but she stayed away from painting anyway because she is sure one painter in the house is enough."

"Through the years there has developed a subtle interchange of ideas between them which is evident in their work. His style of drawing influenced her lace weaving. Some of the characteristics of her lace weaving now run through his drawing. Lace weaving, the name she gives to her variation of the old craft of spraing, is a combination of stitchery, weaving, and knotting. Within a circular frame, she stretches a thin irregular warp and woof. Into these stretched threads she stitches and knots designs--mice, frogs, lacewings, abstract patterns. Usually she uses only black thread and yarn. When hung on

white walls the lace weavings look like drawings.

"Her stitchery is a modern form of embroidery. She uses bits and pieces of yarn, battered pieces of rope, cloth, as many types and textures of fabrics as possible. The insects, frogs and tadpoles, she brought home as a child to her parent's dismay have been translated into designs.

"The Gorskis have two sons. The older son is retarded and lives at the Southbury Training School. The experience of their frequent trips there provoked a number of paintings which Gorski generally refers to as "abandoned figures."

"During World War II, from 1941 to 1946, Gorski served in the Army as a map and a model maker. He made three dimensional scale models of terrain, which at a glance showed the location of mountains, valleys, box canyons, beaches. When the United States dropped the atomic bomb on Hiroshima, he was on Luzon making models of islands to be invaded. 'My initial reaction was relief. I looked at it as another military strategy. I wouldn't have to make any more models. Now I understand the horror of it.'

"The terrain models have served as the basis of relief paintings which he has recently been doing. In these he builds up the surface of the work. Shadows falling across it add another dimension to the image. They approach sculpture and change when the lighting on them is shifted."

[Gorski] "feels that artists are immersed in an age similar to that of Leonardo DaVinci's with its astounding discoveries in the physical and intellectual world. Micro-photography, new types of plastics, space exploration, and experimentation in electronic music all provide artistic stimulation. He reads Scientific American for example as an artist, not a scientist.
Gorski was describing with fascination a recent painting of a retarded individual blowing a dandelion fuzz: "Life is a game you don't win, but in

some ways you enjoy it." This statement reveals the man's philosophy as a looser but as a happy one. It also reflects his self awareness, his characteristic ease for philosophically extracting meaning out of his art. In the following text we will study his canvases, but also carefully listen to his thoughts.

Gorski grew up in Lackawanna, New York, which was an industrial city and a big terminal east to west. As he reminisced of his childhood, his father stood out. As a child, he recalled observing his father dressing up in the evenings, putting on a black tie, and going to work at his tavern. Young Gorski spent time with his father. They visited friends' shops and took long walks, his father holding him by the hand going over bridges and the railroad tracks. "My father would take me across a long bridge," he said, and in Henry's mind that bridge spanned all the way to his father's Russia, from which in 1904 Gorski senior had come as a young boy. His father was happiest, laughing and joking, on weekends. Gorski's mother, who was Polish and Catholic, did not seem to be as outstanding in his reminiscences.

Gorski grew up suffering from a serious speech impediment. It blocked his communicating with others. Maybe it was due to his conflict of cultural identities. Polish was spoken at home and English at school. "I was relieved to be taken out of parochial school, eight to nine years old, to go to public school," where he finished grammar school. Gorski was the only boy from his neighborhood to go to college. His father wanted him to become an engineer. When his high school art teacher told his father that he should go to art school ("I'll get him a scholarship"), his father took Henry aside: "Don't become an artist. You'll starve. They live in attics. You won't make a living. Become an aircraft engineer and I will pay for your whole education." "I insisted to be an artist and we had a real conflict. I loved my father but I loved painting." The speech impediment disappeared in college, as soon as he found his identity as an artist."

Letter to Dr. Levis dated 1982

"I had certain reservations about submitting to your thesis which I feared would attempt to explain my paintings in your collection in terms of my personal odyssey, storm-tossed as it often was. Happily you do make the distinction that the art stands on its own merits, irrelevant of personal experiences.

To your profile on my 'symbolic universe' I would add a significant aspect inherent in my paintings and sculpture: their sense of irony. Often while working in my studio, the photos, drawings, typographic fragments spread on the floor and tables presented accidental happenings, amusing and sometimes ominous imagery. A pervasive sense of joy, release erased any taint of ponderous pedantry dangerously inherent in 'serious' themes.

My one-man exhibition titled 'Painting from the Underground,' at the Spectrum Gallery, N.Y.C. in 1966, included many pieces now in your collection. Robert Newman, director, sensed the spirit of my paintings. He wrote, 'There is a comedy in fear, humor in the strength of self able to face fear. Here a power of visualization goes through its torments with irony, going into haunting sensations. The face is the self, susceptible in the eyes.'

Another satirical exhibition, 'Artists Save Face,' initiated and designed by me in cooperation with artist friends, was held in New Haven in 1971. This exhibition of self portraits as artists saw themselves displayed no naturalistic imagery of ourselves. On the contrary, the self revelations in varied personal styles were conducive to speculation, contemplation and wonder. Indirectly presenting a richer experience to the viewer, irony serves the principle, 'Many a truth is spoken in jest.' The format of the invitational flyer parodies a current tabloid. The photographs of the ten artists are presented as mug shots. Aaron Kurzen, in the exhibition's preamble, perfectly epitomized our sense of irony hung on paradox.

The sense of irony does not imply an impersonal distance but rather enhances a more highly expressionist emotionally colored personal relationship. Irony clears away the debris of practical concretized limitations and becomes an experience of liberation for purposes of expression. It's FUN!

Of course real life situations including the tragedies as deeply felt and lived personal experiences cannot be treated with irony. I feel that existence can be interpreted on aesthetic, ethical and religious levels. The aesthetic level and point of view is the least effective means of coping with real life situations since it really cannot do for the other' (who is suffering). Art can only copy, mimic or interpret the infinite possibilities of experience. At best in my work as artist and teacher, I resort to the joys of irony, much as Socrates. But in my personal life I resort to the absolute imperatives of religion. To quote one of my favorites, Samuel Beckett (also a poet of losers): 'I believe all that blather about a life hereafter; it cheers me up.'

As an artist I must rely on another artist, the writer Abram Tertz, for pointing my way: 'At present I place my hopes in an art in which the grotesque would replace the realistic in the description of everyday life. This is what would respond to the spirit of our epoch.' My work in your collection reflects this viewpoint.

As an artist, reading your psychoanalyst's essay leaves me cold...non-committal as if the lifeless cadaver of me, the artist, was propped up on a slab and examined for clues. Reminding me of a mural by Orozco at Dartmouth College titled, 'Sterile Knowledge,' doctors in varied academic garb examining a human skeleton.

The above comment has nothing to do with my feelings about my paintings in your collection. They merit consideration, solemn or enjoyable, for meanings which can be multi-dimensional in their interpretations on various planes.

To explain my personality in terms of my work strikes me as a formidable and awesome task. I shall have to leave that area of professional competence to you. I am only reminded that Robert Frost's poetry reveals very little of the son-of-a-bitch he was; that Dostoevsky raped a twelve year old, gambled family, friends and himself into hock, etc...that Emil Nolde was a Nazi and Ezra Pound a Fascist.

Henry Gorski"

Letter to Dr. Levis dated 1987

"William Blake's prophetic and apocalyptic poem speaks to our present age of all-pervasive dehumanization:

"My mother groan'd! My father wept. Into the dangerous world I leapt:"

I leapt out of my mother's womb in the back room of a working man's tavern located in a steel town during a world war. My personal odyssey since that traumatic day encompassed half the spinning globe and spanned a depression, another war worth three bronze stars, apprehensions of atomic dissolution as a map maker, still another war which threatened one son, dealing with a severely handicapped hyperactive other son, etc., etc...Painting and art became a defensive shield which cushioned the "slings and arrows of outrageous fortune." What these "interesting" times ("interesting" in the acrimonious sense of cursing an enemy: "May you live in an interesting age!") had wrought to my inner person determined the directions my painting would take.

Interest in other cultures dealing with these inward conflicts and bogey men of spiritual undergrounds took me to Pre-Columbian Mexico, mystical Spain and most recently to Italy. The study of Primitive Art experienced first hand in New Guinea, the island arts of the Pacific, Australia and the West Coast, the anxieties of Kafka and Dostoevsky and the mosaics of Italian basilicas established my particular thrust toward expressing and revealing some dimension of the inner person.

A chance meeting, perhaps a natural gravitation, a confluence of opposite attractions (of Art grafting onto Science) has since developed into a fecund relationship. Albert Levis perceived seemingly parallel directions in my paintings as symbols applicable to his Formal Theory of human behavior-- directions of which I was not consciously aware.

My own comments on my paintings in the following text are, to the best of my memory, the sources of inspiration which motivated them. At times there may be differing, even contradictory responses to my work; but that is the multi-faceted nature of art--that it can present different aspects, evoke varying responses at different times.

Albert Levis in his formal approach to behavior theory, as seen and interpreted through the artist's eye, has enhanced the realm of creative vision which I experienced intuitively as a painter. His new dimension of insight fostered a meaningful relationship between the Formalist and the Intuitionist. This manuscript extends the frontiers of understanding our humanity."

EXHIBIT #2
THE GORSKI RETROSPECTIVE
Deciphering the symbolic language of the unconscious

The Gorski Retrospective, like the other exhibits of the *Museum of the Creative Process*, validates Formal Theory's assumptions on the scientific nature of the creative process by illustrating the formal and physical nature of the symbolic language of the unconscious. The canvases illustrate the core pattern that organizes emotions as a formally interrelated sequence of six role-states and three formal operations.

The canvases confirm the creative process as a conflict resolution mechanism which is the physiological adjustive response to stress. This process follows a distinct path which is a mental-emotional dialectic, departing from a conflict and completing the objective of a resolution. The significance of this finding is the identification of an orderly phenomenon that bridges art and science.

My relationship with Henry Gorski started in 1972 upon the occasion of a lecture on the Formal Theory to the New Haven Medical Association. Seeking to illustrate the formal structure of emotions and the periodic nature of the conflict resolution mechanism, I displayed a dozen of his canvases. Looking at his canvases the audience could understand the concept of the unconscious mind proceeding along the path of three formal transformations and along the six states of the Conflict Resolution Process. Ever since that lecture I have been collecting his art compulsively, challenged by having a record illustrating the creative process as a natural science phenomenon.

Six objectives of the exhibit
My original intention was to illustrate the notion of the three formal operations: reciprocity, negation and correlation. Gorski's canvases using minimalist symbolic language focused on one theme, be that the mouth, athletes and the cross. The simplicity reduces the variables of his work and allows to observe emotions evolve along the three formal operations. The relational distinctions manifest as formal dichotomies clear transformations of the one symbolic reference. Canvases with mouths obstructed evolved to mouths screaming, illustrating passivity and activity.

Absent mouths evolved to multiple kisses, reflecting the difference between antagonism and cooperation. The obstructed mouth is transformed to the accurate portrayals of the artist's own mouth overlapping a cross. This reflects correlation the relation of the person to the world; the artist labels this canvas, *identity*. The Retrospective is continued with totally missing faces in the sports paintings, followed by portraits of the entire face in the sequence of the handicapped period. This reflects further a sense of resolution which at the end of his lifetime work is completed with a cross made of kisses labeled Paradox, symbolizing the reconciliation of opposites, pleasure and pain as the meaning of life.

A second objective evolved to illustrate the six role process: stress, response, anxiety, defense, reversal and compromise. The exhibit presents the three formal transformations and the six role-state process in several sequences of interrelated canvases.

A third objective emerged identifying in the Gorski canvases repetition of the theme of conflict resolution. Indeed we detect six cycles of emotional sequences clarifying the Conflict Resolution Process as a periodic phenomenon.

The fourth objective emerged as the illustration of how the exhibit illustrates perfectly the laws of two scientific natural science phenomena organizing Gorski's symbolic universe.

The fifth function of the exhibit was to illustrate the continuity between the five artistic phases of the Retrospective into a single dramatic totality.

The sixth objective discussed in the conclusion of this volume is to illustrate the nature of the genesis of religion as a normal physiological psychological phenomenon and the importance of religion identifying the normative conflict generating reality surrounding the artist.

Appreciative of the value of this collection, in 1987 I acquired a gallery to display his artwork as *'art to science, a gallery and Forum.'* The same year I also acquired the *Wilburton Inn* to display more art exhibits and to deliver retreats on the scientific breakthrough. In 2005, the Gorski Retrospective was placed in its current home, the *Teleion Holon Retreat and Farm*. *'Teleion Holon'* refers to the Aristotelian concept of the organization of ideas in Greek dramatic plays as a perfect or scientific universe. The Retrospective clarifies this universe of ideas with the canvases of one artist as a dramatic or conflict resolving continuum.

Making sense of the meaning of life; a joint venture of an artist and a scientist
The exhibit demonstrates the orderly nature of the unconscious mind, illustrating and validating the Formal Theoretical premise while making an artist's work more meaningful. The artist pursued meaning independently of the scientist. The title of one Gorski painting: *The Mathematical Proof of the Metaphysical Existence of God* reflects the artist's interest in science, as his own quest for meaning. He sought to identify the interface of religion and science. The artist felt harmony metaphysically and captured it metaphorically in an image of God kissing Adam in which God is the origin of a field that has a direction, from Alpha to Omega, and a structure of sine curves as multiples of pi; the field around the kissing mouth of God is marked with concentric circles in the numbers of 1, 2, 3, and 4. This portrayal of God was scientific but in metaphorical terms.

There is a striking resemblance between Gorski's graphic illustrations and Formal Theory's portrayal of the pendulum oscillation characteristics.

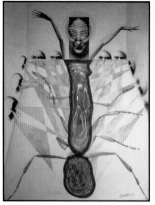

GORSKI'S SYMBOLIC UNIVERSE

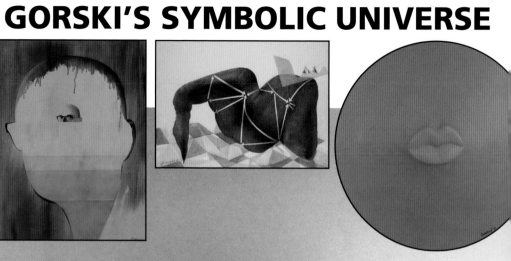

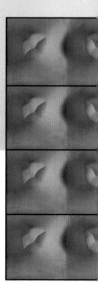

PAIN-THINGS/MOUTHLESSNESS PHASE

THE RIDDLE OF THE KISS

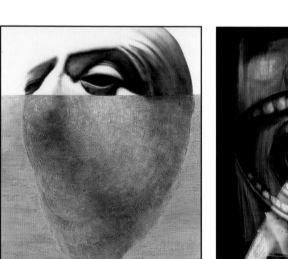

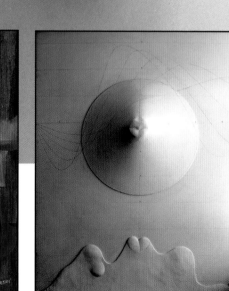

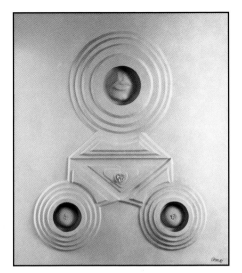

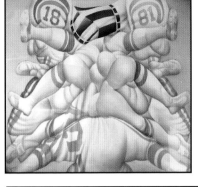

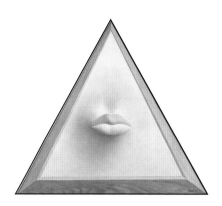

EROTIC/AGAPE PHASE

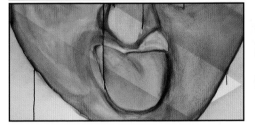

ILLUSIONS/REALITY PHASE

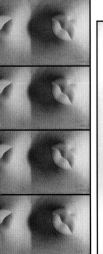

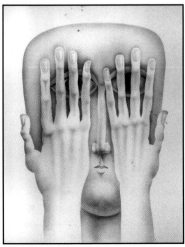

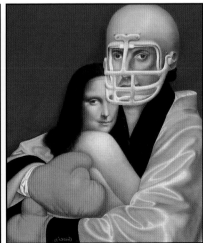

TWO SCIENTIFIC MODELS FOR THE MEASUREMENT AND GRAPHIC PRESENTATION OF THE CONFLICT RESOLUTION PROCESS:

THE PHYSICS OF THE PENDULUM AND THE FORMAL OPERATIONS OF THE SCALE

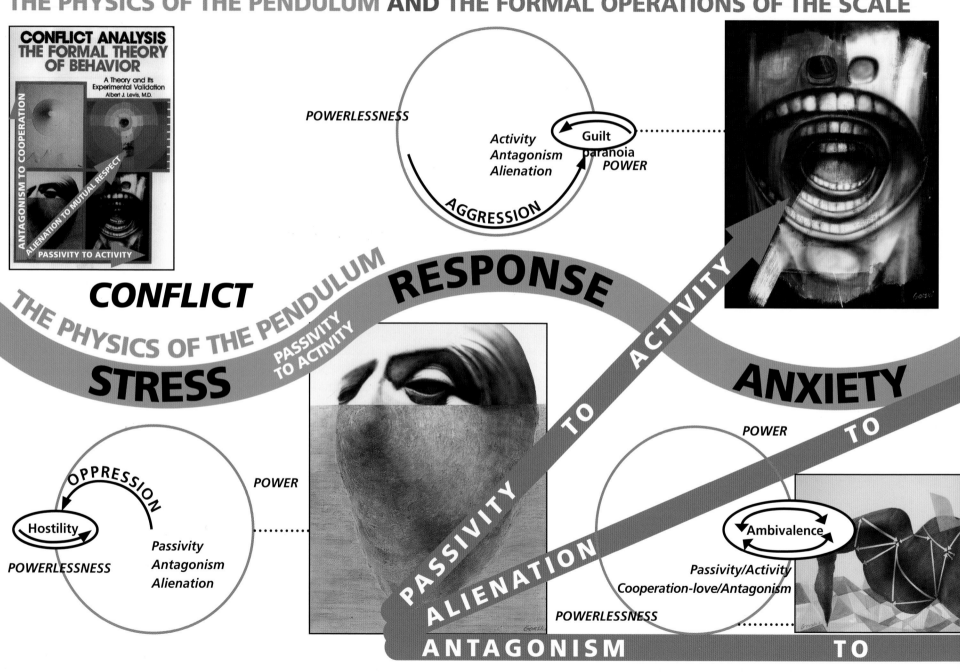

CONFLICT ANALYSIS
THE FORMAL THEORY
OF BEHAVIOR

A Theory and Its
Experimental Validation
Albert J. Levis, M.D.

ANTAGONISM TO COOPERATION

ALIENATION TO MUTUAL RESPECT

PASSIVITY TO ACTIVITY

POWERLESSNESS

Activity
Antagonism
Alienation

Guilt
paranoia
POWER

AGGRESSION

THE PHYSICS OF THE PENDULUM

CONFLICT

STRESS

RESPONSE

PASSIVITY TO ACTIVITY

ANXIETY

TO ACTIVITY

OPPRESSION

Hostility

POWERLESSNESS

Passivity
Antagonism
Alienation

POWER

PASSIVITY TO ALIENATION

POWER

Ambivalence

Passivity/Activity
Cooperation-love/Antagonism

POWERLESSNESS

ANTAGONISM

TO

TO

THE FORMAL OPERATIONS OF THE SCALE

THE CONFLICT RESOLUTION PROCESS, THE UNIVERSAL HARMONIC, THE UNIT OF THE SOCIAL SCIENCES ORGANIZES A SYMBOLIC UNIVERSE

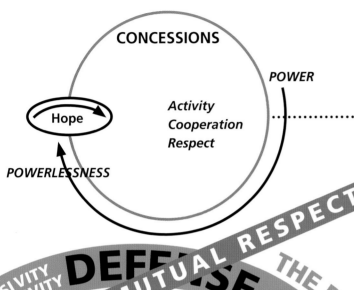

CONCESSIONS

POWER

Hope

Activity
Cooperation
Respect

POWERLESSNESS

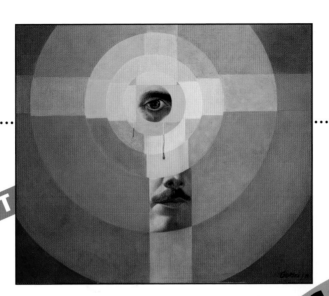

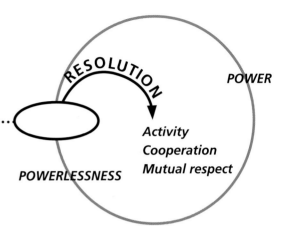

RESOLUTION

POWER

Activity
Cooperation
Mutual respect

POWERLESSNESS

PASSIVITY TO ACTIVITY DEFEAT MUTUAL RESPECT THE PENDULUM OSCILLATION PASSIVITY TO ACTIVITY COMPROMISE

REVERSAL

RESOLUTION

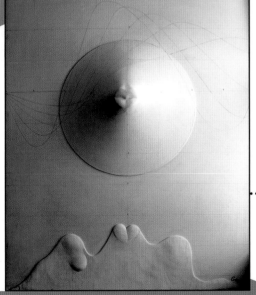

ASSERTION

Activity/passivity
(kissing and being
kissed by God)
Cooperation
Mutual Respect

POWER

Considerateness

COOPERATION

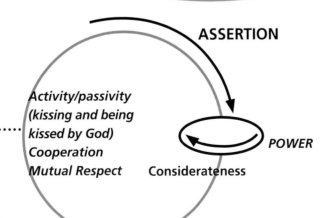

LEGEND

Clockwise Arrow = Cooperation
Counter Clockwise = Antagonism
Ellipses = Psychic System
Circles = Social System
Arrows within Ellipses = Emotions
Arrows within Circles = Behaviors
Diameter of Circles = Power Differential

POWERLESSNESS

THE THREE FORMAL DISTINCTIONS ORGANIZE THE CANVASES

CONFLICT DEFINED AS PASSIVITY, ANTAGONISM AND ALIENATION

RESOLUTION DEFINED AS ACTIVITY, COOPERATION AND MUTUAL RESPECT

POWER = EMERGENCE OF THE MOUTH ENGENDERS COOPERATION , LOVE AND ASSERTION

1965 The Committee

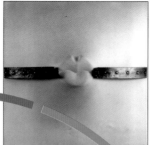

1970 Saja's Secret

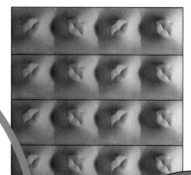

1973 Alliterative Obsession

1967 Body with Vectors

1965 The Ship of Fools

POWERLESSNESS

1966 The Birth of Adam

1974 Eye-dentity

GOD = REST MUTUAL RESPECT

1973 The Mathematical Proof of the Metaphysical Existence of God

POWER

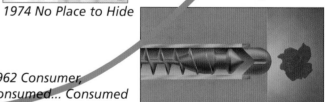

1974 No Place to Hide

1971 Tangerine Kiss

1970 Identity

1965 The Dream

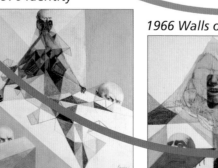

1966 Walls of Fear

1962 Consumer, Consumed... Consumed

1968 The Rape of the Rose

POWERLESSNESS = MOUTHLESSNESS ENGENDERS ANTAGONISM AS HOSTILITY AND AGGRESSION

ILLUSTRATING THE PROCESS AS THE PATH TO CONFLICT RESOLUTION

CONFLICT DEFINED AS PASSIVITY, ANTAGONISM AND ALIENATION

RESOLUTION DEFINED AS ACTIVITY, COOPERATION AND MUTUAL RESPECT

POWER = EMERGENCE OF THE HERO
ENGENDERS COOPERATION
LOVE AND ASSERTION

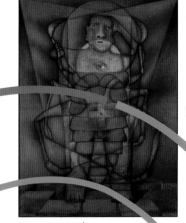

1976 Vestigial Being

1982 Blocked

1982 Scrimmage

1982 Winner Take All

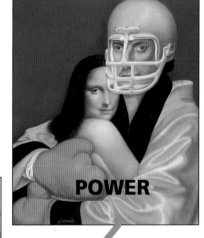

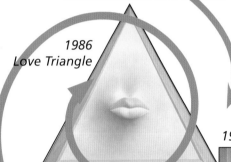

*1986
Love Triangle*

POWERLESSNESS

1984 Shadow Play

SPIRITUALITY = REST
MUTUAL RESPECT

POWER

*1986
Manuel With Bird*

1978 Fumble

*1978
Through
the Hole*

LEGEND

CLOCKWISE =
COOPERATION

COUNTERCLOCKWISE =
ANTAGONISM

**POWERLESSNESS = FACELESSNESS
ENGENDERS ANTAGONISM, HOSTILITY
AND AGGRESSION**

1980 Windup

I used the sine curve to illustrate the six role-states of the process. The cross section of the sine curve was identical to the Power field as a set of concentric normative circles to indicate tension levels as deviations from the acceptable but also allowing me to present the relational variations.

The sine curve graph serves to map the personal journey with canvases. The three formal operations are the compass guiding the mind from alpha to omega, from conflict to resolution. Gorski identified the center of the field with God's kiss, implying tension around religious norms. I identified the center, the rest state, as the secular norm surrounded by concentric tension levels indicating normative deviations, the power field of interrelated behaviors. Our graphs coincided. The sine curves presented the six role state process in the course of the time needed to resolve a conflict. The circumference presents the field of normative deviations, invisible fences that contain the individual within the societal norms. The deviations from the divine energize Gorski's canvases with conflicts and clarify the emotional significance of the Formal Theoretical vectors as corresponding to notions of right and wrong.

Gorski's emphasis on feelings introduced vivid imagery in the place of the cold and rigorous abstractions: passivity as blocked mouths became activity illustrated with screaming mouths, antagonism of screaming mouths became cooperation, represented as kissing mouths. Alienation of early mouthless figures became mutual respect as spiritual kisses portraying the artist's mouth in the background of the cross. Gorski's graph identified the resolution with piety, the transformation along the periodic process as the end of the path of the six emotions.

In my Formal Theory I have been seeking to grasp the emotional process rationally, so I needed the language of emotions to portray the significance of the constructs and formulas. Gorski began with the language of emotions and aspired for abstractions. He was trying to grasp metaphysics as mathematics. I was attempting to put a human face on physics and math.

Gorski's art enlivened *the Formal Theory of Behavior*. The Theory was not only science, it addressed the dramatic essence of psychology. Everyone could follow the unconscious thought process resolving conflict along a distinct predictable path. Gorski pursuing the depiction of his emotions was the illustrator of the scientific process. I was able to identify in the images of his canvases an elegant and eloquent validation of my thesis on the nature of the process. Here we see a human story as a natural science and moral order phenomenon. Emotions are bound tightly with the laws of logic, math and physics. So in this exhibit science as the unit process is validated because it makes the art perfectly meaningful.

Over the years the sequences of Gorski canvases became for me the means for the illustration of abstractions about the organization of emotions. It was the record of the unconscious as an intelligible entity. The art follows the laws of science, confirming the theory that the unconscious is a natural science moral order phenomenon.

The conclusion is that the unconscious manifested as the creative process is an observable physical entity. The process defines moral order as emotional determinism, the path to goodness based on science that is clear reductionism. This entity, the unit of behavior, integrates the two irreconcilable philosophical traditions, determinism and reductionism, art and science. The canvases are the 'mathematical proof' integrating psychology and morality with the rigorous sciences into the exact Moral Science.

The artist and the analyst are partners in this project. The artist, intuitively, and the scientist, rationally, arrive at the same conclusion: there is an order which guides a person's emotions and it is one that we can explain with science. This exhibit leads from art to science, introducing the interpretation of metaphors as the dialectic evolution of emotions.

To confirm this impression the exhibit introduces art side by side with its scientific interpretation as units of conflict resolution. The Retrospective displays the continuum of images interpreted by science in parallel with the formal dialectic of emotions. The sequences evolve from conflicts to resolutions finding at the end the dramatic conclusion, in this case a father reconciled with the reality of his handicapped son as a happy person. This process integrates the five thematically different periods of Gorski's enigmatic compositions into a single lifetime drama. The exhibit then validates the Formal Theory as the means to interpret symbolic systems. It also confirms the process as the atomistic unit of the social sciences.

This exhibit makes history by introducing the conflict resolution process as the psychic mechanism which binds emotional statements, the canvases, into discrete units of meaning. Each canvas is integrated formally to the others and the entire Retrospective is integrated into an emotional equilibrial totality. The exhibit thus demonstrates the meaningfulness of the creative process as a moral order phenomenon. This is the Universal Harmonic, Aristotle's Perfect Universe, his principle of the continuity of action.

The unit process as the object and formal analysis as the method for the study of the social sciences
Psychology and religion never achieved the distinction of science for lack of an object and a method of analysis. This exhibit ushers in this missing object and the elusive method as the formal analysis of the artist's circumscribed periods of conflict resolution. In this exhibit the series of symbolically connected canvases illustrates the object of both psychology and moral order as one and the same. It is the Conflict Resolution Process, a natural science entity, one that abides by the laws of science.

The unconscious is demonstrated as the physiologic equilibrial phenomenon reconciling the individual and society. The dialectic process's mission is the emotional adjustment to a stressor or change.

It is the spontaneous equilibrial mental response to stress. The exhibit illustrates the individual's emotional quest for equanimity, rest, peace, and stability in a tumultuous environment.

This pattern, a pure abstraction, is very significant for psychology. It is the unit entity of the unconscious as both a moral order and a natural science periodic phenomenon; this unit entity redefines and unites the social sciences into the Moral Science. It is the unconscious as the Universal Harmonic. It is the origin of all creativity: literary creations are conflict resolutions; the process is the plot and the moral of stories; it is the structure of all psychological phenomena such as syndromes, diagnostic categories, assessment techniques, and it is the moral order of the religions of the world. This entity is the scientific process that we can use to interpret metaphors be that an artist's retrospective or the study of religions as measurable conflict resolving processes. The process is a trigonometric formula with many resolutions.

The formal analysis of symbolic languages demonstrates the manifestation of a universal order

Science transforms meaninglessness to meaning, cacophony to a pleasant symphonic composition. My task in this exhibit is to integrate art along the conflict resolution process compounding harmony with meaning. Demonstrating meaning validates the theory making the emotions clearer as formally interrelated.

The significance of the Retrospective – besides displaying art – is in interpreting art by detecting meaning overlapping with science. This is the mechanism of the unit process, a clear natural science phenomenon structuring meaning and making behavior measurable and predictable. This scientific interpretation of art compounds

meaning but also validates the six-step and three formal operations structure of associations representing the human unconscious as the equilibrial unit of the social sciences.

I am interpreting the art as the process connecting the canvases of the artist as sequences of conflict resolutions of a lifetime. Does the unit of three formal operations make the canvases more meaningful than seeing them as isolated aesthetic statements? Does the sequence of his self-portraits, introduced as the overarching dialectic of resolutions, make sense as the path to reaching one's spiritual potential?

Figurative Expressionism

There is a focus on science in this exhibit, but one should not overlook the art. The scientific interpretation means to compound the interest and enjoyment of the art for its artistic features and aesthetic and representational qualities.

The Gorski Retrospective is a remarkable collection of a great contemporary American artist. It represents his lifetime works, almost fifty productive years. The exhibit includes a WPA canvas, the *Homecoming*, dated 1946 and includes his last paintings dated 1993. Gorski's themes and techniques of figurative expressionism are representative of the post WWII art culture, a period that valued the symbolic representation of feelings, and of inner conflicts rather than realism. This trend was greatly influenced by the psychoanalytic movement's discovery of the unconscious, promoting attention to the inner reality as opposed to the naturalistic depiction of the environment. The artists of this period redefined the world with symbolic distinctions and invented a range of metaphorical languages to depict their conflicts.

In America, starting in the 1950s--the heyday of Abstract Expressionism and New York's emergence as the center of the artworld – a number of artists decided to return to the figure. But as they were committed to the Abstract Expressionist

way of painting that had been formative of their styles, they would not give it up, choosing instead to adapt it to their need to paint recognizable imagery. Artists like Grace Hartigan, Elaine De Kooning, Lester Johnson, Nathan Oliviera, Richard Diebenkorn, David Parks, and Vera Clement had only this dual allegiance in common.

Gorski's paintings represent riddles, encrypted communications (see *Gorski's Symbolic Universe; The Riddle of the Kiss*). He described his paintings as several sequences of "pain-things" because the canvases reflect his suffering. He used several themes over the years; these represent symbolic languages that changed radically from period to period. His paintings are integrated into three periods of conflict resolution: "Pain-things", including mouthlessness and crucifixions; the erotic and religious imagery phase; and the illusions and reality phase, pp 92-97.

This organization of his work parallels that of the well-known British figurative expressionist Francis Bacon, but there are clear differences between the two artists. Gorski's work progresses to conflict resolution as conformity to norms whereas Bacon's work defies existing norms. He had been seeking social change. While Gorski learns from his single erotic conflict and goes through a phase of crucifixions and transformations, Bacon's art reflects an obsessive repetition of erotic encounters and conflictual themes violating conventions, normative or acceptable behavior. Bacon's studies of crucifixions and evolving self-portraits remain in the domain of intense conflict. Unlike Gorski, Bacon refused to capitulate as a child to his father's spankings, as an artist to norms of painting, as a lover to societal norms, as a mortal to the screaming Pope. Yet he is credited for being a pioneer in portraying and promoting homoeroticism and influencing the revisiting of the norm. (*See Focus Exhibit 3*).

DISCUSSION OF THE EXHIBIT AS THREE TOPICS

Topic 1. The Retrospective as three acts of a drama or of the CRP.
Act 1: The Hero's Values and Conflicts
Act 2: The Hero's Adventure
Act 3: The Hero's Illusions and Reality
Topic 2. The physics of the unconscious process as a natural science phenomenon in its many aspects. The formal relation between variables in formulas of the logic of relations and the Simple Harmonic Motion.
Topic 3; Three Focus Studies on the function of the CRP
  FOCUS STUDY #1: The Healing Function as illustrated by Gorski's evolving self-portrait sequence
  FOCUS STUDY #2: The Normative Compliance Function as illustrated by Gorski's religious paintings and his faith-based gender portrayals.
  FOCUS STUDY #3: The Norm-Changing Function as illustrated by comparing and contrasting the works of Gorski and Francis Bacon.

TOPIC #1: THE RETROSPECTIVE AS THREE ACTS OF A DRAMA

The Formal Analysis of the Gorski Retrospective

The core thesis of the Formal Theory is that the unconscious mind deals with stress by transforming it to a compromise through a process that has a distinct structure and a moral function: the Conflict Resolution Process (CRP). Its structure follows a predictable dialectic of six emotions: stress, response, anxiety, defense, reversal and compromise. This transformation is guided by three inner needs as formal operations seeking comfort and stability, i.e. a state of rest. The operations transform passivity to activity, antagonism to cooperation and alienation to mutual respect.

The first objective of the exhibit is to show how the process integrates the very diverse canvases of the artist into a single drama. We therefore show how the canvases capture the emotional odyssey of the artist through the key conflicts of his life.

The canvases are accompanied by statements of the artist clarifying the feelings portrayed in the respective images. The illustrated annotated collection is a record in art and in words that facilitates the task of interpretation.

The connection between Levis' Formal Theory and the Retrospective is that the art demonstrates the science of the process. The process is illustrated by Gorski's canvases integrated into a single, three-act dramatic continuum. The canvases of the artist thus become meaningful while validating the abstractions of the six role-states and the three formal operations.

The Retrospective is displayed chronologically, retracing Gorski's personal drama as the three acts of Adam/Kafka, his central hero. In each act we see a resolution as a compromise with life's painful realities summed up at the end of each series by one or more of the artist's self-portraits. In the following text we address the conflicts experienced in each period.

Act 1: In the first act of this drama the hero is a family man preoccupied by his concerns about his sons. This phase, entitled by Gorski as "Pain-things," distinguishes Adam/Kafka evolving through two cycles of conflict resolution. The first cycle pertains to conflicts about his elder son's institutionalization as a result of his autism. The second cycle revolves around political matters as the younger son was threatened by the draft into the Vietnam War.

Mouthless paintings in both cycles show the artist feeling overwhelmed by these oppressive conflicts. Two canvases with religious themes illustrate Gorski's devout faith in God. These two cycles are concluded with two self-portraits, both presenting the artist's face emerging from suffocating fingerprints. The first is in the shape of a clamshell, the second, as seen in the self-portrait focus exhibit, is in the shape of the Pentagon.

Act 2 is characterized by Adam's erotic adventure.

In celebrating peace he becomes exuberant with the love culture of the Age of Aquarius. He seeks solace in love but is scared of closeness to women. Eve/Mona Lisa is a dangerous temptress. Unstoppable, he encounters love and experiences guilt for an adventure and seeks expiation in espousing religion; we see his self-portraits as personal crucifixions.

The mouthlessness of the first act is replaced by his obsession with sensuous kisses. The kisses multiply, intensify in color and lead up to *The Rape of the Rose*, the violation of innocence. A canvas labeled *Nowhere to Hide* is succeeded by several crucifixion-associated self-portraits, *Identity* and *Eye-dentity*. They reflect the artist's willingness, with tongue in cheek, to conform to cultural norms.

Act 3 addresses Adam's issues with morality and mortality by presenting sports paintings as alternative crucifixions. Here he is recovering from guilt by identifying with the competitive athletes, victims of our sensationalist culture. Adam, his hero, is escaping the cruel world to the safety of illusions. From the illusions he confronts reality by turning his attention to his tormented autistic son. Gorski completed his Odyssey and drama by identifying the inmates' humanity while also discovering his own freedom of stylistic innovation and spontaneous emotional and spiritual expression.

The sequences of conflict resolution

It is of great interest to analyze the five series of thematically distinct symbolic phases. It is extraordinary to connect these individual resolutions into a single formal lifetime continuum, the three acts of a dramatic play. The artist was unaware of the connection of his canvases until he encountered them hung as an exhibit. Then the artist could see his drama integrating all distinctions of his life gradually completing his search for identity and meaning of it all. The artist and the audience can recognize here the importance of grasping the perfect universe of the process as pertinent for one's healing.

Act one: personal and political quests for meaning

"Pain-things", role oppression (RO) and expressing hostility and anger at the untrustworthy authorities, role assumption (RA)

The first act spans from the end of the Second World War to the end of the Vietnam War. We distinguish here two sets of canvases unfolding in parallel with a similar set of conflicts and resolutions. One is an earlier set related to his first son being an autistic child, *the Child of Darkness*. His son's placement in an institution evoked the depression portrayed in the series of the *Abandoned Figures*. These canvases depart from dehumanized brown constructions weaving their way to mouthless figures on top of game boards. The second set pertains to political developments, the Vietnam War threatening Gorski's second son with being drafted, as in *Portrait of Nick*. Gorski had fought in the second World War and defined it as his formative stress or role oppression experience. This background explained the political focus of the second set of protesting angry and hostile canvases. His unexpressed anger, manifested as hostility in both sequences represented his role assumption. These two cycles encompass the many canvases of mouthlessness reflecting both his depression for his first son and his anger for the dangers to his second son. The *Ship of Fools* is about the recruits on the way to the front.

The role assumption of the personal "Pain-things" cycle presents the mouth opening up with anger in *Consumer, Consumed... Consumed.* The anxiety state presents the blind and mouthless *Odysseus* lost in space behind vertical confining bars, unable to express his feelings, and unable to see. This canvas portrays a sense of futility and alienation. The sequence gets resolved with the emergence of the hero in *Birth of Adam*, a profile emerging from underneath a fingerprint.

In the political "Pain-things" cycle canvases address political themes: space travel, war mobilization, and censorship of the press. *The Man of Letters,* making indecipherable sounds, is muffled by technology. This phase of oppression, as a painful state of passiv-

ity, elicited negative responses from the artist: anger and hostilities targeting the political authorities. The defense portrays the suspicious secretive politicians, *The Committee*, as mouthless authority figures duplicitously staring into space and at each other. Gorski's hostility at the establishment is presented in his Kafka bugs, mouthless canvases and sculptures sprouting three sets of arms as tentacles silently manipulating the world.

Eventually the authority figures sign a peace agreement and shake hands in *The Game*. The negation of personality is reversed with the affirmation of peace treaties. Kindness allows the person, *The Double*, to emerge from his protective shell. Peace as resolution frees the obstructed mouths. The mouth, the icon of emotions, melts the gag and emerges as a kiss in *Saja's Secret*. The peace negotiation process transformed the Kafka bugs into Gorski's set of kissing winged love bugs of 1967. In 1968 Gorski completed several religious pieces, including one of a face with tears, *Small Parts as Tears*, and another, *Crucifixion*, commemorating the assassinations of King and Kennedy, beloved political leaders of the period.

A sense of healing is completed in both Pain-things cycles with the *Birth of Adam* and *The Double*, announcing the person's imminent emergence from oppression, evoking a sense of rebirth and absolution from anger. The timing of these canvases corresponds to the passing of civil rights legislation and of negotiations for peace in Vietnam. In *Zero Mostel as a Kite* we see a mouth opening up to sing as a colorful reverberating canvas.

Act two: Eros versus agape
Temptation and anxiety, anticipation of role reversal (ARR) versus defense as the counter-phobic role assumption (CPRA):

The second act of the Gorski drama unfolds in the mid 1970s, a period of explorations and loss of inhibitions characterized by the age of Aquarius. The phase is a paradox as it started with the purity of love, *Everything with a Kiss*, and was completed

with the ensuing phase which we can facetiously call 'Everything With a Cross.' I united the two symbolic periods as interrelated into the cycle of the erotic conflict resolution. It connects Gorski's transgressions and self-punishment experiences.

The artist's adventure of free expression started with *Saja's Secret*, a call for love that melts the gag of silence. The artist was liberated. He had a voice and passion for life. This period started with the hot kiss melting the metal gag; then his kisses multiplied. He created columns, planes and walls of kisses reflecting the reversal of years of mouthlessness. With his tapestries of kisses he celebrated the discovery of peace and the freedom to love and be loved. His kisses eventually became the red-orange and round kiss of passion, *Tangerine Kiss*.

Next we see its target, the girl in white, *The Hyperbolic Bride*. She is innocent; her erogenous zones are concealed by concentric circles accentuating their magnetic energy. A rose is framed by a triangle in the middle of her torso. The obsession with kisses must have overwhelmed Gorski's capacity for self-restraint. His passion for the girl led to the climactic paintings of *Figure with Vectors* (reflecting his yearning for a kiss). *The Rape of the Rose* followed. Then we detect a reversal of fortune in *Nowhere to Hide*, brought on by remorse and guilt.

This remorse led to a new iconography. Gorski discovered the perfect hiding place: the cross. Upon the interface of the cross and his face we see Gorski's illuminated facial characteristics. In *Eye-dentity* we see a tear of blood coming down his realistic self-portrait. Freedom of expression had backfired and Gorski quickly reverted to choosing pain rather than savoring pleasures.

The erotic phase which started with the liberated kiss evolved to the challenge of an object of affection, the girl as an exquisite rose generating the conflict of abuse of power countered by guilt and expiatory behaviors. The artist perceived the encounter as the violation of innocence; sexual love violated the spirit of agape. Guilt ensued and the artist accepted self-crucifixion and self-sacrifice as his just desserts. *Eye-dentity,* and several other self-portraits as a crucifix, reflected his determination for self-improvement. We identify his willingness to accept deliberately the pain that had suffered passively in the previous cycle.

The series is concluded with the canvas of a face looking like a cross, inscribed *'I will make a man more precious than fine gold.'* Gorski surrendered his individual power to the higher power and adopted a mission of goodness, finding inner peace in faith as the life of sacrifice rather than one of self-indulgence. The second act is therefor completed with a spiritual identity. This confirms the artist's reversal of fortune, from *Everything With a Kiss* evolving to 'Everything With a Cross'. He was more comfortable in the position of crucifixion than as an idol worshiper and sinner. He traded the secret pleasures of sexual love for the conciliatory pleasures of agape. He welcomed expiation as conformity to social norms. His choice was the comfort and the safety of normative behavior. A canvas *The Vows* illustrates a couple reconciled though blocked by dark clouds. It might represent conflict resolution in his strained domestic relations.

Act three: illusions of kisses and the reality of the cross Accepting the responsibilities of a creator, Role Reversal (RR) and finding peace of mind, Compromise Role Assumption (CRA)

The third act of his passion play unfolded in the culture of the '80s undoing the excesses of the liberal '70s. Gorski had found absolution, expiation from his transgression in the spirituality of the crucifixion. In a next phase he was painting sports paintings, the phase of *'Heroic Athletes.'* This series continued with the phase labeled *'Illusions and Reality.'* This series was followed with portraits of institutionalized handicapped individuals as the *'Reality of Being.'*

The third act is replete with Gorski irony. It starts with *The Vestigial Being,* a complex symbolic statement combining the bug figure, a penis as his sexuality, the paranoid self-conscious eye of feeling observed, and

the cross as the awareness of norms and setbacks. These associations are encompassed in the concept of a sacrificial Mexican athlete. The kiss symbolism is missing. Here we have a warrior with the determination to win in spite of dangers and pain. This is a transition canvas generated following a visit to the Yucatan where he learned that at the end of athletic games in Mexico the loser was sacrificed to the gods.

Returning home, Gorski portrayed American athletes as colorful sacrificial victims in the spirit of the Mexican culture. His heroic athletes play all the sports in intense colorful canvases which are glum in depicting concealed suffering rather than the pleasures of sports. The athletes wear masks; they are institutional warriors distinguished by numbers, uniforms and emblems. They represent the battles for victory dramatizing the athletes as heroes and yet the same as victims of the exploitive world of entertainment. The sports heroes become the new crucifixes oppressed by our society. Like Roman Gladiators, they kill each other for the sake of survival and public entertainment.

While the heroic athletes were seeking to emerge beyond being shadows, uniforms and nameless numbers, they remained victims and losers. The series might be corresponding to Gorski's pursuit of success in the art world, and as he achieved it in spite of his expectations of gloom and futility a new emotion occurred in him. Success was experienced as a welcome illusion. His athletes questioning winning are winners. So in a new phase he presents success as an illusion. He denounced victory as illusion in *Winner Take All,* in which Sylvester Stallone holds a naked Mona Lisa on his enrobed lap. He presented this impossible fantasy as the laughable illusion of an athlete who is a dreamer. Irony is laughing at one's fantasies.

Gorski completed the series presenting himself, the artist, as the creator of his symbolic distinctions. He continued with *Manuel with Bird,* presenting an illusion, a happy, retarded youth holding a blue bird in his hand; the reality was that the bird was painted on his shirt. In *Love Triangle,* the painting of a kiss is fooling the eye; the canvas is flat and the frame is part of the canvas

though it is made to look three dimensional. This canvas is alluding to his fantasy of being loved by another woman in a love-triangle relationship.

With these canvases Gorski denounced the reality of his success and his attainment of the objects of desire by showing that reality is illusions. By depicting himself painting kisses on the windows of his prison he accepted responsibility as an artist for being the creator of his symbolic reality or universe. He emerged from painting the competitive world of sports as a winner by declaring that life is the reality of illusions, and laughing at his own erotic aspirations. Upon this realization he entered a new thematic phase dealing with the reality of his handicapped son seeking to be reconciled with pain.

The third act transformed his temptation for power and success as kisses to the admission of the painful reality of the real people and their feelings; he admitted here his self-deception, and came to terms with the cross, the reality of painful emotion without cringing. The third act ends with Gorski's moral activism. He moves from the phase of self-deception, anger and alienation from the world to being content, positive and invested in respecting humanity as the advocate of the handicapped. What was in his heart is seen in the balance of his artwork as portraits of the inmates of the institution, the home of his autistic son. In this concluding phase of his artwork Gorski exclusively painted the painful faces as realistic and expressionistic portraits.

He was no longer painting obstructed mouths or kissing lips. He illustrated the world of his autistic son with his companions as the spectrum of their emotions. It was an uncomfortable reality but he finally came to terms with it writing on the bottom of one canvas: *'OH ALMIGHTY GOD'*! This phase completed his drama and addressed his deepest conflicts, the acceptance of his handicapped son. Upon completion of this series Gorski put his brushes down. He never painted again. He accepted the tragic reality of his personal predicament. The last thematic series affirms reality beyond illusions.

We may be analytical in this series of canvases of the handicapped. On the lower tier, the passivity side of the sequence, we see a series of disabled faces. On the activity or upper tier the faces are idealized and stylized as Mexican gargoyles and they are spiritualized as faces with halos, bodies standing on the illusory cross; the final set of portraits presents individuals with a range of true emotions, contemplation, joy and anger. In the Retrospective, the downtrodden, with their emotions depicted realistically, inherit the limelight. Gorski was playful with the inmates. He constructed faces into kites to hoist in the springtime breeze way up in the blue sky. Gorski here was accepting the cruelty of life serenely.

It is upon the conclusion of this series that Gorski returned to an earlier canvas, *Paradox*, a cross made of kisses on a blue sky and painted his last self portrait with a crown of thorns. He was able to expose the Christian norm of loving selflessly and feeling love. On the back of the canvas we see the original date of completion as 1969, his era of kisses. However on the front of the canvas the date is 1993. This is the last canvas and it depicts what I consider the image of mutual respect, the condition for a conflict to be completely resolved. The title *Paradox* may refer to the reconciliation of "Pain-things" and pleasure-things: the crosses and the kisses. Gorski completed a number of his earlier paintings as noted by hand-written statements pasted on the reverse sides of the canvases. For instance, in 1994 he added a halo to the last canvas of a handicapped youth completed in 1993. So the end of his artistic career culminates in respect for spirituality consoling him for his tragic realities.

There is a tremendous transformation in his painting technique during the phase of the portraits of the handicapped. There is a total departure from the past. The first change was the shift of his attention on the object of his canvases; he departed from the symbolism of the face and emotions through focus on the presence or absence of the mouth etc. to portray the whole face and its genuine emotions. The second change is stylistic in replacing the controlled tech-

niques of the past periods by unleashing his brush-strokes and expressing his feelings and the feelings of his subjects. Also the range of new colors are somber earth tones, dull, dark and terracotta reds. The change coincides with Gorski breaking the norm of what was artistically acceptable. He was painting for himself.

Review of the drama
It is striking how after years of portraying mouthless faces, kisses alone, then crucifixions and faceless athletes that the artist would finally choose to depict portraits of the gloomy institutionalized individuals as the heros of the world. Gorski found in the portraits of the deprived the resolution of his spiritual odyssey. Here he is embracing life however painful. Though these portraits present disturbing images of the human condition he captured them with love and compassion. Gorski portrayed the inmates genuine expressions of feelings; in these portraits we see anger and joy, happiness, loneliness, idiocy, and grandeur. We also see the artist's own feelings of resignation and joy. The happy ending for the painter of losers is showing that the underprivileged of our society are human, that they have a face, feelings and courage beyond the intimidations, discriminations, oppressions and illusions of our world.

The pain, loneliness and despair of these figures cannot be waved away. The portraits of the underprivileged companions of his institutionalized son represent Gorski's respect for humanity but also of the personal sense of freedom in the expression of his feelings. He adorns these figures with halos and crosses, and sees them as spiritualized icons. The eloquent portraits of his unpretentious spiritual heroes became his tribute to the dignity of the powerless.

Gorski felt these canvases had no commercial value. He painted them while visiting his son. The portraits of the inmates were statements about looking at the human condition in an accepting manner, no longer hoping to heal his son's condition, simply accepting it. Here is the emotional significance of compromise. They show the artist respecting the individuals' vibrant emotions, their suffering and their strengths.

Gorski gave me these canvases along with one of his very early canvases, *Homecoming*. He valued our friendship and I valued his gesture. I framed the canvases of the handicapped with expensive frames unlike all other valuable canvases and displayed them at the Special Olympics being held that summer at the Yale Bowl, in New Haven, CT. Strikingly, the Olympics gave handicapped people the opportunity to compete, play and win like the rest of Gorski's heroic athletes enjoying the legitimacy of having fan like their non handicapped peer group. The paintings won the limelight. This series could be entitled "the winners" because they have complete faces while the early sports paintings could be thought of as "the losers" because they do not. It took Gorski a lifetime of painting to deal with his conflicts about his son's condition. Hope for a cure and for rehabilitation generated his internal conflict. The acceptance of reality resolved the conflict and freed him of the sense of hope and failure.

Gorski sequentially dealt with the issue of finding his identity, coping with desires for women and for power, then accepting power and love as an illusion whose resolutions is making peace with the most painful aspects of life. He discovered the freedom of expression and the testing of norms of the acceptability of art.

Connecting these canvases as a series of evolving portrayals of feelings we see Gorski finding at the very end self-acceptance and peace as the healing state of his personal drama. The compassion and respect for his handicapped son became the metaphor of his resolving his conflicts in the normative world of painting. He gave himself the permission to paint for himself, to express his emotions without concern of the public opinion. He experienced healing. If this art is unacceptable to the art world, so what? He did not care. The artist has the right to break the norm of painting for others. He was entitled to paint for himself and face the world with a smile. In his letter to me he stated 'painting was FUN.

Consumer Consumed... Consumed (1962)→

"The mind, fragmented, insecure, seeks substance and form. Man is in a kind of limbo in his attempt at emerging with an identity. He is at the state of becoming. He is experiencing tension between being and not being. The **screaming** person feels anxious."

"Siren-like screams of anger and fear echo against frightening aggression and pain as my second son was threatened with military draft. I had been upset because of the Vietnam buildup. I felt that we were just being driven into this great big mouth, as it were, by the government and big business. Almost every aspect of our lives was largely influenced by this sort of thing, jeopardizing our sense of freedom, that which supposedly we understand here in the West."

RESPONSE

PASSIVITY TO ACTIVITY

unable to communicate

(communicating by) screaming

(without communicating) journeying into a vast unknown

STRESS

ANXIETY

←Child of Darkness (1962-1963)

This is Gorski's autistic son. His face is obscured by darkness and the uncertainty of his feelings. The child's mouth is highlighted but is silent. He is **unable to communicate.**

←Odysseus (1964-1965)

"Inspired by the fervid experiments and ventures into space travel during the early sixties. Symbols of dials, arranged on the black sky function as stars to guide the modern space traveler. The central figure of Odysseus is symbolically fragmented. **Journeying into a vast unknown,** he is driven (the "driver" is driven!) by the tantalizing revelations of new technologies whose ultimate values are not revealed and remain a mystery to the almost blind Odysseus."

The explorer, Odysseus the space traveler, feels trapped. He has many instruments but he is blind. He is driving a vehicle but he is barred. He fears he is a prisoner.

ANTAGONISM TO COOPERATION

←*Walls of Fear (1964)*

"Our **fear of emotions**, our habit of treating normal feelings as deplorably sentimental, and strong emotions as simply hysterical or funny, betrays our fundamental fear of life."

Birth of Adam (1966)→

"A head is rising from the cocoon of amniotic fluid. For man birth is the start of pain, conflict, and repression. To me there is more truth in myth than there is in fact, in spite of the fact that the evolutionists won the fight about creation. This painting reconciles, I think, the Darwinian idea of the early emergence of man from earth and the creationist **emergence** of man from God."

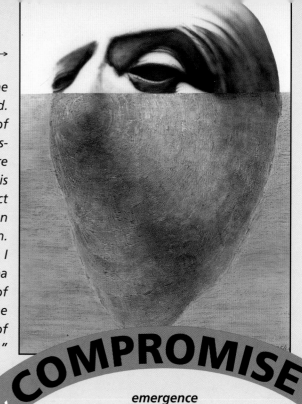

DEFENSE

PASSIVITY TO ACTIVITY

COMPROMISE

fear of
(communicating) emotions

(silence as)
a universal death

emergence
(from silence)

REVERSAL PASSIVITY TO ACTIVITY

The Snare (1969)↓

"Entrapped figure whose tense arms are braced in rigid state of anxiety. A process of depersonalization and loss of identity in a totalitarian world turning into a desert of human emotions, barren of feelings with no room for **individual personality or freedom**."

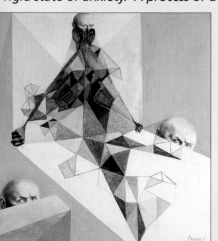

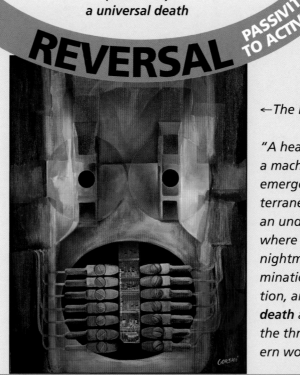

←*The Dream (1964)*

"A head possessed of a machine-like visage emerges from a subterranean darkness, an underground where fear spawns a nightmare of extermination, incineration, and **a universal death** as reflected in the threats of modern world events."

↓*Small Parts as Tears (1967)*

ALIENATION TO MUTUAL RESPECT

1964-1969

POLITICAL COMMUNICATIONS

From war to peace. From antagonism to cooperation

The Ship of Fools (1965)→

This is about the anger experienced by those drafted to the war in Vietnam.

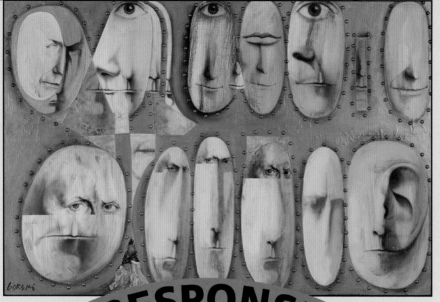

The Committee (1965)→

*"When the power to communicate is blocked, the eyes and the gestures reflect anger, torment, fears, and frustrations. Threats of war were worldwide. Many of the **leaders of the Western nations were playing a game**, trying to maintain a balance that would give them the edge. They wielded enormous power and exercised subterfuges and political ploys. Although the painting was done quite a few years before Watergate, that situation highlighted the work as I had sensed it years earlier."*

RESPONSE

any possible meaning and communication (is) numbing and senseless

PASSIVITY TO ACTIVITY

individual personality or freedom

traveler is trapped

STRESS

ANXIETY

←Man of Letters (1964)

*"Our technological revolution, its blown up reverberations of media information in such profusion and confusion as to render **any possible meaning and communication numbing and senseless**. The human form vaporized into a huge non-being manipulated by machine-oriented excrescences."*

The Cosmonaut (1966)→

*The space **traveler is trapped** in his suit. Like Odysseus, this traveler is a victim of technology, his personal self is completely trapped in the gadgetry of the modern times.*

The Stringed Instrument (1967)→

"Man's constant anxiety triggered by new depersonalized demands upon a diminished self-identity turns the person from prescribed measurements of behavior to a vestigial hulk of his original human form."

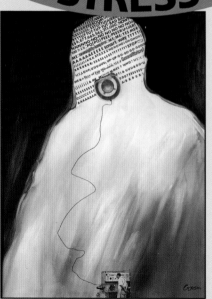

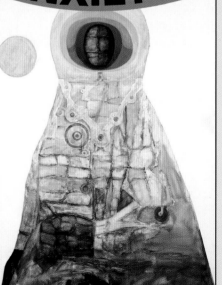

ANTAGONISM TO COOPERATION

The Double (1966)→

"The healthy mind emerges from the amorphous conflicted psyche. Our contemporary life presents a quandary for the individual; who would like to be idealistic but at the same time responds to the demands of reality that go contrary to many ideals. Conflict is created which frustrates any real creativity. The larger aspect of the person, his blank aspect, is negated as the **inner person is trying to find his own identity**, his consciousness, as it were, in the smaller, softer, and more complete self. Unable to focus toward a unified personal identity, this individual is dispersed and fragmented behind various walls or defenses. The true self wants to hide but "there is no place to hide," as the old spiritual tells us."

PASSIVITY ACTIVITY DEFENSE

COMPROMISE

REVERSAL
PASSIVITY TO ACTIVITY

leaders... playing a game

The negation of personality

inner person is trying to find his own identity

5% (1969)→

"Although world leaders, Eisenhower, Adenauer, De Gaulle, and Dulles can only reveal fractions of themselves to others. They are therefore non-persons, giving only a glimpse of themselves. I had been interested in the relief technique, that I could get a double plane image, a recessive image. It took a lot of technical devising and when I finished "5%" I was very pleased with the result, in that it did express a kind of negation. I wanted the figures to sink away from the foremost plane. **The negation of personality** is confirmed by the use of percentages. The person is completely submerged by the use of planes, colors, numbers, and percentages."

Crucifixion (1968)↓ "This centuries-old theme, a form of punishment practiced in many cultures, is here depicted in a modern idiom of contemporary symbols (a DeMille production with images of famous' stars'?) Civilization's periodic need to cleanse itself of imposed horrors on the innocent. Ours is the guilt of racial bias, fear, and hatred."

ALIENATION TO MUTUAL RESPECT →

COMMUNICATING POSITIVE FEELINGS

From innocence to sin. From guilt to expiation. The hero's erotic adventure

The White Kiss (1970)→

"The kiss is a seeking, a reaching outward from the isolated prison of the self. It has been my intent to make the ideal real; to intensify by giving it form in this positive symbol. It epitomizes that perfect tension between inner desire (spirit) and realization (physical touching); **the impulse of life for form; the infinite possibilities of love.**"

Tangerine Kiss (1971)→

"The kiss is the path of release, of shedding psychic shackles, a reaching outward from the isolated prison of self. This is a kind of happy statement. The selection of the tangerine red was an exuberant note. I wanted to explore the emotional impact of brilliant color and of the lips coming forward, reaching out to you. People have called these my lip paintings. I explain that they are not simply lip paintings, they are kiss paintings."

The Rape of the Rose (1976)→

"The theme of this painting contrasts with the theme of love in the Kiss series. The force of mechanical depersonalized power here symbolized as a projectile molding and casting suggests the male sex organ in nature. It contrasts to the Rose symbolizing the soft, beautiful, fragile aspects of life for which we all hunger. This painting evolved from thoughts on the mysteries and complexities of natural and man-made **forces in eternal tension and conflict.**"

RESPONSE

(Release of) gags to my being

PASSIVITY TO ACTIVITY

the impulse of life for form; the infinite possibilities of love

(questionable) symbols of our infatuations

STRESS

ANXIETY

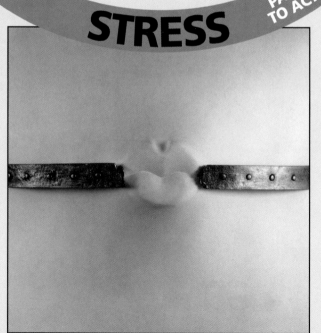

←Saja's Secret (1970)

"Breaking through silence with a revelation. Here a steel band is melting, as it were, by the warmth of a kiss. This image symbolizes the power of love. I have felt the traumas and frustrations of many years in the army, tensions in the career life and family that somehow built up as **gags to my being**. Then the release came. Love, symbolized by the kiss, can break through the many rigid gags symbolized by the steel band which before blocked the mouth."

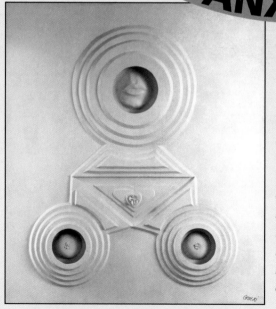

←The Hyperbolic Bride (1969/1970)

"Our technological age is outwardly manifested by beautiful geometric forms and shapes. Our love affair with the machine is here symbolized by the bride "all dressed in white." The two breasts suggest automobile headlights, **symbols of our infatuations.**"

ANTAGONISM TO COOPERATION

"To resolve his conflicts, to emerge into life victorious, man must touch the world and bear the tears that reality must bring. Having come to the realization that my own very sad personal experiences were trials and tribulations, I came around to the realization that I'd find salvation in **compliance with universal truths**. Working on the painting was particularly helpful in my search for the loving God. In my own personal life, I have felt many heart-breaking experiences. In this painting I have felt there is redemption for the suffering. This is revealed in me as light, a faith in a universal being of love and caring. The

Eye-dentity (1974)→

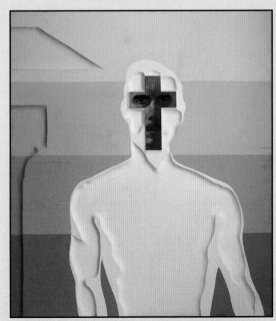

painting is actually a depiction of a salvation and finding of myself. The complete self-portrait is not revealed, but its important aspects are there: The eyes and are exact self-portraits. My eyes are important to see what I understand best. I am a visual person. Through my eyes I understand more. The design of the concentric circles indicates that I am fused with the source of light spreading outward, like waves when a pebble is thrown into the water. To something as abstract as the idea of universal laws and symbols I wanted to impart something as tangible and naturalistic as the lower portion of my features. The tear that starts in the eye is clear, drops below and is transformed into a drop of blood; it is like the feeling of the tragic condition of my son. How does one reconcile this pain with universal love?"

DEFENSE

PASSIVITY ACTIVITY

forces in eternal
tension and conflict

dealing with the
problem of guilt

REVERSAL

PASSIVITY TO ACTIVITY

COMPROMISE

compliance with
universal truths

No Place to Hide (1974/1975)→

"Man suffers oppression and frustration yet fears self-revelation and dares not speak his mind. Man cannot hide from sin, guilt, and fear. The tiny mouth reflects his inability to communicate. This is my first painting **dealing with the problem of guilt**. There is no way to hide our interior, since it will manifest itself in some way. Trying to hide behind the cage of his fingers, the individual finds them transparent. He purses his mouth and still feels as if his scream might betray him."

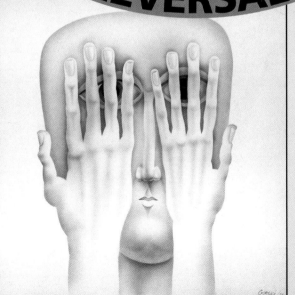

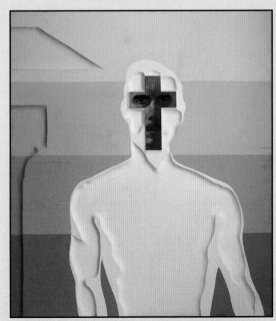

↑Identity (1974)

ALIENATION TO MUTUAL RESPECT

From crucifixion to apotheosis. From alienation to mutual respect.

Windup (1980)→

"The baseball pitcher coiled into a powerful stance ready to strike like the cobra epitomizes the tension of the dancer in absolute concentration and perfection."

Through the Hole (1978)-

"The phenomenon of Sports as games reverberate throughout history. The drive toward the Goal, breakin through defenses, culminating in winning, arouses a ma of hysteria of approbation. In games it was ever thus.

End Zone (1982)→

*"Like Roman gladiatorial spectacles, our age has produced games and exhibitions designed to maim and injure, in which brutality is far more visible than sportsman-like skill. Ours is **a cult of callousness**, a morality of the faceless masked figure."*

RESPONSE

imminent threatening danger

PASSIVITY TO ACTIVITY

ready to strike like the cobra

a fear of exposing the tender, caring, loving aspects of our nature

STRESS

ANXIETY

←Vestigial Being (1976)

*"The eye is the core of the strength, the inner light of man as he transcends his lowly origins. His limbs are intermingled with an insect's. He still stands on unfirm ground. I do believe that the Mexicans have this sense of **imminent threatening danger** in all their pre-Columbian, colonial, and even in contemporary paintings."*

Blocked! (1982?)→

*"Games as drama constantly appear as symbols of our ever-changing culture. The drive to power, domination, and conquest (winning) desensitizes our more human qualities--**a fear of exposing the tender, caring, loving aspects of our nature**."*

ANTAGONISM TO COOPERATION

Compromise 1: Love Triangle (1986)→

"This painting symbolically presents an illusion of three-dimensional reality. The Kiss, the epitome of Love within the perfect harmony of the Triad: the Good, the True, and the Beautiful--a Holy Trinity. **Is the Illusion the Reality of Being?** --aspiring to an apex of infinity disappearing in the mystery of Love."

←Compromise 2: Manuel with Bird (1986)

"One of Dostoevsky's "insulted and injured" born to bear "the slings and arrows of outrageous fortune" against tremendous odds. Perhaps an abiding Faith, symbolized by the bird in his hand (he's got the whole world in his hand) can see him through. Is Faith just a painted bird of hope on the sweatshirt of life? My Faith is the transformation of nature's distortions through shape and color of each painted stroke into a newly perceived beauty in reality."

DEFENSE — COMPROMISE

a cult of callousness

sympathy for the 'loser' and the less fortunate is swept away

Is the Illusion the Reality of Being?

REVERSAL

PASSIVITY TO ACTIVITY

Compromise 3: Shadow Play (1984)→

Winner Take All (1982)→

"To the victor belong the spoils. In a contemporary competitive world which emphasizes power and success, the strong get stronger, their rewards multiply; an unbalanced brutalizing tendency where **sympathy for the 'loser' and the less fortunate is swept away.**"

Fumble (1983)

Human Race (c. 1983)

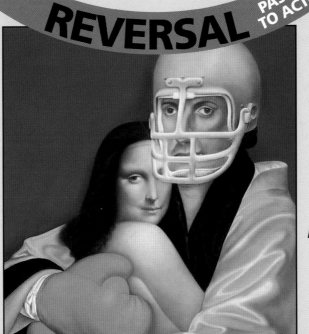

"Shadow Play uses my self-image as a shadow on a plane, empty wall in an empty room symbolizing existential nothingness. This shadow-self transcends the emptiness by the symbolic act of painting. An opening in the upper right through which the sun projects light into the sterile room also serves a symbolic purpose. A source of awareness, enlightenment or inspiration, it can be a window into a larger cosmic reality or a reality as interpreted by the imagination of the creator-artist and/or the viewer.

ALIENATION TO MUTUAL RESPECT →

1991-1993

COMMUNICATING PERSONAL FEELINGS

From spirituality to reality. From self-doubt to self-respect.

Gorski's art revolved around his Christian norms which artificially regulated his gender relations and intensified his desires and fears of women. His art portrayed these desires, fears and resolutions as kisses and crosses. He resolved these desires by elaborating on them using themes of crucifixion, later disguised as sports paintings. He finally dismissed his desires as illusions and was freed from the need for penance or atonement.

He returns to reality, defined emotionally as his preoccupation with his handicapped son. In his last phase of work, liberated from the "Alliterative Obsessions" with kisses and crosses, the artist deals with his unresolved feelings/pain for his autistic son. His career as an artist is completed here with a series of canvases which he identifies as "Pain-things" once again. Chronologically, during the span of three years, he completed a sequence of ten canvases that represent a normative departure from the past in several respects.

Gorski's emotions are also clarified as he designates each named canvas in the series as Painthings I through VI. In 1992 his focus turned to depicting these helpless individuals as Mexican gargoyles, later humanizing them as Christian figures with haloes, and alternatively with the image of a crucifixion.

RESPONSE

PASSIVITY TO ACTIVITY

STRESS

completely helpless with eyes closed

divine gargoyles

eyes pleading for help

ANXIETY

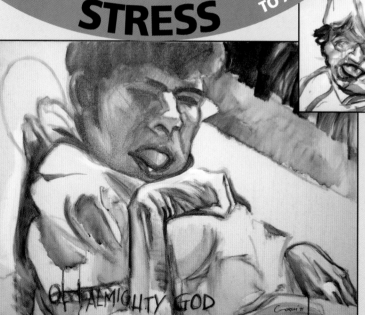

While in the first phases of his work the faces were obstructed by machinery, political power, athletic competition or were illuminated by a crucifix, the final phase zeroes in on the realistic features of the person. The style of these paintings evolve during the course of the three year period. The series begins with three canvases beginning in 1991 that are sketches, tentative outlines of pathetic figures. The emotions of the artist are overwhelming and are literally spelled out in the first canvas of the Painthings series: "Oh, Almighty God" (1991).

ANTAGONISM TO COOPERATION

Pain-things Series (1991)↑

Pain-things Series (1993)↑→ The series ends with two canvases painted in 1993 of the intense emotional expressions of joy and anger. These canvases are not simply studies of pathetic or spiritual subjects; rather they are glorifications of the genuine, spontaneous feelings of admirable, confident human beings emancipated from the stigmatizing status of the mentally ill.

PASSIVITY TO ACTIVITY **DEFENSE**

COMPROMISE

religious/spiritual heroes

whimsical and self-accepting

REVERSAL **PASSIVITY TO ACTIVITY**

human beings with a wide range of emotions

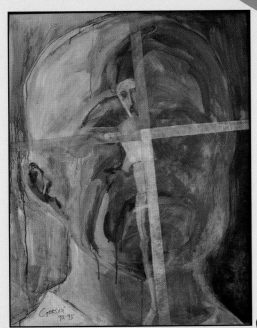

The evolution of these ten portraits illustrate a complete conflict resolution process. It starts with stress as "Oh Almighty God", a state of passivity, antagonism and alienation, and ends with the rethinking of his son as masterful, cooperative and respectable. With the empowerment of his son, Gorski comes to free himself from the pain of his ultimate conflict and amends an older painting of a cross with kisses by adding his self-portrait. Thus he concludes his artistic career.

In this series of canvases we detect the manifestation of the conflict resolution mechanism affirming the assumption that creativity is a healing mechanism that addresses a problem and ends with a masterful compromise. In the context of the Retrospective, this fifth sequence of thematically homogeneous canvases represents the resolution of the first series in which we saw the artist troubled by his handicapped son as illustrated in "Child of Darkness."

Therefore we can establish that the five series of canvases are in a formal relationship to each other as interrelated role-states leading to progressively more encompassing insights.

Cross of Kisses→
(1969, completed in 1993)

Child of Darkness (1962-1963)

ALIENATION TO MUTUAL RESPECT

TOPIC#2:
THE PHYSICS AND LOGIC OF THE CRP

The emphasis in this section is in examining the scientific aspects of the mental process. We detect science in the formal grammar, the verb forms, and the physical syntax, the sequencing of the six role-states, as the process unfolds along the symbolic language of each sequence of the Conflict Resolution Process. The understanding of the unconscious mental mechanism dealing with stress in an adaptive manner along a predictable path is an important new insight in art appreciation. This path is guided by the physics of emotional forces underlying the process (see Panel 2 of the Wizard of Oz Exhibit). Physical corrective forces steer the person from the deviations to the rest state. Feelings of hostility and guilt as conflict, guide the mind to equanimity as conflict resolution. The end result is adaptation, a new identity, an attitude change achievable through the six necessary steps. The common feature of the conflict resolution process is transforming personal discomfort to a social and spiritual identity following three formal transformations along six emotions in search of a rest state.

Formal Analysis of symbolic languages

Science starts by identifying the object of study and the method of the study of this object. The object is the creative process as a circumscribed entity that resolves conflict. The method is two equilibrial systems, the scale and the pendulum oscillation; these are reflected in the symbolic language of the images.

The Retrospective is analyzing a complex symbolic system as a conflict resolution totality encompassing five subsections, repetitions of the periodic process. The formal interpretation of metaphors identifies the process as a simple harmonic and its multiple manifestations. While we integrated the canvases into five harmonic sequences, these are integrated into an overarching unifying process. The Retrospective then is a symbolic universe which abides by certain rules:

the grammar of three formal operations and the syntax of the six role-states. We recognize each period's moral conclusion as the insight that helped the artist to deal with and resolve period-specific conflicts.

The analytical method addressing each segment consists of three steps:
• Identification of a distinction, a symbolic theme or role choice characteristic of each period;
• Identification of the six separate role-states in each thematic period;
• Organization of the sequences as interrelated into a dramatic lifetime continuum.

Gorski's Odyssey sequentially identifies five periods of conflict resolution. Early conflicts dealt with issues of his first-born son: his loneliness, abandonment, alienation, social injustices, powerlessness. Later he dealt with his erotic conflicts and spiritual resolutions, and finally he dealt with issues of competitiveness, identity, age, and human obsolescence. He emerged spiritually affirmed from each encounter with adversity.

Formal distinctions

The exhibit presents the circumscribed segments of the drama as symbolic transformations unfolding as the three formal operations of a key distinction along the six step process. Formally, a conflict is defined as a state of passivity, antagonism and alienation, and resolution as mastery, cooperation and mutual respect. The mind completes a resolution transforming passivity to activity, antagonism to cooperation, and alienation to mutual respect.

Resolution is achieved upon the end of the third oscillation following the completion of the scale's three formal operations restoring the mental rest state. The oscillation stops when the conflict is resolved. The energy of conflict is transformed into resolution, order or meaning. In physics we identify upgraded energy as negative entropy. In psychology we identify it as attitude change and identity formation.

In each phase of his work we distinguish a key symbolic distinction unfolding into a symbolic universe. In the early periods of his pain-things series Gorski was dealing with emotions identified with the blocking of the mouth. The mouth as a form was transformed into its opposites: obstructed versus kissed, its reciprocal forms: obstructed versus screaming, and loved versus loving; its correlative forms: alienation in the world versus identity with religious faith or spirituality beyond faith.

In every cycle of his artwork there are similarly sets of symbols that are formally transformed to represent emotional states in formal relation to each other. Thus in the athletic heroes phase the mouth is replaced by the athletic or sports uniform covering the personal features, the person becomes a number or his uniform: opposites are depicted as blocked versus storming like a hawk, reciprocals as aggressing versus aggressed upon and as admired and admiring; the correlative states of alienation versus mutual respect are depicted as the athlete being faceless or masked, a number and uniform versus being a celebrated face in the case of Sylvester Stallone and Mona Lisa. The correlatives are also presented as a set of desirable illusions versus undesirable realities. Resolutions accept mutual respect in illusions as opposed to the state of alienation experienced in the sports paintings.

Identification of the six separate role-states in each thematic period

The depiction of emotions in his artwork distorts the images from realistic to symbolic statements. This fact allows us to study the formal transformations during thematically distinct phases of his symbolic languages. The descriptions of the canvases by the artist confirm the path of interpretation. Hence we see the six role state process and the three formal operations repeated five times with interrelated images fitting the six role-states. The exhibit shows how the images are in a dialectic relation to each other as suggested by the process. The cycles of canvases make the isolated paintings meaningful and help us to understand the evolution of the artist's feelings.

Organization of the sequences as interrelated into a dramatic lifetime process.

The Conflict Resolution Process organizes emotions in each of the distinct symbolic phases corresponding to the artist's five period-specific conflicts. Identifying these sequences validates the theory confirming the manifestation of the conflict resolution order as the universal underlying dynamic. The five cycles of the Retrospective reflect his lifetime conflicts and their resolutions. We see his relational pattern evolve in increments of wisdom, developing a broader way of thinking and achieving a happier attitude.

The sequences of resolution correspond to broader insights about life as adjustments to the adversities of life. This increase in meaning and positive attitude validates the postulation of conflict resolution as a lifetime progression. His moral growth bypasses reliance on religion. The artist discovered the spiritual power of the creative process, 'the illusions and reality' phase confirming a shift from religious imagery to existential spirituality.

This transformation is the physiology of the mind as a kind of software programming the unconscious mind. We are born programmed to resolve. The brain is bundled at our inception with a set of software necessary for the personal adjustment to social life. This transformational process is illustrated in each of the six sequences of the Gorski Retrospective. The Gorski Retrospective illustrates this process, retracing the artist's lifelong journey, meaningfully uniting the entirety of his artwork through a number of separate symbolic domains. Visitors will recognize the process as a periodic phenomenon reoccurring in five separate sequences unified into the personal lifetime drama conveyed in the sixth series: the self-portraits. The formal transformations are

represented graphically as a sine wave consisting of the six formally connected emotions.

The unconscious thought process as a natural science phenomenon

The process integrates the artist's canvases as several harmonics presenting the Conflict Resolution Process as a six-part-dialectic directed by the three formal operations. The symbolic language of emotions, logic and physics, have parallel dimensions. The intense imagery demonstrates the correlation of emotions both along relational and natural science variables. The mouth marks a deviation from the rest state in relation to other mouths, blocked mouth versus screaming mouths, kissing mouths versus kissed mouths, spiritual neutral crucifix mouths, etc. We also see the symbolism in terms of the physics of the pendulum oscillation as displacements or normative deviation, velocity or deviating acts or behaviors. The acceleration or emotions are corrective forces and energies.

These constructs abide by the formulas of logic and physics: emotions or accelerations are proportional and opposite to normative deviations or displacements. Hostility manifested when the mouth was blocked, *Birth of Adam*, and guilt manifested when the mouth was seeking the forbidden woman's lips in *Figure with Vectors*. Guilt is opposite and proportional to a normative deviation toward power as portrayed in *the Rape of the Rose*; the restorative force is depicted in the next canvas, *Nowhere to Hide, in which* guilt opposes the aggressive behavior of the *Rape*. The force of guilt is decelerating the deviance, and in *Crucifixions* attains the new balance as the resolution.

The Gorski Retrospective's conflict resolution sequences of canvases confirm the mental emotional harmonic as a palpable or measurable formal and natural equilibrial phenomenon. The Retrospective, as five thematically connected series of canvases, illustrates the inherent dialectic of a

lifetime of evolving emotions. The Gorski canvases helped me to illustrate the complex relations of variables in the analysis of the logic and the physics of the process along the formulas of two equilibrial phenomena, the trays of a scale and the oscillations of a pendulum. In the textbook of *Conflict Analysis, the Formal Theory of Behavior*, Gorski's canvases illustrated ten scientific correlations or formulas, i.e. canvases validated the relation between emotions being proportional and opposite to the deviation from the rest state.

The physiology of conflict resolution

The motivational forces steering behavior are corrective forces that are opposing normative deviations. While the deviations are centrifugal, the emotions are centripetal. These forces stem from the physiologic need to adjust to norms or social acceptability. Deviations from the norm are experienced as stress. The same way that we cannot interfere with our heartbeat, we also are at the mercy of the mental beat. All we can do is, like Gorski, tap our creativity and recognize the dramatic evolution that binds our thoughts and conforms to the norms of our culture.

Creativity, captured in the dimensions of a story, reveals this orderly stream of associations. Any sample of creativity will predictably depict the universal process organizing our feelings and actions. The mind blindly complies with the need for adjustment to socially acceptable behavior, whether a person commits a violation of norms or if he feels violated, the conflict is resolved as the person is making a compromise.

The sequences of conflict resolutions of the Retrospective depict the emotional and moral significance of the art as a scientific phenomenon whose purpose is the adjustment of the individual to a social reality or norm. The self-portraits and the conflict resolutions manifested in the rest of the exhibit introduce the process of conflict resolution coinciding with emotional growth. The exhibit attests to the unconscious process guiding the mind along this orderly set of emotional/spiritual steps toward the end state of social adjustment. This is why we identify this process as a unit periodic social adjustment or moral order phenomenon.

The exhibit conceptualizes the unconscious and spirituality as intertwined in a simple natural science phenomenon integrating psychology and morality. Since the process is the necessity of moral order, the conformity to societal norms, the process has been identified as God. God is the symbolic designation of the universality of the process. In drama we know it in the manifestation of the apocalyptic descend of a god on the stage of a Greek tragedy, the *deus ex machina* making normative corrections by punishing the protagonist or antagonist.

Religion, the *deus ex machina*, is the unconscious mechanism of the process. The outcome of a drama instead of validating science has reinforced norms and beliefs in respective deities as rationalizations on the nature of the inner process. Science now redefines the psyche as the formulas of science while gods are redefined as alternative solutions of the formulas. Religions and gods represent measurable culturally distinct conflict resolutions. We also see that the definition of god evolved in the course of Gorski's resolutions to a less dogma based entity and to a more demystified secular spiritual force.

Symbolic distinctions as formal and physical constructs and formulas

A conflict is generated when the state of rest is disturbed, divided by a distinction into opposites, subsequently into reciprocal and correlative forms. The intensity of the distinctions determines the quantity of energy involved in a conflict. The distinctions set off the dialectic evolution of emotions toward the reconciliation of the conflict. Creativity is merely the catabolic, anabolic digestive system of the mind processing distinctions to conciliations. Distinctions gener-

ate energy which leads to the reconstruction of the rest state. This processing is the system of formally interrelated transformation of ideas and energies.

Compromise leads to the rest state and the fusion of the opposites. The uncomfortable system of the split of one key idea as the conflict is reduced unconsciously by the inner motivation to reach the energetically stable rest state. The resolution amounts to the transformation of the unstable energies of emotions into the stability of meaningful concepts, such as spiritual beliefs. The reconstituted rest state entails modified emotions, the sense of justice upon a resolution. The compromise corresponds to a psychological and sociological outcome: the task of the creative process is to assist the individual in finding a social adjustment with emotional integrity, an identity.

For Gorski resolution coincided with evolving compromises: the end of his "Pain-things" traverses a circuitous path through a number of symbolic splits and reconciliations. The absent mouths are corrected with ubiquitous kissing lips. The kisses eventually generate conflict evolving to the crucifixions. The second act's sexual love is transformed into religious values and eventually spirituality. The father in pain for the misfortunes of his beloved son is reconciled with this personal tragedy elevating his son from his misery to identify him with a saint or a crucifix.

There is continuity among all the canvases from the mouthlessness to the crucifixions eventually perceived as the heroic athletes completed with illusions and reality as the admission of his son as a sacrificial human. Resolution for Gorski is admitting love as the ultimate rest state. Desires, pain and loss are subdued as beliefs and hopes. He manages to reconcile himself with his silent and angry son, as the human with a whole range of feelings. The accurately portrayed emotionally liberated but clearly retarded inmates of the

asylum are Gorski's final set of crucifixes. The sight of sadness coincides with the appeal to God as the instant call for resolution. A canvas of the most distorted image of a human spells out the resolution with the inscription of the canvas of *Oh Almighty God!*. Gorski's creative unconscious knows how to accept the norm of pain expressing hurt feelings and advancing to healing, the reduction of conflict.

Energetic ideas, cathexis

In the formal analytic method we recognize the circumscribed phenomenon of a conflict resolution as the object for the study of behavior. The process at another level of methodological reduction is defined as energetic transformations in the continuum of conservation of energy but also of its upgrading from chaos to order, from entropy to negative entropy. Conflict is labile energies; resolution is stable energies. The formal role-states or emotions are defined as energetic quantities gradually upgraded and stabilized as resolution or spiritual rest states. The formal transformations of the key role uniting six thematically distinct phases into three cycles of conflict resolutions is interpreted energetically as leading to the broader resolution of inner and outer justice.

The ten levels of analysis, the formal analysis profile

The exhibit ushers science into the field of psychology and morality. Considering art as a conflict resolution entity, each canvas is a natural science phenomenon with formal and natural science dimensions. Each canvas is defined as a formal transformation and as an energetic one in the context of the sequence. The energetic state is defined in the context of the simple harmonic motion, the oscillation of the pendulum. Gorski's thematic periods are formally related role-states and energies leading to the goal of resolution or ultimate inner outer justice.

We recognize ten levels of analysis of any relational system, each level representing a formula of correlated variables from the realms of logic, math and physics.

Level 1, the formal analysis of symbolic systems: The Formal Theory textbook uses the Gorski canvases to illustrate the ten levels of analysis.

Four canvases on the jacket of the Formal Theory volume illustrated the three formal operations transforming conflict to resolution:
• Reciprocity transforms passivity to activity,
• Negation transforms antagonism to cooperation
• Correlation transforms alienation to mutual respect.

The grammar of forms: The role choice is a symbolic choice transformed into its formal alternatives; the role choice is the mouth and related forms are the absent or oppressed mouth, the screaming mouths, the kiss, Adam being kissed by God's mouth, the artist's mouth forming in the context of the Crucifix. These formal transformations have a predictable order: absent mouths versus angry mouths illustrate the principle of reciprocity, the states of passivity and activity. The mouth oppressed by a fingerprint is opposite to the mouth of Adam kissed by God. The kissing mouths became erotic and they lead to crucifixions, the correlative counterparts. A serene mouth and the eye with a tear of blood capture the drama formally identified with correlation corresponding to portraying alienation transformed to mutual respect.

Level 2-10 the physics of the process: the equivalence between psychological concepts and the constructs and the formulas of physics
The exhibit served me to illustrate the principles of logic as well as the constructs and formulas of physics. The process, like a pendulum oscillation, consists of energetic transformations. The images explain the Aristotelian concept of the continuity of action as coinciding with conservation of energy and continuity of symbolic choices.

In the Formal Theory volume Gorski's art work has been used to examine the laws of physics governing his symbolic system. His canvases illustrate correlations along the laws of the physics of the Simple Harmonic Motion. I examined how the Gorski canvases illustrate the ten formulas of the Formal Analysis Profile, (FAP). The canvases explain the application of the formulas of the rigorous sciences on the symbolic system. The canvases confirm the formulas of logic and physics and the bridging of art and science, of the humanities with the rigorous disciplines of logic and physics.

• Deviations from the rest state as portrayed in the oppressed versus the screaming mouths correspond to the pendulum's displacement from a position of powerlessness to its reciprocal of power. The two reflect the personal sociological status change identified with the physics concept of displacement.

• Emotions proportional and opposite to the displacement or status change are equivalent to the concept of acceleration in physics. Emotions are conveyed in the canvases as anticipated by this formula. They are centripetal forces opposing the centrifugal displacements or deviation from the rest state.

• Behaviors correspond to velocity.

• Conflict corresponds to the construct of physics identified as energy.

• Emotions, status, behavior can be graphically portrayed as interrelated sine cosine curves, just like the concepts of the variables of the Simple Harmonic Motion.

Distinctions generate energy. The energy is conserved and transformed through a series of role-states. The role-states are emotions as energies transformed along the sequence of the continuum of the process. The process is concluded reconciling emotions into the conflict resolution where resolving a conflict coincides with upgrading of order, generating what is called order as negative entropy.

Resolution is negative entropy, the increment of order. The Retrospective helps us to conceive of the creative process as an energetic pump that automatically upgrades order or energy coinciding with resolving conflicts. This energetic transformation from a conflict to a resolution provides the moral structure and the direction to emotions as well as insights. The Retrospective confirms the artist's ongoing personal growth by studying the canvases as a sequence of a progression in abstractions on the nature of meaning.

REVIEW in Seven Days Burlington VT
The Proof Is in the Painting / Eyewitness: Henry Gorski
BY KIRK KARDASHIAN [09.09.09]

Imagine how it might feel to write a novel — only to discover, just before sending it off to the publisher, that someone in your town had made a surreal film that seemed to illustrate all the ideas you'd put in your book. Would you be shocked? Mystified? Elated to find a creative soulmate?

Dr. Albert J. Levis, a psychiatrist who lives in Manchester, probably experienced all those emotions and more when he first met the artist Henry Gorski in 1972. The brainchild of their friendship is a synthesis of art and science — a scientific interpretation of art, and an artistic representation of science — that is displayed at the Chaffee Art Center through October 12.

The exhibit, "Science Stealing the Fire of the Gods and Healing the World," uses what Levis called his "Formal Theory of Behavior" to interpret Gorski's abstract and symbolic oeuvre of oil paintings, bas-reliefs, mixed-media works and sculptures. "He was looking for the mathematical proof of the metaphysical existence of God," says Levis of Gorski. "I was able to show him it was in his art."

The name of the exhibit comes from the Greek myth of Prometheus, who stole fire from Zeus and gave it to mortals. Here, the forbidden "fire of the gods" appears to be knowledge of human nature, which Levis' scientific theory draws from art and translates into a moral framework through which to interpret behavior.

Gorski, 91, was born in Lackawanna, New York. His first artworks were sketches of men drinking beer at his father's tavern. He went on to get a bachelor's of fine arts at the University of Buffalo and then served in the United States military during World War II, making models of islands that would later be bombed. The art on display at the Chaffee — all of which is owned by Levis and permanently displayed at his bed and breakfast in Manchester, the Wilburton Inn — was created between the early 1960s and 1990s. For Gorski, this was a period of intense reflection — about his two sons, the Vietnam War, religion and morality.

Levis, 71, is a Greek-born Jew who lost his father and grandfather in World War II. By the end of that conflict, 96 percent of his Greek-Jewish community had been killed; thousands more Greeks, including some of his friends, died in the ensuing civil war, which Levis witnessed. "I grew up wondering, Why is the world so crazy?" he recalls.

Levis went to medical school in Geneva and Zürich, moved to the U.S. in 1964, and finished his psychiatric training at Yale in 1967. Shortly thereafter, he opened a psychiatric practice, the Center for the Study of Normative Behavior, in Hamden, Connecticut.

It was there that Levis began his research into the nature of human conflicts and their resolutions. He detected a pattern of behavior that starts with an initial stressor and ends with a compromise. Drawing it on paper, he noticed the pattern resembled a wave or a pendulum that swings but tends toward rest — the equivalent of the physical principle of simple harmonic motion. Levis' Formal Theory of Behavior asserts that, unconsciously, we are all moving along this wave, oscillating from stress to response to anxiety to defense to reversal to compromise, and then starting all over again. He calls this the Conflict Resolution Process and contends that the pattern also governs artistic creation and is reflected in works of visual art, literature and mythology.

Preparing to present his theory to the New Haven Medical Association in 1972, Levis sought a visual aid that would make it all less abstract. Someone suggested he visit Gorski's studio, also in Hamden.

When the men met, they both realized there was "a natural gravitation," as Gorski put it in a 1987 letter to Levis, between their art and science. "Albert Levis," Gorski wrote, "perceived seemingly parallel directions in my paintings as symbols applicable to his Formal Theory of human behavior — directions of which I was not consciously aware."

The retrospective at the Chaffee uses the Formal Theory of Behavior to organize Gorski's work, separating it into three "acts" like those of a drama, each composed of about eight paintings. The acts represent phases of Gorski's life, and the artwork seems to be his way of grappling with the challenges that faced him in each.

The first act, for example, entitled "Pain Things," revolves around Gorski's autistic son, whose disability was so severe that he was eventually institutionalized. It begins in Levis' "stress" phase with "Child of Darkness," a dark impression of a boy's face obscured by shadow, his closed mouth highlighted. The "response" phase is embodied by "Consumer Consumed … Consumed," a series of open mouths enclosing each other, all screaming in anger and frustration.

The next phase is "anxiety," represented by the painting "Odysseus," in which Gorski depicts a crazed man grasping a steering wheel through cell bars. "Odysseus is blocked and blind," explains Levis in an interview. "He doesn't see where he's going."

The reaction to anxiety is "defense." In "Walls of Fear," walls at right angles block the mouths of bald heads pictured at the bottom right and bottom left. The center of the painting depicts a small window leading to an open mouth with a trace of a smile. "Our fear of emotions," Gorski wrote about this work, "our habit of treating normal feelings as deplorably sentimental, and strong emotions as simply hysterical or funny, betrays our fundamental fear of life."

The next swing of the pendulum brings Gorski to what Levis calls "reversal," a passive phase of feeling helpless. "The Dream" shows a robot-like head with its mouth agape but barred by transistors and wires. "This is the human predicament in our age," says Levis, "when you feel all the gadgetry and instruments becoming you."

The final stage of the dialectic is compromise. Gorski depicts this resolution with a figure emerging from an abstraction. The first act ends with "Birth of Adam," in which a white head seems to materialize from a thumbprint. "A head is rising from the cocoon of amniotic fluid," Gorski wrote. "For man, birth is the start of pain, conflict and repression." Perhaps Gorski is here evoking the essentiality of compromise, suggesting that life is not full of winners and losers, but survivors.

Gorski was raised a Catholic, and Christian symbolism figures prominently in his work. When his "compromise" paintings don't depict human heads, they usually incorporate a crucifix into a face. Levis interprets this as meaning that, while Gorski is tempted by things like infidelity, he ultimately defers to the moral standards of his religion. He accepts the limits Catholicism places on him and reforms his behavior accordingly.

To highlight this aspect of Gorski's thinking, Levis included in the exhibit some paintings by Gorski's contemporary, Francis Bacon, whom he describes as just the opposite. "Bacon is an aggressive thinker," says Levis. "He challenges the acceptability of homophobia, challenges religion." Levis sees faith as important to the Formal Theory of Behavior because religions have, for so long, caused conflicts by dictating accepted forms of behavior. But they also offer paths to compromise. Unlike Gorski's art, with its Christian focus, the Conflict Resolution Process blends paradigms of resolution from Greek, Asian and Judaic traditions.

On September 11, when the exhibit opens, the dangers of "holy war" are sure to be on people's minds. That's no coincidence, says Levis. He believes his theory "explains how we can get out of this war, conceptually." Whether Levis' notions about conflict are truly "fire from the gods" or just common sense, their pairing with Gorski's art is inspired.

TOPIC #3: THREE FOCUS STUDIES ON THE FUNCTION OF THE CRP

FOCUS STUDY #1: The Healing Function as illustrated by Gorski's evolving self-portrait sequence

Two hypotheses to validate:
Self-consciousness leads an artist to complete self-portraits. Expression is art and reflects emotions. If the Formal Theory is correct, the sequence of self-portraits must portray the evolution of emotions towards a conflict resolution.

Throughout his career, Gorski completed self-portraits. Examining the evolution of these images we detect an entire conflict resolution process binding these paintings. The self-portraits for the dramatic sequences correspond to the resolutions of each of the five thematically distinct periods. Indeed the five sequences are integrated by the cycle of self-portraits into the sixth and overarching Conflict Resolution Process.

The self-portraits sequence illustrates the emotional significance of each role-state and of the entire harmonic of emotional transformations in the continuum of one symbolic variable; the image of the artist. The self-portraits sine curve illustrates the artist's lifetime emotional growth captured by the transformation of his very own image. The evolving self-portraits clarify the abstractions of the three formal operations and the six emotional role-states of the unit process. Gorski's evolving images define the formal and emotional dimensions as a scientific phenomenon. Each of the six self-portraits illustrate the formal operations as six transformations of the artist's face. Each portrait identifies one of the six role-states and its formal relationship to the other role-states.

The Self-portraits Study is of extraordinary scientific significance as it integrates the disconnected images separated by thematic phases and multiple years. Remarkably, the self-portraits are in the anticipated formal relation to each other. The series begins with Gorski's identity emerging in the first act from political powerlessness, a state of passivity, to a post-war era of peace and love, from oppression and mouthlessness to kisses. The next self-portraits capture Gorski's anxiety about kisses and his resolution of the erotic conflict, as he identifies himself with a crucifix. This illustrates his cooperation and compliance with Christian norms. The final act portrays Gorski experiencing the third formal operation, mutual respect, in two ways: he is the creator of kisses in *Shadow Play*; and in *Paradox* he sketches himself in 1993 on a cross of kisses that is also being kissed. The evolution of these self-portraits leading to this positive outcome demonstrates the healing function of the creative process. Thanks to his artwork, Gorski adjusted well to the painful adversities of his life.

The First Act
The first role state is stress. Stress identifies Gorski as a person flattened by a fingerprint across his entire body. Only his head, hands and feet escape the obliteration of the self. **The first formal operation, passivity transformed to activity, presents the changes from the stress state to the next, the response state**, which identifies him as a hesitant diplomat with his hand outstretched seeking mutual respect from a bunch of untrustworthy politicians, the mistrusted authority figures. Upon this phase of progressive reconciliation with authorities the artist is liberated from negativity toward them, and these further transform his *Kafka Bugs* to kissing *Love Bugs*.

The Second Act
Figure with Vectors illustrates his **anxiety role state** upon the encounter with a kiss. This canvas presents him afraid of his desires for women. **Transforming antagonism to cooperation, the second formal operation,** he becomes hopeful of love from God in the *Mathematical Proof of the Metaphysical Existence of God*. In the ensuing **defense** role state, having surrendered to temptation during this phase, he portrays himself in realistic detail expiating. 'Identity' and '*Eye-dentity*' portray him illuminated in his interface with the cross. The '*Eye-dentity*' canvas portrays him as a wise eye with a tear of blood streaming from his eye down his cheek and his mouth and chin as the axis of the cross. The centered eye is surrounded by luminous halos.

The Third Act
The state of **reversal** depicts the outcome of the person's emotional adventure, in this case the afterthoughts from his erotic, religious and athletic or post religious existential experience. The self portrait presents him as '*Shadow-painting.*' Here Gorski's faint profile image is painting kisses in the window of a prison cell. This image shows that he is accepting responsibility for being the creator of his illusions, his symbolic universe.

His compromise state is captured again in a cross but a very different one. This original cross consists of sculptural white kisses suspended on a clear blue sky. The three dimensional kisses are directed outwards. Gorski's face is sketched on the lower kiss image of this cross as though he is kissing the world. Then in the center of the cross there is a depression where the cross is kissed, kissing lips are imprinted inwardly at the center of the cross.

Viewing the self portraits historically let us remember their inception and unfolding. Upon the stress phase, the first canvas of the series, he portrayed himself flattened by a finger print. Upon the last portrait he depicts himself kissing and being kissed. My interpretation of this canvas is that the artist is in peace with himself and with the world. He loves and also feels loved. **This combination of passivity, activity states and of cooperation illustrates the third formal operation, mutual respect. This reconciliation between two dispositions represents the completion of the process. This operation was missing in the prior paintings**. The cross of kisses was constructed in 1969 as dated on the back of the canvas.

FOCUS STUDY #1: THE HEALING FUNCTION OF THE CRP
as illustrated in Gorski's evolving self-portraits

CONFLICT	STRESS	RESPONSE	ANXIETY	DEFENSE	REVERSAL	COMPROMISE	SELF-PORTRAIT
ACT 1: THE HERO'S VALUES AND CONFLICTS							Gorski's evolving identity
1960-1970 Communicating negative feelings: From suppression to emergence. From passivity to activity.	Unable to communicate	(Communicating by) Screaming	(Without communicating) Journeying into a vast unknown	Fear of (communicating) emotions	(Silence as) a universal death	Emergence (from silence)	
1970-1975 Political communications: From war to peace. From antagonism to cooperation.	Any potential communication is numbing and senseless	Individual freedom	Traveler is trapped	Leaders playing a game	The negation of personality	Inner person trying to find his own identity	
ACT 2: THE HERO'S ADVENTURE							
1975-1980 Communicating positive feelings: From innocence to sin. From guilt to expiation.	(Release of) gags to my being	The impulse of life for form; the infinite possibilities of love	Symbols of our infatuations	Forces in eternal tension and conflict	Dealing with the problem of guilt	Compliance with universal truths	
ACT 3: THE HERO'S MORALITY AND MORTALITY							
1980-1986 Existential communications: From crucifixion to apotheosis. From alienation to mutual respect.	Imminent threatening danger	Ready to strike like the cobra	Fear of exposing the tender, caring, loving aspects of our nature	A cult of callousness	Sympathy for the loser and the less fortunate is swept away	Is the illusion the reality of being?	
1986-1995 Communicating personal feelings: From spirituality to reality through the expression of emotions. From self-doubt to self-respect.	Completely helpless with eyes closed	Divine gargoyles	Eyes are pleading for help	Spiritual heroes	Whimsical and self-accepting	Human beings with a full range of emotions	

But the self portrait superimposed on this cross was completed in 1993 as signed in the front of this canvas. Interesting that the artist identified with this compromise only after the end of his last series, the paintings of the handicapped; mutual respect is the condition for the completion of a conflict. This self portrait is a scientific testimonial for the validation of the theory.

The self-portrait sequence alerts and informs the viewer of the exhibit about the scientific nature of the emotional process. This process, symbolized by the sine curve, is the testimonial on the spontaneous and syndromal organization of emotions. The resolution manifests itself in this sequence of thematically bound canvases. The self-portraits sequence clearly unites the successive sequences of conflict resolution into an overarching pattern that clearly reflects the emotions of the artist coinciding with the six-role process as predicted by the theory. It is difficult to deny the existence of the pattern as binding the individual canvases into the lifetime sequence. Predictability is defined as periodicity and it attests to the presence of science. This phenomenon is mind-boggling, but again this is what we can expect from science: predictability surpassing probability.

The self-portraits series allows us to review his entire artwork at a glance and to recognize the continuity across all canvases of his Retrospective. This affirms the human condition as both an emotionally balanced and impressively predictable and measurable entity confirming the marvelous connection of art to science. The passage is smooth as we identify the conflict resolution template meaningfully connecting a lifetime of symbolic imagery into an emotional totality that evokes sympathy.

While each phase of his work represents a conflict resolution of interrelated canvases, the overarching totality is the most intellectually convincing and emotionally compelling statement. It affirms that underneath all the symbolic disguises we can recognize the continuity of an emotional cathartic experience. The series of self-portraits affirms that despite the thematic discontinuity of his artwork the entirety of his creations reflects the dramatic continuity of emotions the unconscious compels completing one's personal conflict resolution.

FOCUS STUDY #2: The Normative Compliance Function as illustrated by Gorski's religious paintings and his faith-based gender portrayals

The entire series of self-portraits affirm Gorski's compliance with Christian norms as the reconciliation of kisses and crosses, pain and pleasure. Norms determine the experience of conflict; they regulate behavior inducing conflict. Conflict is the perception of the distance from the norm, the emotional experience of a normative deviation. Resolution is the equilibrial adjustment, i.e. one's reconciliation with the societal norm. Norms determine the distinctions of right and wrong. Deviations entail consequences.

The formal analysis of the Retrospective addresses the issues of norms by examining how the artist is affected by norms and how he personally rebels and alternatively conforms to them to resolve his conflicts. In Gorski's early work he was fighting the political normative system. In his religious phase he was violating and then conforming to the religious norms. At the completion of his artwork he finally broke free from one norm, his traditional aesthetic; he transformed his painting style, and thus completed his symbolic universe with a new resolution.

Deviation from religious norms generate conflicts
The conflict resolution process is an equilibrial phenomenon seeking balance between the individual and society. Balance is established as the individual conforms to societal norms. The individual begins the process breaking a norm, i.e. by challenging the system, and ends the process by conforming to the system's norms. Gorski's self-

perceived transgression, illustrated by *The Rape of the Rose,* challenged the system and then espousing religion and spirituality, he conformed to it.

The Retrospective gives us the opportunity to examine the religious norms generating conflicts in Gorski's universe. It also compels us to consider how science may have a role in rethinking these norms by determining them based on the scientific understanding of the process following the three formal operations.

Religions are metaphors of conflict resolution; science studies the Conflict Resolution Process perfectly from conflict to resolution abiding by formulas; religions are partial discoveries of the Universal Harmonic. They are solutions of the formula as narrow discoveries of how to resolve conflicts. Religions have identified and mystified alternative paths to conflict resolution. Science integrates and reconciles the many religions of the world as complementary discoveries of the process.

The scientific knowledge of the process of conflict resolution introduces the missing objectivity on norms and challenges the subjectivity of diverse faiths. Science allows us to objectively determine norms based on the three principles of conflict resolution. Hence, science establishes moral consensus, the prerequisite to healing the person and the world.

The conflict begins when an individual challenges a norm. Israel means *to wrestle with God*, which entails welcoming criticism between parties in conflict, while Islam means *to submit or to accept an authority without debate*. These are two cultural norms generating different emotions about expressing oneself and hence leading to different cultures and values. The individual breaks a norm and compromises by reconciling with the norm or by effectively changing it. The process has two components, the phase of fighting the system and the phase of yielding to its authority. The individual may prevail and negotiate the societal norms by

1960-1995

THE PATH TO WISDOM

The evolution of self-protraits in search of self-actualization.

The canvases of the sixth sequence integrate Gorski's lifetime of partial conflict resolutions into a higher order resolution. This sequence reflects the cumulative value of partial resolutions as a real progression of insights into wisdom.

The partial resolutions illustrated by self-portraits are emotions in the suggested formal relation to each other reflecting attitude changes leading to the final compromise following the inner adjustment to the most painful experience of his life, coping with his feelings about his handicapped son.

The final cycle, the evolving self-portraits as the formal transformations of the face, integrates the artist's work into a dramatic totality which documents his search for comfort and his attaining it as wisdom.

←Committee (1971)

**Activity
Cooperation
Duplicity**

↓*The Game (1973)*

↑*Lovebugs I and II (1967)*

The progression to love

RESPONSE

Gorski emerging from oppression

PASSIVITY TO ACTIVITY

from a handshake to a kiss

hoping to be loved and feeling loved

STRESS

ANXIETY

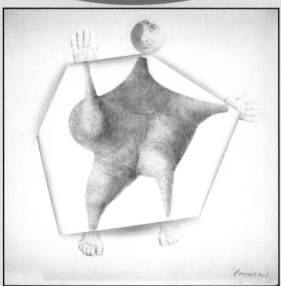

↑*Fragment of a Head (1967)*

←*The Birth of Gorski (1966)*

**Passivity
Antagonism
Alienation**

↑*Figure with Vectors (1967)*

**Passivity
Cooperation
Respect**

*The Mathematical Proof of the
Metaphysical Existence of God (1973)*→

ANTAGONISM TO COOPERATION

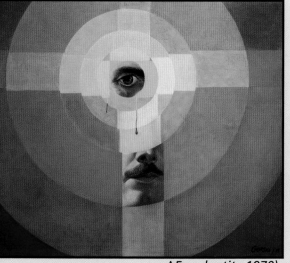

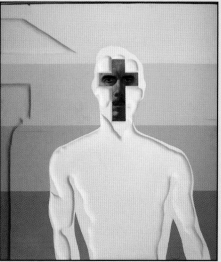

↑Eye-dentity 1970) and ↑Identity (1974)

Cross of Kisses→
(1969, completed
in 1993)

**Activity,
Cooperation
Mutual respect**

**Activity
Cooperation
Respect**

Gorski as the creator of his universe

DEFENSE

loving as agape

REVERSAL

**PASSIVITY
ACTIVITY**

**PASSIVITY
TO ACTIVITY**

COMPROMISE

mutual respect... loving and being loved

Shadow Play (1984)→

**Activity
Cooperation
Respect**

The measurability of Gorski's emotional transformations

Moral Science is validated by effectively making the canvases of the entire Retrospective meaningful by integrating them into the single formal transformational continuum. This method of interpreting art, i.e. creativity unfolding predictably as a unit entity, organizes our thoughts and reflects formal dimensions.

Each canvas then is qualified as a segment of the harmonic which is both a natural science and the moral order phenomenon. Each canvas represents an attitude that has physical dimensions defined by its relation in the evolutional context of the conflict resolution process. The captions beside each canvas identify the measurement of the respective attitude.

ALIENATION TO MUTUAL RESPECT

bringing about change. Alternatively, the submissive individual, like Gorski, can be very vulnerable and receptive to conforming to the norm.

The second focus study examines the role of norms in the generation and resolution of conflicts and discusses legitimacy of the norm-making authority in regulating behaviors. We review the significance of religious norms in the creation of Gorski's conflicts and art by paying special attention to his canvases with religious themes and also how religious norms affected his portrayals of gender relations.

Gorski's work is replete with religious iconography: Biblical references, images of God, Lazarus, Crucifixions, the good Samaritan and the Apostles. This focus exhibit underscores the importance of Christian norms in shaping Gorski's symbolic language and the intensity of his preoccupations with sexuality, stemming from its taboo nature. We see this in his portrayals of the man-woman relationship. Women are blinding lights, scintillating temptations, dangerous spiders, mysterious contraptions and radioactive boxes, they are cats playing with mice. Men are portrayed as victims: Kafka bugs, suffering saints, faceless athletes and handicapped inmates.

Gorski's norm as the Kiss of God

The Retrospective illustrates Gorski's struggle with norms and authorities. We clearly see the awareness of boundaries and deviations on a canvas that is identified as *The Mathematical Proof of the Metaphysical Existence of God (pp 88)*. The artist is very conscious of norms as mild deviations from the rest point which is the kiss of God to Adam. Here we have the space divided by fine lines and sine curves. The horizontal line starts with alpha and is completed with omega. The vertical lines identify 1, 2, and 3 as the levels of tension marked as concentric circles around the mouth; a set of sine curves within the field are identified as pi 1, pi 2, and pi 3. The numbers on this canvas, as scientific boundaries, are an abstraction to a sym-

bolism present throughout his artwork with the reference to game boards. We see the artist's preoccupation with rules and regulations in his very early canvases (e.g. *Endgame*), and again later in his athletic canvases beginning with *Vestigial Being*. Gorski's normative boundaries become more intensely dramatized in his sports canvases. His subjects are represented as numbers and uniforms.

Finally, the halo and the symbol of the cross serve as the representation of omega, symbolizing his identification with the Christian norm, and his experience of saintliness, (e.g. *"I will make a man more precious than fine gold"*). In this sense of boundaries Gorski's art is a manifestation of issues of conflict resolution as awareness of power management, the careful move into the allowed boundaries. The canvas of the *Mathematical Proof* is remarkable as an indicator of the artist's awareness of the importance of the love of God controlling his normative liberties.

This relationship of man to God is about normative compliance as the condition for resolution. The highlight of the second act of Gorski's drama is the result of violating the norm of chastity and innocence, the distinctions of right and wrong as defined by religious values regarding sexuality.

Norms defining gender relations in the Gorski triptych

There is among his works **a** triptych which illustrates Gorski's perception of the Christian norm regulating gender relations. This presents the intense conflictual relationship between the genders generated by sexual interests. The portrayals illustrate the consequences of his moral injunction on gender relations. Sexual interests generate intense anxiety and defenses against women perceived as dangerous. His men are mesmerized, scared and hostile towards the powerful, irresistible, woman, the *Lady Bug*. This woman is the powerful, seductive Mona Lisa; she has a secret: passion. *Saja's Secret* is the canvas of the hot kiss melting the plate of steel in front of the mouth.

The central image presents a woman, *Lady Bug*. She has a Mona Lisa face but is a strip tease dancer with scintillating body mesmerizing her audience of entranced men. These men are pathetically scared at the spectacle. Their faces are half-hidden by the nightclub table. Deprived of mouths, they grow tentacles out of their eyes. The bug-eyed prehensile eyes become beams of light searching the space and dissecting it into a game board. Men without mouths seem preoccupied with desire, anxiety and hostility. There is no room for trust and love here. There is no happy ending coming out of this encounter of the genders. Yet *Lovebugs* are only a few brushstrokes away and then we have the phase of the world of kisses. *Alliterative Obsession* is a wall of kisses, the major billboard for the quest for love.

The central canvas of the triptych presents the confrontation of the genders and is complemented with the portrayal of a man on the left and a woman on the right. These images clarify the qualities of the players. The man is an upright Kafkaesque bug with his mouth obstructed with proliferating tentacles. Gorski is consistent in his portrayals of men during this artistic phase all of which feature mouthless men with multiple layers of defenses and three symmetrical sets of prehensile extremities. By contrast, the woman on the right has a beautiful, sensuous, enigmatic, kissable, seductive mouth, more powerful than Mona Lisa's famous lips. Her outstretched arms with black hair remind us of a spider's web waiting for the bug to become entrapped. The hair appears pubic and alludes to the possibility of an equally dangerous encounter. The attractive feminine image is threatening like potential sin and eternal damnation.

This triptych gives us clues about the normative definition of gender relations inspired by religious norms; it implies "lead us not into temptation." The three canvases display the consequence of the intensified normative separation of the genders which demonize and complicate gender relations. Forbidding a feeling of trust, alienation ensues between men and women and the result is intense conflict.

In the *End Game* the body of a woman is a game board covering the entire canvas. The body of the woman is rigged with zapping gadgets. On this game board men are like pawns and the woman is a queen in a game of chess being watched by a crowd. A depression on the rigid canvas portrays the unconscious reality captured metaphorically as a cat and mouse encounter on a kitchen floor. Man is the vulnerable trapped mouse; the woman is the menacing cat. In another canvas a group of women are depicted as silhouettes with their heads covered with *Lampshades;* this is Gorski's discovery of a colorful head-cover or hijab symbolizing his discomfort with his desires for women.

Gorski's respect for gender norms inspired him to compose the lyrical portrayal of the beauty and mystery of the feminine nude, but only in his sketchbooks. The only woman he portrayed is the Mona Lisa. His love of women is seen as repetitions of agape symbols, manifested in his multiple sculptured kisses. Kisses are gentle portrayals of women. In one of his charcoal etchings a round kiss expands to cover the naked person like an open umbrella held horizontally. The kiss, as agape, sanitizes the discomfort of sexuality of *The Rape of the Rose.* Hence, Gorski's many kisses may be equated with the forbidden nakedness.

Kisses neutralize one's forbidden sexuality, the frail wishes for love. The well-formed plastic wall of Kisses are compromises. They are representations of women free of the glare of their scintillating bodies. The kisses are making men feel loved, disarmed of their conflictual desires. The spread sheets of kisses present the artist's preoccupation with women as the alliterative search for agape healing the artist of his unacceptable feelings of lust. Kisses are the safe, spiritual representations of God's love. Kisses illustrate agape as the idealized relationship permitted by the Christian set of norms.

There is but one canvas illustrating harmony between a man and a woman, called *The Vow.* It presents the wedding couple with the bride and groom standing next to each other. Their bodies are ethereal and nearly transparent. They portray the elusiveness of love. Dark clouds give this image a mysterious unreality. Then there is another canvas which I call *The Diamond;* it presents the glow of a sliced geode, a brilliant diamond cut in half as an explosion of light without any reference to gender relations. I consider it the symbolic diamond held in *The Vow* and the portrayal of the allowed cosmic bliss.

Under the influence of the 'Make Love not War' spirit of the post-Vietnam war era, Gorski's mouths emerged from innocence to the sinful pursuit of the pleasures of an erotic kiss, and eventually of the ensuing intimacy. The drama of this encounter caused by reaching out to resolve the dangerous polarization between the genders backfired. This kiss was the serious moral lapse, the *rape* of innocence, the violation of the norm of chastity.

The artist felt that he had become a sinner. The ensuing multiple crucifixions attest to his need to repent and expiate. Gorski's subsequent men became crucifixes, competitive athletes who were losers, and finally innocent retarded youth. While Gorski's men eclipse themselves into self-sacrificial roles, his women, the appealing agape kisses became a phase in history after the experience of the rape. The norm of love evolved to the illusions about love in the *Winner take all* encounter of a fictitious Stallone embracing Mona Lisa and the triangular imaginary kiss, *Love Triangle.* Illusion was the artist's choice of conforming to the Christian norm as the acceptable boundary in love relations yet still dreaming of kisses. As opposed to illusions of sensuality we see the portrayal of sacrificial athletes and the portraits of the handicapped heroes. The portrayal of the handicapped became the end game scenario of Gorski's normative religion-based distinctions.

We may conclude that religious norms on morality have erected for Gorski the tall boundaries to the flow of feelings. Initially these dammed up feelings threatened the dam. The related tension was experienced as anxiety in the *Figure of Vectors* upon the encounter with the forbidden kiss. It reflects the manifestation of threatening concerns. The damming up of intense emotions was the factor distorting his perceptions of genders in the triptych. The imagery of men and women reflects the polarization of the man woman relationship under the influence of moral injunctions affecting the artist's sense of right and wrong. Religion's demonizing the man woman relationship intensified the perception of danger in the relationship between the genders.

FOCUS STUDY #3: The Norm-Changing Function as illustrated by comparing the works of Gorski and Francis Bacon.

To amplify the Formal Analytic method we can contrast the works of Henry Gorski to those of Francis Bacon, a figurative expressionist whose canvases have puzzled the world with their audacity, violence and sexual explicitness. The comparison of the two artists' symbolic languages helps us to recognize the universality of formal distinctions. The two artists evolved in diametrically opposite directions dealing with the same contemporary norm-challenging issues of love, sex and God. Inserts in the path of the exhibit demonstrate the similarities and differences in the parallel treatment of these subjects by the two artists. The images differ dramatically but they portray clearly the formal alternative choices in the same thematic and symbolic continua.

By contrasting the two artists' canvases we confirm the symbolic choices reflecting the artists' different ways of resolving conflict along the three formal operations: passivity versus activity, antagonism versus cooperation and alienation versus mutual respect, which characterize the transformation of a conflict into a resolution.

GORSKI'S VARIATIONS ON THE THEME OF CRUCIFIXION

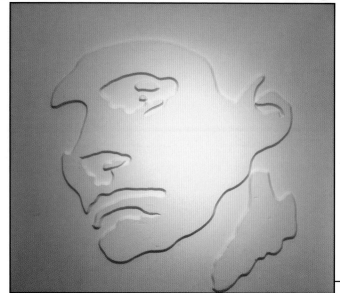

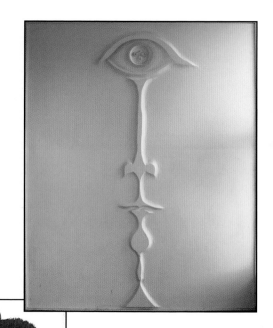

CRUCIFIXIONS: 1964-1968

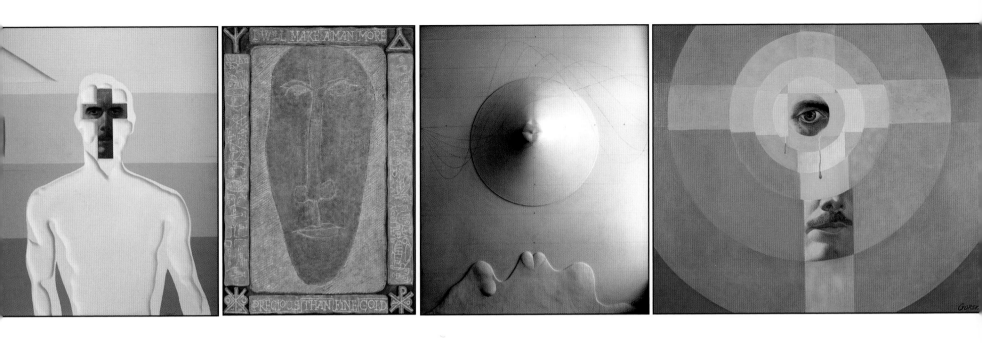

CRUCIFIXIONS: 1970-1993

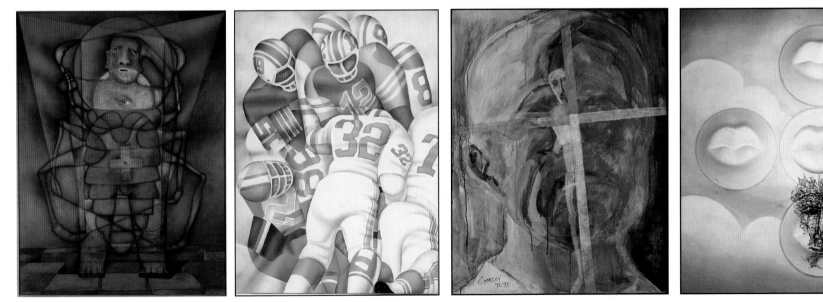

CULTURAL NORMS: FAITH-BASED GENDER DISTINCTIONS

Gorski's religious values define eroticism as frightening to men. His men as bug figures are hostile and manipulative, then portrayed as violators (*Rape of the Rose*), later atoning as crucifixions, next as heroic athletes and victims of an exploitive world, and finally as emotionally expressive but helpless, institutionalized inmates.

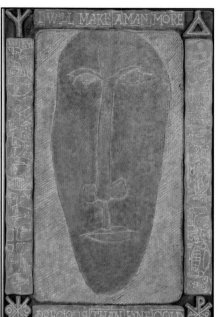

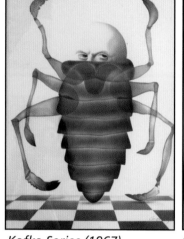

Kafka Series (1967)　　　　*The Vow (1970)*

"I Will Make A Man More Precious Than Fine Gold" (1971)

"Conditions for developing human maturity necessitate the cultivation of exquisite sensitivity and incomparable tenderness; the need to affirm the primacy of the person in daily living."

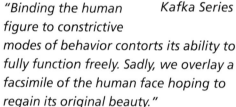

Figure with Vectors (1967)

"Binding the human figure to constrictive modes of behavior contorts its ability to fully function freely. Sadly, we overlay a facsimile of the human face hoping to regain its original beauty."

Homage to Kafka I (1972)

"Man emerged without any light of consciousness, dehumanized, retreating like a turtle within his shell. This is one of a series of sculptures that I wanted to try in ceramic of the theme of man being split in two forms. His head and eyes are reminiscent of 'The Committee,' while his mouth is covered by his business suit which conceals and reveals. It reveals the ultimate dissolution of his identity. As he is trying to wrap himself up in the safety shell, he submerges himself into this bug-like configuration reminiscent of Kafka's metamorphosis. The partial facial image revealed only as a fragment, is being transformed into something less than human; pinned like an insect onto a game board symbolizing 'the game of life.'"

Homage to Kafka II (1972)

"Man is ensnared in a machine-like insect form, unable to express himself, yet desperately trying to manipulate the world around him."

Heroic Athlete

Triptych I, II and III (1967) portray the man/woman relationship. *Triptych I* portrays man as a mouthless Kafkaesque bug figure.

Gorski's religious values define eroticism as dangerous. Women are symbolically transformed from sexual and erotic figures (spiders and radioactive chambers) to asexual and safe abstract forms (kisses).
In that formalized identity of kisses Gorski reveals his fascination with women
as an obsession for love.

Lady with Lampshades (1960)

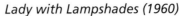

Alliterative Obsession (1973)

"The kiss is a seeking, a reaching outward from the isolated prison of the self. It has been my intent to make the ideal real; to intensify by giving it form in this positive symbol. It epitomizes that perfect tension between inner desire (spirit) and realization (physical touching); the impulse of life for form; the infinite possibilities of love."

Lovebugs I & II (1967)

Endgame (1967)

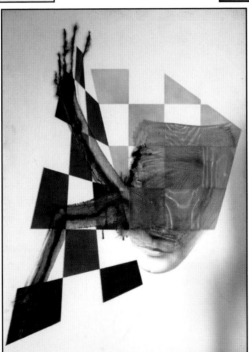

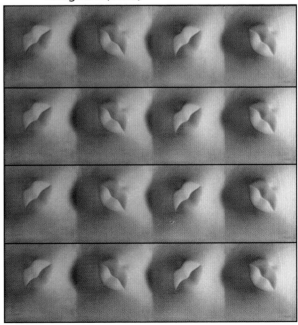

Triptych II presents the bug-figured men mesmerized by the golden spider.

Triptych III portrays the woman with an intact mouth and prehensile hairy appendages.

Alliterative Obsession (1973) shows man's preoccupation with yearnings for loving women.

Choices along the spectrum of the three operations reflect alternative relational modalities. The juxtaposition of the alternatives explains the simplicity of the underlying formal grammar, the three formal operations or distinctions, and the formal syntax, the six-part emotional dialectic processing of conflicts.

The contrast also illustrates the consistency of alternative personal styles in resolving conflict, the manifestation of artists' different relational modalities. These are the brand new diagnostic categories, the relational syndromes of normal behavior. Everyone fits into one of these formal alternative relational patterns. These are meaningful and relevant as they reflect personal distortions and responses and further indicate the modalities, relational strengths and weaknesses.

The comparison of the two artists clarifies that the symbolic imagery of an artist reflects formally interrelated choices and that these are personally determined alternatives along the three formal operations. Variations in these three operations define the personality types as alternative ways of resolving conflict. Symbolic choices reflect the relational modalities determined by the artist's personality, hence by observing art we may diagnose the respective artist's personality, which accounts for the consistency in imagery, the same themes dealt with by the two artists (Peppiatt, 2008).

The antithetical conceptions along these themes attest to these two artists' completely different normative choices and personality types. Accordingly, we may diagnose Gorski as a submissive-cooperative, mutually respectful person. In contrast, we may conclude that Bacon is a dominant-antagonistic person, comfortable in his alienated relationship with a number of mainstream norms. The respective relational modalities account for the differences between the images of the artists.

Comparison of the two artists

Gorski and Bacon are creatures of the 20th century, only a few years apart in age. Both had intense relationships with their respective fathers. They were both exposed to a Christian moral upbringing and values. Both men experienced the vicissitudes of WWII. Both dealt with parallel norm-testing issues like sex and god. The differences are of significance for the science of interpretation as reflecting cultural homogeneity but personality variation. The differences reflect the personal relational modalities as completely opposite and complementary responses to life's identical stressors.

This discussion contrasts the art of Gorski with that of Bacon along a lifetime of emotional dialectics that has been used in deploying the Gorski exhibit as three acts of a play and six role-states of passivity-activity sequences of interrelated emotions.

Act One: stress/response

One of the common themes that manifested early with both artists is the portrayal of crucifixions showing the artists' awareness of moral norms. Gorski experienced the crucifixion as his identification with pain, accepting it rather than expressing anger, or yielding assertively to temptations and pleasures. His early crucifix presents the features of a face as a cross shedding mechanical tears, reflecting his sense of alienation. Another *Crucifixion* (1964-1969 Phase of Political Communications, pp. 107), depicts political figures that have died in the service of social justice. Christ is besieged by women, both as worshipers and as temptresses illustrating Kazantzakis' *Last Temptation of Christ* (Kazantzakis, 1960); ascetically he is containing desire, while literally being bombarded by coquettish female planes that surround the cross, savoring his drops of blood on wafers.

In stark contrast, Bacon's early crucifixion, a triptych, depicts angry, violent, screaming, biting

monsters in the form of male genitals in the process of erection. The early study of phallic figures with open, hungry, menacing and screaming mouths is succeeded by the next crucifixion, completed in the year 1946. It presents a most disturbing image of inhumanity and cruelty. An unfeeling man – a devilish authority figure with a black umbrella – is callously sitting below the carcass of a big animal, human or bovine, his face indifferent to the bloodshed. Explaining his strange painting Bacon said it evolved by itself; he started painting a bird with wings spread out and this unconsciously evolved to the bizarre image. The canvas was not preconceived. We may conclude that his unconscious was comfortable with antagonism, extreme aggression, and alienation.

Act One is concluded with the response images to the identified religious norms. These are reflected in both artists in the portrayal of human heads with clear differences in emotional choices as their solutions to life's moral dilemmas. The heads reflect the artists' relational philosophies that will become clear in the canvases that follow.

Gorski's faces are identified as "Pain-things." Their features are obstructed. The sensory organs and apertures, eyes, mouth and even nostrils are blocked by mechanical devices or an ominous fingerprint that suffocates the face. The heads evolved to represent one signature image, a mouthless, intense Kafka-esque bug. Kafka is the tormented character of the terrifying world war who is persecuted and tortured for no reason. He is society's eternal victim. His mouth is obstructed by a fingerprint or a level of submersion. The bug's feelings are expressed with a multiplicity of arms reflecting a wish to manipulate the environment.

In the Gorski Retrospective there is only one canvas that features open and biting explosive mouths, *Consumer, Consumed... Consumed*; the artist had discarded it in the attic and sold it to me at the value of its canvas. In obvious contrast, all of Bacon's faces are showing angry open mouths with piercing, menacing teeth. Bacon's mouths are screeching and screaming, while Gorski's are ominously silent. Bacon's heads took on the identity of a Pope which he said were inspired by a Velasquez painting. Bacon's Popes are also screaming. The heads are not submerged but rather elevated in box-like pedestals.

Act Two: anxiety/defense
Both artists used triptychs to depict the conflicts in process. Gorski's single triptych depicts his unresolved man-woman power play, with men threatened by women's power of seduction. Gorski's women are portrayed as blinding lights in *Virgins with Lamps*, as threatening Mona Lisas in *Winner Take All*, and as cats toying with men as mice cornered on the kitchen floor in *Endgame*.

The middle phase of the artists' work represents the Erotic phase followed by guilt and self-consciousness. Gorski's mouthlessness gave rise to the opposite, the gradual emergence of the mouth. At its inception it was an evolution of his Kafka bugs kissing, *Love-Bugs I* and *Love-Bugs II*. The ensuing period focused on the mouth as a multiplicity of kisses. One canvas introduces discreet erotic symbolism, *The Hyperbolic Bride*, in which a woman's mouth and breasts are delicately concealed. This canvas was followed by the erotic encounter perceived as the violation of innocence, denounced by the artist as *The Rape of the Rose*. It depicts a penis-like plaster injection syringe menacingly directed to a red rose. This is the apex of his erotic assertion.

Following this experience the artist surrendered the desire-pursuing behavior immersed in remorse. The next canvas, *Nowhere to Hide,* portrays his guilt. The last canvases in the cycle portray how Gorski discovered the safety of the cross as his *Identity*, and *Eye-dentity*; his eyes and his mouth now surrendered to the cross. These

are self-portraits overlapping with the cross. His discomfort with sexuality and his remorsefulness reveal Gorski as a shy person who presents erotic issues gingerly as safe kisses, and defensively assumes *agape* instead of sex.

Bacon also entered an erotic phase which follows the screaming Pope heads with canvases portraying graphically depicted acts of intercourse between men. He violated Catholic norms in spite of the Pope screaming at him. These depictions of sexuality are offensive to those espousing conservative norms. While Gorski was remorseful for the minor transgression of a kiss, and repents symbolically, Bacon continued with his explicit depictions of homosexual men copulating in a multiplicity of triptychs. His paintings feature no inhibition for public scrutiny of his culturally unacceptable sexuality. His triptychs depict self-consciousness as fears of being observed. In spite of this self-consciousness Bacon remains undeterred in his depiction of sexuality, violence, blood, and multiple relations. The acts of copulation are breaches of norms. The only sense of remorse or guilt is depicted as being observed or intruded upon by uninvited guests: primordial authority figures, observers, stone faced onlookers. Instead of Christian remorse his next crucifixion duplicates the violence of *Crucifix 1946*.

Act Three: reversal/compromise
Reversal and compromise present the men productive in their work but admitting feelings as paramount. The third act represents the existential phase in the artists' lives. They deal with issues of winning versus losing, and of mortality versus immortality.

Gorski surrenders his prowess to an abundance of self-portraits with the cross eventually transforming to colorful athletic or sports paintings. The athletes are Roman gladiators aggressing or being victims of the game, but they are fierce players. They are society's victims, hurting others

and themselves in order to entertain the public.

In spite of being the self-described artist of the losers, as Gorski started winning an audience with his sports paintings he denounced his success as an illusion and began to deliberately paint illusions, portraying the unreality of the objects of his affection. In Gorski's *Shadow Play*, the artist is the creator of his emotional options. He presented his ambivalence in a modified kiss, *Love Triangle*, a totally spiritual reference covering up the sexually risqué insinuation of a man in love with two women. He ended his drama with portraits of reality, the images of his handicapped son's companions, presenting them as empowered by their emotions of joy and anger.

Bacon, by contrast, indulges himself in endless depictions of sexual encounters and his self-consciousness associated with them. He demonstrates his choice of immortality as reflected in his choice of stories from Greek Mythology: the Erinies haunting Orestes as they menacingly enter his bedroom where he is with a lover; Carrion birds attack Prometheus; Oedipus bleeding while conversing with a frozen Sphinx. His canvases present spirituality but also violence and paranoia offset by memories of his lost lover.

Gorski proceeds to conflict resolution through the series of sports paintings wherein the athletes are alternative victims. Gorski's last self-portrait is spiritual; he depicts himself in a cross made of kisses. This self-portrait reflects an evolution from oppression to resolution, i.e. mastery, cooperation and mutual respect.

Bacon's multiple self-portraits evolved to reduce distortions and assaults on the face and soften substantially, depicting personal emotions and the whole body of the person contorted but content. His self-portraits are aesthetic statements, not moral distinctions.

ACT 1: HEROES, CONFLICTS AND VALUES; Gorski's Kafka/Adam hero; Pain-things with obstructed mouths and crucifixions (1962-1970)

Crucifixion 1968

Child of Darkness 1962

Consumer 1962

The Dream 1964

Birth of Adam 1966

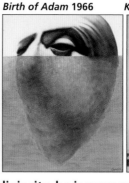

Kafka Bug 1968

Birth of Gorski c.1968

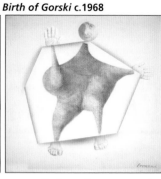

ACT 2: THE HEROES' ADVENTURE, EROTIC CONFLICTS AND GUILT; Gorski's shyness and religiosity, he is remorseful and surrenders to religion; (1967-1976)

Triptych: *Homage to Kafka, Mona Lisa as Ladybug* 1967

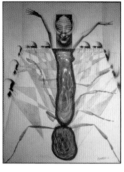

Saja's Secret 1970

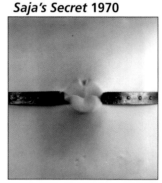

Tangerine Kiss 1971

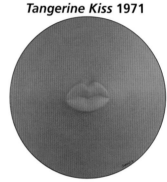

Rape of the Rose 1968-?

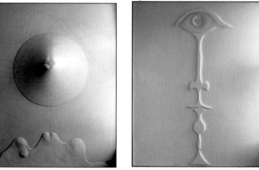

No Place to Hide 1974

Identity 1970

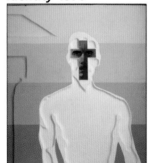

Eye-dentity 1974

I'll Make a Man... 1971

The Proof 1973

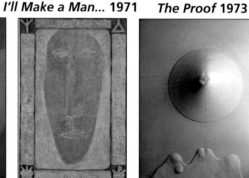

Eye of God 1967

ACT 3: THE HERO'S MORALITY AND MORTALITY; Gorski's realities & illusions (1979-1993)

Through the Hole 1978

Blocked! c. 1979

Winner Take All 1982

Shadow Play 1984

Painthings 1993/94

Paradox 1993

ACT 1: Bacon's Pope hero and heads with screaming mouths, eroticism as crucifixions (1944-1953)

Three Studies For Figures At The Base Of A Crucifixion 1944   *Crucifix 1946*   *Head III 1949*   *Pope's Heads after Velazquez* 1949-1953

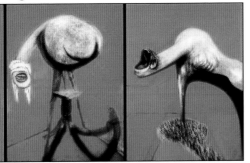

ACT 2: Bacon's explicitness and paranoia explain his triptych presentation; he rebels against religion but is self-conscious and feels intruded upon (1953-1976)

Two Figures 1953   *Three Studies for a Crucifixion 1962*   *Two Figures Lying on a Bed with Attendants 1968*

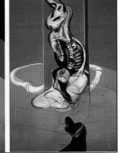

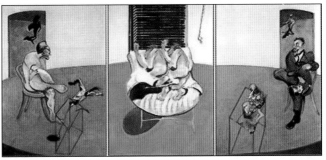

Triptych May-June 1973   *Triptych 1976*   *Three Studies for Self-Portraits 1976*

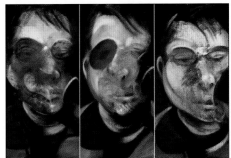

ACT 3: Bacon's eroticism, mythic struggles and uncompromising irreverence (1974-1987)

Triptych 1974-77   *Self Portrait 1982*   *Human Body 1984*   *Oedipus & Sphinx 1984*

Self-portraits

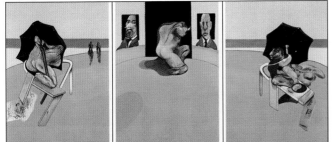

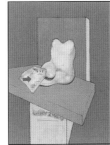

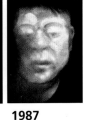

1979   1980   1987

Reversals and compromises, mutual respect as sadness, and mortality come to haunt the artists. Gorski and Bacon mourn life's decline and paint their dear ones. Gorski is haunted by his son and Bacon by images of his deceased lover. A sequence of portraits are again identified as pain-things. Triptychs realistically portray Bacon's lost lover, Peter Dyer, who committed suicide. Pools of blood and states of sickness reflect that Bacon too expresses loss, acknowledging the loss of his loved one.

his identity, coping with desires for women and for power, then accepting power and love as an illusion whose resolution is making peace with the most painful aspects of life. He discovered the freedom of expression and the testing of norms of the acceptability of art.

Connecting these canvases as a series of evolving portrayals of feelings we see Gorski finding at the very end self-acceptance and peace as the healing state of his personal drama. The compassion and respect for his handicapped son became the metaphor of his resolving his conflicts in the normative world of painting. He gave himself the permission to paint for himself, to express his emotions without concern of the public opinion. He experienced healing. If this art is unacceptable to the art world, so what? He did not care. The artist has the right to break the norm of painting for others. He was entitled to paint for himself and face the world with a smile. In his letter to me he stated 'painting was FUN.'

Henry Gorski died peacefully in 2010 at the age of 92, six months after the death of his beloved wife.

Conclusion
In this study of patterns we see the conflict resolution process manifested clearly throughout the Gorski exhibit, and in parallel meaningfully binding Bacon's art. The two artists' canvases share the process, integrating their distinct images across a number of phases of their work into two complete lifetime dramas. The Formal Analysis introduces objectivity and meaning into the symbolic languages of the two very different symbolic universes. It deepens our appreciation of the artists while acquainting us with new ideas about the nature of the psyche as an adaptational mechanism that varies from person to person according to their relational modality.

The Gorski exhibit and the Bacon corollary illustrate the path of the language of the unconscious as a formula that finds complementary resolutions reflecting the emotional disposition of the artist, thinker, person. The science of the creative process introduces a new way of looking at art as the formal organization of emotions as sequences of six role-states driven by three formal operations. This outlook helps to measure meaning as the relational modality of the respective artist. The scientific interpretation of symbolic languages throws a completely new light in art appreciation, making art meaningful for the artist and the public, but especially for the psychologist and the educator.

While submissiveness leads Gorski to introspection and compliance with norms, Bacon's dominance approach to conflict resolution has the individual prevailing over the social system. Instead of kind Gorski conforming to the system, the dominant Bacon seeks to change the system. We may object to his choice of imagery or his radical way of confronting our sensitivities, but Bacon's dominant-aggressive mode of relating has contributed to changing our homophobic world.

DISCUSSION OF SYMBOLIC DISTINCTIONS
The two artists' conflicts were inspired by religious norms, but also by their relational modalities. Behavior is affected both by culture and by personal relational proclivities. These two factors determine the choice of symbolic systems of the artist. Science provides insights to understand the individual's adjustments to stressors.

Gender conflicts in Gorski and homosexuality for Bacon, central to their dramas, are brought about by religion's obsession with sexuality. This obsession dates from the monotheistic, father-son alliance against the pagan, matriarchal goddesses of antiquity, the temptresses. The Abrahamic religions demonized the pagan goddesses and their power of sexuality, erecting distinctions and mortifying punishments for transgressors.

The political or ethical system of the land determines societal norms on conflict and resolution. The individual is expected to adjust to these norms yet individuals and societies have changed norms and our contemporary world has evolved from the early definitions of monotheism. But for many, especially the fundamentalists of the world (Gorski may be viewed as one of them), religion still regulates behavior and identifies the norms which induce and reduce conflicts.

Here we wish to raise the issue of who is entitled to determine norms? Is it the political authority of civil rights legislation or is it the church advancing discrimination of genders and of sexual practices? The issue on the legitimate authority determining norms is relevant for our times marked by the strife between rigidity of religious beliefs on gender relations versus liberal views on sexual behavior. This country and the rest of the world is affected by fundamentalists. While the radical Islamists are extremists attacking liberal West, the majority in the American public feel violated by the notion of same-sex marriage, abortion and primal cell research. We are witnessing the world, caught between alternative normative ethical determinations.

What is the role of Moral Science? Its relevance is in determining the norms of conflict resolution objectively. The three formal operations lead to conflict resolution. These values are innate in the human unconscious and are based on the objectivity of observing the process. Dogma-based determinations stem from a historical developmental phase of civilization when the world had very little else to establish moral order other than divine revelations. The world has not yet discovered the scientific nature of the unconscious mind and it is only redefining justice based on litigation rather than science. Legal authority introduced civil rights, but law is less important in the mind of believers than the wisdom of the imperious god. Science may tip the balance for making normative distinctions.

Science can prevail by identifying the three principal operations of the conflict resolution process as the moral imperative in determining the key norm of conflict resolution; science gives the exact dimension on deviation from the rest point. Moral Science's principles of conflict resolution: activity, cooperation, and mutual respect in partnerships may be relied upon as the criteria determining interpersonal norms and moral values. Conflict resolution can then be determined by science as moral order phenomena remain outside of the realm of the supernatural. Religious norms need and should be revised in accordance with the scientific analysis of the process simply because they are counterproductive in their impact on the public as well as the adjustment of the clergy.

The new shift in paradigms is exchanging the point of conflicts from issues of control of women's sexual behavior to issues of power. Relations on power historically were focused on sexual behaviors. This was a symbolic choice. Communism shifted focus of conflicts into eco-

nomic distinctions as capitalists unjustly exploiting the proletariat.

The Moral Science redefines morality and restructures relationships merely on issues of power and relations. Power implies the capacity for normative deviation. Introducing mutual respect between partners focuses on power sharing and bypasses the sexualization of power. The issue of power diffuses gender and class as moral distinctions. The gender polarity or distinction was established during the patriarchal era, men prevailing over the promiscuous women. One-god religions prevailed over polytheism or paganism but in reality this distinction was applied on matriarchy's promiscuous moral ethics.

The financial polarity between classes was brought about by the communist revolution and dismissed by the fall of this ideological distinction. We are living in a world defined by more inclusive distinctions, such as individual civil rights and relational power choices determined by personality and not by gender, race or sexual preference. These need to be dealt with at that personal level. The process as the unit of conflict resolution changes the distinctions of the prevailing paradigm. Gender and financial distinctions are a phase in history.

The common issue throughout the Retrospective is gender relations and consequences. The new norm of mutual respect reduces the barriers in communication and allows the spontaneous flow of associations to work on the resolution of gender differences along the three principles of conflict resolution. Parity between partners levels the boundaries and diminishes the censoring of feelings and the ensuing distortions of reality. Communications reduce tensions. They cure the couple and the world of the energetic intensity generated by the overregulated gender distinctions. The Universal Harmonic has the physiologic homeostatic function of bringing about social change as well as emotional adjustment to what cannot be changed.

Gender wars and sexual preference choices have been artificial moral fixations. Normative changes can defuse the heightened energy generated in the canvases of the artists. Incomplete resolutions generate norms that are unfair and unjust, incompatible both with the scientific definition of moral order and the civil rights laws.

Science 'steals the fire of the gods' by introducing new concepts in determining norms. It emancipates the world from norms that do not resolve conflict according to the three principle operations. Science then addresses the conflicts of 9/11 and of other religion-incited conflicts, such as those of the Catholic priests' pederastic behaviors, by showing that moral order is a natural science phenomenon that can be defined on the basis of relational rather than theistic, dogma based, moralist distinctions and premises. Moral values may and should be defined by universal natural science relational principles.

The anthropology of conflict resolution as the evolution of normative paradigms
In another exhibit of the Museum of the Creative Process, the Sculptural Trail through the history of religion, religions are portrayed evolving along the dialectic progression of awareness of the conflict resolution process. We recognize religions as pioneering scientific discoveries of the nature of the unit process. The science of the process integrates them just like it integrates the canvases of Henry Gorski as moral and scientific discoveries. This Sculptural Trail on the grounds of the Wilburton Inn is introduces what is missing in the Abrahamic religions: awareness of the importance of mutual respect between partners, here men and women, parents and children, as the condition for conflict resolution. This development deliberately pursued could lead to the Healing of the World.

The Trail addresses the inequity advanced by the Abrahamic religions on the treatment of women as a lapse in the thinking of religions. It is intelligible as related to the historical evolution of gender relations. But this lapse needs to be reviewed in the context of the scientific understanding of moral order. Religious determinations evolved through the centuries as the battles of the genders. They represent determinations that are now seen as differing from the scientific norms.

Dated norms as partial resolutions of conflict are unjust to the genders and are polarizing the gender relations and the world. Religions are misleading the world and mesmerizing it to believe their normative distinctions as God's truth. Religions are inflicting psychological conflicts and perpetuating social injustices in the world by disrespecting civil rights and leading to adverse results. Religious norms are stifling the world's emotional growth, making it impossible for individuals to deal with their feelings and the world to find peace and moral consensus.

Science reconciles religions to the scientific understanding of conflict and the determination of norms

Gorski's and Bacon's art help to rethink psychology and moral order using the concepts of conflict resolution to understand the mind, god, psychology and religion. The scientific interpretation of art helps us understand cultural conflicts and the evolution of gender relations and the conceptualization of moral order. The religions of the world evolved spontaneously redefining the institution of the family and the conceptualization of moral order. The world needs to confront its sanctified paradigms as counterproductive by placing moral order on a scientific foundation.

Science steals the authority from religions in determining norms in the name of parity, justice and cultural effectiveness. Science diagnoses the inequity of the prevailing social norms discriminating women, demonizing sexuality and discouraging communication of feelings and relaxation of tensions. Gorski's mouthlessness and kisses and Bacon's screaming mouths and obses-

sive sexuality are formally-related emotional distinctions. Science defends the sacredness and inviolability of the principles of resolution.

Though science is challenging religion, science is the friend of religions. It completes the task of religions aspiring for peace in the person and the world. It is obvious that religions have failed to deliver peace. They are the cause of inner and of cross-cultural conflicts and they are inspiring artists and inciting terrorists and priests to unacceptable conduct. Science assists the task of providing the scientific foundation of morality by assisting religions in correcting their conflict-inducing distortions on normative behavior.

The Gorski exhibit explains the impact of religion on the psychology of communications and perceptions. Science can enhance understanding psychology and delivering emotional and values education. This redefinition of morality and of relations entails challenging the legitimacy of religions in determining moral order since religions resolve conflicts inadequately and since their perceptions are distorted. The exhibit then becomes an opportunity to propose activism for a conceptual revision of what is moral by launching a far-reaching rethinking of the social sciences in the service of healing the world from the divisiveness of religions.

The exhibit reinforces the relevance of the Moral Science in the healing of the world polarized by normative systems that do not comprehend the underlying issues. We need to revisit norms, their origin and their psychological and sociological impact on our societies. Science promotes the discovery of the spontaneously self-regulating unconscious which seeks conciliation rather than an unconscious stifled by fears flooded and obsessed by threatening desires leading to loss of control.

The Formal Theoretical Analysis is pertinent to our times of moral confusion. It contributes a

shift of paradigms from the dogmatic content of stories, the many sacred Scriptures, to the credibility of the universal plot of all stories as a scientific phenomenon. This shift of paradigms entails a change of moral values from sanctified normative models to the recognition that moral values are the three formal operations underlying the formula of conflict resolution.
The formalization of morality entails that religions be held accountable to science. Upon this anniversary of 9/11 we may consider this exhibit a confirmation that the Moral Science steals the fire of the gods and that it can heal the world.

Conclusions

THE SIX OBJECTIVES FOR THE GORSKI RETROSPECTIVE

The first objective was to illustrate the notion of the three formal operations: reciprocity, negation and correlation. Gorski's canvases illustrate the three formal operations as dichotomies using the symbolic language of the mouth. Canvases with mouths obstructed evolved to mouths screaming, then to kisses, then to accurate portrayals of the artist's own mouth. The Retrospective is continued with totally missing faces in the sports paintings, followed by portraits of the entire face in the sequence of the handicapped period.

The second objective, to illustrate the six role process: stress, response, anxiety, defense, reversal and compromise was achieved presenting the three formal transformations and the six role-state process in six sequences of interrelated canvases.

The third objective, to identify emotional sequences that predictably resolve conflicts as a periodic phenomenon was illustrated with study under the Topic one exhibit, presenting the lifetime canvases as a three act drama. The retrospective illustrated the ongoing upgrading of order, meaning and attitude.
Topic exhibit two addressed the fourth objective, the illustration of the laws of two natural science phenomena organizing Gorski's symbolic universe.
The fifth function of the exhibit was to illustrate the continuity between the five artistic phases of the Retrospective into a single dramatic totality.
The sixth objective discussed in Focus exhibit two the importance of relational modality in responding to normative injunctions. The exhibits focus studies 2 and 3 addressed the two points. Focus study two addressed the normative identity for Gorski and focus study 3, the comparative study, illustrated the relational modality variations in resolving conflict. Gorski's submissive modality accounted for his deference to religion's norms. The study also clarified that religion is a normal physiological psychological phenomenon.

The conclusion upon leaving the Retrospective should be that the creative process is a natural science moral order phenomenon, the unit of the social sciences and

that norms and individual relational modalities determine the nature of conflicts experienced.

The Moral Science allows us to introduce objectivity into the study of the process since the unconscious is the origin of moral order and of all religions. The redefined unconscious should use the unit order integrating the humanities: psychology and religion, into the exact Moral Science, the Science of Conflict Resolution.

This realization entails the need for moral revisionism respectful of the scientific principles leading to fairness in the resolution of conflicts. This is the solution for the contemporary drama of our world in search of meaning. Based on the scientific analysis of conflict, science is entitled to spell out the optimal conflict resolution norms based on the formal operations of moral order as conflict resolution. The world needs the new paradigm to reconcile its religions leading to the equitable handling of relations to decrease personal and cross cultural conflicts.
We may conclude with this study that all creativity is unified by the inner need to adjust to stress or pain. The Retrospective viewed as a totality of conflicts and normative resolutions confirms that the creative process is an emotional adjustive and healing equilibrial mechanism. It corrects conflict, the symbolic, emotional and energetic division of ideas, the inner disturbances of the rest state, by processing emotions and energies dialectically. The mind automatically transforms emotions into symbolic systems, reflecting the underlying process of energies. The end is resolutions as spiritual and social growth.

The disturbance, or conflict, be that a deficiency of status that needs to be corrected or a transgression, as usurpation of power that must be punished, the process spontaneously leads to the rest state. Hostility and guilt, love and loss of love are corrected with emotional and intellectual growth; the keys to resolution are the three formal operations of the processing of emotions. A conflict is only resolved when ideas or parties are reconnected on the basis of the shared experience of mastery, cooperation and mutual respect. These qualifications represent the conditions for the

restoration of the rest state, the correction of the normative deviation, be that loss or undeserved gain. Compromise entails resolution as the state defined by one's attitude corresponding to the set of feelings described above. We may conclude that the Gorski Retrospective, a complex symbolic system, validates the theoretical premise introduced in the analysis of the thought process.

Resolutions as compromises are a mental trade-off or bargain. The individual experiences a loss but offsets it with a spiritual gain, a morally uplifting experience. This emotional equilibrial phenomenon, being a conserved energetic entity, the process is shown to abide by the set of formulas of natural science .

The healing of the world

The Retrospective introduces the concept of the scientific nature of our thinking. It also raises the issue of contrasting the Moral Science versus religion. Science clarifies the importance of norms but also the psychological and political determination of norms. Science reduces behavior to the rigorous unit process and to manageable normative parameters, determined by the principles of conflict resolution. The Science of Conflict Resolution steals the power/fire of the gods in determining norms. Morality becomes the purely scientific phenomenon of resolving conflicts. Religions are reduced to respectable partial resolutions.

The world will heal as reason prevails over faith and that the norms determined by the innate moral order are adopted to deliberately improve our narrow cultural paradigms of conflict resolution. The exhibit clarifies moral order and the nature of normative determinations. Science revamps the social sciences and leads to new concepts and practices. Universal moral values, based on scientific principles lead us to a moral consensus and may thus heal the world.

Religions and the love of God are not about divine figures but about the calculus of managing power respecting the necessary formal transformation of resolving conflict.

EXHIBIT #3
THE WIZARD OF OZ PANELS
The Conflict Resolution Process as the Integrative Paradigm of The Social Sciences

INTRODUCTION

Lyman Frank Baum's Wizard of Oz story illustrates the typical unfolding of ideas as a conflict resolution. It depicts the journey or drama of naïve humans struggling to reach the great magician Oz. They receive his healing message only to discover that Oz is a deceptive human and the healing is in their spontaneous transformation. It is the journey that has transformed them. They reach their objectives without the magic of the wizard. If it is not the Wizard, who is responsible for this outcome? What are the secrets of this spontaneous magic guiding force?

The Oz characters have healed themselves from their anxieties, self doubts, feelings of defectiveness and inferiority but the rest of the humanity still expects healing to come from God. We need an explanation and the Formal Theory introduces it by carefully examining the structure of this story. Though the story is children's level entertainment its metaphors embrace the key existential issues of humanity, the quest for meaning and resolution beyond the sacred authorities.

We study this story here because its four metaphors illustrate the four complex aspects of the Conflict Resolution process: epistemology, psychology, assessment as psychoeducation; and morality or religion. The four key metaphors illustrate the social sciences and their integration into the new Moral Science.

The interpretation of these four metaphors as aspects of the story (the plot, the characters, the adventure of transformation and the moral of the story), confirm the universal manifestation of the Conflict Resolution Process. Each metaphor and realm allows us to explore the unit of conflict resolution as it elucidates a different social science as a parallel symbolic system.

The information on the study is delivered in the 12 Wizard of Oz panels. The panels systematically present the interpretation of the four metaphors of the Oz story. These are suspended on the exterior walls of the Sanctuary. Three panels on each aspect of the pavilion focus on the wisdom of one metaphor and its implications for one social science. The pertinent information about each discipline is displayed on one of the four exterior walls of the square Sanctuary (see graphic opposite).

The exhibits introduce the scientific interpretation of metaphors and demonstrate the orderly process underlying the four social sciences

In the formal analysis of the Oz story we identify the Conflict Resolution Process as the moral order underlying all metaphors. Science clarifies the magical world of the metaphorical language as the issues of formal relations. The metaphors humanize the abstractions of science, and organizes the information meaningfully; the model reduces the complexity of each respective realm of knowledge into a user-friendly construct.

Four metaphors in a story present the process as the integrative paradigm

The process is a transformative entity readily identifiable in all samples of creativity confirming the theoretical assumption on the scientific and moral organization of emotions. The Oz exhibit provides us a different challenge; in this story we observe the process in four different metaphors of the texts and each metaphor represents a different aspect of the story:

The yellow brick road is interpreted as the entirety of the concept of the plot; it is the metaphor of the journey as an adventure that begins with a conflict, the needs of a set of heroes and ends with the resolution, the healing. The plot as an inert object may be interpreted as the epistemology of the unit process and used to introduce the scientific concepts pertaining to the abstract nature of the process.

The four heroes walking the road are interpreted as metaphors of four personality types, as alternative ways of resolving conflict. So these characters as metaphors pertain to psychology's diagnostic categories.

Killing the witch is a metaphor of the need to overcome fears and to dare challenge injustices. This is a metaphor of personal transformation as experienced in effective personal transformation, education and therapy.

Facing the ominous frightening wizard and evolving pity for the magisterial authorities pertains to dealing with moral authorities and seeing them demystified. Oz is a metaphor of demystifying religions and being lucid about the optimal ways of resolving conflicts as just ways of managing power.

The formal interpretation of each metaphor of these four sheds light to one of the social sciences rethinking each as another manifestation of the same orderly process. The plot, the characters, the adventure in encounters with the witch and with the wizard, the four aspects of the story reflect four topics of study, four social sciences. We recognize them as epistemology, psychology, psychotherapy and religion; these are here united by the same process underlying all of them at the same time. The analysis of this story then addresses the process as the integrative paradigm integrating the social sciences into the Moral Science, the Science of Conflict Resolution. Epistemology studies the science of the concepts, psychology studies diagnostic categories, therapy studies the measurement of personality, and religions study the nature of moral order.

1. The Yellow Brick Road is a metaphor of the conflict resolution process as the proverbial

THE SANCTUARY OF THE WIZARD AND WISDOM
LOCATION OF EXHIBITS:
THE METAPHORIA MURALS, THE WIZARD OF OZ PANELS, SCULPTURAL CYCLES 1 AND 6.

journey. The journey alludes to the structure and direction of the psychic mechanism. Epistemology studies the scientific method: The unit is identified with constructs and formulas from the rigorous sciences. I.e. displacement in the Simple Harmonic Motion corresponds to normative deviation in behavior; acceleration corresponds to emotions, and velocity to behaviors. In the physics of the pendulum acceleration is bound to displacement by a formula, which now applies to behavior. Acceleration is proportional and opposite to the displacement, and emotions are similarly proportional and opposite to normative deviations. If a person is oppressed he is going to be proportionately emotional, hostile, resisting the oppression. If a person aggresses, he will feel guilt as emotions opposing his/her own normative deviation, etc. The mental oscillation, like that of the pendulum, is about energetic transformations. Unlike the mechanical oscillation the mental process achieves resolution upon the third oscillation coinciding with the transformation of conflict to a resolution, and of chaos energy to ordered energy. This physical transformation coincides with a formal relational one. Conflict as passivity, antagonism, and alienation is transformed to resolution as mastery, cooperation and mutual respect.

2. The four characters walking the yellow brick road are metaphors of four alternative ways of resolving conflict. They identify each one of the key relational modalities. Psychology studies the unit process as the unconscious rollercoaster of interrelated emotions clinically identifiable as a syndrome and qualified as a set of relational modalities. There are four relational modalities corresponding to four personality diagnostic categories of wellness: i.e. dominance and subordinacy syndromes modified by cooperative and antagonistic relational variations.

3. Killing the witch is a metaphor of risk taking and personal transformation. It refers to the transformation of dependency needs to self-sufficiency and maturation. This is achieved through psycho-education. A psycho-assessment, *Conflict Analysis Battery* facilitates tapping on creativity for self-knowledge and personal growth. It measures the unit entity. The unit is readily assessed through an inventory and a set of projective tests. This instrument has diagnostic, therapeutic and educational functions. It measures the way of resolving conflicts combining a relational inventory and a set of projective techniques. The testing is user friendly; it can be administered equally well by the educator and the clinician. It generates protocols, which lead to the development of personal insights connecting emotions and experiences into a dramatic totality constituting a very meaningful and well illustrated clinical record. This record is equally useful to the student and the teacher, the patient and the clinician.

4. Understanding the Wizard of Oz is a metaphor for God, religions and morality. Moral order studies the conflict resolution process as the origin of religious thinking. The religions of the world constitute descriptions of the innate need for conflict resolution and the quest for peace; they identify peace, the rest state, as norms regulating interpersonal relations along a particular paradigm of conflict resolution. Deviations from the norm have been conceived as sins and compliant relating as virtues. Religious norms discovered alternative types of conflict resolution and mystified and deified the natural science process. Now the science of the process integrates the religions of the world into the Moral Science, the study of the calculus of power management and reveals the true essence of the wizard.

Formal Epistemology:
On the southern wall we interpret the Yellow Brick Road as the metaphor of the unit process. The journey is frequently used as the abstraction of the story as a drama.

The Yellow Brick Road is the metaphor for the plot of stories. It is connecting the episodes of the journey as the six role-states of the Conflict Resolution Process. Thus the Road presents the process as a natural science phenomenon that allows us to introduce the **epistemology** of the well-known constructs and formulas of two equilibrial phenomena into the study of emotions.

Formal Theory interprets the Road as a natural science phenomenon identified as an equilibrial, periodic entity, identical to the Simple Harmonic Motion and the equilibrial scales. The postulation of this equivalence introduces the constructs and formulas from the rigorous disciplines of logic, physics and math into the now rigorous field of behavior. Behavior becomes predictable, graphically portrayable and measurable.

Psychology, Psycho-diagnosis and Personality types:
On the eastern wall I present the concept of syndromes, the psychology of the relational modalities as alternative types of conflict resolution. I discuss the four characters as the metaphors of these four alternative syndromes of relating or resolving conflicts following the two formal choices: dominance versus submission, and cooperation versus antagonism. The well-known characters of the four heroes of the story illustrate four syndromal diagnostic categories, the relational modalities as the essence of psychology.

The characters personify the four relational modalities, i.e. the four syndromal personality types: Dorothy is the dominant-cooperative; the cowardly Lion is the dominant-antagonistic; the Scarecrow is the submissive-cooperative; and the Tin Man is submissive-antagonistic. This personality typology pertains to the essence of psychology as a predictive science of wellness. These relational modalities predict behavior for the well and the diagnosed persons alike.

Psychoeducation and Psychotherapy

On the northern wall we interpret the metaphor of the killing of the witch as dealing with dependency needs. By taking risks through tapping creativity one is led to self-discovery and transformation. Here we discuss issues of psychoassessment, psychoeducation and therapy. Conflict Analysis resolves dependency needs by helping a person become self-aware and responsible. Provided one is willing to do the work, this is an attainable goal.

The killing of the witch is a metaphor that may be interpreted as the emotional work involved in overcoming the dependency needs of the maternal authority, and by extension to any other patterns leading to personal maturation, individuation, and transformation. This is an appropriate metaphor of the task of emotional education. The killing of the witch dramatizes the significance of emotional growth, the inner transformation which accompanies any valuable psychoeducation; therapy or education should facilitate outgrowing one's fears, attachments and habits.

Self-discovery transforms the negative aspect of one's thinking by dispelling anxieties and addressing conditions inhibiting a person's growth. Outer and inner negativism is defeated as in the simple vanishing of the witch into smoke. The positive side of the mind is strengthened and one is enabled to resolve internal conflicts. One can then proceed with new insights, enlightenment and wisdom to transform one's attitude.

Formal Moral Values

The western wall features the formal interpretation of the Wizard of Oz as a metaphor pertaining to religion and spirituality. The Formal Theory understands and respects religions as the reality of the process. The science reinterprets the religious postulates: Maimonides' Ten Articles of Faith and the Ten Commandments are equivalent to the three principles of conflict resolution, the

postulates of holistic thinking.

Science respects the notion of prayer as meditation, the experience of the spirit of trust in the process as the alternative to god; god is the process and we can be pious about it. The prayer redefines the quest for God as the universality of the quest for conflict resolution or the restful state.

Finally, Oz is all about the magic of the healing power of the intangible process which generates the spirituality of all faiths. In the many distorted perceptions of the deceptive authority of the Wizard of Oz we may recognize the many faces of religious authorities.

These four metaphors then, as simultaneous manifestations of the Conflict Resolution Process, pertain to four social science disciplines which have been studied separately from each other and are now brought together as the inseparable composites of the unit order. The social sciences are integrated in the one Moral Science.

CRITIQUE OF THE OZ STORY

There is a difference in the way the story dismisses religion as a fraudulent Oz and the Formal Theory's explanation of the concept of god. The Formal Theory regards gods as distortions of the process, but the process is a reality that cannot be dismissed like a fraud. The ultimate authority behind the magician is the science of the process. It has the features of god: it is universal; it commands authority as the moral order which binds parts into meaningful totalities. Thus, the analysis of this set of metaphors rediscovers the benevolence and the ubiquity of the process/god in the science-abiding human unconscious.

The conceptualization of the process as a unit has far-reaching implications for the scientific rethinking and practice of psychology. The process represents the scientific interpretation of metaphors, the relationship of parts in a totality. The

formally interrelated episodes lead to a conflict resolution. The Formal Theory's approach to analysis utilizes the relational method.

The propositional method, the 20th century's rational humanism focused on the content of stories as the total truth

Oz was identified in the story earlier as the projection of the hopes and fears of the four young explorers, a metaphor for God. This reference to Oz as God is defeated as the grand illusion at the end of the story. He is revealed to be an impostor. This implies that God and religions are delusions. Indeed, 20th century scientists dismissed God and religions as misconceptions and mere projections of our own making without any substance. Rational people challenged the irrationality of faith.

The dismissal of the Wizard, methodologically speaking, is a concrete, propositional statement, not a relational one. While Baum grants Oz the role of a god, by dismissing him as a fraud he implies that we can denounce God as a mere illusion. Toto's innocent unveiling of Oz is like demystifying God and reducing him to a benevolent or malevolent figure. God is presented as a monolithic entity.

Religion is not just an illusion, a projection, a public misperception of a higher authority, but the reality of an innate, conflict resolving dialectic. Religions have the substance of conflict resolution and correspond to particular ways of resolving conflict. They are natural science phenomena with clear dimensions, their norms regulating human socialization. The Oz Panels take issue with the concept of redefining God along this relational perspective.

The conclusion that Oz is a fraud and consequently that religions are fabrications of our imaginations was a typical turn-of-the-century perception of religion. Scientists in the 20th century seeking truth were using the propositional method of analysis. They identified the truth in the content of the story or by telling a new story rather than recognizing the formal organization of emotions in all stories. They thus dismissed religions as unscientific, inaccurate and unbelievable stories. Thinkers of those days dismissed religion for its incorrect content like Genesis's account of creation dismissed by Darwin's Theory of Evolution. Science of those days attempted to correct the content of stories with new stories, those of the pseudo-sciences of psychoanalysis, Marxism and evolution as it pertains to religion.

False assumptions

Innocent Toto is the spirit of the times. Scientists of that era were asking irreverent questions about God, social order, physics, race and economics. Scientists were dismissing the sacred truths of the past. The thinkers of the 20th century were rebelling at religion's incorrect information on creation as well as its harmful effect on cross-cultural relations. Genesis's version of creation was questioned and banned from the classroom. Rational humanism, embraced by many thinkers of the beginning of the 20th century, was replacing the irrational content of stories with the new but equally arbitrary semitruths: Freud's Oedipus Complex defined the unconscious; Darwin's Theory of Evolution ended the reign of God; Marx's manifesto attacked the capitalist class; and Einstein's Theory of Relativity ended the Newtonian era.

Science's deceptive assumptions of reality represented the century's methodological mistake, the use of propositional thinking

Rational humanist philosophies of the 20th century were abandoned upon the end of the century as psychoanalysis failed the West and communism failed the East. Christian Europe and Islamic Afghanistan, religions as beliefs in God, defeated communism's rational humanism. Battles based on the content of stories failed to yield the needed moral paradigm. Rational and irrational humanism and religions have alternated between being the moral and political philosophies prevail-

ing in Emerald City. Oz is still reigning supreme inspiring the public with his machinations in the beginning of the 21st century.

The reality upon the beginning of the 21st century is that the world, disenchanted with pseudoscience, is returning to religion. The world interprets moral stories prepositionally, once again embracing the supernatural. East and West are restoring religion to its primacy relying again on stories. The science of moral order, hinging on the formal interpretation of stories, escapes the public's awareness. Reality remains hidden. Calamity has befallen Thebes as the world cannot interpret the riddle of the Sphinx and extricate itself from the concrete nature of moral order.

The alternative to this dichotomy of focus on stories as true or false is to identify the truth about moral order in the formal analysis of stories. The formal interpretation of metaphors respects religions as alternative types of conflict resolution. Religions have evolved as abstractions on the nature of the process. Their problem is that they deify the process and take it away from the science of psychology. Religious constructs are close to science. The Moral Science replaces the vague notions of religions with clear concepts of the Conflict Resolution Process.

What is lost in the dismissal of the Wizard of Oz as a mere fraud is the recognition that religions and gods represent the holistic interpretation of metaphors. The point is that the plot of stories is the bigger picture than the content of stories. 20th century philosophies evolved truisms as ideologies rather than understand analytically the formal structure of the mental process as the universal common denominator in all ideologies. The century missed the transformative conflict resolving process as the core paradigm of all stories surpassing the issue of the truth versus falsity of stories.

Shift of methodologies in the interpretation of metaphors

The riddle of the Sphinx was 'what walks on two, three and four?' Oedipus missed the significance of the interrelation of the three phases of life as parts of a dramatic process that need to be managed. He missed the significance of the equilibrial relationship of the three phases of life and disrespected old age by killing his father. The correct answer to the riddle of the Sphinx and the interpretation of metaphors was not in the Freudian observation of the universality of the Oedipus Complex defining the human unconscious as sexual and violent.

The essence of the dramatic process as described by Aristotle observing the plot of Greek tragedies as a perfect universe is relational. Hubris deserves to be punished, while good behavior gets rewarded. Using the Formal Method, the human unconscious is redefined as the need to resolve conflict and depart from the antagonism to achieve cooperation, to depart from the passivity and choose the mastery, and to depart from alienation to achieve mutual respect. To avert the tragic end of Oedipal relations, the parts of the play and the phases of lifetime must be clarified as formally interrelated episodes of a totality.

The challenge of our times is to recognize the interrelationship of behaviors in dramatic totalities as having a predictable structure and a conflict resolution outcome. The holistic interpretation of the riddle of the Sphinx should address the power issues of Greek domestic relations, the dominant antagonistic pattern of the Greek culture, the arrogance or hubris that inspired Greek tragedies. Oedipus was not the hero for solving the riddle. He was the victim of a misinterpretation of the riddle. He left the riddle unresolved and so did Freud.

The 20th century's thinkers committed the same mistake as Oedipus. They played into the Sphinx's power game. They knocked the Sphinx off its pedestal to attain the prize of incestuously marrying Iocasta, the matriarch of Thebes; they married power rather than the analysis of power play.

This misinterpretation of the riddle inspired the conflicts of the two World Wars and the Holocaust. As a result the 20th century, the era of rational humanism, became the most self-destructive world ever. Disaster befell the world because the thinkers of the century did not use the correct or scientific way of understanding behavior and religion.

The Oz story is relevant because its metaphors exemplify the formal method of interpreting the dramatic process. The world needs to understand the Conflict Resolution Process as universal in all stories and develop an awareness of the unconscious thought process. Humanity needs to recognize and respect the inherent mental and societal faculty of resolution of conflict. It needs to become deliberate in addressing the equitable management of power.

Experimental validation of the Formal Theoretical assumption:
Formal Theory's premise is that the unconscious mind resolves conflict along three formal operations, transforming passivity to activity, antagonism to cooperation and alienation to mutual respect. The Relational Modality Evaluation Scale was constructed to examine the manifestation of these relational choices as four alternative resolutions of conflict submissive and dominance, cooperation and antagonism, as diagnostic categories, the relational modality syndromes, and a fifth, measuring neuroticism, psychic tension as reflective of the third relational operation, alienation to mutual respect.

Dr Karras, professor of statistics in the Department of psychology in Southern Connecticut, examined 100 protocols of the relational assessment. His findings identified the coincidence of the scales with relational modality diagnostic categories confirming the formal theoretical assumption of the three relational distinctions.

CSU   A unit of The Connecticut State University

SOUTHERN CONNECTICUT STATE UNIVERSITY

501 Crescent Street • New Haven, Connecticut 06515

Telephone: 397-4515   November 22, 1985

TO WHOM IT MAY CONCERN:

       I conducted Item Analysis, Reliability, and Validity Studies of the Conflict Analysis Battery which was constructed by Dr. Albert Levis.

       The reliability study of the battery indicates that the different scales have high reliability coefficients to be used in individual diagnosis. The Dominant Cooperative, Dominant Antagonistic, Submissive Cooperative, Submissive Antagonistic, and Psychic Conflict Tension scales have reliability coefficients which range from .88 - .96. The Antagonistic/Cooperative Scale has a reliability coefficient of .79. This is due to the fact that it is the shortest scale. It has only ten items. The different reliability coefficients are much higher than those of the MMPI scales.

       The different validity studies of the battery indicate that the scales have enough evidence of validity for its purpose.

       In addition, factor analysis was conducted on the battery items. The factors which were extradicted highly overlapped the original scales. The results of factor analysis are indicative of the factorial validity of the different battery scales.

       The battery is comparable to the best available personality inventories in construction, reliability and validity. Also, it measures important personality dimensions based on Dr. Levis' Theory of Behavior. By continuing research, the battery will gain prominence in personality assessment.

Yours Truly,

Shawky F. Karas, Ed.D.
Professor & Director of the
Research & Measurement Program

EXHIBIT #3: THE WIZARD OF OZ PANELS

THE INTEGRATION OF SOCIAL SCIENCE DISCIPLINES INTO THE MORAL SCIENCE

The interpretation of four metaphors clarifies the four social sciences:

1. **The Yellow Brick Road as the Epistemology of patterns**

2. **The four characters as Psychology's diagnostic categories**

3. **The killing of the witch as the science of Psychoeducation**

4. **The unveiling of Oz as demystifying Religion and Morality**

THE SANCTUARY OF THE WIZARD

The Sanctuary of the Wizard is divided into four sections, each pertaining to one metaphor from the Wizard of Oz. Each metaphor corresponds to one of the social science disciplines and helps to evolve insights. The Yellow Brick Road is the metaphor of the process. The characters walking the road represent personality types. Killing the witch pertains to personal transformation, assessment, and therapy. Oz corresponds to understanding morality.

Side One: EPISTEMOLOGY
The Unit defines the unconscious as a periodic, measurable, moral order upgrading phenomenon by utilizing scientific constructs. It is the abstract constructs and formulas, the logic, physics and the mathematics of the mental oscillation; hence the Unit bridges the humanities and the sciences. It is the creative process organizing thoughts in myths, dramas, metaphors and art.

Side Two: PSYCHOLOGY
The Unit is the predictability of psychology's relational syndromes as four diagnostic categories of wellness.

Side Three: ASSESSMENT & EDUCATION
It is the art and associations of diagnostic instruments that serve to quantify, qualify, and modify the Conflict Resolution Process of the creator.

Side Four: MORALITY & RELIGION
The Unit is the cultural norms and principles which govern relationships. The Unit is the formulas of conflict resolution; its resolutions correspond to the many evolving religions and images of God.

FORMAL ANALYSIS OF THE WIZARD OF OZ STORY
The four sides of the Sanctuary correspond to the four aspects of the Process:
Epistemology, Psychology, Psycho-education and Morality

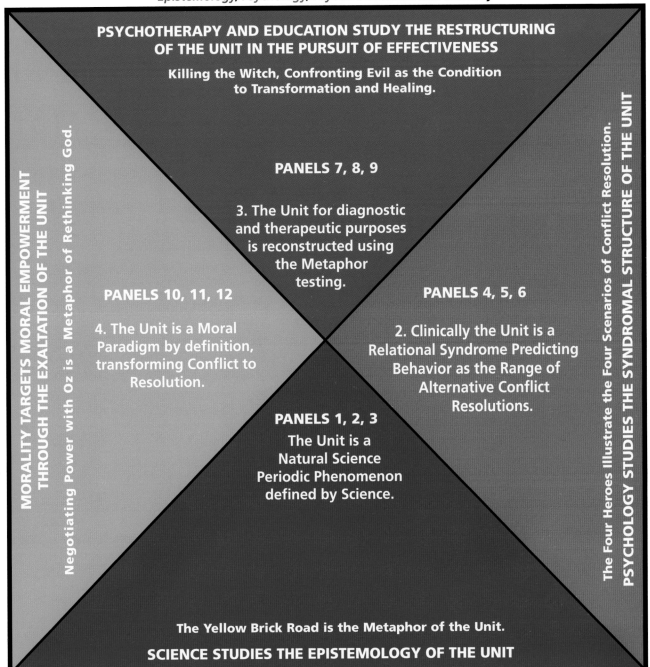

PSYCHOTHERAPY AND EDUCATION STUDY THE RESTRUCTURING OF THE UNIT IN THE PURSUIT OF EFFECTIVENESS

Killing the Witch, Confronting Evil as the Condition to Transformation and Healing.

PANELS 7, 8, 9

3. The Unit for diagnostic and therapeutic purposes is reconstructed using the Metaphor testing.

PANELS 10, 11, 12

4. The Unit is a Moral Paradigm by definition, transforming Conflict to Resolution.

PANELS 4, 5, 6

2. Clinically the Unit is a Relational Syndrome Predicting Behavior as the Range of Alternative Conflict Resolutions.

PANELS 1, 2, 3

The Unit is a Natural Science Periodic Phenomenon defined by Science.

The Yellow Brick Road is the Metaphor of the Unit.

SCIENCE STUDIES THE EPISTEMOLOGY OF THE UNIT

MORALITY TARGETS MORAL EMPOWERMENT THROUGH THE EXALTATION OF THE UNIT

Negotiating Power with Oz is a Metaphor of Rethinking God.

The Four Heroes Illustrate the Four Scenarios of Conflict Resolution.

PSYCHOLOGY STUDIES THE SYNDROMAL STRUCTURE OF THE UNIT

The Unit of the Conflict Resolution Process, a Natural Science Phenomenon as the Secular Paradigm of Moral Order.

In the Wizard of Oz* story, the Yellow Brick Road is a path uniting Dorothy's adventures into a totality with a beginning, a middle and an end. According to the Formal Theory, this path of surprises and adventures is an example of a perfect abstract and predictable system of transformations dictated by the unconscious, redefined as the Unit of the Conflict Resolution Process.

The secrets and the magic of psychology and religion are revealed by understanding this measurable and predictable unconscious mechanism which, like the Wizard of Oz, governs our lives and determines our fortunes. In uncovering this unconscious and universal moral order, the Formal Theory demystifies psychology and morality and makes life less scary and more manageable for Dorothy and mankind.

*THE WIZARD OF OZ
L. Frank Baum
Illustration by H.M. Brock

The stress state above is the first of six interrelated parts of the dramatic totality.

"The poor Scarecrow was left clinging to the pole in the middle of the river"

FROM ART TO SCIENCE, FROM CONTENT TO PROCESS, FROM A DRAMA TO A UNIVERSAL MORAL ORDER, THE FORMAL ANALYSIS OF A MODEL SYMBOLIC SYSTEM.

Science interprets the periodic phenomenon of the Greek creation stories into a 6-role formal transformation process that resolves conflict.

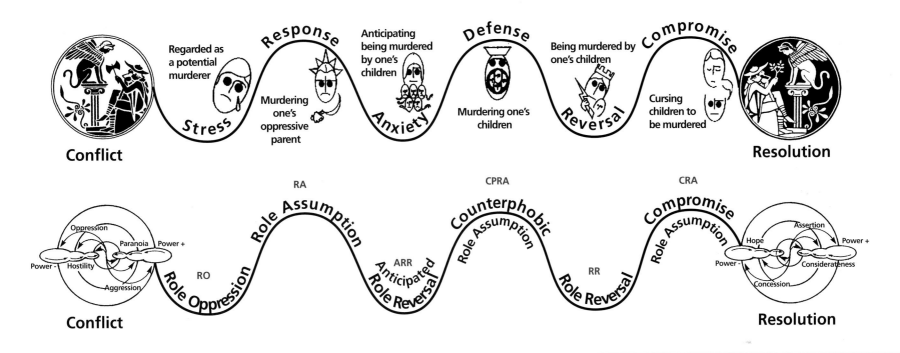

The Sanctuary of the Wizard Elucidates the Four Manifestations of the Unit.

THE UNIT IS A SEQUENCE OF SIX INTERRELATED ROLE-STATES: STRESS, RESPONSE, ANXIETY, DEFENSE, REVERSAL AND COMPROMISE

It is an unconscious stream of associations that predictably transforms chaos to order, and conflict to resolution.
• This six-role sequence is the heartbeat of the mind.
• It is the metaphor underlying all metaphors.
• It is the key that opens the doors to all symbolic universes.

The Sanctuary of The Unit presents the systematic study of the Unit. Each of its four walls addresses one aspect of its manifestation:

Science, Psychology, Education and Morality. Panels on the exterior walls introduce the concepts. Murals on the interior walls illustrate the same with case studies.

• Science Studies the Epistemology of the Unit. Panels 1, 2, 3: The Unit defines the unconscious as a periodic, measurable, moral order upgrading phenomenon, by utilizing scientific constructs. The Unit is the abstract constructs and formulas, the logic, physics and the mathematics of the mental oscillation. Hence the Unit bridges the humanities and the sciences.

• Psychology Studies the Syndromal Structure of the Unit. Panels 4, 5, 6: The Unit is the creative

process organizing thoughts in myths, dramas, metaphors and art. The Unit is the predictability of psychology's relational syndromes.

• Psychotherapy and Education Study the Restructuring of the Unit in the Pursuit of Effectiveness. Panels 7, 8, 9: The Unit is the art and associations of diagnostic instruments that serve to quantify, qualify, and modify the Conflict Resolution Process of the creator.

• Morality Targets Moral Empowerment Through the Exaltation of the Unit. Panels 10, 11, 12: The Unit is the cultural norms and principles governing relationships. The Unit is the many and evolving images of God.

Myths and Religions, Art and Drama, Psychology and Science as Mankind's Quests for Meaning, for the Hidden Moral Order.

Mankind has created myths, religions, philosophies and theories of psychology to make life less scary and unpredictable. Like the Wizard of Oz, these magical forces govern our lives. Originally these forces were attributed to external entities like heroes and gods. Gradually we turned for answers to the examination of internal demons, like Freud's Id struggling with the Ego and the Superego.

The Formal Theory demystifies psychology and morality by redefining the Freudian unconscious as a purely abstract totality – the Conflict Resolution Process. This totality consists of six role-states which are interrelated like the oscillations of the pendulum, in the Simple Harmonic Motion.

The only difference between the unconscious mind and of the pendulum motion is that the mind interrupts this cyclic repetition of events by seeking conflict resolution and rest. Unlike the pendulum going back and forth forever, Dorothy and her friends walk the Yellow Brick Road twice to confront and conquer mankind's fears by transforming conflict to resolution, or in formal terms, by transforming passivity to activity, antagonism to cooperation and alienation to mutual respect.

The Formal Theory translates the dialogue between the characters into an ongoing predictable, personal dialectic.

"You ought to be ashamed of yourself, a big beast like you!"

FROM ART TO SCIENCE, FROM CONTENT TO PROCESS, FROM A DRAMA TO A UNIVERSAL MORAL ORDER, THE FORMAL ANALYSIS OF A MODEL SYMBOLIC SYSTEM.

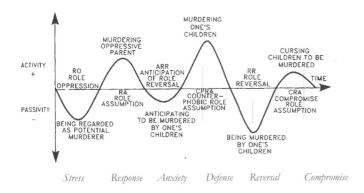

Stress   Response   Anxiety   Defense   Reversal   Compromise

The Formal Theory Portrays the Conflict Resolution Process as a Harmonic, Mental Oscillation

The Greek cosmogony myth, interpreted as a Conflict Resolution Process, has inspired the key theoretical assumptions of the Formal Theory:
1) the formal dialectics of the ideational process;
2) the process as a purely natural science phenomenon;
3) the process as a particular kind of emotional, social structuring of relations, the dominant antagonistic pattern prevalent in the Greek culture.

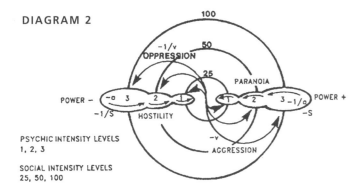

DIAGRAM 2

PSYCHIC INTENSITY LEVELS
1, 2, 3

SOCIAL INTENSITY LEVELS
25, 50, 100

The Formal Theory's Concentric Circles Model: The Power Field is the Cross Section of the Mental Oscillation.

By using the key role relation to describe the three variables, those of norms, behaviors and feelings, any given system's complexity attains the conceptual simplicity of a natural science phenomenon. Psychosocial phenomena then may be analyzed along natural science variables and correlations or formulas.

The Scientific Definitions of the Unit.

THE CONFLICT RESOLUTION PROCESS IS A SIX ROLE-STATE PERIODIC SEQUENCE THAT CONVERTS CONFLICT TO RESOLUTION
Scientifically speaking, this sequence is an abstract entity in which the role-states are interrelated forms. It is also a natural science entity in which the role-states are intertransformable modalities of energy whose sum total is conserved.

ACCORDING TO THE LAWS OF LOGIC the Unit is defined as an equilibrial totality seeking conflict resolution through three formal transformations: reciprocity transforms passivity to activity, opposition transforms antagonism to cooperation and correlation transforms alienation to mutual respect.

ACCORDING TO THE LAWS OF PHYSICS
the unit is a mental oscillation of intertransformable energies which gravitates to stability or negative entropy, defined as the diminution of chaos and the increase of organization or order.

FOLLOWING THE PRINCIPLES OF BIOLOGY
the Unit may be defined as a homeostatic mechanism that unconsciously regulates psychological and sociological experiences by personal attitude and promoting social change. It is pursuing increased personal adaptation and social justice.

GRAPHICALLY, THE UNIT IS AN OSCILLATION PORTRAYABLE AS A SINE CURVE AND AS ITS CROSS-SECTION: THE POWER FIELD
The Power Field is seen as three concentric circles representing levels of tension. The Field's parameters are qualifiable and quantifiable. Two sets of ellipses reciprocally placed at the Power Field represent the psychic system of an individual's Self-Other dynamic or the psychic systems of two interacting individuals in a social transaction portrayed through formally and physically quantifiable vectors representing behaviors and emotions. These vectors also correspond to the role-states of the six-role state sequence.

3

Finally the Quests for Meaning find in the Unit the Science-based Paradigm of Moral Order.

Toto exposed the ominous Oz as a person controlling an interactive audiovisual effects machine. Similarly the Formal Theory demystifies psychology and morality by unveiling the rational organization of mental operations. The Formal Theory unmasks the unconscious as a mental heartbeat identical to the Simple Harmonic Motion (SHM). There is only one difference between the two. The equilibrium of the Conflict Resolution Process is tipped against cyclic repetition by favoring resolution.

With this difference aside, the Formal Theory suggests parity between the moral-mental and the mechanical oscillations. This parity bridges the gap between the humanities and the rigorous sciences and introduces the natural science constructs and formulas into the disciplines of psychology and morality.

Passing the Golden Cap corresponds to the empowerment of an authority figure fulfilling the unconscious need for justice or moral order.

"You must give me the Golden Cap"

THE CONFLICT RESOLUTION PROCESS

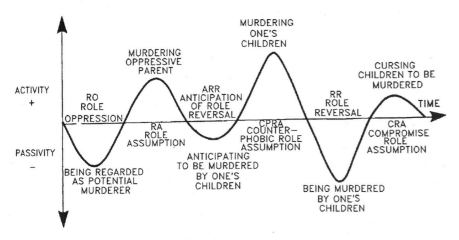

Diagram 1: The Oedipus myth, expanded by the formal analysis of the Greek cosmogony myths, has evolved into a key theoretical challenge for the Formal Theory: (1) It illustrates the formula of the dialectics of Ideational process. (2) It is the model of purely natural science processing of energetic disturbances. (3) The myth illustrates a particular kind of emotional, social structuring of relations, the dominance antagonism pattern prevalant in the Greek culture.

THE MODEL OF THE GREEK CREATION MYTHS

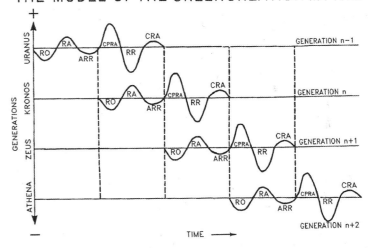

Diagram 2: The pattern repeats itself in 5 consecutive generations of the Greek cosmogonal family. We note that a lifetime sequence starts with the phase of role oppression. Fathers of the prior generation (generation n-1), afraid of being deposed by their children, murdered or oppressed them *(CPRA* generation n-1 coincided with *RO* generation $n)$. When the oppressed children of generation n came of age, they killed their father *(RA* generation n coincided with *RR* generation n-$1)$. When the generation n children became fathers, they anticipated they would be killed by their own children *(ARR* generation $n)$. Because of this fear, they counterphobically oppressed or murdered their children *(CPRA* generation n coincides with *RO* generation n+$1)$. Eventually generation n+1 grew of age and killed their fathers (generation $n)$. The life cycle ended when the generation n parent cursed his or her children to experience the same predicament, that the (generation n+$1)$ in their turn be killed by their children, generation n+2 *(CRA* generation n coinciding with *ARR* generation n+$1)$.

The Scientific Laws Underlying Moral Order were Derived by Equating the Unit, a Social Science Periodic Phenomenon, with the Simple Harmonic Motion and the Equilibrial System of a Scale

Level 1: Formal Analysis

POSTULATE 1: THE PROCESS IS AN EQUILIBRIAL SYSTEM OBEYING THE LAWS OF MATHEMATICAL GROUPS.
The elements of an ideational universe are formally interrelated ideas as determined by the laws of mathematical groups and the logic of relations.

The Laws of Inverse:
Opposite States:
cooperation + antagonism,
cancel each other out:
a+(-a) = 0

Reciprocal States:
activity and passivity,
yield the totality:
a x 1/a = I

The Ten Levels of the Conflict Analysis Profile

Logic: Laws of relational logic
Group theory of mathematics: Law of Inverse:
In every mathematical group, for every element, there is an inverse element, which, combined with the first, yields the identity element
Under the operation of addition, the inverse elements are opposite
a + (-a) = 0

Under the operation of multiplication the inverse elements are reciprocal
a • 1/a = 1

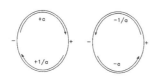

A Natural Science Periodic Phenomenon: The Simple Harmonic Motion (SHM)

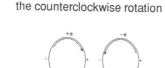

Inverse constructs:
Opposites are the clockwise vs. the counterclockwise rotation

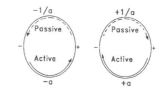

Reciprocals are the two same directional rotations distinguished as the passive and the active alternatives

A Social Science Periodic Phenomenon: The Unit of the Conflict Resolution Process (CRP)

Opposite constructs: cooperative (marked as positive) vs. antagonistic (marked as negative)

Reciprocal constructs: Direction for the scoring of antagonism (-) vs. cooperation (+) passivity (1/S) vs. activity (S)

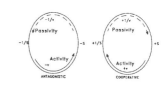

Level 2: Physics of the Process

POSTULATE 2: THE PROCESS IS A NATURAL SCIENCE EQUILIBRIAL PHENOMENON OBEYING THE LAWS OF PHYSICS. The Conflict Resolution Process may be conceptualized with the constructs and formulas of the Simple Harmonic Motion.

The Constructs of Physics:
Displacement: S = Power, Social Status.
Acceleration: a = Motivational Force
Velocity: v = Behaviors,
Mass: m = Emotional Investment
Opposite States: cooperation + antagonism, cancel each other out: a+(-a) = 0

Level 2
Variables
Analysis

Physics
Variables of the SHM

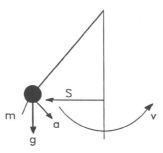

The Simple Harmonic Motion is conceptualized as a function of the following symbolically identified variables:
Displacement= S
Maximum displacement=A (amplitude of the oscillation)
Velocity=v

Acceleration=a

Force= F gravity = g
Mass= m
Energy= E

The 6-role sequence is conceptualized as a function of the following behavioral variables equivalent to physics:
Normative Deviation= Status Differential= S
 (-S status of aggression; -1/S status
 of being a victim of aggression)
Social conduct =v
 (-v murdering
 -1/v being murdered)
Motivational Force= a
 (-a wishing to murder;
 -1/a fear of being murdered)
Dependency Needs=g
Involvement = m
Conflict = Energy = E

POSTULATE 3: THE PROCESS IS AN ENERGETIC PHENOMENON
Conflicts are energetic quantities whose intensity is determined as the product of the subject's dependency needs times this individual's displacement from his/her equilibrial position.

POSTULATE 4: THE ENERGY OF THE PROCESS IS CONSERVED
The oscillation of the Conflict Resolution Process consists of the intertransformation of energetic modalities whose sum total is conserved.

POSTULATE 5: THE PROCESS IS DEFINED AS A FORCE DIRECTLY PROPORTIONAL AND OPPOSITE TO AN EQUILIBRIAL DISTURBANCE
The motivational force (acceleration: a) that a person in conflict experiences is proportional and opposite to the social status shift from the position of rest (displacement: S).

POSTULATE 6: THE PROCESS IS DEFINED AS A PERIODIC PHENOMENON
The Conflict Resolution Process, the six-role dialectic pattern, is the periodic trigonometric function of its three covariant constructs : emotions (a), behavior (v) and displacement (S).

POSTULATE 7: THE PROCESS MAY BE PORTRAYED GRAPHICALLY
The Conflict Resolution Process may be portrayed as a sine curve and its cross-section, the Power Field as a circumference. Ellipses in the Power Field Circle illustrate one individual's set of mental Self-Other representations or a set of interacting individuals in reciprocal relationship to each other orbiting the Power Circle.

Level 3: Energetic Analysis, Conflict is Energy
$E = F \times S$ Conflict is the product of
F = Dependency or Motivational Needs times
S = Social status shift = displacement

Level 4: Transformation of Energies Analysis
Law of Conservation:
$E_{total} = E\ dynamic + E\ kinetic + E\ momentum$
$E_{total} = E_{psychic} + E\ social + E\ Biological$

Level 5: Conflict Analysis
The Force vs. Displacement
Relationship: $a = -1/2\ K \times S$

Level 6: Syndromal Analysis
The Periodic Nature of Behavioral Phenomena
$a = -ac \sin H \bullet v = vc \cos H \bullet s = a \sin H$

Level 7: Graphic Analysis
The Graphic Portrayal of Behavior
The Structural & Longitudinal Drawings

Graphic illustration of trigonometric variables as function of time:

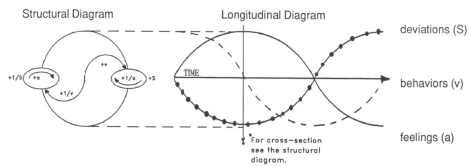

Structural Diagram   Longitudinal Diagram

POSTULATE 8: THE FORMAL VARIATIONS OF THE PROCESS LEAD TO A TAXONOMY OF FOUR SYNDROMAL ALTERNATIVES: From this perspective we distinguish clinically four key alternative relational syndromal modalities.

Social Science Phenomenon

1. Direction of circular velocity cooperation (clockwise) vs. antagonism (counterclockwise)
2. Direction toward pole of dominance or subordinancy.

Level 8: Diagnostic Analysis
Relational Modality Analysis

The Syndromal Organization of Behavior
Dominance vs. Subordinancy
Antagonism vs. Cooperation
Alienation vs. Affiliation

POSTULATE 9: THE ENERGETIC INTENSITY OF THE PROCESS IS MEASURABLE: The *Conflict Analysis Battery* of psychological tests leads to the qualitative and quantitative determination of the individual behavioral variables.

POSTULATE 10 : THE PROCESS MAY BE QUALIFIED BY ITS EFFECTIVENESS: The four Relational Modalities differ among themselves in terms of the interpersonal effectiveness they confer to the individual and the culture.

Level 9: The Quantification of Behavior
Conflict Analysis Battery:
RMES, the Inventory and the set of Metaphor tests

Level 10: The Qualitative Evaluation of Behavior
Efficiency = n = E useful / E total = Effectiveness

The Unit as a Syndrome, a Sequence of Formally Interrelated Exchanges.

In real life the six-role Unit process (Stress, Response, Anxiety, Defense, Reversal and Compromise) becomes a sequence of interrelated events, thoughts, emotions and behaviors that illustrate the personal relational Conflict Resolution Process. Dorothy and her three companions, the Lion, the Tinman and the Scarecrow represent alternative ways of resolving conflict as the choice of relating varies from one character to another.

Animal personalities with their distinct characters serve well to highlight particular patterns of relating. The *Animal Metaphor Test* guides a person to identify his/her relational pattern by drawing two animals and by composing a conversation between them. The person's choice of animals and the ensuing exchanges help to diagnose the person's relational modality. This is illustrated in the animals' identities and their exchanges as an individual's Conflict Resolution Process.

The Formal Unit Process manifests itself as the exchanges of a sample metaphor story.

The formal Unit process manifests itself as the dialectic evolution of associations in a sample metaphor construction exercise. By using the key role relation to describe the three variables, those of norms, behaviors and feelings, any given system's complexity attains the conceptual simplicity of a natural phenomenon. Psychosocial phenomena then may be analyzed along natural science variables and correlations or formulas.

In the *Animal Metaphor Test* the choice of animals and their conversation reveals the relational modality of its author. Animal choices and the animals' exchanges have formal characteristics and natural science dimensions.

CONFLICT ANALYSIS BATTERY
©1984 Albert J. Levis, M.D.
ANIMAL METAPHOR TEST #1 (AMT#1)

Name:_____
Date:_____ Age:_____

This test offers you the opportunity to be imaginative and create a story featuring two animals. To do this, follow these steps:

Step 1: Draw two animal figures in color. *Please use pencil or pen to outline and color in using crayons, pencils, or magic markers.*

Step 2: Fill in the blanks. *Please use a pen.*

ANIMAL #1
Type of animal: Mountain Lion
Age in human years: 48
Animal's sex: Female
Describe the animal's personality by listing 3 or more traits:
Viscious
Calculating
Controlling

ANIMAL #2
Type of animal: Turkey
Age in human years: 34
Animal's sex: Female
Describe the animal's personality by listing 3 or more traits:
Naive
Gullable,
Lost

32

Step 3: The animals are having a conversation. What are they saying to each other? Indicate the sequence referring to the animals by their identity number.

#1 "You will do just what I tell you — as I tell you."
#2 "Okay Lion — I am only a turkey and you can have me by the throat."
#1 "That's right. Glad you know your place."
#2 "Okay. Thank you powerful almighty Lion." "Thanks for letting me live — what else may I do for you?".
#1 "Stay out of my sight also — you annoy me — do nothing to serve my purpose."
#2 "May I fly away?"
#1 "No — that gives you too much freedom, pleasure and sense of self." "Stay around in fear and hide if you must — but be here for me to kick around or I will eat you!"
#2 "Yes great Lioness."

Step 4: What were the animals doing and saying before the conversation just recorded? The Lioness was terrorizing some other animal close by. The turkey was pecking at bugs quietly.

THE *CONFLICT ANALYSIS BATTERY*

The Battery is a theory-based self-assessment instrument consisting of both a relational inventory and a set of standardized projective creativity tasks measuring the Unit Conflict Resolution Process. They diagnose, qualify and quantify the variables of one's syndromal relational modality. It is diagnostic, therapeutic and educational.

The tasks guide a person to create metaphors usually by inventing two characters who then have a conversation. The conversation's exchanges clarify the individual's six-role state sequence, his/her personal Conflict Resolution Process or relational modality. A number of projective tasks allow the reconstruction of the symbolic universe of the test-taker.

THE SYNDROMAL ORGANIZATION OF EMOTIONS

The Unit process organizes associations as well as behaviors and emotions into a predictable six-role Conflict Resolution Process. Thus if an individual felt loved by his father (Stress), he would be prone to love his father (Response), he therefore would anticipate love from his children (Hope = Positive Anxiety), and would be loving to them (Defense), therefore he would be probably loved by his children (Reversal) and he would wish to bless them in return, that they too would enjoy love from their own children (Compromise).

Syndromes vary qualitatively, i.e. (dominance vs subordinary and cooperation vs. antagonism) reflecting a particular personal relational modality, and they vary quantitatively reflecting the intensity of the individual's emotional and sociological state. These attributes of syndromes are measurable and may be assessed by observing one's stream of spontaneous thoughts.

The Syndromally Interrelated Exchanges of the Conflict Resolution Process are the Measuring Rod of the Social Sciences.

EXAMPLE OF FORMAL ANALYSIS OF A SYMBOLIC SYSTEM

The Gorski Retrospective represents an ideal symbolic universe which we have studied consisting of five sequences of formally interrelated canvases.

The four Henry Gorski canvases (seen at right) illustrate with formal transformations of the features of the face how the unconscious evolves from a state of passivity to one of activity (left to right), from a state of antagonism to one of co-operation (from bottom to top) and from a state of alienation to one of mutual respect (diagonally from left to right).

These formal distinctions occur in all samples of creativity connecting images and emotions into the six-part Conflict Resolution Process. This process is experienced clinically as a syndrome and the prevalence of one of these formal choices determines the diagnostic category of the symbolic universe.

The function of the testing is to generate a symbolic system for the test-taker in which we can detect the person's conflict resolution choices.

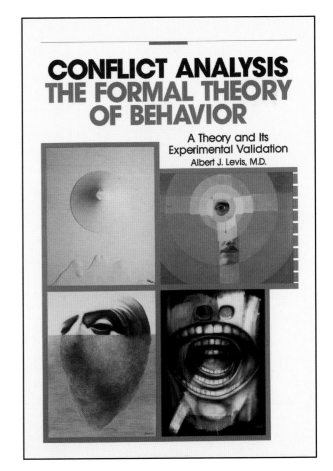

CONFLICT ANALYSIS
THE FORMAL THEORY OF BEHAVIOR

A Theory and Its Experimental Validation
Albert J. Levis, M.D.

5

The Formal Range of Four Relational Modalitie as Alternative Responses to Stress and Related Distortions of Reality.

Individuals differ in the way they resolve conflicts. Their differences may be identified as qualitative distinctions along the two key principles of relating. Accordingly in dealing with stress usually an individual unconsciously chooses to be either passive or active, and either antagonistic or cooperative. His/her relational choice determines a person's expectations or anxieties and subsequent defenses, reversals and compromises.

Dorothy and the Lion illustrate the dominant-cooperative and the dominant-antagonistic modalities, the Scarecrow and the Tinman, the submissive-cooperative and the submissive-antagonistic relational alternatives. The Oz heroes exemplify the four relational syndromes.

Their respective role choices entail different passivity states, hence expectations and distortions. Dorothy who chooses to be a thinker (activity) saw Oz as an enormous head (her passivity or anxiety state). The Lion who threatened others with his roar perceived the Wizard as a fierce fireball. The Scarecrow who was kind perceived Oz as a kind lady. The Tinman who could not love, perceived Oz as a most terrible beast (see Panel #11).

Eventually confronting their passivity or anxiety states, their relational distortions, helped the Oz heroes to overcome their weaknesses, to see reality without distortions, thus to transform their conflicts into true resolutions.

RO:	Role Oppression Stress
RA:	Role Assumption Response
ARR:	Anticipated Role Reversal, Anxiety or Distortions
CPRA:	Counterphobic Role Assumption

SOCIAL SYNDROMES				
	Subordinacy		Dominance	
	Cooperative	Antagonistic	Cooperative	Antagonistic
	RA / RO	RO / RA	RA / ARR	ARR / RA
Diagnosis	Passive Dependent	Passive Aggressive	Active Dependent	Active Aggressive
Transactional Analysis	Child	Adapted Child	Nurturing Parent	Critical Parent
Formal Relating	RO-Accommodating RA-Trusting	RO-Withdrawing RA-Hostile	RA-Demanding CPRA-Nurturing	RA-Controlling ARR-Distrustful
New Situation	Looks forward to	Resigned to	Afraid of	Paranoid in
Degrees of stress:				
Degree 1	Happy Follower	Reluctant Follower	Social Leader Fights for Oppressed	Individualistic Leader Limit-tester
Degree 2	Blames self. Holds negative feelings in. Apologetic.	Blames the leader.	Blames others. Portrays self as victim.	Blames everybody. Denies hurt feelings.
Degree 3	Seeks help	Is tense but helpless	Manipulates Threatens to abandon system	Abandons system

Each Oz hero illustrates a particular type of syndromal relating or modality of resolving conflict.

The Formal Range of Relational Modalities Constitutes the Spectrum of Normal Personality Categories.

THE FORMAL THEORY DISTINGUISHES FOUR PRINCIPLE RELATIONAL MODALITIES ACCORDING TO HOW A PERSON RESOLVES CONFLICTS ALONG THE PRINCIPLES OF RECIPROCITY AND OPPOSITION

Along the principle of reciprocity a person may unconsciously choose to be dominant or submissive, and along the principle of opposition one may choose to be antagonistic or cooperative. The combination of the two relational alternatives leads to four relational modalities or syndromes; the dominant cooperative and the dominant antagonistic, also the submissive cooperative and submissive antagonistic. These modalities may vary along a third relational principle: correlation, according to whether a person chooses to be alienated vs. affiliated or respectful.

Personality differences along the dominance -subordinancy way of relating seem to be genetically determined. The other two qualifying distinctions seem to be determined by one's developmental experiences and cultural values.

Cultural systems, like individual personalities, differ along the syndromal range of formal relational modalities. This is demonstrated by contrasting four culturally distinct variations of dealing with temptation as conveyed by relational variations of the metaphor of the apple of temptation.

Relational modalities as deviations along the resolution sequence may be regarded as incomplete conflict resolutions spontaneously evolving toward increased conflict resolution. This evolutional determinism manifests both in one individual, also in one culture and cross-culturally. It may be detected by observing consecutive samples of creativity as in the four Gorski canvasses on the jacket of the volume: *Conflict Analysis - The Formal Theory of Behavior*, (Panel #4) and as in the four cultural solutions of the "forbidden fruit" as illustrated in Mural #6.

The ways of dealing with temptation differ from culture to culture. Parallel cultural moral paradigms involving the apple metaphor illustrate four relational alternative choices. Mural #6 illustrates how cultural paradigms evolved progressively upgrading interpersonal effectiveness. The Formal Theory's Unit Conflict Resolution Process represents the science-based, malleable paradigm of moral order.

6

Complete Conflict Resolution as a Paramount Objective.

Relational modalities, as attitudes, are modifiable by completing the entire Conflict Resolution Process, that is by outgrowing one's relational limitations through confronting one's fears or anxieties. Pursuit of complete conflict resolution and personal transformation guided the four companions to encounter the Wizard of Oz, who in turn challenged them to kill the Wicked Witch of The West.

To acquire the desired qualities of courage, a heart, a brain and going back home, the companions had to pursue a new six-role journey. Along this journey they transformed the Stress of their needs, to a Response, their new adventure. They overcame their fears, (Anxiety), by taking risks, and thus defeating the Wicked Witch, (Defense). Empowered by this victory, they were able to confront Oz, demystify his identity and reverse roles with him, (Reversal). Oz departed from the Emerald City and the companions succeeded him by assuming his roles of leadership (Compromise). Along this six-role-process our heroes were able to resolve their conflicts by transforming oppression to mastery, antagonism to cooperation and alienation to mutual respect.

Risk taking is the means to overcome one's fears.

"Giving a great spring, he shot through the air'"

Therapy and Psychoeducation as the Deliberate Pursuit of Complete Conflict Resolution.

The Continuum of Psychopathology and Health

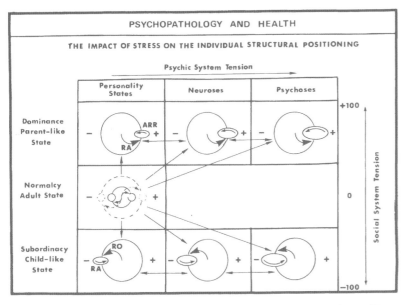

Psychopathology may be viewed in terms of increased conflict along the relational and energetic variables, the dimensions of relational states.

The Evolution of the Patient-Therapist Relationship

DIAGNOSIS	TRANSFERENCE	CONTRACTUAL RESTRUCTURING	RESOLUTION
Active Aggressive / Antagonistic / ARR=Distrust			
Active Dependent / Cooperative / ARR=Demandingness			
Passive Aggressive / Antagonistic / RA=Hostility		THERAPIST: firm assertive supportive	GOALS: Reduction of social and psychic tension, appropriate role reversibility. Increase in cooperation and communication.
Passive Dependent / Cooperative / RA=Resignation		PATIENT: Expected to be cooperative ○=THERAPIST	⬭=PATIENT

This figure presents the evolution of the patient-therapist relationship along the three principles of conflict resolution: moderation, cooperation and mutual respect.

RELATIONAL MODALITIES DIFFER IN THE DEGREE OF INTERPERSONAL EFFECTIVENESS THEY CONFER. Individuals and cultures increase their effectiveness by spontaneously evolving across the spectrum of relational modalities toward increased conflict resolution. Incomplete conflict resolution leads to psychopathology and sociopathology.

By contrast, complete conflict resolution leads to wellness and may be attained by deliberately pursuing the principles of conflict resolution. Cultures reinforce and regulate resolving conflict through their educational, legal, artistic, spiritual and psychotherapeutic institutions.

THE STUDY OF CREATIVITY ATTESTS THAT BOTH INDIVIDUALS AND CULTURES INCREASE THEIR EFFECTIVENESS SPONTANEOUSLY PURSUING THE THREE OBJECTIVES OF CONFLICT RESOLUTION: moderation, cooperation and mutual respect. This moral determinism may be detected at the cultural level by observing the evolution of the world moral paradigms and at the individual level by observing the evolution of an artist's spontaneous creations. This determinism may be easily validated experimentally by monitoring a test-taker's or patient's conflict resolution strategies in the course of one's education or therapy by using the *Conflict Analysis Battery* (See Murals 7–12).

Creativity & Power Management, the Journey of Self-Discovery and Personal Transformation.

The Wizard of Oz story may be seen as a sample of the *Creativity and Power Management* course. This course deliberately taps creativity to capture the personal symbolic system in metaphorical language for diagnostic and therapeutic objectives. The adventures of the heroes in the Oz metaphorland herald what occurs in the Power Management training. The adventures lead first to self-discovery and then to personal transformation.

Like the book of the Wizard, the training creates awareness of the unifying central path, the rollercoaster of the Unit Process. Then it organizes along this path one's experiences and thoughts as a pattern of relating. Next it explores the restructuring of one's relating. Finally the training addresses the rethinking of morality. It departs from the static notions of an external authority figure by promoting awareness of the dynamic intrapsychic principles of conflict resolution.

Power Management differs from the Oz book merely in that it is about one's own symbolic universe and about the abstract redefinition of moral order stemming from one's very own unconscious.

The three days and four nights of reconstruction work is reminiscent of Genesis' six days of creation and the day of rest. This time-frame runs parallel to the 6-role state Conflict Resolution Process leading to the reconstruction of one's symbolic universe.

"The tinsmiths worked for three days and four nights…"

FROM ART TO SCIENCE, FROM CONTENT TO PROCESS, FROM A DRAMA TO A UNIVERSAL MORAL ORDER, THE FORMAL ANALYSIS OF A MODEL SYMBOLIC SYSTEM.

Creativity and Power Management, a Comprehensive and Concise Program of Emotional Education.

CREATIVITY AND POWER MANAGEMENT, THE CONFLICT ANALYSIS TRAINING MODEL

The Battery is a standardized comprehensive emotional education and a brief psychotherapy program that targets insight and wisdom that leads to increased personal and interpersonal effectiveness.

The program addresses three objectives:

• Understanding the Unit for integration of knowledge.

• Understanding the Unit's personal manifestation for self-knowledge.

• Understanding the moral structure of the Unit for personal inspiration and spiritual empowerment.

KNOWLEDGE - The training includes a cognitive or didactic component, a series of lectures targeting understanding the unit of the six-role process intrinsically connecting thoughts, behaviors and emotions, pursuing conflict resolution, that is moral order (see the poster portrayed at right).

SELF-KNOWLEDGE - The training includes a self-assessment, the *Conflict Analysis Battery*, constituting the experiential, insight generating component. Creativity exercises guide the trainee to identify how she resolves conflict. Trainees integrate their metaphors composing a poster reconstructing the Unit's personal manifestation in their symbolic language. They also compose an essay recognizing the conflict resolution principles as moral values guiding their personal style. Power Management toward self-realization and self-improvement.

MORAL GROWTH - The training includes an interactive component targeting moral and social growth. Trainees practice skills of Conflict Resolution consciously targeting the choices of mastery, cooperation and mutual respect.

THE CREATIVE PROCESS IS THE UNIT THAT INTEGRATES ALL KNOWLEDGE

IT IS THE **KEY** THAT UNLOCKS ALL DOORS

Humanities	Emotions Behaviors	Stress Response Anxiety Defense Setback Compromise	stress / response CONFLICT RESOLUTION PROCESS
THE CREATIVE PROCESS INTEGRATES		EMOTIONS AND BEHAVIORS INTO THE	
Science	Forms Numbers Energies	Passivity Activity Antagonism Cooperation Alienation Affiliation Energies Dynamic Kinetic Momentum/Psychic Social Biological	Passivity / activity FORMULAS
THE CREATIVE PROCESS INTEGRATES		FORMS & ENERGIES INTO	
Religion & Politics	Dominant Moral Paradigms	Matriarchy Patriarchy Daughter Power Son Power Father & Son	father / son MODEL OF DOMESTIC JUSTICE
THE CREATIVE PROCESS INTEGRATES		MORAL PARADIGMS INTO THE	
Psychology	Pattern of Relating	Submissive & Dominant Cooperative & Antagonistic Tension	assertion / trust SYNDROMAL CATEGORIES
THE CREATIVE PROCESS INTEGRATES		RELATIONAL MODALITIES INTO	
Personal Creativity	Levis Metaphors Testing	Memories Family Portrait Masks 1&2 Metaphors Dream Short Story	Memories / Mask 1 PERSONAL PATTERN
THE CREATIVE PROCESS INTEGRATES		ALL PERSONAL METAPHORS INTO A	
Psycho Education	Stuctures of Power	Cooperation Moderation Openness Independence Reversibility	moderation / cooperation PRINCIPLES OF EFFECTIVENESS
THE CREATIVE PROCESS INTEGRATES		KNOWLEDGE & SELF KNOWLEDGE INTO	

THE MUSEUM OF THE CREATIVE PROCESS

● Introductory WORKSHOP
● Integration of Knowledge SEMINAR
● Creativity for Self Discovery RETREATS
● Sightseeing with Insight, Tours & Hikes
● Unlocking the Outdoors ● Programs based on
CONFLICT ANALYSIS THE FORMAL THEORY OF BEHAVIOR

The Unit as the Superhighway to Wisdom.

Similarly to the Wizard of Oz story, the Power Management adventure leads to composing and integrating metaphors into two complementary Conflict Resolution Processes. The first leads the author/trainee to find out about oneself and the second to pursue the restructuring of one's metaphors to correct one's relational deficiency by becoming positive in one's outlook and self-esteem. The first sequence is diagnostic and the second therapeutic.

The Diagnostic Sequence proceeds from Stress to Compromise:

1. Stress: Dorothy and friends feel damaged, defective and deprived.

2. Response: Dorothy and friends as four relational alternatives set off on the road of adventure.

3. Anxiety: They share a general fear of authority figures.

4. Defense: The four companions are bonded by surviving several challenges.

5. Reversal: The group is entranced by Oz as a set of individual distortions.

6. Compromise: The companions are determined to pursue their objectives through deliberate risk-taking.

In Panel Six we talked about the second transformation sequence. Upon its conclusion, the four heroes have been transformed from being in conflict, defined as feeling oppressed, antagonistic and alienated to experiencing resolution, defined as feeling mastery, cooperation and mutual respect.

The Soldier with the Green Whiskers is an appropriate symbolization of the trainer utilizing the Conflict Analysis Training workbook guiding his students through the streets of the Emerald City, the integrated images of their own metaphor world.

"The soldier with the green whiskers led them through the streets of the Emerald City"

Self-Knowledge is Achieved by Identifying One's Personal Conflict Resolution Process.

UNLIKE OTHER PSYCHOASSESSMENT INSTRUMENTS, THE *CONFLICT ANALYSIS BATTERY* IS A THEORY-BASED COMPREHENSIVE SELF-ASSESSMENT THAT COMBINES BOTH AN INVENTORY TEST AND A SET OF PROJECTIVE TECHNIQUES.
Both types of testing target the determination of the Unit process as one's relational modality or Conflict Resolution Process. While the inventory determines one's relational modality, the projective tests reveal the symbolic language of the personal drama.

The personal Conflict Resolution Process is recognized, first through microanalysis of each metaphor test as a totality of reciprocal choices reflecting how a person evolves from a conflict to a resolution, second through macroanalysis as the tests of the entire Battery are integrated into reconstructing the personal lifetime Conflict Resolution Process revealing how a person has evolved along a key conflict from childhood to the present.

Accordingly, the personal Conflict Resolution pattern is reconstructed by sequencing the metaphor tests into a conflict resolving dialectic in the context of the six-roles: Stress is depicted in the *Conflictual Memory Test* and the parental Family Balloon Portrait, Response is depicted by the Transparent Mask I and The Marital Family Balloon portrait. Anxiety is depicted in Mask II, and III, Defense by The

Animal and The Fairy Tale Metaphors, Reversal by the second Animal Metaphor and the Dream Metaphor. Compromise is depicted in the Short Story Metaphor.

UNLIKE OTHER PSYCHOASSESSMENTS, THE *CONFLICT ANALYSIS BATTERY* BESIDES BEING DIAGNOSTIC IS THERAPEUTIC AND EDUCATIONAL.
Reconstructing the Unit enlightens the individual by yielding a great number of personal insights and by validating the formal theoretical premise on the nature of the unconscious. The trainee identifies how s/he resolves conflicts and the significance of the conflict resolution objectives. This self study facilitates personal growth both within educational and therapeutic settings.

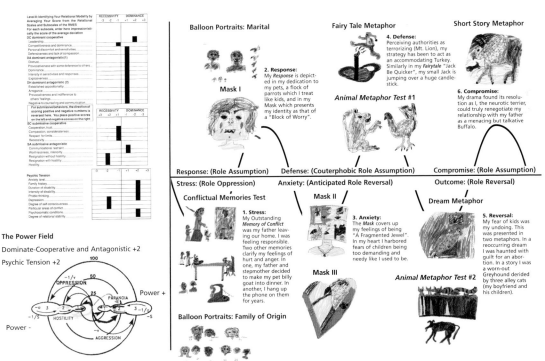

FORMAL ANALYSIS PROFILE

THE METAPHOR PROFILE

The Unit Integrates Knowledge, Self-Knowledge and Clarity of Values.

The second sequence of six roles is the healing or transformational one. It leads to the restructuring of roles with Oz by perceiving him now as a benign and benevolent authority figure. Following the Power Management workbook, the creator of a sequence of metaphors, becomes insightful about his/her pattern, and less intimidated by his/her fears, and thus more capable of coping with reality. S/he feels empowered and becomes responsible for one's life. S/he is enabled to rethink his/her moral dilemmas by evolving a positive attitude, becom-

ing more self-confident, kinder and less prone to be conflicted by blind inner emotional forces and less vulnerable to Oz-like arbitrary self-righteous moral authorities.

Creativity has determined mankind's moral evolution during the history of civilization as epics and religions have redefined moral standards and God. Heroes of cultural paradigms have evolved from cruel judgmental and punitive authorities to ones who are understanding, benevolent and forgiving.

Upon the completion of the voyage the creator of one's metaphors has the courage to introduce oneself as a student of life, comforted at seeing the dreaded wizard as an unmasked and vulnerable trembling human.

"I am Oz, the Great and Terrible,' said the little man, in a trembling voice."

Consolidating Relational Changes by Respectfully Accepting One's Social Roles and Responsibilities.

Power Management starts from knowledge, cognitive information, continues with self-knowledge, attained experientially through the testing, (development of insights and the identification of goals for change) and is finally concluded by clarifying the significance of the three relational principles toward effectively achieving Conflict Resolution.

IDENTIFYING ONE'S UNCONSCIOUS WAY OF RESOLVING CONFLICT, A TRAINEE REALIZES THE IMPERFECTIONS OF ONE'S WAY OF RELATING AND THE IMPLICIT NEED TO IMPROVE ONE'S EFFECTIVENESS.
This is possible simply by deliberately shifting one's relating from polarization to moderation, from antagonism to cooperation, from alienation to mutual respect. Restructuring relationships relieves one of psychopathology.

THE CONSCIOUS AND DELIBERATE PURSUIT OF MORAL ORDER IS REINFORCED BY ADOPTING THE CONFLICT RESOLUTION PRINCIPALS AS SPIRITUAL VALUES AND BY PRACTICING THESE VALUES IN ONE'S DAILY LIFE.
Correct relating reinforced by socialized rituals helps one to feel cared for, then one can care for others: one's family, one's community and peers. The essence of empowerment is active participation in cultural institutions, providing the individual opportunities to enjoy feeling cared for and also to assume leadership in caring for others.

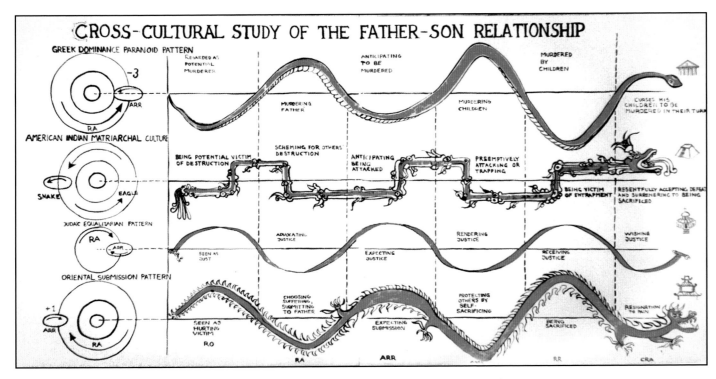

Individuals, like cultures, are characterized by their relational syndromal alternatives. These relational choices, reflected in their moral order paradigms, (see mural #6) determine the acceptable power structure of their authority-subordinate relationship.

Piety as Respect of the Universal Moral Order.

The Oz story represents a typical search for meaning. It is a manifestation of the inner need for conflict resolution which has inspired over the ages the search for God, for a set of inviolable rules and for a rational psychology. It is this inner need for order that drives a person to seek affiliations with communities such as a religion, a nation, a college fraternity and a school of thought. Religions and philosophies have traditionally inspired the public with values; but global consensus on the definition of God, or of a moral system, has been impossible to arrive at. The Oz story is a turn of the century attempt at ghost busting, by metaphorically demystifying and rationalizing moral order. By contrast the Formal Theory advanc-

es the scientific understanding of the unconscious by evolving the relational interpretation of metaphors as stemming from an unconscious need for moral order. This assumption regards the religions of the world as intuitive conflict resolutions that have evolved through a global unconscious search for justice and peace or conflict resolution. Whereas each moral paradigm has finite dimensions, the evolutional sequence that binds them dialectically together is shown to constitute a completely abstract Conflict Resolution Process. This observation shifts mankind from divisive partial truths to science as an awareness of the underlying universal moral order.

Since anticipations are determined by one's relational modality correcting our relational modality can improve our perception of God and inversely a benevolent God can inspire us with an improved attitude

"The Scarecrow saw...a most lovely lady."'

Reconciling Faith and Reason through the Formal Analysis of Yigdal, Maimonides' Thirteen Articles of Faith.

YIGDAL, MAIMONIDES' THIRTEEN ARTICLES OF FAITH

ON THE NATURE OF GOD

1. There is a Creator who alone created and creates all things.

2. He is the One, unique.

3. He has no body, no form.

4. He is eternal.

5. He alone is to be worshipped.

ON PROPHETS

6. The words of the prophets are true.

7. Moses was the greatest prophet.

8. The source of the Torah is Divine.

ON THE CREDIBILITY OF THE SCRIPTURES

9. The Torah is immutable.

10. God knows the deeds and the thoughts of men.

11. God rewards and punishes.

12. The Messiah will come.

13. God forever praised will resurrect the dead.

FORMAL THEORTICAL COMMENTARY ON GOD AS THE UNIT OF THE CONFLICT RESOLUTION PROCESS

1. Religions represent Power Management models, each religion contributing a moral discovery intuitively inspired by the global unconscious need for conflict resolution.

2. Religions have evolved dialectically along the sequence of role transformation contained in the entirety of the Unit Process. Accordingly religions evolved from Matriarchy to Patriarchy, from Daughter Power (Moon Goddess) to Son Power (Sun Gods), from Father and Son Monotheism to Mother and Child Messianism.

3. In its conceptualization of God, mankind has evolved from concrete toward abstract perceptions of moral order,e.g.,from pagan worship to moral philosophies like Buddhism. Now it is possible to define God scientifically as a periodic, predictable, measurable, graphically portrayable Conflict Resolution Process dynamic phenomenon coinciding with the human unconscious. This entity consists of a system of purely abstract formal and energetic transformations.

4. The moral truth is not defined by the content or dogma of religions but by the universal structure underlying all moral paradigms: the Conflict Resolution Process. This structure reflects the formal and natural science properties of the Unit process.

5. The only moral authority to command our loyalty and respect are the totally abstract and universal scientific principles that dictate the nature of the universal moral order. These principles are identified in the definition of the Unit Process.

PROPHETS AS INTUITIVE THINKERS

6. Prophets, artists and scientists alike are guided intuitively by their unconscious need for Conflict Resolution.

7. Moses intuitively recognized the value of the universal Principles of Conflict Resolution as ones that people should deliberately adhere to in order to resolve conflicts.

8. All moral scriptures, literature and creativity reflect the profound unconscious need for moral order.

SCRIPTURAL MORAL DISCOVERIES INTUITIVELY PERCEIVE THE TRUTH

9. There are many sacred scriptures. They represent metaphorical, intuitive attempts to capture the nature of moral order and to present it as the divinely inspired absolute truth. Only science can capture the universal laws of order. The Formal Theory applies the conflict resolution principles to the realms of Behavior and Moral Order.

10. Emotions, behaviors and biological states are organized as syndromal sequences which abide by the laws of science. Hence behaviors and emotions are predictable.

11. The four alternative syndromal ways of relating differ in their effectiveness in resolving conflicts. According to one's handling of power, one may experience happiness or unhappiness, sanity or madness.

12. Only the scientific understanding of the Unit Process can free humanity from prejudice and divisiveness and unite all the cultures of the world through a universal moral order.

13. Science reconciles all moral paradigms into an evolutional continuum of moral discoveries which have contributed to the dialectic development of awareness of the nature of moral order.

Rethinking the Commandments, Rediscovering the Unconscious, Redefining God as the Unit.

Like Toto who drew open the curtain to expose an interactive audiovisual machine, Formal Theory unmasks the Ten Commandments by reinterpreting them as the set of three conflict resolution principles that underlie the human unconscious.

The unveiling of the relational substance of the Commandments represents a major scientific breakthrough in the fields of psychology and morality. While psychology in the past disqualified itself from dealing with metaphysics, the Formal Theory has adopted the Ten Commandments as defining the atomistic Unit of the social sciences. The rational understanding of the unconscious as a moral dynamic makes the science of relations the expert authority in the realms of psychology and of moral order. Religions are rediscovered as the precursors of scientific psychology and as confirming the universality of the transformation principles in the service of improving both the person and mankind.

"Who are you?"

"I am Oz, the Great and Terrible," said the little man in a trembling voice, "but don't strike me-please don't! - and I'll do anything you want me to."

Our friends looked at him in surprise and dismay.

"I though Oz was a great Head," said Dorothy.

"And I thought Oz was a lovely Lady," said the Scarecrow.

"And I thought Oz was a terrible Beast," said the Tin Woodman.

"And I thought he was a Ball of Fire," exclaimed the Lion.

"No; you are all wrong," said the little man, meekly. "I have been making believe."

"Making believe!" he said; "don't speak so loud, or you will be overheard - and I should be ruined. I am supposed to be a Great Wizard."

"And aren't you" she asked.

"Not a bit of it, my dear; I'm just a common man."

Do not strike God out of the total picture. Oz or God is clearly defined as distortions of reality determined by one's anticipations, themselves, a function of one's relational modality. But we need to rediscover God, by redefining him objectively as an abstraction; the Unit does it.

"Don't strike me-please don't!"

Reconciling Psychology and Religion: The Formal Analysis of the Ten Commandments Shows that the Divine Injunctions Coincide with Psychology's Principles of Conflict Resolution.

The Mosaic Commandments as Conflict Resolution Imperatives
1. Thou shalt have no other gods before me.
2. Thou shalt not take the name of the Lord in vain.
3. Thou shalt not make unto thee any graven images.
4. Remember the Sabbath Day and keep it holy.
5. Honor thy father and thy mother.
6. Thou shalt not kill.
7. Thou shalt not commit adultery.
8. Thou shalt not steal.
9. Thou shalt not bear false witness against thy neighbor.
10. Thou shalt not covet.

The Three Conflicts Resolution Principles as Science Based Moral Values

Formal Operation #1
  Reciprocity: Transformation of Passivity to Activity

Formal Operation #2
  Opposition: Transformation of Antagonism to Cooperation

Formal Operation #3
  Correlation: Transformation of Alienation to Affiliation or Mutual Respect

Formal Commentary on The Relational Nature of the Mosaic Commandments

All Commandments guide the process, along reciprocation, as transforming passivity to activity, (Reciprocity: Formal Operation #1).

All Commandments emphasize the importance of cooperative as opposed to antagonistic relating as the principal basis of a just social order. (Opposition: Formal Operation #2).

The first five Commandments address how the individual relates to the community transforming Alienation to Affiliation or Mutual Respect as the paramount condition of one's faith, (Correlation: Formal Operation #3).

Commandment #1 is exacting total commitment.

Commandment #2 is limiting anger and pleading for moderation.

Commandment #3 is seeking total abstractness vs. concreteness or idolatry.

Commandment #4 seeks periodic reinforcement of the principles by experiencing the week as the reconstruction of the dialectic structure of the Unit of the creative process.

Commandment #5 extends the positive attitude of respect and conflict resolution to one's parents.

Commandments #6-10 emphasize moderation in acts of mastery or reciprocity.

Depoliticizing Prayer by Endorsing the Unit as the Secular Moral Paradigm.

Only humans are capable of deliberately reducing mental and interpersonal tension. Through a prayer and meditation, as positive thinking, we can reach the state of complete conflict resolution or peace of mind.

Yet prayer, tainted with political bias, has been banned from American public education. This development has overlooked the healing function of this old institution. The Formal Theory, advancing a secular moral paradigm, rediscovers prayer as the apolitical or universal pursuit of positive thinking, that is of conflict resolution. Now education can reclaim the apolitical prayer to help the student to proceed to the search both of inner peace and of global harmony.

Prayers Maybe Demystified by Redefining God as the Unit.

"Hear my prayer, O Lord, and let my cry come unto thee."

PRAYER IS A PROFOUND INTERNAL DIALOGUE, A SEQUENCE OF BEHAVIORS AND EMOTIONS TRANSPIRING IN THE CONTEMPLATIVE REALM, LEADING TO THE ULTIMATE STATE OF CONFLICT RESOLUTION. ONE HAS A SENSE OF SAFETY BASED ON GENERATING MODERATION, COOPERATION AND A SELF-OTHER MUTUAL ACCEPTANCE. The individual by admitting powerlessness finds mastery, by advocating cooperation and respect finds empowerment. By loving, one feels enabled to become loving and forgiving. Deference to a benevolent God shapes one's positive attitude to all.

Adon Olam, in Hebrew 'Master of the Universe', is a prayer whose empowering value becomes universally acceptable by substituting the controversial, multi-defined concept of God by the scientifically redefined moral Unit phenomenon, the Conflict Resolution Process, also known as the Creative Process.

The Creative Process gives birth to every living thing.
When all was made as the Process ordained,
Then only It was known as the Creator and Master.
When all is ended the Process will reign alone in awesome majesty.
The Process was, is and will be glorious in eternity.
Peerless and unique is the Process, with none at all to be compared.
Beginningless and endless, the Process's vast dominion is not shared.
The Creative Process is our Master, our life's Redeemer, our Refuge in distress,
Our shelter sure, our cup of life, its limitless goodness.
I place our spirit in its care, when we wake as when we sleep.
The Process is with us.
We shall not fear, body and spirit are in its keep.

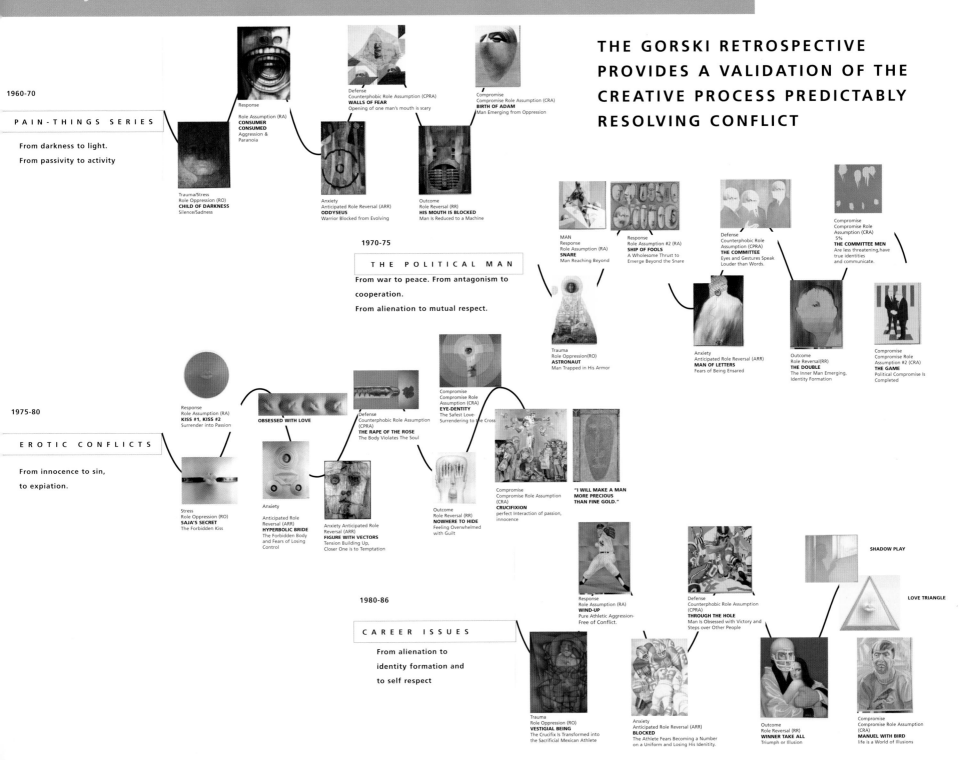

THE GORSKI RETROSPECTIVE
PROVIDES A VALIDATION OF THE
CREATIVE PROCESS PREDICTABLY
RESOLVING CONFLICT

1960-70

PAIN-THINGS SERIES

From darkness to light.

From passivity to activity

Trauma/Stress
Role Oppression (RO)
CHILD OF DARKNESS
Silence/Sadness

Response
Role Assumption (RA)
CONSUMER CONSUMED
Aggression & Paranoia

Anxiety
Anticipated Role Reversal (ARR)
ODDYSEUS
Warrior Blocked from Evolving

Defense
Counterphobic Role Assumption (CPRA)
WALLS OF FEAR
Opening of one man's mouth is scary

Outcome
Role Reversal (RR)
HIS MOUTH IS BLOCKED
Man Is Reduced to a Machine

Compromise
Compromise Role Assumption (CRA)
BIRTH OF ADAM
Man Emerging from Oppression

1970-75

THE POLITICAL MAN

From war to peace. From antagonism to cooperation.

From alienation to mutual respect.

MAN
Response
Role Assumption (RA)
SNARE
Man Reaching Beyond

Response
Role Assumption #2 (RA)
SHIP OF FOOLS
A Wholesome Thrust to Emerge Beyond the Snare

Trauma
Role Oppression(RO)
ASTRONAUT
Man Trapped in His Armor

Defense
Counterphobic Role Assumption (CPRA)
THE COMMITTEE
Eyes and Gestures Speak Louder than Words.

Compromise
Compromise Role Assumption (CRA)
5%
THE COMMITTEE MEN
Are less threatening, have true identities and communicate.

Anxiety
Anticipated Role Reversal (ARR)
MAN OF LETTERS
Fears of Being Ensared

Outcome
Role Reversal(RR)
THE DOUBLE
The Inner Man Emerging, Identity Formation

Compromise
Compromise Role Assumption #2 (CRA)
THE GAME
Political Compromise Is Completed

1975-80

EROTIC CONFLICTS

From innocence to sin, to expiation.

Response
Role Assumption (RA)
KISS #1, KISS #2
Surrender into Passion

Stress
Role Oppression (RO)
SAJA'S SECRET
The Forbidden Kiss

OBSESSED WITH LOVE

Anxiety
Anticipated Role Reversal (ARR)
HYPERBOLIC BRIDE
The Forbidden Body and Fears of Losing Control

Anxiety Anticipated Role Reversal (ARR)
FIGURE WITH VECTORS
Tension Building Up, Closer One is to Temptation

Defense
Counterphobic Role Assumption (CPRA)
THE RAPE OF THE ROSE
The Body Violates The Soul

Compromise
Compromise Role Assumption (CRA)
EYE-DENTITY
The Safest Love- Surrendering to the Cross

Outcome
Role Reversal (RR)
NOWHERE TO HIDE
Feeling Overwhelmed with Guilt

Compromise
Compromise Role Assumption (CRA)
CRUCIFIXION
perfect Interaction of passion, innocence

"I WILL MAKE A MAN MORE PRECIOUS THAN FINE GOLD."

1980-86

CAREER ISSUES

From alienation to identity formation and to self respect

Trauma
Role Oppression (RO)
VESTIGIAL BEING
The Crucifix Is Transformed into the Sacrificial Mexican Athlete

Response
Role Assumption (RA)
WIND-UP
Pure Athletic Aggression- Free of Conflict.

Anxiety
Anticipated Role Reversal (ARR)
BLOCKED
The Athlete Fears Becoming a Number on a Uniform and Losing His Idenitity.

Defense
Counterphobic Role Assumption (CPRA)
THROUGH THE HOLE
Man Is Obsessed with Victory and Steps over Other People

Outcome
Role Reversal (RR)
WINNER TAKE ALL
Triumph or Illusion

Compromise
Compromise Role Assumption (CRA)
MANUEL WITH BIRD
life is a World of Illusions

SHADOW PLAY

LOVE TRIANGLE

CHAPTER TWO: RELIGION

STEALING THE FIRE: RELIGIONS INTEGRATED AS COMPLEMENTARY DISCOVERIES OF THE PROCESS

THE EVOLVING NATURE OF RELIGIONS
Science integrates religions as partial and complementary discoveries of the process
In the first chapter observing three exhibits as samples of creativity we demonstrated the Conflict Resolution Process as a natural science moral order phenomenon. The fire of the Gods is in our possession by identifying moral order not as a metaphysical but as a scientific demystified measurable entity. Now humans may associate moral order with science rather than with religion. Moral order is hence a scientific phenomenon that we can be objective about.

While moral order is a natural science phenomenon, religions are not fairy tales. We view them as metaphorical discoveries of conflict resolution. They are forerunners of the science; they discovered aspects of the natural science phenomenon; they described it with metaphors; deified it, mystified it and worshiped it. Their shortcoming has been that they grasped moral order partially, intuitively/metaphorically, and rigidly.

The scientific understanding of the moral process places science ahead of religion. Science comprehends religions as particular moral orders, as solutions of the abstract, equilibrial calculus of power management. While science is formulas true for any value of their variables, religions are solutions of the formulas for specific relational choices. Science determines that for every action there are six interrelated emotions and

behaviors, the syndromal context of any conflict resolution. So, for every choice there has been a story and a religion which people accept as the total truth. The scientific moral paradigm, the unit of the social sciences, is the measuring rod of religions as conflict resolutions. This analytical capacity of science corresponds to stealing the fire, the moral leadership of the gods.

In the second chapter we show that science, understanding conflict resolution perfectly, integrates the religions of the world as a progression of discoveries on the nature of the unconscious process. Furthermore science now completes the unfinished business of religions. It attains the objective of religions of perfecting the equitable adjustment of all members of the family, the complex but basic social system.

Religions aspired for peace or conflict resolution but never attained it. They evolved models of structuring role relations in the domestic system but never achieved equitable conflict resolution for all domestic partners. Science identifies the characteristics of the optimal structure of relations. It clarifies the perfect moral end as well as determining a formula with multiple solutions. The formula is the calculus of power management. It leads to the ideal moral order for the fairest structure of domestic systems but also accounts for any system as a particular solution of the formula.

The Sculptural Trail establishes continuity between religions as the progression to abstraction
The definition of the unconscious as the unit orderly sequence of emotions allows the formal analysis or interpretation of all religions as measurable metaphors of conflict resolution. We recognize religions as insights in the scientific nature of the six-role state process. The sculptural trail, the fourth art exhibit of the Museum of the Creative Process, retraces the evolution of religions as a progression of quasi-scientific discoveries or insights of increasing abstraction on the

nature of the underlying scientific order of the mental process.

The Sculptural Trail provides the scientific interpretation of religions as formally interrelated resolutions of conflict integrated into the emotional dialectic of the process. The religions represent the progression ending with science as the final abstraction on the nature of the moral order as a process. This progression overcomes the current impasse between alternative paradigms.

This exhibit shows that religions have been pioneers in the scientific search for moral order as justice in the evolving system of domestic relations. It validates the process, reconciles the religions, and completes the discoveries to the point of the scientific abstraction on the nature of moral order.

The sculptural exhibit presents science integrating religions into a continuum of moral discoveries ushering in Moral Science
Science, clarifying perfectly the Unit Process, steals the fire of the gods by understanding religions and psychology as imperfect conflict resolutions. The Sculptural Trail retraces the history of religion by illustrating how the people of the world evolved institutions of conflict resolution. The Trail presents the evolution of religions as alternative ways of resolving conflict permeating all cultural institutions.

We detect these resolutions as partial discoveries of the Conflict Resolution Process as a scientific phenomenon. We detect these partial discoveries in their explanations of the cosmic creation reflecting a model of role relations structuring the family system and characterizing the qualities of divine rulers. The Trail organizes religions as a dialectic continuum of ever-improving domestic relations models but also as deepening insights on the Conflict Resolution Process identified with God.

The Formal Theory promotes that cultures evolved dialectically from one to another as formally interrelated resolutions. Each one contributes a discovery of an aspect of the universal and abstract conflict resolution unconscious. As different and spontaneous as these religions may be, science integrates them as the continuum of the three formal paths to resolve conflict. Three major religions as resolutions evolved along the three principles of conflict resolution by seeking mastery (Greece), cooperation (India) and mutual respect (Judea).

Science then emerges to integrate the religions of the world as the complement of formal alternatives unified dialectically in the abstract process, the comprehensive and over-arching paradigm. Moral Science is then the ultimate and definitive abstraction on the nature of moral order.

While the Gorski Retrospective focused on the formal interrelation between canvases as particular resolutions integrated dialectically into totalities of conflict resolution, the Sculptural Trail studies religions as discovering complementary aspects of the process integrated into improved global moral abstractions and accounts for improved conflict resolutions.

The Gorski canvases were juxtaposed to show the formal transformation generated by the mind of the artist. Now the Sculptural Trail reconstructs the continuity between religions. For instance, the Epics of the Goddess is a cycle of evolving sculptural images of women, reestablishing the natural continuity of the process' three formal transformations. These unite the cultures of the world into a single conflict resolution continuum. Hence both the Retrospective and the Trail demonstrate the manifestation of the three formal operations leading to the completion of the task of conflict resolution.

The exhibits also demonstrate the scientific assumption on the nature of the process as energetic leading to the advancement of order as increments of negative entropy. Unlike what happens to energy in the mechanical inorganic world, in behavior energy is upgraded into negative entropy. Order is translated into the state of fairer resolutions and progress in conceptual abstractions. Creation of order is the objective of morality, technically defined as conflict resolution.

This growth in abstraction and interpersonal effectiveness is manifested in the history of religion as increased clarity on the nature of the unit process coinciding with the improvement of domestic relations and the redefinition of the divine. The Moral Science represents the cumulative wisdom of the growth of religions modeled in the restructuring of domestic relations and the refinement of attributes on the nature of God.

Religions evolved as progress to abstraction. The historical evolution of religions corresponds to incremental awareness of the unifying Conflict Resolution Process as the ultimate "divinity." This moral order was captured in Judaism in its metaphors of monotheism, Genesis, the Ten Commandments, the yearly cycle of festivities and the insights on psychological diagnosis. Judaism is the religion closest to science for the following innovations:

• **Genesis** is a good metaphor of the six-part entity of the Conflict Resolution Process leading to resolution as the state of rest.

• **Monotheism** reflects the recognition of science's single cause-effect principle that we ascribe to the process. Unity is the perfect universe as it abides by the laws of science.

• **The Ten Commandments** spelled out as the voice of God describe the three principles of conflict resolution as injunctions in resolving conflicts in interpersonal relations.

• **The four children of the Haggadah ceremony** of the Jewish Passover/Easter celebrating the Exodus from Egypt identify the four relational syndromal modalities as how four types of children ask information about 'what is special about this night?'

There is compatibility then between science and religion. The difference is that science is abstract and dry in its symbolic language. However, the implications of science are important as its language entails the universality of natural law, whereas religions fragment the world into cultures of revealed law. Thus true believers stay alienated from each other and from the ultimate nature of the moral order and how it should affect interpersonal relations.

The language of science – constructs and formulas from the realms of logic, math and physics – introduce objectivity and expand the applications of moral order to new insights on the nature of psychology, epistemology, assessment and moral values.

The Trail unites the many goddesses and gods as the anthropomorphized ascriptions of insights on the process. Gods reflect the dialectic and dramatic evolution of insights on the nature of the moral process. The Trail unites these sanctified magical divinities as complementary phases of spirituality evolving toward the scientific abstraction of the entire process. At the same time, upon the end of moral discoveries attributed to religion, the Trail presents science as clarifying the process, taking us beyond where religions have brought humanity to the unifying spirituality of the physics of the harmonic.

Science not only integrates religions, it also contributes the Harmonic as the integrative denominator of religions and psychology. With its clear insights on the process as the scientific unconscious, science addresses the current impasse of religious conflicts. All religions identify the nature of moral order. This is the reason for the allusion of science 'stealing the fire of the gods.' Science, as more abstract and universal, is more credible than religions.

History of the Sculptural Trail

The idea of the Sculptural Trail started in 1982 as a family project enacting the history of the Bible conceived of as a trail of ten stations. This project was meant to educate my daughter, Tajlei, upon her bat mitzvah. The stations were initially marked with signs placed on flimsy posts. A good friend, artist Karl Tremper, painted the signs and I planted them around our home's back yard. The stations of the trail in the history of the Bible were dramatized with musical skits, a sort of minstrel show.

The exercise of a journey through history was the inspiration for the Sculptural Trail at the Wilburton Inn. The study of Biblical history expanded to retrace the history and future of religions. The first segment of the Trail identifies the quest for meaning examining a paradigm shift from the content of stories to the plot of stories. The middle segment reviews the history of religions as a continuum from matriarchy to patriarchy, from pagan religions to monotheism. The third segment celebrates the new moral paradigm as monuments to the process and educational technology targeting emotional and moral literacy.

Upon its completion the Trail retraces the history of religion beginning with the scientific discoveries of the process, continued with the conceptual discoveries of the many religions of the world integrated into the cycles of matriarchy and the cycle of patriarchy, and ending with the discoveries of the two key concepts of the Moral Science: the process, its six part structure and the moral direction of the three formal operations.

The design of the Sculptural Trail

With the gestalt or template of the plot of stories in mind inspired by my studies of the Greek Creation myths, I started installing sculptures on the grounds of the Inn. I fondly remember one flatbed delivery that brought three major art pieces from a sculptural studio in Connecticut; this was my educational "luggage" for the fledgling cultural center.

One of the sculptures delivered that day was an exact copy of an Easter Island head; this would eventually become the Sad Wizard standing in front of the Sanctuary to be erected behind it. There were also two heavy excavating scoops which would eventually represent the beginning of the path and reflect the most intense family conflicts as the Sun and the Moon of the Aztec culture; according to the Aztec myths a brother, the Sun, is protecting mother Earth from his sister, the Moon. He is dismembering her every day upon sunrise. The third sculpture on the flat bed was the massive white cubes erected on the hill which eventually became the metaphor of the worship of the story, as the Bride and the Groom. The bride is referring to the love of the Bible as the word of God. The bride is the Book worshiped by the Groom as the People of the Book. This sculpture eventually became one of the monuments on the cycle of the Scriptures of the One God.

I placed the three stations as far apart from each other as I could on diametrically opposed locations across the estate with the help of an excavator and a long crane. These three stations became the reference points on the grounds of the inn for a tapestry I wove with stations of meaning over the next 22 years of owning the inn.

Art capturing the structure of the unconscious process the trail evolved to consist of six cycles of sculptures. Each cycle is a story helping to understand the importance of the plot of stories as the new moral paradigm. The Sculptural Trail evolved gradually as a work of art. The science and intuition on the process guided me as the artist-scientist from the original concept of the template of conflict resolution to reconstruct the anthropology of religion. The mid-section of the Trail uses the process to bind the many cultures into two units of resolution: the cycle of Matriarchy and the cycle of Patriarchy.

The formal integration of disparate cultures represents a validation of the Formal Theory. The Trail integrates the religions of the world into the affirmation of a new world moral order.

The significance of establishing this fact is enormous. It has many practical applications; it recognizes continuity of all cultures as scientific discoveries of the process, thus reconciling the different world views but also introducing the need for change in the norms of orthodox cultures. The discovery of the process as the science of religion is important for the moderation of extremist fundamentalist movements. The new concept is of paramount significance not only in reconciling religions but also in its multiple applications in the fields of psychology and education.

The Trail does justice to science and religion as the progression of knowledge on the nature of the human mind. The cycles of the Trail have grown slowly, establishing continuity between fragments of truth, similar to the tedious work of reconstructing a broken vase and restoring it to its original beauty. The sculptures reconstruct the world drama following the template of the Universal Harmonic process and integrate religions into a set of scientific formulas.

The Sculptural Trail is the path to abstraction on moral paradigms; it presents the history of paradigm shifts leading from the stories to the plot of stories; the process is celebrated as the overarching moral order, the scientific moral paradigm; the trail makes us conscious of the orderly unconscious.

The Sculptural Trail exhibit graphically presents the difference between religions as stories and the process as the universal plot of stories. We see the difference between stories, the individual philosophies, and the plot of stories as the process, the abstract dramatic totality. We realize the outstanding type of resolution, one needed as concession or compromise. It is a resolution for civil rights. It has been won politically by minorities, and has been recognized in contemporary society but has not been accepted by religious traditions as these are unable to evolve, frozen upon dated moral paradigms and norms. The major impasse in religions' determination of norms is conflict resolution in the area of gender parity; the Trail explains the lack of resolution in gender relations as hinging on the lack of mutual respect between the genders. The Trail makes history as science is accounting for this impasse and addressing the resolution of this conflict that has handicapped the Abrahamic religions. Science identifies a sociological problem as a formal, relational, conceptual one that has a clear solution. Science introduces the missing formal operation, mutual respect between the genders, as the means to correct the current injustice. Mutual respect completes the norm of gender parity and conflict resolution in family relations.

The Trail integrates all religions, the forerunners of science, leading to the confirmation of the scientific process. It meaningfully reconciles the religions of the world clarifying the abstract definition of the process as the ecumenical moral paradigm; the process is validated as the flexible calculus of power management. Science 'steals the fire of the Gods' meaningfully integrating the diversity of religions. Science's process is the integrative abstract paradigm.

THE TRAIL AS A THREE-ACT DRAMA

The sculptures of the Trail are arranged in six cycles corresponding to the three acts of a drama. Each act consists of two cycles illustrating the interrelated passivity and activity states. Each act of the sculptural drama begins with a gate; we have three gates marking the phases of the sculptural drama. The Trail, as a drama, becomes more meaningful by referring to the Promethean struggle with the gods. The first gate, science, clarifies the orderly nature of the process as 'the fire of the gods'; the second gate pertains to the integration of religions by science as 'stealing the fire of the gods', and the third gate corresponds to the resolution, education, clarifying emotional and moral education as 'giving the fire to the mortals.'

GATE 1: SCIENCE
"The fire of the gods" as the science of the Conflict Resolution Process

The first gate is about the scientific understanding of the creative process. The importance of science is conveyed by the shift of focus from the diversity of contents of stories to the universal plot of stories as an innate adaptive scientific mechanism.

CYCLE ONE: The shift from stories to the plot of stories, from dogma to reason.

The trail begins with an Easter Island Head shedding a tear of blood; the head is the wizard, the author of all stories of the world; he is expressing the stress experienced by today's world: 'How come after all  my stories the world is not living happily ever after?' Next to him stands a scale, representing science which responds to the Wizard: 'Do not despair the secrets to happiness are in all stories, but instead of believing the stories as the total truth consider what is universal in all stories, the plot of stories.' This dialogue between art and science, between the wizard and the scale, introduces the shift of paradigms and clarifies the plot as the scientific paradigm, which will provide meaningful answers to the wizard in pain.

CYCLE TWO: Science identifies the secrets to "happily ever after"

The answers, the scientific paradigm, are presented in the next cycle of the trail, a fairy tale, the sculptural story of a lady and three dragons.

It progresses to 'happily ever after' as the sculptures of 'the kiss' and 'the embrace.' Happily ever after corresponds to the scientific secrets of conflict resolution, the three transformative operations of the conflict resolution process: mastery, cooperation and mutual respect.

This triple transformation clarifies the scientific nature underlying all dramatic stories; it is the plot of stories, the Promethean fire. This is the unit process; it integrates the many stories and establishes the universality of the moral authority of science. The formal interrelation of conflict and resolution are made obvious by contrasting the initial and final segments of the story as a conflict resolution. We then detect the three formal operations turning passivity to activity, antagonism to cooperation and alienation to mutual respect. These are the secrets to living happily ever after.

Walking the Trail, we encounter the progression toward enlightenment. First we come to understand the plot of stories, the human unconscious as the creative process, the conflict resolution mechanism as the origin of all moral thought. It is both a moral entity and a scientific phenomenon.

GATE 2: RELIGION
"Stealing the fire of the gods" as science understanding the conflict resolution process

The second gate, act two, on religion, refers to Prometheus stealing the fire of the Gods; it consists of two cycles, the Epics of the Goddess and the Scriptures of the One God, a dramatic evolution finding its completion with the help of science. This is the most important segment of the trail as it presents the history of religions as a dialectic sequence of partial and complementary discoveries of conflict resolution integrated into a meaningful dramatic continuum. Each sculptural station introduces the discovery of a norm or covenant which restructures family relations and also redefines the external moral authorities regulating the sanctified covenants/norms.

The story of religions begins with a cycle integrating the pagan religions as sculptures of the epics of the goddesses. It is completed with a second cycle integrating the scriptures of the One God. This cycle is completed by the reconciliation of the process and the story, represented by the Labyrinth, a scientific structure providing the drama's resolution, mutual respect between the genders.

The second act, the gate of religions, begins with matriarchy: men are victims, and continues with patriarchy, men are the challengers, and is completed with new insights from science. Matriarchy, the first segment, is about the epics of the Goddess. The sculptures are a circle of the heroines of the epics, the goddesses. These illustrate the evolving images of women retracing the epics as gender wars resolved by social contracts and covenants progressively restructuring domestic roles, rethinking societal norms, and redefining women and gods.

These covenants improved the family institution and redefined the divine as an increasingly abstract external monitoring authority. Science integrates the pagan religions as partial but complementary discoveries of the process. Each religion discovered a formal operation as the complementary path to resolution. The epics represent a continuum of resolutions which rethink norms, regulate domestic relations, and transform the role of women from that of the wild mother of the jungle, as matriarchy, into the domesticated monogamous, loyal, self-sacrificing, spouse of patriarchy.

The cycle is completed with Judaism and the spiritual triumph of the father-son covenant, the alliance of men overcoming the power of the mother, the goddess, by adopting monotheism. This alliance of men neutralized the power of women, protecting them from seduction. The cycle of the scriptures of the One God evolved as the struggle between the father-son covenant challenged by a new posturing of women, the mother-child alliance.

The rule of the father-son discriminating against women was undermined by the messianic rebellions symbolized in the mother-child alliance of Christianity and Islam's Crescent and the Star. The Messianic religions represent the highlight of the drama of domestic role relations of the Abrahamic religions.

It is the task of science to intervene and interpret dogma in the context of historical developments and offer the solution in the context of the scientific moral imperative. To achieve resolutions one must abide by the three formal operations. Religions have failed to find a unifying moral order. This occurs in the fourth cycle of this Sculptural Trail. Science, in this drama, steals the fire, by reconciling the traditions discovering the resolution of domestic conflicts by introducing mutual respect between the genders. Science, in this trail, provides information and solves the conflicts of the Abrahamic religions. Science's contribution, mutual respect between the genders, is the condition for all partners in a system to arrive at conflict resolution. Science completes this drama, still unresolved in our times, through the shift of paradigms from the stories we believe to the universal plot of stories.

The second segment/act is about science stealing the fire of the gods by understanding religions as alternative ways to resolve conflict. Two cycles integrate the religions into a continuum of conflict-resolving discoveries. Science continues beyond where religions have taken us and proceeds beyond their wisdom to resolve their conflicts by integrating them into the Moral Science.

We retrace the history of religion as conflict resolutions that are, with the help of science, integrated and reconciled as the cumulative insights into the scientific nature of the process. Goddesses and gods evolved throughout the history of religion and developed and sanctified new patterns of relating. These addressed the many conflicts in domestic relations and promoted the establishment of ever more equitable family institutions.

CYCLE THREE: Matriarchy as the *Epics Of The Goddess*, the "Taming Of The Shrew"

This third cycle is about the Matriarchy challenged by men as reported in the Epics of the Goddess.

2. RESPONSE Greece: *The Iliad* and *The Odyssey*	4. DEFENSE Japan: Tao and Zen	6. COMPROMISE Israel: The Scriptures Monotheism
The Sphinx and Penelope	*The Dragon & The Geisha*	*Virgin Mary Broken Joy, Sarah, Hagar*
1. STRESS Mexico: Codicil Tablets and the Aztec Calendar	3. ANXIETY India: Upanishads and Buddhism	5. REVERSAL Mesopotamia: Gilgamesh Epic
The Sun and the Moon, The Aztec Figurines	*The Waxing and Waning Moon, Siva and the Inner Child*	*Ishtar, the Seductress of Babylon*

The epics of the goddess represent gender wars leading to the transformation of the role and the portrayal of women. Each culture advanced an alternative mode of how to resolve conflicts by pursuing the principles of one key formal operation: mastery in Greece, cooperation in India and mutual respect in Israel.

CYCLE FOUR: From Patriarchy through the Scriptures of the One God to the Moral Science

The fourth cycle is about Patriarchy challenged by Matriarchy leading to the conflicts between the Scriptures of the One God.

2. RESPONSE *The Abrahamic Family's Covenant*	4. DEFENSE *Bride and Groom as the Father-Son relationship*	6. COMPROMISE *The Labyrinth: Paradigm shift as mutual respect between men and women*

1. STRESS *Bar Mitzvah Sarah's Concession*	3. ANXIETY *Exodus from Egypt, Moses' Ten Commandments*	5. REVERSAL *Virtual Jerusalem, Messianic religions as Women's rebellion*

This cycle is about Judaism's abstract conceptualization of the process. Nevertheless it still fails to satisfy one of the requirements of conflict resolution: mutual respect between men and women. The cycle presents the father-son alliance and how this was challenged by Messianic religions' mother-child alliance. This reflects the gender conflicts in Judaism as intensified by the Greco-Roman influence during the Hellenistic times. These parent-child alliances remain unresolved in our times.

The huge Biblical sculptures present the hubris of this drama as the discrepancy between men and women. The three patriarchs tower over four matriarchs and two concubines. This sculpture, celebrating the father-son covenant, represents an injustice, the over-correction of the power of matriarchy through the oppression of women.

The Bride and the Groom intensifies this conflict as the bride is not a woman, it is the Scriptures illustrating that women have been replaced by the word of God.

The installation of *Virtual Jerusalem* represents the reversal in the fortunes of patriarchy. At this point women are rebelling and asking for equal rights, claiming that God is with the mother and child and not with the father and son.

Science resolves this drama by shifting paradigms from the many stories in conflict to the universal plot of stories which require compliance with the three formal operations, including the rule of mutual respect. This conflict is presented sculpturally with the final installation contrasting the metaphors of the content of stories versus that of the plot of stories. In *How To Be A Bird,* three sets of birds represent the content of stories as three different ways to resolve conflict. In *The Labyrinth: Finding Out What Kind Of Bird One Truly Is* represents the plot of stories. This sculpture also introduces the concept of mutual respect with the story of Theseus and Ariadne. Ariadne gives Theseus a thread so he can navigate the labyrinth, kill the Minotaur, the monster child of Matriarchy, and find his way out again.

Science completes the abstract understanding of the moral process. It shifts the focus from arbitrary father-son/mother-child covenants to an understanding of the Conflict Resolution Process. It also identifies the need for mutual respect between domestic partners to achieve resolution of conflicts within the family system.

Science shifts from many stories/Scriptures to the universal Conflict Resolution Process, entailing mutual respect established in the father-son covenant now expanded to the relation between men and women. This paradigm reconciles men and women and cancels the need for revelation, dogma and metaphysics. This development corresponds to science stealing the fire of the gods and assuming moral leadership.

GATE 3: EDUCATION/HEALING
"Giving the fire to the mortals" by advancing moral and emotional literacy

The end of the Trail presents how science reduces the diversity and complexity of religions by promoting the heuristic effectiveness and deductive elegance of the process. Religions evolved in the course of the history of civilization as complementary discoveries of the natural science Conflict Resolution Process. The process now, the universal plot of stories, the scientific answer to the divisiveness of the many messages of the sacred stories, defines the new moral order.

The third segment/act of the Trail celebrates the validation of the scientific paradigm with monuments to the process illustrating the features of the structure and the moral function of the unit process. It consists of two cycles of modern art, two installations, one celebrating the new moral paradigm and another its utilization as creativity for self-discovery, self-knowledge and self-help.

The third segment/act is about education, giving the fire or wisdom of the Conflict Resolution Process to the mortals. We are now able to convey the knowledge in the classroom about the scientific process which reconciles morality, psychology and science to achieve the elusive goals of education:

integration of knowledge, self-knowledge and clarity of moral values.

This third set of cycles presents science as triumphant and as relevant to social and educational reform. Giving the fire of the gods to the mortals is the power of science to implement and enforce change by understanding that all moral order stems from the formal mental operations. Science empowers the public.

The Trail celebrates the discovery of the process with two cycles pertaining to the relevance of the new paradigm for education.

CYCLE FIVE: The cognitive segment; moral literacy as reconciling science and religion

The fifth cycle recognizes the importance of the process. Two monuments celebrate the new moral order as the unit of the social sciences. Another monument celebrates the principles of the unconscious that automatically transforms conflict to resolution.

Redefining Genesis as the helix	*Demystifying the Ten Commandments as the three formal operations, moral values*
 *The Teleion Holon Genesis* as the parts of the process and Sabbath the day of rest or resolution 	Reciprocity transforming passivity to activity Negation transforming antagonism to cooperation Correlation transforming alienation to mutual respect 

This cycle is also about abstract art celebrating the scientific concepts and principles of conflict resolution. The choice of biblical titles for these monuments, *Genesis* and *The Ten Commandments*, offers continuity between science and religion and pays tribute to the traditional biblical discoveries. *Genesis* represents the Teleion Holon, the holistic examination of the process. A second set of sculptures represents the three mandatory, unconscious, equilibrial principles of conflict resolution, and identifies them as *The Ten Commandments*.

CYCLE SIX: The Experiential Segment: Emotional literacy reconciles psychology and science

The sixth cycle targets emotional literacy. It consists of four sculptures which were created with the help of the metaphor generation exercises. The four sculptures on the pediment of the Sanctuary present examples of creativity used for self-discovery and personal transformation.

This final cycle presents the *Animal Metaphor Test* used for self-discovery. The sculptures, suspended on the pediment of the Sanctuary, are metaphors executed by a trainee seeking marital counseling. They reflect his journey to conflict resolution in three stages.

Adam's Temptation, a Case Study

Pecker pecked: The metaphor represents the hero's activity – having an affair – as a beak pecking; and his passivity state – feeling attacked by his wife – as a fish bone being pecked.

Tug-of-war between the characters of the drama: the hero at center with his mistress on left and his wife on right, with two sets of beaks, one pecking on him and the other talking to the lawyers, the wise goat.

Internalization of the conflict and wondering which side is up: the hero's conscience pinching his shirt and the fish bone becoming dollar signs.

Resolution as the way of the clown: the hero left his wife, felt content with his mistress and reconciled with the world.

Emotional and moral literacy become attainable goals for the education of the public through this program. Art and science united can make the public conscious of the moral unconscious and help people evolve personal insights on how to manage power.

The model promotes the modification of relations into equitable systems and practices. Science, recognizing moral order as an orderly innate process, can alleviate the fears of religious people in departing from the comfort of religions to explore the broader moral paradigm. Moral Science does not preach agnosticism or atheism; rather it promotes a new Gnosticism and the clear definition of God as the conflict resolution moral order that stems from the human unconscious as a physiological response to stress. Science reverses the frightening moral vacuum of Darwinian materialism as it applies to human relations.

The process as the over-arching order is manifested in many aspects of the sculptural trail

The six-role state process is validated as the meaningful dialectic integration of parts in a dialectic relation with each other into the over-arching moral totality. This dialectic process manifests at multiple levels of the sculptural trail uniting religions, as sculptural stations:

• First, the sculptural trail consists of six cycles of sculptures.
• Second, the epics of the Goddess are stations in the six-role state dialectic connection to each other.
• Third, the Sculptural Trail is another installation that may be seen as a dramatic totality.

At all these levels of the Trail, religions, as discoveries of resolutions, are integrated as the six dialectically connected role states or emotions into the unit dramatic process. This exercise of integration retraces the evolution of religions and makes each one more meaningful as related to the other religions and to the scientific process. The progression reveals what is changing and what is outstanding in the current state of the art in the world of religions.

The Trail, by retracing history, clarifies that religions have evolved as adaptive sociological models first by resolving interpersonal relational conflicts restructuring family relations and second by redefining the moral authorities. Divinities have functioned as role models of religious norms and as monitors of the evolving norms.

The human drama: from the epics through the scriptures, and on to the Moral Science

The family institution evolved with men gradually limiting the sexual freedom of matriarchal women, while defending this freedom for themselves. *The Iliad* and *The Odyssey* are epic battles of the genders, demonstrating how patriarchy assumed power over promiscuous Helen of Troy and also other matriarchs like Circe, Calypso and Nausica seeking power over Odysseus and his crew.

India, in the Upanishads, and later Buddhism discovered cooperation, restrain of desire on the part of men, as the means to reduce inner and social conflicts.

Judaism contributed the Father-Son covenant's mutual respect between father and son, with the exclusion of women from positions of power, in the place of the Grecian Oedipal father-son antagonism and men's dependence on women. This restructuring of the father son mother relationship was possible as Abraham was able to reassure Sarah and the women of Judea to trust fathers. This trust entailed the reduction of the negative influence of the mother over her sons against the father.

The improvement of family relations in the Judaic family coincided with the redefinition of the moral authority. In Judaism, God is an abstract authority. The oneness of God is identifiable with the process. God is left unnamed and defined as the process, 'what was, is and will be.' The six-day phenomenon of Genesis, meaning creation in Greek, parallels creativity's six-part Conflict Resolution Process. Resolution is celebrated as the Sabbath, the day of rest.

While mutual respect was introduced by Judaism it was applied as a principle in the father-son relationship only. The gender relations conflict remained unresolved. Female sexuality, identified with pagan religions, remained dangerous and

God was called upon to protect men from temptation, succumbing to female seduction. However, in spite of all warnings the kings of Jerusalem, David and Solomon did succumb to temptation. King David erred in falling in love with Bathseba. Solomon discovered love of women in his relationship with Sheba.

A sculpture highlights the triumph and the downfall of the Abrahamic religions

The inception of the drama of the scriptures is highlighted in one massive installation by Judith Brown. This installation stood in 1984 at the Lincoln Center in New York City. It consists of three eighteen foot tall golden Pharaohs, four diminutive women and two Horus birds as the bookends of the installation. I identify this sculpture with the Abrahamic family. The three tall Pharaoh figures are the patriarchs, Abraham, Isaac and Jacob sitting on thrones; the four little women standing in front of them holding libations represent the four matriarchs serving the masters. The two stout birds, the Horuses, represent the nameless concubines, the other women with beaks to peck on the wives.

I see this as a political sculpture addressing the strengths as well as the deficiencies of the Abrahamic moral paradigm directly responsible for the unresolved conflicts of our times: our culturally divergent ways of dealing with women. This sculptural station celebrates a milestone in the history of civilization; the significance of the Judaic moral contribution, the discovery of the father-son covenant, introducing for first time mutual respect in the historically antagonistic father-son relationship; the sculpture also accurately portrays the change of the man-woman relationship. We have here an asymmetrical relationship both in numbers, six women versus three men, as well as size, men are eighteen feet tall while the women are less than four feet tall.

The discrepancy reflects first a change of the attitude of women, who instead of undermining the father-son relationship, trust the fathers with their sons. They are able to accommodate that relationship and step down from their powerful matriarchal and traditionally antagonistic controlling disposition. But this stepping down dramatizes the dangerous predicament of the Judaic women. In it we observe the disparity between men and women as the limitations of this moral paradigm. This sculpture explains the contributions and the moral failures of Judaism.

We may conclude that the mutuality and parity between father and son introduced monotheism, coinciding with the cooperation of womanhood; it eliminated the parity of the twelve Olympian gods and goddesses of democratically-minded Greece. Thus faith in God diminished women's power in the family system. The struggle between the genders is discretely manifested in the Abrahamic family as mothers promoted their favorite sons and undermined the paternal authority. For example, Sarah's defense of Isaac over Ishmael, Rebecca's promotion of Jacob over Esau, Rachel's favoring Joseph over his eleven siblings, etc..

In *The Iliad* the Greek men contained Helen's, and by extension all women's, sexual freedom or promiscuity but did not change their antagonistic attitude. The Judaic culture reconciled father and son by transforming the antagonistic relation between men and women through gaining the trust of mothers. Women remained aggressive but motivated not by lust and selfish power but by the desire to bear children in the service of God. The concession of power to God, and to men, eventually became the basis for oppressing women. This gender oppression motivated women under the pagan Greco-Roman influence to rebel against the Judaic discrimination of women by promoting the mother-child alliance of the Messianic religions. This alliance initially offset the misogynistic, oppressive father-son covenant.

The Messianic movements meant to protect oppressed women. This dialectic is illustrated

with another sculptural installation, *The Virtual Jerusalem,* in which the women on the ramparts of Jerusalem rebel and claim 'girls are as good as boys' while another sculpture of a virgin and child states 'God is not with the father and the son but with the mother and the child.'

The problematic Judaic and Messianic man-woman relationship is resolved through science shifting paradigms from the ever-changing content of stories to the universal plot of stories and the discovery of the importance of mutual respect as the condition for complete or perfect conflict resolution. Sculpturally this is conveyed by the installation of *The Labyrinth*, which illustrates the plot of stories, having a beginning, middle and end, versus three sets of birds illustrating 'how to be a bird' as the divergent values of the content of the scriptural injunctions. This installation contrasts the universal plot of stories versus the divergent content of stories. It clarifies the advantages of science and provides a uniform and objective message.

Science is triumphant over religions in this final installation showing the difference between the content and the plot of stories. Science, the plot, the underlying scientific order, reconciles the three contradictory messages as three complementary but incomplete moral solutions. This illustrates how the content of stories provides alternative injunctions which confuse the public: Islam=submit, Israel= wrestle with God, Christos= be good. This installation presents the unresolved conflicts of our times which inspire the solution: the reconciliation of people by shifting to the scientific paradigm. In this paradigm the moral values coincide with the formal conflict resolving principles.

Covenants as resolutions or compromises establishing norms

The two sculptural cycles, about pagan and then monotheistic religions, present the dialectical evolution of resolving the conflicts of the family

as the key civilization-creating institution. The dialectic induces mutuality between the partners of the family system, mother, father and children.

The pagan goddesses of Matriarchy promoted polygamy and polytheism. The scriptures of the One God changed that norm. Judaism promoted the father-son covenant, regulating women's role and sexuality, while tolerating polygamy for men, norms sanctified by a powerful idealized male god, the God of monotheism. The Messianic religions countered the father-son covenant with the new norm, the mother-child alliance, initially tolerating women's sexual rights but then these religions became more oppressive to women's rights than Judaism. The Messianic norms favored two alternative ways of dealing with women and gender rights: Christian sexual abstinence versus Islamic monogamy for women and polygamy for men.

The Trail completes the drama of the scriptures with science providing the answer to reconciling the three Abrahamic resolutions. Science contributes the missing element toward achieving the primary task of religions, peace on earth. The missing element is the new norm of mutual respect between the genders and parity in sexual behaviors. Science integrates all members of the family into the egalitarian, mutually respectful association of individuals independent of gender and age.

Mutual respect between genders and generations as partners is the missing formal operation necessary to achieve the state of conflict resolution, the coveted state of shalom/peace. This moral order is not revealed by external metaphysical authorities. It is identified in the analysis of the creative unconscious as the natural science moral order entity, the ultimate moral authority completing the elusive task of religions.

The process is validated by reconciling the religions as a continuum of resolutions. They foster interpersonal justice, protected by the sacredness of the scientific integrity of the homeostatic, natural science moral mechanism. The new moral order respects creativity as a spiritual practice, which demystifies psychology and religion and deals with the unconscious conflict resolution as the personal and societal adjustment mechanism. Science identifies the process as the individual adjustment mechanism and puts an end to the quest for the meaning of life. Morality is driven by the inner need for social justice; it is pursued automatically by the innate physiological response to stress.

Review

The Sculptural Trail exhibit, as the analysis of metaphors, eliminates the divide between faith and reason. The new science-based insights on moral order introduce reason and objectivity into the study of morality. Religions are respected for pioneering insights and sanctifying them as aspects of the natural science phenomenon ahead of the social sciences. Religions are criticized here for mystifying this process, promoting faith over reason and causing confusion in the world by advancing alternative norms and alternative stories and gods as the total truth.

FORMAL THEOLOGY
On norms and Gods

The Formal Theory identifies the abstract Conflict Resolution Process, moral order, by studying the formal organization of emotions in the structure of ideas in any story. The rediscovery of the process in samples of creativity validates the Formal Theory into the Moral Science. Research confirms the unconscious as a universal, conflict-resolving, natural science moral order phenomenon. The formal conceptualization introduces scientific respectability to the study of religions and spirituality. The Moral Science redefines norms as power management distinctions and god as the universal formal operations which guide us to resolutions as social and emotional harmony; norms and gods are natural science phenomena defined and quantified as resolutions of the universal formulas.

All creativity and all religions may be interpreted as metaphors of conflict resolution; metaphors are measurable entities. Cultural metaphors determine the structure of the domestic partnership as a type of resolution dictated by the culture's norms and the characteristics of the respective divine authority. By interpreting norms and the descriptions of the divine in cultural metaphors as conflict resolutions we may look critically at the contributions of particular religions in capturing aspects of the abstract process.

Reviewing the range of norms and deities we may note that the Judaic religion contributed immensely in the area of conceptualization of the moral order. Yet we must acknowledge that Judaism is just a stage in the quest for scientific wisdom. Its pitfalls are the conceptual limitations in understanding the process beyond its metaphorical definitions as Genesis, its worship as the one God, and his Ten Commandments, etc.. The world has evolved and it therefore needs the evolution of religions beyond metaphors to the precise deductive abstractions of the formulas of science.

Norms consist in making distinctions in symbolic systems, the right and wrong polarities; the unconscious Conflict Resolution Process helps individuals adjust to these distinctions. It organizes emotions and shapes associations on the way to the normative rest state. Norms qualify and quantify cultural systems and religions. These may be portrayed graphically as the interrelated six role-states of the dialectic entity, each with its distinct relational dimensions.

Religions, ahead of psychology in understanding conflict resolution, have made us conscious of the unconscious need to resolve conflicts. But religions have deified and mystified norms and deities as the definitive moral authorities generating psychopathology and socio-pathology. They have generated psychic and cross-cultural conflicts. It is to be expected that as dogma-based rigid institutions they will also resist change and fight insights into the scientific clarity of emotions, norms and divinities. They resisted scientific insights into astronomy and they are bound to resist insights into their non-scientific moral paradigms.

Normative rigidity, the problem of our religions

Religions having discovered aspects of moral order have monopolized them as sacred and everlasting. They have sanctified partial conflict resolution choices as metaphysically determined through revelation, as the absolute and definitive insights into the universal order. Thus they have been trapped in their visions, unable to deal with change and progress to abstraction. They face the problem of having advanced the absolute and being unable to retract their tightly held views of reality. Hence they are deprived of the capacity to evolve and adapt to change. Their symbolic distinctions become the culture's closed reality system of dated norms and anthropomorphized divinities. Identifying norms rigidly, they themselves cannot tamper with them. Religions are prisoners of the past and their appeal is the power of an idealized symbolic universe.

Norms of the interpersonal relations and the attributes of god may be contrasted to the scientific CRP as the standard to judge specific religions' contributions to humanity and their deviation from current secular conflict resolution norms. The challenge for thinkers is identifying the merits of the formal conceptualization. The public may evolve beyond the religions and their stalemates. Some may recognize this evolution in the transformation of cultural metaphors and allow the possibility that their personal paradigms may evolve to the secular scientific norms and abstract spirituality.

We have witnessed transformation in the archaic

Aztec metaphor of the eagle devouring a snake, which symbolizes the overwhelming inequity between extremely polarized partners. This tension has been resolved by local cultural developments. The snake at the mercy of the eagle, his powerful partner, a metaphor illustrating the Aztec cultural conflict, shows the powerless, passive, antagonistic and alienated state of the citizen of this culture. This state of conflict was resolved as Quetzalcoatl, the feathered serpent, reflecting the symbolic merging of the two opposite identities into one, the bird and the snake as the dragon with wings.

More improvements in the relational asymmetry of the Aztec metaphor occurred with the influence of another culture. The matriarchal Goddess, Quatlique, an eagle-like monster threatening the extinction of the world, could only be appeased with live human sacrifice. Under the Christian influence she was transformed into the mother of God as the Virgin of Guadeloupe. The cult of the matriarchal goddess upstaged the Judeo-Christian child God. These symbolic evolutions reflecting cultural rethinking of relations gives us hope that the anthropomorphic god figures may be transformed into the abstraction of the unit, the rigorous universal Conflict Resolution Process.

Conflict Resolution, science, does not cancel moral order. It redefines it and allows its evolution. New, kinder religions have supplanted archaic cruel ones. Religions evolved as a sequence of complementary conflict resolutions, as partial discoveries of the unconscious process; this progression to abstraction is completed by science as the discovery of the transformational unconscious adaptive mechanism.

The evolving images of god
The formal analysis allows the appreciation of cultural features in the context of the scientific definition of cultural solutions. The spontaneous restructurings of conflict resolution are manifested in cultural stories as the progression of relations between members of the family system. It is also duplicated in other relational systems such as the relation of a hero and his rivals in stories, athletic games, the relation between cosmic entities like mother earth and father sky, the sun and the moon. Moral order in the era of moral reason will be determined not as empirical accomplishments that are questionable and subjective but as the optimal, the fairest formal restructurings of relations.

The cultural distinctions may then be contrasted as variations of the unit process, the science-determined state of conflict resolution, the abstract concept of moral order. Awareness of the scientific nature of the unit order transforms behavior into the orderly realm of the Moral Science, the Science of Conflict Resolution, and reduces religions to discoveries of measurable alternative entities.

Metaphors of the divine evolved by defining moral order as the supernatural anthropomorphic entities located in inaccessible places. The formal analysis voids all theism. It dismisses Creationism and refutes the need for the concept of God. Gods are merely projections of the intra-psychic need for powerful external regulatory entities.

The father-son covenant and Monotheism is a shift of paradigms and norms which restructure the Oedipal, Grecian norm of father-son antagonism and the polytheistic view of the supernatural. The Abrahamic norm/metaphor resolves the father-son conflict and redefines God as the definitive moral paradigm, whereas it is not. It is only a partial solution and as we mentioned earlier it is an unjust and immoral conflict resolution given the contemporary norms of gender relations. Judea established mutual respect between fathers and sons but not between men and women. It left unresolved gender relations perpetuating an inequity. Abraham deprived women from equal status. All political power and rights were granted to men. This resolution precluded mutual respect necessary for complete conflict resolution in the system of family relations. The Messianic religions addressed this inequity, yet they too were unable to sustain the momentum of the emancipation of women. This has happened in the West finally during the 20th century.

Judaism deserves praise but also awareness as discovering partial aspects of the universal order and promoting them as the definitive set of truths. We may praise Judaism for introducing the Abrahamic model of domestic relations but also reproach it as responsible for the oppression of women and the eventual advent of the Messianic religions as a reaction to how Judaic norms treated women. The unresolved issues of the Abrahamic family relations underlie the world's current political and theistic conflicts.

We may thank Judaism for monotheism, identifying single cause-effect reasoning, for the metaphor of Genesis as insights on the conflict resolution creative process, for the Ten Commandments as insights on the three conflict-resolving formal operations, for the identification of the four children asking what is special about the Passover night as the metaphor of the four syndromal ways of resolving conflict, but we may not praise Judaism for being afraid and defensive of women and for discriminating them as inferior to men.

Cultures invented gods to sanctify normative conflict resolutions, structuring gender/domestic relations, thus freezing progress. Science now restructures relations and rethinks the moral authority identified with the universal laws of the well-informed conflict-resolving unconscious. Science, like Prometheus, prevails and steals the fire of meaning from the idealized gods of cruel, divisive and unjust resolutions.

The political relevance of the Moral Science
Thus the Sculptural Trail evolved from the Bible

Walk to encompass a dramatic continuity of science's struggle with religion. Science has prevailed by demystifying religion while clarifying spirituality as the path to conflict resolution. Science gives the skills of enlightenment to the mortals by reforming education, psychology and religion.

The Trail guides us successively through these three phases of the Promethean path. The scientific information on moral order is drawing its insights through analysis of the creative process or the plot of stories, whereas religions have advanced their insights through revelation, the modification of the content of stories. Change is needed now as religions are at war again with each other in our very sophisticated modern times. Science helps usher in change by guiding humanity beyond the multiplicity of stories to understand the universal process as the physiological adjustment to change.

This process is made obvious by simply observing the plot of stories. Now understanding moral reason is the scientific prerequisite to resolving the religious conflicts of our times. Science goes beyond religions in dealing with the integration of knowledge.

In walking the Trail, we come to appreciate that the thought process is a natural science, physiological, psychological and moral order phenomenon. It is the human adaptive response to stress, the unconscious faculty that has helped humanity gradually deal with loss and pain, make changes and grow. This fathomable and universal process is the abstract unit of the social sciences; it is manifested in the arts and it is our resource for coping with spiritual matters.

Creativity is the predictable, formal interrelation of emotions into dramatic totalities of conflict resolution. It is the mind's automatic response to stress. The process serves two tasks:
1) The unconscious resolves conflict as a physi-

ological adjustment with personal compliance;
2) It contributes to social normative changes.

Moral Science

The mid-section of the Trail, Gate 2, retraces the history of religion as the evolution of discoveries of how to resolve conflicts within the family institution. Monuments along the Epics of the Goddess and the Scriptures of the One God present the milestones of these moral discoveries progressing from the matriarchal times through the patriarchal era and now finally addressed by the Moral Science.

The Sculptural Trail presents variations of the moral harmonic as a series of stories to become gradually aware of the exact nature of the plot of stories as the unconscious, motivational mechanism. The six cycles of the trail represent the six role state dramatic process. The path is experienced as a drama commanding its resolution. The six role process is particularly clear in the cycle of the Epics of the Goddess in which each sculpture of a goddess reflects the moral discovery of a culture transforming the role and image of women. Here six cultures, each presented by the emotional statement of a story and a sculpture illustrate the ongoing transformative CRP.

The sculptures as discoveries of conflict resolutions reflect that religions ahead of psychology studied this process and evolved insights in the essence of moral order as the key variable in human behavior. The Moral Science shifts awareness to the common denominator of all stories as the plot of stories, an abstraction summed up in the harmonic of the six role-state process.

The second chapter of this book is an exercise in the validation of the Formal Theory. We see the science of the process integrating religions as complementary discoveries into the total entity of the unit process. By predicting and demonstrating the validity of its predictions the Moral Science improves the current understanding of moral order

and religion. It demystifies religions as particular solutions to the formula. Science promotes respect for religions which can now be integrated into an irrefutable abstraction on the unit process as the essence of human psychology.

Religion as an art form

While respecting religions we must remember that religions are metaphors not formulas and that they suffer limitations in conceptualizing moral matters fairly. Even the Judaic discoveries became frozen in dogma written in stone as a story told by God and not as the formal understanding of the process. Moral Science studying the creative process as the harmonic entity of the plot of stories captures the nature of moral order better than religions.

Inversely, religions are stories while science is merely the plot of stories, the abstractions about what is universal in all stories. The Moral Science studying the plot of stories evolves new insights on the nature of moral order but loses some of the poetry and humanism of human interaction. Science detects the formulas of conflict resolution, true for all values of its variables, but religions present dramatic stories which deify alternative ways of resolving conflicts. Science integrates them in the fairness of a formula, but gods, the anthropomorphic metaphors of the Conflict Resolution Process are inspirational.

Religions made considerable progress in capturing the process as an abstract universal order. We mentioned earlier about Monotheism, Genesis and the four children of the Haggadah. For instance the Ten Commandments captured the injunction directing people to avoid and to resolve conflicts. The ritual of Yom Kippur, the Day of Atonement is about admitting transgressions and fasting in order to expiate for such conduct. This ritual holy day emphasizes the myriad ways of transgressing and the many ways of repenting and denouncing abnormative or unacceptable conduct. This annual religious tradition is pure science but also poetry and ritual targeting conflict resolution. Religious rituals and holy days reinforce knowledge and fine tune skills in managing power in order that the person averts the experience of extreme conflict.

Science is now able to understand the discoveries of religions as partial insights on the process, as historical contributions in exalting moral order as the virtues of conflict resolution but science integrates and surpasses these insights. Also, science completes the unfinished quest of religions to understand the nature of moral order abstractly. Science discovers the process as formulas and demystifies religions thus clarifying conflict resolution as an equilibrial phenomenon restoring inner peace.

Social changes
Science steals the fire of the Gods by understanding religions as natural science phenomena abiding by the laws of science and by integrating them as a continuum of complementary discoveries of the universal process. So science unites the religions as the many solutions of the one formula that defines justice as an equilibrial process.

Science is about espousing consciously and deliberately the values of moderation, cooperation and mutual respect stemming from the unconscious described by the analysis of the thought process as it manifests in all samples of creativity. Religions are about morality exalted, as revealed by the voice of god, a supernatural entity. Both science and religion have their role in the marketplace of moral education.

The Conflict Resolution Process commands now the moral imperative rather than any one divinely sponsored role model. But gods have the charisma of heroes. They represent the partial knowledge of the process but the wholesome effectiveness of exaltation of values that cannot be generated by science alone. The Moral Science rediscovers religion by clarifying moral order as founded on the universal laws sacred because

they are based on natural law. Science worships formulas, but also understands the arts as the spirituality of metaphorical presentations.

Reconciling science and religion
Concluding this section we review our impressions. The new theory establishes several equivalences between religion and science and cautions people about the limitations of the traditional religious thinking though it respects religions as art forms.
• Science translates God into the unity of the Conflict Resolution Process
• Science understands Genesis as the structure of the dialectic of the thought process and the Ten Commandments as the three relational principles guiding the unconscious mind to conflict resolution.
• Science establishes spirituality as the respect of the creative process by interpreting metaphors correctly as the universality of the conflict resolution process.
• Science integrates religions as the evolution of insights on how to resolve conflicts in the family institution and determines the evolution of domestic role relations to strengthen the family institution.
• Religions progressed by evolving norms regulating the sexual freedom of women and have shifted worship from the promiscuous Goddesses to the one male God identified in the Father Son covenant avoiding temptation.

Religions, limited by their foundation on revelation, have not been able to evolve and to resolve domestic conflicts as the world advanced civil rights. Dogma makes religions mutually incompatible cultural world views and in conflict with current civil rights laws.

The Moral Science introduces new clarity in the field of moral order and suggests the needed changes that religions and cultural institutions must make to resolve their conflicts and advance their wisdom from dogma to respect for natural moral law. This is the condition required so that we achieve moral consensus across cultures.

Thus science steals the fire of the gods by placing the humanities on the firm rational foundation. Science understands religions, integrates them, clarifies their differences and reconciles them with morality and psychology. The Moral Science solves the current conflicts of the Abrahamic religions identifying the importance of mutual respect between partners as the condition to resolve conflict. It is this underlying variable that has escaped the Abrahamic religions and has led to unfairness, inequity between genders leading to the oppression and the subsequent rebellion of women.

Moral development has centered on the role of women in the family system
The key conflict of cultures has been the development of the family institution, resolving conflicts in the partnership of men and women in sustaining a relationship able to resolve conflicts between many individuals, husband and wife, parents and children, men and women at large in society.

The Epics of the goddess is about the domestication of women, the gradual reduction of women's sexual freedoms. In Greece, sexual Helen of Troy evolved into asexual Penelope in the Odyssey. In the orient Indian Goddess Kali evolved into China's shrinking liberties culminating into Japan's compliant Geisha culture. In Middle East promiscuous Ishtar of the Gilgamesh epic evolved into the subordinated partners of Sara, Esther, Ruth and Naomi, and the asexual Virgin Mary (Mitchell, 2004). The cycle of gender wars led to an over-correction on the power of women depriving them of equal civil rights with men. The partnership of father and son in prayers to the almighty was established at the expense of women's rights. The Abrahamic family allowed polygamy for men but dictated chastity for women.

Patriarchy's scriptures of one God define the role of women as inferior to that of men. This inequity is unfair and source of conflicts that have been resolved in alternative ways in each Abrahamic culture. The oppression of women led to the rebellion of women under the Greco roman influence as the mother child covenant of the Messianic religions challenging the father-son patriarchal covenant. Moral Science intervenes here to diagnose the inequity in the Abrahamic religions mired in conflict and to address its correction.

If the religions truly wish to establish justice in the world they must address the unfinished business of the Abrahamic family. Science rectifies this inequity guiding the conflicted Abrahamic religions as the inherited drama between men and women to its equitable resolution introducing the formal operation missing in the Abrahamic religions, mutual respect in the woman man, father mother relationship.

The trail presents the importance of recognizing the origin of religions as the quest for peace in the family relations retracing its history from the times of Matriarchy when women did not have to account to a husband. The trail retraces the journey of humankind through many religions as philosophies of relations restructuring family relations. We notice how in this journey women have lost out in rights. The trail makes us aware of the need to evolve beyond the Abrahamic covenant discovering the scientific nature of the Conflict Resolution Process and the demystification of morality.

Science suggests morality's ultimate correction:
• First, a shift in paradigms from the study of revelation to the study of the plot of stories and natural law.
• And second, a shift from the inequitable to the equitable treatment of women.

Introducing science into religion addresses the inequity in the Abrahamic family while placing on scientific foundation the metaphorical notions of

God, Genesis, and the Ten Commandments.

God is redefined as the process. God is a word encompassing the wisdom of the natural order of the Conflict Resolution Process. The unit concept, all its constructs and formulas, account for all religions. The formula of moral order integrates the religions but also the social sciences meaningfully into enlightenment.

The single most important cultural change needed for peace in the world is recognizing women's civil rights as equals in all aspects of our society. It is not ethical to treat women as an inferior cast and as responsible for sinfulness or as the guardians of virtue. The secret to happiness is in proper handling of power for both genders and in all relations. Power management is equally important for men and women. Ethics and virtues may be measured in how individuals and cultures handle power.

The Trail ends with the recognition of the importance of the principle of mutual respect and pays tribute to the assertive modality in resolving conflicts. It also recognizes respect for the process as the universal mental moral mechanism eliciting the same emotion for the process as we have been experiencing for God.

The trail presents the continuity of respect as piety initiated by religions founded on revelation but continuing in the phase of scientific knowledge pursuing the quest for harmony facilitated by recent findings. We may increase our abstractions and universality of reason without loosing the general awe that religions have inspired as faith. Redefining God scientifically as formulas governing our thoughts should not diminish but should increase the sense of piety inspired by the all knowing authority that has indeed created the symbolic and the cosmic universe as an orderly system. The new knowledge confirms the sacredness of creation and of the creative process.

The Trail's cycles of stories clarify the journey of humankind discovering the simplest language to address managing power as the secrets to happiness. The new knowledge increases the sense of respect for moral order as the drama of implicit retribution motivates a person to be thoughtful in one's heart and in one's mind. The new awareness increases our understanding of the formidable moral imperative shaping our destiny.

The presentation unfolds like a real drama, addressing the problems of our times as the struggle between stories we believe in versus the science of the process as the plot of stories. Science yields enlightenment on values as well as useful personal insights and skills on how to resolve conflicts.

The Trail's task, retracing the world's journey through many moral paradigms, is imparting awareness of the nature of love relations by making us conscious of the unconscious as a conflict resolution process. This process integrates the religions of the world and clarifies the relevance of this discovery for the public's emotional education as the condition for finding personal happiness and peace in the world.

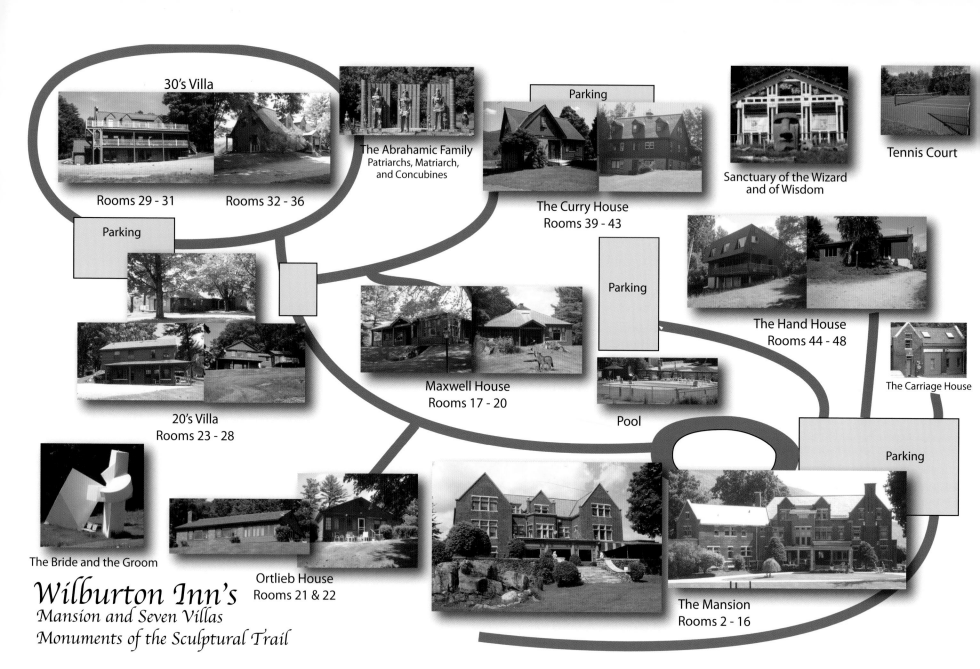

30's Villa

Rooms 29 - 31   Rooms 32 - 36

Parking

The Abrahamic Family
Patriarchs, Matriarch,
and Concubines

Parking

The Curry House
Rooms 39 - 43

Sanctuary of the Wizard
and of Wisdom

Tennis Court

Parking

The Hand House
Rooms 44 - 48

The Carriage House

Parking

20's Villa
Rooms 23 - 28

Maxwell House
Rooms 17 - 20

Pool

The Bride and the Groom

Wilburton Inn's
Mansion and Seven Villas
Monuments of the Sculptural Trail

Ortlieb House
Rooms 21 & 22

The Mansion
Rooms 2 - 16

WILBURTON INN'S SCULPTURAL TRAIL OF THE HISTORY OF LOVE
THE THREE SEGMENTS OF THE SCULPTURAL TRAIL: SCIENCE, RELIGION AND EDUCATION

Science: Paradigm shift The Sad Wizard discovers the scientific secrets of living happily ever after in the wisdom of the plot of stories as a conflict resolution mechanism: mastery, cooperation, and mutual respect.

Religion: The epics of the Goddess as complementary discoveries of conflict resolution. Greece, mastery, India cooperation, and Judea mutual respect between father and son. The cycle of the Scriptures of one God as the drama completed with mutual respect between men and women.

Education: Monuments to the Scientific Moral Paradigm: Studying the physical structure and the moral function of the conflict resolution process, and sampling creativity for self discovery.

6. CREATIVITY FOR SELF DISCOVERY

Judea
Abraham and his women
Hagar as a Camel
Broken Joy
Abraham did it!

1. SANCTUARY OF THE WIZARD AND OF WISDOM

The Abrahamic Family and the altar for the test of love

The Gilgamesh Epic In pursuit of mutual respect

Virgin Mary

Naomi

The perfect universe

Three equilibrial principles (mastery, cooperation, and mutual respect)

Moses

5. MONUMENTS TO THE SCIENCE OF CONFLICT RESOLUTION

4. THE SCRIPTURES OF THE ONE GOD

Penelope the loyal wife

Japan The Dragon and the Geisha

3. THE EPICS OF THE GODDESS

Sarah and Isaac

The Embrace

The Kiss

India Siva stepping on the inner child

The Bride and the Groom as the book and people of the book

Christ and the Apostles

Iliad's Helen of Troy The fight and flight response.

2. THE FAIRY TALE

The power of Mother Earth

"God is not with the father and the son, but with the mother and the child"

"Girls are as good as boys"

Eureka! The process as the scientific moral paradigm

The lady and the dragons

Don Quixote and Dulcinea

Cruel matriarchy in Mexico

Virtual Jerusalem Father son vs. Mother and child

Three scriptures define how to be a bird (in a cage, free to fly, and becoming chicken soup for the soul)

The Labyrinth as the sculpture of the plot of stories, and of the Conflict Resolution Process.

The sun kills his sister, the moon

THE SCULPTURAL TRAIL OF THE HISTORY OF LOVE AS THE DIALECTIC EVOLUTION OF INSIGHTS INTO THE UNCONSCIOUS CONFLICT RESOLUTION PROCESS

Three gates: science, religion and education, with two cycles of sculptures each, constitute the Trail in the History of Love. The stations represent discoveries on the nature of the creative process as the scientific entity of the Conflict Resolution Process. This concept is clarified at the first gate, it integrates the religions of the world as partial and complementary discoveries of the process at the second gate and provides modern art monuments to the scientific paradigm as the fairest way of relating and the most abstract conceptualization of the psyche as the God of Love upon the third gate. This display of concepts as sculptures demystifies and reconciles the mental process and the progression of its awareness through the evolution of religions.

GATE ONE: SCIENCE
The paradigm shift from art to science introduces the process as a natural science phenomenon.

CYCLE ONE:
The Wizard, an Easter Island Head with a tear of blood running down his face, and Wisdom, as a Scale representing science, are carrying on a dialogue about the secrets to happiness; this is an an installation by Levis; 'The secrets are not in the stories we believe in but in the universal plot of stories, the Conflict Resolution Process.'

CYCLE TWO:
The secrets to happily ever after are conveyed by examining the plot of a fairy tale: the *Lady and the Dragons*, installation by Albert Levis 2a, 2b, the princess, and the ceramic dragon, by Barbara Kaufman illustrate the nature of conflict; it is described as a state of passivity, antagonism and alienation. Juxtaposed to *The Lady and the Drag-*

ons is the resolution, the happy ending of every fairy tale, 'living happily ever after', as *The Kiss*, 2c, and *The Embrace* 2d, by Bill Harby and *Don Quixote and Dulcinea, as the Possible Dream*, 2e, by Suzan Benton. The resolution is characterized scientifically as the state of mastery, cooperation and mutual respect.

GATE TWO: RELIGIONS INTEGRATED INTO THE MORAL SCIENCE
Two cycles, matriarchy and patriarchy, present the evolution of family relations as two cycles of ongoing dialectically connected religions as discoveries of covenants or conflict resolutions.

CYCLE THREE:
Matriarchy, the epics of the Goddess
The epics of the goddess are about heroic struggles or wars between men and women as a dramatic negotiation for power leading to the restructuring of family relations. Powerful and aggressive women are challenged by power pursuing men. Men are progressively subduing women.

Matriarchy starts with women in dominant social roles. They are either hideously ugly, scary, threatening extinction, like Mother Earth of the Aztecs, or irresistibly beautiful, like Helen of Troy. The cycle ends with women transformed to angels. At the end of the cycle, in Judea, Mary, a mother, is viewed as a virgin. Upon the resolution women's appeal is not outer beauty or power but inner beauty: kindness, compassion, hard work and wisdom. Virtue for a woman is to be willing to sacrifice her power, be that her sexuality or her child.

The religions redefine the concept of 'living happily ever after' as several measurable and interrelated resolutions restructuring the power balance of domestic relations. Each culture resolves conflicts with women along a different combination of the three formal or relational operations: mastery, cooperation and mutual respect.

The Homeric Epics in Greece present men masterfully domesticating women;
The Upanishads and then Buddhism in India men discovered inner restraints, amounting to respect of and cooperation with women;
In Judea men failing to achieve mutual respect between men and women discovered the father son relationship by neutralizing the importance of women.
This cycle's major artist is Barbara Kaufman; her ceramic sculptures enliven the evolving identities of the Goddess.

Stress
3a, The Propane Tank as mother earth's Torpedo Breast, Earth's milk by Levis
3b, Matriarchy's most terrifying mother is the Aztec Quatlique, cruel mother Earth sending her son Huitzilopochtli, the sun god, to kill mother's rival, her threatening daughter, the moon goddess Quayatsakli, gender war epic #1, Lippincott, installation by Levis.

Response
In the Homeric epics men set limits to matriarchy by challenging women's original uninhibited sexuality. Women loose the right of sexual freedom but still retain pride in their gender. The Homeric Epics, *The Iliad* and *The Odyssey* gender war #2, start with Helen of Troy, 3c as the Sphinx. She does not resolve conflicts; she is the 'fight and flight woman. This woman is transformed to the ideal wife as Penelope, 3d, by Barbara Kaufman. Penelope is the subdued matriarch; she restrains her self; she is married to Odysseus who also steered himself past temptations listening but not surrendering to temptation.

Anxiety
In the Hindu story of Kali and Siva, Gender War epic #3 roles were reversed in India where men discovered the operation of cooperation.
There is a connection between India and Greece. Women in Greece were unhappy. Ios, a mistress of Zeus, was cursed by Hera, his wife, to become

a cow; with the help of Hermes she escaped from the guardian husband, Argos Panoptes. She jumped over Bosporus, 'the jump of the cow', to Asia Minor and found her way to India, where cows are sacred. She became there the Moon Goddess Kali. 3d, An installation presents three big wheels waxing and waning in which each wheel has Kali's six arms.

In front of the three wheels is 3e, *Siva*, Kali's consort, the god of creation and destruction. He is balancing himself on a little child underfoot, a demon. This demon is our own demanding inner child respectful of the authorities above him. The image represents how men are learning to repress their desires by pursuing a delicate inner balance, breathing deep to relax the inner needs and to align the six erogenous zones or chakras as energies to the spiritual seventh chakra on top of one's head.

The sculpture of Siva is mounted on a pedestal of gears with multiple cogs. It emphasizes how man in India has discovered how to become a cog in the wheel rather than remain the arrogant Greek big wheel. We may recognize in these behaviors the discovery of cooperation central in the inception of Buddhism. In Hinduism and in Buddhism, man is a cog of the wheel rather than the big wheel.

Defense
In Japan, and China men emerge from being demons underfoot to become dragons revered as the sun gods. While men emerge, women lose power; in China they have their feet bound and in Japan they have their ego reduced by becoming geishas, selfless servants at the disposition of men. This is a radical reversal in gender roles from the Indian role structure.

3f, The installation presents this new structure as a dragon, the Sun God, respected by his wife, *The Geisha* 3g. An engine block is the little dragon reminding us of the highly cooperative and col-

laborative Japanese and Chinese family. Characteristically the installation reflecting cooperation and massive respect for God lacks mutual respect between the genders.

3h, Buddha in a Lotus position reflects the values of the culture as introspection, control of desires and serenity rather than the pursuit of pleasures and societal reform. It expresses the acceptance of serenity as the key societal value. Buddha is the example of the philosophy of cooperation, kindness and self-restraint; Levis

Reversal
From Japan to Mesopotamia there is again a reversal of roles in the man and woman relationship. *The Gilgamesh Epic*, 3i, installation presents the empowered woman as a seductive voluptuous nude princess Ishtar and her lover, a groveling snake with a smiling face. This represents the mirror image of the Japanese family. The Mesopotamian beauty, the powerful whore of Babylon cures the self-effacedness of the geisha and the snake reduces the self assuredness of the dragon. The Japanese dragon was reduced to a groveling snake. It is this humbling relationship that was questioned by prince Gilgamesh, as princess Ishtar sought to seduce him. He rejected Ishtar's advances reminding her of her promiscuity. This epic struggle marks the quest for mutual respect in the Mesopotamian culture, as men seek to redefine the man-woman relationship. This epic inspired Bible's Adam and Eve story and the father-son covenant. 3i, Ceramic sculpture by Barbara Kaufman, installation by Levis.

Compromise
3j, *Broken Joy* is the installation of broken sculptures representing Abraham's war, his assaulting women's licentiousness by breaking his father's pagan idols, sculptures of Grecian naked women. Symbolically a wheel is introduced, representing almighty God's Genesis, as the periodicity of science's Conflict Resolution Process. Two statues introduce the Messianic rebellion of women as

the alliance of the mother and the Son against the traditional inequitable father son alliance. The Messianic believers worship the mother child alliance; the prophets are viewed as divine. In Islam this is presented in the configuration of the crescent, the compromised moon goddess, and the star, her child. This symbolism may be seen to correspond to the alliance of Hagar and Ishmael.

Hagar 3k, is a camel on a dune promontory, as a beast of burden with war toys, a ceramic sculpture by Barbara Kaufman. The camel commemorates Hagar's anger at Abraham for consenting to Sarah to dismiss her, with his first born Ishmael, to the desert. Ishmael presented by his war toys illustrates his anger at his brother Isaac for stealing his birth-right.

Another mother-child alliance is seen with *Virgin Mary and the Martyr*, 3l, sculptures by Barbara Kaufman, presenting the Christian woman reduced to an angel. She is a saintly virgin, a non-sexually threatening partner. Helen's external beauty has become transformed into the inner beauty of kindness, the capacity to resolve conflict in a cooperative manner.

3m, *Naomi*, 'I'll go whether thy go' symbolizes the Judaic woman, as a devout worshiper of the one God.

CYCLE FOUR:
Patriarchy as the Scriptures of the One God
This cycle dramatizes the alliance of men and God, the covenant alliance discriminating against women. They are oppressed and they rebel under the influence of the Greco-Roman cultures to seek power by declaring an alliance of the mother and the child in the Messianic religions. The drama of men and women comes to an end as science shifts paradigms from the stories, which divide people to the plot of stories, which unifies diversity and clarifies the principles of moral order.

Stress

4a, The cycle begins with *Sarah*, a vessel like woman, by B. Kaufman, and the *Bar Mitzvah Boy*, learning about the Bible and respecting rules like the Kosher cuisine. *Sarah*, the lady of the nipples, or chicken soup is ready represents the image of the Biblical woman concealed by a burqa, but trusting her husband in spite of lack of mutuality in power. *Bar Mitzvah Boy*, 4b, says 'slow' reflecting that he has learnt to restrain his reactions. The signs on the wall sum up his education on the history of biblical history.

Response

4c, *Moses,* by Alfred Lippincott, exits Egypt across the Red Sea and wanders in the Sinai, the triangular field. A porcupine sculpture, presents Moses advancing, his mouth is open to capture manna; his hair stands up straight, as antennas to detect the voice of God.

4d, *The Apparition in the Desert of the Abrahamic Family* is a sculpture of the Biblical family by Judith Brown. It presents the three Patriarchs Abraham, Isaac, and Jacob, as three gigantic pharaoh figures sitting on thrones, illustrating the father-son covenant or alliance, a historical breakthrough in family relations. The sculpture also portrays the four matriarchs as four diminutive figures contributing libations to the giant men, and two Horuses representing the concubines as birds, or chicks, with beaks to peck on the wives. The covenant was facilitated by women inspiring their children to respect their fathers and to study the Bible. The supremacy of men represents imbalance of power. This male arrogance is the hubris of the Biblical cycle. This woman-man-children configuration will be challenged by the Messianic religions.

4e, *The Altar for the Sacrifice of Isaac* by Bill Harby or the test of love, Split Copper Beech by Bill Harby. This sculpture commemorates the test of love initiated by Abraham, who according to Levis tested both Hagar's and Sarah's willingness to let him sacrifice their sons. According to this interpretation Sarah trusted Abraham, while Hagar did not.

Anxiety

4f, *Joshua*, the whodunit in the desert, represents Joshua warning the Jews in the desert about the danger of electing kings, military leaders, who might abuse the power delegated to them. Levis 4g, a big house with two lions in front of it represents the *Kingdom United*. *Kingdom United* is the big building representing the foundation of Jerusalem with a temple for the worship of the one God, and the palace for the great king of the Jews. The kings committed transgressions and they were punished.

4h, Two houses, *Kingdom Divided,* represent the Jewish Kingdom divided into Samaria and Judea; the scattered implements remind us of the agrarian society of the Biblical times.
The hill below represents exile in Babylon.

Defense

4i, Jews in exile in Babylon published the Bible, the record of the covenant between the Jews and God. *The Bride and the Groom* is a monumental sculpture representing the importance of the relationship between the Bible as the bride, and the people of the book, as the groom. The Jews love the book, kiss it, study it, dance with it, are ecstatic about it as the voice of God. They enjoy understanding and interpreting it. The book holds the secrets of living happily ever after. While the book is representing the bride, the women of this culture are politically eclipsed by the love of God's book.

4j, *The Eruv*, is the string suspended between trees delineating the boundaries for self-discipline and spiritual limits. A thousand regulations are implicit in this fine line between right and wrong.

Reversal

4k, *The Chariots of Alexander* in front of the ramparts of *Virtual Jerusalem* show how the city is besieged by ideas of faith and reason. *The Chariots* reflect on the pronounced influence of the Greek culture on the Judaic men and women in rethinking norms and beliefs. Installation by Levis.

4l, the tall debarked and ominous looking tree in front of the circle of trees, hit by lightning, reminds us of the *'the Wailing Wall.'*

4m, the area delineated by tree stumps and a circle of tall pine trees is our *Virtual Jerusalem*. In the center of the circle of tall pine trees is a table and chairs. The table and the chairs around it symbolize *Men Studying the Law*, Levis. On the table is the sculpture of 4n, *Moses Standing on the Tablets Gazing at the Moon*, Lippincott.

4o, Several figures sitting on the ramparts of Jerusalem complaining are *Unhappy Women* by Phyllis Kulmatiski. They are the oppressed women of Jerusalem protesting. One 4o, is featuring a banner stating that *'Girls are as good as boys.'* Another features on her forehead an inscription, *'to be born a female is a death sentence.'*

4p, one has a baby boy standing on her lap. We may assume that the mother figure is telling us: *'God is not with the father and the son, but with the mother and the child.'*

Compromise

A complex installation contrasts the story versus the plot of stories as two alternative paradigms. Its two parts describe the confusion on the nature of the truth conferred by religions versus the clarity on the nature of moral order conferred by science thus addressing the query of the perplexed Wizard at the inception of the trail. Stories tell us *'How to be a bird'*, the plot of stories, our stories, tells us *'what kind of bird we are.'*
4q, *'How to be a bird'* is an installation of three birds reflecting the Messianic messages of how to deal with power or temptation as three different instructions: The three kinds of birds

illustrate how the scriptural messages differ as Israel, Islam and Christos. Israel means 'to wrestle with God' two big birds are free within an arch; Islam means 'to submit' a bird is in a gilded cage. Christos means to be compassionate: The bird is suspended like a crucifix by a crown of thorns being cooked to become chicken soup of the soul.

4r, A turkey is flying down the driveway of the inn. It is the free-thinking person as the turkey that ran away before Thanksgiving Day, representing the fourth option in handling power.

4s, *The Labyrinth* is a sculpture that illustrates the creative process following a universal path leading to self discovery. Through the use of the *Animal Metaphor Test* we can find out how we resolve conflicts.

The Labyrinth features many animals on its path, a chicken and a rooster, a cow and a pig, two little pigs with wings and a Pegasus, 4t, at the center of *The Labyrinth*. The pigs discuss 'There will be peace in Jerusalem when pigs fly' and the other pig objects, 'Peace is on the way.' It comes as science inspiring people's understanding of the unconscious mind. The world will heal as there will be one truth for all believing people.'

The Apostles, 4u, as '*How to Be a Fish*' describe the diversity of interpretations of who is Jesus, by Sarah D'Alessandro.

GATE 3: EDUCATION; THE SECRETS TO HAPPINESS ARE IN THE SCIENTIFIC ANALYSIS OF THE PLOT OF STORIES, THE SCIENCE OF CONFLICT RESOLUTION

CYCLE FIVE:
Moral Science, the key concept of the Formal Theory
5a, *The Wolf Howling in the Desert* is about my discovery of the Helix, the unit of the Teleion Holon, or perfect universe of thoughts in a story. The plot of stories is a unit that in six steps com-

pletes a conflict resolution.

The Marble Reflections, 5b, by Bill Harby, are also Formal Theory's *Self -Reflections*, manifesting the composition of the Teleion Holon as the six parts of the total conflict resolution process. Three clusters, the three acts of a play, represent the continuum leading to a large single stone, the state of rest. The sculptural installation could also be named Genesis, the creation, reminding us of the six days of creation and the day of rest.

Modern Art 5c, Mich Syd's suspended stones illustrate Formal Theory's three formal conflict resolution operations: *The Oscillating Stone* honors the physics of the pendulum, as the reciprocal operation, transforming passivity to activity; the *Spinning Marble* honors the operation of negation, transforming antagonism to cooperation; *Stone Suspended at a Vertical Axis* reminds us of the operation of correlation, the shift from alienation suspending the stone on the bottom of the post, to mutual respect in the middle and arrogance on the top.

CYCLE SIX:
Validation of the Formal Theory through creativity for self-discovery
An infidelity conflict is a set of sculptures generated through a workbook by an artist working through a classical triangular relationship drama. The spontaneously evolving sequence chronicles the unfolding process progressing predictably to resolution.

6a, STRESS RESPONSE ANXIETY: *Pecker Pecked*, shows the activity of pecking in juxtaposition to the passivity of being pecked. The activity marks the distinction defining this symbolic system.

6b, ANXIETY AND DEFENSE: The family feud represents the several parties engaged in this domestic conflict.

6c, REVERSAL: The conflict is internalized; his

head is spinning and his conscience pinches his shirt. This reflects the state of inner pain.

6d, COMPROMISE: Two clowns, in symmetrical arrangement, are smiling while a hand is extended to the world reflecting resolution, compromise and mutual respect.

Conclusion:
The Wizard, seeing this orderly development to happiness, laughs again with great relief.

7a, The goddess of democracy, *Lysistrata*.

7b, The Gorski aspiration, '*I Will Make a Man More Precious Than Fine Gold.*'

7c, The Logo, giving a branch of olive tree to the sphinx; the answer is in mutual respect and collaboration.

EXHIBIT #4: THE SCULPTURAL TRAIL
STEALING THE FIRE OF THE GODS

How the world became conscious of the unconscious as a conflict resolution process; a scientific, moral order phenomenon:

GATE 1, SCIENCE: "The fire of the gods" as the science of the process

Cycle 1. The object of study of the science as a paradigm shift
from the content to the plot of stories

Cycle 2. The relational method to study the plot of stories from propositional to relational and identifying three relational operations as the scientific secrets of living 'happily ever after'

GATE 2, RELIGION: "Stealing the fire" as demystifying religion

Cycle 3. The process integrates the Epics of the Goddess as
gender wars leading to the creation of the family institution

Cycle 4. The process resolves the drama of the scriptures of the one god by
introducing mutual respect between men and women

GATE 3, EDUCATION: "Giving the fire to the mortals" as amoral and emotional education

Cycle 5. Monuments to the Conflict Resolution Process as celebrating the new moral order

Cycle 6. Utilizing creativity for self-discovery as the new spirituality

GATE 1, SCIENCE: THE FIRE OF THE GODS AS THE SCIENCE OF THE PROCESS

CYCLE 1:
THE WIZARD AND WISDOM: A DIALOGUE BETWEEN ART AND SCIENCE, FOCUS ON THE PARADIGM SHIFT FROM THE STORY TO THE PLOT OF STORIES

The Conflict Resolution Process, the foundation of morality, is a natural science phenomenon. It consists of six roles/emotions guided by three formal transformations.

The importance of the totality as a Conflict Resolution Process.
The first cycle is a dialogue between an Easter Island head, the Wizard, and a scale, science. The Wizard has a tear of blood running down his cheek representing religions in pain.
The Sad Wizard, in conflict, asks:
  "How come after all my stories the world is not living happily ever after?"
The Scale, as the science of the Harmonic, responds:
  "Do not despair! The secrets to happiness are in all stories, but instead of believing them, look for what is universal in all of them. It is the plot of stories, the conflict resolution mechanism. The plot is the object for the scientific study of behavior."

The Trail integrates all the sculptures as six stories progressively reflecting more clearly the nature of the plot of stories as features of the Conflict Resolution Process.

RESPONSE

Conflict

PASSIVITY TO ACTIVITY

STRESS

ANXIETY

THE FAIRY TALE IDENTIFIES WHAT IS UNIVERSAL IN ALL STORIES, i.e. THE PLOT OF STORIES.

The tale begins with a conflict: a lady is confronted by three dragons.

The resolution: the sculptures of a kiss and an embrace as 'living happily ever after.' The lady and the dragons, a fairy tale, defines the plot of stories as the path from conflict to resolution. Conflict is scientifically defined as the states of passivity, antagonism, and alienation. Resolution is defined as mastery, cooperation and mutual respect.

This information sums up the discoveries of Moral Science. The fairy tale demonstrates the universality of the conflict resolution mechanism.

The Lady

Three Dragons

Conclusion: The fairy tale confirms that the plot of stories is a circumscribed conflict resolution entity with a predictable structure and the moral function of 'happily ever after.'

Science: Here we witness the conflict between the lady and the dragons, defined as a state of passivity, antagonism and alienation, transform to a state of activity, cooperation and mutual respect as illustrated by the sculptures *The Kiss* and *The Embrace*.

The first two cycles of the Sculptural Trail impart the scientific information on moral order as the innate Conflict Resolution Process. We are shifting the focus from the story to the plot of stories in order to inform the visitor that the plot is a conflict resolution mechanism with certain key characteristics.

In this first segment of the Trail, Cycles 1 and 2, science introduces the definition of morality as the abstraction underlying all stories. The fairy tale interprets metaphorical language as a sequence of formal operations within the circumscribed

phenomenon of the plot of stories. The implication at the outset is that morality is a natural science, a physiological phenomenon that stems from the unconscious and does not originate in apocalypse or divine revelation.

A second fairy tale, *Don Quixote, with Dulcinea and Sancho Panza*, his loyal friend. The couple finally live happily ever after at the Wilburton Inn's Museum.

The Kiss

The Embrace

GATE 2: ON RELIGION: SCIENCE STEALING THE FIRE OF THE GODS DEMYSTIFIES RELIGIONS AS A PROGRESSION OF DISCOVERIES OF CONFLICT RESOLUTION

CYCLE 3, ANXIETY: MATRIARCHY, THE EPICS OF THE GODDESS AS GENDER WARS LEADING TO DISCOVERIES OF THREE TYPES OF CONFLICT RESOLUTION

INTRODUCTION: The Epics of the Goddess is a cycle of sculptures of powerful women evolving towards the discovery of alternative and complementary ways of resolving conflict as a series of battles between the genders.

The Epics of the Goddess represent gender wars leading to the gradual formation of the family institution. Matriarchy, being the first phase of the development of the institution was fraught with tremendous conflict. We see evidence of that in the Aztec civilization's mythology of the most cruel mother Earth who exacts live sacrifices to avert the fifth destruction of the universe. She is the eagle struggling with the helpless snake, her partner in the family.

Progressively, women lose the right over their sexual freedom, establishing the biggest trade-off, men's respect for their offspring. The Epics of the Goddess clarify the six role-states as six moral discoveries of how to resolve conflicts. Each culture in the epics represents a gender war altering the power balance of the spouses and the children in the evolving institution of the family.

Religions evolved dialectically along the Conflict Resolution Process, resolving domestic conflicts sequentially. They discovered mastery, cooperation and mutual respect as the variables of conflict resolution which change the norms of acceptable behavior and redefine the divine. The Harmonic presents the evolving identities of women as interrelated goddesses and heroines.

Stress: The Aztec monster matriarch was transformed in Greece to the fight-and-flight Sphinx, the Homeric mighty Helen of Troy and the seductresses of the Odyssey. The Greek Mother Earth is portrayed as the Sphinx, a humanized eagle, who kills those who fail to interpret her riddles. She is the mother, Iocasta, who wishes to marry her son and kill her husband. She is the women of the Odyssey such as the sirens, who seek to possess and destroy Odysseus.

Response: In Greece, the Iliad and the Odyssey present men united to subdue the matriarch Helen. Perseus decapitated Medusa. Orestes and Electra killed their promiscuous mother, Clytemnestra. The mighty Helen was transformed into the loyal but oppressed Penelope. The Greek religion resolved conflicts in domestic relationships by men dominating women, exercising the principle of **mastery by transforming the state of passivity to one of activity.** Greek men managed to kill the monster mother and replace her with the loyal and faithful Penelope, the dominated spouse (Graves, 1960).

Anxiety: The oppressed Greek woman was emancipated in India as Kali, the sacred cow, inspiring cooperation as the philosophy of Buddhist men. India rescued the Greek woman, transformed into a cow by making it sacred and thus commanding respect from men. India discovered the importance of cooperation for the improvement of domestic relations. Hinduism's Siva is portrayed as stepping on his inner child, defining the state of cooperation. Buddhism emphasized the same concepts with its Four Noble Truths: life is suffering, suffering springs from desire, eliminate desire to eliminate suffering, enlightenment follows the eight-fold **path of moderation and cooperation.**

Defense: China and Japan reversed the power roles for the genders. Men became powerful, like dragons, and women became powerless. The power of the woman was reduced from Moon Goddess to that of the compliant geisha, while the power of the men grew to that of the mighty dragon Sun god. The religions and cultures of India, China and Japan resolved conflicts in domestic relationships by **introducing cooperation in the man-woman relationship.**

Reversal: In Mesopotamia the Japanese geisha becomes a promiscuous woman. Prince Gilgamesh challenges Ishtar **seeking mutual respect between man and woman.** Ishtar's promiscuity caused women to be regarded contemptuously and punished. Eve, inspired by Ishtar's story, was blamed for humanity's exile from paradise.

Compromise: The cycle of the Epics is completed with the Virgin Mary, a woman who was able to sacrifice her sexuality and her only child for the glory of the father. Finally, Judea contributed a new dimension to the improvement of domestic relations by introducing the concept of mutual respect between the father and the son. In the process, women lost power but gained the security of the safety of their offspring. The power of women is neutralized by the alliance of the father-son covenant. Abraham smashed the effigies of beautiful women and exalted the one loving male God as the alternative to worshiping conflict-arousing goddesses. The Judaic religion discovered the importance of mutual respect between father and son as the means to resolve conflict.

The Contemporary Bride

The Geisha

Girls are as good as Boys

God is not with the father or the son but with the mother and the child

Ruth/Naomi

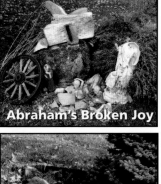
Sarah in a burqa

Abraham's Broken Joy

Hagar as the beast of burden

The Virgin Mother

The Sphinx as Helen - the fight and flight response

Penelope

Aztec matriarchs

Ishtar the Seductress, aka Eve

THE EVOLVING IMAGES OF THE GODDESS

CYCLE 3: THE EPICS OF THE GODDESS
THE ROLE OF WOMEN IN THE PAGAN RELIGIONS

RESPONSE: The Greek epics of the Iliad and the Odyssey are interpreted as men at war with matriarchal women. These conflicts are resolved with men dominating or overpowering women. The resolution of conflicts has men as incestuous sons breaking the alliance with mothers against the fathers, killing the mother overcoming her power of seduction, and setting limits to women's heroic demands in tragic poems. Men fought the histrionic Maenads and frightening Erinies, the fight and flight Sphinx, as Iocasta and Helen of Troy, unfaithful murderous Clytemnestra, patricidal and infanticidal Media, the powerful Phaedra, the hypnotic Calypso, Circe, the sirens, and Nausica, all powerful seductive matriarchal women testing Odysseus capacity to resist their nefarious appeal. These women of many namesake Greek tragedies are defeated or punished. Women are transformed into the new culture's virtuous heroines, the faithful wives Hera and Penelope, the dedicated daughters Antigone, Ariadne and Iphigenia and the virginal wise and hardworking Athena.

Response:
The Oddysey's
Penelope
The loyal wife/
domesticated woman

Anxiety/Defense:
Buddhism's four noble truths

RESPONSE

Mexico's matriarchy

Greece's patriarchy

India's Moon goddess

STRESS

ANXIETY

The torpedo breast

Stress:
The Iliad's Helen of Troy as a Sphinx
The fight/flight matriarchal woman

STRESS: Codicils tablets and the Aztec calendar of Mexico define matriarchy
The pre-Columbian figurines

The struggle of the sun killing the moon, a brother killing a sister threatening to the mother. The eagle devouring the snake

Anxiety: India's Upanishads
The stages of the moon • The Siva on gears
Discovery of cooperation with women in charge in India

ANXIETY: The Oriental epics and philosophies present men transforming antagonism to cooperation with women. In India men respected women as the roaming sacred cows and the powerful magical Kali whose power is reflected in her three sets of arms; she is the creator and destroyer; men discovered cooperation as self-control, the power of suppression of desire, as the virtue of this culture. Cooperation is symbolized in the image of Siva, Kali's castrated partner balancing himself on one leg stepping on a content child-like figure, which we may we assume is representing his inner child, his suppressed desires transformed into a good attitude with his predicament. This homunculus may represent Buddhism's noble truths about accepting pain and restraining desires to achieve the state of Nirvana or non rebirth. DEFENSE: In the Chinese and Japanese cultures men assumed the dominant role in the cooperative relationship. They identified themselves with Sun Gods, dragons, and delegated the role of subservience to women defined as with bound feet in China and as geishas in Japan.

Compromise: Hagar as camel

Biblical/Messianic religions as conditional respect for women

Virgin Mary

Ruth/Naomi

Defense: Japan, Tao and Zen
The dragon and the geisha • Mastery and cooperation of men with women in Japan

Broken Joy/Idols
The end of the era of the goddess

PASSIVITY ACTIVITY DEFENSE

COMPROMISE

REVERSAL PASSIVITY TO ACTIVITY

Japan's Sun god

Mesopotamia's seductress

Israel's Father-son covenant

Reversal: Gilgamesh epic Ishtar the seductress of Babylon, Israel's bible

REVERSAL: In Mesopotamia the Gilgamesh Epic is about a man seeking mutual respect with seductress Ishtar and finding it instead in the relationship with a father figure fighting women and temptation. Ishtar did not offer a long-lasting exclusive relationship to the prince. In an epical war with her and promiscuous women the prince lost his partner Enkidu. Inconsolable he spent his life seeking his dead friend as the pursuit of immortality and knowledge of the hereafter. COMPROMISE: This epic inspired both the Adam and Eve story and of the Father Son Covenant of the Bible. Women were viewed as responsible for the loss of Paradise associated with enjoying sexuality, the forbidden fruit. Eve, Vashti, and Delilah are examples of non virtuous women, while the heroines Sara, Ester, Naomi, Ruth and the asexual Virgin Mary as well as the repentant Magdalene were respected as virtuous. Virtues for women were asexual love, agape, and the selfless commitment to others. This resolution entailed modesty for women, the concealment of women's attractiveness and the banning of nudity. Modesty obliged them to hide their physical appeal and beauty. Sexually free Abrahamic women were and still are punished by their own family men and an unforgiving culture.

CYCLE 4: DEFENSE AS PATRIARCHY, THE SCRIPTURES OF THE ONE GOD, A DRAMA COMPLETED BY SCIENCE WITH THE DISCOVERY OF MUTUAL RESPECT

Abrahamic patriarchy's conflict between the monotheistic and Messianic religions represents the continuation of the struggles of patriarchy versus matriarchy. These are disguised now as the conflicts between the father and the son versus the mother and child. The son is deified in Christianity and Islam thus introducing a new set of values and role models into the Messianic religions and leading to the differences between the faiths. The conflict in these religions represents the unresolved drama in the Abrahamic family relations.

This conflict can only be defused by introducing a broader and finer understanding of moral order. This order must address the origin of the conflict between the religions as stemming from the lack of mutual respect between men and women in the Judaic family. The science of the process as advanced by the Moral Science completes the discoveries on the scientific nature of the process with a shift of focus to the holistic understanding of dynamics. Science clarifies the significance of mutual respect between partners as a requirement for the resolution of conflict in the gender relations.

The fourth cycle dramatizes the man-woman relationship of the Abrahamic family. Science as the *deus ex machina* intervenes in this drama to guide religions to a shift of paradigms and to the completion of conflict resolution in domestic relations. A number of sculptures present the family's unresolved conflicts as redefined battle lines; the new gender wars involve the alliances between father and son versus mother and child:

• Stress: The cycle starts with the Bar Mitzvah ritual representing the father son covenant as a mother severs controls over her son allowing him to join the pious men's congregation preaching male domination and decrying female power as temptation to desires.

• Response: The golden Pharaoh sculpture is the sculpture of the Abrahamic family presenting three patriarchs and four diminutive matriarchs and two chicks, big birds, representing the nameless concubines. It shows how patriarchy overcorrected the power of matriarchal women by delegating to them subservient roles, depriving them of sexual rights, while it allowed men to practice polygamy.

• Anxiety: Moses is the conscience of Judaism. The awareness of the Commandments passed harsh judgement on the behavior of the kings. The Jewish kings strayed into forbidden love relations and lapsed into paganism. They were punished with the destruction of the temple and their exile in Babylon.

• Defense: The Bride and Groom sculpture presents the love relationship between the Jews and the Bible; the bride is the Bible, the groom is the people of the book. The sculpture presents the intensity in the love of the story literally conceived as the word of God representing the total truth.

• Reversal: The installation identified as the virtual Jerusalem introduces the conflicts of the Abrahamic family as the powerful clash between men and women with two sets of strategically positioned sculptures. Men, gathered in the center of the city, talk about the Law, while women on the ramparts of Jerusalem complain. Women empowered by the Greco-Roman cultural influence are emancipated and seek rights. The installation presents the Christian era messianic rebellion of women, as the mother child alliance challenging the father son covenant. A single woman wears a banner stating 'Girls are as good as boys' and a mother is protesting silently holding onto a child: 'God is not with the father and the son but with the mother and the child' representing how the father son covenant is challenged by the mother child Messianic alliance. In Islam this alliance is affirmed in the image of the Crescent and the Star symbolism of that faith.

• Compromise: The final installation contrasts metaphors of the content of the three scriptures versus the plot of stories. The scriptures are symbolized by three sets of birds each defined by the respective injunctions as 'How to be a bird.' Israel means to wrestle with God and the birds are tall and free, Islam means 'to submit' and the birds are confined in gilded cages, Christos means 'to be good' and the bird is a crucifix alluding to the virtue of the bird as being cooked to become chicken soup of the soul. The alternative to the content of the stories is recognizing the universality of the plot of stories. Sculpturally this is defined as the Cretan Labyrinth as the path to transformation identified metaphorically as 'to learn how to fly.' The trail is featuring two little winged pigs, 'if pigs could fly?' at the starting gate of the Labyrinth. Pegasus is the message in the center of the Labyrinth, a mythic winged creature. The Labyrinth is the sculpture of the process, the plot of stories, also a story introducing mutual respect as a requirement for conflict resolution. The story is that of an Athenian prince, Theseus, and a Cretan princess, Ariadne, collaborating to kill the Minotaur, a monster child, the symbol of the Matriarchal era, of a woman in love with a bull. Mutual respect is the missing conflict resolution principle in the Abrahamic family and its attainment completes the drama of this cycle and delivers the key transformation of religions to the Moral Science.

Conclusion: The Moral Science demystifies religion suggesting a shift of paradigms from the stories we believe in to the plot of stories as a conflict resolution mechanism. The Moral Science identifying the unit process as the origin of all religious moral order is stealing the fire of the gods. The unit process demystifies religions as natural science partial conflict resolutions. Science diagnoses religions as alternative structures of conflict resolution in the family institution. Science introduces the new paradigm and resolves the conflicts of the Abrahamic religions suggesting the correction of religions' moral arbitrariness and perpetuation of the cultural unacceptable norm of inequities in the area of gender relations. The implications of Moral Science are identifying morality as a scientific phenomenon integrating religions. Morality is defined as the process completed by the three principles of conflict resolution: mastery, cooperation and mutual respect. The labyrinth as the plot of stories is the path of creativity for self-discovery and self-knowledge. The prerequisite to happiness is the adoption of abstract and insightful thinking about conflict resolution and power management.

Religions examined as metaphors are viewed as particular ways of resolving conflicts. Science guides conflict resolution beyond the particular to the universal understanding of resolutions. It reconciles and integrates them into an evolutional continuum of discoveries ending upon the identification of the process as an abstraction abiding by the formulas of logic and physics; this then is the ultimate definition of moral order. Science is able to clarify moral order beyond the particular religious discoveries and guide religions to address their unresolved conflicts and to identify the changes they need to make to resolve their cross-cultural differences.

Religions explored the universal moral order of the Conflict Resolution Process but as a metaphysical phenomenon attributed to external anthropomorphic moral authorities identified as gods. Now science assumes the task of demystifying religion as the ways of the unconscious resolving conflicts. Science grasps the process and reduces religions to natural science relational and energetic measurable phenomena. Religions represent sanctified paths to conflict resolution.

Abrahamic family as a milestone and a hubris for a drama that still remains unresolved.

The altar for the sacrifice of Isaac, or the monument to the test of love.

CYCLE 4: DEFENSE AS PATRIARCHY, THE SCRIPTURES OF THE ONE GOD

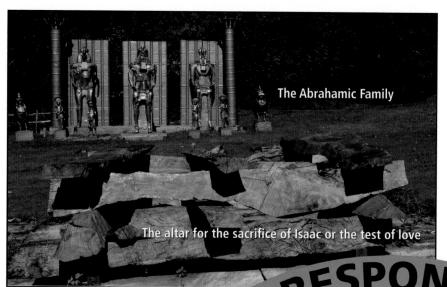

The Abrahamic Family

The altar for the sacrifice of Isaac or the test of love

RESPONSE: Defining Judaism as the Abrahamic sculpture. It presents the Abrahamic family as the three pharaoh-like figures, representing the patriarchs, Abraham, Isaac and Jacob, towering over the four matriarchs and two symbolic concubines presented as birds. The discrepancies between men and the women, who are presented much smaller in size and inequitably in terms of numbers represents hubris, the arrogance of men.

The pyre in front of the Abrahamic family is the altar for the sacrifice of Isaac. We identify it as the test of love that Abraham devised to test Sarah's capacity to respect his relationship with Isaac, and Isaac's capacity to honor God.

Levis is suggesting that when Sarah asked Abraham to give up his first-born son, Ishmael, and his mistress Hagar, that he extracted a concession on the part of Sarah to accept his uncompromised relationship with Isaac, even to the extent of his having the right to sacrifice Isaac to the Almighty.

RESPONSE

Bar mitzvah as mother yielding her son

The father-son covenant oppressing women

The Ten Commandments

STRESS

ANXIETY

STRESS: The Bar mitzvah commemorates the sacrifice of Isaac, a mother surrendering her son to his father for a potential immolation to God; 'slow' pertains to the son learning self restraint. A mother trusting a father for the care of their son is a breakthrough in the history of family relations.

ANXIETY: Moses as the voice of God conveyed to the Jews both the leadership for the Exodus from Egypt and the Ten Commandments, the imperatives of conflict resolution for the survival as a nation. The Bible captures the evolution of the new nation as it is enduring the travesties of the journey through the desert on the way to the Promised Land. This phase in the history of Judaism formed the character of the nation, like childhood developmental experiences shape the personality.

Moses, the voice of God, the conscience of Judaism

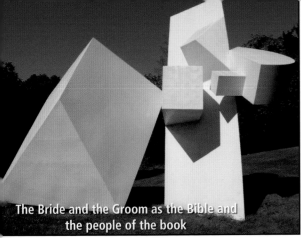

The plot of stories is metaphorically represented by a labyrinth.

Islam means "to submit" and the birds are in cages.

Israel means "to wrestle" and the birds are tall with their mouths open.

Christos means "to be good", and the bird is defined as the chicken soup of the soul.

The Bride and the Groom as the Bible and the people of the book

DEFENSE: The sculpture represents The Bride and the Groom, referring to the Bible as the bride and the people of the book as the groom. In this development women are of symbolic value but in reality they are excluded from social political activities.

COMPROMISE: This installation presents the resolution of the conflicts of the biblical religions by juxtaposing the metaphor of the content of stories versus the plot of stories. The scriptures, literally interpreted, are metaphorically represented by three sets of birds. They are prescriptive, defining humans 'How to be a bird.' The plot of stories is metaphorically represented by a labyrinth. The path, defined as 'to learn how to fly', hence using one's imagination weaving a story and finding out what kind of bird one is.

The school of fish represents the many versions of Christ.

DEFENSE · REVERSAL · COMPROMISE

The Bible as the Bride

The Messianic mother-child alliance

Moral Science's mutual respect

The conclusion of this sculptural cycle presents the shift of paradigms as necessary for religions to resolve their conflicts. The implication is double: moral order is the science of conflict resolution and conflict resolution is predicated upon the recognition of the importance of mutual respect between the parties in conflict. Science completes the task of religions, points out to the evolution of gender relations and promotes peace by recognizing the need for the emancipation of women and according them mutual respect as equal partners in the family dynamic.

This installation represents the virtual Jerusalem, the circle of pine trees and tree stumps represent the ramparts of the Holy City. In the center of the circle the white table and chairs represent the gathering of men discussing the Law. Women are sitting peripherally on the ramparts complaining/rebelling.

'Girls are as good as boys'

'God is not with the father and the son but with the mother and the child'

REVERSAL: In the history of Judaism the Messianic religions represents a dramatic reversal of fortune. The Greek influence emancipated men and women from faith to reason. The Messianic religions represent the rebellion of women in alliance with their sons against the oppressive patriarchal father-son covenant.

Genesis/Teleion Holon as the six parts of the process, and the Sabbath, the day of rest and resolution

Bill Harby's 'reflective stones' represent Genesis or the Teleion Holon process, a six-part structure leading to a single megalith, the resolution. This sculpture celebrates respect for the Conflict Resolution Process

GATE 3, EDUCATION: GIVING THE FIRE TO THE MORTALS AS EMOTIONAL EDUCATION

Having identified the fire of the Gods with the scientific paradigm of moral order, and having used this paradigm to integrate the religions of the world as ushering in the Moral Science, at this point science assumes moral leadership over the range of religions and psychological theories in conflict, thus bringing the fire of the gods to the mortals.

In Cycle 5, Reversal, we celebrate the new scientific moral paradigm as the phase of a breakthrough in the quest for meaning. Here we present a monumental sculpture illustrating the dialectics of the process of creation, and three individual sculptures identifying the three equilibrial principles of the unconscious.

In Cycle 6, Compromise, we present the application of the Formal Theory by utilizing the creative process for the generation of metaphors and for the person, as the creator, to interpret the metaphors and become self-aware.

CYCLE 5, REVERSAL CELEBRATES THE DISCOVERIES OF THE MORAL SCIENCE: THE COGNITIVE / EDUCATIONAL COMPONENT

This is the cognitive segment summed up as learning about the process and the three formal operations. The fifth cycle consists of two sets of abstract sculptures celebrating the process and the principles of conflict resolution as clarity in the nature of the key concepts of the Moral Science.

Introducing these abstract concepts as monuments the trail diminishes the focus on dated icons of religion and enhances enlightenment as science providing the new paradigm.

Bill Harby's 'reflective stones' shown on the opposite page represent the Teleion Holon process, a six-part structure leading to a single megalith, the resolution. This sculpture celebrates the Teleion Holon, or Genesis, as respect for the Conflict Resolution Process.

Another set of sculptures, Mitch Sid's three equilibrial stones, represent the three equilibrial one directional principles of conflict resolution as the distinctions that we may equate with the Ten Commandments. The Biblical titles of these sculptures suggest continuity between intuitive religions and science. The monuments of this cycle celebrate the Perfect Universe and its formal operations while paying tribute to the traditional intuitive biblical equivalent concepts. Science is presented merely as the formalization of the propositional constructs of religion.

The pivoting rotation of the sculpture represents the formal alternatives of co-operation and antagonism

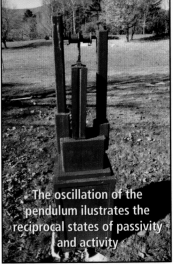
The oscillation of the pendulum ilustrates the reciprocal states of passivity and activity

Levis (the wolf) Howling in the Desert, EUREKA! The helix, the shape of the process as a DNA molecule or tendril

The three equilibrial sculptures by Mitch Sid clarify the Commandments as the conflict resolution imperatives

The position of the stone on the vertical axis, totem pole, illustrates the notions of alienation vs. mutual respect

CYCLE 6, COMPROMISE: CREATIVITY FOR SELF-DISCOVERY, THE EXPERIENTIAL COMPONENT OF THE PROGRAM

STRESS RESPONSE ANXIETY: Pecker pecked Recognizing the physical and social nature of conflict as passivity, antagonism and alienation

REVERSAL in social terms Conflict as the tug of war between the characters of the drama

The REVERSAL in terms of inner conflict, the personal drama: internalization of the conflict wondering which side is up?

COMPROMISE: Resolution as the way of the clown, the compromise of discovering a new attitude about life: A smile as mastery, a handshake as cooperation and mutual respect . A whacker as lots of fun in love life.

The *Animal Metaphor Test* as pecker pecked

The individuals involved in the conflict as a tug-of-war

The internalization of the conflict as his head spinning and his conscience pinching his shirt

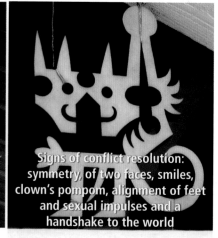

Signs of conflict resolution: symmetry, of two faces, smiles, clown's pompom, alignment of feet and sexual impulses and a handshake to the world

Adam's education in dealing with temptation Utilizing *Creativity And Power Management* to study his personal symbolic universe for insights and enlightenment, self discovery and self-improvement.

These sculptures represent the application of the formal theoretical concept of using creativity to generate metaphors to identify one's own relational patterns. The sculptures were metaphors in which the trainee identified his feelings in conflict and their evolution to satisfactory resolution. In them the creator, seeking marital counseling to deal with his dominant wife, identified a certain relational pattern. The first sculpture represents his key conflict of marital infidelity as "pecker pecked," a bird's beak complemented with a fishbone body was his *Animal Metaphor Test*. In the second and third sculptures, he recognized the characters in conflict and the internalization of the conflict. In the fourth sculpture he recognized his conflict resolution, both in his relation with his wife and with his own sense of anger and guilt toward her.

CYCLE 6, COMPROMISE:

In Cycle 5 we reiterated the findings of the process by celebrating the new reality.

In the final segment of the Trail, Cycle 6, Compromise, we present the application of the Formal Theory by utilizing the creative process for the generation of metaphors and for the person, as the creator, to interpret the metaphors and become self-aware.

Here we have an example of tapping creativity for self-discovery and acquiring insights for self-improvement.

The standardized program of emotional education is presented here with a case study as sculptures suspended from the pediment at the entrance of the Sanctuary. These were generated with Power Management, the concise program of emotional education based on studying creativity for self-discovery.

The sculptures are metaphors executed by a trainee seeking marital counseling identifying his difficulties in dealing with his dominant wife's power and escaping this predicament as his choice conflict resolution pattern. These sculptures represent the application of the formal theoretical concept of using creativity to generate metaphors to identify one's own relational patterns.

Self-discovery facilitates the outcome of psychotherapy available to the well public as emotional education leading to a new literacy. Learning about oneself improves one's skills in managing power and maximizes one's chances of attaining happiness.

CHAPTER THREE: EDUCATION

GIVING THE FIRE: A CONCISE PROGRAM OF EMOTIONAL EDUCATION

The first act of the Promethean drama identified the fire as the science of the process. The second act dealt with the process integrating religions, corresponding with stealing the fire of the gods, or the credibility of religions. The third and final act of the Promethean drama, giving the fire of the gods to the mortals corresponds to educating the public on the scientific nature of morality. Giving the new knowledge amounts to emancipating humans from their bondage to dogma, the abusive reign of the uninterpreted metaphors controlling believers like puppets, or dogs within invisible fences.

Religions are responsible for normative regulations that generate intense personal conflicts that are not in the interest of the public welfare. This realization leads to the conclusion that the current presentation of moral paradigms is misleading and responsible for the conflicts experienced within and between faiths. The Formal Theory, clarifying the conflict resolution process as the universal, equilibrial and homeostatic physiological mental mechanism, introduces the scientific understanding of morality and psychology.

This harmonic and universal moral order has been identified by religions as the moral authority of gods; in reality Gods and religions are merely projections of this psychic process. Gods evolved in the history of religion as alternative ways of resolving conflict. From many mean and scary creatures gods evolved to become the one kind and compassionate justice sponsoring moral authority of monotheism.

Religions are intuitive and metaphorical studies of conflict resolution. By interpreting metaphors scientifically the Moral Science studies religions as discoveries of conflict resolution. Now the Formal Theory clarifies the scientific nature of the moral order as mathematical and physical abstractions, as formulas of the rigorous sciences and the mere calculus of power management. The calculus completes the task to abstraction and universality. The Moral Science goes a long way beyond the imperfections and narrow moral choices of religion and dogma-based conflict resolutions.

A new mandate for education

Thus the Moral Science completes the unfinished task of religions by showing that the foundation of all moral laws is natural law. It establishes the importance of the creative process as the unit of moral order, the unit of the social sciences. This unit integrates epistemology, psychology, assessment and morality with the rigorous sciences making behavior into the exact Moral Science. This rational science revamps religions, psychology and education.

The realization that psychology and morality have become a science entails the need for a new model of education including instruction about the process and its personal relevance. We should distinguish here two different tasks for this type of education. The first task is instruction on the science of the process. The second task is instruction about self-discovery by identifying how the individual resolves conflict.

Introduction of Creativity and Power Management

The first task, **moral education**, may be achieved by a thorough study of the creative process as introduced by the five exhibits at the Museum. The second task, **emotional education**, may be achieved through the use of the *Conflict Analysis Battery*, relying on creativity for self-discovery.

Moral education, as the scientific understanding of

the process and of the evolution of religions corresponds to enlightenment. Emotional education complements and targets self-knowledge and clarity of values, leading to wisdom. Self-knowledge is about identifying one's relational modality as the particular way of resolving conflicts. Wisdom is judicious power management hinging on understanding relational power choices and consequences and deliberately making the right choices.

Moral and emotional literacy as a civil right

Moral and emotional education may be considered as a civil right tantamount to regular literacy. The concise program of emotional education based on the Moral Science leads to this literacy, which equips the student intellectually and emotionally with the knowledge and basic skills necessary to cope with our culturally and psychologically complex world.

This civil right allows for the correct interpretation of metaphors as alternative ways of resolving conflict and thus understanding both religions and emotional realities. Emotional literacy is the right to self-knowledge and clarity on moral values. This literacy reconciles differences, eliminates fragmentation, and diminishes cross-cultural conflicts.

The current educational theory respects the right for political correctness because it regards all religions as equally legitimate. The new understanding of moral order recognizes religions as particular and imperfect ways of resolving conflict and evaluates their effectiveness and fairness. Political correctness, which suspends critical analysis of religions, is dangerous to the public. The public has the right to rebel at being treated as thoughtless puppets controlled by the strings held by the religious traditions. The era of moral reason entails a revolution; the fire of Prometheus is knowledge which emancipates humans from the bondage to narrow moral paradigms, unfair norms regulating thoughts and behaviors.

The history of civilization confirms the trend of gradually restructured domestic roles in parallel to the redefinition of the nature of god. This historical precedent entails that religion be extrapolated to the Moral Science. The new society will identify the principles of conflict resolution as the universal and definitive moral values. The civil right for emotional and moral literacy should begin by establishing clarity on the scientific nature of the unconscious thought process and continue with the study of the history of religion as evolving norms as conflict resolutions in the area of domestic relations coinciding with redefinitions of God.

Knowledge of the Conflict Resolution Process ought to be imparted to the public as the foundation of all education. This knowledge is the right for all citizens to think clearly and critically about the realities of our normative environment free from prejudice.

The Formal Theory reconciles art and science to provide the content and direction to reshape the curriculum of education. It provides the guidelines for a conceptual reform that revamps education and takes the public beyond the current stalemate between evolutionists and creationists, the science of biology versus mythology. The Moral Science unifies the messages to be advanced by educators, clergy and therapists alike by interpreting metaphors as ideational symbolic systems resolving conflict.

Science does away with controversial issues that religions have sanctified as dogma, the arbitrary theistic criteria, the mandate of revealed moral righteousness. Science goes beyond the boundaries established through partial understanding of the moral process. It departs from favoring a particular configuration of power, such as the Father-Son covenant versus the mother-child alliance, to found moral order as an abstract process establishing fairness in all relations, i.e. the proportionate and appropriate management of power.

The third chapter, promoting education in the new science is about giving the fire, the Moral Science, to the mortals and healing the world. This role is captured through the effective delivery of the new knowledge to the public. The challenge of the Formal Theory is achieving its role as the guiding philosophy, inspiring personal transformation and social change.

Giving the fire is about introducing moral order as a scientific phenomenon dissociated from the ambiguities of religion and the concreteness promoted by agnostic psychologies. Giving the fire is achieved through studying creativity as the scientific moral paradigm integrating knowledge. This objective has been addressed by developing and delivering a concise program of moral and emotional education. This program reconciles science with psychology, emphasizing the need for justice, or moral order, as the inner compelling drive determining emotions and behaviors. Morality becomes the central human need determining social change and the attainment of the coveted objectives of peace of mind and peace in the world.

The program begins by educating the student about the physiology of the unconscious as the origin of all morality in the service of adjustment. Science fulfills the need for meaningful explanations providing clarity to the nature of the moral unconscious and its role as the integrative paradigm. Science delivers the clear conceptual language, new diagnostic categories of wellness, new and effective technologies for assessment, and clarity on relational values as the principles of conflict resolution.

Giving the fire is alerting the public and the academia about perceiving the unconscious as moral, seeking justice, and as predictable instead of as agnostic/amoral and unpredictable; the scientific unconscious is the origin of all moral order. Giving the fire is redefining morality as a clear natural science phenomenon. Objectivity

on moral order is the beginning in freeing the world from the divisive and inaccurate partial truths, the narrow restrictive norms advocated by religions.

In this chapter on giving the fire we explore the significance and relevance of the scientific constructs for the many fields of the social sciences: from education and psychology, to religion and politics. Here we will explore implementing the Moral Science in two key areas behavior/education and religion/politics.

We will discuss an emotional education program *Creativity and Power Management* to achieve the objectives of enlightenment, insight and wisdom. The basis of the program is the systematic study of the creative process clarifying concepts of the new science, their relevance for psychology, religion, and self-knowledge.

EMOTIONAL EDUCATION: *CREATIVITY AND POWER MANAGEMENT* TARGETS PERSONAL INSIGHTS AND ENLIGHTENMENT

The challenge now is to inform the public about the integration of psychology and moral order into the exact Moral Science. How do we convey that psychology has moral grounding? How do we establish that religions are about emotional psychological and sociological solutions? The goal is to inform the public about the new interpretation of the human essence free of metaphysical beliefs and magical thinking, respectful of causality, science and spirituality bound together by a harmonic that seeks conciliation, humility and stability.

We have explored the delivery of this information with a concise and comprehensive program of emotional and moral education: *Creativity and Power Management*. At this point in the volume we will review the new knowledge as a program of emotional education. Besides educational reform we need to learn how to deal with the religious institutions seeking their cooperation in making adjustments to the norms of science and freeing the public from compliance to their dated and pathogenetic norms stemming from another cultural era.

Science, stealing the fire, gains credibility in its expertise on moral matters and improves our understanding of psychology and moral order. The case study exhibit presents the concept of conflict resolution as the foundation of a program of moral and emotional education clarifying how we can give the fire to the mortals in the form of personal insights and an integrative meaningful education as enlightenment with the objective of healing the world.

Creativity and Power Management

The practical relevance of the Formal Theory is that we can use creativity as the compass to organize cultural realities and to reconstruct the personal relational system. *Creativity and Power Management* is a concise program of moral and emotional education consisting of studying the creative process as a scientific and moral order phenomenon, the unit of the social sciences. The unit clarifies the cultural and personal styles of power management demystifying religion and the many schools of psychology. The Moral Science answers questions about the nature of moral order. It also introduces the technology of creativity for self-discovery.

The *Conflict Analysis Training* workbook presents a manual-driven integrative psychotherapy, and alternatively, a comprehensive program of emotional education.

The program has three components: a cognitive, an experiential and a skills development segment. Creativity becomes the means to achieve the elusive objectives of education, the integration of knowledge, self-knowledge and clarity on moral values.

• The first component is educational or cognitive; it targets enlightenment, the bridging of the humanities and the sciences as well as the integration of psychology and morality into the Moral Science. Enlightenment is the understanding of the moral process and the evolution of religions as norms and divinities. The creative process is the healing response to stress. It is also the religious response as the individual's discovery of the sanctification of conflict resolution.

The art exhibits of the Museum of the Creative Process validate the Formal Theory highlighting the Universal Harmonic as the formal organization of emotions into units of conflict resolution. The Harmonic becomes clear as the unconscious equilibrial unit present in all symbolic systems, be those of Greek Myths, Gorski canvases, or patients' metaphors.

• The second component is experiential, i.e. diagnostic and therapeutic, and targets self-knowledge or insight. Insight is defined as understanding one's emotions and responses as related to one's relational modality. Learning about creativity is not a passive experience managed by educators and high priests. We learn about moral order in an experiential manner, by creating symbolic systems and observing the harmony established to detect wellness, pathology and healing.

The experiential part consists in completing, *The Conflict Analysis Battery*. This is a novel psycho-assessment instrument that taps creativity for self-discovery and insights. It facilitates personal transformation. *The Conflict Analysis Battery* consists of Formal Theory-based tests combining inventory and projective techniques. The metaphors generated in this workbook are used in correspondence to the six role-states template to reconstruct the Conflict Resolution Process, the personal drama or pattern.

• The third component is skills development along the pursuit of the spirituality of conflict resolution: it targets the introduction of clarity on moral values as the three scientific principles of conflict resolution and the implementation of these principles in one's life. A student may monitor his/her patterns of relating and pursue self-improvement being aware of the broader definition of spirituality as the art and science of conflict resolution.

Wisdom is defined as judicious power management skills hinging on understanding one's relational modality. We learn to appreciate religions but also to distance ourselves from them with the compassion of examining their integral choices in conflict resolution as bound to history. We can detect in religions and literature the drama that will need more than our sympathy; it requires our active intervention.

All three segments of the training may be attended separately or consecutively. All three segments are recommended for those interested in enlightenment, insight and wisdom. Fathoming the creative process makes it possible to identify the unconscious for educational, diagnostic and therapeutic objectives. Psychology and morality become the two inseparable components of the mental process.

As foouncded on one unified science the program can efficiently deliver emotional education to the well public, and therapy to those who are clinically diagnosed. This emotional education is suitable for the classroom and therapy settings alike.

They represent a thorough training program suitable for the general public and professionals interested in introducing emotional and moral education in their respective settings.

THE EDUCATIONAL/COGNITIVE SEGMENT
THE PURSUIT OF ENLIGHTENMENT ATTAINABLE THROUGH A REVIEW OF THE INFORMATION DOCUMENTED WITH THE MUSEUM EXHIBITS AS PRESENTED IN THIS BOOK

The cognitive or educational segment reviews the three topics pertaining to the Universal Harmonic as the scientific moral paradigm. Using the Promethean metaphor we review the concepts advanced along its three distinctions: the fire as science; stealing the fire as the integration of religion and science; and giving the fire as the discussion on matters of healing the person and the world.

Topic 1: Science/Fire
The first three exhibits present the nature of the CRP as a purely scientific, moral order phenomenon totally unrelated to religion.

Topic 2: Religion/Stealing the fire
The Sculptural Trail shows how the unit order integrates religions as a continuum of moral discoveries completed with their integration with psychology and science into the Moral Science clarifying the scientific nature of moral order.

Topic 3: Healing/Giving the fire
Here I have presented the concepts of the program of emotional education exemplified with the case studies of *Creativity and Power Management*.

The review of the three chapters
Upon completing the guided tour of the exhibits or reading this guidebook the visitor or reader may ask oneself the following questions:

Reminding us of the pertinent facts summing up the message put forward by the exhibits book. They address first the concept of the process, second the integration of science with psychology and religion, and third the educational reform targeting an emotional and moral education.

?

Do I understand the fire as the unconscious Conflict Resolution Process encompassing psychology and moral order into a natural science phenomenon?

?

Do I understand stealing the fire of the gods as science integrating religions, by reducing religions to alternative and partial but complementary discoveries of the unit Conflict Resolution Process?

?

Do I understand giving the fire to the mortals as delivering an emotional education program to effectively introduce enlightenment, insight and wisdom?

TOPIC 1:
SCIENCE/THE FIRE

Do I understand the fire as the unconscious Conflict Resolution Process encompassing psychology and moral order into a natural science phenomenon?

About the scientific moral paradigm as the fire
We introduced the Promethean fire as the metaphor of the unit of the CRP, the scientific moral paradigm, by exploring the impact of this discovery in the interpretation of metaphors, all creativity. The Museum exhibits validate the CRP by showing that it organizes information meaningfully in all realms of creativity. The presence of this organizing pattern across all realms attests to the fact that science-based moral order is a universal natural phenomenon. The exhibits highlight the importance of shifting the study of morality from the metaphysical and metaphorical domain to the realm of the natural sciences as the formal analysis of samples of creativity.

The Formal Theory advances the unit order and transforms the humanities into a natural moral science. The realm of analysis is the formal interrelation of emotions as role-states; the method of analysis is formal distinctions among the set of ideas/emotions in a symbolic universe. This symbolic system is a circumscribed unit entity. It is the Conflict Resolution Process, a homeostatic phenomenon restoring the personal sense of balance whenever this is disturbed by a stressor. The outcome is compromise an improvement in the quality of the conserved energy of emotions. The mind predictably processes emotions/role-states, and energies progressing to the moral end of a resolution as the upgrading of energy, the change of attitude through the generation of meaning.

Creativity as a natural science phenomenon
The first objective of the exhibits of the Museum of the Creative Process has been to illustrate and

validate Formal Theory's premise on the scientific structure and moral function of the creative process as a natural science phenomenon, a perfectly abstract universe, the Teleion Holon. The Metaphoria Murals, the Wizard of Oz panels of the Sanctuary and the Gorski Retrospective introduce and validate the theoretical assumptions of the process. These three exhibits, as orderly symbolic universes, highlight the process as the unit order, the Universal Harmonic, organizing information as a predictable, and measurable unit order. These exhibits demonstrate the unit order, bridging art and science, psychology and morality and introduce the Moral Science as a well-articulated field of knowledge.

The three art exhibits identify the circumscribed sequences of formally related art events, pursuing the completion of the Conflict Resolution Process. Conflict resolution is shown to be a periodic phenomenon, the unit entity of behavior. The holistic entity represents the object for all observers to study behavior and evolve consensus on the nature of the psyche as the unit of moral order reconciling morality and psychology with the lucidity of the rigorous sciences. Thus we may conclude that science has the answers to the mysteries of psychology and religion.

Conflict resolution as the circumscribed phenomenon of holistic thinking changes the way we look at art. The new art appreciation focuses on the relational context, which binds art pieces as formally related symbolic transformations within the totality of a story. The relational context has been demonstrated as the six-step harmonic and the three formal transformations. It is not difficult to detect this Conflict Resolution Process in dramas and novels; the Gorski Retrospective makes it clear in the graphic arts. The Museum's art exhibits demonstrate this holistic continuity unfolding in a predictable manner in all symbolic universes.

We observe art not as isolated objects of aesthetic significance, but as ideas integrated by the dialectic of the process, the unit Harmonic of the social sciences. Myths, canvases, stories, and religions are reduced to conflict resolution units of predictability and scientific analysis. The unit paradigm is pertinent in rethinking psychology: it allows us first to adopt the clear conceptual language of the rigorous sciences for the study of behavior; second, to reconceptualize diagnostic categories on purely dynamic parameters; third, to evolve new and accurate psycho-assessment techniques; and fourth, to rethink psychotherapy, psycho-education, religion and spirituality by improving our capacity to manage power in order to resolve conflicts optimally.

The exhibits illustrate the new way of looking at art as units of conflict resolution. They shift our awareness from fragmentation of reality to the perception of meaning as the purposeful connection of fragments into conflict resolving totalities. The exhibits shift our focus from the content of stories to a determinist/moral and reductionist/scientific process. They help the viewer, reader or observer to reflect on this process as conflict resolution, the meaning of life. The holistic unit order rethinks psychology and moral order as abiding to the laws of science.

The exhibits rediscover the process in all samples of creativity. Accordingly they examine the relationship between six consecutive emotions as canvases, sculptural stations, mural tiles, pieces of art and associations in compositions of metaphors. We also examine the repeated series of conflict resolutions as recorded in the evolution of ideas in the symbolic universes of cultures and the works of one artist. The purpose of the exhibits is to demonstrate the universal process as the way the mind and civilizations resolve conflicts evolving ever-improving abstractions on the nature of the process.

The exhibits of the Harmonic proceed like a permanent poster show, systematically examining the premise of the theory and arriving at the same conclusion. Yes, we have a universal entity, a mental heartbeat, which organizes information meaningfully as a conflict resolving process. The exhibits concur on the universality of the process and the structure of the unconscious both as moral and rational. The Harmonic helps observers emerge from being divided and fragmented by contradictory belief systems to evolve consensus on moral values as the scientific principles of conflict resolution: moderation, cooperation and mutual respect.

The Harmonic in the Metaphoria Murals

The 12 Murals in the Sanctuary present studies of the predictable conflict resolution totality as the universal plot of stories. The murals identify the Harmonic with six tiles representing the six parts of the unit process. This process allows us to introduce continuity and reason where there was fragmentation and alienation.

The Harmonic is clearly marked in every mural as the sequence of the conflict resolution unit's six role-states: stress, response, anxiety, defense, reversal and compromise. The murals feature the Unit order in sample symbolic systems. Each mural displays the structure and function of the Conflict Resolution Process binding parts, be those cultural metaphors or experimentally elicited, personal creativity tasks. Seven of the murals illustrate and validate the theory through the experimental study of the creative process by using the theory's assessment instrument, the *Conflict Analysis Battery*.

The Metaphoria Murals demystify religions as alternative ways in resolving conflict

Murals one to six present the evolution of cultural stories into clarifying the unit of conflict resolution.

Mural 1 illustrates the Harmonic integrating six episodes in the life cycle of the Greek Gods as described in the Cosmogony, the Greek creation story. This mural depicts the cruel transactions of the Greek Cosmogony as stories reflecting the antagonistic pattern of relations in the Greek family. This antagonistic pattern is prevalent in the glorious culture's myths, tragedies, epics, politics and dramas.

Mural 2, presents the process reconciling the multiple competing moral paradigms of the world.

Mural 3 illustrates 10 Biblical Commandments identified as the three principles of conflict resolution. These account for the variations in relational modalities of the three Abrahamic religions.

Mural 4 shows how the Harmonic integrates experimentally generated metaphors to detect the personal conflict resolution pattern. In the second set of murals, #7-12, the Harmonic is shown to again integrate personal metaphors for diagnostic and therapeutic purposes.

Mural 5 shows how the Harmonic integrates cultural metaphors as formally interrelated discoveries of how to resolve conflicts.

Mural 6 contrasts four cultures as alternative ways of resolving conflicts that is in dealing with temptation or power.

The Harmonic and the Gorski Retrospective

The Harmonic is confirmed by uniting the canvases of the Henry Gorski Retrospective into a set of symbolically distinct sequences of conflict resolutions. Thus, the exhibit illustrates the six-role process integrating all canvasses as evolving relationally around a key role-state, in Gorski's case, pain. Each cycle illustrates the circumscribed, formally interrelated sequences of canvases as the episodes of a dramatic play with a beginning, middle and moral end. This exhibit highlights the presence of formal operations by making obvious the relational transformations, which connect the disparate canvasses into a lifetime dramatic or transformational continuum.

Indeed, the five sequences are summed up in the respective self-portraits. The interrelation of the self-portraits as resolutions reflects accurately his evolving identity. The portraits as resolutions represent a progression of improved attitudinal or conflict resolving adjustment to the adversities of life. This increase in positive attitude is the proof, which validates the postulation of the process as the self-healing and as an innate adjustment mechanism. A dramatic confirmation of the Conflict Resolution Process is in the final self-portrait canvas of the Gorski Retrospective integrating the kiss and the cross into a cross made of kisses and his last self-portrait superimposed on it. The title of that canvas clarifies the surprise in the reconciliation of pleasure and pain, he calls the canvas: *The Paradox*. The emotional growth is confirmed by the comments of the artist, clarifying the evolution of his disposition. The Gorski Retrospective is also useful in portraying the laws of the formal and physical transformations, the science of epistemology, as the study of the scientific structure of the Unit, the ten levels of the Formal Analysis Profile.

The Harmonic and the Wizard of Oz Panels

The Oz Panels show how the Harmonic underlies and integrates the four key metaphors of the Wizard of Oz as pertaining to the four aspects of the study of conflict resolution, and how it integrates these aspects as social sciences into the cohesive Moral Science.

To this effect, the external Oz Panels and the interior Metaphoria Murals are arranged on both sides of the same four walls of the Sanctuary so that the abstractions articulated on the exterior panels, the Oz story, are illustrated by corresponding clinical case studies on the interior. Thus theory and practice corroborate information to address the issues of one discipline at a time and four disciplines sequentially.

Accordingly, the southern wall illustrates the discipline of epistemology, using the metaphor of the Yellow Brick Road to represent the Harmonic as a natural science phenomenon. This postulation of the process introduces rigorous constructs and formulas into the field of behavior. Behavior becomes predictable and measurable. Oz Panel 2 sums up the Formal Analysis Profile as the equivalence of natural laws and the social sciences observations. The murals on the interior side focus on the equivalent themes of creation stories and religion as combining psychology of the unconscious, creativity and morality with science, predictability and measure.

The eastern wall presents the discipline of psycho-diagnosis using the four characters of the story to clarify the Harmonic as a clinical syndrome manifested as the four relational modalities: dominant-cooperative (Dorothy); dominant-antagonistic (the Cowardly Lion); submissive-cooperative (the Scarecrow); and the submissive-antagonistic (the Tin Man). These key relational modalities predict behavior for the well and the diagnosed persons alike.

The interior wall introduces two wellness and two clinically diagnosed case studies of alternative personality types, subordinacy and dominance. The two are wellness cases. They are contrasted in one mural in the brief evaluation process. The two non-well cases are presented with their respective metaphors as unfolding in the course of long-term therapy reflecting the process as a series of improving resolutions.

The northern wall presents the killing of the witch as the metaphor for the discipline of psychotherapy or power management. The metaphor of killing the witch is useful in representing the challenge of taking risks for emotional growth including overcoming one's dependency needs. Risk taking leads to personal growth and healing. We see the four heroes resolve the conflicts of their damaged identities.

The murals on the interior illustrate the use of creativity through the generation and organization of metaphors for self-discovery and how the process is diagnostic, therapeutic and effective. These murals clarify the nature of symbolic systems, how to interpret images, their formal transformations and redeployment, the significance of the images' directionality. Mural 9 presents the remarkable therapeutic effectiveness of completing the mere assessment process.

Finally, the western wall represents the discipline of Moral Order, using the Wizard as the metaphor of moral authorities leading to the analysis of ethics, morality and religions. On the interior of the wall we study the nature of the moral process both as the personal discovery of moral order, Mural 4, and also the study of religions and cultures as the evolution of restructuring family relations and redefining God as improved abstraction on the nature of moral order, (Murals 5 and 6).

Critique of rational humanism

The Wizard of Oz story is an epic tale of the 20th century's emboldened humanism demystifying religion. The story's metaphors define the road, the journey of life, the characters, the range of relational modalities, the adventures of the heroes struggling with their own uncertainties and identities in front of the parental and cultural authorities. The story starts with a child in conflict with a powerful abusive parental authority, the child's wrestling with the parental authorities, good and bad, the witch and the wizard, as intimidating powerful figures. The witch goes up in smoke; the Wizard is unveiled as a fraud. The Wizard's departure is good for the human characters' empowerment as they are freed from their fears and as they accept responsibility of the Emerald City. The story ends with the tormented persons transformed and healed as cured patients. The healing conflict resolution experience starting with a conflict and ending at a resolution addresses enlightenment at a number of levels, conceptual, psychological, therapeutic and moral.

But one may wonder the significance of the unveiling of the Wizard in its pertinence, implication to religion and Gods as dismissible figments of our imagination. Baum presents Oz as a magical authority equivalent to God. He indicates the relational distortions of Oz's image by each of the heroes corresponding to his attitude; the mild-mannered Scarecrow perceived him as a fair lady, the hostile Tin Man as a bolt of lightning, etc.. The distorted perceptions validate Formal Theory's relational modalities as the respective anticipations being fulfilled. The problem I have with the story is that Oz, and by extension religions, are perceived as fraudulent and completely dismissed. This outcome, in my opinion, reflects the antireligious sentiments of the beginning of the 20th century representing rational humanism's position that science disproved the existence of God. I object the summary dismissal of Oz as I regard him as the impersonation not only of all divinities but also of the conceptual reality of the Conflict Resolution Process, the underlying scientific phenomenon.

Conclusion

The positive message of the three exhibits is that we have identified the unconscious, a circumscribed entity, as a psychological and moral observable natural science phenomenon. This is the creative process as an object for the scientific analysis of behavior. Science is now enabled to interpret our cultural metaphors, to qualify, quantify and dialectically integrate them. We need no longer be held hostage to religions' singular claims of representing the total truth. We can feel comfortable with the Conflict Resolution Process as the science-based moral mechanism underlying all creativity and reconciling psychology's patterns with science's constructs and formulas.

The art exhibits constitute a formidable intellectual challenge promoting the scientific conceptualization of the creative process, the integration of the social science disciplines and the development of a model program of emotional education. Suddenly it is possible to integrate knowledge, fathom self-knowledge and elucidate moral values. The formal conceptualization of the unconscious as the Unit of the Conflict Resolution Process reconciles the sciences and the humanities; it unites the social science disciplines into the cohesive Moral Science.

The exhibits are of practical importance. They introduce creativity as the object of the study of psychology. They demonstrate that creativity holds the secrets to the scientific understanding of behavior, but also that it is the key to accessing the unconscious in order to achieve diagnosis and healing. The formalization of the unconscious constitutes a breakthrough with vast ramifications for both psychotherapy and prevention.

The Unit process clarifies the concepts of behavior. It allows for the formulation of wellness diagnostic categories and wellness education. The Unit allows the development of accurate and meaningful instruments of self-assessment and personal growth as well as the means to streamline moral and emotional education. The theory represents the culmination of the integration of the humanities and the rigorous sciences.

This conclusion is powerful. We are neither at the mercy of Gods nor of psychological approximations, neologisms or mere empirical observations. But also we have no sympathy for agnostic science. Formal Analysis becomes the means to understand moral order as a universal Harmonic providing meaning to psychology, religion and science. The new concept informs us about wellness and is the compass to navigate moral dilemmas. We recognize personalities as relational modalities. This distinction frees us from the phenomenological diagnostic categories of the established descriptive non-dynamic classification system, (Diagnostic Statistic Manual or DSM). It provides us with the means to understand and measure our ways of relating and to evaluate and perfect our relational approach without being diagnosed as emotionally disturbed or as entering therapy.

The four conceptual social science identities of the Harmonic

Unlike other grand theories, because the Formal Theory introduces scientific constructs and formulas into the realm of behavior, this theory may be tested and validated by examining the structure of symbolic systems.

Do the exhibits confirm the manifestations of the Conflict Resolution Process? Do they attest to a six role-state sequence consisting of three formal operations transforming conflict to resolution? Does the process integrate diversity into an overarching and universal realm of mental and moral order? The personal sampling of mental and moral order and the art exhibits help to answer these important questions affirmatively. The exhibits are validations of the key concept.

The Harmonic is the plot of stories as the unit of moral order. It is the roller coaster inner dialogue and the adventurous negotiation between the individual and the environment unfolding as a dramatic struggle. This definition describes the unconscious as a natural science homeostatic phenomenon. It is the compass guiding behavior to stay within acceptable or normative boundaries.

The exhibits generate awareness of the holistic Unit process organizing ideas in the symbolic universes of each one of the four social sciences. In each of these disciplines the same process is recognized in alternative identities and functions.

• Epistemology: the Unit of the Conflict Resolution Process may be conceptualized as a natural science and formal equilibrial system with the rigorous constructs of the sciences. The exhibits demonstrate the hypothesized scientific order underlying all samples of creativity. They illustrate the six role-state structure and the conflict resolution function throughout the symbolic systems displayed.

• Psycho-diagnosis: the Unit may be qualified and

thus yields a new set of psychodiagnostic categories, the syndromal relational modalities, as the alternative ways of resolving conflict. The exhibits illustrate the new range of diagnostic categories, the relational modalities.

• Psycho-assessment: the Unit is a measurable dramatic process identified with the use of a self-assessment technology based on tapping the creative process to identify how one person resolves conflicts. The instrument of psycho-assessment, a workbook, is called the *Conflict Analysis Battery*. The exhibits illustrate how the Battery measures the Unit process. *Creativity and Power Management*, this theory's manual-driven psychotherapy, uses the Battery to lead to insights, learning and attitude modification.

• Moral Order: the Unit is the scientific moral paradigm and moral solutions vary by modifying the variables of the three formal operations that resolve conflict. The exhibits help to understand moral order. Science provides the secular paradigm of moral order. The Conflict Resolution Process inspires us to goodness and peace on earth. The exhibits redefine morality in universally acceptable scientific terms thus reconciling the religions of the world.

Summing up Formal Theory's attributes of the unit process

The unit of conflict resolution shows that psychology and morality are inherently intertwined in the unit process introducing meaning as scientific clarity in the field of metaphors. Science confirms that religions have observed and described the conflict resolution order, especially in Judaism's principles of faith, the attributes of an external magical but benevolent force.

• The Formal Theory identifies the CRP as the object of scientific analysis of psychology and moral order.

• The CRP is the organization of ideas in all

samples of creativity. We know it as the plot of stories. It is a moral order periodic entity abiding by the laws of the natural sciences; as such it is the unit of the social sciences; Aristotle identified it as the Teleion Holon, the perfect universe, in the study of Greek dramatic plays.

• The CRP is a mental equilibrial conflict resolving, moral order phenomenon manifested in samples of creativity, whether they are stories, plays, canvases, epics or religions, as the universal predictable and measurable natural science formal organization of ideas.

• The CRP is defined as six emotionally/energetically charged role-states bound by a set of three formal operations into a periodic unit entity. The six role-states are: stress, response, anxiety, defense, reversal and compromise. The three formal irreversible operations are passivity transformed to its reciprocal activity; antagonism to its opposite, cooperation; and alienation to its correlate, mutual respect.

• The CRP is an abstract, formal and energetic equilibrial process abiding by the laws of natural science phenomena like the trays of a scale and the pendulum oscillation. This correspondence allows us to import scientific constructs and formulas from logic, physics and math into the study of behavior. Accordingly, the CRP may be represented as a six-part or three-cycle Harmonic, and its cross-section as a circle, the field of power distinctions.

• Moral Science recognizes alternative ways of resolving conflict as four wellness diagnostic categories, the relational modalities; these categories are very meaningful as alternative personality types predictive of their strengths and weaknesses. The public benefits by identifying their relational modality, its strengths and weaknesses.

• Moral Science measures the CRP with a self-assessment instrument, the *Conflict Analysis Battery*, which is diagnostic, therapeutic and educational.

• The CRP, as the unit of the social sciences, integrates them into the Science of Conflict Resolution, the Moral Science.

• *Creativity and Power Management* is an educational program, targeting moral and emotional literacy. We advocate this literacy as a new civil right. Education on the Moral Science is introduced with the art exhibits of the Museum of the Creative Process. The art exhibits demonstrate the universal Harmonic as the Unit of the CRP.

TOPIC 2:
RELIGION/STEALING THE FIRE FROM THE GODS

Do I understand stealing of the fire of the gods as science integrating religions, by reducing religions to alternative and partial but complementary discoveries of the unit Conflict Resolution Process?

Stealing the fire as departing from metaphors to identify reliable science integrating religions meaningfully into the Moral Science

The second objective of the study has been to demonstrate the CRP integrating religions and integrating them into the Science of Conflict Resolution. The process has been the tool to fathom religions as metaphorical discoveries of the unconscious Conflict Resolving Process. The Formal Theory integrates them by recognizing them as a progression of conflict resolution entities establishing continuity between them and the Moral Science. Hence we recognize that religions advance moral order as justice, yet the optimal state of resolution and justice for all is clarified best by science. Science completes the unfinished task of religions.

Moral Science stealing the fire does not invalidate religion as suggested by Darwinian theoreticians. Neither do we dismiss Genesis as Creationism; on the contrary we acknowledge it as an accurate metaphor of the six-role state Conflict Resolution Process. Moral Science respects reli-

gions as having pioneered alternative conflict resolutions ahead of contemporary psychology. Religions are honored as promoting models of conflict resolution through metaphors. As such, religions have relational dimensions; the Moral Science goes beyond metaphors, interpreting them as natural science phenomena and is critical of religions as frozen partial insights in the science of the process and thus as counterproductive in many moral matters.

The Harmonic and the Sculptural Trail

The Sculptural Trail presents the evolution of awareness on the mental Harmonic by retracing the history of religion through six cycles of sculptures, each telling a story, integrated into the unit process. The trail starts with the process. It continues integrating religions as discoveries of the process and finally it introduces the process as the new moral authority. The trail's six cycles are interrelated as steps in a process of resolution. They shift our attention from metaphors of particular ways of resolving to the abstract and scientific understanding of the creative process as a conflict resolving mechanism, the unit of the social sciences.

The sequence of the six cycles of the trail progressively clarify the scientific structure of the plot of stories:

Stress: the dialogue between the sad wizard and the scale, wisdom, shifts our focus from the content of stories to the plot of stories;

Response: the fairy tale clarifies the Conflict Resolution Process as the scientific secrets of living happily ever after.

Anxiety: the epics of the Goddess as cultural gender wars shaped the family institution, clarifying pagan religions as discoveries of alternative and complementary ways of resolving conflict but ended with the oppression of women by monotheism.

Defense: the scriptures of the one god retrace the conflicts of the Abrahamic religions as domestic power struggles between the father-son covenant and the mother-child alliance. These are reconciled by the scientific moral paradigm requiring mutual respect between partners in the family system for the resolution of a conflict. The labyrinth is a sculptural rendering of the plot of stories, the reduction of stories into the universal Conflict Resolution Process.

Reversal: The moral CRP is celebrated as the new reality. Abstract art pays tribute to the creativity as the sacred scientific process. One installation illustrates the process as a three-part continuum. Another installation honors the simple principles of conflict resolution with three equilibrial sculptures. The last segment of the trail affirms continuity between science and religion with the set of abstract sculptures celebrating the notions of Genesis and the Commandments as sculptural constructions.

Compromise: finally, four sculptures of one student celebrate the use of creativity for self-discovery by identifying one's Conflict Resolution Process as the means for emotional education. These realtional operations are the secrets of happiness. They are also the measurable dimensions of the Conflict Resolution Process reflecting knowledge on behavior and oneself.

The Sculptural Trail presents religions as evolving complementary scientific discoveries, a sequence completed by the Moral Science

The Sculptural Trail presents the evolution of awareness on the mental Harmonic as the nature of the unconscious as a natural science and moral order phenomenon. The trail does so by retracing the history of religion through six cycles of sculptures, each telling a story, which increasingly clarifies the scientific nature of the plot of stories. The trail's six cycles shift our attention from historical metaphors to the abstract and scientific understanding of the creative process as a conflict resolving mechanism, the unit of the social sciences. The secrets of happiness are the measurable dimensions of the Conflict Resolution Process reflecting knowledge on behavior and oneself. The Trail shows how the progressive awareness of the Harmonic integrates the religions of the world into the rigorous process and how the use of the process leads to the Moral Science.

The sculptural trail retraces the history of religion. Indeed in the mid segment of the trail science completes the task of religions by identifying their ongoing progression to fairer norms and increasingly abstract definitions of the divine. In the cycle of the scriptures the harmonic integrates the episodes in the history of Judaism into a drama that finds its resolution by resolving the perennial gender relations conflicts through the introduction of mutual respect between all the members of the family.

All six sculptural cycles of the trail evolve into resolutions at higher levels of abstraction reflecting the universal quest for meaning as increasingly founded on reason. This quest with the trail ends in the discovery of the unit process as the ultimate moral paradigm useful for personal insights and societal emotional and moral growth.

The Sculptural Trail presents many stories that evolved independently of each other as a sequence to provide the world with increasingly meaningful moral messages. The unit is the ultimate insight on the nature of moral order and the unconscious is introduced as the ultimate moral authority. Conflict resolution is predicated on the transformation of conflict as passivity, antagonism and alienation to mastery, cooperation and mutual respect between partners. It is important that the world examine our belief systems in the context of the history of religion as the quest for domestic happiness. It is imperative to consider the evolution of paradigms from polytheism to monotheism and now to science.

Moral Science, the Science of Conflict Resolution
While respecting religions, the new science criticizes religions for promoting faith ahead of reason by endorsing partial knowledge, i.e. metaphors as the ultimate reality. Religions, because of their limited capacity to comprehend the process, have distorted causality by introducing dogma-based explanations. We have shown how the process reconciles religions as a dialectic progression of alternative modes of resolving. Science completes their progression with the scientific understanding of the process as an equilibrial phenomenon following the laws of the Simple Harmonic Motion.

Science demystifies moral order and empowers morality as a natural science phenomenon guided by the personal need for social justice as the equitable treatment of all members of a social system. Thus, science emancipates believers from the reign of uninterpreted metaphors and guides them to the alternative, moral reason, as the study of complete conflict resolution. Science does not dismiss religions and moral values; rather it empowers the public to understand religions critically evaluating their contributions to the process while all the same recognizing their incompleteness and ethical arbitrariness.

Conflict Analysis-the Formal Theory of Behavior, published in 1988, presented a scientific breakthrough and its validation without claiming its role in the politics of knowledge. The volume introduced the scientific study of the unconscious as the formal organization of ideas, the atomistic Unit of the social sciences having a distinct structure and serving a physiological, homeostatic function. The process was exemplified with the formal analysis of samples of creativity, myths, canvases, dramatic stories, patients' artwork and metaphors.

The Formal Theory's contribution may be summed up as science identifying the unconscious as the master key to knowledge. Conflict Analysis was about the science of this key that opens all doors. In great contrast to the first publication, *Stealing the Fire of the Gods, Art*

as Evidence of Science places the emphasis on the Universal Harmonic as the science-based as opposed to dogma-based moral paradigm. The emphasis in this book is contrasting Moral Science to religions. Moral Science's formalized way of conceptualizing moral order is validated as the means to understand and integrate religions.

This book introduces the Moral Science as having an activist agenda, antagonistic to religions by promoting a perspective that deserves to win respect as the cure from the everlasting interfaith conflicts, the perennial wars of metaphors. Science advocates conflict resolution as the adjustment process, which can address the deficiencies of the current moral conceptualizations. Traditional paradigms are misleading the faithful and are mishandling justice; they are sacrilegious in the sense that they violate science, generate excruciating personal conflicts, domestic conflicts and abuses of power in the name of a misunderstood God. God is the reality of the innate human process.

Science with a heart, a cause and a mission
The Harmonic is not simply a scientific phenomenon, a spiral, an inert, equilibrial, circumscribed dialectic, a master key that opens all doors. It is the compass for societal conformity with universal laws. It provides hope for moral justice in a world in excruciating religion-evoked turmoil. The paradigm is not merely factual information on the structure of the process; it is about the cause of conflict resolution, a war of values to be won by defining morality abstractly as the Science of Power Management. The Moral Science helps religions to respect natural law as adequate in defining moral order. Natural law neutralizing revealed law. Scientific reason is able to question faith.

Moral Science's task is to define morality as the physiologic innate mental mechanism. The new paradigm is useful in saving and improving lives; it demands a confrontation with the current moral authorities to alert them that they lack pertinent knowledge and that Science can give it to them. The Moral Science then is not only about science; it is a science with the mission to advocate conflict resolution to correct injustices and attain lucidity across the universe of meaning seekers.

Stealing the fire should be qualified as science delivering to humans the capacity to redefine moral order and improve social justice. Science claims the epistemic language defining moral order as a natural science phenomenon. Moral order was delegated to the gods based on metaphysical explanations in the times when humans were unable to reason and in times of lack of sophistication on matters of science. Aristotle could not reason beyond basic laws of logic and physics. Now, as humanity is becoming conscious of the unconscious as a science-based moral message, believers may realize that the traditional formulations and explanations on the creation of the universe by gods have been inaccurate and incomplete understandings of cultures, psychology and science.

As confidence increases in the science-based moral order the public will understand that morality is a phenomenon that is abiding by the rigorous laws of science. The desirable outcome of scientific integrity is that the secular world may establish moral consensus and inspire believers to the advantages of science.

The unit order, as scientific knowledge, represents politically sensitive information that can dramatically alter the way we define reality. The Promethean paradigm of stealing the fire reflects the shift of power in control, from the tyranny of metaphors to the joy of redefining moral authority as the inner yearning for conflict resolution. Science upstages religion by assuming the credibility of formulas. Science, as reason, is prevailing over faith, but also encompasses it.
The Moral Science has general advantages. It is

the science that redefines psychology; the moral paradigm is the unconscious; it identifies scientific concepts in the study of behavior, the diagnostic categories of wellness, moral values, and the assessment methods of the unconscious process. Moral Science sponsors the norm of conflict resolution as the state of mastery, cooperation and mutual respect. This norm is the moral paradigm reinforced in the analysis of all samples of creativity. This equilibrial, unconscious process, the spontaneous path to justice, becomes endorsed as the standard by which all metaphors can be interpreted and judged.

The affirmation of science through the arts increases the credibility of the new concepts; this entails that science assume the leadership to inspire and to advocate changes, reconceptualizing the social sciences as the unified Science of Conflict Resolution, the Moral Science. This science can have a dramatic social impact as it introduces justice and dignity for all, rectifying inequities in the area of gender roles and power management in all relationships, domestic and political. Science sanctifies the norms of a new social order. Following the shift of paradigms, the Moral Science becomes the authority on the psychology of the unconscious as the scientific nature of moral order. So now science is responsible for determining normative or socially acceptable behaviors.

TOPIC 3:
GIVING THE FIRE/HEALING/EDUCATION

Do I understand giving the fire to the mortals as delivering an emotional education program to effectively introduce enlightenment, insight and wisdom?

Having stolen the fire now science has established the credibility of the new moral order and we are ready to deal with the challenge of finding a receptive audience of mortals interested in the fire, the precious new mind-liberating information. We want to enlighten the public by clarifying the

nature of the unconscious which integrates the wisdoms of the world, clarifies the many aspects of psychology, inspires people to be creative and examine their creativity for insights and personal transformation. Science elucidates issues of morality and the psychology of power management as unified and reconciled. Another aspect of education is the development of skills related to art appreciation as a scientific spiritual experience.

With the above thoughts as a preamble of this closing section let us return to the third objective of the book as giving the fire to the mortals. We pursue this task through the introduction of the Formal Theory into education as well as psychotherapy. *Creativity and Power Management*, the model study of the creative process, is the means to enlightenment, insight and wisdom.

We introduce the well-balanced concise program of emotional education addressing both moral and emotional literacy. Creativity, as conflict resolution, is the object of our studies. The program explores the nature of the process using the art exhibits of the museum or this guidebook. The means for healing is tapping creativity for an inward journey of introspection. The program uses the *Battery* to tap creativity for self-discovery and personal transformation. The program includes the analysis of one's metaphors with holistic exercises, processing information in the context of personal growth. Exhibit #5 presents the experiential segment with seven case studies.

The fifth exhibit illustrates the effectiveness of the use of creativity for self-discovery. It consists of seven murals presenting creativity in the service of self-discovery. The murals illustrate art generated in the course of the training program, utilizing the *Conflict Analysis Battery*, the application of the creative process for self-discovery and self-help.

The fifth exhibit, creativity for self-discovery (Murals 7-12)
To illustrate the experiential segment of the pro-

gram I presented seven case studies demonstrating the ease of reconstructing the personal drama as the template of the mental heartbeat, a simple harmonic integrating images of metaphors and the related personal emotions. The seven cases focused on processing information generated by the *Conflict Analysis Battery*.

Mural 4, *My Metaphors, Myself*, introduces the correspondence of the six role-states of the Harmonic with six tests from the metaphors of the *Battery*.

Mural 7, *The Aesthetics of Metaphors*, illustrates the formal operations manifested in the symbolic transformations as states of passivity and activity presented in parallel metaphors.

Mural 8, presents the Physics of Imagery as the language of the unconscious, which abides by the formulas of physics. The mural illustrations clarify how to interpret the physical orientation of the animal metaphors reflecting the trainees' emotions.

Mural 9, presents the effectiveness of the healing function of the metaphor testing. In this case the patient was cured of perennial anxieties, depression and guilt related to her childhood Holocaust experiences. This therapeutic outcome transpired over the course of three sessions.

Mural 10, focus on differentiating the diametrically opposite scenarios of two relational modalities. The mural contrasts the profiles of two students, one dominant and one submissive, reflecting the differences between the two relational syndromal diagnoses.

Murals 11 and 12, present two long-term therapy outcome studies monitored with metaphor testing using two different methods. We witness the ongoing growth of the patients during the therapeutic process. In the first study the patient repeated the metaphor exercises of the entire Battery. In the second study the patient completed the single *Animal Metaphor Test* in successive sessions. By comparing these cases we observe how therapy reflects phases in the maturation of both patients. The tests reveal the difficulty in repressing verses in expressing feelings. Both dominant and submissive persons learn to manage power and improve

in their communications and adjustment. Gladys evolved from an original fear of expressing anger and destroying a her family as a "flame-throwing dragon" to being able to "express feelings and still being friends." The murals clearly convey the phases of therapy as the challenges and objectives to be accomplished during the sessions. The two cases reflect on the importance of long-term therapy and the significance of the monitoring process in mapping out its course.

These cases also reflect on the emotional growth of the individual dealing with moral conflict. The seminarian is a case in point; he chose to become a priest to deal with his homosexual urges and early traumas, which he felt were humiliating experiences. The issues of right and wrong were so intense that he was motivated to become a priest to cure himself of bad feelings by fighting the devil and thus assisting others.

Art is more beautiful and meaningful as we learn to appreciate the weave of the process. Art illustrates the conflicts and art appreciation may be enhanced through scientific analysis of the emotional and aesthetic experience. We seek to recognize in the aesthetics of art the structure of the conflicts of the artist and the respective consequences. We experience all creativity as orderly harmonics just as when we listen to music as an abstract experience. This happens as we develop skills in the interpretation of the creative process.

The range of these activities reinforces our new perspective coinciding with the spirit of the Harmonic. We now can recognize the orderly process in all symbolic universes: we can predict the universality of natural laws; we can anticipate conflict resolution as the meaning of life. Moral Science is not sterile knowledge; it is the wisdom founded upon the laws of nature, which facilitate personal growth and social change. As we study the process by interpreting metaphors we validate the theory and expand our appreciation of the universality of order; our conviction grows that there is order and

justice in human affairs. The arts guide us to the spiritual experience to witness science diminishing suffering and promoting wellbeing. We may have lost the sense of the existence of god but we gain confidence in the orderly laws governing humanity's mental and moral universe.

THE EXPERIENTIAL SEGMENT
'CREATIVITY AND POWER MANAGEMENT' TARGETS PERSONAL INSIGHTS THROUGH CREATIVITY FOR SELF-DISCOVERY

The Harmonic and the Case Studies
Promoting awareness of the process, the exhibits advance the scientific and moral paradigm that both psychology and religion have needed for the scientific study of behavior and the humanities. The Formal Theory revamps psychology as an applied and spiritual science, the Moral Science. Psychologists now may explore the domain as a rigorous field but also assume spiritual leadership as experts in the fields of morality. The Formal Theory shifts our attention from the multiple, mystifying moral and theoretical paradigms to the rational universal process as the dynamic unit underlying all paradigms: religions, conceptualizations, classifications and testing technologies. The Unit process, as the most abstract paradigm, reconciles our less abstract, theoretical and moral paradigms.

The pursuit of creativity for self-discovery and healing is a spontaneous response
We have argued that stressors stimulate creativity to spontaneously achieve healing, which coincides with a state of moral discovery. We have encountered this in Greek tragedies as the *deus ex machina*, the apparition of an emissary of gods delivering the verdict for the punishment of the hero. The divine intervention completes the inner need for conformity and freedom from conflict. This is the function of the role state of compromise. The intensity of conflict is proportionate to the depth of the resolution as a spiritual or religious experience.

The task of the teacher is to cultivate the analytical skills of the student through the scientific understanding of creativity to detect one's conflicts in the symbolic language of his/her art. This creativity allows us to become better observers, more empathetic and insightful. We learn to adopt the objectivity of an analyst or psychotherapist who puts the creative process on the couch as the object of analysis. The program educates the student to observe meaning as a universal order. The instruction begins with the case studies exhibit. Of course this is a model or work that needs to be completed by the student. Nothing is as personally meaningful as the study of one's own metaphors. But here are cases introducing the technology of the experiential program.

THE CASE STUDY EXHIBIT

The Sanctuary of the museum presents seven murals of case studies based on the use of the *Conflict Analysis Battery*, the self-assessment workbook. The workbook identifies one's personal Conflict Resolution Process using the simple metaphor testing technique of completing creativity tasks. Such scrutiny readily allows the detection of the orderly process underlying one's stream of associations.

One of the *Conflict Analysis Battery* creativity tasks, the *Animal Metaphor Test*, instructs the student of behavior to draw two animals and then to listen to their conversation. The sequence of exchanges of the animals reflects the person's six role-state Conflict Resolution Process. The exchanges become the prototype of the personal drama, and are in the predictable formal interrelation to each other as parts in the universal formal totality.

This simple creativity task departs from art and demonstrates science first as the six formally interrelated exchanges of one's unconscious dialectic. Second, following three formal operations, the exercise demonstrates that the unconscious

pursues activity with moderation, cooperation and mutual respect, the universal objectives. This finding validates the postulation of the innate unconscious need for the conservation of the emotional state of stability or rest as the key motivational imperative.

SEVEN MURALS AT THE SANCTUARY ILLUSTRATE CASE STUDIES OF CREATIVITY FOR SELF DISCOVERY

The case studies are of great importance in validating the theory and in demonstrating that the theory-related testing delivers a user-friendly emotional education program. The implication of the use of this battery is that we have here a reliable instrument to standardize and expedite psychotherapy cost-effectively, but also a concise program of wellness emotional education that can benefit the anyone, informing him/her about behavior, self-knowledge and clarity of values. This is the happy ending of this dissertation. The Formal Theory gives us hope that humanity can be educated and healed from its confusion on psychological and moral matters.

MURAL 4 (pp. 82-83 and p. 235), 'My Metaphors Myself' introduces the metaphor creation process which leads to the reconstruction of the personal conflict resolution pattern. The trainee completes the exercises of the workbook and arranges them in a dialectic manner to reconstruct the six role-states of the process. There is correspondence between the metaphor tests and the six role-states of the process. This correspondence serves us well in organizing information meaningfully along the dramatic process reflecting how a person resolves conflicts.
Stress is revealed in the *Conflictual Memory Test* and the *Balloon Portrait of the Family of Origin*.
Response is captured in the *Transparent Mask Test*, and also in one's Marital Family Balloons Portrait.
Anxiety/hopes, the hidden emotions are portrayed in the image behind the mask and in the third mask illustrating what is in a person's heart.

Defense is presented in the *Animal Metaphor* and *Fairy Tale Test*.
Reversal is revealed in the Dream Metaphor and the Intensified *Animal Metaphor Test*.
Compromise is identified in the *Autobiographic Short Story Test*. This exercise informs on a person's attitude.

MURAL 7 (pp. 236-237) presents the very painful and dramatic story of an adult woman who as an adopted child was physically and sexually abused. The mural demonstrates the healing dynamics of the unconscious process by contrasting side-by-side formative traumatic childhood experiences with the formally-related corresponding adult experiences and/or fantasies. This demonstrates the healing of the person manifested in the formal reconfiguration of the parallel symbolic systems. The mural's imagery demonstrates the formal structure of emotions underlying conflict and resolution.

We examine each test reflecting a childhood experience in the context of another reflecting her adult experiences. We see the formal restructuring of childhood traumas with adult developmental adjustments. We observe a continuum of formally-related states of passivity, antagonism and alienation experienced in childhood as connected to the formally rearranged states of mind in adulthood along the principles of mastery, cooperation and mutual respect. We perceive these developmental experiences in a formal relationship with the states of resolution. The artwork presents the three formally related reversals within each one of the equivalent symbolic systems.

Balloons of the Family of Origin* versus *Balloons of the Marital Family; This juxtaposition shows how the family balloons are colored, placed with short strings at a distance from each other in the *Family of Origin*, while the *Marital Balloons* are held together with long strings.

EXHIBIT #5: CASE STUDY MURALS
CREATIVITY AND POWER MANAGEMENT;
A CONCISE PROGRAM OF EMOTIONAL EDUCATION

Mural 4:   Reconstructing the process using personal metaphors

Mural 7:   The healing process as a formal directional transformation

Mural 8:   The physical dimension of emotions

Mural 9:   Effectiveness of the process of self-discovery

Mural 10:   Contrasting relational modalities

Mural 11:   Utilizing the *Conflict Analysis Battery* to monitor therapy outcome

Mural 12:   Utilizing the *Animal Metaphor Test* to monitor therapy outcome

The baby balloon overlaps the maternal balloon reflecting the mother's protective stance toward her child. This image also reveals the mother's discomfort at being emotionally drained from being overprotective.

The Mask of True Feelings, reflects the traumas of her childhood as a landscape of mishaps offset by the cover-up of "a mask of serenity."

Her *Dream Test* corrects a trauma of her childhood, her mother intruding into the bathroom to slap her while she was sitting on the toilet in sight of her father. This trauma is corrected in a dream about her second husband and protector who attacks her first husband perceived as cruel as her mother. The ex-husband is sitting on the toilet being attacked by the second husband holding Cinderella's glass slipper in his hand.

Her *Animal Metaphor Test* depicts her experience of abuse in her childhood versus her assuming a protective stance rescuing an animal from a garbage bag in her *Short Story Exercise*. The experience of abuse is offset by acts of kindness as she saves life.

MURAL 8 (pp. 238-239) is the case of a young seminarian in a routine screening for emotional pathology. The mural is valuable in reflecting the meaningfulness of the direction of the animals in the five sets of drawings. The aesthetics of the artwork, the directionality of forces, reflect the nature of his emotions coinciding with those of the pendulum oscillation. The directions of the movements of the animals in the artwork introduce information about the emotional phenomena as physical forces. Right-directed faces and bodies correspond to impulsivity, competitiveness and aggression. Here the story pertains to collaboration in a homosexual outing. Left-directed animals portray depression and introspection, the metaphor here is of the "Prodigal Horse" returning to the farm. Forward-facing animals reflect anxiety; this metaphor reflects concerns about issues of

right and wrong originating in his homosexual experience.

MURAL 9 (pp. 240-241) is about the speed of the insights generated through the testing contained in the workbook. This is the touching case of a holocaust survivor who by completing the workbook worked through her feelings of childhood drama to come to terms with her guilt about the loss of her overprotective grandparents. This patient's comments about her testing experience are to be found on page 230.

MURAL 10 (pp. 242-243) is about the two opposite relational modalities. Two students in training reveal the opposite personality types, the two major relational modalities. Here, side by side, we see the differences in relating manifested in the relational scales and artwork of two trainees. The metaphors of Melissa show her dominant, competitive and anxious personality while the metaphors of Chris show the counterpart disposition, his tendency to be submissive, hostile, intolerant and how he could lose control of his well-restrained anger.

MURALS 11 AND 12 (pp. 244-247) are about monitoring the progress of two patients in long-term therapy utilizing the metaphor testing; one is a dominant woman who completed five workbooks. She is dealing with her aggressiveness and paranoid fears. The other is a submissive woman struggling with communicating her hostile feelings. She suffered from an eating disorder and was also terrified of losing control of her anger. She enjoyed creativity utilizing only the *Animal Metaphor Test*.

The last four case studies exemplify with artwork the diagnostic differences of the relational modalities determining the respective social adjustments and emotional pathologies. These cases also exemplify the process of their therapeutic evolution to healing and wellness. All seven cases reflect the reliability of the *Conflict Analysis Battery*.

MURAL 12 IN MORE DETAIL (pp. 246-247)
Gladys completed metaphors practically for each one of her many therapy sessions. These are reconstructed in a mural showing the progress in her therapy along four rows of metaphors integrated into four phases of growth.

The first row reproduces the evaluation documents, presenting the sequence of metaphors generated upon the initial phase of therapy. We identify here the nature of her conflict as an eating disorder with two of her tests: the *Conflictual Memory Test* presents her feeding her mother and her grandmother objecting to her choice of a multi-layered sandwich. The first Mask presents her being feminine with lots of make-up.

The second image, what is underneath the mask, presents her with her mouth blackened; it is the 'black hole' reflecting her binge-purge eating disorder; in the third mask we see the problem as a communication blockage. We see a moat separating smiles and bunnies from tears and dark clouds, lightning, and heavy rain, all signs of anger and depression. This difficulty in communicating feelings was the issue underlying her eating disorder. Gladys, a submissive person, could not cross the moat.

The block symbolized her inability to vent her feelings. The problem of communications was confirmed in her first *Animal Metaphor* of a dog and a cat turning their backs to each other. The difficulty in venting her feelings was explained in the last metaphor, the Short Story which presents a dragon breathing out fire burning her family. Expressing her anger was perceived as dangerous and unacceptable.

The deep-seated communication problems were determined by her submissive antagonistic relational modality. Therapy helped her work through the expression of her emotions and the metaphors attest that she achieved substantial growth.

The second phase of metaphors, the moat series, presents animals in conflict in either side of the moat. The counterpart animals evolved as it became easier to express herself. She is transformed from a scared bunny stuck with big animals, to an ostrich with her head in the sand, and then at the end state she is an eagle soaring.

The third series is about a phase of intensification of her eating disorder of anorexia and bulimia; this recurrence manifested upon a stressful encounter. This phase was characterized as a cycle of intense binge-purge behaviors worked on symbolically as the conflicts between a vulture and a snake battling each other. At the end of this series her new identity is a tiger. The tiger kills both the snake and the vulture. Gladys evolved to a new identity, distancing herself from the self-destructive pattern.

The fourth series of her metaphors describes communication conflicts with the several key figures in her life spelling out her feelings honestly. The particular individuals start with her mother and end with her husband. She is able to finally communicate with him. The end metaphors represent two giraffes talking to each other, representing herself and her husband. The exchanges are pertinent: 'we can disagree and still be friends', the two giraffes face each other and are symmetrical which corresponds to mutual respect. What a transformation from the initial metaphor of a dog and a cat, turning their backs to each other and to the viewer and stating in a hostile manner 'who cares about your feelings?'

THE EFFECTIVENESS OF POWER MANAGEMENT IS DUE TO THE CONCEPTUAL ELEGANCE OF THE UNIT PHENOMENON WHICH INTEGRATES EPISTEMOLOGY, DIAGNOSIS, PSYCHOASSESSMENT AND MORAL ORDER

GRAPHIC ANALYSIS OF THE PERSONAL EMOTIONS IN THE SOCIAL CONTEXT

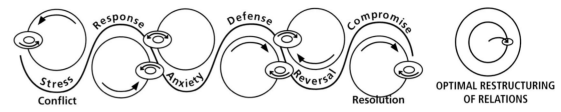

• The graphic analysis of the metaphors helps the trainee to understand the relationship between behaviors and emotions in a social context and the benefits of appropriate behavior modification.

THE TEMPLATE OF THE HARMONIC AS A PENDULUM OSCILLATION

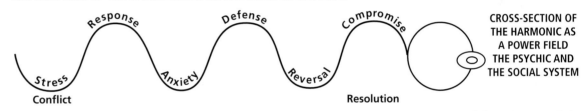

• Emotions, status, behavior can be graphically portrayed just like the concepts of the sciences of the equilibrial machines, the pendulum oscillation and the balance of the trays of the scale.

PSYCHOASSESSMENT AS RECONSTRUCTING THE PERSONAL HARMONIC

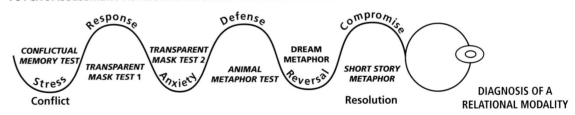

• The *Conflict Analysis Battery* helps to reconstruct the personal Conflict Resolution Process and reach both a diagnosis and a plan of therapy.

In the case study murals found in the next pages we have arranged the Metaphor Test (images and insights) according to the template of the Conflict Resolution Process. The template above indicates the correspondence between role-states and the various tests of the Conflict Analysis Battery.

TRANSCRIPT OF AN *ANIMAL METAPHOR TEST*

To complete this test, simply print this screen and complete the drawing. Fill answers in the space provided.

Step 1: In the space below, draw two animal figures in color. Please use pencil or pen to outline and color w/ colored pencils, or magic markers.

Note from author:
This sample test was generated by an uncoached college student following the instructions of the *Animal Metaphor Test*. This test is ypical of other projective tests included in the *Conflict Analysis Battery* available in the *Conflict Analysis Training Workbook*.

The above protocol illustrates the remarkable insights evoked by this assessment instrument. The following case studies, as illustrated in the Murals presented in the next pages under exhibit #5 represent the summation of metaphor tests also contained in this assessment instrument.

Instructions:
Step 1: Draw two animal figures

Step 2: Identify them

Animal #1.
Type of Animal: Elephant
Age in human years: 17
Animal's sex: Female
Describe the animal's personality by listing 3 or more traits:.
Curious, Independent, Bold, Impulsive, Assertive

Animal #2
Type of Animal: Deer (fawn)
Age in human years: 7
Animal's sex: Male
Describe the animal's personality by listing 3 or more traits:
Cautious, Sensitive, Affectionate (when feeling at home), Anxious, Responsive

Step 3: The animals are having a conversation. What are they saying to each other? Indicate the sequence referring to the animals by their identity number
1. If you're so worried about hurting yourself, why do you sleep under apple trees?
2. I don't know... it's just what- (gets interrupted)
1. Not only do you have to sleep on round, hard, lumps, which can't be comfortable, but, apples can fall and bonk you on the head while you're sleeping!
2. It's just what I've always done. I mean, I think this tree forms a nice canopy. Plus, in the winter I get to make a sort of nest in the snow and munch chilled, fallen apples before curling up asleep.
1. But you do get bonked on the head...
2. Yes... but it's okay, really. I don't mind. Not at all!
1. You're weird.
2. This system works for me. You don't have to like it, but I do, okay?
1. Yeah, whatever.
2. Wait... what are you doing?
1. Nothing... I just thought I'd reach up with my trunk and shake these apple-laden branches a bit.
2. Don't! Please don't, stop! You aren't supposed to do that!
1. Why not? It's fun.
2. They'll fall when they're ready to fall.
1. Wow. You're just no fun. Ha- you're a no-fun apple-fawn! pause Hey, what's over there?
2. Where? Oh umm... you can't go over there. Nope. Not allowed.
1. Sure I can. What, are you worried about getting in trouble? What are you, like 7?
2. Umm, actually, yes.

1. Oh.
2. I just don't think it's a good idea. Besides, you can just stay here and play with me. Hey, would you like an apple? They're quite yummy.
1. No thanks.
2. You could shake the branches if you want a really fresh one...
1. I know that. I don't need your permission- I'm older and bigger than you!
2. You don't want to go over there... there's barbed wire tangled in among the pricker-bushes and there are swarms of biting bugs, and sink holes of mud and...
1. So? I'm big, and my skin it pretty tough.
2. But you're also heavy ... you could be swallowed up by the mud after one false move!
1. I'll be fine. Listen, would you come if I promised to go first? Then I could shield you from all of the briars, and I can swish away bugs with my tail.
2. I guess I could. I mean, you really shouldn't go all by yourself, anyway.
1. You sound like my Mom, hurry up!
2. Okay, okay I'm coming!

Step 4: What were the animals doing and saying before the conversation just recorded?
The elephant came by, exploring and smelling new things. The fawn was nestled under an apple tree, at the edge of a field. The tree is in a brushy area that transitions to swampland. It is in this ecotone that the two animals meet. The elephant is not shy. She doesn't know the fawn at all, but asks all sorts of questions. The fawn doesn't mind, though he would never have been as forward and talkative as this young elephant, especially to someone he'd never met before. After they talk for awhile, the elephant want to play. The fawn is reluctant to roughhouse with an animal so much bigger than himself, and is hesitant to move from his cozy spot in the shade. It is at this moment that the dialogue begins.

Step 5: What did your animals do and say after the initial conversation?
The newfound friends make their way towards

the other side of the swamp. Soon the moist, foamy ground gives way to a rockier forest floor carpeted with pine needles and crackling leaves. The fawn discovers a new tree that he likes even more than his Apple. The elephant becomes less annoyed with the fawn's many insecurities, and the fawn grows more comfortable and less shy as they continue to wander further and further from home.

Step 6: Give a title to the story: The Elephant and the Apple-Fawn

Step 7a: What conflicts are these animals experiencing between themselves?
The elephant is adventurous, curious and cannot really understand why anyone would rather stay home than go out and experience new things. For her, the world is a playground, an obstacle course to overcome—she lives to face these obstacles and problem solve. In contrast, the fawn is a homebody, a worrier (not a warrior). He doesn't like change and has difficulty making transitions. Though he knows he should try stepping outside his comfort zone, the idea of doing so is overwhelming and upsetting.

Step 7b: What are the conflicts between them and their world? Elaborate.
The elephant is impulsive. She proceeds without thinking about future repercussions of her actions or behavior. Her inability to adjust her behavior to accommodate the feelings and actions of others creates unnecessary disorder and conflict with the creatures around her. While she is friendly and loves company, her tendency to act without thinking isolates her, and so she is always seeking attention and companionship. The fawn is overly cautious: everything and everyone remotely unfamiliar threatens his organized understanding of the world and the creatures in it. While the specific characteristics of the familiar home he loves are inspiring and comforting, incorporating new things into this fixed framework is too disruptive for him, and,

as a result, this framework (his apple tree nest) is rather limited and stagnant. The world around him often bumps up against his isolated apple-bubble, and when it discovers how resistant this little deer is to change, it often bypasses it and continues on, not wanting to exert the effort required to help this fawn experience new things.

Step 8: What changes should these animals make to resolve their conflicts?

Both animals would benefit from being more mindful. The elephant bases too many decision on her rational mind, she thinks, " I can do that. Why not? All I need to do is this, this and this." She needs to take into consideration the emotions she is experiencing and acknowledge that, just because she wants to do something (and technically can do something), doesn't mean she should or must do that thing.

The fawn's emotional reasoning counteracts any rational thinking. He is working on this inability to change his daily routine. And, in the conversation above, one can see that by the end of this snippet of dialogue, the fawn has challenged some of his initial decisions, which he probably would not have done without the elephant's persistent challenging of his assumptions and fixed ideas about what can and cannot be done.

Step 9a: Which animal do you identify with the most? Elaborate.
I can relate a great deal to the fawn, though I think I have come a long way from where he is and where I once was. I've never dealt well with change, and though I do make necessary transitions, it takes me much longer than anyone else to become comfortable and at home in that new setting. In the past, I have learned to cope by making my own isolated home within that

larger setting, which I can then retreat to and feel safe in, despite being in an overwhelming, larger world full of people who I often assume will not be able to appreciate why I may be homesick.

Step 9b: Who do you identify with the counterpart animal? Elaborate.
The elephant echoes many people in my life: my boyfriend, my friends, and even the part of me that often criticizes my own hesitancy and shyness. Juxtaposed to the fawn, the elephant appears to be kind of a bully, but, one could also say that she is just trying to help the fawn overcome simple obstacles which the fawn could not have passed on his own. The fawn makes molehills into mountains, something my boyfriend often says I do, which I think is very true.

Step 10: How does this animal drama pertain to you?
If people hadn't constantly challenged or pointed out my cognitive distortions to me, I would not have learned to do so and perhaps would never have moved away from "home" in the literal and abstract sense. Having guidance and company is very important for me to make successful transitions. The fawn would never have gone out to explore the swamp by himself, but, the elephant talks him into it because she promises to be right there. I worry about being alone, because when I feel overly isolated and lonely, I isolate myself further by building walls that I cannot deconstruct on my own.

Step 11: What changes should you make to resolve your conflicts?
I think being calm and relaxed enough to train myself not to worry and ruminate and obsess over all the things that could or will go wrong will be enough to completely change my approach to life. This is obviously easier said than done; but, if I work on accepting that there are things I cannot control and remind myself

that worrying accomplishes nothing, I think I will begin to resolve conflicts in a much healthier, mindful way. I think I don't take care of myself as much as I should, though my tendency to avoid change and conflict masks itself as being a measure of self-protection, though it tend to further isolate and alienate me from new things.

Step 12: In life we repeat ourselves. Present an incident similar to what transpired in your metaphor story to illustrate your particular pattern.

I have difficulty making decisions. Even if I made a decision that I've since come to regret, it's very difficult for me to rethink things, and change things around. This is a rather trivial example of this, though at the time it did not seem to be: I declared an English major, though proceeded to take mainly Religious Studies classes. I found myself in the fall of my junior year having taken 2 English classes, meaning I would need to take 8 more before I graduated in spring 2012.

Also, the English courses offered in this time period were not ones I really wanted to take, and I was devastated, and crippled with dread, already defeated. All my friends urged me to just change my major to Religious Studies, because I'd almost completed the requirements for the major without even trying! I'd become so wedded to being an English major, however, that even thinking about the process of un-declaring and re-declaring was overwhelming and frequently brought me to tears. I felt as though I'd made a choice, and thus couldn't go back or change my path. Little things like this happen all the time, and even though I'm aware my of distorted point of view, I convince myself that any other point of view will just present the same awful and grim situation slightly differently.

Step 13: Reviewing this incident, describe your relational pattern, that is, how you relate with other people, and how you set things up to get yourself in trouble.

I convince myself that things are true and rigidly fixed, whether I am facing an inevitable year of grunt work, or deciding that an entire group of people in the dining hall is morally corrupt and full of bullies. I cannot make a decision without constantly second guessing myself. So, when it comes to assessing people I don't know, I choose not to waste my energy wondering whether or not they are good or bad people. I just decide, because, what have I got to lose? This has been a pattern for me, but I am very aware of it now, and, now that I am less depressed, I really am changing the way I relate to people, whether I know them well or not.

I don't like feeble and artificial friendships (well, I suppose no one does); because I hate the idea of phony friendliness, I can appear to be quite unfriendly, though this is certainly not my intention. I don't pretend to be friends with people I barely know, but prefer to develop genuine and close friendship that are important and meaningful. This means that I know fewer people, and, I guess, that I am more socially isolated. Because I'm not one to quickly make "best-friends", it takes time for me to accept people who I often feel, at least initially, have very little in common with me. Some of my closest friends are individuals I disliked and dismissed based on our first few encounters, but have since come to really love. When this transformation happens I realize that I could have been closer to people much sooner if I had been open to the possibility that I would, someday, be able to relate to them.

I guess I tend to be on guard, not wanting others to think I'm their friend when I might not be, and protecting myself from people building artificial relationships. This constant vigilance is exhausting and can make every interaction into a competition or test. I have moved away from this pattern, or ...am very much in the process of moving. I have worked hard to be less judgmental, and more aware of my irrational tendency to categorize people without knowing anything about them. Because I tend to judge others, I tend to assume that others are judging me in the same way, which makes me feel incredibly insecure and disliked, even though my only basis for this assumption is rooted in my own judgmental behavior.

Step 14: What changes are you willing to make?

I want to enjoy life, not survive it. I am willing and eager to make the changes I know to be necessary for me to do that, though I know such changes will not and cannot happen all at once. I need to take care of myself. I'm in the process of healing; the last few years have been very rough emotionally and physically, and I am only beginning to feel that there is hope of mending again. The changes that come with mending are the ones I need to make first; I will reassess them and adjust them as I go.

The following are comments volunteered by a well college student completing two tests of the self-assessment battery unassisted by an educator or a therapist. Her comments point out that the testing can be meaningful and useful to the well public within the context of an emotional education.

'My immediate reactions after completing these two tests were those of wonder and insight. These tests challenged me to really think introspectively. The first test, the survey, (the personality inventory identified as the Relational Modality Evaluation Scale, RMES), was a very good explicit test that was interesting and very detailed. I think that it kind of sets the scene to try to make one seem all good and wonderful to a viewer's eye, whereas the *Animal Metaphor Test*, challenges one to think in a different perspective in a more artistic sort of way.

I found the *Animal Metaphor Test* to be an especially interesting implicit test. I have never done a test like this but have definitely read about them through psychology courses. I think that it has its own special spin to it though that really encourages one to put effort and thought into each response. The artistic aspect accompanied with the narrative allows one to really express their inner selves in a way that simply talking or brain imaging cannot detect. I like the way that it forces one to address some inner conflict in their current lives and then at the end, how to take immediate action for the betterment of life and resolution of conflicts. The section where it explains that we repeat ourselves and to describe a situation where the certain conflict has happened really puts into perspective our own actions. Most times we are either unaware or reluctant to admit when we are causing conflict, which can bottle up inside and disrupt at a given moment. Since the person is recognizing their flaws and conflicts themselves, and not hearing it from a friend or therapist, they will do much more to change these flaws.

I also like the concept of drawing an animal to represent oneself. With so many different varieties to choose from, an animal representation is a really interesting way to gain insight to a person's personality. Overall, I though the tests were very interesting and informative to both the person taking the test and the experimenter distributing the tests.'

The following comments were contributed by patients about the effectiveness of the self-assessment experience (Insights are generated by connecting role states; to convey this connection the patients are identified with the forms of a key relational issue):

Patient#1
THREATENING AS A STEP-CHILD AND FEELING THREATENED BY HER STEP-CHILDREN
This patient wrote an essay about her therapy experience upon the completion of two books of tests; the original was for a four-session evaluation, the second was completed during a therapeutic phase. Her original *Animal Metaphor Test*, two animals and dialogue is transcribed on the Oz Panel #4. Her completed battery is presented as a Metaphor Profile integrating all testing on Oz Panel #8. This patient identified as "The Turkey who became a Terrier", reports on the completion of and interpretation of the second battery of tests.

Patient: a 33 year-old anxious woman suffering from panic-attacks and depression Diagnosis:
Axis I Depression - Anxiety
Axis II Dominant-cooperative
Length of Therapy: 4 Sessions evaluation completing one set of tests, followed by ten sessions of group therapy.

Patient essay
"As a 33 year-old woman, I went through this therapeutic evaluation to find the cause of my panic attacks and my severe anxiety I began to experience whenever my boyfriend's children would come to visit him at our shared apartment. I was no stranger to therapy. In fact for at least 20 years (perhaps more?), I have suffered from depression, two suicide attempts, hospitalizations, fragmented interpersonal relationships, hypochondria, migraine headaches, asthma and a host of other no doubt psychologically related maladies.

The first battery of tests, allowed me to bring forth through a sequence of revealing drawings and statements, my innermost fears, traumas and conflicts. After completing the testing, I felt a sense of mastery realizing the rational nature of my conflicts in a non-threatening way. By drawing the metaphor exercises I came to realize my problematic tendencies manifested in images and dialogues.

In my first book, I made illustrations of a strong predatory animal and one which gets preyed upon: Mouse and a Hawk, Red-Riding Hood and The Wolf, a Shark and a Sea fish, A tired Greyhound dog and Three mocking Alley Cats. During the training that followed, the structure of my relationships repeated itself in the second battery series: a Mountain Lion and A Turkey, Jack Jumping over the Candlestick and A Basking Shark and tiny Plankton and finally a Terrier and a Buffalo.

The implications of my exercises were meaningful in looking at myself. The integration of the testing revealed that, the anxiety I experienced from encounters with my step-children as illustrated in the tired Greyhound derided by three Alley Cats was related to the hostility I felt against my own stepmother. The artwork and commentary helped me to realize the deep seated anxieties about my step children as the mirror image of my hostile unexpressed attitude at my stepmother (Mouse vs. Hawk in the first series) and (Turkey vs. Mt. Lion in the second).

Adjusting my feelings toward my Father as in the Short Story of 'The Terrier and the Buffalo,' helped me to feel less threatened by my boy-friend's children's visits. I felt less threatened by them, my stepchildren. After the second testing experience I felt more resolved in my relationship with my Father and my Stepmother.

The two self-studies provided me with an over-view of my present in the context of the past. I depicted my immediate family, their charac-teristics, strengths and failings. The drawings helped me to review my past family life and my subsequent responses, anxieties and defenses in a logical, rational progression instead of solely as non-connected emotional outpourings as it occurred in other therapies I have experienced. I now recognized my underlying hostile and antagonistic disposition whereas I always felt victimized, "devoured", preyed upon in relation-ships. And all this information about the past and about my perceptions came to bear on my current interactions with my parents as well as my boyfriend and his children. It explained how I perceived them as hostile and demanding like I had felt as a restrained stepchild.

Some of my behavior/s had been touched upon in prior therapy programs ---- but none of them made connections, never so quickly and concisely as in this experience. What I have achieved is a clearer and better springboard from which to ei-ther continue therapy or work some conflicts out on my own. Without these insight-generating diagnostic instruments and change-generating processes I would not have been able to iden-tify the sources of my current conflicts so easily, quickly and logically. These insights helped to modify my attitude and to experience less anxi-ety. Medication alone would have postponed dealing with the conflicts as opposed to dealing and permanently trying to resolve them.

I used anti-depressants for awhile but I experi-enced the brief exposure to the Power Manage-ment therapy as a 'user-friendly, psychological education which allowed me to diagnose myself

and to work towards evolving a clear under-standing of connecting my past attitude and my current fears. It is a positive program for self-realization that is needed in order to change attitudes and overcome symptoms. I wish I had had an opportunity to work through my conflicts early in life before my personality developed into inescapable life patterns which sadly followed me into adulthood."

I recommend bringing Power Management into the classroom, the school system, where it might provide a 'User-Friendly', systematic, psychologi-cal venue in which to diagnose and work towards resolution of conflicts in today's youth. It is a positive program for self-realization and young people need self-realization in order to master their feelings early on in life. Before their own personality conflicts cripple or fix them into ines-capable life patterns, which would sadly follow them into adulthood.

Patient #2
THE HOLOCAUST SURVIVOR
This case study, mural #9, illustrates the self-diagnostic, self-healing therapeutic value of the completion of the metaphor testing, and the minimal need for professional services for the adequate generation and interpretation of the testing battery.

Patient comments
The patient recently came to the Center request-ing my help to prepare a brief regarding her childhood experiences documenting her status as a displaced person as needed to qualify her for restitution as compensation from the Ger-man government. Besides taking down the facts, I asked her to complete the set of metaphor exercises of the *Conflict Analysis Battery* as a way of providing me with pertinent information reflecting the emotional impact of her extraor-dinary experiences in her life-long emotional adjustment for me to communicate my findings to the German authorities and also to help her

to explore the significance of these events in her lifelong emotional adjustment.

She was born in 1933 to a Jewish mother and a German father. Also her parents were divorced when the patient was only 6 years old. Her father was killed in action on the Russian front while her mother attempted suicide following being raped by German soldiers. Her mother was hospitalized, deported and finally committed suicide when she returned from a concentration camp. Her maternal grandparents who were her guardians were also deported. She survived, first being placed in a foundling home then living with her aunt and then with her paternal grand-parents. She was persecuted along with her pa-ternal grandparents because of her mixed ethnic background until finally that family escaped from Austria to Switzerland.

Her set of metaphors illustrated her unresolved conflictual issues such as her guilt feelings for having experienced a childlike sense of relief when her grandparents were deported to an alleged labor camp. Evidence of her distrust of herself is depicted in her *Mask Test*; evidence of her sense of resolution is depicted in her recent dream test presenting her reconciliation with her deceased maternal grandmother.

Patient
Age 62, Married woman Holocaust Survivor
Diagnosis: Well person, seeking documentation of her status as a Holocaust survivor for potential compensation from the German government.
Length of Therapy: Three visits
Outcome: According to the patient, she gleaned a lot from therapy, which helped her to under-stand life-long difficulties and symptoms related to her traumatic childhood experiences.
Essay following three sessions titled by the pa-tient: My "$5 Session of Psychotherapy"
"This system of metaphors works by itself. It has been a therapy and my mind has become clearer. This way you get an answer and it is a

logical one. Congratulations! You have something there. I was amazed. I will be drawing my dreams if I want some explanation."

"Whenever I had time, whenever thoughts struck me... I did it. It took some time. I couldn't decide. Finally it all came through in a whimsical way. It clarified itself and it made sense. It is amazing how much you find out about yourself. You have a dynamite process. It makes me feel better about my mind. It is something that gives you answers to the system and gets answers out of your own mind. It is a feeling of security I haven't had in years."

"The original purpose of my examination by Dr. Levis was the existence or non-existence of leftover psychological scars caused by my childhood experiences during the Nazi time. I was uncertain that any concrete proof of them could be established at all, and it appeared even more unlikely that it could be done within a short period of time. But that was before I knew of Dr. Levis's method. I was uncertain that any concrete proof of them could be established at all, and it appeared even more unlikely that it could be done within a short period of time. Dr. Levis's method was to complete several creativity exercises. I was allowed to take the first part of the *Conflict Analysis Battery* with me as homework since I live some distance away.

Sitting at my kitchen table (a familiar nonthreatening environment) I confronted a series of tests (in many ways similar in format to tests I had faced at school except that the only preparation I needed was having lived my life.). The tests are about memories from my childhood, portraits of the family, dreams, animal and fairy tale metaphors. They started with a drawing and continued with a series of thought provoking questions. The tests led me to painful memories, and to thinking of how to represent them. The questions about them (i.e. who was there? How did you feel about that person?) helped me to be

analytical rather than to relive them alone. I had to keep my concentration within that experience quite clinically for a longer period of time, than I think I ever had before. I was led through the series of questions to a solution of my own. I began to enjoy the unfolding stories and final answers. I found that I could not predict them, they wrote themselves, one reply leading to another. I began to understand what I had heard writers say, 'that characters behaved as they wished to, once they were conceived.'

Dreams had always been difficult to analyze on my own; I have tried. They reminded me of onions, one layer uncovered another, until I got quite confused. Suddenly a dream I had attempted to unravel for the past 53 years, whenever I thought of it, became a simple matter when subjected to Dr. Levis's method. Perhaps the act of creating a physical image gave it a more concrete reality in my mind. Whatever... it worked! Whenever I finished my assignment, the doctor received it asking additional questions or helping me see a missed clue. After three sessions he knew more about me than long-time friends and I had gained valuable insights, an unexpected bonus for me. I feel more secure now, because I know that my own mind can provide the answers to all my problems. I can follow the method of dealing with them.

As a member of an organization called Holocaust Child Survivors of Connecticut, Inc., I attend commemorative services for the slaughtered Jews during the reign of terror of the Third Reich. This is the first year I could look at it calmly as something like the honoring of veterans of wars or tortured prisoners and not as an invitation to relive a terrible time. (See the attached recent memory drawings and process). The healing fallout of my therapy is not in yet.

Had the high school psychologist, who called me into his office after I became a student in America put a *Conflict Analysis Battery* of tests

in front of me, I could not have gotten away with a simple "yes" to his question of "Are you happy?", when I was not at all. My husband had abdominal pains which doctors believed to be psychological during the early years of our marriage, which sent him to a psychiatrist. He was very uncommunicative in his sessions, which I found out when the doctor told me after calling me in, in order to get some more information. My husband stopped going to him soon after. Luckily the pain episodes abated and ceased altogether within two years. He probably would have completed Dr. Levis's tests (he told me when I showed him the ones I did) since they fitted into the pattern of testing he was used to from school rather then his image of a lunatic who is asked strange personal questions by a man he hardly knew. I feel that the fact of having to reveal highly personal data in Dr. Levis's tests is masked by having to perform an introspective solitary task first with you alone as a witness. When the doctor reads back your material, he is telling you your story, and you make corrections or additions only, distracted from the realization that you have just confided in him.

As a person who recently completed a testing series with Dr. Levis, I am greatly impressed by the possibilities of his system. Judging from my experience it is a superior vehicle for screenings, such as for kids in a school and for conflict in the work place. The testing can be used for a fast, accurate psychological assessment or for a self-assessment at any point in time of a person's life. It reflects clearly one's state of mind. In psychotherapy or psychoanalysis it can be taken to whatever detail is desired or necessary, greatly reducing the time required for the completion of therapy and the hours spent with a professional. This in turn reduces the cost providing a larger population with access to therapy.

In my last job as a budget analyst for the state, my boss had the belief that all problems presented could be reduced to asking what? why? how?.

Dr. Levis's final process question is "how will I use this experience to change my behavior?" To my knowledge this question is absent from much of modern therapy. My New York City college roommate was still having weekly sessions, 15 years after I left the city, when our correspondence ended. Each test included in the battery I took, ended with the question "How will I change my behavior to avoid a conflict of this nature in the future?" This answer is that I have made peace with myself. One big burden, hate and guilt have been lifted from my mind. I feel better about myself, resolved with my experiences. I am more spontaneous in my emotions and more open in my expressions.

In conclusion I can only say that I can glimpse a wide highway of uses for Dr. Levis's tests and that it travels a long way towards my generations' cry of "What the world needs now is a $5.00 psychoanalytic session."
"I want to share an example of being spontaneous in my emotional expression."

Appended to the letter; a recent memory, drawing and process.
"Chava Alberstein sang Israeli and Yiddish songs including the plaintive theme from Schindler's List which I know every note of but I only remember the often repeated "Kinderle" from the words. Her powerful responsive voice resounded through the Bethel Temple and I was aware of little else but that wonderful noise. I remember thinking how excellent her singing was, when I realized that I was crying and I didn't really know why. My emotions were rising and ebbing with the music that pervaded me and I stopped caring that I was making a spectacle of myself. Lest you think that I am always that emotional, let me hasten to say that I only did that once before, and that was at home listening to a record many years ago in my twenties. Though I don't know Yiddish, I knew the melodies of many of the songs. Did my mother or grandmother sing these songs when I was little? Or grandfather play

them on his violin? The answer to this question will have to be added to the many mysteries of my early childhood.

Patient #3
THE OWL AND THE PUPPY DOG, CONTROLLING AND LOSING CONTROL
This case is a testimony of the power of insights generated by the testing. A single test led to profound personal insight that evoked a radical attitude change, which eradicated severe psychopathology in the shortest period of time.

Patient: a 29-year old male college student
Diagnosis: Axis I, severe chronic Insomnia-Depression,
Axis II Dominant-Cooperative relational modality.
Length of Therapy: seven visits.
Outcome: The insomniac patient was able to sleep without medications.
History: This college student had suffered from severe chronic insomnia for 15 years. He had been on a variety of medications, none of which appeared to be successful. He came to the Center requesting to be hospitalized because he had been deprived of sleep for a week. Seven weeks later the patient was able to sleep without medication and he experienced a dramatic psychosocial adjustment, a remarkable personal transformation, after having been dysfunctional for years.

Patient's essay #1
Picture this, a very dark day begins. It's 7:30 AM. The sun is shining, the birds are singing and the dew is rising off the trees but not for me. For me this is just another extension of a day that has not ended. For several days it is painful to see the sunrise, for it means I have not slept for another night. Barely having the strength to continue, I move forward in what seems a worthless life, which I wish I could leave. Pain is all around me, my head hurts, my body aches, my eyes so heavy that I do not understand why they will not stay closed. Every minute I welcome death. I will not

take my life but I wish for death to either come or go away. My life is a living hell. No one understands and people say things like 'you just need to work a little or be more tired.' Little do they realize I have physically and mentally worked straight with no sleep for more than four days. My sanity slowly comes and goes. I worry about what I will do sometimes but I must remember to remain strong. The sun sets for another day. I am petrified, for this signals the beginning of my personal hell. Days aren't so bad, but nights are extreme pain, every minute slowly ticking by and me wondering 'can I make it through another night?' Tears begin to swell in my eyes as I know this will be another sleepless night. This is painful to write. I had to hide it after I wrote it. It represents so much pain. I let my fiancée' read it. Last few nights the hopelessness is not there. I am close to being able to sleep on my own, but yet it seems far.

Patient's essay #2
1. When I first came to see Dr. Levis I was not sleeping and I had a sense of hopelessness. Dr. Levis used some drawings I had made to unlock the meaning of my animal metaphors. The first drawing I made, a picture of an outdoor setting with an owl and a puppy dog. The owl was my grandfather and the puppy was myself. My grandfather had died about a year and a half ago and Dr. Levis pointed out that I was following my grandfather like a puppy and when my grandfather passed away I had become the owl in the picture and that I was controlling everything around me and that I needed to stop controlling and start trusting people. I immediately could see that I had become the owl and that I was controlling people. As I left the office that day I felt tons lighter and saw things differently.

2. It did not take me long to start to realize I had been controlling all the people in my life. I did not like this and I started to trust people and not control them. I must admit, it was a huge difference in the way I looked at the world. Instead of

trying to control events around me, I would just let them happen and trust. I realized for many years I was controlling my younger brother. My brother had died several years ago in an auto accident. So one person I could never stop controlling was him because he is gone. Dr. Levis knew I was controlling my brother by another picture I had drawn. In this drawing I was much younger and was getting out of my bed to shut a light off that my brother had turned on earlier. Back and forth my brother and I would compete and me always trying to control him. I would do things like break his collarbone when he beat me at a soccer game, smash him in the face for touching my truck and on and on. I wish I could apologize to him.

3. I knew I would have to talk to my parents and fiancé about the ways I was trying to control them. It wasn't easy but I confronted them one at a time to let them know I am sorry and I am another person now. My father was the least receptive. He was angry and said 'everyone has problems' and continued to unload on me. But I knew this would happen because I had not been honest with him in the past. Although he was angry, I felt better because I told him. At the same time, I went into relapse Thursday and Friday. I did not sleep at all. Saturday I got drunk and slept a few hours. Sunday and Monday I had not slept at all and Tuesday I was exhausted. During these sleepless nights I cannot say it wasn't difficult. But something was different. I did not feel as hopeless and I became very close to sleeping but just could not go that extra inch or two needed to fall asleep.

4. Wednesday I came to see Dr. Levis and explained to him about the relapse. I wrote some things down on a piece of paper and I was instructed to sit down in the chair and kick back and relax. It took a few minutes but then I felt myself fall into the grasp of the comfortable chair. I was told about a pendulum on a clock and the ocean waves coming in and out. This was extremely relaxing and a breathing pattern began to emerge, a different pattern from before, a more relaxing pattern. As I awoke I felt much better and I think another piece to my puzzle has been put into place.

Patient #4
THE MAD POSTAL EMPLOYEE, AGGRESSION, PARANOIA AND MORE AGGRESSION
The following comment was generated by an individual with the relational syndromal diagnosis of dominance. The patient's comments tell of the significance of the testing for evolving insights and for better understanding the need for changes.

Age 49, Postal employee fired for committing theft of a tape.

Diagnosis: Hospitalized following a suicide and thoughts of murdering his family.
Axis I- Schizo-Affective Disorder.
Axis II Equivalent Dominant/Antagonistic relational modality.
Length of Therapy: Three visit-evaluation.
Outcome: the three visit evaluation was successful

Patient comments:
"I would like to reply to the test given by Dr. Levis. I have seen the doctor three times and when I was working on the test and drawings I found it to be very helpful in dealing with my aggression attempting suicide and thinking of harming my family.

The Balloons have helped me deal with my childhood and realize that aggression started in my younger years. This testing is a much better way of dealing with a patient as one could sit and talk to the doctor and never get to the scope of the problem. This is also a very good way to get to the problem much quicker. This type of testing will also help decide the exact type of therapy, which will be most beneficial to me, the patient.

I have never had this type of therapy before and have found it to be very helpful in getting to my problem sooner. This test also helps one to analyze oneself.

I did feel under pressure with thoughts as I really did not want to release feelings, but the drawings helped even though I do not like to draw. I have been through therapy before and it did not work with just talking to the doctor as I was not able to reveal my true feelings. I would like to see this test expanded to other patients as it has started me to think positive and less negative. This test has also given me a different outlook on life as SUICIDE is not the answer."

Patient #5
BUILDING WALL'S AROUND ONE'S HEART AND BEING AFRAID OF THEM COLLAPSING
This case illustrates the thematic continuity between the metaphor drawings helping to establish insight into a consistent relational pattern.

Patient: a 40 year-old divorced nurse.
Diagnosis: Axis I Chronic Depression,
Axis II Relational Diagnosis: Submissive - Antagonistic Personality
Length of Therapy: Total of 5 Sessions
Outcome: Symptom free and also able to pursue life goals.

Patient comments:
"Therapy here is different, it is more structured. It is not just winging it. There is a beginning, a middle, and an end as opposed to free flow of comments like "what is going on this week? and trying to raise the self-esteem of the patient by making things that have happened look better."

"The focus is what YOU have to do better to relieve symptoms rather than 'I did the best I could do at the time.' It is not about what makes you feel better for the moment like an ice cream cone. It is not instant gratification. It is about what to do to feel better in the long run."

Patient #6
COMPETITIVENESS AND THE FEAR OF FAILURE
The patient was a college student who quit school several times in anticipation of failing grades.

After four weekly sessions the patient did not feel paralyzed by her fears of failure, she was able to enjoy peer relations and feel good about herself.

Patient comments:
"I've gained more insight on my own doing the drawings. It brought out a lot of hidden meanings. I am able to be more aware of how to gain inner peace by making an effort. I realize that there is a build-up of experiences throughout my life that show how I conducted myself being competitive, obsessed with grades and how I got constantly depressed. I have caused myself to be that way."

The patient's parents' comments:
"Dear Dr. Levis,
I wanted you to know how grateful we are to see our daughter's progress and her happier and more confident disposition. In a short time you have already given her some valuable and long-lasting "tools" to use throughout life. Thank you for your professional interest in our daughter and your courtesy to us. Appreciatively..."

Patient #7
LOSING TRUST AND TRUSTING AGAIN
This case reveals the facilitation of the program in enhancing openness and the development of trust. The patient is a 56 year-old business man who suffered from insomnia for the last 30 years, ever since his first wife left him for another man. He had been in therapy and on a variety of sleeping and antidepressant medications several times. After five visits he terminated feeling secure about his recovery and the improvement of his sleeping pattern.
Diagnosis: Axis I: Chronic insomnia and also panic about the inability to sleep.
Axis II: Relational modality, Dominant/Cooperative
Length of Therapy: Five Visits
Outcome: Relief of symptoms, able to sleep without dependence on medications, self-confidence.

Patient Comments:
"This time I opened up a lot more--- not only here but to my wife, my children and others. I have talked to them about my difficulty sleeping, whereas before I kept it from them. When I went to my family doctor, then a psychiatrist, they gave me pills to make me sleep. Here I learned to become self-reliant rather than depend on somebody else's authority and advice to fix me. I have learned to be communicative... it is all right to talk about my feelings... insomnia is not an insurmountable thing.

I did the artwork when I was feeling bad and it helped me to express feelings that I otherwise wouldn't have faced. I am happy to have made this progress. I feel confident that I can handle my fears of insomnia from now on without panicking. I am having more and more good nights and days without medication ... I have to trust people more. Not to be too careful. Let it happen."

Patient #8
THE SUN AND THE UGLY TROLL
"Looking back at the past few years of my life, it seems as if I were a different person from who I once was, and almost the opposite of who I would hope to be."

The horrible things I have done to myself have reinforced my self-loathing and have left emotional scars on my family. I am sickened and embarrassed by my behavior: screaming tantrums, cutting and scarring my skin, biting myself, hitting myself, suicide scenarios and quasi-attempts to kill myself, fleeing and hiding from my family, swearing, throwing knives at the wall, tying my hair in knots, refusing to bathe. Who was that person, and how did she get that way? During therapy, I have been able to identify contributing factors to my state of emotional distress. Some of these were: a controlling mother, a critical father, a self-perceived guilt for the death of my aunt, an uncommunicative stepfather, a criticizing grandmother, a marriage of false pretext, a series of rapes, a severely mentally ill mother-in-law, failure to attain the job I had planned for and an extremely stressful work environment.

The feelings arising from my response to these factors in my life have created the horrible monster I became. If asked to describe myself, I would say bad, stupid, lazy, ugly, fat, mean, bitter, unwanted, worthless and a burden to those around her -better of dead.

So, after five hospitalizations for suicidality, a series of medications and countless therapy sessions, has anything changed?

Yes – in degrees. I have not cut myself in quite a while, and think of it infrequently. I do not believe that I would actually kill myself, nor seriously threaten to again. I am becoming more involved in my daily family life and responsibilities. I am able to care for my young stepdaughter, niece and nephew. I am not becoming overwhelmed by the major changes in my life – moving to a new home and opening a store. I am looking forward to my new job, and feel I can handle it. How did I begin to get better?

I am still learning to live with myself, but I think I can, I think I can, I think I can…"

4. MY METAPHORS, MYSELF: 1983

Validation #2: Here six metaphor creation tests help to reconstruct the personal six-role Conflict Resolution Process. The experimentally derived sequence validates the theory by showing that parts are formally interrelated within the dramatic totality. This totality also tells how its author, Dr. Levis, evolved from a stress, "The War of the Metaphors", through his response, anxiety, defense, reversal, to the compromise of "The Reconciliation of the Metaphors".

2. RESPONSE is identified by the MASK TEST which reveals a person's identity. I chose the image of the runaway Pinocchio, the wooden puppet lying about his identity, fleeing the killer whale of hot ideologies pursuing naive consumers.

4. DEFENSE is identified by the ANIMAL METAPHOR TEST. Here the Formal Theory Oedipus is offering the Sphinx an olive branch, conflict resolution, as the new answer to the everlasting riddle on the nature of man.

6. COMPROMISE is identified by the SHORT STORY TEST. My Judaic passion for justice and my Greek respect for reason as the fiddler on the temple roof unite the world metaphors in the cosmic dance of a universal moral order.

1. STRESS is identified by the MEMORIES TEST. It represents my recollection of World War II as "The War of the Metaphors", the war of multiple cultural conflicts endangering everybody's survival.

3. ANXIETY is identified by the BEHIND THE MASK TEST. It presents Pinocchio trapped in the stomach of the killer whale with his creator, Geppetto. My Pinocchio is showing to a puzzled Gepetto the unit of the Conflict Resolution Process which has transformed him into a true human.

5. ROLE REVERSAL is identified by the DREAM TEST. It presents the daydream of my family working as a team delivering hospitality and wisdom to fellow travelers on the patio of my Art to Science Project, the Wilburton Inn.

7. THE FORMALLY INTERRELATED METAPHORS YIELD THE PERSONAL SCENARIO OR SYNDROMAL POWER MANAGEMENT STYLE.

The CONFLICT ANALYSIS BATTERY elicits art & DREAMS. The upper tier presents the reciprocal activity states, the MARITAL CONFLICT RESOLUTION PROCESS here that of "Cinderella", a 34-year-old SUR text along the opposite polarities of certain themes. The lower tier features passivity FAMILY, a MASK, the ANIMAL, FAIRY TALE and SHORT STORY METAPHORS. vivor of childhood abuse. states, the PARENTAL FAMILY, MEMORIES OF CONFLICT, HIDDEN EMOTIONS Contrasting Passivity vs. Activity states we reconstruct the PERSONAL

— MASTERY CONFLICT RESOLUTION | PHASE — ACTIVITY — COOPERATION — | RESPECT

2. THE MARITAL FAMILY BALLOONS portray the dramatic manifestation of closeness as balloons tightly held together their string art long and tightly interwined. Indeed the infant is overlapping the maternal balloon.

4. MASK I Depicted as "Serenity" is a cover up of feelings. "I hide my feelings to appear unaffected. I have done so for so long. I don't recognize my feelings anymore."

6. DREAM - Slapping her ex-husband, a mother surrogate, while he was sitting on the toilet. "I pulled out a dress slipper made of emeralds. It tinkled. My boyfriend said that's it. I'll get him with that!!!

8. RECENT MEMORY illustrates the patient escaping, hiding with baby while her foster mother is directing her husband to go after her and the baby.

10. ANIMAL METAPHOR TEST th Shepherd vs. Kitten metaphor represents the depressed client resenting her demanding infant.

12. SHORT STORY — She is rescuing a kitten thrown in the garbage. "Oh look at the poor thing. It is a Kitten. It is just real sick. I am going to take it home and make it better."

CHILDHOOD CONFLICT INDUCTION | PHASE — PASSIVITY — ANTAGONISM | — ALIENATION

1. PARENTAL FAMILY BALLOONS portray the abusive mother as a black and the abused client as a small blue balloon. Family members are far apart from each other and have short independent strings.

3. MASK II illustrates "anger, frustration, confusion, sorrow, hopelessness and emptiness." THE HEART is labelled 'Beauty With Mishaps.'

5. CHILDHOOD MEMORY OF ADOLESCENCE "My foster mother entered the bathroom and slapped my face while I was sitting on the toilet. I was embarrassed to be seen by my father helpless and exposed."

7. RECENT MEMORY OF CONFLICT illustrates first husband abusing "Cinderella".

9. ANIMAL METAPHOR TEST-INTENSIFIED CONFLICT This Metaphor illustrates a passivity state her foster mother's abusive conduct. She is a vicious, manipulative, dominant Lion. The patient is a timid, loyal, humble puppy.

11. CHILDHOOD MEMORY Portrays foster brother in his bed with patient underneath the covers. "I was two years old. He placed me between his knees and told me it was a baby's bottle. He didn't care about me, he used me as an object."

MURAL VII: THE FORMALLY INTERRELATED METAPHORS
YIELD THE PERSONAL SCENARIO OR SYNDROMAL POWER MANAGEMENT STYLE.
THE *CONFLICT ANALYSIS BATTERY* ELICITS ART AND TEXT ALONG THE OPPOSITE POLARITIES OF CERTAIN THEMES.

The lower tier features passivity states, the PARENTAL FAMILY, MEMORIES OF CONFLICT, HIDDEN EMOTIONS and DREAMS.
The upper tier presents the reciprocal activity states, the MARITAL FAMILY, a MASK, the ANIMAL FAIRY TALE and SHORT STORY METAPHORS.
Contrasting Passivity vs. Activity States we reconstruct the PERSONAL CONFLICT RESOLUTION PROCESS of "Cinderella", a 34-year-old survivor of child abuse.

MASTERY CONFLICT RESOLUTION PHASE • ACTIVITY, COOPERATION, AND RESPECT.

2. *THE MARITAL FAMILY BALLOONS*
Portrays the dramatic manifestation of closeness as balloons tightly held together their strings are long and tightly intertwined. Indeed the infant is overlapping the maternal balloon .

4. *MASK I*
Depicted as "Serenity" is a cover up of feelings. "I hide my feelings to appear unaffected. I have done so for so long. I don't recognize my feelings anymore."

6. *DREAM*
Slapping her ex-husband, a mother surrogate, while he was sitting on the toilet. "I pulled out a dress slipper made of emeralds. It tinkled. My boyfriend said that's it. I'll get him with that."

8. *RECENT MEMORY*
Illustrates the patient escaping, hiding with her baby while her foster mother is directing her husband to go after her and the baby.

10. *ANIMAL METAPHOR TEST*
The Shepherd vs. Kitten metaphor represents the depressed client resenting her demanding infant. "Would you stop licking me?" vs. "No I won't." "Why not?" vs. "Because it feels good." "To whom?" vs. "To both of us." "I don't want you to bother me." vs. "Then I'll lay next to you." vs. "Okay."

12. *SHORT STORY*
She is rescuing a kitten thrown in the garbage. "Oh look at the poor thing. It is a kitten, it is just real sick, I am going to take it home and make it better."

CHILDHOOD CONFLICT INDUCTION PHASE • STATES OF PASSIVITY, ANTAGONISM, AND ALIENATION.

1. *PARENTAL FAMILY BALLOONS*
Portrays the abusive mother as a black and the abused client as a small blue balloon. Family members are far apart from each other and have short independent strings.

3. *MASK II*
Illustrates "anger, frustration, confusion, sorrow, hopelessness and emptiness."

The HEART is labelled 'Beauty With Mishaps'.

5. *CHILDHOOD MEMORY OF ADOLESCENCE*
"My foster mother entered the bathroom and slapped my face while I was sitting on the toilet. I was embarrassed to be seen by my father helpless and exposed."

7. *RECENT MEMORY OF CONFLICT*
Illustrates first husband abusing "Cinderella."

9. *ANIMAL METAPHOR TEST-INTENSIFIED CONFLICT*
This Metaphor illustrates a passivity state her foster mother's abusive conduct. She is a vicious, manipulative, dominant Lion. The patient is a timid, loyal, humble puppy.
Lion: "You rotten mutt, you do what I tell you or I'll eat you up. I'll crush your little bones, etc."
Puppy: "No, no... please don't hurt me. I'll do anything you say. Please stop, you are hurting me."

11. *CHILDHOOD MEMORY*
Portrays foster brother in his bed with patient underneath the covers. "I was two years old. He placed me between his knees and told me it was a baby's bottle. He didn't care about me, he used me as an object."

8. THE PHYSICS OF AESTHETICS: THE ART CONFIGURATIONS HAVE SOCIAL EMOTIONAL MEANING AND NATURAL SCIENCE DIMENSIONS.

ball oscillating in a morally polarized magnetic field whose right pole coincides with power, and left pole with powerlessness. As figures oscillate to power like a pendulum ball, we see their profiles representing the state of kinetic or action energy, when the figures face forward they represent potential or emotional energy. We then read his METAPHOR PROFILE as the motion of a sinner to power, a transgression, where he experiences anxiety, guilt, and anger and from where he oscillates back to powerlessness, repentence and social service.

The evolving direction of metaphor figures of the "tempted seminarian" confirm the formal thesis that the self is like a pendulum

2. RESPONSE -MASK I

The mask conveys the Seminarian's damaged identity as he, the youth, has become a bearded, grough man paradoxically labelled "Mona Lisa". A bug on the mask's cheek reflects a further blemish of his identity, his impression that he has become both effeminate and evil.

-S (displacement)
-v (velocity)
-1/s (acceleration)
a = -1/2 KS

4. DEFENSE- ANIMAL METAPHOR TEST I
Assumption: The imbalance of two animals directed to the right corresponds to a person seeking power or taking liberties and experiencing anxiety.
Validation: His eagles transgress. Top Eagle: "Let's fly over there- this is fun, huh?"
Bottom Eagle: "Yeah this is fun! Let's go over here. But it is kind of dangerous."

Evil Power : -S
Exploration : -v
Guilt : -1/a
The pendulum shift to the right coincides with repeated transgressiveness or homosexual explorations. This shift guarantees anxiety as experiencing "danger".
Formula : E=a x S
Energy side moving figures correspond to social action or kinetic energy.

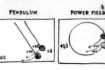

Commentary: Prodigal Horse concession making. Backswings coincide with transformation of psychic/potential energy, repentence or guilt to social or kinetic energy expiation behaviors and hope.

E Total = E (social or kinetic energy).

6. COMPROMISE - SHORT STORY:
Assumption: Two left directed animals reflect introspection and depression.
Validation: The "Prodigal Horse" didn't want to plow and followed the evil horse to another field where food was plentiful without having to work. But this food "poisoned his insides". Repenting, this Horse, returns home to plow.

1A. STRESS - THE CONFLICTUAL MEMORY TEST
reveals that his adolescent homosexual play generated guilt: "I always assumed the more female role which felt perverted."

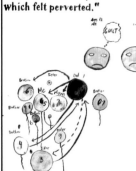

Antagonism = (counter-clockwise move) :- (minus)
The power position = status of evil as a significant normative deviation :-S (displacement)
The behavior of transgression is :v (velocity)
The ensuing emotion experienced is guilt = 1/a (acceleration)
The sinful transgressive behavior is experienced as guilt a state of high potential energy : E potential

1 B. STRESS - THE PARENTAL FAMILY PORTRAIT
is titled "Berlin Wall". It reflects the tremendous polarization, and lack of communication between the father and the members of the family, entailing elevated psychic tension experienced by the seminarian. This state corresponds to a pendulum ball suspended in a maximal left deviation as the state of maximal potential or emotional energy.

Status of Powerlessness
Oppression is experienced as : -1/S (displacement)
emotional state of hostility : -1/v (velocity)
: -a (acceleration)

The Formula of Energy (E) as equal to Force (a) times Displacement (S) informs us on the intensity of the conflict experienced.
(E) Energy =Force (a) times Displacement (S)
Conflict (E) = Dependency Needs (a) times Status Deviation (S)

3. ANXIETY- MASK II Reflects hope that a smiling and winking face magically gets rid of the sense of guilt, the bug, seen descending below.

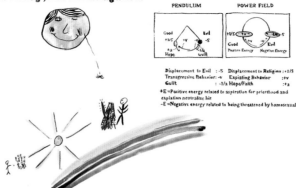

Good — Evil
+1/S — -S
+v — -v
+a — -1/a
Good — Evil
Hope — Guilt
Positive Energy — Negative Energy

Displacement to Evil : -S Displacement to Religion : +1/S
Transgressive Behavior: -v Expiating Behavior : +v
Guilt : -1/a Hope/Faith : +a
+E =Positive energy related to aspiration for priesthood and expiation neutralize his
-E =Negative energy related to being threatened by homosexual

THE HEART ILLUSTRATES THE TOTAL FORCE SYSTEM: ANXIETY AND HOPE as a rainbow reflecting his alternative identities. On the right end of the rainbow(-S) the evil power tries to control him. He feels guilty (-1/a). On the left end he surrenders to God (+1/S), and feels empowered (+a) as a preacher saving people from evil and sin.

5. REVERSAL - FAIRY TALE METAPHOR
Assumption: The imbalance of two animals partially facing forward reflects different degrees of anxiety and action.
Validation: Bugs Bunny is a big bully setting the pig up for humiliation brandishing his menacing phallic carrot. (Hostility). While Porky Pig on the right field is moving to the left, and redfaced looks forward (guilt) and humbly admits being "a spineless impressionable individual who should put a spine in himself so he can believe in his worthiness."

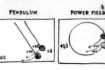

Bugs Bunny, the Seducer, forward directed indicates self-consciousness or anxiety. Pig turning to the left but facing forward is yielding power and feeling embarrassed.

E total = E potential and E kinetic

Both animals reflect high potential energy. The pig reflects a mixture of anxiety and action energies.

PENDULUM POWER FIELD
Bugs Bunny — Porky Pig
-1/S — -S
-a

5. ROLE REVERSAL - INTENSIFIED CONFLICTUAL ANIMAL METAPHOR
Assumption: Forward directedness coincides with maximal psychic tension or anxiety.
Validation: The monkey, the good energy, defies the bossy gorilla, the evil power. Like a hero he picks up the sword and slays the mighty gorilla.

Gorilla — Monkey Punishment — Ambition
-1/S — -S
-a

Forward Directedness : High Emotional Energy

Revenge to Justified Action of Vindictiveness +t Death to Evil : -1/s
Action of Revenge : +S Punishment : -S
Assertion : +a Expiation : +1/a

Commentary: Facing forward coincides with the point of maximal hesitation, corresponding to the maximal potential energy = emotional tension. The compromise total is not of expressing of guilt.

E total = E psychic or potential

MURAL VIII. THE PHYSICS OF AESTHETICS:
THE ART CONFIGURATIONS HAVE SOCIAL EMOTIONAL MEANING AND NATURAL SCIENCE DIMENSIONS.

The evolving direction of metaphor figures of the "tempted seminarian" confirm the formal thesis that the self is like a pendulum ball oscillating in a morally polarized magnetic field whose right pole coincides with power, and left pole with powerlessness. As figures oscillate to power like a pendulum ball, we see their profiles representing the state of kinetic or action energy when the figures face forward they represent potential or emotional energy. We then read his METAPHOR PROFILE as the motion of a sinner to power, a transgression, where he experiences anxiety, guilt, and anger and from where he oscillates back to powerlessness, repentence and social service.

1A. STRESS -
CONFLICTUAL MEMORY TEST
reveals that his adolescent homosexual play generated guilt: "I always assumed the more female role which felt perverted."

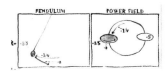

1B. STRESS
PARENTAL FAMILY PORTRAIT titled "Berlin Wall."
It reflects the tremendous polarization, and lack of communication between the father and the members of the family, entailing elevated psychic tension experienced by the seminarian. This state corresponds to a pendulum ball suspended in a maximal left deviation as the state of maximal potential or emotional energy.

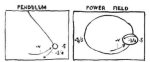

2. RESPONSE
MASK I
The mask conveys the Seminarian's damaged identity as he, the youth, has become a bearded, gruff man paradoxically labelled "Mona Lisa." A bug on the mask's cheek reflects a further blemish of his identity, his impression that he has become both effeminate and evil.

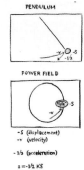

- S (displacement)
- v (velocity)
- 1/a (acceleration)

a = -1/2 KS

3. ANXIETY
MASK II
Reflects hope that a smiling and winking face magically gets rid of the sense of guilt as the bug, seen descending below.

THE HEART ILLUSTRATES THE TOTAL FORCE SYSTEM: ANXIETY AND HOPE as a rainbow reflecting his alternative identities. On the right end of the rainbow(-S) the evil power tries to control him. He feels guilty (-1/a). On the left end he surrenders to God (+1/S), and feels empowered (+a) as a preacher saving people from evil and sin.

4. DEFENSE
ANIMAL METAPHOR TEST
Assumption: The imbalance of two animals directed to the right corresponds to a person seeking power or taking liberties and experiencing anxiety.
Validation: His eagles transgress. Top Eagle: "Let's fly over there- this is fun, huh?"
Bottom Eagle: "Yeah this is fun! Let's go over here. But it is kind of dangerous."

5. REVERSAL
FAIRY TALE METAPHOR
Assumption: The imbalance of two animals partially facing forward reflects different degrees of anxiety and action.
Validation: Bugs Bunny is a big bully setting the pig up for humiliation brandishing his menacing phallic carrot. (Hostility). While Porky Pig on the right field is moving to the left, and red faced looks forward (guilt) and humbly admits being "a spineless impressionable individual who should put a spine in himself so he can believe in his worthiness."

5. ROLE REVERSAL
INTENSIFIED CONFLICTUAL ANIMAL METAPHOR
Assumption: Forward directedness coincides with maximal psychic tension or anxiety.
Validation: The monkey, the good energy, defies the bossy gorilla, the evil power. Like a hero he picks up the sword and slays the mighty gorilla.

6. COMPROMISE
SHORT STORY
Assumption: Two left directed animals reflect introspection and depression.
Validation: The "Prodigal Horse" didn't want to plow and followed the evil horse to another field where food was plentiful without having to work. But this food "poisoned his insides." Repenting, this Horse, returns home to plow.

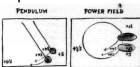

9. THE METAPHOR PROCESS IS A COST-EFFECTIVE VEHICLE FOR SELF-DISCOVERY AND SELF-HEALING.
THE WORKBOOK GUIDED HANNA, A 62 YEAR OLD HOLOCAUST SURVIVOR TO RECOGNIZE AND RESOLVE HER CONFLICTS.

IN ONLY THREE SESSIONS SHE WAS ABLE TO MAKE PEACE WITH HERSELF TO GET RID OF HER MASK AND TO FEEL ALIVE, VULNERABLE AND PASSIONATE AGAIN.

2a. RESPONSE. *In her MARITAL BALLOON PORTRAITS she admits anger in her marital family.*
My husband agreed to forgo his share so that his sisters could get more of the inheritance; we were all very angry.

#1 "Get away thief, the catch is mine."
#2 "No way, by right, it's mine."

2b. RESPONSE. *She hid her emotions behind strength.* "Inscrutable", is the face of a 40-year-old woman who does not want to admit to weakness; this face is a well controlled mask.

4a. DEFENSE. *Her ANIMAL METAPHOR TEST reveals her emerging from victimization by identifying with the aggressors' dominant behaviors.*

#1 "We shall see about that!"
#2 "Roar, growl, Grrr!"
#1" Grrr, grrr: They continue to growl and fight."

One lion killed an antelope. Another encroached on his territory. They must kill to live, they are territorial. I identify with the lions. The lions could be nations or persons who think they should have something somebody else has. It goes on constantly and I have to join it if I want to survive.

4b. DEFENSE. *Her FAIRY TALE METAPHOR reconciles her with an unpleasant reality.* This fairytale is about Joshua, a 10-year-old boy. His friend Cerberus, an adventurous, trusting, wise, changeable, flying ageless dog is guiding him to the land that never ends. The boy is myself. The dog represents my grandfather.

Joshua: Will you take me to the land that never ends?
Cerberus: A strong belief of enough people propelled me into being again.

Cerberus: It's a wondrous realm; continents appear and vanish. That happens when believers and naysayers are just about even. Evil philosophies sometimes gain ascendancy and destroy gods and heavens. The guiding principle is to have balance.

6a. COMPROMISE. *Her SHORT STORY METAPHOR reveals her successfully restraining dominant and anxiety provoking strivings.*

Ava: My niece was on a farm this summer and when they wanted milk they went to Bessy the cow instead of the store.
Allan: This is the day I want to meet my first cow!
Ava: How much is the fare to the country? It is more than I've got.
Allan: There are a lot of dames with cash!
Ava: You would not dare! There will be other weekends for cows.

Allan appears to be the bold unconventional facet of my personality. Ava keeps me honest and out of jail.

6b. COMPROMISE. *In A THANK YOU NOTE she shared her losing control and experiencing a profound emotional release.*

CHAVA ALBERSTEIN

A mezzo-soprano sings to celebrate the Israeli Independence Day. I broke down sobbing and made a fool of myself, but I did not care. Her voice filled me with peace. I felt alive again.

1a. STRESS. *Three MEMORIES OF CONFLICT reveal a proneness for power and guilt.*
a. German soldiers forced the door, they took my mother to another room. I heard her crying and shouting. The next morning my mother had tried to hang herself. I felt guilty.

c. I was taken to a foundling home. At night I tackled the way to the bathroom past waterbugs and cockroaches. Every morning the nuns combed each child for lice. Every day I got sick. I was a spoiled brat unable to cope with the new reality.

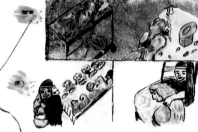

TEARS

b. My grandparents were deported to Auschwitz, I thought to a "work-camp". Some part of me felt glad to be rid of their loving control. Later, when I realized they went to a "death-camp", I felt like a terrible person for enjoying a slight feeling of freedom.

1b. STRESS. *In her ZOO FAMILY PORTRAIT she contrasted her Jewish mother's and her German father's families and wondered* "Can we understand some of our persecutors and if so are they innocent?"

Parrot: Uncle G., indoctrinated, idealistic, Nazi.
Owl - Maternal grandmother: Enterprising; clever; outgoing
Unicorn- Maternal grandfather: Honest, trusting, patient
Coyote-German father: Liked garlic, tossed me up into the air
Mule- Myself: Analytical, polite, Private.
Songbird- Mother: Emotional, mezzo-soprano, vegetarian
Porcupine: Aunt, critical. They made lame excuses for murdering 12 million people.
Ostrich: Grandfather, in denial.

I may have inadvertently encouraged it. Before I died, I began to question all the stuff they taught me.

If I wish real hard maybe I can erase the Holocaust and take what I see at face value.

3a. ANXIETY. *In her TRUE FEELINGS MASK she denounced herself as deceptive.* She was a "Perfect Looking Poison Fruit"

3b. ANXIETY. *In WHAT IS IN YOUR HEART DRAWING she denounces her good motives but then dismisses these concerns.*

My heart is full of good intentions that pave the road to hell. I take things too seriously. It helps to laugh at your pain and confusion.

5a. REVERSAL. *Three DREAM METAPHORS reveal her fears of the impending destruction of her universe and of herself.*

A CHILDHOOD DREAM: 9-years-old. A large black sinister crow sat on a wooden fence next to three sunflowers. Above the moon and the sun shone at the same time. This meant the end of the world the way I knew it. I was terrified. The sunflowers represent my mother and hope.

5b. REVERSAL. *In a memorable DREAM AT AGE 40 she finally met her fate, death:* I remember being dead. I was killed but don't know how, and I was waiting for something to happen and nothing did. I told myself there is nothing after death afterall and kept watching the preparations for my funeral.

5c. REVERSAL. A RECENT DREAM *gave her relief, her grandmother had not died in Auschwitz. She was alive and well.*
Grandmother is still alive in Prague in a government shelter. She has not written me because she doesn't know my address.

MURAL 9. THE METAPHOR PROCESS IS A COST-EFFECTIVE VEHICLE FOR SELF-DISCOVERY AND SELF-HEALING.

The workbook guided Hanna, a 62-year-old holocaust-survivor to recognize and resolve her conflicts.
In her three sessions she was able to make peace with herself to get rid of her inscrutable mask and to accept feeling alive vulnerable and passionate again.

1a.STRESS
3 MEMORIES OF CONFLICT reveal a proneness for power and guilt.
a. German soldiers forced the door, they took my mother to another room. I heard her crying and shouting. The next morning my mother had tried to hang herself. I felt guilty.

b. My grandparents were deported to Auschwitz, I thought to a "work-camp." Some part of me felt glad to be rid of their loving control. Later when I realized they went to a "death-camp", I felt like a terrible person for enjoying a slight feeling of freedom.

c. I was taken to a foundling home. At night I tackled the way to the bathroom past waterbugs and cockroaches. Every morning the nuns combed each child for lice. Every day I got sick. I was a spoiled brat unable to cope with the new reality.

1b. STRESS
ZOO FAMILY PORTRAIT
She contrasted her Jewish mother's and her German father's families and wondered "Can we understand some of our persecutors and if so are they inno-cent?"

Unicorn- Maternal grandfa-ther: Honest,trusting, patient

Owl - Maternal grandmother: Enterprising, clever, outgoing
Ostrich- Paternal grandpa: Strict, fair, strong work ethic.
Mule- Myself: Analytical, po-lite, private.
Songbird- Mother: Emotional, mezzo-soprano, vegetarian
Porcupine- Aunt : Critical, protective
Griffin - Uncle : Scientific, versatile, loving.
Coyote-German Father: Liked garlic, tossed me up into the air
Parrot - Uncle G.: Indoctri-nated, idealistic, Nazi

1. Unicorn:
Shouldn't we have learned something since?
2. Owl:
The wounds are emotional.
3. Mule: If I wish real hard maybe I can erase the Holo-caust and take what I see at face value.
4. Porcupine:They made lame excuses for murdering 12 million people.
5.Ostrich: I may have inadver-tently encouraged it.
6. Parrot: Before I died, I be-gan to question all the stuff they taught me.

2a. RESPONSE
In her *MARITAL BALLOON PORTRAITS* she admits anger in her marital fam-ily. My husband agreed to forgo his share so that his sisters could get more of the inheritance; we were all very angry.

2b. RESPONSE
She hid her emotions behind strength. "Inscru-table", is the face of a 40-year-old woman who does not want to admit to weakness; thisface is a well controlled mask.

3a. ANXIETY
In her *TRUE FEELINGS MASK* she denounced herself as deceptive. She was a "Perfect Looking Poison Fruit."
This image reflected my being suspicious, alterna-tively gullible, that is tak-ing things at face value.

3b. ANXIETY
In WHAT IS IN YOUR HEART DRAWING *she denounces her good motives but then dismisses these concerns.*
My heart is full of good in-tentions that pave the road to hell. I take things too seriously. It helps to laugh at your pain and confusion.

4a. DEFENSE.
Her ANIMAL METAPHOR TEST reveals her emerging from victimization by iden-tifying with the aggres-sors' dominant behaviors.

#1 "Get away thief, the catch is mine."
#2"No way, by right, it's mine."
#1"We shall see about that!"
#2"Roar, growl, Grrr!"
#1" Grrr, grrr. They continue to growl and fight."
One lion killed an antelope. Another encroached on his terri-tory. They must kill to live, they are territorial. I identify with the lions. The lions could be nations or persons who think they should have something somebody else has. It goes on constantly and I haveto join it if I want to survive.

4b. DEFENSE. *Her* FAIRY TALE METAPHOR *reconciles her with an unpleasant reality.*
This fairytale is about Joshua, a 10-year-old boy. His friend Cerberus, an adventurous, trust-ing, wise, changeable, flying ageless dog is guiding him to the land that never ends. The boy is myself. The dog represents my grandfather.

Cerberus: A strong belief of enough people propelled me into being again.
Joshua: Will you take me to the land that never ends?
Cerberus: It's a wondrous realm, continents appear and vanish. That happens when believers and naysayers are just about even. Evil philosophies sometimes gain ascendancy and destroy gods and heavens. The guiding principleis to have balance.

5a. REVERSAL
Three DREAM METAPHORS reveal her fears of the im-pending destruction of her universe and of herself.
A CHILDHOOD DREAM: 9-years-old. A large black sinister crow sat on a wooden fence next to three sunflowers. Above the moon and the sun shone at the same time. This meant the end of the world the way I knew it. I was terrified. The sunflowers represent my mother and hope.

5 b. REVERSAL
In a memorable DREAM AT AGE 40 she finally met her fate, death: I remember being dead. I was killed but don't know how, and I was waiting for something to happen and nothing did. I told myself there is nothing after death afterall and kept watching the prepa-rationsfor my funeral.

5 c. REVERSAL
A RECENT DREAM *gave her relief, her grandmother had not died in Auschwitz. She was alive and well.* Grandmother is still alive in Prague in a govern-ment shelter. She has not written me because she doesn'tknow my address.

6a.COMPROMISE
Her SHORT STORY META-PHOR reveals her success-fully restraining dominant and anxiety provoking strivings.
Ava: My niece was on a farm this summer and when they wanted milk they went to Bessy the cow instead of the store.
Allan: This is the day I want to meet my first cow!
Ava: How much is the fare to the country? It is more than I've got.
Allan: There are alot of dames with cash!
Ava: You would not dare! There will be other weekends for cows. Allan appears to be the bold unconventional facet of my personality. Ava keeps me honest and out of jail.

6b. COMPROMISE.
In A THANK YOU NOTE she shared her losing control and experiencing a pro-found emotional release.
A mezzo-soprano sings to celebrate the Israeli In-dependence Day. I broke down sobbing and made a fool of myself, but I did not care. Her voice filled me with peace.
I felt alive again.

10. THE EVERY DAY PSYCHOPATHOLOGY OF THE DOMINANCE AND SUBORDINANCY RELATIONAL MODALITIES ILLUSTRATED WITH THE METAPHOR PROFILES OF MELISSA AND CHRIS, MY FIRST TRAINEES IN THE SUMMER OF 1992.

THE DOMINANCE SCENARIO: THE DOMINANT PERSON EASILY PANICS AND COMPROMISES. MELISSA'S *STRESS* WAS GUILT EVOKED BY HER EARLY MISCHIEF. HER *RESPONSE* WAS BEING HERSELF, SINGING HER FEELINGS LOUD AND CLEAR. HER *ASPIRATION FOR* ATTENTION GENERATED ANXIETY AS FEARS OF RUNNING OUT OF TIME. HER *DEFENSE* WAS BEING MORE DEMANDING OF HERSELF AND OTHERS. HER *REVERSAL* WAS LOSING HER VOICE AND BEING IMMOBILIZED INTO THE SILENCE OF AN *ABANDONED MERMAID*. IN HER *COMPROMISE* SHE ADJUSTED HER COMPETITIVENESS BY BECOMING COMPLIANT TO HER WISE AND CONFORMIST GRANDMOTHER. SHE, THE VOYEURISTIC CHILD, BECAME THE VULNERABLE, NAKED CLASSICAL FEMININE SPIRIT.

FAMILY BALLOON PORTRAIT: "My pattern is established from childhood. I am fattened on attention and praise. My job is to sing, eat and make people happy."

CONFLICTUAL MEMORY: "Desiring attention from a boy I had a crush on, I got my friends together and walked in on him while he was going to the bathroom."

TRANSPARENT MASK: "Wanting to make sure people notice me, I make a bold appearance, though it sacrifices prettiness. I come on very strong, full of color, energy and life."

UNDERNEATH THE MASK, WHAT IS IN MY HEART: "I am always aware of time however. Always tense beneath the gaiety and fun. I am very competitive with my friends and family. Very aware of who is ahead of me and time/youth running out. Still at the center is love, kisses and my love of music."

AMT I: "Though I have every resource I need, I pray on the modest unassuming vegetable patch. I envy their productivity and self-reliance. I push them, charm them, demand they help me and give me what I want."

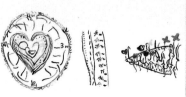

FAIRYTALE METAPHOR: "As a child my mother read me Hans Christian Anderson's Little Mermaid. She gives up her voice for the ideal boy but it doesn't work. Sad and lonely she watches as he marries another, though not as special as she is. The other girl gets him."

SHORT STORY: "The compromise is the desexualized Birth of Venus who is me being haunted by my grandmother over the competitive and proper social and professional goals. It is also me haunting my old, innocent boyfriends, pestering them, singing songs about them and not letting them ever leave my reins."

DREAM: "I would dream that I could fly doing the breast stroke and swimming through the air. I would fly to the Arts Center up the long wooded driveway."

AMT II: "The Bird of Paradise, wild, free and hard, blends with Sweet Peas-messy and free and soft, demands the Daisy's sunlight. Realizing it is being ridiculous, she asks for low key friendships, compromise and help."

THE SUBORDINANCY SCENARIO: THE SUBMISSIVE PERSON CAN BE HOSTILE AND EXPLOSIVE. *STRESS* - CHRIS'S CHOICE MEMORY DEPICTS HIM VICTIMIZED AND RESENTFUL. HIS *RESPONSE* SHOWS HIS ASPIRATIONS FOR BEING A WISE, YET SAD KING. HIS *ANXIETY* IS HOPE AND FEAR OF CHILDLIKE INNOCENCE. HIS INTOLERANCE TO INNOCENCE AS A BADGER MENACING A RABBIT. IN HIS *REVERSAL* THE BADGER IS OUT OF CONTROL, DEVOURS THE RABBIT AND AS A MONSTER HAUNTS HIS CHILD HOOD DREAMS. HIS *COMPROMISE* SHOWS THE SAD AND RESIBLE KING BEMUSED BY AN UNPRETENTIOUS JANITOR.

FAMILY BALLOON PORTRAIT: "It seems that I am envious of the attention my mother gives my little sister. She is 13 y.o. and attempts to attract attention. She discovered that the family is more likely to take notice of her when she speaks as if she were dumb - a skill she is rapidly mastering."

CONFLICTUAL MEMORY: "Held underwater by another child, I chose to go along with him. I planned to pretend to be drowned, hoping to make him feel guilty. This was a key incident, as it established the themes of resignation (submission) and intellectual "power" (planning and subtle manipulation." **STRESS**

MASK 1: "This haggard face represents my assuming the "role" of resignation to pain as my identity. I identify this state with the acquisition of knowledge, to be wise is to be sad in my mind. An important detail here is the crown, which shows my attribution of nobility and power to this outlook." **RESPONSE**

MASK II & III: "This mask depicts a state opposite to that of sadness and wisdom. It's delight and wonderment. The child faces are equated with innocence or ignorance. My subconscious belittles this outlook caused by envy of my little brother. The connection is that happiness is possible only through the attainment of knowledge." **ANXIETY**

AMT I: "My Animal Metaphor Test shows my defense against the anxiety of the previous stage. The rabbit here stands for "happy ignorance" transformed defensively from the "happy innocence" of Mask II. The Badger is hostile and wise, but retains some respect for the Rabbit's happiness, enough to refrain from eating him. I identify with the Badger, who longs to be happy himself, and therefore both envies and resents the Rabbit."

FAIRYTALE: "The evil, deceptive, cruel and merciless White Witch threatens Ashland the benevolent, tough and noble Lion. The Lion is the behavior I want to emulate, however I often fall into the rut of acting like the witch." **DEFENSE**

DREAM: "Monster chases me down the hallway of my house. As I reach the kitchen he grabs my feet, I hold onto the door. I try to yell but my voice does not come out."

AMT II: "This is the setback stage. The Badger no longer feels the respect for the Rabbit's happiness which held him back before. He knows only hate and resentment, and so pounces on the Rabbit, devouring him. It appears here that wisdom, pain and resignation will continue to accompany one another. Luckily, the final stage above, shows that this is not so." **REVERSAL**

SHORT STORY: "This scene shows my resolution to the conflict in this process. The wise king of this story finds that when the burden of power on him becomes too great, he feels better after talking to his friend, Manny, the Janitor. Here, wisdom and innocence/ignorance not only coexist in harmony, but actually complement one another. Wisdom alone leads to sadness; innocence alone leads to superficiality. When one becomes capable of experiencing both, true and substantial happiness follows. This is my resolution.." **COMPROMISE**

10. THE EVERYDAY PSYCHOPATHOLOGY OF THE DOMINANCE AND SUBORDINANCY RELATIONAL MODALITIES ILLUSTRATED WITH THE METAPHOR PROFILES OF MELISSA AND CHRIS, MY FIRST TRAINEES IN THE SUMMER OF 1992.

The dominance scenario: the dominant person easily panics and compromises. Melissa's stress was guilt evoked by her early mischief.
Her response was being herself, singing her feelings loud and clear. Her aspirations for attention generated anxiety as fears of running out of time.
Her defense was being more demanding of herself and others. Her reversal was losing her voice and being immobilized in the silence of an abandoned mermaid.
In her compromise she adjusted her competitiveness by becoming compliant to her wise and conformist grandmother.
She, the voyeuristic child, became the vulnerable, naked classical feminine spirit.

1. STRESS- FAMILY BALLOONS
"My pattern is established from childhood. I am fattened on attention and praise. My job is to sing, eat and make people happy."

1. STRESS- CONFLICTUAL MEMORY TEST
"Desiring attention from a boy I had a crush on, I got my friends together and walked in on him going to the bathroom."

2. RESPONSE - MASK I
"Wanting to make sure people notice me, I make a bold appearance ... though it sacrifices prettiness. I come on very strong, full of color, energy and life."

3. ANXIETY - MASK II
"I am always aware of time however. Always tense beneath the gaiety and fun. I'm very competitive with my friends and family. Very aware of who is ahead of me and time/youth running out. Still at the center is love, kisses and music is my love."

4. DEFENSE- ANIMAL METAPHOR TEST
"Though I have every resource I need, I pray on the modest unassuming vegetable patch. I envy their productivity and self-reliance. I push them, charm them, demand they help me and give me what I want."

5A. REVERSAL - AMT II
"The Bird of Paradise, wild , free and hard, blends with sweet peas--messy and free and soft, demands the daisy's sunlight. Realizing it is being ridiculous, she asks for low key friendships, compromise and help."

5B. REVERSAL - FAIRY TALE METAPHOR
"As a child my mother read me Hans Christian Anderson's Little Mermaid. She gives up her voice for the ideal boy but it doesn't work. Sad and lonely she watches as he marries another, though not as special as she is. The other girl gets him."

COMPROMISE - SHORT STORY:
"The compromise is the desexualized Birth of Venus who is me being haunted by my grandmother over the competitive and proper social and professional goals. It is also me haunting my old, innocent boyfriends, pestering them, singing songs about them and not letting them ever leave my reins."

5C. REVERSAL - DREAM:
"I would dream that I could fly doing the breast stroke and simming through the air. I would fly to the Arts Center up the long wooded driveway."

The subordinancy scenario: the submissive person can be hostile and explosive. Stress- chris's choice memory depicts him victimized and resentful.
His response shows his aspirations for being a wise, yet sad King. His anxiety is hope and fear of childlike innocence. His intolerance to innocence as a
badger menacing a rabbit. In his reversal the badger is out of control, devours the rabbit and as a monster haunts his childhood dreams.
His compromise shows the sad and risible king bemused by an unpretentious janitor.

STRESS - FAMILY BALLOON PORTRAIT: "It seems that I am envious of the attention my mother gives my little sister. She is 13 y.o. and attempts to attract attention. She discovered that the family is more likely to take notice of her when she speaks as if she were dumb - a skill she is rapidly mastering."

STRESS - CONFLICTUAL MEMORY: "Held underwater by another child, I chose to go along with him. I planned to pretend to be drowned, hoping to make him feel guilty. This was a key incident, as it established the themes of resignation (submission) and intellectual 'power' (planning and subtle manipulation."

RESPONSE - MASK 1: "This haggard face represents my assuming the 'role' of resignation to pain as my identity. I identify this state with the acquisition of knowledge, to be wise is to be sad in my mind. An important detail here is the crown, which shows my attribution of nobility and power to this outlook."

ANXIETY - MASK II: "This mask depicts a state opposite to that of sadness and wisdom. It's delight and wonderment. The child faces are equated with innocence or ignorance. My subconscious belittles this outlook caused by envy of my little brother. The connection is that happiness is possible only through the attainment of knowledge."

DEFENSE - ANIMAL METAPHOR TEST
"My Animal Metaphor Test" shows my defense against the anxiety of the previous stage, The rabbit here stands for 'happy ignorance' transformed defensively from the 'happy innocence' of Mask 11. The badger is hostile and wise, but retains some respect for the rabbit's happiness, enough to refrain from eating him. I identify with the badger, who longs to be happy himself, and therefore both envies and resents the rabbit.
FAIRY TALE: "The evil, deceptive, cruel and merciless White Witch threatens Ashland the benevolent, tough and noble Lion. The Lion is the behavior I want to emulate, however I often fall into the the rut of acting like the witch."

REVERSAL - ANIMAL METAPHOR TEST II DREAM: "Monster chases me down the hallway of my house. As I reach the kitchen he grabs my feet, I hold onto the door. I try to yell but my voice does not come out."

This is the setback stage. The badger no longer feels the respect for the Rabbit's happiness which held him back before. He knows only hate and resentment, and so pounces on the Rabbit, devouring him. I appears here that wisdom, pain and resignation will continue to accompany one another. Luckily, the final stage above, shows that this is not so."

COMPROMISE:
SHORT STORY: "this scene shows my resolution to the conflict in this process. The wise king of this story finds that when the burden of power on him becomes too great, he feels better after toalking to his friend, Manny, the Janitor. Here, wisdom and innocence/ignorance not only coexist in harmony, but actually complement one another. Wisdom alone leads to sadness; innocence alone leads to superficiality. When one becomes capable of experiencing both, true and substantial happiness follows. This is my resolution."

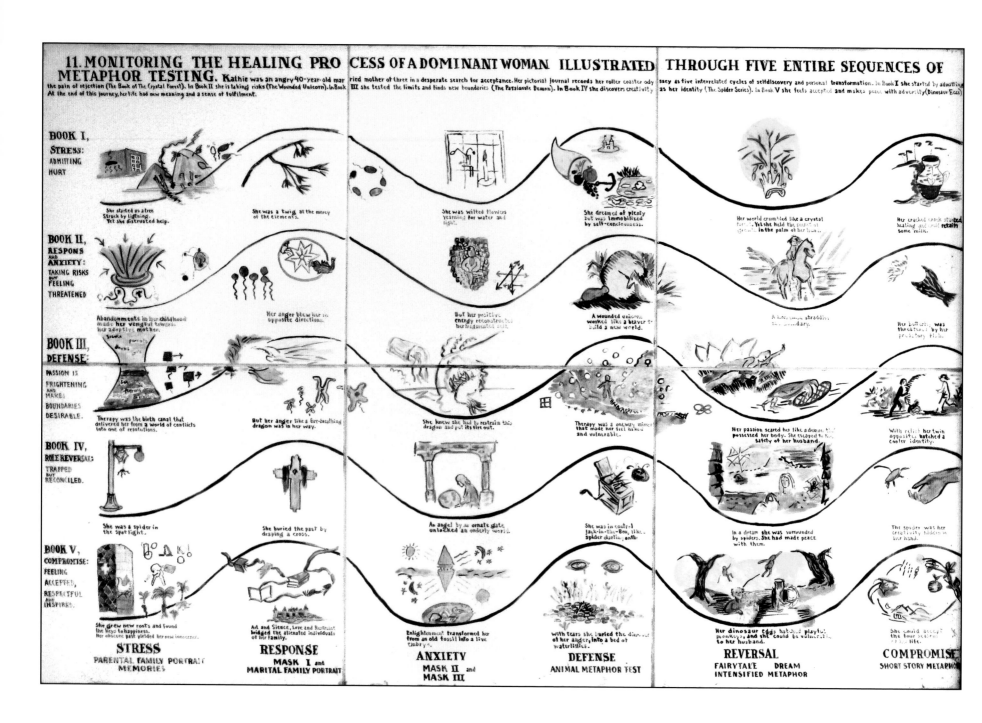

11. MONITORING THE HEALING PROCESS OF A DOMINANT WOMAN ILLUSTRATED THROUGH FIVE ENTIRE SEQUENCES OF METAPHOR TESTING.

Kathie was an angry 40-year-old married mother of three in a desperate search for acceptance. Her pictorial journal records her roller coaster odyssey as five interrelated cycles of selfdiscovery and personal transformation. In Book I she started by admitting the pain of rejection (The Book of The Crystal Forest). In Book II she is taking risks (The Wounded Unicorn). In Book III she tested the limits and finds new boundaries (The Passionate Demon). In Book IV she discovers creativity as her identity (The Spider Series). In Book V she feels accepted and makes peace with adversity (Dinosaur Eggs). At the end of this journey, her life had new meaning and a sense of fulfilment.

BOOK I, STRESS: ADMITTING HURT

She started as a tree struck by lightning. Yet she distrusted help.

She was a twig at the mercy of the elements.

She was wilted flowers yearning for water and light.

She dreamed of plenty but was immobilized by self-conciousness.

Her world crumbled like a crystal forest. Yet she held the secret of growth in the palm of her hand.

Her cracked crock started healing and could retain some milk.

BOOK II, RESPONSE and ANXIETY: TAKING RISKS but FEELING THREATENED

Abandonments in her childhood made her vengeful towards her adoptive mother.

Her anger blew her in opposite direction.

But her positive energy reconstructed her fragmented self.

A wounded unicorn worked like a beaver to build a new world.

A horseman straddled the boundary.

Her butterfly was threatened by her predatory fish.

BOOK III, DEFENSE: PASSION IS FRIGHTENING AND MAKES BOUNDARIES DESIRABLE.

Therapy was the birth canal that delivered her from a world of conflicts into one of resolutions.

But her anger like a fire-breathing dragon was in her way.

She knew she had to restrain this dragon and put its fire out.

Therapy was a oneway mirror that made her feel naked and vulnerable.

Her passion scared her like a demon that possessed her body. She escaped to the safety of her husband.

With relief her twin opposite, hatched a cooler identity.

BOOK IV, ROLE REVERSAL: TRAPPED but RECONCILED.

She was a spider in the spotlight.

She buried the past by draping a cross.

An angel by an ornate gate unlocked an orderly world.

She was in control Jack-in-the-Box, like a spider dancing on the...

In a dream she was surrounded by spiders. She had made peace with them.

The spider was her creativity hidden in her hand.

BOOK V, COMPROMISE: FEELING ACCEPTED, RESPECTFUL and INSPIRED.

She grew new roots and found the keys to happiness. Her obscure past yielded her new innocence.

Art and Science, Love and Restraint bridged the alienated individuals of her family.

Enlightenment transformed her from an old fossil into a live embryo.

With tears she buried the dinosaur of her anger, into a bed of waterlilies.

Her dinosaur eggs hatched playful monkeys, and she could be vulnerable to her husband.

She could accept the four seasons of her life.

STRESS	RESPONSE	ANXIETY	DEFENSE	REVERSAL	COMPROMISE
PARENTAL FAMILY PORTRAIT MEMORIES	MASK I and MARITAL FAMILY PORTRAIT	MASK II and MASK III	ANIMAL METAPHOR TEST	FAIRYTALE DREAM INTENSIFIED METAPHOR	SHORT STORY METAPHOR

11. MONITORING THE HEALING PROCESS OF A DOMINANT WOMAN ILLUSTRATED THROUGH FIVE ENTIRE SEQUENCES OF METAPHOR TESTING.

Kathie was an angry 40-year-old married mother of three in a desperate search for acceptance.
Her pictorial journal records her roller coaster odyssey as five interrelated cycles of self-discovery and personal transformation.

BOOK I, STRESS: ADMITTING HURT

She started as a tree struck by lightning. Yet she distrusted help.	She was a twig at the mercy of the elelments.	She was wilted flowers yearning for water and light.	She dreamed of plenty but was immobilized by self-consciousness.	Her world crumbled like a crystal forest. Yet she held the secret of growth in the palm of her hand.	Her cracked crock started healing and could retain some milk.

BOOK II: RESPONSE AND ANXIETY: TAKING RISKS BUT FEELING THREATENED.

Abandonments in her childhood made her feel vengeful towards her adoptive mother.	Her anger blew her into opposite directions.	But her positive energy reconstructed her fragmented self.	A wounded Unicorn worked like a beaver to build a new world.	A horseman straddled the boundary.	Her butterfly was threatened by her predatory fish.

BOOK III: DEFENSE: PASSION IS FRIGHTENING AND MAKES BOUNDARIES DESIRABLE.

Therapy was the birth canal that delivered her from a world of conflicts into one of resolutions.	But her anger like a fire-breathing dragon was in her way.	She knew she had to restrain this dragon and put its fire out.	Therapy was a one-way mirror that made her feel naked and vulnerable.	Her passion scared her like a demon that possessed her body. She escaped to the safety of her husband.	With relief her twin opposites hatched a cooler identity.

BOOK IV: ROLE REVERSAL: TRAPPED BUT RECONCILED

She was a spider in the spotlight	She buried the past by draping a cross.	An angel by an ornate gate unlocked an orderly world.	She was in control like Jack-in-The -Box, like a spider darting on the web.	In a dream she was surrounded by spiders. She had made peace with them.	The spider was her creativity hidden in her hand.

BOOK V: COMPROMISE: FEELING ACCEPTED, RESPECTFUL AND INSPIRED

She grew new roots and found the keys to happiness. Her obscure past yielded her new innocence.	Art and Science, Love and Restraint bridged the alienated individuals of her family.	Enlightenment transformed her from an old fossil into a live embryo.	With tears she buried the dinosaur of her anger into a bed of waterlillies.	Her dinosaur eggs hatched playful monkeys and she could be vulnerable to her husband.	She could accept the four seasons of her life.

Stress (RO)	Response (RA)	Anxiety (APR)	Defense (CPRA)	Reversal (RR)	Compromise (CRA)
Parental Family Portrait And Conflictual Memories Tests	*Mask I and Marital Family Portrait Tests*	*Mask II and Mask III Tests*	*Animal Metaphor Test*	*Fairytale, Dream and Intensified Metaphor Tests*	*Short Story Metaphor Tests*

12. MONITORING THE HEALING PROCESS OF A SUBMISSIVE BULEMIC THROUGH THE REPEATED USE OF THE ANIMAL METAPHOR TEST.

PHASE 1: IN THE EVALUATION PROCESS GLADYS EVOLVED FROM A CHILD CHASTISED BY HER GRANDMOTHER TO A FIRE-BREATHING DRAGON AFRAID OF HURTING HER LOVED ONES.

Family of Origin Balloons

Memory: "You are a bad girl." Grandma: You can't bring that stupid sandwich to your sick Mother.

Marital Family Balloons

Mask I: "Perpetual Shutting out sadness with a smile and outrageous makeup.

Mask II: "Blackout" Unable to express emotion, she was also unable to stop eating.

Mask III: "The Moat" The Moat separates her true feelings of anger and sadness from the happy surface of bunnies, flowers and sunshine.

Animal Metaphor: "Who will listen, Will you?" Cat: You can't really hear me can you? Dog: Why should I hear what you do have to say?"

Dream: "Running Late"... Can't find clothes that fit... but I can hide my fat body in a submarine.

Short Story: "Dove or Demon" I'm reliable, considerate, dull; she turned into a fire breathing dragon, hurt those around her. Then wept.

PHASE II: IN THE MOAT SERIES THE PROBLEM WAS CLARIFIED AS A POWER IMBALANCE AS SHE EVOLVED FROM A DUMB BUNNY TO A FREE, SOARING EAGLE.

"Run Rabbit Run" Gilla: Rabbit, you are the proverbial dumb bunny. You are gullible, inane and spineless.

"A Ray of Sunshine" Griffin: Hey ostrich, it's nice to see you without your head in the sand. You say others don't hear you, but you never listen to ME, your inner self.

"Mermaid and Centaur" (M): I am nothing. I am vulnerable, unclothed. (C): I care not to hear you speak of sadness, I don't want to hear such things. I am a centaur/you a fish.

"Lamb and Bull" Why don't I know you? Why have you fenced me in? Why do I have my back to you? Why can't I ever figure out how I feel about you?

"The Feckless Fawn", Deer: Your big teeth and claws scare me, You might hurt me. Bear: You're making me mad. Get over here before I lose my temper and bite you.

"Feathers & Claws" 'Here I am soaring upward. Why haven't I been here before?' The eagle flew beyond the mountains and the bear waved good-bye.'

PHASE III: IN THE SNAKE/VULTURE SERIES THE PROBLEM SHIFTED TO AN EATING DISORDER AS SHE RESPONDED TO STRESS CONTROLLING AND LOSING CONTROL OF FOOD. SHE EVOLVED FROM A SNAKE HISSING AT A VULTURE TO A JAGUAR DESTROYING (BOTH

"Feast or Famine" Snake: I can hiss at you and, if I choose, bite you with my venom-filled fangs.

"Venom for the Vulture, Feathers For The Snake" Vulture: I am not sure I am ready to die. I can still fly away. A failed attempt to become a whole.

"Dealing with a stressor A Storm Approaching". Snake: You have me up against the wall in a storm. Am I safe in the eye of the storm?

"After the Storm". The vulture won the battle. She ran amok and ate... the snake grew weary and weak.

"Now or Never" Snake: If you keep feeding me the way you are, I'll die. Rabbit: The only thing I know to do is cry.

"Life is Not Binge or Purge" Jaguar destroys snake and vulture. And says, 'I'll win. My patience has run out. The snake and the vulture must die.'

PHASE IV: IN THE FINAL PHASE OF THERAPY SHE RECTIFIED POWER IN A NUMBER OF RELATIONSHIPS. SHE EVOLVED FROM BEING REJECTED FROM HER MOM'S KANGAROO POUCH TO ADMITTING TO HER HUSBAND HER NEED FOR A TRUE PARTNERSHIP.

"No Room For Two" Mom Kangaroo: Why are you eating so much? Soon you'll be fat and ugly. Child: I eat for solace so you'll be aware of me.

"Wake up and Live" Armadillo says to Porcupine: You are not bound by convention. You can color outside the lines.

"Jaguar vs. Hippo" Jaguar: You're so obese and ugly, You must stuff food and drink in your cavernous mouth all day and night.

"How very dull". Bobcat self says to bighorn sheep husband: You never wanted to change anything nor do you want me to change. There is no joy to look forward to.

"An unveiling" Girland to Girpoise: Neither of us express anger. We have to tell each other when, why we're angry. People can have disputes and be friends again.

"Who Am I?" Dolphin: I enjoy companionship. What are you? Pigagu: A "we" and not an "I". The pig eats too much, the jaguar desires control and the seagull wants freedom.

STRESS	RESPONSE	ANXIETY	DEFENSE	REVERSAL	COMPROMISE

MURAL XII. MONITORING THE HEALING PROCESS OF A SUBMISSIVE BULIMIC,
50-year-old Gladys, through the repeated use of only one protocol - the *Animal Metaphor Test*.

PHASE I: GLADYS EVOLVED FROM A CHILD CHASTISED BY HER GRANDMOTHER TO A FIRE-BREATHING DRAGON AFRAID OF HURTING HER LOVED ONES.

Memory:	Mask I:	Mask II:	Animal Metaphor:	Dream:	Short Story:
"You are a bad girl." Grandma: You can't bring that stupid sandwich to your sick mother.	"Perpetual Smile" Shutting out sadness with a smile and outrageous makeup	"Blackout" Unable to express emotions she was also unable to stop eating.	"Who will listen, will you?" Cat: You can't really hear me can you? Dog: Why should I hear what you do have to say?"	"Running Late" Can't find clothes that fit...but I can hide my fat body in a submarine.	"Dove or Demon" I'm reliable, considerate, dull; she turned into a fire breathing dragon, hurt those around her. Then wept.

PHASE II: IN THE MOAT SERIES. THE PROBLEM WAS CLARIFIED AS A POWER IMBALANCE AS SHE EVOLVED FROM A DUMB BUNNY TO A FREE, SOARING EAGLE.

"Run Rabbit Run"	"A Ray of Sunshine"	"Mermaid and Centaur"	"Lamb and Bull"	"The Feckless Fawn",	"Feathers & Claws"
Gilla: Rabbit, you are the proverbial dumb bunny. You are gullible, inane and spineless.	Hey ostrich, it's nice to see you without your head in the sand. You say others don't hear you, but you never listen to ME, your inner self.	(M) : I am nothing. I am vulnerable, unclothed. (C): I care not to hear you speak of sadness, I don't want to hear such things. I am a centaur/you a fish.	Why don't I know you? Why have you fenced me in? Why do I have my back to you? Why can't I ever figure out how I feel about you?	Deer: Your big teeth and claws scare me, You might hurt me. Bear: You're making me mad. Get over here before I lose my temper and bite you.	'Here I am soaring upward. Why haven't I been here before?' The eagle flew beyond the mountains and the bear waved good-bye.'

PHASE III: IN THE SNAKE/VULTURE SERIES THE PROBLEM SHIFTED TO AN EATING DISORDER AS SHE RESPONDED TO STRESS, CONTROLLING AND LOSING CONTROL OF FOOD.
She evolved from a snake hissing at a vulture to a jaguar destroying both snake and vulture.

"Feast or Famine"	"Venom for the Vulture, Feathers For The Snake"	"Dealing with a stressor A Storm Approaching."	"After the Storm."	"Now or Never."	"Life is Not Binge or Purge"
Snake: I can hiss at you and, if I choose, bite you with my venom-filled fangs.	Vulture: I am not sure I am ready to die... I can still fly away. A failed attempt to become a whole.	Snake: You have me up against the wall in a storm. Am I safe in the eye of the storm?	The vulture won the battle. She ran amok and ate... the snake grew weary and weak.	Snake: If you keep feeding me the way you are, I'll die. Rabbit: The only thing I know to do is cry.	Jaguar destroys snake and vulture. And says, 'I'll win. My patience has run out. The snake and the vulture must die.'

PHASE IV: IN THE FINAL PHASE OF THERAPY SHE RECTIFIED POWER IN A NUMBER OF RELATIONSHIPS.
She evolved from being rejected from her mom's kangaroo pouch to admitting to her husband her need for a true partnership.

"No Room For Two" Mom	"Wake up and Live"	"Jaguar vs. Hippo"	"How very dull."	"An unveiling"	"Who Am I ?"
Kangaroo: Why are you eating so much? Soon you'll be fat and ugly. Child: I eat for solace so you'll be aware of me.	Armadillo says to Porcupine: You are not bound by convention. You can color outside the lines.	Jaguar: You're so obese and ugly. You must stuff food and drink in your cavernous mouth all day and night.	Bobcat self says to bighorn sheep husband: You never wanted to change anything nor do you want me to change. There is no joy to look forward to.	Girland to Girpoise: Neither of us express anger. We have to tell each other when, why we're angry. People can have disputes and be friends again.	Dolphin: I enjoy companionship. What are you? Pigasu: A "we" and not an "I." The pig eats too much, the jaguar desires control and the seagull wants freedom.

Stress (RO)	Response (RA)	Anxiety (APR)	Defense (CPRA)	Reversal (RR)	Compromise (CRA)

CONCLUSION

MORAL SCIENCE HEALING THE WORLD

The Difference Between Religion and Moral Order: Religions are Out, Moral Order is In
'Conflict Analysis, the Formal Theory of Behavior' addressed the methodological issues for the conceptualization of the unit in the study of behavior by identifying the object and method for its analysis. It advanced the process as a self-regulating periodic mental mechanism responsible for adjustments to the normative or acceptable behavior but also accounting for the individual challenging the normative. We identified adjusting to the normative as moral order. 'Science Stealing the Fire of the Gods and Healing the World' uses the art exhibits of the 'Museum of the Creative Process' to demonstrate and validate this premise of the Formal Theory.

The exhibits serve as evidence of the moral mechanism as a scientific phenomenon. They identify the universality of a natural science periodic phenomenon with a conflict resolution, social adjustment or moral function. The emotional process is the mechanism of the moral transformation. The new unconscious as a mental equilibrial homeostatic phenomenon, the atomistic unit of the social sciences, encompasses psychology and moral order into the exact Science of Conflict Resolution, the Moral Science.

The art exhibits demonstrate the process as a universal predictable and measurable entity showing how the individual and also cultures deal with change preserving stability but allowing adjustment through transformation or growth. The process, a simple harmonic or dialectic of emotions reconciles opposites into unities, oneness through its finite dialectic of six emotions evolving through three formal operations. By understanding this conflict resolving process as

how nature spontaneously seeks adjustment by transforming negative to positive emotions, science understands the mind as well as cultures as ever-evolving patterns of self-improvement. The moral evolution does not need external intervention; it does not require either theistic interference or biological foundation.

By understanding the mind and cultures as self-organizing systems science steals the fire of the gods, the credibility of external supernatural regulatory authorities. Science establishes the scientific foundation of moral order and dismisses Gods and religions; they loose their magical power as moral order is now attributed to the intrapsychic mechanical transformative process constantly seeking peace of mind predicated on social justice.

The exhibits book presents examples of the merger of moral order and science as the sine curve or the Universal Harmonic. This implies that a trigonometric formula integrates meaningfully opposite forces, emotional and social states in conflict, and guides them to resolutions. This finding reflects on the unconscious programed by a software that is adjustive, which seeks inner and outer transformations as the necessary end of all symbolic universes.

Each exhibit reinforces the premise of the universality of conflict resolution:

• The Metaphoria Murals introduce the pattern in three creation stories. The Greek religion emerges upon the end of the murderous interactions of the five cycles of the Cosmogony; the conclusion of the cycles of infanticidal and patricidal transactions between the five generations is that a son, Erichthonius, builds a temple to his mother, Athena, and that his mother grants Athens her blessings, a wise owl and an olive tree. Here it should not be overlooked that this creation story of one of the most significant civilizations coincides with the worship of a domestic

relations resolution celebrating the virginity of a mother figure.

• The last painting of the Henry Gorski Retrospective sums up the function of the process: the canvas titled 'Paradox' displays a cross made of kisses, four kisses going outwards, the central fifth kiss going inwards. A drawing on the lowest kiss presents the artist's final self-portrait wearing a crown of thorns. The interpretation of this imagery is an affirmation of the unconscious motivational force reconciling opposites, here the conflict between pleasure, the kiss, of sexuality, with pain as symbolized by the cross.

• The Oz story is concluded with a new world order: the dreaded Wizard of Oz, an effigy of God, is dismissed by a group of empowered mortals. Dorothy's defective and scared friends are emotionally and socially transformed to become the leaders of the Emerald City.

• At the end of the Sculptural Trail, installed on the pediment of the Sanctuary of the Wizard and of Wisdom, there is a set of sculptures generated with the self-assessment instrument illustrating and validating the transformative power of the unconscious Conflict Resolution Process. The sculptures confirm the use of creativity for self-discovery, the deliberate use of the process as the path leading to insight, emotional growth and social changes. In this case again we see the restructuring of a social and emotional system coinciding with power balance in a domestic relations system.

• Creativity is highlighted in each case study of the fifth exhibit as the path leading predictably to self-discovery, self-help and personal growth. The process leads to self-awareness, as personal insights and as inner transformations consisting of finding inner peace and social adjustment.

The exhibits of the *Museum of the Creative Process* demonstrate the mind guided by a wise, equilibrial unconscious Conflict Resolution Process. This is a natural science phenomenon and the unit of the social sciences. This phenomenon bridges the big divide between moral order, the humanities, psychology and the rigorous sciences: physics, logic and math. The Moral Science is the paradox of reconciling the mechanical and the spiritual, the two opposites, the pleasure of 'knowing' with the pain of sacrifices. The conflict resolution process is a compromise between pleasure and pain amounting to personal growth. It assists humans to manage power, be that arrogance, righteousness, or injustices in order to experience relief as peace of mind and peace in the world.

The art exhibits show the formal structure of associations in every sample of creativity as the circumscribed six formally interrelated emotions transformed from a conflict, a state of passivity, antagonism and alienation to the resolution, a state of mastery, cooperation and mutual respect. This process, Aristotle's Perfect Universe, reconciling opposites, pleasure and pain, also reconciles now at the end of this volume, religion and science. It accounts for universal order, the meaning of life accounted for by respect of natural laws.

Here we need to differentiate religions from moral order. Religions are imaginative stories explaining and promoting moral paradigms, Gnostic religious stories reconciled now with science. The universal moral order, the unit of the Moral Science is a natural science phenomenon.

Science clarifies conflict resolution as the key to the transformation of conflict, of negative feelings, of entropy or chaos, to meaning, positive feelings, moral order, wisdom and civilization. In the art exhibits we have identified this inner structure of the process as the Universal Harmonic representing the three formal inter-trans-formations of the key action as a well-structured system in every sample of creativity.

The exhibits show moral order as the circum-scribed dialectic of the six emotions transformed by three measurable formal operations. In detecting the universal order religions as partial truths loose credibility. On the contrary moral order as a universal science based process gains in credibility. It represents the integrity of formulas. We identify here both the formal dimensions of the unit process and the physics of the emotional oscillation defined by the constructs of the Simple Harmonic Motion. This structure of the process allows us to introduce measurement in the study of behavior. We can measure the relational variations, be it of an individual or of a cultural entity, through the quantifiable and qualifiable relational choices unfolding predictably within any symbolic system.

The formal interpretation of art makes creations meaningful and validates the thesis of the dialectic emotional growth. The conclusion from this study is that religions are partial truths, while moral order is the universal truth. Hence we may affirm that religions are history and the future belongs to the Moral Science.

The coincidence of psychological and sociological meaning with scientific order represents a major scientific breakthrough. The unconscious is redefined as the motivational, homeostatic, organizing force seeking normative compliance, and meaning as rest, defined as normative consensus. Conflicts represent deviations from social norms, the acceptable power positions, leading to resolutions as conforming or challenging but finally agreeing on norms.

In this context moral order is a sociological and psychological phenomenon. The process bridges art and science, the psyche and the societal system leading to the affirmation of the existence of a universal order. Psychology and religion merge to become the exact Moral Science, the Science of Conflict Resolution.

The formal theoretical, conflict-resolving un-conscious, is a peace striving psychic, physiological mechanism completely different from the conflict-generating Freudian unconscious. This circumscribed entity proceeding from a conflict to its resolution, an equilibrial oscillation, is the abstract unit organizing psychological and sociological systems. The unit order is the mental heartbeat and the unit of the social sciences, the integrative paradigm of religion and psychology, of the humanities and the rigorous sciences.

The Moral Science puts an end to metaphysical quandaries. Methodologically we must note that this scientific phenomenon pertains to the organization of emotions as purely symbolic systems. As such these entities are conceptually pure and independent of the brain, of neurological influences, and of metaphysical supernatural determinism. The harmonic of emotions represents the process as the object of study of psychology and religion, revamping conceptually the spectrum of the social sciences.

The unit process does not only affect our perception of religions. It also impacts our range of psychological theories. The Moral Science introduces a scientific epistemology, new diagnostic categories of wellness, clear assessment technology, innovative psycho-education and therapy techniques; science clarifies moral order as an orderly phenomenon and religions as pioneers in discovering partial aspects of this process. The unit of Conflict Resolution integrates the diversity of our fragmented reality, the plethora of social sciences into the one predictable and measurable meaningful Universal Harmonic.

Beyond religion and on to the Moral Science
Will things change as science has unmasked the wizard? Does it suffice for science to pull the curtain for all of us to look at gods as the machinations of the unconscious? Will the world remain entranced, captive of its grand illusions generated by the emotional machine and defended by the well established theistic institutions, religions, be-

lief systems entailing unchanging norms, normative rigidity?

The problem is that believers and cultures have great investment in continuing at the status quo, no matter what moral reality is about. Gods are the patterns we worship and religions is the music we live by. Science, though, makes the stagnation to the status quo very difficult. Reason is a popular alternative to belief in unreason. If the explanations work practically the world will have great incentives for making drastic changes. Especially as the world now is helpless, attacked left and right by fundamentalists, the true believers, it is possible that religious people might question orthodoxy and react to being manipulated and violated by entrenched dictatorial religious traditions.

The Formal Theory reduces theism, while it promotes moral order as an exact science

While the Darwinian science questioned religions misunderstanding moral order as a scientific phenomenon, dismissing gods and religions, the Moral Science as the physics and logic of emotions, hence of the process, recognizes the scientific and moral nature of associations as overlapping. The exhibits have served the purpose of showing that the machine of moral order, Aristotle's *deus ex machina*, is the autonomous psychic mechanism, our unconscious responsible for the creation of gods; this mechanism is the foundation for a new moral order beyond religions.

Understanding theogony as a scientific psychological phenomenon

The unconscious is a closed system of power positions evolving from stress to response, from anxiety to defense, to the inevitable reversal of fortune and then to a compromise. At the reversal state the person needs help, a release from the grips of self induced terror, the self-fulfillment of one's prophecies, manifested in nightmares, illness, abandonments, failures, defeats, and one's anticipated demise. The mind in the phase

of compromise generates associations of divine interventions, it invents gods. The creative process, Genesis means creation in Greek, does not create the cosmos; it creates the perfect totalities of stories, of conflict resolutions; some of these stories are about cultural heroes we identify with gods and religions; story telling demonstrates the scientific emotional need for moral order stemming from the unconscious. The physiological and psychological process eventually manifests itself as the sociology of religions. The origin of all gods, the nature of theogony, is inherent to the psychology of the unconscious creative process.

Gods are imaginary friends, wizards, emotional inventions of partners to whom the person is willing to make concessions to, contract covenants with, so that they rescue the person from his/ her state of distress such as the impending end of life. Gods rescue a person from his inner demons, fears, the downturn of dramatic lifetime journeys. Gods then are creations providing the conditions for our need for immortality, thus achieving the happy ending of conflict resolutions, and an attitude change, from despair of a loss we celebrate entering eternity.

Religions and gods evolve from unique private distortions to shared universal beliefs. The evidence is that individual patterns mold the divine, which once conveyed to others becomes a cultural reality, a shared belief, a religion. Religions predict outcomes because they are self fulfilling.

Gods are inherent part of the closed symbolic systems

Conflict resolutions generate norms, covenants, compromises. The world perceives different gods depending on the humans' relational choices. Religions and gods are popular myths, projections that become real because they are interpersonal in nature. Patterns shape transactions as consistent, repetitious and predictable. They become shared so myths that people believe in become realities. Throughout history and throughout the

entire globe people have sanctified their idealized divinities, have erected temples worshiping the Gods' and their normative patterns as the ultimate ethical reality. Humanity like the four heroes of the Wizard of Oz has evolved its perceptions of the Wizard.

Kavafy, in his poem 'Ithaca' shared a warning: 'The angry Poseidon, the Lestrigones, the Cyclops, you are not going to see them unless you are erecting them in front of yourself.'

We recognized the evolution of religions as a progression to fairness in dealing with domestic conflicts and as a progression in the abstract conceptualization of the nature of the divine concluded with the process defining the conditions for fairness and the ultimate definition of god as the process. Now humanity should espouse reason and extricate itself from counterproductive patterns and the predicament of abiding by ineffective and unfair norms.

Religions explained. Biology contradicted the belief in creation but did not explain the nature of moral order. Religions thrived while science was morally and philosophically irrelevant. Biologically founded psychology and metaphysically grounded beliefs, religions, have collided as two contradictory and incompatible perceptions of the human condition. Now the Moral Science has a better explanation on moral order than religions. But the new concept does not contradict religions; it understands them as resolutions of the same formula. There is a good chance that Moral Science will prevail as the optimal alternative to religions, socially disruptive theism and fundamentalism. The new science reconciles psychology and moral order. It understands the unconscious as the object for the study of both realms.

Any field to become a science must avail simplicity in its concepts, the reduction of complexity to an atomistic unit entity, a predictable periodic and measurable phenomenon. For science to understand psychology and religion we needed a concept pertaining to the individual and to his/her moral or normative social system. The concept of the unit process accounts for the two realms, the person and the social system, the internal and the external reality determined by psychic initiatives, not by supernatural forces.

Psychology understands the individual within the moral or normative context of sociology, morality; the normative or sociological, determines conflicts and resolutions constituting the psychological make up of the individual. The psyche and the moral do not require two different domains of knowledge. Science is about deviations from the moral or normative. Psychologists can clarify the moral order, thus becoming objective in their assessments.

The formal theoretical message reassures the public that has been torn between psychologists advancing an amoral psychology and preachers advancing rigidly moral mandates. Now we only have one set of rules for good behavior; ethics is proper equitable power management. The Formal Theory integrates the two isolated realms, the theistic and the psychological models into the dynamic interchange between the two in the concept of a shared universal moral and scientific pattern.

The pattern pertains to the individual and the societal as a single, simple ideational system, the emotional dialectic of the Conflict Resolution Process. The Process pertains to the individual emotions in the context of the societal norms; a person is conditioned by the parental input and is transmitting this pattern to the filial generation. The trans-generational interaction generates the personal and the social reality in the same symbolic language, its grammar and syntax, its physics and logic.

The personal pattern procreates/propagates/

perpetuates itself; it generates social, cultural patterns. The social pattern shapes the individual and the individual shapes the social. The pattern generates the emotional and the social reality. The individual psyche is in a formal relational balance with the social reality by engaging each other into a dramatic self-fulfilling interaction. Patterns determine psychic and social reality; prophets are individuals who create the cultures that emerge as religions.

Patterns, cultures and religions evolve; injustices are gradually rectified. Looking back in the history of civilization, we may retrace the history of moral paradigms as discoveries of improved ways of resolving conflicts; we see new covenants finally leading to the understanding the creative process as the scientific morality generating mechanism.

Understanding the process as patterns helps us to reconcile the religions, the evolution of gods and also the normative boundaries as covenants or conflict resolutions between humans. Understanding the process or pattern as a unit entity explains the moral and the physical or mechanistic and the metaphysical or spiritual nature of psychology and of faiths.

Science identifies the process as a natural science moral and social order-generating phenomenon. This equilibrial emotional dialectic becomes the unit of behavior and accounts for all psychological and sociologic/religious experiences. The new unconscious is different from the psychoanalytic unconscious and different from the moralist theistic determination of right and wrong.

The process becomes the unit of behavior and determines how the individual adjusts to the social system but also how the individual alters or reshapes the system. Humans seek justice as the most abstract understanding of something universal. Psychology then is about the unit order of the individual in the social or normative

context. It studies how the individual adjusts to society but also how s/he is responsible in reshaping reality. The healthy individual conforms to norms but also questions norms in pursuit of a more just and equitable order. The disturbed individual provokes the social order and the social order seeks to prevail and manage the deviant by disciplining him/her.

Moral Science emancipates humanity from the tyranny of gods yet enjoys respect from religions
Prometheus compromise is in that he was able to give the fire of the gods, may be simple moral order, to the unfortunate mortals with the blessings of the gods. Gods, mainly Zeus, respected him because he had the gift of foretelling, which saved Zeus's life. Similarly science will be respected by religions/gods/the clergy, because of its capacity to foretell. Foretelling frees humanity from the unpredictability of gods while empowering the Moral Science that predicts accurately and reliably. Science places moral order on a scientific foundation while allowing gods to enjoy respect as the integrated Pantheon of world religions. Each religion like an Olympian god has contributed insights and wisdom on the human faculty of resolving conflicts.

In the past science identified with forays of biology, dismissed gods and did not distinguish between morality and divinity. Scientific research on religion focused primarily in utilizing evolution to disprove Genesis, the creation story, and hence invalidating the existence of a magical Creator of the cosmic universe. This position dismissed religions lumped together as the Abrahamic' Gods' domain of mysticism. Biology's dismissal of gods and religions has been bad science. It did not enlighten us about the nature of religion, of gods or of the nature of the moral unconscious. Biology introduced atheism dismissing lightly all moral and spiritual, all sociological and psychological issues.

Atheist science based models have focused on

disproving the Abrahamic God as representative of all religions. Yet the concept of god is much wider than the Abrahamic God and the Biblical myth of the Creation of the cosmos and of humans; this misperception of the devine represents a big methodological mistake since there are as many creation stories as religions and gods.

God is seen as the evolving concept of the divine
The Formal Theory studies god as the continuity of the divine identified in the diversity of faiths current and historic. God is seen as the evolving concept of the divine; there we can detect the trend to the restructuring of domestic relations coinciding with the abstraction on the nature of the divine. We see this clearly as polytheism evolved to monotheism and beyond to philosophers' philosophies. Religions gradually discovered God as the process, a unit entity identified as Monotheism translatable as the worship of the unit, monas, coinciding with the theistic perception of the process. The Formal Theory continuing the march of redefinitions of god, transformed the Aristotelian concept of the unity of action into a natural science equilibrial and moral order mechanism.

The Moral Science perceives gods and religions as complementary, alternative, measurable insights on the scientific moral phenomenon
Science respects religions as an evolutionary continuum leading to the awareness of the unconscious as an emotional dialectic seeking inner balance and social justice. The ultimate definition of God coincides with that of the Conflict Resolution Process as a physiologic natural science equilibrial phenomenon abiding by the laws of science, natural law.

Conflict resolution is implicit in all theistic religions; they promise peace on earth. Science regards religions as measurable conflict resolution phenomena; the ultimate emotional objective then of religions and of science is the same but religions have deified peace as a magical entity

while the Formal Theory has validated the notion as the unit of the social sciences, a measurable phenomenon.

Science measuring religions identifies gods as very different narrow and highly regulated ways of resolving conflict; the human unconscious is programmed to strive for peace as conflict resolution following a universal well-structured pathway, the six role states or emotions connected by three formal operations. While the innate need for peace and justice is a well-defined phenomenon, the nature of the divine as redefined by religions corresponds to many variations in conflict resolution.

We recognize four syndromal alternatives organizing human behavior and identify them in the range of religions differing from each other as a set of alternative relational modalities. The study of the tangible process allows us to differentiate religions and to measure the elusive divine as abiding by alternative scenarios of relating.

Religions discovered conflict resolutions ahead of science; with several paradigms they promoted conflict resolution with one difference from science: religions narrowed the norms on resolving conflict thus diminishing the process's social effectiveness and they ascribed the imperative of resolution and management of justice to external authorities, divinities, gods rather than the human unconscious and its homeostatic function.

The Formal Theory reverses this double deficiency of religions
The Formal Theory shifts the object of study from the debate on the content of stories to the formal analysis of the universal plot of stories and regards the emotional cascade as a natural science phenomenon; it also attributes the process to the unconscious and not to gods. This discovery enhances respect for the science and reduces religions' moral authority on human affairs. Science steals the fire of the gods; it cancels their monopoly of virtue. The formal process understands moral order as

an intrapsychic process generated as a homeostatic adjustment mechanism but this process is also interactional or interpersonal; the innate mechanism connects the individual with his social counterparts as a measurable psychological and sociological phenomenon. The formal method allows us to measure sociological phenomena like religions' along the same relational dimensions as individual relational choices. We may hence evaluate religions as how moral and insightful they are as compared to the scientific prototype. Do they promote fairness in resolving conflicts in relations? Are their divine figures abstract concepts or anthropomorphized entities?

Science addresses the contributions of religions as a progression in conflict resolution, as the continuum of covenants or norms regulating domestic and intergenerational relations. It also examines the level of abstractness of religions' conceptualization of the divine as the attributions on the nature of the process. Rethinking the essence of all gods as the Conflict Resolution Process science reduces the power ascribed to any one 'God.'

Science, like Prometheus, foretells
The Moral Science understands the nature of moral order abstractly and thus upstages religions as the expert authorities in human relations. Science defines the perfect resolution as the set of three formal operations. Divine figures are exalted but they remain ineffective in solving the problems of our world.

Until now science, especially psychology, could not venture into morality delegating it to metaphysics and abstaining from the analysis of religions espousing the position of Political Correctness. The Moral Science ventures forth with the definitive insights on a new psychology based on conflict resolution. The new psyche as the process is then the purveyor or guardian of moral order.

We finally understand morality scientifically and we can analyze religions as imperfect resolutions and as limited insights in the nature of the process. It is the unconscious that seeks the social adjustment of the individual and it is this mental faculty that seeks to conform or to change norms and that suggests redefinitions of the self-divine relationship. The unconscious pursues the ideal resolution, formulas seeking the optimization of interpersonal relations coinciding with the concept of the perfect conflict resolution; scientific perfection is what we attribute to God. The truth though, as we pointed out, is that religions and gods sponsor imperfect conflict resolutions. The new definition of god is the set of the scientific formulas of moral order.

Upon the era of globalization the cultures and religions of the world collide with each along their contradictory paths to peace and wisdom. Religions identify different norms for domestic relations denying awareness of the evolution of civil rights. Though they evolved promoting the restructuring of domestic relations they represent authoritarian regimes that are intolerant of progress. They do not tolerate criticism and do not allow growth and change. It is this rigidity in normative choices that complicates global relations and the formation of a secular society. The religions of the world inspire their respective constituents with sets of moral solutions, which are mutually incompatible paradigms blocking the development of moral consensus.

Religions perpetuating dated values offer injustices as righteousness, resist change and obstruct progress as immoral; this cultural dissonance inspires the faithful to be intolerant of other civilizations and to undermine the alternative values as unacceptable lifestyles; faithful people become terrorists like the ancient gods who mistreated Prometheus and his rebellious mortals. These cultures regard progress as a blasphemy and sacrilege to their theistic orders. Inversely science objects to religions' power as manipulation of the public with consequences that are adverse to the public's interests. Science aspires to reconcile the religions

and to integrate them with the ultimate moral order that they have all aspired for but never achieved. The Moral Science moves humanity beyond religions as the limited paradigms of moral order into the science founded moral consensus.

Moral Science sheds light in the origin of morality. It is founded on the unconscious set of relational variables as the correct moral distinctions in managing power. Thus while science respects religions it also criticizes them as promoting obsolete norms and absolutist self-righteous authoritarianism controlling the minds of the naïve public. The faithful are reduced to puppets controlled by uninterpreted metaphors of dated norms or conflict resolutions. Religions' empowerment and current rekindling of normative wars demonstrates their ineffectiveness in bringing about peace to our divided global civilization. Science, like Prometheus, seeks to rescue humanity from the cruel self righteous gods and emancipate it from the conceptual limitations of religions.

Religions interfering with the public's best interests need to be managed by science
While religions originated in the need for improved family relations they are blocking the progress of family relations based on misunderstanding the principles of conflict resolution, the history of gender relations and the nature of the divine. Frozen in the past they defend inequitable and unfair normative models of relations and promote shortsighted definitions of the divine. They harm the world by regulating sexuality and procreation exacting a high toll on the health of the global society. They perpetuate maladjusted norms in the name of god and vehemently object to healthy norms as injustice and immorality.

Religious traditions induce global cross-cultural conflicts and easily start wars between observing and non observing or emancipated populations. The public must understand now that religions represent evolutionary societal experiments, ideologies like communism, which have their

positive and negative influences but which are of time limited value. As the world evolves through its societal experiments we note that religions are outgrown and gods redefined and forgotten. We are now at an era of the scientific redefinition of moral order.

It is not so long ago that humans discovered that the Earth is not the center of the universe, and that drugs control disease. It is not so long ago that humans exited the jungle to become self-aware and aware of societal relational solutions. Humans evolved norms and conventions and sanctified them with religions based on their understanding of seeking social and emotional stability. Suddenly humanity may find the scientific aspects of psychological abstractions rather than staying captive in the era of magic, theism, original sin and paradise lost.

The new era does not dismiss norms. It addresses the issue of right and wrong in the management of power. Power disturbances in family relations and cultural systems are the topic of the new moral order. The new norms are the formal operations leading to conflict resolution. They enhance a power-balanced psyche and the role system of family relations. Education and psychology are empowered to deliver moral and emotional education as the fair management of power.

Humans have delegated to religions too much power and religions have abused it. Science's norms facilitate reducing the sacredness of religions and reduce religions' self-righteousness and lack of accountability. The Moral Science providing clarity on moral matters diminishes the dependence of the public on religions as the monopolies of virtue.

Perpetrators or abusers of power victimize themselves
The Moral Science, the Science of Conflict Resolution or of Power Management provides clear guidelines to assess abuses of power and to clarify

how abuses automatically backfire on the perpetrators.

1. The Catholic Church's perverse attitude on controlling people's sexuality, a serious abuse of normative power, has been the church's downfall in its impact on the clergy manifested in the prevalence of child abuse in all countries where Catholicism is practiced; the massive delinquency of the clergy and its impact on the faithful is not reflecting individual psychopathic conduct, but rather a culturally-induced psychopathology. It is Catholicism's obsession with controlling the sexual behavior of the public that has made the clergy suffer multiple neuroticisms around sexual conduct.

2. The Islamic culture's lack of openness on moral matters generates tensions in their family relations besides deepening the normative divide between this culture and the West. The Islamic culture's intolerance toward openness has generated extremism in its populations, fanaticism, intolerance of other culture's customs and beliefs, and it has also alienated some of its own scholars as dissidents and infidels.

The scientific objectivity of the new moral paradigm promotes a new civilization, conferring consensus on moral matters, reconciling the divided paradigms into a clear new order with its many advantages: Science improves the realm of psychological insights, and services, revamps education, also promotes creativity and highlights the arts. Moral consensus inspires a new norm, emotional and moral literacy, the capacity to understand right and wrong determined by the new moral values, the three scientific principles of conflict resolution.

While science releases people from the inordinate obsessions and guilt inducing norms of religions that demonize sexuality and rigidly ritualize behavior, new norms regulate people's behavior and engage them in a normalcy of moderation based on cooperation and mutual respect. Moral order is now free of the intense sense of sin and virtue and norms inflicting guilt and fear.

The key norm sponsored by the Moral Science is balance through openness to all systems allowing for self-assessment and self-adjustment. This openness will undo the oppression of women and the lack of freedom of expression characteristic of theistic cultures. It can correct the dysfunction of global world conflicts. Believers are puppets of their systems unwilling to examine alternatives. The current world tensions represent the pathology of cultures as people of faith perpetrate atrocities in the name of God. The Arab Spring is one example of the puppet revolution against repressive norms and values.

The new moral order will not be without norms
The center of moral gravity is shifted by the new science. The Moral Science introduces new norms; deviations from them will evoke the range of feelings we identified characterizing the process. Religions are moral deviants and at this point they need to experience guilt and become motivated for substantial self-adjustment before they earn the world's confidence again. Following the new norms we may expect peace between people and comfort between family members. We may expect less power play and polarization between people in authority and subordinates, be that in the military, the business organization or the family.

We may expect reverence and harmony expressed in a number of non-religious institutions, while the religious traditions might open to introspection and pursue the new alignment with each other, with history and science. Peace in the world, harmony in relations, less focus on sexuality will help the world to become a happier and more considerate society. Celebrating creativity, the new spirituality, will heal the world.

THE GENESIS OF RELIGION

RELIGIONS AS AN INTEGRAL PART OF PSYCHOLOGY EVOLVED IN THE SEARCH FOR EMOTIONAL REST AND SOCIAL JUSTICE

The art exhibits of the Museum of the Creative Process capture the inner Conflict Resolution Process as the Universal Harmonic. They offer evidence that the process reduces conflict. They confirm it as a natural science phenomenon abiding by the laws of the equilibrial oscillation of the pendulum, the Simple Harmonic Motion and that of the balance of the trays of the scale. Thus the museum art exhibits demonstrate the coincidence of physiology, psychology, moral order and social justice with the rigorous sciences. They present the process in the analysis of all phenomena of creativity as the harmonic, which leads to the generation of moral, religious and spiritual thinking.

Now we will show that it is the process that has generated religions; inversely religions discovered the Conflict Resolution Process partially and metaphorically before contemporary psychology. With the discoveries of the Moral Science psychology outgrows the era of religion by definitively clarifying the nature of morality as a scientific phenomenon and reclaiming it from the realm of metaphysics.

The exhibits of the *Museum of the Creative Process* establish that the foundation of moral order is an orderly, unconscious physiological phenomenon; they establish morality/conflict resolution a physiological adjustment mechanism as the driving force behind all thinking. The motivation to morality coincides with the need to achieve the emotional rest state as conformity to or rethinking of norms; all emotions gravitate to morality as social justice, as the magnetic North.

We conclude that the unconscious moral order is the motivational entity of behavior, and hence the process becomes the mental emotional structure for the analysis of behavior as the unit of the exact Moral Science. Science recognizes the homeostatic function of the unconscious as the emotional adjustment of the individual to his/her normative societal environment. By becoming aware of this process we learn how to be deliberate and conscious in managing power and resolving conflicts. Religions evolved as deliberate ways of resolving conflict, but now science reinforces this natural intention with clarity on issues of conflict resolution. Scientifically established principles clarify moral values; these are more refined directives than those of religious mandates.

The clarity of Formal Theory's injunctions stems from the recognition of the natural and moral organization of the unconscious thought process as a holistic entity, a periodic natural science that is both a predictable and quantifiable phenomenon like the pendulum oscillation and the equilibrial trays of the Piagetian-Kleinian scale of four formal operations.

The exhibits of the *Museum of the Creative Process* are clinical case studies of the unconscious mind, which validate the formal theoretical assumptions. They introduce the formal analysis of symbolic languages of the unconscious as a conflict-resolving phenomenon. Indeed, the exhibits attest that this process is manifested in all samples of creativity as a predictable and universal entity. They demonstrate the scientific and moral organization of the unconscious creative process and thus successfully validate the Formal Theoretical assumptions.

We conclude on the structural characteristics of creativity and hence on the unconscious: associations are bound by three formal transformations which complete conflict resolution in six exchanges making the process a natural equilibrial phenomenon, the unit of the social sciences. The research also affirms that we can sample creativity as the object of scientific analysis for the

evaluation of one's personal strategy for resolving conflicts. The creative process reflects the unconscious as the emotional equilibrial process, as the scientific foundation of psychology and morality.

Religions, forerunners of the Moral Science, evolved from concrete to abstract concepts in the realm of norms and gods. Moral order has been defined by religions with norms that determine acceptable behavior and divinities that monitor human conduct. Religions evolved introducing norms increasing fairness in structuring interpersonal relations and increasing abstraction in defining the divine. They evolved from the magical thinking of African and American Shamans worshiping animal-like gods, to the Greeks and Romans worshiping the twelve immortal Olympian Gods, to the Judaic monotheism, eventually to the Messianic religions deifying the prophets and the Oriental religions as philosophies of life. Religions evolved from concrete stories gradually grasping the elusive scientific abstraction of the process.

This evolution is completed by science introducing totally abstract reason as constructs and formulas defining the process of moral order as a natural science phenomenon. We conclude that stories of moral order originate in the normal psyche and manifest as we show in the predictable weave of emotions and thoughts. We have known the process all along as the plot and the moral of stories. Religions and gods are integrated and redefined by the scientific formulas of moral reason; natural law and moral law are shown to coincide.

From religion to science, from faith to reason, religions and gods demystified as solutions of the formulas of the process
In the Metaphoria Murals exhibit we observe the Greek creation stories dramatizing the struggle between generations and genders in the conflicts of the family of Greek gods. Resolution of

conflict followed a progressive rapprochement between gods in conflict and the alienated humans. The conflicts between Gods and Goddesses in Greece were reduced generation after generation in parallel to the distance between Earth and the Sky. Father Sky and Mother Earth were brought closer as conflicted Chronos and Rea. Chronos, a Titan, symbolized as a star, also means time. He and Rea evolved in the next generation to the Olympians, Zeus and Hera, humanizing Mount Olympus. The Olympians in turn were succeeded by the virgin goddess Athena, a noble woman born from Zeus' head; she was associated with the hill of the Athenian Acropolis. Erichthonios, Athena's son, who was fathered by impetuous Hephestus, became the king of Athens. He in turn revered his virgin mother from the polis, the city of Athens. He built Parthenon, the temple of the Virgin, for his mother, Athena on Acropolis, the fortified promontory of the wise city.

The evolution of progressive closeness and conciliation between divinities and humans conveys metaphorically the evolution of increased self-awareness of the powerful unconscious driving mechanism. Science shifts the origin of wisdom from the Polis to the human unconscious. Religions evolved in the quest for peace, rest, resolutions, permanence, immortality all countering the inevitable demise of the person. Stories were invented offering explanations for all phenomena, making life meaningful. Gods evolved from mystifying complexity to the simplicity of providing role models of family relations. The transformational process is the common theme to all generations. Finally we avail explanations identifying the scientific mechanism as the key to the interpretation of all prior stories as metaphors of the underlying emotional dialectic.

The new level of abstraction reconciles morality and psychology with the sciences completing humanity's long-term quest for meaning. The validation of the formal analysis of metaphorical thinking confirms the definition of the human unconscious creative process as a natural science phenomenon. Abstract thinking now accounts for psychology and morality, poetry and religion. Science compels, commands, inspires. It does not cancel God; it simply redefines Him as the abstract order present in the formulas governing the creative process.

Religions progressed as discoveries of conflict resolution within one culture, like in the Greek Cosmogony, but they also evolved from culture to culture. We may consider Judaism as the next level of abstraction of the unconscious process continuing the discoveries achieved by Greece. Below are the set of the central constructs of Judaism, which we interpret as metaphors of conflict resolution, identifying continuity between religion as metaphors and the analytical concepts of the new Moral Science.

By comparing science and religion we recognize parallels or equivalences between Judaism's basic premises: Monotheism, Genesis, the Ten Commandments, a relational typology of personality and the Conflict Resolution Process as the unconscious organization of thought:

• Monotheism corresponds to science's single cause, cause-effect reasoning.

• Genesis' six-day structure leading to the Sabbath, the day of rest, is equivalent to the six-step Conflict Resolution Process, ending with the celebration of the state of resolution. The week is a periodic phenomenon like the CRP, the unit of behavior and the social sciences; hence Genesis is a metaphor of conflict resolution as the structure of symbolic conflict resolving universes.

• The Ten Commandments are the descriptive identification of the three formal conflict resolution principles guiding the moral transformations of the unconscious. We identify these as the universal moral values of moderation, cooperation and mutual respect. The natural science moral directives are like commandments in that they are helpful in averting the generation of conflicts. The scientific moral imperatives of the creative process, the three principles of conflict resolution, the voice of the unconscious, may be equated with the voice of God that guided Moses.

• The four children identified in Passover's Haggadah coincide with the four relational modalities, as the four complementary ways of resolving conflict, Formal Theory's four syndromal personality diagnostic categories.

• Religious catechism, the religious education based on the study of the Bible and holidays that are timed as multiples of seven, remind us that the evolution of spirituality is an ongoing progression of insights into the Harmonic. This education parallels the celebration of discoveries of the secrets of happiness occurring in our emotional education program identified as *Creativity and Power Management*. The study of the Bible on a yearly cycle represents a typical moral and emotional education program that, provided one interprets its metaphors relationally, can be delivered to the general public to provide the needed moral and emotional literacy.

Becoming conscious of the unifying unconscious

The study of the unconscious as a moral order phenomenon allows us to develop clarity in understanding both psychology and religion; we have been able to evolve a new comprehensive science, the Science of Conflict Resolution and undo the damage of the traditional separation of the many disciplines in the study of human behavior. Moral Science yields meaningful insights in the human mind. These are useful for the public to know and of significance to undo the divisiveness incurred by the split between the two realms, psychology and morality and between the many religions and the many social sciences.

The Moral Science is the final phase in the historical evolution of religions as moral paradigms
Science completes the task of religions to achieve meaning, optimal norms, moral role models and by providing an understanding of the nature of the universal unconscious as the moral authority, the calculus of power management. Science gives people insights into the consequences of making choices; the assumption is that the educated person will make the best power or relational choices.

Religions delivered useful explanations, practical philosophies, helpful norms, inspirational role models and great rituals of passage, but by using metaphors, which offer only a very narrow window into the range of possibilities for resolving conflicts. Science conceptualizes the moral organization of emotions as pursued automatically by the human unconscious but now steered deliberately by the educated, self-aware, self-conscious mind. The exhibits attest that the unit process is both a natural science and a moral order phenomenon independent of religions. Religions have guided people's choices but the public can now use moral guidelines inspired by science as well as by the classical spiritualities.

So the conscious mind, by observing one's own creativity, becomes self-aware and can examine how the unconscious is conducting itself. It can understand the unconscious moral response as the adjustive mechanism organizing emotions and associations proceeding automatically, spontaneously to settling intrapsychic and interpersonal transactions. We witness how the innate process, externalized in samples of creativity, is the reliable agency seeking order by organizing emotions, perceptions and transactions, resolving psychic but also interpersonal conflicts, seeking the state of rest; the mind is the compass to moral order as the magnetic north. All the same sampling one's own creativity reflects and reveals the personal pattern of resolving conflicts.

The Moral Science represents the conclusion of religions

Finally science shifts our focus from metaphors, art, to the formal structure of the creative process as the source of moral order and identifies the universal moral values as scientific principles. The process, integrating mankind's stations along a long journey of discoveries, allows us to evolve consensus in understanding the unconscious as an orderly and moral unit process. Science demonstrates that the unconscious seeks goodness and social adjustment following a rational path. This message clarifies motivation and emotions following the path of self-improvement. The unconscious promises rewards for those who embrace the normative concept and multiple punishments for those who defy it.

The Formal Theory's unit process is the final phase in the evolution of abstraction on matters of behavior and morality. It retraces the evolution of thinking from metaphors, approximations on the nature of the Conflict Resolution Process, to the formal understanding of the thought process as a natural science phenomenon. Religions as moral discoveries of particular solutions are reduced to resolutions of the abstract formula of conflict resolution. While religions improved conflict resolution strategies, they never came to understand moral reason as a science. Science comprehends morality and completes religions' quest for meaning. How do we conceptualize this inner mechanism that evolves to religious thinking?

The moral logic of emotions

The conclusion drawn from science contradicts the notion of metaphysical revelation, the delivery of moral order by external moral authorities such as God handing to Moses the Ten Commandments and the prophets recording God's own words in the scriptures. What then, we may wonder, is the relationship of the unconscious to religion? 'How did religions evolve as believable and inspirational stories stemming from the unconscious?' Religious thinking is an integral part of human psychology. The Moral Science explains the sense of revelation as stemming from the structure of the six-step conflict resolution physiological adjustment mechanism. The science of the process elucidates the nature of religions as projections of the individual's alternative types of conflict resolution onto external authorities exacting reciprocal conduct from the individual.

The Conflict Resolution Process as the self-reflexive emotional processing of information determines the way we think about others, gods as rescuers, relations, reality, causality and morality. The gods mirror human conduct and make people accountable. Science clarifies theism and morality/determinism through the reductionist make up of the unconscious as a six-role sequence and makes gods and religions accountable to science and humans.

Religions evolved universally as intuitive, metaphorical discoveries of conflict resolution. The process of stress leads to a response. This role choice is then evolving as anticipations of role reversal, anxiety versus hope identifiable as prophesies. The person defends oneself from the anxieties and goes along with the hopes. Subsequently the person fails or succeeds and attributes one's anticipations as prophecies to external authorities. These authorities become real reinforced by distortions of reality. There is a consequence in having a God or authority holding a person accountable. Accordingly a person moderates one's behavior by wishing the authorities to become kinder and more benevolent. While the individual prays the authority figures are consolidated in his thinking. Divine supreme authorities evolve delivering deserved retributions for the actions of the individual. This is the point of the distinctions of hell and paradise.

The psychological factor, the paranoid response, from anxiety to defense, role reversal and compromise, the intrapsychic mechanism responsible for religious thinking

There are two issues to consider here: first the psychological origin of moral order and second, the sociological factors reinforcing beliefs. We may identify this personal discovery of god and religion following the process of conflict resolution. We then witness the paranoid, moral or religious mental response. This response discovering religion is part of the psychology of the conflict resolving process. It represents the third cycle of the process, the states of role reversal and compromise. The Formal Theory explains religious thinking, a universal psychological phenomenon, as stemming from these two role states.

The emotion of anxiety as anticipated role reversal becomes fear upon the state of reversal. It is experienced in the reversal/compromise or paranoid phase of the unconscious process associated with guilt, and vulnerability, feelings of being observed by a severe external authority. We know this as the Yom Kippur state. Upon the state of role reversal the mental process automatically attributes in a paranoid manner power to an external moral authority. This entity punishes but also rewards. It is a rationalization that eventually becomes shared and reinforced within a community as a factual reality. This process is intensified in the mind of the psychotic individual, who hears voices, god talking to the person, and eventually expanded with delusions that one is god.

The paranoid phase is followed by the compromise role state as surrender accompanied with willingness to negotiate with this overwhelming but eventually merciful and revered authority. The person automatically is willing to repent, to make concessions and offer sacrifices to the imaginary friend or enemy, the supreme moral authority. In the role reversal state the arrogance of the fighter is transformed to respect of the universal external reality associated with the compromise of the spiritual individual. Religiosity becomes then philosophical spirituality and eventually respect and trust of predictable and manageable science.

The unconscious process is a morality and religion generating mental mechanism. The personal discovery of resolution becomes a religion as the person seeks validation, public acceptance for one's compromise response. Religions are a quest for meaning but also of shared validation of a belief. The process is the underlying mechanism. It is the universal physiological moral response. The individual mind under stress discovers God on its own.

This internal emotional need to resolve conflicts has evolved in the maturing individual and cultures from a cruel God, unpredictable and threatening, evoking mistrust and fear, commanding total surrender as we have witnessed in early religious thought, to a benevolent, trustworthy loving self sacrificial god, a loving and caring parental authority comforting the compliant supplicant as a well-behaved child. The paranoid response evolved from the cruel goddess of matriarchy in Mexico to the friendly protective One God of the Jews. The Mexican version of the cruel mother Earth evolved subsequently to the caring and forgiving Virgin of Guadalupe. Psychoanalysis identified the change from the punitive to the friendly super ego. Religions evolved as humans learned to converse and negotiate with their inner self, the paranoia generated creatures.

Religions are organized societal responses originating in the need of the individual to compromise and adjust socially to a normative society. The law of beliefs is that emotions evolve from the original sense of pain/stress to the proportionate willingness to sacrifice, believe and trust the divine.

The Conflict Resolution Process organizes emotions and ideas in every symbolic universe by completing compromises as the acceptance of an external authority overruling the individual dealing with his stressors, pain, loss, and survival. This entity as a natural scientific phenomenon abiding by the laws of science is the building block of emotional and social reality as the entity organizing relations and meaning. The process is the origin of religious systems and of the redefinitions of God. Hence it is this orderly psyche that has been programmed into religions that can be reprogrammed with freedom from external constraints into responsible behaviors knowing the consequences of power choices.

The sociological factor as the search for consensus and consonance

Conflict resolution is the human faculty dealing with loss and pain by advancing personal transformation and emotional growth enabling the person to adapt to social changes in a collaborative manner. Sacrifices as tokens of compromise represent the path of emotional concessions furthering one's societal adjustment. The unconscious moral mechanism consolidates the personal path to addressing the societal paranoia and the needs for expiation as the conventions of compliance to the agreed upon belief system.

Conformity as moral self-sacrificial conduct reduces anxiety. Religions require consensus on most positions; they reinforce distortions as the normative system of beliefs that shape the orderly moral reality. The personal paranoid subjective emotion conforms to the powerful institutionalized bureaucratic convictions spelled out in the respective faiths. Thus religions become the powerful political institutions that inspire conformity, command control of the public opinion, and compel to self-sacrifice in cultural matters.

Religions depart from individual exemplary conduct to become tribal rituals of resolving conflicts expanded to institutions of organized worship with temples and yearly routines of festivities, concessions, offering sacrifices in exchange for emotional relief. Thus religions evolved as stories of conflict resolution responding to existential questions healing personal and societal conflicts. Religions evolved as conflict resolutions offering explanations about the mysteries of life, generating solace to the suffering individual and sanctification to the critical passages of life.

The art exhibits provide us with pertinent information about the genesis of religions. Religions evolved as alternative ways of resolving conflict. We have seen how Greece resolved conflicts with mastery, India with cooperation and Israel with focus on mutual respect. Resolutions having particular dimensions generated alternative divinities. Religions evolved alternative value systems reflecting the personalities of their storytellers but also cultural mentalities. Religions like personality types represent rigorous science moral order phenomena that have particular dimensions; they represent alternative ways of resolving conflict and applying these modes to diversity of symbolic choices.

Moral order is the *deus ex machina* present in every sample of creativity as the inherent dramatic resolution. This is amply demonstrated throughout the five exhibits. Religion, and moral order without religious references, is an extension of physiology and psychology. The formation of moral solutions as religion is an integral part of the human thought process. The exhibits demonstrate not only the existence of moral order but also the propensity of the unconscious mind to generate stories leading to the development of religion and spirituality.

The inner reality projected outwardly seeks to validate itself transforming outer reality into a particular moral philosophy with consonant patterns. Moral orders as we see them in all samples of creativity simply reflect the unconscious quest for meaning. All religions begin as personal emotional discoveries; these evolve into sociological substantiations. We see evidence of the birth of religion as a universal phenomenon intimately connected to the creative process.

Through the dialectic of this process the individual adjusts to and changes or conforms to his environment. Personality types vary in the power play between the individual and the system. The personal and cultural adjustments are determined by relational modalities. The same variables characterize the personal and the cultural relational models. Religions reflect a leader's personal relational preferences expand his values into moral philosophies defining the norms of the society. The divinity's relational modality determines the cultural order as the normative behavior of the religion.

The art exhibits explain morality in the universality of the structure of stories as the six-role state Conflict Resolution Process. They validate the process as a natural science phenomenon, which integrates disparate components into a predictable entity that is measurable, qualifiable, quantifiable, graphically portrayable, socially relevant and personally compelling and meaningful.

Science clarifies the nature of moral order as mathematical and physical abstractions, formulas of the rigorous sciences, constituting the calculus of power management. The process is software organizing associations, emotions and behaviors into the equilibrial or adjustive mechanism. The process is predictable transformations of emotions and interactions seeking to restore a disturbed equilibrial state with fairness to both parties involved in a conflict. The conflict resolution mechanism is an emotional roller coaster experienced as relief, justice and meaning.

In their respective norms religions have evolved partial but complementary discoveries on how to resolve conflicts. The world has adopted stories and has grown to believe them as the total truths about moral order. Science now understanding psychology also understands the origin and the development of religions. Religions have evolved as the sociological component of the psychology of conflict resolution. Morality is implicit in psychology as normative adjustments, the unconscious response to stress as deviation from the norm.

Concluding we postulate that religions stem from the personal conflict resolution disposition grounded in the unconscious need to feel safe in one's societal adjustment. They represent personal relational moral choices redefining societal norms. The new universal God is the formulas of conflict resolution providing alternative solutions symbolically represented by suitable relational characteristics. Moral Science identifies these figures as solutions of the formulas underlying all symbolic universes. Religions are the range of solutions of the formulas of moral order for different values of the key variables.

The benefit of this study is that psychology and religion are integrated into a cohesive single scientific domain and hence that we can study psychological and religious issues as natural science phenomena. Accordingly we can diagnose, analyze and consider changes as needed. Behavior being adjustment responses to stress it is of interest for both the individual and society to understand the nature of their respective perspectives in order to interface and reconcile differences. Resolution at the individual level is sanity and at the societal level is peace in the world.

RESOLVING CONFLICTS FAIRLY IN DOMESTIC RELATIONS: EPIMETHEUS, PROMETHEUS AND ATLAS DEALING WITH ZEUS' GIFT PANDORA, RELIGIONS VERSUS SCIENCE

Religions testing science and science responding exploring self-discovery
Zeus giving Pandora to Epimetheus may be viewed as religion challenging human wisdom in dealing with women. Pandora is the experiential version of the riddle of the Sphinx. The issue is freeing oneself from possessive mothers and managing power in the new relation with women as equal partners. Relating to women has been the core task of religions.

Our hero, Prometheus stole the fire and was bound on a rock. Science or forethought was useful to Prometheus, an alternative Joseph; he counseled Zeus about his predicament, his relationship with a woman. He foretold Zeus that he was going to be killed by her son. Zeus chose another partner and out of gratitude released Prometheus from the rock.

Prometheus' name forethought represents the capacity to predict, to anticipate the future; in this case he predicted the evolution of a relationship. Prometheus, Mr. Forethought was not a wizard; he was the scientist of relations, he knew about patterns that repeat. Zeus's, religion's response to science, was testing Prometheus's wisdom, his expertise in relations with women in general. So it is not surprising that Zeus chose to gift a woman to Prometheus' s brother, Epimetheus, Mr. Afterthought; Epimetheus may be conceived as Prometheus' double; and his name Afterthought implies wisdom after the completion of a transaction, the gift of Pandora as the challenge of solving domestic conflicts.

"Beware of Greeks bringing gifts" is a relevant adage. Zeus's gift was a wife named Pandora, her name meaning 'all gifts.' She symbolizes the challenges of conjugal partnerships combining pleasures with relational problems. Her box contained hope and despair. Pandora is the box of many gifts. The box is a metaphor for the many qualities one finds in (Greek) women.

Most Greek dramas bear the names of complex women or are about them: Helen of Troy, Klitemnestra, Electra, Iphigenia, Phaedra, Medea, Bachae, the Trojan Women, etc. Pandora, all gifts, the gift to 'Brothers Wisdom' represents Zeus's revenge. It is religion's challenge of science's wisdom in properly dealing with women.

The best test for a wizard is giving him a woman as a present and checking what religion he is going to invent to justify his marital strategy. If Prometheus and company symbolize 'science' then the Pandora project is the test of science by Zeus and religions' prescriptive way of managing women. How can science determine the optimal mode of relating to find happiness?

Here emerges the significance of the third brother, Atlas. He is the one who carries the whole world on his shoulders. I interpret the world as the metaphor of the 'perfect universe' of a story or a drama as identified by Aristotle, highlighting the importance of a key behavior in all dramas, and the continuity of actions. According to Aristotle the key action or role became the self-reflexive choice coming back to the initiator of the action as his role reversal, the reversal of fortune past the phase of recognition. Atlas then represents the formal integration of Prometheus, and Epimetheus as the totality of the myth, the story.

Atlas's burden, portrayed as the globe, is the entirety of all stories as choices and dramatic consequences; it is the stories' plot as the necessity for order and justice. The completion entails the axiom of making optimal choices in dealing with women. It is the Universal Harmonic uniting the fragments or episodes into meaningful totalities; in Atlas's virtual monitor we can see the depictions of the varieties of conflict resolutions, all the scenarios. The globe then that Atlas proudly holds on his shoulders is the mythos, the entire story, the dramatic reality of the human journey, a reminder of the unforgiving syndromal nature of power choices. Atlas's role is that of a scientist of mythology, he who observes and connects the before with the after into the wisdom of patterns. With his Globe/monitor he reminds us of the mythos, the reality of the total story, of the process with a beginning, middle and the moral or deserved end.

Atlas unites Prometheus' forethought and Epimetheus' afterthought as the divine justice inherent in the world as a harmonious elegant predictable spiritual totality that unfolds along the alternative pathways of power management. Prometheus introduced science as wisdom; wisdom is tested with Epimetheus, living with the god-sent Pandora, the complexity of domestic conflicts, anticipating peace and harmony in the love relationship, but knowing too well the curses, the unending strife of the many pitfalls of relations.

Pandora's box contains the range of relational alternative as ways of dealing with women and temptation. Humankind has been contending with Pandoras, family relations conflicts, since the inception of civilization. In Mural 6 of the Sanctuary, we reviewed the range of relations as cultural resolutions of power management in dealing with temptation. The range is illustrated in the solutions of the moral dilemma of the apple metaphor. We saw four alternative societal/cultural responses to the issue of dealing with temptation and power.

Atlas's globe flickers and tells us what scenarios are in the box as alternative resolutions:
• The submissive antagonistic response is illustrated in the Mexican animal metaphor of the Eagle devouring the snake. Humans are sacrificed and their bleeding hearts are the apples that belong to the gods. This conflict between the powerful eagle and the snake was resolved in this culture by the eagle merging with the snake into a new creature, the Quetzalcoatl, the feathered serpent.

• The submissive cooperative response is illustrated by the Indian culture's powerful Kali, the apple as the sacred cow. It was dealt by the culture as the philosophy of enduring pain and consistently suppressing desire, illustrated by Siva dancing on his inner child, the homunculus under his foot. Accepting one's predicament has sustained in India

the parallel coexistence of four casts.
• The dominant antagonistic response was Greece's apple inscribed 'to the fairest' culminating in the Trojan War. Helen wanted unlimited power and so did the women pursuing the golden apple. Helen was punished. The outcome of greed and arrogance was the tragic hero's punishment, i.e. Oedipus is a typical hero, whose punishment was very cruel.

• The dominant cooperative response was illustrated by the Judaic choice of Eve as a temptress and learning to abstain from the forbidden fruit averting the fate of Adam, since surrendering to temptation entailed suffering the consequence of the exile from Paradise. On the contrary behaving respectfully entailed being the Chosen People, and being given the Promised Land.

Atlas, suspending high the wisdom of afterthought complementing forethought, confirms the need for wisdom as the psychology of proper power management. The key word in the three brothers' identities is 'mythos' like in mythology referring to stories that explain. So what the world needs to cope with Pandoras, women as the opportunities of dealing with power or managing temptation, is mythology, or its contemporary alternative, the science of psychology, the Moral Science, and the related emotional education that prepares a person for life.

Moral Science challenging religion by addressing normative choices as the calculus of power management

The four categories identified above pertain to both cultural and personal ways of managing power. We have recognized these as personality types in the four heroes of the Wizard of Oz story. We have also identified them as the four canvases on the jacket of the Formal Analysis textbook. Our world is confused with these cultural alternative competing unintegrated model stories or myths of power management. Now these icons may stand to represent lessons in the program of a new emotional and moral education we identify as Power Management. The icons represent personality determined relational modalities. The education examines the alternatives and recommends the optimal choice.

Which paradigm should the naïve humans listen to for guidance? The mortals espouse the values of their cultures as the only normative system that is acceptable. Science on the contrary is about the science of patterns. The Universal Harmonic unifies the stories by studying the plot of stories explaining moral issues as alternative solutions of a set of formulas. The exhibits demonstrate and confirm the scientific nature of the Conflict Resolution Process as the unit of psychology and moral order.

Observing creativity as the structure of the thought process we note its stability but also its attitude-changing function leading to spiritual and religious reasoning. We conclude that the unconscious dialectic process is a spontaneous healing moral process that is reflecting cultural and personal relational preferences but which also may flow to the optimal and most fulfilling of choices. The insight is that we need to make good choices. We need to evolve an ethical code of conduct that surpasses in wisdom the diverse traditional moral paradigms and that becomes the universal safe paradigm.

Paradigms evolve. We detect this trend for ethical and conceptual evolution at the personal and the cultural levels. At the personal level we detect evolution to spirituality beyond religion in the Gorski Retrospective and the Kazantzakis case study. At the cultural levels we detect it at the many stations of the Sculptural Trail and the Metaphoria Murals. All exhibits demonstrate ongoing transformation, new insights and related increased level of abstraction. Hence we may conclude that the exhibits confirm the unconscious process as a natural science adaptive or healing transformational phenomenon with a moral end

satisfying humanity's quest for meaning but also its needs for adjustment.

Religions are philosophies of power management, which anchor their thinking to particular ways of resolving conflict. Psychology as science identifies these through the analysis of stories, and is able to quantify and qualify with a set of formulas the optimal direction in resolving conflicts, following the principles of conflict resolution: mastery, cooperation and mutual respect. The public needs to be educated on the scientific nature of the conflict resolution process and the range of normative alternatives. Science cuts the strings manipulating the public like brainless puppets by interpreting metaphors and freeing people from traditional sacrosanct cultural relational choices.

THREE CASE STUDIES OF DEALING WITH POWER/TEMPTATION LEADING TO RELIGIOUS RESOLUTIONS: GORSKI, KAZANTZAKIS AND BACON

Temptation and limits, forethoughts and afterthoughts evolved into epics, dramas, and religions. Religions represent the range of moral resolutions. Religions are the unconscious response to stressors and how to handle women has been the big stressor of all cultures. The answers have been the many religions. We will see some cases of how the mind handles temptation generating a religion as response to an intense stressor. Odysseus fought hard to not yield to women's power. Greek drama continued the struggle of individuals with women in the multiple tragedies named after key women of their mythology. Judaism dealt with women in the Abrahamic story and found a solution in controlling the power of women through the father son alliance.

In the following segment we will review the moral responses of Henry Gorski a visual graphic artist, and for Nickolas Kazantzakis, a prolific writer in dealing with this core theme of all religions.

A. HENRY GORSKI, THE MORAL DEVELOPMENT OF A NORM-RESPECTING ARTIST

The Gorski Retrospective presents the search for meaning identifying the divine and then aspiring for science and spirituality. Several of the exhibits illustrate and confirm the religious or paranoid response. The unconscious adjustment process in the phases of reversal portrays self-consciousness and in the next phase of compromise the images of the divine.

Paranoia as self-consciousness is presented as self-portraits. Compromise as images of the divine, the theistic phase, illustrates the projective attribution of moral authority to God figures. The Gorski exhibit's self portraits demonstrate the paranoia, as *Nowhere to Hide* and then the compromise a series of self portraits coinciding with the cross or the crucifix, eventually evolving to the sequence of the sports paintings symbolically presenting crucifixions. All five of his conflict resolution sequences lead to religious paintings. (see the *Eye-dentity* canvas as well as the final self portrait, presenting his conflict resolution as a cross/pain made of kisses/ pleasure, religion turned to spirituality, on which he designed his last self portrait, his last quest for resolution and personal identity.)

The combination of *Nowhere to Hide* as the role reversal and of *Eye-dentity* as the compromise role state constitute the third cycle of the three cycle six role state sequence. This cycle represents the paranoid, moral or religious response to stress as the discovery of comfort in the reconciliation of the individual with society's norms. Religion has been rediscovered here as the healing or adjustive phases of the six role state process. To understand the generation of religion we may continue observing Gorski's moral discoveries manifested in his artwork.

The personal religious experience is generalized by being inclusive of the heroes of the era. In *Crucifixion*, his most magnificent and complex canvases, Gorski presented the crucifix with allusions to contemporary heroes. In *Crucifixion* he introduces dramatic contemporary conflicts: it includes the road sign of Martin Luther King's march to Alabama, faces of Robert Kennedy, John Lennon and of astronauts gathered below the cross. On the other side of the cross are famous contemporary women: we recognize Elizabeth Taylor and Jackie Onassis lamenting the death of the cultural heroes merged into the Christ concept. Women are also portrayed as fleeting airborne temptations, seductive, playful Lucky Strike ladies compassionate and coquettish seekers of Jesus' drops of blood on their wafers.

This canvas, full of irony and symbolism, presents personal eroticism in conflict with Jesus' and Gorski's asceticism. In these canvases the personal religious solution embraces the societal and political reality of the times. The personal choice of Christian values is promoting awareness of them as the values of the national culture. Personal conformity is expanded to exalt the icon of sacrifice as the universal value.

The theme of religion as social justice inspires Gorski to ground moral order onto a more solid foundation than religious and political themes and dramatic sensuous kiss symbolism. In search of universal laws to justify what he senses as universal truths on harmonious relations, to capture the notion associated with the divine, Gorski turns to science as the purest language, the most reliable symbolism to explain the perceived order. Then he paints this order with symbolism combining kisses and mathematics as portrayed in his sculptural canvas of God kissing Adam solidified with simple harmonics and graphic elements intensifying the father son covenant with references to laws of physics and math; we see concentric circles, pi symbols, numbers, and multiple harmonics accounting for the title of the painting, *The Mathematical Proof of the Metaphysical Existence of God.*

B. FRANCIS BACON, THE AESTHETIC DEVELOPMENT OF A NORM-CHALLENGING ARTIST
Another affirmation of the normalcy of the religious response
Francis Bacon's canvases are relationally the counterpart conflict resolution approach compared to Gorski's. But the canvases of both artists may be viewed as dramatic three act totalities: The first act presents the heroes and the conflicts; the second, the drama at its peak as the challenge of the norm, as the erotic adventure; the third act presents the spiritual resolution. Though Gorski's and Bacon's relational choices are diametrically opposite, we see their stories unfold in a parallel way to their resolutions. Gorski seeks normative compliance identifying with the cross. Bacon seeks normative change denouncing the Pope and defiling the crucifixion highlighting his sexual preference as his personal favorite choice. Bacon too presents self portraits but they celebrate his emotional turmoil features rather than Gorski's spirituality of inner peace.
SEE THE COMPARATIVE TABLE OF GORSKI AND BACON CANVASES

C. NIKOS KAZANTZAKIS, THE RELIGIOUS AND MORAL DEVELOPMENT OF A NOVELIST
Kazantzakis' religious response
To explore moral dilemmas in the generation of the religious response, and to expand on our observations of the spiritual experience portrayed in Henry Gorski's canvases of crucifixions, I am introducing here for analysis Nikos Kazantzakis' moral dilemma. His case study parallels Gorski's leading to his discovery of religion. They both dealt with the theme of the Last Temptation of Christ. The canvases of the Greek author articulate Gorski's sentiments, those of the inner voice guiding the person to the relief of conflict.

Here we have the opportunity to observe a famous author/artist as a case study. He presents his conflicts and their resolutions for us to experience the trials and tribulations of a human developing spirituality and religion as the means to cope with his intense moral conflicts. The limited analysis of his case study suffices to shed light on the religion making process manifested here in the literary retrospective, identifying the conflicts that the conflict resolution pattern organizing the collected works of a celebrated contemporary author.

The case study is illustrating the relation between psychology and religion in a parallel manner to the study of the Gorski exhibit. Kazantzakis was so conflicted that his inner struggle gave birth to both a religious manifesto and a series of novels dramatizing his moral dilemmas pursuing the inner healing of his intense personal conflicts. Here we have a picture of the creative process evolving in a parallel manner along two directions. The first was his religious response as a manifesto of abstract principles or basic assumptions; the second was his creative response, spontaneous creativity for self-discovery and emotional growth or healing. The two choices shed light on the Conflict Resolution Process as a mental faculty, which processes personal conflicts to evoke either religiosity or art and scientific insights.

In the presentation of the evolution of religions we discussed the man-woman relationship as conflictual and leading to the generation of new norms regulating sexuality and family role relations. Kazantzakis discovers god upon struggling with an erotic conflict and choosing asceticism as his coping mechanism. At an early point in his life he composed a book on asceticism, which he entitled *The Saviors of God*. In it we see the fight for a life dedicated to God as opposed to his surrendering to temptation.

The Saviors of God includes the following declaration of faith:

1. I believe in one God, defender of the borders, of double descent, militant, suffering, of mighty but not omnipotent powers, a warrior at the farthest frontiers, commander in chief of all the luminous powers, the visible and the invisible.

2. I believe in the innumerable, the ephemeral masks which God has assumed throughout the centuries, and behind his ceaseless flux I discern an indestructible unity.

3. I believe in his sleepless and violent struggle which tames and fructifies the earth as the life-giving fountain of plants, animals and men.
4. I believe in man's heart, that earthen thrashing floor where night and day the defender of the borders fights with death.

5. O Lord, you shout: Help me! Help me. You shout, o Lord and I hear.

6. Within me all forefathers and all descendants, all races and all Earth hear your cry with joy and terror.

Blessed be all those who hear and rush to free you, Lord, and who say: Only you and I exist. Blessed be all those who free you and become united with you, Lord, and who say: You and I are one And thrice blessed be those who bear on their shoulders and do not buckle under this great, sublime, and terrifying secret: THAT EVEN THIS ONE DOES NOT EXIST!

The biographical information clarifies what the author experienced prior to his religious declaration. Kazantzakis was writing a book on Buddhist values of containment of desire when he was personally tested by his attraction to a charming Viennese woman. He had set up a date with her, which precipitated a bout of disfiguring eczema. Handicapped by the eczema he kept postponing the encounter but the eczema nonetheless worsened until he removed himself from Vienna and the temptation. Moving to Berlin made his illness disappear. Instead of completing the book on Buddhism he started the book on asceticism as the resolution of his conflicts. He wrote The Saviors of God in 1922; he was in his thirties. He

completed it as a resident of a Greek monastery.

His conflict with women is exemplified in another anecdotal story related by his translator. Accordingly Kazantzakis experienced erotic yearnings for a French elderly innkeeper courtesan. He enjoyed a platonic relationship and proved the endurance of his asexual love of this woman by fulfilling a pledge of perseverance to meet her 8 years later. He managed to keep this date with her just before she passed away.

The two stories affirm the intensity of Kazantzakis' conflicts in dealing with temptation. He sought religion to free himself from unacceptable desires. His primitive earthly self, the Greek animal of lust in him collided with his Christian, Buddhist and communist idealisms. The mature Kazantzakis was consistent in demonstrating the position of love as a spiritual commitment rather than as a sexual entanglement. He demonstrated his values with the choices of his heroes holding dear the uncompromised sense of Christian agape fighting lust or alternatively surrendering to lust for life.

To restrain desire and passion as the devil's calling he needed God in 1922 as his helper and healer. But in 1922 nobody believed in god; those were the atheist times when the world was inebriated with rational humanism. God was weakened for lack of believers. God and religion were being attacked by communism on the left, psychoanalysis on the right, and by philosophers and scientists in the middle; he had translated Nietzsche in Greek, and knew about the death of God. Also he was a student of Bergson, who substituted God with the vital force, élan vital. In spite of this atheistic philosophical moral perspective he proclaimed faith in God. This was prompted by his ascetic choice.

The book's title, The Saviors of God, was qualified by the translator with the subtitle Spiritual Exercises. This translation reduced the author's

emphasis in the Greek subtitle, Asketiki, which I translate as The Manual to Asceticism. This distinction is significant because it conveys the author's focus on one particular spiritual choice, the pursuit of asceticism as the denouncement of sexual urges, indiscriminate eroticism as promiscuity, the forbidden self-indulgence.

Kazantzakis' creative response as the healing process The Saviors of God defined Kazantzakis' normative distinctions, his views on sexual role relations. It introduced the conflicts that evolved his literary universe, which consisted of classic heroes Jesus and Odysseus, personifying his unresolved issues through alternative identities. His conflict resolution philosophy dictated the characters' identities reflecting the author's opposite set of fantasies, the strength to resist temptation and the intense passion of surrendering to it. His characters dramatized the alternatives of asceticism versus the scruple-free Grecian lust for life. Abstinence was attributed to Jesus, sexuality to his Greek heroes Odysseus and Zorba.

I wish to explore here Kazantzakis' distinctions on sexuality and why he experienced such a tragic conflict between alternatives, asceticism versus lust. His definition of sexuality is portrayed in the film The Last Temptation of Christ as Jesus witnessing the abhorrent promiscuity of a whore. He adores Magdalena yet keeps his distance from her. This is his choice of a woman that the devil will tempt him to pursue as the alternative to his suffering for the world on the cross.

In the fantasy of indulgence that unfolds quasi realistically he is guided down from the cross to marry her. Mysteriously she vanishes and then other serial relationships with women ensue. Scruples occur at that point as Judas reminds him of his moral mission. At the dramatic closure of the story Jesus distances himself from lust to return to the ascetic cross representing Kazantzakis' optimal mode of conflict resolution.

So asceticism is the reciprocal of lust. These distinctions are based on his personality of a shy person who is deathly afraid of the normal expression of feelings. From this perspective of repressed emotions he judges the intensity of his passion as unacceptable dangerous lust. He projects his own urges upon women whom he perceives as reprehensible whores victims to lust.

We witness these extremes manifested in the attributes of his heroes as alternately resisting and yielding to temptation, as spirituality versus embracing women in an existential thrill, free of inhibitions. We witness the binge-purge dilemma of anorexia bulimia, manifested in the realm of sexual relations. There is proportionality between the intensity of his preoccupation with religion and with its counterpart, his forbidden sexually abhorrent fantasies. Both are attributed and acted out by the opposite characters of his novels.

The heroes' conflicts reflect and heal his own dramatic choices that troubled him in the Vienna of his 30s; he was torn like Jesus on the cross of his novel between the pleasures of lust and his heroic commitment to self-sacrifice. Alternatively Odysseus, Jesus' counterpart in his novel on the Odyssey, departs from Ithaca to confront the gods rather than obey them; he loosens himself from the mast of self-restraints to party with the sirens. At the end of this journey the wise hero finds salvation in asceticism again.

Zorba the Greek represents the healing phase in his handling temptation (Kazantzakis, 1953). Here we see compassion mixed with intolerance. Zorba, representing a diluted version of Odysseus, is teaching his young inhibited companion, a daring Jesus figure, the power of dance, and the joy and exuberance of life free of sexuality yet full of existential intensity. The dance is the purity of a spiritual, non- conflictual élan vital. In this compromise Zorba is a character, who weaves a love story for the decadent, elderly courtesan Bubulina, now a sick woman who simply needed to feel loved. Zorba offers her the illusion of love, just as Kazantzakis had accomplished with the old innkeeper courtesan.

In this novel Zorba is gracious and loving in spite of the reputation of the woman, however he cannot conceal his doubts about her trustworthiness. Her unaccountability in the moralist Greek society is reflected in the cruel end of her life; we see the unforgiving moral rigidity of the island's women who invade her apartment to plunder her belongings while she agonizes helplessly in her deathbed. Men's intolerance is reflected in the condemnation and stoning of her youthful counterpart, a young and promiscuous widow.

Kazantzakis' idealist socialist, self-sacrificial Christian identity collided with his Oedipal, selfish, Greek ecstatic non-conformism. He was afraid of this Grecian inclination for limitless individual power, the pursuit of immortality, this Dionysian lust for life, the heroic celebration of the moment as a dance sweeping one's awareness into ecstasy at the expense of responsibility and accountability to the past and the future and he dramatized these values in the eyes of his scared self and the modern viewer of alternatives.

These extreme alternative colliding choices appeal to the public inhibited but seeking freedom from inhibitions, through mundane compromises, human limitations and societal controls. This blend of pure asceticism and unmitigated pleasure for life, his élan vital represents the unresolved qualities of his emotional reality projected to his literary heroes, constituting a symbolic universe appreciated by the public who too suffer of ambivalence on values. The state of ecstasy as oneness is experienced by both his ascetic religious and his sensuous pleasure loving characters. His drama is resolved as he seeks to merge, to become one with God and end his erotic, ecstatic abandon with women as Jesus or Odysseus.

Neuroticism versus wellness

The tone of *The Saviors of God* is declarative, like Marx's political manifesto, another sample of moral imperatives in this case influenced by a Judaic value system, advancing a doctrine to reinforce the author's determination to resist temptation while defending his passion for life. The book reinforces asceticism, his Christian- Buddhist cultural identity over his pagan Greek- Oedipal, Dionysian, uninhibited self. But are these distinctions to be entertained by the public as religion? Certainly this religion is propagating conflicts rather than resolving them. The benefit of drama is catharsis as sympathy, identifying with the hero's transgression, but also relief from not suffering, being punished like him.

Kazantzakis' perceptions of women are either pure idealism or alternatively demonic/erotic. These are cultural and personal distinctions, but they are incorrect distinctions for the optimal structuring of gender relations. Should we follow his neurotic reasoning or seek to change the religious response to a different resolution? We can, and society has, redefined gender relations and the free expression of feelings.

Kazantzakis' books do not resolve the world's problems of fairness in the troubled man-woman relationship. They simply reflect the author's problematic disposition toward women compatible with the set of dated norms punishing women for freedom in their sexuality. Kazantzakis was an extremist, promoting virtue as restraint of desire, a warrior fighting his strong urges to yield to temptation by espousing Buddhist and Christian asceticism. We may wonder if Kazantzakis suffered like our culture from the polarization in matters of sexuality inducing the extreme responses of sinner versus saint, the binge versus purge uncontrollable behaviors. Are our heroes helpful in comprehending our contemporary adversaries, the very inspired Talibans, as the contemporary saviors of God? Their struggle for identity started with the war of liberation from the godless communists.

Religion and the Moral Science

Kazantzakis' choice of asceticism is an example of how religion originates as a response in dealing with personal conflicts by looking outward for self-regulation. Kazantzakis wished to strengthen his will by seeking God to define moral order as a motivating factor to deal with his obsession with forbidden desires. Reaching for god was a desperate plea for help. It was especially difficult as it occurred during the turmoil of the beginning of the 20th century. He was caught in a time of cultural transition.

On the one side there was the perseverance of the Victorian era, and on the other side there were moral revolutions in progress. We may sum up the conflicts of these days as ideologies of theism versus atheism. Kazantzakis chose a path, which reconciled secular philosophies like communism, psychoanalysis and evolution with religion and tradition. His inclination was with theism, but at the same time he recognized that religion was an emotional reality bordering an illusion. Following a century of wanton atheism our world is returning to the illusion of desperate theism. We are witnesses of humanity's struggle between reality and illusions. The Moral Science comes strategically to shift the world from the sexual conflicts and clarify the alternatives of power choices.

It is relevant to experience how quickly and effectively our insights allow us to reach an accurate understanding of the complex symbolic universe of a prolific author. The exercise increases our appreciation of art and its creator, but also clarifies the generation of religious and spiritual thought and its limitations and pathology.

The effectiveness of understanding art, psychology and religion can expand from the individual case to entire cultural systems. The analysis of individual moral dilemmas does not differ from the analysis of the contemporary world suffering from unresolved moral conflicts. We need the analytical insights as the means to resolve cultural conflicts affecting us today and to understand the behavior of very religious people, who in the name of god generate the real conflicts of our times instead of finding new effective resolutions for their emotional quandaries.

We can understand religions' conflict resolutions gone awry as doctrines, e.g. Holy War/Jihad, the Crusades, etc. seeking institutional survival but not affording introspection. The Muslim concept of Jihad literally means 'struggle' and has a moral mission in its combative aspirations. It is founded on the paranoid religious response, the unconscious compelling a person to social activism in the defense of a set of moral values. Saint Augustine is credited as being the first to promote a "Just War" theory within Christianity in the 7th Century, whereby war is justifiable on religious grounds. Saint Thomas Aquinas elaborated on these criteria and his writings were used by the Roman Catholic Church to regulate the actions of European countries and to justify the cruelties of the Crusades.

Exploring Kazantzakis' world gives us an opportunity to question religion and to feel reinforced to steal its fire as responsible for eliciting neurotic and inefficient responses that have outlived their usefulness and that endanger the true believers. The analysis of this case connects us to people who have difficulty distancing themselves intellectually or emotionally from faith.

Kazantzakis' ordeal is reexperienced by the catholic clergy, victims of their own asceticism and uncontrollable lust that has manifested with the scandalous behavior of respectable individuals. More a natural behavior is artificially repressed more that behavior comes to haunt the mind and evoke behavioral imbalance. This behavior is no longer an individual's prerogative, or the church's choice in moral values; it represents pathology that is dangerous and massive and a societal violation of civil rights that is incompatible with moral principles and international law.

Religions as social educational institutions affect the public health generating intense conflicts with their powerful distinctions. Ultimately they are accountable for these messages distributed in the name of god to the naïve public. They should be held accountable when epidemics of misconduct occur in their ranks. Using their monopolistic power they have abused the public trust. They have inflicted pathology to the individual wellness and the general public health by determining norms that are unfair and unhealthy.

Catholic clergy have suffered of the demonization and oppression of sexuality. Islamic clerics have inspired suicidal behaviors and massive protests to suppress public and private criticism and opinion. These antisocial behaviors, of sexual aggression and of outward uninhibited militancy violate the believers and the infidels. They necessitate a deliberate public organized response to restrain religions' immunity to criticism as a powerful secular institution.

Religions are institutions that suffer pathology and must be made accountable to science and the public for their normative choices. Their policies and conducts must be considered as subject to analysis and correction. The world must terminate their outrageous breaches of societal ethics. Religions must be managed to respect psychology as well as international law and jurisdiction.

This series of case studies reminds us of the necessity to recognize that our world needs to be enlightened on the nature of religion and to become critical of institutional value systems. Religions should not be immune to criticism or unaccountable to worldly authorities and reason. The Formal Theory offers clear concepts on the nature of morality that cannot be manipulated by any artist or dogma. Science can remind the modern martyrs of the latitude/longitude of their position in the universe and offer them relief from their inspired missions.

MORAL SCIENCE CONCLUDES THE ERA OF RELIGION AND PROMOTES A NEW MORAL PARADIGM AS A CIVIL RIGHT

The path from art and religion to science, from conflict to resolution, has been established. The mind follows a predictable and universal path to moral order. The initial emotional expression is conveyed utilizing a symbolic language; this is followed by the scientific deciphering of symbolism; insights emerge confirming the predictability of the emotional dialectic. The shift of paradigms rediscovers piety as respect of the scientifically defined moral order. We depart from art/ metaphors to encounter the plot as the abstraction, the science of spirituality whose sacred symbol is the Universal Harmonic.

Art as creativity reflects the feelings, the state of mind; science maps the feelings. Art grounds us dramatically into the reality of sensations, childhood memories, existential terror, hope for salvation. Science generates respect for the interrelation of experiences into a perfect universe, as the bigger reality, the abstraction of the formal order. The student of this order experiences spirituality as a profound sense of reverence.

Science defines wisdom as the study and practice of the universal process. The unit process is the measuring rod of stories. Interpretation makes stories more meaningful so they appeal both to the heart and to the mind. Science explains diversity but identifies the optimal way of resolving conflict. It can borrow the wisdom of religions to inspire piety, but pious people are encouraged to be inspired by science more than by religion. They should be cognizant of the Greek tragedies to remind the public of the punishment of arrogance; they should use Judaic moderation and oriental detachment. They can rediscover piety as respect of the unit process, as the optimal conflict resolution leading predictably to a kinder attitude, mindfulness, the ultimate spirituality.

Science generates respect for moral order as unconditional trust in universal laws. We may pray with the same reverence to the scientific unit of moral order, the universal peace monitoring harmonic, as to the many gods we are familiar with. Science is redefining God as the unit. But this is what monotheism means. Monotheism may be interpreted as Greek for the worship of the one God or the worship of the unit, monas.

The unit concept provides the clear language validating spirituality as quantification and predictability. This integrative paradigm is the object of study equally meaningful to all perplexed humans. It embraces all stories and all social sciences. It reduces all stories to the abstraction of the formulas of the harmonic movement completed in three oscillations guided by the three principles of conflict resolution.

Moral Science is a politically relevant scientific discovery pertinent to our world divided by its multiple religious metaphors. It helps to interpret metaphors as alternative conflict resolutions, as the process and confers enlightenment and insights useful in dealing with inner and outer conflicts, interfacing the personal with the multicultural value systems.

The challenge of our times is to inform the public about religions as imperfect ways of resolving conflicts while inspiring the public with the perfection of the scientific moral order. The abstract language of science, the analytical method, introduces moral reason in the place of the prevailing compartmentalized and alienated divisive faiths.

The mega merger
Uncertainties about the definition of God and wisdom are resolved in the reliability of the Moral Science. God as process, as the unit order, by definition heralds peace; the unit is not only science but moral and mental order with a wide range of applications. God is the equilibrial principles predictably evolving to resolutions, peace, a new interpretation of Sabbath. The unit process clarifies elusive concepts like morality, the unconscious, diagnostic categories and assessment of creativity.

The process, the universal harmonic, has extraordinary importance in bridging the humanities and the sciences, in reconciling religions among themselves, in clarifying psychology and defining morality. Science integrates religion and psychology with science into a single domain of knowledge. The three realms merge into a meaningful totality. They are intrinsically connected. The new concept of moral order is a formula valid for all religions and all mental states. Religions and psychology are solutions of the formula for alternative values of its variables. The Formal Theory offers a completely integrative view of reality: the psychology of morality or the calculus of power management.

Science assumes the normative authority
The new theory has political relevance and great pertinence to our times of normative cultural conflicts. The essence of this communication is of strategic importance for our times. The creative process is literally the mental moral order. Here we are not talking of another paradigm, but of the unit of the social sciences interfacing and bridging the humanities and the sciences. This claim has been validated by practice and research, statistics and multiple experimental studies. The images of the Museum of the Creative Process demonstrate art as evidence of this science.

The scientific paradigm redefines morality; it does not cancel it; it unifies the old paradigms, exposes their limitations as partial understandings of the universal order and integrates them into an evolutionary continuum. Religions represent the evolving awareness of social justice as sanctifications of alternative configurations of the domestic relations system.

As partial truths the paradigms identified morality, which eventually was identified with immorality. This is the case of the Abrahamic family; the sculpture commemorates that the big breakthrough of the father son covenant coincided with the unfair, inequitable relation between the genders. Three 18 feet tall men, the patriarchs, four little women and two concubines, the chicks, they are not even human, the sculpture illustrates dramatically the inequity between the genders of the Abrahamic family. This image was sacred for thousands of years but we may regard it now as immoral or unfair from our normative perspective valuing the parity of genders.

The new paradigm does not eliminate the old paradigms; it reconciles them as steps into the abstraction of formulas. So the new paradigm is not alienating the world of religions, it simply offers a more elegant and universal abstraction on what religions have been trying to grasp poetically and intuitively. The redefinition of God as the Universal Harmonic makes sense. The priests are redefined as the psychologists, the scientists of moral order; clergymen should be preachers on the evolution of religions to the Unitarian Moral Science. Politicians should be the only legislators of morality. They have been struggling to give legitimacy to civil rights frequently opposed by the churches.

A case in point, in liberal, feminist France, the head scarf of the Islamic women was banned as incompatible with the current perception of the gender relations. This religious norm was overturned by the political power commanding in this country the emancipation of women mandated by the authority of the government.

We need science to give us perspective in the evolution of norms in order for the world to heal from the divisive belief systems and to respond effectively to the contemporary crisis of values. The discrepancy in perceptions of reality have led us to the War on Terror, a simple clash of norms on the role of women. Moral divisiveness will not go away until science prevails over the entrenched beliefs, misleading the public with convictions worth dying for. The only path to lasting peace is introducing science, the language that is respected by all, the scientific paradigm, to reconcile our many paradigms. The process, the Universal Harmonic, is simple and effective; it has multiple rewarding applications. Besides paving the road to peace confronting and reconciling religions, it can enhance education and revamp psychology.

The Formal Theory interprets metaphorical language using analytical thinking and understands religions integrating them into the broader perspective of the psychology of power management and complete conflict resolution. This reconciliation helps the person attain wellness, spirituality and the world to achieve peace. The implication is that we have in science a reliable clear moral paradigm and that science assumes the moral leadership over the multiple disunited religions.

Formal Theory's approach to moral order transcends religions by speaking the universal language of science. The world evolves from the many religious metaphors to the science understanding the unconscious mind, from which originated all belief systems and ideologies.

Science offering the abstract conceptualization of the emotional process can inspire and unite the cultures of the world. The remedy to our cultural problems is the acknowledgment of science defining the new moral paradigm. The new paradigm gives credit to religions but lifts the world to the intelligence of understanding the origin of all morality. The process gives meaning to the diversity by comprehending the underlying unifying values. Science offers this quantum leap interfacing our diverse cultures and flattening our ideological and cultural differences, so instead of beliefs dividing the world, the common denominator, conflict resolution, may unite, secure and reconcile the intelligent people of the world.

The quest for meaning ends with science understanding the unconscious proceeding spontaneously, predictably from art to science, from the particular to the universal, from emotions to insights. The abstraction as the automatic pursuit of conflict resolution has a synonym, mindfulness or kindness.

The process as the integrative paradigm of the social sciences

The unit order shifts respect from the story to the plot of stories. The unit deciphers the mysteries; it is the key to interpret metaphors scientifically as conflict resolution phenomena. This interpretation frees people from the idolatry of the story, the misperception of the story as the whole truth.

The truth is not in any one solution of the formula, not even the solutions advanced by the sacred scriptures; the truth is in the formal order of the universal moral phenomenon underlying and integrating all stories, all faiths. Conflict resolution as a natural science phenomenon, as a formula true for all variables, is sacred; it is the essence of the multiple contradictory religious stories as resolutions of the formula; it is the universal moral process, the plot of all stories, underlying all thinking.

Evidence establishes the creative process as a natural science periodic phenomenon. This is the unit, the integrative paradigm. It consists of a six-role state and three formal operations entity that transforms a conflict to a resolution.
• Epistemologically we know this phenomenon as the perfect universe, the plot and moral of stories as a symbolic universe that may be interpreted as a Conflict Resolution Process abiding by the laws of science's orderly Simple Harmonic Motion and the equilibrial scale. The social science phenomenon adopts the natural science's

constructs, formulas and graphic presentation as a three-cycle harmonic and its cross section as a set of concentric circles.

• Psychologically we identify the conflict resolving process as the unconscious, the homeostatic or self-corrective response to stress. This physiologic natural science phenomenon as a syndromal sequence of emotions and behaviors has been identified with diagnostic categories of wellness, the relational modalities. We recognize a set of four key diagnostic categories of wellness, the dominance and subordinacy, cooperative and antagonistic relational modalities.

• The unit is measurable; we avail a user-friendly self-assessment, the *Conflict Analysis Battery*; it yields information directly to the test-taker and the protocol establishes a clear personal symbolic system as a meaningful record. The battery is diagnostic, therapeutic and educational.

• Morally the process is identified with three principles of conflict resolution. These are underlying the traditional moral paradigms such as the Ten Commandments. The process is the scientific moral paradigm.

A science-based spirituality

The Moral Science books represent a historical turning point in the conceptualization of the social sciences. Eras begin with a new explanation, a new paradigm, and the Formal Theory introduces such a paradigm. This is the scientific paradigm of moral and mental order. It manifests in all samples of creativity and it is used to interpret metaphors. The books begin the era of moral reason.

The Formal Theory expands on the nature of the unconscious as a scientific process organizing the associations in samples of creativity. As a result thinkers may reach consensus on what is the nature of a universal science based moral order and at the same time understand the human unconscious as the scientific phenomenon for the study of behavior. Moral Science ushers in both a scientific motivational dynamic psychology and

the rigorous definition of moral order.

The new science has pertinence in the conceptualization of the unconscious but also its manifestation as religions and as the normative regulation of interpersonal relations such as the configuration of the family institution. The science has impact on conceptual, sociological and political matters. It emancipates the public from the reign of religions as uninterpreted metaphors; it frees the public from the unfair constraints of religious norms.

Science conceptually corrects the alienation between psychology and morality but also between dated and contemporary normative conduct. Science determines that moral thinking becomes the principle motivational force, as the need for interpersonal effectiveness and fairness. Religions have discovered solutions. Earlier solutions interfere with progress.

Psychology and religion are about evolving fairness in interpersonal relations. Religions reinvented themselves to accommodate the need for resetting norms; science of moral psychology rethinks concepts but also norms without addressing changes in belief systems. Science determines the flow of norms rather than capitulate like religions to the dated norms and incomplete understandings of the nature of interpersonal relations.

Currently the world is helpless at the mercy of diverse moral imperatives, unintegrated knowledge, uninterpreted metaphors on the themes of the psyche and God, unprocessable information since our intelligence does not recognize a clear object of observation and the appropriate method in organizing conceptual information along the path of reason and abstraction. The world has made progress in all areas of science and technology but has had difficulty in understanding the psyche and God and agreeing on what are the acceptable concepts on behavior

regulating institutions in a modern society.

Religions have established territorial control as belief and normative systems that erect barriers to progress. Religions object humanity's enjoying the fruits of the tree of knowledge. They deprive the believers from basic intellectual freedoms and demand total emotional compliance. The secular political correctness position of 'do not ask and do not tell' regarding matters of faith cordons off the humanities from the critical sciences and allows the coexistence of questionable practices as political rights.

The new publications reconcile reductionism and determinism and free a new understanding of the psyche and God. The Formal Theory and the Moral Science books identify the scientific path to meaning that integrates, interprets, bridges, categorizes, assesses, reconciles, and raises questions, but mostly that harmonizes respectfully the information on psychological and moral matters. It represents a radical departure in the field of the humanities and achieves all that with a single very simple concept, the Conflict Resolution Process.

The key paradigm shift of the Moral Science departs from the many stories we believe in to recognize the plot of stories as a conflict resolution mechanism, the universal process. Isolating the object and identifying the scientific method, appropriate for the analysis of this object, challenges the last frontier of knowledge.

The new science object and method identify the universal order in the soft sciences as a six-part dialectic, the Universal Harmonic. This harmonic departs from the particular story to identify the universal as forms transformed, energies conserved but upgraded, conflicts predictably resolved as increased order and meaning, a more positive attitude. This shift of paradigms integrates all stories and binds art to science. The plot of stories becomes formulas of physics and logic and the creative process becomes the tool to penetrate the frontiers blocking humanity from the wisdom of abstract thinking.

The tool of creativity is metaphors that we now can interpret with the formulas of science elucidating the nature of harmonics. We are so comfortable interpreting metaphors that we have developed a technology of creativity for self-discovery, to measure the individual personality and to examine cultural patterns. Understanding the creative process introduces scientific organization in all humanities. The exhibits of the Museum of the Creative Process are case studies of how to depart from the arts, to identify the universal harmonic in every symbolic system. The process establishes continuity wherever there has been fragmentation.

As the dust settles, as the fog concealing new ideas disperses, the new theory will be respected as establishing connections between alienated knowledge. The world will wake up to a new landscape, a clear horizon that lets you see forever. Wherever we look, whatever we examine will be meaningful, orderly, and clear. The Moral Science ushers the era of the broadest explanation. We will no longer feel walled off, fragmented and alienated. We will be able to understand the universe, cultures, religions, mythologies, magic, history, leaders and followers, the genders, the language of art, the symbolic language of dreams and of literature, of music all reinforcing one concept, the Harmonic of conflict resolution.

The Harmonic is the new single truth, the new spirituality. It processes all information meaningfully as the evolving equilibrium between individual needs and societal constraints. The Harmonic is orderly and believable. It is simple. It has formulas we can understand and graphics we can recognize and interpret at a glance. The Harmonic is of universal pertinence. It is the plot of stories. It is drama. It is syndromes. It is religions and it is the evolving philosophies of life;

all diversity is unified in the spirituality of the creative process.

Conflict resolution reconciles the parallel claims of alternative truths. It is the reality behind all metaphors. Science interprets metaphors and reconciles the alienated disciplines in the field of the social sciences. Psychology is about morality and both are about science. In the process we find ourselves in harmony with all our emotions and life episodes. In it we find our patterns, our partners and our children. Everything becomes predictable, measurable and meaningful. Everything becomes orderly. The world can communicate across metaphors and borders. We feel enlightened and insightful.

This paradigm reconciles, integrates and formalizes psychological and moral knowledge, the range of the humanities. The books on the process incorporate mythology and embrace science, capturing in between psychology, diagnosis, assessment and morality. The same volumes integrate wellness and illness, education and therapy. The new psychology has the simplicity and depth to appeal to the great public as user-friendly popular knowledge, targeting, enlightenment, insight and clarity of values.

The Moral Science is not for the church green alone. It is entering Main Street as a theory that is validated and that introduces a new concept clearly illustrated in the art exhibits of a Museum, that generates a new language useful for the integration of knowledge to be delivered in the classroom, the training center and even the churches. The workbook represents the state of the art in assessment technology. *Creativity and Power Management* introduce a concise program of emotional education and psycho-education for all ages. The expertise and competence of this science spans the arts, mythology, psychology, religion, science and education.

Activism in healing the world: A new moral imperative, managing religions' political power, their nomothetic faculty

The key issue in this volume is science versus religion. The realm of moral order currently is monopolized by the normative or nomothetic power of religions. We have identified the scientific nature of the moral process, how it reconciles religions as partial discoveries of the Conflict Resolution Process and completes their mission as the science of the Conflict Resolution Process, the Moral Science. The imperative of healing the world is moral power management rethinking what is optimal normative behavior.

We need here to explore the political power of rational normative determinations, the power to make distinctions between what is right and wrong. Moral Science affects the religious traditions by informing the public about the limitations of religions. Humans need to be educated to judge religions as cultural paradigms in the context of the wider perspective of relating, or resolving conflicts, using the principles of formal analysis. This education is bound to be delivered as scientific knowledge on behavior integrating psychology, moral order and the sciences and providing the public with new clarity on the nature of morality and norms.

Emotional and moral literacy, a new civil right as education on the formal interpretation of metaphors

One way of protecting the public from the powerful impact of religious distortions of the truth is insisting in the adoption of this education. Education must address the discrepancy between religious and science-based information especially in what regards norms which evoke psycho- and socio-pathology. Scientists and educators not only may, but they should warn the public about religious thinking and norms in view of the Science of Conflict Resolution. Religions like cigarettes should be labeled on their packaging: 'Belief systems may be hazardous to your health.'

While our world is helpless in containing religions the public has access to information and to preventative emotional education. A new civil right is emerging, that of emotional and moral literacy. The public needs the fundamental civil right to learn to read and write, but it also has the right to freedom of reason suppressed by religions. Emotional literacy is equivalent in scope with the right to conventional literacy. Education can achieve this by integrating information on the subjects of psychology and morality coinciding with science.

The Science of Conflict Resolution, as a factual study, is a field of knowledge suitable for the public's basic education. Information on the process should be delivered in the classroom to clarify the evolutionary nature of moral paradigms and norms but also to inform the individual on the psychology of relational modalities. This scientific information is desirable to provide the individual with personal insights as enlightenment in the area of moral psychology and its relevance for personal relational insights. The school student must study relational modalities as well as the evolution of belief systems, domestic norms, and contemporary norms identified as civil rights.

The legitimate way to protect the public's health is to promote the civil right of emotional and moral literacy, as the study of optimal ways of resolving conflict through a curriculum of moral and emotional education. The public needs sociological cultural enlightenment and information leading to personal insights. Moral Science entails the obligation, the moral imperative of this literacy. The focus of this education of the public is the formal interpretation of metaphors and the study of optimal power management.

Activism
Besides educating the public on issues of managing personal power the issue arises on how to deal with the existing normative power of

religions. The Moral Science inspires us to rethink culturally dictated norms as these may represent polarizing dichotomies generating conflicts in the person and the respective cultures. Religions in our times as political self-righteous institutions endanger world peace as well as the mental wellness of the believers. Politicians, educators, psychologists and the clergy themselves are alarmed but helpless in dealing with religion associated socio- and psychopathology.

The issue is how does the world protect the public from abuses of power on the part of religions as normative political institutions. Religions have their own needs of self-preservation. Their absolute power is in defining norms based on their dogma. Thus they affect wellness and peace without being accountable to any authorities. The responsible representatives of the world are the priests of science. The public defenders are scientists, educators and legislators. Science makes religions accountable to the moral authority of the conflict resolution principles. Science alone has the secrets to moral values as scientific principles, and the defenders of science have the responsibility to initiate reforms. They must intervene to contain the power of religions on the basis of respect for the public by alerting people on religions' abuses of power and informing the public on the science based spirituality.

Religions have tremendous social impact. They are powerful institutions but the Moral Science representing objectivity and sound reasoning is entitled to more respect than religions. Religions represent subjectivity and speculative reasoning, and are political normative institutions that must be made accountable to external civil authorities. Their dogma-based values are no longer acceptable as compatible with reason. Reason demystifies religions as fathomable mental normative structures and entails that they are not immune to criticism. They are no longer sacred and may no longer escape the public's reason-bound norms of social conduct.

Identifying religions' normative fallacies leading to cultural pathology
Below we review some of the religion associated socio- and psychopathology adversely affecting the vulnerable, naïve and gullible public.

1. Issues of the Catholic religion
The Vatican has avoided recognizing the pedophilia endemic among its clergy. The church and the press have been preoccupied with the cover-ups criticizing the priests and the church's hierarchy managing the erring priests rather than acknowledging the cause-effect relation of doctrine and practices affecting adversely the clergy and the public. The church and the press have not linked pedophilia with the religion's doctrine. The church leadership seems determined to dissociate its doctrine as the cause of pathology. The public remains impervious to the obvious connection of the pathogenetic impact of the religion's treatment of sexual conduct and the incidence of pedophilic misconduct.

The problems of psychopathology generated by the focus on controlling sexual behavior are much more widespread than the cases of pedophilic clergy. The damages to the health of the public surpass the isolated episodes of pedophilia. The culprit is Catholicism's obsession with controlling the public's sexuality. In doing so the church is demonizing sexuality into something very conflictual. The conflicts consume the individual's preoccupations and generate defensiveness, obsessions, which precipitate severe psycho- and socio-pathology. We may witness the measure of this pathology in the incidence and prevalence of the pedophilic behavior among catholic clergy. The incidence of clergy's pedophilic behavior has manifested universally, wherever the church preaches. Pedophilia then is church-evoked behavior that needs to be addressed with rethinking the church's norm toward sexual behavior.

There are many other areas where the church intrudes in the personal lives of the public in matters of sexual nature such as the issue of birth control and termination of pregnancy. Do churches have the right to establish norms controlling people's sexual lives or is it upon the consumers of Christian ethos to determine rules for proper management of their sexual behavior?

Who is in charge of managing these pathogenetic sexuality doctrines and policies? Does the church have the right to associate sexuality with evil? Does a church have the right to severely upset the believers and the clergy given the devastation this behavior has caused to the innocent youth trusting their priests? Does the church have the right to impose the rule of celibacy and abstinence to its clergy given the associated well-documented, statistically significant incidence of pedophilic deviance among the priests?

2. A second religion, Islam, must be held accountable for generating pathology with its well- established norms. The influence of individual behavior by religious norms marked the traumatic beginning of the new millennium with the striking immorality of 9/11, scarring the universe with an act inspired by religious people in the name of their spiritual leader. The same mentality manifested itself in the nefarious attack on the monuments of Buddha and has inspired the multiple suicidal bombers destroying life indiscriminately insulting the values of civilized people. Islamist militant theism endangers peace in the world. How will Islam reform itself without a popular uprising among the faithful wishing to truly improve their institution?

Morality in Islam is associated with the inequitable treatment of women, discriminating on the rights of women, expecting women to wear head-scarves and burkas and depriving them of equal rights and roles in their societies. These norms are incompatible with the innate rules of conflict resolution and reflect dated sociological evolutionary phases in the development of the family institution.

Where is this pathology stemming from? It is associated with the unacceptable norms of the suppression of the freedom of expression and the imposition of thought control in promoting rote learning rather than analytical thinking. Deviants of these norms, intellectuals inspired by the need for change, are threatened with Fatwas, summarily pronounced death sentences. Controlling free speech for authors and cartoonists is an antisocial autocratic domineering disposition that is extremely counterproductive for the health of the culture.

This norm is undermining growth within the culture and affects the compatibility of this culture with others that are more progressive. Lack of freedom to express criticism, obsessive indoctrination in a set dogma based way of thinking, intolerance of alternatives, are traditions and norms that lead to irrational reasoning, to militant theism, hostile conduct, self and others destructive mentality.

Depriving the freedom of speech, forbidding public debate on religious and normative issues is a fundamental pathogenetic religion related norm that needs to be reversed. Changes will be difficult as the religion justifies these behaviors as God given inviolable injunctions. But these norms and values may be deemed as pathogenetic, considered as immoral or abnormative, needing to be addressed by the science based perspective. Again the question is on who has the authority to judge religion generated psycho- and socio-pathogenetic behavior? Is there an agency to represent the pubic and to protect it from the self-righteousness of dogma?

3. Judaism is burdened with hundreds of moral injunctions completely controlling the orthodox Jews' lifestyle. Orthodoxy represents a small minority of this religion, yet it is very difficult for them to even consider rethinking their rigid and regulated belief system and narrowly ritualized practices.

4. Buddhism is another religion that needs monitoring. It subjects believers to the total suppression of desire through numbing thought control. Meditation workshops target training people to silence for days, weeks and months at a time. Expressing one's legitimate emotional and physical needs is discouraged. Silencing the person's needs by subjecting oneself to painful rituals is viewed as desirable. Is this view of profound asceticism the ultimate moral objective in the moral education of the public?

5. The polarization of espousing pain versus pleasure may be recognized in Hinduism evolving from asceticism of Ganges to the sensualism of Karnak.

HEALING THE WORLD BY CONTAINING THE NORM-SETTING POWER OF RELIGIONS
Science as the superior moral authority must make religions accountable to natural law.
Moral Science ushering in the scientific conceptualization of psychology and morality as the integrative unit entity is stealing the fire of the gods winning the struggle for meaning between science and religion. The scientific conceptualization of behavior and religion and their integration into the exact Moral Science empowers the public while in parallel it diminishes the power of religions to determine the norms of proper behavior. The universal moral order defined by reason frees the mortals from the dependence on questionable dated explanations, misleading beliefs, metaphors that are advocated as realities stifling cultural progress.

Religions are manufacturers of spiritual and normative products deviating from the science-based moral or conflict resolution norms. Religions should be subjected to analysis of their ways of resolving conflict and held accountable like so many other industrial institutions in the ways they are affecting the physical and mental health of consumers. The public using science may hold religions liable for their adverse impact.

How free can religions be in ruling the globe with impunity by commanding divine entitlement for their inequitable power management preferences? They will be as free as the civilized people tolerate the adverse normative power of religions. Because of the Moral Science religions no longer have immunity from analysis, from the critical evaluation of their practices, from criticism of their malpractices and impunity for their abusive and conflict evoking behaviors and policies.

Misdirected idealism: The dynamics of the politics of meaning, fundamentalism as the post-communism quest for a new moral paradigm
The world of the 21st century is in a phase of ideological transition. The bankruptcy of national socialism, communism and psychoanalysis has left a spiritual and ideological vacuum that has been filled in the East and West by traditional theistic value systems. We are witnesses to the reversal of the rebellious agnostic humanism and atheism of the 20th century replaced by the rampant theism and fundamentalism of our times. The public from communists and capitalists are now redeployed along their incompatible religious beliefs. The new virtue is to worship respective dogma based inspirational paradigms. Fundamentalism is the new world norm. It has been espoused as militant religion among many contemporary groups.

Contemporary fundamentalists are the passionate "Saviors of God." Unable to find meaning in dealing with moral ambiguities in our confusing times the public has espoused stories about ultimate moral authorities. There are many examples of "escape from freedom," as Eric Fromm described in his book, explaining the surrender of individuals and of populations' moral judgment to that of questionable alternative "higher authorities."

In America, the Christian right has been seeking to influence government policies. In Israel, Jewish fundamentalists seek control in starting settlements in Arab lands justifying this with their scriptures. We all know the excesses of the inspired Islamists. The question arises: Can science have a chance to succeed in this theocratic political climate?

The new insights on religion represent a radical ideological departure in the balance of power of reason versus faith. Religions are deeply implanted in our traditions as sacred. It is difficult to awaken the world to moral order as a scientific phenomenon. But due to the fact that religions have become self-righteous and divisive institutions causing untold human suffering, mental turmoil, ongoing wars and cross-cultural conflicts, they have incurred attention to themselves as irrational entities that the world needs to contend with and potentially seek to reform and regulate.

Moral Science criticizing religions unlike evolutionism does not dismiss moral order. On the contrary science introduces clarity on the object of study and the method of analysis of moral order. Moral order, redefined as a natural science phenomenon that has inspired the emotions identified universally as religions, emerges with inspirational values of its own. The respect of spirituality provides the alternative to religious fundamentalism, so while science threatens the power of fundamentalism, it does not deprive the public from the needed clarity on the nature of morality and meaning.

9/11 marked the highest point of ugly theistic activism. After this assault at civilization by a theistic group of young, intelligent, well educated, and heroic individuals the world was alarmed at the adverse power of religion. The intensity of faith driven inspirational conduct against humanity has stimulated thinkers to ponder on the nature of religion and God. But so far the assault of civilization by a religious group has not elicited outrage at religions; on the contrary other religions inspired a counteroffensive as political alliances engaged in a war between cultures.

The scientific premise determines what is sacred
The conceptual impasse of the biological science on religion limited the effectiveness of religious criticism. Psychologists unable to understand religion have abstained from engaging in the dialogue on religions as their expertise is in understanding behavior rather than morality. Reporters, Radio and TV journalists have paid tribute to spirituality ignoring the malevolent extremism of ideological positions. The insights on religion so far have been shallow and inadequate to puzzle through the problem of conceptually or legally effectively containing the self-righteousness of religions.

The major difficulty has been the lack of conceptual understanding of psychology and of religions. The press initiated criticism but has been paralyzed by the uninformed religion inspired public expressing intolerance and indignation at criticism. America enjoys freedom of speech but here too we suffer of the politization of religious values.

Until now morality has been defined by religions. It has been in the jurisdiction of religions to determine what is acceptable or virtuous; religions have forever dictated distinctions between what is morally right and wrong. Biologically based scientists questioning religious dogma have questioned moral order espousing atheism without redefining moral order. Atheism versus theism is a distinction of the past, when there were no moral alternatives between believing and understanding morality as a natural science phenomenon. The analysts of conflict change the power balance in this discourse. The public now may seek justice and question the authority of religious paradigms as unfair and inaccurate, as counterproductive and misleading systems inspiring ugly miscarriages of justice.

The new science helps to address the contradictory stories and to explore the advantages of science's unifying moral paradigm

Presently the public's quest for meaning is served by either numbing atheism or paralyzing theism. The theistic choice inspires many religious groups of our times to strive for strict lifestyles and compliance to orthodoxy accompanied by intolerance to openness and change. But the silent majority of the atheist public consists of spiritual people alienated by the unreason of dogma and trusting reason and science. This segment of the public will welcome the insights of the Formal Theory. Scientists might then be 'the saviors of humanity.' One thing is clear; the world needs a new moral paradigm but has been unable to identify the nature of ethical power outside of religions. It can do this with the help of the Moral Science.

Scientists now can understand the orderly nature of moral order better than religious moralists and evolution's biologists. Science provides objectivity in conceptualizing moral and psychological order. Conceptual clarity is the prerequisite for the public to stand up against the normative thought control assumed by religions. The consequence is that social scientists become the experts of moral law founded on natural law, while the clergy and biologists are exposed to espousing inequitable and alternatively amoral paradigms.

Science as the moral paradigm will eventually prevail because of its rational moral relevance. The unit process is inspirational to all. The Moral Science message emancipates humanity from the tyranny of religions as uninterpreted metaphors. Religions appealing to the emotions are powerful, but ultimately reason and science prevail. So at this point, religions as moral institutions are upstaged by science. Reason prevails over religion and we may expect the development of an interfaith tribunal empowered to judge the religions questioning their arbitrary normative authority.

Science as Conceptual Correctness may put an end to the free for all Political Correctness. Moral authorities monitoring consumers' interests will intervene to protect the public from the self-righteousness of religions. Religions then might be subjected to re-licensing like radio and TV stations, like the many professionals who have to attend continued education to qualify them for re-credentialing. At that point religions and spokespeople of God, could be screened in evaluating their ideologies as responsible for crimes against humanity.

The Moral Science introducing the notion that religions have natural science dimensions can help the public to reexamine the charters of churches. Demystified and demesmerized as God's representatives the religious institutions to survive will need to become aware of their impact on society. The public will vote by walking away from noxious religions to alternative moral institutions. We will then have new moral institutions as the informed consumers follow the ultimate moral perspective. Why would they attend a church that is dangerous to their mental health when there is a healthier place for worship and socialization?

It is the informed public that has the power over religion, so the political option at this point is to educate the public and empower it in dealing with the religious institutions. The public empowered will fight for justice in the same manner as it has brought restrain to the industrial and the political institutions affecting the rights of the individual.

The battle of science versus religion: legal activism, class action suit against religions

In the past protected by the constitutional right to freedom of religious beliefs, and further because of lack of criteria to judge the religions qualitatively the public resorted to the principle of political correctness. The law and the spirit of democracy has protected this freedom provid-

ing tolerance to religious beliefs with immunity from criticism and political impunity. The abuses of religions and the empowerment of the public require the change of attitude toward tolerance of religious freedom. The principle emerges that religions are free but as social institutions they are subject to legal regulation and respect of societal norms and scientific concepts.

The world is waking up from being mesmerized by misinformation as beliefs. The informed public is bound to defend itself from the dictatorship of faiths. The public united may address the injustices of all Abrahamic religions gender discriminating norms and obsession with controlling sexual behavior, their unrealistic family planning policies in the context of generating social adversity and unrealistic demand on the limited resources of the planet. These religions must encourage the equity of genders, the use of birth control to avoid the impending population explosion in the age of the depletion of resources.

The world is suffering because of religious beliefs and the public needs to defend itself from the dictatorships of faiths by suing religions as accountable to reason and as responsible and liable for social adversities. The public might seek changes to protect those victimized by religious institutions. We may conceive on that basis that a class action suit may be brought by the oppressed, defenseless public susceptible to religious doctrine and normative regulations, against religions as responsible for their plight.

Religions represent powerful institutions comparable to financial industrial monopolies producing products that may be beneficial but also detrimental to the public's welfare and mental health. Religions may be viewed as for profit industrial institutions that are liable for their impact on the consumers or believers morally susceptible to their indoctrinations. Religions then may be brought to courts as liable to and responsible for the damages inflicted on the citizens/

consumers of beliefs and the institutions should be responsible to indemnify the public for their suffering.

Organizations, such as the tobacco industry, food and drug industries, financial institutions, and accounting firms have been made accountable for their products' and services and they have been punished by the courts for hurting the public. Courts have inflicted penalties to industries and have demanded reforms from the institutions. They have asked for warnings to be given to the consumers concerning the impact of their products. Should not religions as well be scrutinized when their impact on the public's welfare determines the conflicts of their lives? Should they not worn the public about their claims as subjective, metaphorical assertions, and not as the absolute and final truths.

Moral literacy as a new civil right as important as the right for religious freedom empowers people to interpret metaphors and free themselves of moral dictatorships. It is conceivable that people coordinate their grievances in a well-organized web site about their personal suffering inflicted by their religions. I imagine such information and related blogs could provide constructive criticism and eventually empower the consumers to lodge legal action questioning the moral authority of religion in view of a well-established Moral Science.

Social networking and legal activism will restrain the power of religions

The difference in our times upon the publication of this book is that the public has achieved empowerment as a new reality of abundance of information and synergy among consumers. The era of the social media empowers justice for all, and the science empowers the public in recognizing and criticizing tyrannical authorities. The public then has new choices in the politics of power management. It is able to rally and collaborate in addressing social injustice on its own.

For instance, the public can get organized and lodge a campaign to make religions accountable to the scientifically established concepts of morality. The public has the right to restrain religions' powers. In preparation for a class action suit the social media could serve the public to rally support for specific coordinated issues. A Moral Science web site could organize people to offer information about personal adverse impact of religious injunctions so that the public becomes aware of the problems of religions as the preparation of class action suits to effectively restrain religious doctrine as the faulty monopolies of virtue.

The public acceptance of concepts on moral order is a certainty; the prevalence of science over religion vindicated Galileo in spite of the resistance of the church. What is questionable is the speed of the shift of paradigms. The speed will be accelerated given that the world is currently in a state of perpetual crisis generated by religious terrorism.

The new concepts enable addressing religious biases. The Moral Science offers insights on the rigorous definition of moral order and it provides the Conflict Resolution Process as the moral and scientific alternative to the cacophony of multiple religions and psychologies. Power Management as an emotional education integrates religions, psychology and science securely providing this valuable information in the classroom where it can generate enlightenment and personal insights without ambiguity.

Progress has entailed innovations in the history of civilization. The tradition is reforms occurring as new religions overruling dated moral standards, or normative behaviors. Emperor Constantine moved the center of the Roman Empire away from Pagan Rome to Constantinople the capitol of a new faith in the ancient world. A parallel shift is overdue. As the world is becoming a singular global society we suggest a shift of paradigms from theism to relational formalism, conceptual abstraction and social fairness. We also suggest the shift of centers of culture from theistic divisive Jerusalem to abstractly thinking culturally integrating, creativity based spiritual New York City. The World Trade Center, the Tower of Babel, victim of fanaticism must be rebuilt with the spirit of the new Temple of Jerusalem, representing the healthy power of abstract spirituality uniting the world.

The churches and schools, psychotherapists and clergy should impart and reinforce one message for the public, ethical power management. Religions should survive transformed into presenting the same message with alternative solutions aware of their value choices and their limitations. All religions should recognize the humanistic origin of religion and that Gods and religions are part of the human psychology and that religions are subject to the same power management pathology we encounter in individual behavior.

Change is outstanding. It is upon educated people to understand the concept and advocate growth. It is the duty of clergy and academics, teachers and psychologists to become the apostles of the new science-based moral order by interpreting metaphors as alternative resolutions entailing awareness of the universality of the process but also of the variation in resolutions. Evolution of paradigms required four centuries of testing for Christianity to prevail over the pagan religions and finally to become the norm of the Byzantine empire. The technologically advanced world may be can reduce the time for the needed moral transformation of our society.

The power of the Moral Science

The power of the Moral Science is in its capacity to reconcile religions, psychology and science and deliver moral consensus, a new kind of wisdom. Science defeats theism by elucidating the psychology of the religious response and by identifying the unconscious as the origin of moral order.

Science is showing that religions are partial and complementary discoveries of the scientific nature of the process. Science reduces religions to observable measurable natural science phenomena. Science helps religions to increase their effectiveness by endorsing conflict resolution concepts including scientific principles as moral values clarifying the virtues of optimal power management. The Moral Science introduces the set of concepts, the process as a natural science phenomenon that allows thinkers and consumers to found a critical position from which to judge normative determinations.

Currently the Moral Science is merely an aspiring new conceptual initiative. It is a science-based theory of behavior and moral order. It needs significant critical mass to establish its legitimacy and its viability beyond the life of its author. But this science-based voice represents the conceptual reform that integrates the social and the rigorous sciences. To succeed the new science needs multiple endorsements, legitimacy granted by scientists and the moral empowerment granted by public opinion.

Religions our revered sociological, psychological adjustive responses to life stressors mean well but know little else other than their institutional wisdom conveyed through metaphors and transmitted with the power of ritual and community consensus. Religions may benefit by recognizing their relational choices and related distortions and consequences; becoming open minded they could modify some practices and convey through their teachings respect for the universal moral order. They could deliver services that reconcile paradigms and help the healing of people and relationships. All religions should converge in promoting the path to power management in personal and cultural matters.

The discoveries of the Moral Science introduce the needed objectivity in making ethical distinctions: morality and religion can no longer be victim to simplistic creationists and hostile evolutionists. Science confers multiple advantages. The Moral Science is the conceptualization that integrates all religions. Integration of religions can make sense to everybody as objectivity and functionalism.

The unit process imparts clarity to the field of the social sciences and also to religions. Science as the truth about moral order may be unbound by religions as Prometheus was by Zeus. Religions have an interest in giving the fire to the mortals, reconciling themselves with each other and with society assuming a new role in peace making and in furthering wellness. After all this has been their mission statement.

EPILOGUE

The Formal Theory identified the unconscious as a Conflict Resolution Process, a moral order and natural science phenomenon. This premise of the Formal Theory was validated using the *Conflict Analysis Battery* and the art exhibits of the Museum of the Creative Process. The Formal Theory thus became the Moral Science.

The Moral Science regards religions as forerunners of the Science of Conflict Resolution. They identified particular conflict resolutions as metaphors of relating, as normative definitions of family relations attributed to corresponding role model divinities, the deifications of the unconscious natural science phenomenon.

The Moral Science reconciles psychology and religion with science and frees the public of the tyranny of partial truths, metaphors presented as the total truth. The science also provides norms based on the scientific principles of conflict resolution, hence the process is conceived as the ultimate moral authority.

The plot of this book metaphorically follows a conflict resolution, the mythic struggle between Prometheus and Zeus, which culminated in Prometheus, unbound, becoming the fire-giver, the benefactor of the mortals. Science in a parallel manner identifies the fire of the gods, the origin of all moral order, as the orderly unconscious establishing the scientific foundation of psychology and morality. This concept demystifies religions as types of conflict resolution, as partial discoveries of the natural science unconscious. The new science departs from this discovery's advocates like Prometheus seeking social change and advocating a new civil right to emotional and moral literacy. This literacy frees the public from the arbitrariness of religious dogma, the rule of the uninterpreted metaphors by promoting an emotional and moral education program, *Creativity and Power Management*, for the formal interpretation of metaphors.

The Promethean dramatic struggle with the gods is a good metaphor for the modern struggle between science and religion. The mortals like puppets are controlled by their sanctified metaphors to fight an endless civil war of metaphors. The Promethean Science brings fire, insights, teaching the public how to interpret metaphors and free themselves from the tyranny of their cruel gods.

Science as Prometheus begins the era of a change of paradigms from stories we believe in to the process, the plot of stories as moral clarity. Science makes a distinct contribution of both taking the power away from the gods and giving it to the public. The power is in using the creative process as a scientific technology, introducing the laws of the rigorous sciences into the study of psychology. The process is measurable and graphically portrayable. The unconscious may be readily captured and measured in samples of personal creativity. This technology may be used for educational, diagnostic and therapeutic objectives.

The key to science is objectivity so that everybody can observe a phenomenon and reach the same conclusions. The key to making behavior into a science is detecting the unconscious as a universal periodic and moral order phenomenon. The most important contribution of the Moral Science is establishing objectivity on psychological and moral matters, like clarifying the nature of the psyche and of god and by determining societal norms, the distinctions between right and wrong.

This book is about objectivity by identifying the unconscious through its projection in all creativity as a measurable mechanism that resolves conflicts. Therefore to study the unconscious we observe the arts, canvases, myths and metaphors, religions, and we identify there a natural science moral order entity.

The three chapters of this book reflect the struggle between science and religion, in terms of objectivity versus subjectivity. First science like Prometheus clarifies the importance of the scientific understanding of the unconscious as equivalent to the fire of the Gods. The contentious 'fire' corresponds to the scientific understanding of the unconscious as a conflict resolving process, the origin of all moral order. Next science wrenches the fire from religion by interpreting religions as evolving metaphors of social justice. The notion of 'stealing the fire from the gods' is about understanding religions scientifically as incomplete discoveries of the conflict resolution process and science achieving the definitive objectivity on the language of conflict resolution, clarity on moral values and practically achieving peace on earth offering people a new civil right emotional and moral education.

'Giving the fire to the mortals' corresponds to improving education through studying the creative process, integrating religions with psychology and science as the Science of Conflict Resolution. Science gives new knowledge clarifying insights and moral values, demystifying religions and delivering a technology utilizing the creative process revolutionizing respectively the fields of psychology, religion and education. Science interprets metaphors into quantifiable and graphically portrayable conflict resolution entities and identifies this order integrating knowledge into enlightenment, insights and wisdom.

Creativity is the Rosetta Stone of the unconscious mind. It demonstrates the coincidence of emotions as art symbolism with the science of formal operations leading to a moral or conflict resolution outcome. Thus we witness how the simple symbolic language of any sample of creativity following three formal transformations of the key symbol binding a set of six emotional states evolves exactly as predicted along the six role state sequences of conflict resolution. The overlap of art, science and morality makes art works meaningful and validates the concept of the orderly and moral unconscious, the Formal Theoretical thesis. The exhibits thus reconcile the arts, psychology and moral order with science, and affirm the moral and scientific nature of the unconscious. Formal Theory's unconscious becomes the atomistic unit entity studied now by the exact Science of Conflict Resolution, the Moral Science. This conceptualization introduces science into psychology and morality, but also integrates religions as partial and complementary discoveries of the conflict resolution process into an evolutionary continuum progressing toward fairness and abstraction presently completed by the Moral Science.

Conflict resolution by definition reconciles opposites into unities. The reconciliation entails the formal transformation of the original two positions into a compromise adaptational end state. In this volume we pursued reconciling science and religion leading to the Moral Science, their merger doing justice to both. The new science is the effortless seamless integration of science and religion based on demonstrating the scientific and moral nature of the unconscious as the predictable mindful weaver of feelings and thoughts into the Conflict Resolution Process. This measurable unconscious becomes the integrative paradigm not only of religion and science, but the atomistic unit order of all the social sciences.

In this volume we have achieved a milestone, a major scientific breakthrough, the reconciliation of science and religion. This requires modifying the original positions of both realms. Originally science understood religion from the propositional logic perspective as a set of unreasonable assumptions incompatible with the facts of biological evolution. Science hence dismissed scientific explanation of religions defining them as meta-physical; creationism and prophetic revelation accounted to a second magisterium or an alternative type of reasoning. The Formal Theory changes science's methodological approach. The truth does not depend on axiomatic statements but on the formal interrelation of parts in wholes.

Science discards the biological axiomatic perspective of the Darwinian focus on the interpretation of Genesis. It introduces the relational method studying order in the formal correlation of parts in totalities. This method observes the interrelation of emotions in the processing of conflicts following a distinct path of formal transformations. The Formal Theory recognizes the mental emotional totality in all samples of creativity as a conflict resolving mechanism. This constitutes a set of six emotions guided by three formal operations. The Conflict Resolution Process becomes the scientific unit of the social sciences. This phenomenon represents a natural science periodic and equilibrial mental entity. Science evolves insights in this phenomenon as a formal and physical mechanism. Another aspect of the process: Conflict is evoked by transgressions as normative deviations accompanied by corrective emotions. The process spontaneously corrects the emotional discomfort through the change of attitude leading to normative compliance or normative adjustment. The resolution represents psychic relief, emotional stability also identified with the state of rest.

Formal Theory's methodology changes science's object and method for the study of behavior. The nature of truth shifts from the axiomatic assertions on the truth or falsity of the content of stories to what is universal in all stories, the formal structure of emotions in the plot of stories. From this perspective all thought is motivated by conflict resolution, the need for moral order. This assumption, the process coinciding with moral order as a scientific phenomenon, closed the gap between psychology, religion and science.

The new Moral Science is predicated on the iden-tification of the unconscious as a predictable and measurable adaptational homeostatic physiological mechanism. This has been the role of the exhibits of the Museum of the Creative Process. By demonstrating the universality of a harmonic of emotions they validate the physical structure and the moral function of the unconscious as a natural science equilibrial phenomenon. The exhibits validate the Formal Theory and transform it into the Moral Science. By validating the assumption of the formal interrelation of emotions progressing from a conflict to its resolution moral order is shown to exist in all thought independently of religions. Science identifies morality as the natural science phenomenon of the unconscious, the mental heartbeat. Thus the Moral Science establishes the fact that psychology is inseparable from morality and from the study of religion and that both realms abide by the laws of the rigorous sciences. This finding affirms that moral law coincides with natural law.

The exhibits also show that religions evolved toward the Moral Science; they are fathomable entities of conflict resolution representing insights into the unconscious process; they are metaphors of conflict resolution that can be interpreted as quantifiable and graphically portrayable natural science phenomena. Indeed, Genesis is rehabilitated as the apt insightful metaphor of the six-part Conflict Resolution Process coinciding with both Aristotle's six-part dramatic process and with Hinduism's six chakras bound by the seventh on top of a person's head. The interpretation of metaphors vindicates religions as forerunners of science; they have identified partial but complementary aspects of the unconscious process. The Moral Science changes the method of analysis of religions. The content of stories becomes irrelevant. We can analyze dogma precisely as particular ways of resolving conflict. Religions may be understood with the physics of equilibrial systems promoting variations of conflict resolution as formally interrelated alternative relational modalities. Religions correctly perceived conflict resolution but they have espoused alternative resolutions, unfair norms, and concrete attributions of the process.

Science, thus, evolved from biology to the formal logic and physics of conflict resolution and religions changed from stories of creation to be redefined as alternative ways of resolving conflict. This method of analysis bypasses the controversial issues of disputing religion's cosmic creation and determining the nature of the divine. It suffices for the Moral Science to understand the unconscious as a natural science phenomenon and as the origin of moral order.

The Moral Science reconciles religions with each other as evolving complementary insights in the Conflict Resolution Process. Their resolutions have led to norms regulating human conduct, in particular women's sexuality. They have regulated with norms the structure of domestic relations and reinvented the divine to justify these norms. The evolving religions redefined resolutions/norms in the realm of the family. Norms and gods evolved as belief systems.

Religions were correct about a universal moral order but they have been limited in the norms and the suggested attributions of the divine. Religions evolved along a historical progression of redefining norms improving justice in domestic relations and improving abstraction on the nature of gods. Judaism reduced the multiple gods of the pagan religions into the one loving and just God who was not a person but a process, responsible for all order and justice in the universe; this God was indefinable. He was merely the process, 'He who was, is and will be.' But was this Jewish God fair to women? Was the concept of this elusive God as abstract as the scientific notion of the process?

Like Prometheus who gave the fire to the mortals, Moral Science advances a program of emotional and moral education. This program, *Creativity and Power Management*, studies creativity to clarify the key concept and to enable us to utilize it for multiple theoretical and clinical applications. We can use it to understand the mind and to measure it, also to educate the public, inspire it by providing it as a moral alternative to religions. The Moral Science does not cancel spirituality. It provides a new type of faith consisting in trust in conflict resolution. This construct avails clarity in the meaning of life as enlightenment, as personal insights, as skills in managing power and as clarity in the nature of moral values. Meaning along these objectives is attainable by the concise and comprehensive program of emotional and moral education. Power Management studies the nature of the unconscious creative process as a science-based catechism. The effectiveness of this education demonstrates the practical advantages of the new science as the means for changing the human predicament of uncertainty about psychology and religion.

Power Management versus religious catechism
Like religious catechism, the science-based education program has two components, the cognitive or educational and the experiential. The first we identify with moral education; the second as emotional education. The exhibits of the Museum represent the cognitive segment imparting the moral education. The exhibits demonstrate the mechanics of the Conflict Resolution Process as a natural science moral order phenomenon. They illustrate also the evolution of religions as partial and complementary insights leading to the discovery of the underlying scientific paradigm of moral order.

Here we may revisit the parallels between moral education based on religion and alternatively on the scientific study of the creative process founded on the formal interpretation of metaphors. Power Management's cognitive segment is comparable to religious catechism but offers the clarity of scientific concepts. We may see parallels between religious education based on the stories of the Bible contrasted to our study of the creative process as presented in the Museum exhibits. For instance we may compare the Wizard of Oz story with the Passover Haggadah, the festivity celebrating the Exodus from Egypt. Both stories unfold as journeys and both have a set of four parallel constructs, a model of science, the characters, norms and the divine power, which we may compare for their meaningfulness.

Science: In the journey out of Egypt but also in Genesis, the six-day story of creation, we recognize the process symbolically representing transformation as a six part emotional sequence leading predictably to rest, or peace. Alternatively the yellow brick road represents the transformative journey as the metaphor of the process. Unlike the relativity of religious metaphors the process is now clarified as a reliable rational formula identified as the six role state Universal transformative Harmonic, the unit of the social sciences.

Characters, the psychology of attitudes: Both the Haggadah and the story of Oz identify four characters with different attitudes. These correspond to Formal Theory's diagnostic categories. The four Oz characters more clearly than the four children questioning 'what is special about this night?' identify four relational modalities. The Formal Theory makes these clear as alternative ways of relating, each generating life-time self-fulfilling scenarios and particular cultural environments.

Dealing with norms: The Passover ceremony does not identify directly women as witches but the bible leaves females out of the father-son covenant. The Judaic tradition emphasizes the father son primacy discriminating but not vilifying women. Judea unlike Greece resolved the gender rivalries by gaining cooperation from women. Biblical women were resigned to subordinacy to men as their social predicament. They trusted their husbands with their children but devoted themselves to secondary roles. In great contrast the Oz story has the four creatures killing the witch. This allows us to address the perennial antagonism of the genders, the power struggle between mothers and fathers. We may interpret the challenge of a child having to kill a woman as the condition of outgrowing one's dependency needs to mothers, seeking the reversal of the Oedipal disposition. The Greek cultural antagonistic relationship between father and son was fueled by the unresolved domestic power struggle. The Greek cultural concern with women is reflected in the Promethean paradigm about Pandora as the dilemmas surrounding women as gifts associated with curses. While the Bible modified the domestic relations system, the Formal Theory encourages awareness of the lingering power imbalance in domestic relations.

The divine: The Passover exodus is motivated by the grace of a powerful benevolent loving god, rescuing enslaved Jews from the unjust oppressive rule of a Pharaoh. The Passover ritual honors god as the magical loving just almighty who is able to rescue the Israelites, who loves them, guides them, gives them his ten Commandments and the Promised Land. In the Oz story four ailing humans seek personal transformation from a magical but deceptive moral authority. The Oz story deconstructs the divine authority as deceptions and projections. The Formal Theory objects to the deconstruction of moral authority; it delegates this authority to the process. Its real force stems from the unconscious directing behavior to conflict resolution as the magnetic north.

But besides clarifying cognitively the nature of moral order, the key component of *Creativity and Power Management* is its experiential segment based on the *Conflict Analysis Battery*. While religions seek personal soul searching as in the Yom Kipour Day of Atonement Power Management's battery effectively identifies the

personal pattern and related issues. It is a self-assessment instrument that uses the creative process for educational, diagnostic, and therapeutic objectives. The self-assessment leads a person to pursue the needed personal changes. We observe multiple therapeutic benefits through the completion of the battery. The person realizes upon the conclusion of the self-assessment the importance of the personal attitude in shaping the sequence of emotions as conflict resolution self-fulfilling prophecies. The implication is that the individual chooses to modify one's attitude and thus achieve peace of mind and effectiveness in relations. Because of its user friendliness and effectiveness the assessment technology is relevant for the educational and therapeutic needs of the well as well as the clinically diagnosed public.

The Moral Science conclusively represents the science of the unconscious. It transforms religions from arbitrary moralist systems rigidly regulating social norms to the awareness of the process. This entails that religions modify their injunctions misleading the public, dictating wrong norms and preaching the theistic perception of the Conflict Resolution Process. Religious norms need to be corrected redefining the role of women in society. Moral Science frees the mortals from the confining normative moral paradigms of religions and from the idolatrous worship of theistic authorities associated with the particular moral orders.

The discovery of Moral Science clarifies in a definitive manner first the requirements for the optimal normative structuring of relations and second establishes reverence for the qualities of a non-theistic, abstract role model of power management. The new model inspires piety as respect for the Universal Harmonic and the associated principles of mastery with moderation, cooperation and mutual respect. But furthermore the new outlook combines reverence of fairness with corrective self-knowledge. It

enhances self-awareness, self-respect and optimism in espousing the correct modality of conflict resolution. The new spirituality instills trust in the process as the alternative to blind faith in God. The human unconscious predictably resolving conflict inspires hope for justice and goodness; the spirit projected to the loving god is reclaimed by the humans through honoring the positive attributes of the unconscious.

Prometheus was a hero challenging religion punished, handicapped and immobilized but eventually unbound and freed to enlighten. Now it is science empowered conceptually that is the hero that comes to rescue humanity from the misconceptions of moral order. Power Management discovers moral order as a natural science; it builds faith in reason and trust in the universal process and the individual assumes responsibility in the realm of interpersonal relations.

Science explains and foretells; it interprets symbolic languages into the universal language of constructs and principles. Promethean science offers objectivity bridging the metaphorical languages of subjectivity. It is politically empowering. People may evolve moral consensus that is, enjoy the identical perception of reality. Clarity bridges the artificial divisions, misconceptions of norms and gods. This conceptual reconciliation promises to finally confer the most significant conflict resolution, peace in the world. The biblical quotation: 'I will make a man more precious than fine gold' attributed to God may now be heard as the echo of the human unconscious seeking justice and self improvement. The new science grounded spirituality may be as emotionally empowering and as politically influential as traditional inspirational faith.

COMMENTS ABOUT THE HARMONIC AS THE NEW PARADIGM
This book changes the way we look at art, understand behavior, the unconscious, the way we regard or disregard religions, the concepts of

god and moral values, of norms, breaches of norms, the entitlement of religions versus science to determine norms, the way we make clinical diagnoses and conduct personality assessment and therapy; it changes the core topic of education and our expectations from education for enlightenment, self-knowledge, clarity of values and skills in power management.

This book introduces a new concept that radically changes psychology, religion and education. Its effectiveness is communicating a message visually by observing the abstract but qualifiable Universal Harmonic manifested in all the exhibits of the Museum of the Creative Process.

In visiting the exhibits of the Museum as well as reading the book about them we experience a profound emotional relief as we recognize a simple continuity to justice. The universal harmonic is a broader truth that integrates the fragmented world into a reassuring and reliable pathway to healing. It is present in all samples of creativity as a conflict resolving mechanism that represents the orderly evolution of emotions. The harmonic reconciles myths, the epics, the scriptures based on the predictability and the wisdom of science. It is a new moral order making the world meaningful and rescuing it from its moral confusion, its multiple divisive conceptual fixations. We feel deep appreciation for order and meaning, integrated knowledge, conveying the happy ending to our travesties.

The Universal Harmonic integrates fragments into totalities, isolated artwork be that canvases, metaphors, religions, stories within a dramatic context, into a totality that is predictable and meaningful. The Harmonic is science in the domain of emotions, it is the creative and moral unconscious; it is the atomistic unit of psychology unifying the social sciences into the Science of Conflict Resolution. The universal harmonic is the reasoning path of the unconscious seeking the normative adjustment of the individual in society either by the individual changing his attitude or by the individual changing society's norms. The Harmonic is the transformative pathway that the world has been searching for in Genesis, in Cosmogony, in the yellow brick road to the wizard, the magic of the plot of stories that leads to the happy or just end, it is the sacred path of moral values and spirituality. It is now a simple sine curve of interrelated emotions organized by the unconscious. It is formulas of physics and logic. It is the essence of all religions and of psychology. It is also the core message to be clearly conveyed in the classroom.

Science in this book wrestles with all gods and wins the struggle by identifying predictability as the nature of unconscious justice freeing the public from the supernatural and from associated dated norms advanced by religions, paradigms that conferred social justice at one point in history, but which are holding the world captive in its social adjustment.

The conceptual breakthrough is of enormous significance. It generates enlightenment, the integration of fragmented knowledge into the wisdom of a science founded moral order. The concept is of tremendous practical value as we can see science in art but also use art to identify the dimensions of the individual. We can tap the creative process as the means to identify the personal pattern of resolving conflicts. Insights thus become readily available.

The exhibits of the museum validate the Formal Theoretical unconscious as the universal core structure of all thinking manifested in all samples of creativity; it is the physiology of a reflex adjustment to stress. It is psychology as the many ways we relate, the relational modalities, diagnostic categories of science. It is a natural science equilibrial phenomenon; it is formulas, it is the plot of stories, it is the moral paradigm integrating all religions, this process makes sense; it makes the world predictable and measurable.

Creativity becomes the tool to education; science becomes user friendly and manageable.

This unit order deciphers metaphysics and psychology, metaphors and art and translates them using natural law, the simple formulas of physics. Having broken the code of the social sciences we may now unify the arts, psychology and religion into a single rigorous exact science; we call it the Moral Science; it examines the unconscious as a natural science measurable moral order phenomenon.

Enlightenment is being able to see multiple domains in harmony with each other. The fire stolen from the gods is the common denominator of all knowledge, the unit of the social science disciplines; it sheds light to psychology, religion, all creativity at the same time. We see through all humanities the same harmonic integrating parts into totalities of meaning, a simple universal order, a circumscribed harmonic, embracing all domains and ourselves at the same time and find the same order, moderation cooperation and mutual respect.

We call the new order science; people talked of it as God, others as the psyche; we know it as the unit mental heartbeat. Science establishes moral order as the superhighway to wisdom, as the innate mental mechanism, a natural science moral order or conflict resolution mechanism. It is the creative process. Suddenly we have the key that opens up all doors. All religions are integrated as a sequence of resolutions gradually evolving self-awareness and justice in relations.

The ultimate spirituality is when a formula explains everything and also gives us guidance. The formula makes information intelligible; it helps to decipher symbolic languages with objectivity and to interpret metaphors as measurable order.

The unconscious mind is not an erratic, non

rational, conflict generating libidinal and aggressive instinct; on the contrary, it is the orderly engine of conflict resolution, the source of emotional processing of negative to positive feelings, leading to attitude change, to the willingness to deal with pain and to compromise one's egotism. It is an equilibrial energetic entity, a rational quantifiable and graphically portrayable scientific automatism, a natural science mechanism transforming conflict to resolutions; it is the dramatic process that anabolizes energy like chlorophyll and binds it into wisdom. It is a homeostatic innate faculty processing emotions seeking normative compliance and emotional stability transforming conflict to insights and constructive resolutions to new civilizations.

Religions are neither fairy tales nor divine revelations. They are scientific discoveries of the wise unconscious attributed to gods. The unconscious resolves conflicts generating culture and personal wisdom. Now science discovering the unconscious is able to appreciate the wisdom of religions but also see their shortcomings, and to integrate them into a continuum of discoveries reconciled with psychology and physics into the ultimate Moral Science the true psychology of human behavior, an exact science.

The reconceptualization of the unconscious entails revamping education from agnostic to Gnostic, from distant to religion and psychology, to placing the scientific study of the moral unconscious as the core of the curriculum. Education can and must deliver in the classroom besides encyclopedic knowledge the essence of meaning; psychology, and morality, the scientific study of the unconscious projected on the creative process, may be respected as explaining the generation of meaning.

The Conflict Resolution Process through its projection in all samples of creativity yields knowledge on the nature of the psyche and god as a scientific phenomenon. The process reveals the nature of enlightenment, insights in oneself, self knowledge and clarity on the scientific nature of moral values.

The Harmonic integrates the fragmented knowledge into meaningful continua, conflict resolutions as the dramatic or Conflict Resolution Process; this is the mental and moral imperative. It interfaces all sciences, like the humanities and the rigorous sciences, religion and psychology, religions among themselves. It connects symbolic entities, diverse artwork of any artist into the simple drama symbolized by the universal harmonic. The harmonic is formulas of physics, it pertains to the rigorous sciences, it is the organization of emotions in the plot of any book, the emotions expressed as ideas in a sample story, it connects the religions of the world as they have evolved from concrete explanations of the meaning of life to the detection of the scientific and moral nature of the unconscious, creating meaning.

LEVIS HOWLING IN THE DESERT: EUREKA!

Howling in the Desert
A sculptural epilogue:
One final reiteration of the Art to Science theme

The Sculptural Trail's most recent installation notes the danger of misleading ideologies, and, in contrast, emphasizes the advantages of the unit process. Behind the massive two white cubist structures, *The Bride and the Groom*, which are a memorial to the Bible and symbolize the power of the story as the words of God, I am erecting a new installation that dramatizes the critical texts of the 20th century and the paradigms that these books inspired. This exhibit presents Marx, Freud and Hitler and their respective books, and addresses the bankruptcy of their social/moral paradigms. These thinkers and their texts justified arbitrary political movements as science-based truths. In contrast to these failed endeavors, the fourth station represents the Formal Theory's ability to introduce the rigorous Moral Science.

Each of the four stations identifies the author with a bust, and his perspective with a symbolic representation of his universe: Freud's emphasis on human sexuality is symbolized by a set of old-fashioned claw-foot bathtubs; Marx's proletariat with a Russian Armageddon monument and National Socialism with a swastika emblazed on an ominous rusty furnace. In contrast to these stations, I have installed two abstract monuments of the Universal Harmonic that promote scientific objectivity on the nature of moral order: one monument is my *Wolf Howling in the Desert*, the other is a spiral staircase going two floors up into space, *Jacob's Ladder*.

BIBLIOGRAPHY

Aristotle, & Butcher, S. H. (1961). Poetics. New York: Hill and Wang. Print.

Baum, L. F., Denslow, W. W., & Hearn, M.P. (1983). The Wizard of Oz. New York: Schocken. Print.

Brainerd, C. (1978). Piaget's Theory of Intelligence. Print.

Cavafy, C., & Boegehold, A.L. (2008) Cavafy: 166 Poems. Mount Jackson, VA: Axios. Print.

Dershowitz, A.M. (2001). The Genesis of Justice. New York: Warner. Print.

Dews, P. (1999). Habermas: a Critical Reader. Oxford, UK: Blackwell. Print.

Dougherty, C. (2006). Prometheus. New York: Routledge. Print.

Dreyfus, H.L., & Hall, H. (1992). Heidegger: a Critical Reader. Oxford, UK: Blackwell. Print.

Fish, S. (18 Apr. 2011). "Does Reason Know What It Is Missing? - NYTimes.com." Opinion - Opinionator - NYTimes.com. Web.

"Frankfurt School." (18 Apr. 2011). Wikipedia, the Free Encyclopedia. Web.

Freud, S., & Strachey, J. (1977). Introductory Lectures on Psychoanalysis. New York: Norton. Print.

Gay, P. (1988). Freud: a Life for Our Time. New York: Norton. Print.

Graves, R. (1960). The Greek Myths. London: Penguin. Print.

Hartman, D. (2009). Maimonides: Torah and Philosophical Quest. Philadelphia: Jewish Publication Society. Print.

"Henry Gorski Art Exhibit | VPR Image Gallery." (20 Apr. 2011). Vermont Public Radio: Home of VPR News and VPR Classical, and Vermont's NPR News Source. Web.

Ingram, D. (2010). Habermas: Introduction and Analysis. Ithaca: Cornell UP. Print.

Kazantzakis, N. (1960). The Last Temptation of Christ. New York: Simon and Schuster. Print.

Kazantzakis, N. (1953). Zorba the Greek. New York: Simon and Schuster. Print.

Kazantzakis, N. (1960). The Saviors of God; Spiritual Exercises. New York: Simon and Schuster. Print.

Klein, F., Hedrick, E. R., & Noble, C. A. (1932). Elementary Mathematics from an Advanced Standpoint. New York: Macmillan. Print.

Kol Ha-neshamah: Ãˆrev Shabat = Kol Haneshamah : Shabbat Eve. (1993). Wyncote, PA: Reconstructionist. Print.

Levis, A.J. (1988). Conflict Analysis: the Formal Theory of Behavior : a Theory and Its Experimental Validation. Manchester Village, VT: Normative Publications. Print.

Levis, A.J. (1988). Conflict Analysis: the Formal Theory of Behavior: a Theory and Its Experimental Validation. Manchester Village, VT: Normative Publications. Print.

Levis, A.J. (1988). Conflict Analysis Training: a Program of Emotional Education. Manchester Village, VT: Normative Publications. Print.

Levis, A.J. (1977). Contributions of the Formal Theory of Behavior. Hamden, CT: Normative Publications. Print.

Lloyd, G. (1996). Routledge Philosophy Guidebook to Spinoza and The Ethics. London: Routledge. Print.

Maurer, N. (6 Oct. 1968). "Artist Gorski and His 'Pain-things'" New Haven Register [New Haven] Print.

Mitchell, S., & Margaret, B.J. (1995). Freud and Beyond: a History of Modern Psychoanalytic Thought. New York: Basic. Print.

Mitchell, S. (2004). Gilgamesh: a New English Version. New York: Free. Print.

Norris, C. (1987). Derrida. Cambridge, MA: Harvard UP. Print.

Peppiatt, M. (2008). Francis Bacon: Studies for a Portrait : Essays and Interviews. New Haven [Conn.: Yale UP. Print.

Piaget, J., & Garcia, R. (1989). Psychogenesis and the History of Science. New York: Columbia UP. Print.

"Prometheus." (18 Apr. 2011). Wikipedia, the Free Encyclopedia. Web.

Royce, J., Smith, J.E., & Kluback, W. (1988). Josiah Royce: Selected Writings. New York: Paulist. Print.

Sacks, J. (2009). [Sidur á¸Kˀoren] = The Koren Siddur. Jerusalem: Koren. Print.

ABOUT THE AUTHOR

Dr Albert Levis, a Yale-trained psychiatrist, born in 1937, in Athens, Greece, began his research as his own healing process from his childhood experiences of WWII and of the Holocaust writing a play, *The Argives,* about the genocidal War of Troy. Researching Greek mythology he stumbled across the Greek Cosmogony stories and observed that a pattern was transmitted across the five generations of the Greek Gods. By studying periodicity as reflective of science in the realm of behavior he detected the formal structure and the moral function of the pattern as reflecting the unconscious as an orderly conflict resolution mechanism.

Examining samples of creativity, art exhibits, metaphors, stories, led to the confirmation of his theoretical analysis of conflict. It was thus established that the unconscious was a Conflict Resolution Process, a natural science and moral order entity, the unit integrating psychology and moral order with the rigorous sciences.

In 1988, Dr Levis published his findings in *Conflict Analysis, the Formal Theory of Behavior* and acquired the Wilburton Inn, to evolve there a training center and the forum for the scientific study of psychology and religion. There he installed art exhibits, which eventually became the Museum of the Creative Process. The exhibits reviewed in this volume illustrate and validate his theoretical assumption on the nature of the unconscious by studying samples of creativity. The entire sequence of his writings addresses the subject of the existence of a Moral Science, the Science of Conflict Resolution.

FIVE FORMAL THEORETICAL VOLUMES OF THE NORMATIVE PUBLICATIONS

There are five volumes on the Formal Theory; each has a different function and audience. Each publication stands on its own, but the five together represent knowledge on the Science of Conflict Resolution, the Moral Science. The new science integrates the social sciences into a continuum whose object is the unconscious studied through its manifestation as the creative process using the method of the formal analysis. The books may be acquired as a set, each contributing new information and having a complementary function. Below we review their individual contributions to the field of the humanities:

Volumes one, two and five, represent scholarly readings. They introduce the theory, its experimental validation and its application to the fields of assessment and therapy. They methodically integrate a great deal of information. They should be of interest to scientists, the academic public, scholars and students.

The workbook and the exhibits book, volumes three and four, on the other hand will be very popular with the general public including student populations at various levels of education. They present the cognitive and the experiential segments of a training program, *Creativity and Power Management.* The exhibits book presents the concepts of the theory and their relevance for a moral education. The workbook allows utilizing creativity for self discovery as a personalized emotional education.

The entire sequence of volumes will appeal to those interested in the popular fields of psychology, religion and philosophy as the books integrate these fields, reducing a tremendous amount of discordant information into the elegant simplicity of the Universal Harmonic. The five volumes provide enlightenment and personal insights. They are the guide to wisdom. Reading the volumes and viewing the exhibits, completing the training provides conceptual lucidity to the question of the meaning of life, while helping the person to look at oneself. Conflict resolution founded on the existence of a rational and moral unconscious, a homeostatic mechanism, explains humanity's pursuit of justice and abstraction.

1988, TEXTBOOK, VOLUME ONE:
CONFLICT ANALYSIS, THE FORMAL THEORY OF BEHAVIOR

In ten chapters this book introduces the key concepts of the Formal Theory. It departs from the observation that the unconscious is a natural science moral order phenomenon. The pattern is illustrated using the Greek creation story and Henry Gorski's art to illustrate and demonstrate order and predictability in behavior as the Science of Conflict Resolution. The ten chapters include detailed study of methodology, the development of the key assumptions of the theory, applications of the theory in conceptualizing personality development, psychodiagnosis, evolving an assessment instrument, the *Conflict Analysis Battery* and its use in structuring psychotherapy and deliberating on ethics along the lines of the new conceptual model.

1977, VOLUME TWO:
THE CONTRIBUTIONS OF THE FORMAL THEORY

This booklet sums up ten innovations contributed by the Formal Theory in the field of psychology. In particular it introduces the graphic portrayal of the process and its multiple applications.

1988, VOLUME THREE:
CONFLICT ANALYSIS TRAINING, A PROGRAM OF EMOTIONAL EDUCATION: THE WORKBOOK, A MANUAL-DRIVEN PSYCHOTHERAPY

The workbook contains an introduction to the concepts of the theory, as information on the process and the *Conflict Analysis Battery*, a comprehensive self-assessment. The battery contains both an inventory and projectives complementing each other as theory based assessment instruments. The workbook provides processes to organize and interpret the information. The assessment is diagnostic, therapeutic and educational. It may be repeated to evaluate ongoing pathology and to monitor therapy outcome.

2011, VOLUME FOUR:
SCIENCE STEALING THE FIRE OF THE GODS AND HEALING THE WORLD
This publication reviews the art exhibits of the Museum of the Creative Process examining the presence in a number of art exhibits of the formal organization between ideas as emotions with a distinct scientific structure and moral function.

The metaphor of Prometheus "stealing the fire of the gods and giving it to the mortals" is used to integrate the presentation of information in three chapters as a conflict between science and religion coming to a happy resolution as psychology and morality are shown to coincide in the unconscious Conflict Resolution Process and as the object of study of the new Moral Science.

The first chapter of the book identifies "the fire of the gods"; morality as a scientific phenomenon independent of religion by presenting and discussing three art exhibits.

The Moral Science, the science of the process, is about an orderly, abstract and demystified conflict resolution mechanism that transforms conflict from a state of passivity, antagonism and alienation to a state of resolution characterized as activity, cooperation and mutual respect.

The second chapter, "stealing the fire of the gods" presents the Sculptural Trail showing how the Conflict Resolution Process integrates the diverse religions of the world as conflict resolution entities that progressively evolve in fairness and abstraction; the process integrates them with psychology and science.

The third chapter "giving the fire of the gods to the mortals" introduces an emotional education program that may be delivered in the classroom. This is illustrated with case studies presented in seven murals.

The Moral Science postulates that morality and psychology are inseparable aspects of the same natural science phenomenon. Psychology is inconceivable without the driving force or motivation for restoring order as conflict resolution. The book is concluded recognizing that religions as partial and complementary discoveries of the Conflict Resolution Process are the forerunners of science. As science-education this knowledge must be imparted in the classroom. The public has the civil right of emotional and moral literacy, the right to interpret metaphors and understand morality and oneself in terms of relational choices of power management.

2011, VOLUME FIVE:
MORAL SCIENCE, THE SCIENTIFIC INTERPRETATION OF METAPHORS
This volume consists of a number of theoretical essays and clinical case studies refining the development of the scientific theory of behavior, while connecting the Formal Theory to other theories of psychology and psychotherapeutic modalities. The essays address the topics of science, religion and education along the Promethean metaphor; they expand on the same issues.

Regarding science we have two principle studies: One essay discusses the Conflict Resolution Process amplifying the communications presented in the murals exhibit.

A second lengthy essay discusses the process as the integrative paradigm expanding on the information provided in the Wizard of Oz Panels on each one of the four social science disciplines.

Regarding stealing the fire several essays discuss the sculptural trail and introduce the formal theoretical insights on religion.

In the education chapter I present essays on the topics of therapy, comparing the Formal Analysis to other psychotherapeutic modalities.

The Horowitz essay compares the conceptualization of a version of the process, its difficulties with concepts that are not formalized, the diagnostic distinctions of personality types that are not clear, the assessment metaphor creating technology that is cumbersome and therapy outcome that is protracted and inconclusive.

Another essay discusses therapy outcome presenting case studies and the effectiveness of the assessment instrument in imparting clinical insights and facilitating transformation.

An essay compares the Alcoholics Anonymous therapies with the Power Management therapy as both deal with spirituality and self-help. The essay presents the advantages of the Power Management approach over the theistic AA approach.

A final essay discusses the need for emotional literacy and presents its advocacy as a new civil right. So the Moral Science volume contains complementary studies on the creative process systematically presenting evidence and documenting the record of the new notion in its versatile manifestations and applications introducing order and enhancing meaning in the field of the humanities.

CREATIVITY AND POWER MANAGEMENT TRAINING
Power Management is a concise program of moral and emotional education; it is educational, diagnostic and therapeutic at the same time. It is suitable for the general public as well as for the training of professionals interested in the scientific understanding of psychology, moral order and one's own personality. It is helpful in understanding concepts and achieving personal insights. The program combines the presentation of the theory and evidence validating it, with use of creativity for self-discovery.